The New Spurgeon's Devotional Bible

Year One of Two
Using the English Standard Version
and Updated for Today's Reader

by Charles Haddon Spurgeon

updated & revised by Roger McReynolds

Originally Published (circa 1887) as
The Interpreter
or
Scripture for Family Worship

being selected passages of the Word of God for every morning and evening throughout the year, accompanied by a running comment and suitable Hymns

From a review in *The Christian Family* (circa 1890): "The impress of Mr. C. H. Spurgeon's genius is observable in the very felicitous arrangement of the passages of Scripture as well as in the characteristic running comment, in which latter, by the way, Mr. Spurgeon's theological views come prominently to the front."

Unless otherwise indicated, "Scripture quotations are from the ESV® Bible (The Holy Bible, English Standard Version®), copyright © 2001 by Crossway Bibles, a publishing ministry of Good News Publishers. Text edition: 2016. Used by permission. All rights reserved."

Copyright © 2016 Roger McReynolds
All rights reserved
ISBN: 1540495809
ISBN-13: 978-1540495808

Permission is granted to use up to 300 words from this book without prior permission. When using entries from this book in bulletins and Power Point presentations, etc. please include proper credits.

Scripture references should include (ESV) unless otherwise indicated. Example: "1 Timothy 3:16" should be "1 Timothy 3:16 (ESV)" and "© Roger McReynolds" or "Copyright Roger McReynolds" should follow the quote.

Abbreviations

NASB—The New American Standard Bible
NKJV—The New King James Bible

Acknowledgements

My sister, Laura, proofread every entry. May every writer have such a wonderful, skillful, critical, and encouraging proofreader. It is safe to say that she has contributed thousands of changes to this finished work.

My wife, Patti, read the daily entries as a reader and not an editor. She also made corrections and offered suggestions to keep the work readable. Thank you for your encouragement and patience.

Our daughter, Amber, designed the cover. More importantly, and more time consuming, she brought her tech prowess to bear to transform her father's Pages documents into this book format. If you saw what she had to work with you would appreciate her dedicated work as much as I do.

A special thank you to my brother-in-law, Burt, and my friend, Tim. They received daily emails of what were supposed to be final copies and caught a few things that even five proofreadings missed. Burt died of cancer on January 18, 2016. He read through Year Two, January 16 before being placed in hospice care.

You five have been my greatest supporters in this five year effort. Our readers appreciate you more than they will ever know. You have been "tools in God's hand."

Also Updated by the Editor
Charles Haddon Spurgeon

According to Promise: The Lord's Method of Dealing with His Chosen People

All of Grace (including Large Print 16-point font)

John Ploughman's Talk: (Winter 2019-20)

Most Things Spurgeon: A Daily Devotional

Peace and Purpose in Trial and Suffering

Spurgeon's Catechism: Updated for Today's Readers with Proof Texts in the ESV

The Clue of the Maze: 70 Daily Readings for Conquering Doubt + 3 Sermons on Doubting

The Gospel of the Kingdom: Spurgeon's Commentary on the Book of Matthew Updated & Expanded (Spring 2021)

The Imprecatory Psalms from The Treasury of David

The New Spurgeon's Devotional Bible: Year Two & Complete in One Volume

The Penitential Psalms from The Treasury of David (Summer 2020)

The Soul Winner

Spurgeon's Sermons Series

3:16: Thirteen Selected Sermons

A Defense of Calvinism: Including 7 Sermons on the Doctrines of Grace

A Sower Went Out to Sow: Nine Sermons on The Parable of the Sower

Lost and Found: 10 Evangelistic Sermons

The Wise and Foolish Builders and Other Parables of Jesus (July 2021)

Other Works

Sermons of D. L. Moody: 21 Sermons

The Fear of God, by John Bunyan

The Reformed Pastor, by Richard Baxter

Contact Information
MostThingsSpurgeon@gmail.com

Introduction

Charles Haddon Spurgeon was born in 1834 and born again in 1850. Soon after his conversion he became the pastor of a small village church. At the age of 19 he was called as pastor to the church meeting at the New Park Street Chapel in London, England. Seven years later, the congregation moved to their new building named The Metropolitan Tabernacle. Spurgeon preached there to audiences of 6,000 hearers until his death in 1892. There were no electronic amplification systems in those days, but everyone was able to hear him clearly.

During his 39 years in London his sermons were printed each week across the world and in many languages. He also began a college for pastors, established an orphanage, wrote over 100 books, edited a magazine called The Sword and the Trowel, provided living accommodations for widows in their church, supported workers called colporteurs who went door to door selling inexpensive Christian literature and Bibles as well as holding Bible studies, and began a Society of Evangelists for the preaching of the gospel.

Mr. Spurgeon originally produced The Interpreter for family devotions. I like it because it has so much Scripture along with explanatory comments designed to keep the reader in God's Word. In fact, the entire work contains about 35% of the Bible.

Family Devotions: Over the years I tried several ways to have a devotional time with my young family. Reading from the Bible, reading a daily devotional with a Bible verse and a short page of thoughts on the passage, and even a book or two I thought our children would enjoy or at least sit still for. All of my attempts failed. Either our children didn't like it or I didn't like it. I never tried what was then called Spurgeon's Devotional Bible because the Scripture was in the King James Version and Spurgeon used 19th century British English. I hope families will find the English Standard Version and Spurgeon's comments updated into 21st century American English helpful. Each reading takes about five minutes to read aloud. Another ten minutes for discussion and prayer, and your children have had to endure less time than it takes for advertisements in a one-hour television program and hopefully will occasionally learn something of lasting value.

Personal Devotions: Even though Mr. Spurgeon wanted to help parents with family time, I suspect most who use this are like me and read it for personal devotional time. It is an excellent way to read a large portion of the Bible without getting bogged down with all those genealogies. I strongly believe in the importance of reading the Bible completely and regularly and without explanatory notes. I also believe something like Spurgeon's Devotional Bible can be a refreshing, although infrequent, change of pace.

Translation Choice: Crossway has very graciously given permission to use their translation. The English Standard Version is my first choice. It combines both the smooth reading found in many Dynamic Equivalence or thought-for-thought versions with the accuracy of Formal Correspondence or more word-for-word translations.

Footnotes: I hope readers will not be distracted by my footnotes. Spurgeon's original work did not have footnotes. So why does this edition? It was only during my third reading that it finally dawned on me that virtually every title of every day's reading was a Bible verse. I thought that deserved a footnote. He will often quote the Scriptures while commenting on the Scriptures. I thought that deserved a footnote too. Then there were big words that I believe should be kept in the Christian's vocabulary, but that newer Christians and young readers might not yet be familiar with. Words like, "omnipotence," "omniscience," "intercessor," "ordinance," "propitiation," and "type." Hopefully, these footnotes will help a parent answer a child's questions as well as help a newer Christian who is unfamiliar with them. Spurgeon said, "All through the work we have gathered from every available source" and I have included some short biographical notes about some of the people he quotes in this book as well as updated many of those quotes and used the English Standard Version where they quote Scripture.

Illustrations: Here and there I have added an image I thought might be helpful as well as images of some of the men Spurgeon quotes. I have also included images with captions to highlight some of Spurgeon's life. I have made use of the world wide web, but have tried to avoid using any images I thought might be copyrighted.

Hymns: Spurgeon concluded almost every reading with a hymn to be sung by the family. I have left these out. Most are not familiar to today's church attender, there is no musical score, and updating poetry is definitely not part of my skill set.

January 1
The Lord Is My Light[1]

Reading the Holy Scriptures more often will not help us unless the Holy Spirit shows the truth to our souls. Let us pray, as we begin this year's Family Reading, that he who commanded the light to shine out of darkness will shine into our hearts and allow us to know the full meaning of his word. We shall begin at the opening page of God's revelation to us.

Genesis 1:1-5

1 In the beginning, God created the heavens and the earth. 2 The earth was without form and void, and darkness was over the face of the deep. *(We are dark by nature. Therefore, all of our powers are out of balance because of sin. We are nothing but confusion and emptiness.)* And the Spirit of God was hovering over the face of the waters.

The Spirit of God is the first person mentioned in the new creation. He visits the dead and dark heart, and begins the work of salvation inside us.

3 And God said, "Let there be light," and there was light. *(Wherever God gives his grace, he looks on it with pleasure)* 4 And God saw that the light was good. And God separated the light from the darkness. *(Grace also separates, "for what partnership has righteousness with lawlessness?"[2])*

5 God called the light Day, and the darkness he called Night. And there was evening and there was morning, the first day.

It is interesting to notice how the apostle John opens his gospel in the same way that the Old Testament begins, with "In the beginning." Let us continue our reading with the first fourteen verses of John's Gospel. Jesus, the Lord our Savior, is called "the Word," or the spoken mind of God.

John 1:1-14

1 In the beginning was the Word, and the Word was with God, and the Word was God. 2 He was in the beginning with God. *(Jesus already existed when creation began. He was with God before the world was made. Jesus worked together with the Father because he is also truly God.)* 3 All things were made through him and without him was not any thing made that was made. 4 In him was life, and the life was the light of men. *(If we live for God, and have any spiritual light, it is because Jesus Christ makes it happen.)* 5 The light shines in the darkness, and the darkness has not overcome it.

6 There was a man sent from God, whose name was John. 7 He came as a witness, to bear witness about the light, that all might believe through him. 8 He was not the light, but came to bear witness about the light.

9 The true light, which gives light to everyone, was coming into the world.

No one can get true light from any other source, and all who desire light may have it from him.

10 He was in the world, and the world was made through him, yet the world did not know him. 11 He came to his own, and his own people did not receive him. *(The Jews, who were his own kinsmen, rejected him. Sadly, too many children of godly parents also refuse the Savior. May it not be so in this family.)* 12 But to all who did receive him, who believed in his name, he gave the right to become children of God, *(This is the heart of the gospel. Christ is the giver. We are only receivers. Faith agrees to accept Christ, and with him we have the special right to be adopted into his family.)* 13 who were born, not of blood nor of the will of the flesh nor of the will of man, but of God.

14 And the Word became flesh and dwelt among us, and we have seen his glory, glory as of the only Son from the Father, full of grace and truth.

May the Lord allow us to receive his grace and to know his truth. Amen.

January 2
Create in Me a Clean Heart[3]

Genesis 1:6-13

6 And God said, "Let there be an expanse in the midst of the waters, and let it separate the waters from the waters.

---

[1] Psalm 27:1
[2] 2 Corinthians 6:14
[3] Psalm 51:10

The atmosphere separates the clouds above from the waters below. Martin Luther used to be amazed at the sky, because it has no visible support. He saw in it a lesson for his faith, teaching him that the Lord could hold him up by his unseen power. He who creates with a word can hold us up in the same way.

7 And God made the expanse and separated the waters that were under the expanse from the waters that were above the expanse. And it was so. *(In one verse the Lord commanded all land to come into being and for the oceans to separate them. In the next he accomplished it. In the same way one Scripture commands us to believe and another tells us that faith is the work of God.)* **8** And God called the expanse Heaven. And there was evening and there was morning, the second day.

9 And God said, "Let the waters under the heavens be gathered together into one place, and let the dry land appear. And it was so.

Notice how often we see the words, "And it was so." Learn from this. If God makes a promise, it will happen. If he makes a threat, it will not fail to take place.

10 God called the dry land Earth, and the waters that were gathered together he called Seas. And God saw that it was good.

God took care in naming "day" and "night," and "earth," and "sea." This should teach us to call things by their right names. Let us never call sin pleasure or the Lord's service drudgery.

11 And God said, "Let the earth sprout vegetation, plants yielding seed, and fruit trees bearing fruit in which is their seed, each according to its kind, on the earth." And it was so. **12** The earth brought forth vegetation, plants yielding seed according to their own kinds, and trees bearing fruit in which is their seed, each according to its kind. And God saw that it was good.

When God has put light into a soul and separates its sin from its new life, he next looks for fruit, and before long it grows to his glory.

13 And there was evening and there was morning, the third day. *(So far, we have seen the second and third day's work of creation. This is a good place to remind ourselves that our Lord Jesus was there, and "without him was not any thing made that was made."[4]) Let us read about him in:*

Proverbs 8:22-36

22 "The LORD possessed me at the beginning of his work,
  the first of his acts of old.
23 Ages ago I was set up,
  at the first, before the beginning of the earth.
24 When there were no depths I was brought forth,
  when there were no springs abounding with water.
25 Before the mountains had been shaped,
  before the hills, I was brought forth,
26 before he had made the earth with its fields,
  or the first of the dust of the world.
27 When he established the heavens, I was there;
  when he drew a circle on the face of the deep,
28 when he made firm the skies above,
  when he established the fountains of the deep,
29 when he assigned to the sea its limit,
  so that the waters might not transgress his command,
  when he marked out the foundations of the earth,
30   then I was beside him, like a master workman,
  and I was daily his delight,
  rejoicing before him always,
31 rejoicing in his inhabited world
  and delighting in the children of man.
32 "And now, O sons, listen to me:
  blessed are those who keep my ways.
33 Hear instruction and be wise,
  and do not neglect it.
34 Blessed is the one who listens to me,
  watching daily at my gates,
  waiting beside my doors.
35 For whoever finds me finds life
  and obtains favor from the LORD,

---

[4] John 1:3

36 but he who fails to find me injures himself;
   all who hate me love death."

Listen to Christ Jesus, "who became to us wisdom from God, righteousness and sanctification and redemption,"[5] and find life and kindness in him.

January 3
Praise the LORD![6]
Genesis 1:14-23

14 And God said, "Let there be lights in the expanse of the heavens to separate the day from the night. And let them be for signs and for seasons, and for days and years, 15 and let them be lights in the expanse of the heavens to give light upon the earth." And it was so. *(There was light before the appearance of the sun or moon. God created them to proclaim his glory. He could have done without them, but he chose not to. He could enlighten men's minds without his ministers or his church, but he chooses to use them as light in the world. Let us be thankful for them and pray for them.)*

16 And God made the two great lights—the greater light to rule the day and the lesser light to rule the night—and the stars.

A chaos of light was changed to order. Order is a law of God. Families need order for happiness.

17 And God set them in the expanse of the heavens to give light on the earth, 18 to rule over the day and over the night, and to separate the light from the darkness. And God saw that it was good.

God gave the day as a proper time for work. He gave the night as a suitable time to rest. Both are "good" for us in many ways. We should adore the goodness of God for his wisdom.

19 And there was evening and there was morning, the fourth day.

20 And God said, "Let the waters swarm with swarms of living creatures, and let birds fly above the earth across the expanse of the heavens."

The Lord's work of creation progressed to higher levels each day. Grace works much the same way. God will continue to give us greater mercies.

21 So God created the great sea creatures and every living creature that moves, with which the waters swarm, according to their kinds, and every winged bird according to its kind. And God saw that it was good. 22 And God blessed them, saying, "Be fruitful and multiply and fill the waters in the seas, and let birds multiply on the earth." 23 And there was evening and there was morning, the fifth day. *(The incredible numbers of fish and birds in the earth show how powerful this ancient blessing was. Let the Lord bless his church in the same way and her converts shall be "as many as the stars of heaven."[7] Such wonders of creation should not to be mentioned without a song of praise. Therefore let us therefore turn to:*

Psalm 148

1 Praise the LORD!
   Praise the LORD from the heavens;
      praise him in the heights!
2 Praise him, all his angels;
      praise him, all his hosts!
3 Praise him, sun and moon,
      praise him, all you shining stars!
4 Praise him you highest heavens,
      and you waters above the heavens!
5 Let them praise the name of the LORD!
      For he commanded and they were created.
6 And he established them forever and ever;
      he gave a decree, and it shall not pass away.
7 Praise the LORD from the earth,
      you great sea creatures and all deeps,
8 fire and hail, snow and mist,
      stormy wind fulfilling his word!
9 Mountains and all hills,
      fruit trees and all cedars!
10 Beasts and all livestock,
      creeping things and flying birds!
11 Kings of the earth and all peoples,
      princes and all rulers of the earth!
12 Young men and maidens together,

---
[5] I Corinthians 1:30
[6] Psalm 148:1

[7] Hebrews 11:12

old men and children!
13 Let them praise the name of the LORD,
    for his name alone is exalted;
    his majesty is above earth and heaven.
14 He has raised up a horn for his people,
    praise for all his saints,
    for the people of Israel who are near to him.
    Praise the LORD!

Let us praise God with our hearts, words, and actions throughout this day; because he has been very kind to us as a family. Bless his name.

January 4
Your Maker is Your Husband[8]

Genesis 1:26-27, 29, 31

The Lord first prepared the world for man and then placed him in it. He furnished the home before he made the occupant. This is an example of God's thoughtful care for mankind.

26 Then God said, "Let us make man in our image, after our likeness. And let them have dominion over the fish of the sea and over the birds of the heavens and over the livestock and over all the earth and over every creeping thing that creeps on the earth."

Notice the words, "Let us make." The three divine persons of the Godhead held a meeting. Let us learn to adore Father, Son, and Spirit, as the One God. Man was the greatest work of the six days of creation. He was created in a special way and was made to rule over the world. If the animals now rebel against man, it is because man has rebelled against his God.

27   So God created man in his own image,
    in the image of God he created him;
    male and female he created them.

29 And God said, "Behold, I have given you every plant yielding seed that is on the face of all the earth, and every tree with seed in its fruit. You shall have them for food." *(Before he sinned man did not kill animals, but lived on fruits. Every meal that includes meat should remind us of our fall.)*

31 And God saw everything that he had made, and behold, it was very good. And there was evening and there was morning, the sixth day.

Genesis 2:7-10, 15-18, 21-25

7 Then the LORD God formed the man of dust from the ground and breathed into his nostrils the breath of life, and the man became a living creature. 8 And the LORD God planted a garden in Eden, in the east, and there he put the man whom he had formed. 9 And out of the ground the LORD God made to spring up every tree that is pleasant to the sight and good for food. The tree of life was in the midst of the garden and the tree of the knowledge of good and evil.

10 A river flowed out of Eden to water the garden, and there it divided and became four rivers.

There was food and drink in abundance. The variety was delightful and virtually unlimited. The garden was a paradise of comfort. "No herb, no flower, no tree was lacking there that might be for ornament or usefulness; whether for sight, or for scent, or for taste. God's generosity was far more than necessary. It provided for comfort and recreation."[9]

15 The LORD God took the man and put him in the garden of Eden to work it and keep it. *(Some kind of work is necessary to be happy. Lazy people would not enjoy even the garden of Eden itself. A perfect man is a working man.)*

16 And the LORD God commanded the man, saying, "You may surely eat of every tree in the garden, 17 but of the tree of the knowledge of good and evil you shall not eat, for in the day that you eat of it you shall surely die."

This was an easy restriction. Only one tree out of thousands was denied him as a test of his obedience. The Lord's commandments are not harsh.

18 Then the LORD God said, "It is not good that the man should be alone; I will make him a helper fit for him."

---

[8] Isaiah 54:5

[9] We believe this is a quote from Bishop Joseph Hall (1574-1656).

Before Adam knew that he wanted a companion, his tender Creator knew it and had already decided to provide him one. The Lord looks into the future and his grace supplies our needs in advance.

²¹ So the LORD God caused a deep sleep to fall upon the man, and while he slept took one of his ribs and closed up its place with flesh. ²² And the rib that the LORD God had taken from the man he made into a woman and brought her to the man. ²³ Then the man said,

"This at last is bone of my bones
    and flesh of my flesh;
she shall be called Woman,
    because she was taken out of Man."

We should love our mother, our wife, our sister, and our aunt very much. These dear women add very much to our happiness. Boys and young men should always treat women with tender respect.

²⁴ Therefore a man shall leave his father and his mother and hold fast to his wife, and they shall become one flesh. ²⁵ And the man and his wife were both naked and were not ashamed.

We should never be proud of our clothes, because it is our imperfection that makes us need them. They prove that we are sinful, because we are ashamed to be seen without them on. May Jesus clothe us with his glorious righteousness.

Bishop Joseph Hall (1574-1656)

January 5
Jesus Christ is Lord[10]

Our last reading showed us man fresh from the hand of his Maker. It will be good to pause and consider the Lord's goodness to the human race. We cannot find a more suitable passage for today's reading than David's joyful and classic hymn.

Psalm 8

1 O LORD, our Lord,
    how majestic is your name in all the earth!
  You have set your glory above the heavens.
2   Out of the mouth of babes and infants,
  you have established strength because of your foes,
    to still the enemy and the avenger.

It is a part of the excellence and glory of God that he glorifies himself by using seemingly unimportant little ones. Though his name is excellent in all the earth, even babies may praise it. Though his glory is above the heavens, infants may declare it. It requires a great speaker to convince people to admire a questionable man; but the Lord

---

[10] Philippians 2:11

is so much more glorious, that even a child's tongue is enough to confuse his enemies and delight his friends.

3 When I look at your heavens, the work of your fingers,
    the moon and the stars, which you have set in place,
4 what is man that you are mindful of him,
    and the son of man that you care for him?

The heavens are so infinite and man is so small. The moon is so bright and man is so dull. The stars are so glorious and man is so insignificant. Lord, how can you stoop from the magnificence of heaven to visit such a nothing as man? The study of astronomy humbles the mind as well as expands it. Examining the heavens should excite adoring gratitude when we see how generous the Lord's love is to such insignificant creatures as ourselves.

5 Yet you have made him a little lower than the heavenly beings
    and crowned him with glory and honor.

Since man is mortal and angels are immortal, man is a little lower than they are right now. But in the future that will change when we are crowned with glory and honor. Then it shall be seen that angels are actually servants to the saints and that all creatures work for their benefit.

6 You have given him dominion over the works of your hands;
    you have put all things under his feet,
7 all sheep and oxen,
    and also the beasts of the field,
8 the birds of the heavens; the fish of the sea,
    whatever passes along the paths of the seas.

Mankind either tames these creatures or uses them for food. They all fear humans. Their power over the animal kingdom is less because of the fall, yet we still walk among the inferior animals with something of that awe, which, as a poet said, "doth hedge a king."[11] In Adam's innocence, his rule of the animal kingdom was no doubt complete and delightful. One imagines him leaning on a lion, while a fawn frisks at the side of Eve. In the Lord Jesus, however, we see humans given the highest place of honor. We know that the situation of our Lord Jesus represents the situation of all his people, because he is the Head and we make up his body. In Jesus we are indeed "crowned…with glory and honor."[12] It is both our duty and our privilege to rise above all things of earth. We must be careful to keep the world under our feet and animals in their proper place. Let none of us allow having pets to become a snare to us. We are to reign over them. We must not allow them to reign over us.

9 O LORD, our Lord,
    how majestic is your name in all the earth!

*"Lord, what is man, or all his race,
    Who dwell so far below,
That you should visit him with grace,
    And love his nature so?*

*That your eternal Son should bear
    To take a mortal form,
Made lower than his angels are,
    To save a dying worm?*

*Let him be crowned with majesty
    Who bowed his head to death;
And be his honors sounded high
    By all things that have breath."[13]*

---

[11] William Shakespeare's *Hamlet*

[12] Hebrews 2:7
[13] From Dr. Watts Psalms and Hymns.

Dr. Isaac Watts (1674-1748)

January 6
Rest in the LORD[14]

We have grouped together a few of the texts that refer to the Sabbath, so that we may cover the subject in one reading. In the history of the creation, the sacred day of rest is established.

Genesis 2:1-3

[1] Thus the heavens and the earth were finished, and all the host of them. [2] And on the seventh day God finished his work that he had done, and he rested on the seventh day from all his work that he had done. [3] So God blessed the seventh day and made it holy, because on it God rested from all his work that he had done in creation.

This ancient tradition was repeated at the giving of the Law on Mount Sinai. Therefore it has the same sacred approval as any of the other Ten Commandments.

Exodus 20:8-11

[8] "Remember the Sabbath day, to keep it holy. [9] Six days you shall labor and do all your work, [10] but the seventh day is a Sabbath to the LORD your God. On it you shall not do any work, you, or your son, or your daughter, your male servant, or your female servant, or your livestock, or the sojourner who is within your gates. [11] For in six days the LORD made heaven and earth, the sea, and all that is in them, and rested the seventh day. Therefore the LORD blessed the Sabbath day and made it holy."

We are not, however, to think that this law forbids us from doing works of love, kindness, or necessity. Our Lord Jesus has given us full liberty on these points. He corrected Jewish error and taught us not to make the day of rest a day of slavery.

Mark 2:23-28

[23] One Sabbath [Jesus] was going through the grainfields, and as they made their way, his disciples began to pluck heads of grain. [24] And the Pharisees were saying to him, "Look, why are they doing what is not lawful on the Sabbath?" [25] And he said to them, "Have your never read what David did, when he was in need and was hungry, he and those who were with him: [26] how he entered the house of God, in the time of Abiathar the high priest, and ate the bread of the Presence, which it is not lawful for any but the priests to eat, and also gave it to those who were with him?" [27] And he said to them, "The Sabbath was made for man, not man for the Sabbath. [28] So the Son of Man is lord even of the Sabbath."

Our Lord performed many of his most impressive cures on the Sabbath, as if to show that the day was especially made to glorify God by helping mankind. If at one time more than another the healing goodness flows freely from our Lord, it is on that one day in seven that is reserved for holy uses. It is called "the Lord's day."[15] In the passage that we are about to read he shows how right it is for a holy day to be crowned with holy deeds of mercy and love.

Luke 14:1-5

[1] One Sabbath, when he went to dine at the house of a ruler of the Pharisees, they were watching him carefully. [2] And behold, there

---

[14] Psalm 37:7 NASB (ESV - "Be Silent Before the LORD")

[15] Revelation 1:10a, "I, John,... was in the Spirit on the Lord's day."

was a man before him who had dropsy.[16] ³And Jesus responded to the lawyers and Pharisees, saying, "Is it lawful to heal on the Sabbath, or not?" ⁴But they remained silent. Then he took him and healed him and sent him away. ⁵And he said to them, "Which of you, having a son or an ox that has fallen into a well on a Sabbath day, will not immediately pull him out?"

January 7
The Wages of Sin is Death[17]

Today's reading of Scripture includes the sad story of the Fall. This is the story of how we all fell through the sin of our first parents, Adam and Eve.

Genesis 3:1-19

¹Now the serpent was more crafty than any other beast of the field that the LORD God had made.

He said to the woman, "Did God actually say, 'You shall not eat of any tree in the garden'?" *(The devil often begins as if he were just curious about something.)* ²And the woman said to the serpent, "We may eat of the fruit of the trees in the garden, ³but God said, 'You shall not eat of the fruit of the tree that is in the midst of the garden, neither shall you touch it, lest you die.'" *(Eve should have been more precise. God did not say, "lest you die," but "you shall surely die." Error begins with little changes in the truth.)* ⁴But the serpent said to the woman, "You will not surely die. ⁵For God knows that when you eat of it your eyes will be opened, and you will be like God, knowing good and evil." *(Satan cruelly lies about God. He hints that God was afraid that man would grow too great.)*

⁶So when the woman saw that the tree was good for food, and that it was a delight to the eyes, and that the tree was to be desired to make one wise, she took of its fruit and ate, and she also gave some to her husband who was with her, and he ate. *(Notice how sin grows. She listened, she saw, she took, she gave to Adam. If Eve had acted wisely, she would have immediately turned and walked away.)* ⁷Then the eyes of both were opened, and they knew that they were naked. And they sewed fig leaves together and made themselves loincloths.

⁸And they heard the sound of the LORD God walking in the garden in the cool of the day, and the man and his wife hid themselves from the presence of the LORD God among the trees of the garden. ⁹But the LORD God called to the man and said to him, "Where are you?" ¹⁰And he said, "I heard the sound of you in the garden, and I was afraid, because I was naked, and I hid myself." ¹¹He said, "Who told you that you were naked? Have you eaten of the tree of which I commanded you not to eat?" ¹²The man said, "The woman whom you gave to be with me, she gave me fruit of the tree, and I ate." *(He throws the blame on God for giving him a wife. How sad! What miserable ungratefulness.)* ¹³Then the LORD God said to the woman, "What is this that you have done?" The woman said, "The serpent deceived me, and I ate." *(Sinners are ready with excuses and yet they never have a good one. Openly confessing our wrong is far better.)*

¹⁴ The LORD God said to the serpent,
"Because you have done this,
  cursed are you above all livestock
  and above all beasts of the field;
on your belly you shall go
  and dust you shall eat
  all the days of your life.
¹⁵ I will put enmity between you and the woman,
  and between your offspring and her offspring;
he shall bruise your head,
  and you shall bruise his heel."

We find a blessed promise here, like a pearl in a shell. The curse on the serpent is a blessing for us, because it includes a prophesy about Jesus our Savior.

¹⁶ To the woman he said,
"I will surely multiply your pain in childbearing;
  in pain you shall bring forth children.

---

[16] *dropsy* or *edema* - a condition characterized by an excess of watery fluid collecting in the cavities or tissues of the body.
[17] Romans 6:23

Your desire shall be contrary to your
husband,
and he shall rule over you."

17 And to Adam he said,

"Because you have listened to the voice
of your wife
and have eaten of the tree
of which I commanded you,
'You shall not eat of it,'
cursed is the ground because of you;
in pain you shall eat of it all the days of
your life;"

Notice that the curse falls indirectly. God harms the ground rather than man. God's mercy is indeed wonderful.

18 "thorns and thistles it shall bring forth for
you;
and you shall eat the plants of the field.

19 By the sweat of your face
you shall eat bread,
till you return to the ground
for out of it you were taken;
for you are dust,
and to dust you shall return."

Therefore, "sin when it is fully grown brings forth death."[18]

January 8
The LORD is Our Righteousness[19]

The New Testament is the key to the Old. We find in it an explanation of the position of Adam in relation to all mankind. He represented all of us and we all share the sad effects of his transgression. He was the door through which both sin and death entered into our world. The apostle Paul teaches us this in:

Romans 5:12-21

12 Therefore, just as sin came into the world through one man, and death through sin, and so death spread to all men because all sinned— *(All have sinned in Adam who represented them, and therefore all die.)* **13** for sin indeed was in the world before the law was given, but sin is not counted where there is no law. **14** Yet death reigned from Adam to Moses, *(It is clear that there was sin in the world before the law was given because people died—that sin came as a result of the fall.)* even over those whose sinning was not like the transgression of Adam, *(even infants die through Adam's sin though without personal guilt.)* [Adam] was a type of the one who was to come. *(Jesus is the second head of the race, the second representative man. As we fell by our union with Adam, so if we are in Christ we shall rise because of our union with the Lord Jesus. He is, "the one who was to come." He is the Head and Leader of a believing people. The great question is, are we believers in him?)*

15 But the free gift is not like the trespass. For if many died through one man's trespass, much more have the grace of God and the free gift by the grace of that one man Jesus Christ abounded for many. *(Salvation is not given to us because we deserve it. It is a free gift. God's grace outruns human sin. The apostle speaks of "much more," as if he meant, more likely, more easily, more abundantly. It was God's strange work*[20] *when he condemned the race for Adam's sin, but it is his delight to accept people for the benefit of his dear Son.)*

16 And the free gift is not like the result of that one man's sin. For the judgment following one trespass brought condemnation, but the free gift following many trespasses brought justification. *(One sin destroyed us, but grace covers over many sins.)* **17** If, because of one man's trespass, death reigned through that one man, much more will those who receive the abundance of grace and the free gift of righteousness reign in the life through the one man Jesus Christ. *(We were ruined by one man's sin. We are restored by one man's righteousness. The victory will be greater than the defeat.)*

18 Therefore, as one trespass led to condemnation for all men, [so also through

---

[18] James 1:15
[19] Jeremiah 23:6

[20] *Strange Work.* This is a reference to Isaiah 28:21. God's work of judgment is called *strange* or *alien* because it is his nature to extend grace and mercy. However, he "will by no means clear the guilty (Exodus 34:7).

the obedience of the One will the many be made righteous.][21]

All fell by Adam. All who are in Christ are restored by Christ.

19 For as by the one man's disobedience the many were made sinners, so by the one man's obedience the many will be made righteous.

This is the basic and core teaching of the gospel. Jesus makes us righteous because he is righteous. God the Father accepts us because his Son is righteous.

20 Now the law came in to increase the trespass. *(The law of Moses makes us aware of sin. It shows us our evil thoughts and actions. The blessed Holy Spirit uses the law to drive us away from believing that we, by ourselves and by our own strength, can keep the law. He compels us to look to the grace of God in Christ Jesus.)* But where sin increased, grace abounded all the more, *(The floods of grace win out over the mountains of our sins. Almighty love paints a rainbow on the blackest clouds of human sin.)* **21** so that, as sin reigned in death, grace also might reign through righteousness leading to eternal life through Jesus Christ our Lord.

Happy are those who have been given grace and have spiritual life growing within them. That same grace will strengthen, increase, and perfect that life until it is glorified in heaven. Are all the members of this family saved in Christ Jesus? Every one of you should think seriously about the answer to that question. Let us all agree about this and follow the Lord together. And, may we all meet in heaven.

January 9
Lord, Save Me[22]

Our last reading taught us our own connection with Adam's fall. We will now give careful consideration to a passage of Scripture that shows the depravity[23] of human nature flowing throughout all times and all places.

Romans 3:9-26

In this portion Paul quotes the words of several Old Testament authors, puts them all together, and presents them to us as a terrible, but accurate, description of fallen man. The Jews loved to brag about their ancestry. The apostle asks the question,

9 What then? Are we Jews any better off? No, not at all. For we have already charged that all, both Jews and Greeks, are under sin. *(As an old commentator puts it, "whole evil is in man, and whole man in evil."[24])* **10** As it is written;

"None is righteous, no, not one;
11 no one understands;
no one seeks for God."

Paul begins by quoting David in Psalm 14 and applying his words to the whole human race. Whether Jew or Greek, human nature is always the same. There is no hope of finding anyone who is naturally righteousness.

12 All have turned aside; together they have become worthless;
no one does good,
not even one."[25]
13 "Their throat is an open grave;
they use their tongues to deceive."[26]
"The venom of asps is under their lips."[27]
14 "Their mouth is full of curses and bitterness."[28]
15 "Their feet are swift to shed blood.
16 in their paths are ruin and misery,
17 and the way of peace they have not known."[29]
18 "There is no fear of God before their eyes."[30]

Notice that in our character and nature, the disease of sin has affected us. We are sinful in every way; inside and outside, in mouth, feet, heart and eyes. We may not have committed all the evils mentioned here,

---

[21] William Hendriksen's translation was used here. ESV reads, "so one act of righteousness leads to justification and life for all men." - *editor*
[22] Matthew 14:30
[23] *depravity* - sinfulness

[24] John Trapp (circa 1656)
[25] Psalm 14:1-3
[26] Psalm 5:9
[27] Psalm 140:3
[28] Psalm 10:7
[29] Proverbs 1:16' 3:15-17
[30] Psalm 36:1

but they are all in our nature. Our situation and our education may prevent us from being as bad in practice as we are in our heart, but as the poison is in the snake even though it does not bite, so sin is always with us.

What bloodstained sins these are that infect us! How divinely powerful must the medicine be that can cure us from such deadly diseases.

After this charge against human nature, there follows a declaration that no one can be saved by the works of the law, because everyone is already guilty. The evidence of their guilt and damnation is already made clear in the book of the law.

19 Now we know that whatever the law says it speaks to those who are under the law, so that every mouth may be stopped, and the whole world may be held accountable to God. **20** For by works of the law no human being will be justified in his sight, since through the law comes knowledge of sin. *(We use the law correctly when it convinces us of sin and forces us to the Savior. However, we completely abuse and distort the law if we hope to be saved by obeying it.)*

21 But now the righteousness of God has been manifested apart from the law although the Law and the Prophets bear witness to it— **22** the righteousness of God through faith in Jesus Christ for all who believe. For there is no distinction.

There is no difference. All are guilty. It is impossible for anyone to be worthy of salvation. Justification by faith is the only way.

23 For all have sinned and fall short of the glory of God, **24** and are justified by his grace as a gift, through the redemption that is in Christ Jesus, **25** whom God put forward as a propitiation by his blood, to be received by faith. This was to show God's righteousness, because in his divine forbearance he had passed over former sins. **26** It was to show his righteousness at the present time, so that he might be just and the justifier of the one who has faith in Jesus.

What a precious gospel verse. May every member of this family understand it and have a part in the substitution of the Lord Jesus. We are all fallen. May every one of us be justified freely by God's grace through faith in the blood of the Lord Jesus. Let us sincerely pray to be cleansed by the atoning death of Jesus, who suffered the curse of the law for his people.

John Trapp (1601-1669)
English Anglican Bible Commentator

January 10
Love is from God[31]

Genesis 4:1-15

1 Now Adam knew Eve his wife, and she conceived and bore Cain, saying, "I have gotten a man with the help of the LORD." *(She probably hoped that this was the Messiah. Oh, how often parents' hopes are not realized. It was not a man after the heart of God to whom Eve gave birth, but a man of sin, a child of the wicked one.)*

2 And again, she bore his brother Abel. *(Abel means "Vain" or "Unsatisfactory." Evidently, Eve did not value him much, but he was precious in the sight of the Lord. What mistakes we make about our children.)* Now Abel was a keeper of sheep, and Cain a

---

[31] I John 4:7

worker of the ground. ³ In the course of time Cain brought to the LORD an offering of the fruit of the ground, ⁴ and Abel also brought of the firstborn of his flock and of their fat portions. And the LORD had regard for Abel and his offering, ⁵ but for Cain and his offering he had no regard. *(Cain had no faith and no concern for the blood of atonement. Abel had both. These should be the main concerns of our Christian activities.)* So Cain was very angry, and his face fell. *(Cain was not angry with himself, as he should have been, but with his brother and with God.)*

⁶ The LORD said to Cain, "Why are you angry, and why has your face fallen? ⁷ If you do well, will you not be accepted? And if you do not do well, sin is crouching at the door. Its desire is contrary to you, but you must rule over it." *(It is sin that stands in the way of our fellowship with God.)*

⁸ Cain spoke to Abel his brother. And when they were in the field, Cain rose up against his brother Abel and killed him. ⁹ Then the LORD said to Cain, "Where is Abel your brother?" He said, "I do not know; am I my brother's keeper?" *(We will either be our brother's keeper or our brother's murderer. If we do not work to save others, we will be guilty of their blood.)* ¹⁰ And the LORD said, "What have you done? The voice of your brother's blood is crying to me from the ground. ¹¹ And now you are cursed from the ground, which has opened its mouth to receive your brother's blood from your hand. ¹² When you work the ground, it shall no longer yield to you its strength. You shall be a fugitive and a wanderer on the earth."

¹³ Cain said to the LORD, "My punishment is greater than I can bear." *(Cain does not confess his sin. He only complains about his punishment. We know many who think the same way. They object to hell and stubbornly continue in sin.)* ¹⁴ "Behold, you have driven me today away from the ground, and from your face I shall be hidden. I shall be a fugitive and wanderer on the earth, and whoever finds me will kill me." ¹⁵ Then the LORD said to him, "Not so! If anyone kills Cain, vengeance shall be taken on him sevenfold." And the LORD put a mark on Cain, lest any who found him should attack him.

This ancient story of the first murder is used by the apostle John as a picture of the life of unbelievers in all ages. Love marks the children of God, but hate is the sure sign of those who will inherit the wrath of God. The beloved apostle writes:

1 John 3:10-15

¹⁰ By this it is evident who are the children of God, and who are the children of the devil: whoever does not practice righteousness is not of God, nor is the one who does not love his brother.

¹¹ For this is the message that you have heard from the beginning, that we should love one another. ¹² We should not be like Cain, who was of the evil one and murdered his brother. And why did he murder him? Because his own deeds were evil and his brother's righteous. ¹³ Do not be surprised, brothers, that the world hates you. ¹⁴ We know that we have passed out of death into life, because we love the brothers. Whoever does not love abides in death. ¹⁵ Everyone who hates his brother is a murderer, and you know that no murderer has eternal life abiding in him.

Oh for grace to remove from our hearts all anger, envy, desire for revenge, and bitterness of every kind. Oh for grace to be like Jesus who is full of love and gentleness.

January 11

Abide in Me[32]

Our reading leads us to think about that famous saint of the church who lived before the Great Flood of Noah's day. Enoch, the great-great-great-great-grandson of Adam.

Genesis 5:21-24

²¹ When Enoch had lived 65 years he fathered Methuselah. ²² Enoch walked with God after he fathered Methuselah 300 years and had other sons and daughters. ²³ Thus all the days of Enoch were 365 years. ²⁴ Enoch walked with God, and he was not, for God took him.

---

[32] John 15:4

It is worth noticing here that the sacred writer says once that Enoch "lived;" but then he changes the word and writes Enoch "walked with God." This teaches us that fellowship with God was the most important thing in Enoch's life. Fellowship with God should also be the most important thing in our lives. Enoch was not a mere talker about God, but a walker with God. This holy patriarch[33] lived in unbroken fellowship with the Lord for three hundred years—not visiting with God now and then, but constantly walking with him. This is not an easy thing to do. To remain in unbroken fellowship, "this is the work, this is the labor."[34] Yet the Holy Spirit can enable us to accomplish even this. Continued fellowship is what we should aim at. We should not be satisfied with anything short of it.

Some excuse themselves from seeking after unbroken fellowship with God because of their job, or their surroundings, or the many things they think need to be done. Enoch had to care for his family and he was also a public preacher. Yet he kept up his walk with God. No business or household cares should make us forget our God. A close relationship with God keeps the saints safe. It is their comfort and delight. It is their honor and crown. Fellowship with God should be desired more "than gold, even much fine gold."[35] Enoch was happy to enjoy it so sweetly and so continuously. The long relationship of this good man with his God ended in his being taken away from earth without dying, to that place where sight outshines faith. He did not live like others and therefore he did not die like others.

Paul[36] tells us a little more concerning this holy man, and we will gather up the pieces of his history that remain in the Bible so that nothing will be lost.

Hebrews 11:5-6

⁵ By faith Enoch was taken up so that he should not see death, and he was not found, because God had taken him. Now before he was taken he was commended as having pleased God. ⁶ And without faith it is impossible to please him, for whoever would draw near to God must believe that he exists and that he rewards those who seek him.

Enoch's fellowship with God came from his faith in God. Works do not make us walk with God, but faith brings us into his presence and keeps us there. It is very likely that Enoch's holy lifestyle did not please others, but that did not matter much to him because it pleased God.

From Jude we learn that Enoch looked for the coming of Christ. The pure in heart see God. They are the truly enlightened people of their generation and look far into the future. What Enoch saw he proclaimed for the warning of others. It is our duty to do the same, so that sinners may be led to flee from the wrath to come.

Jude 14-15

¹⁴ It was also about these that Enoch, the seventh from Adam, prophesied, saying, "Behold, the Lord comes with ten thousands of his holy ones, ¹⁵ to execute judgment on all and to convict all the ungodly of all their deeds of ungodliness that they have committed in such an ungodly way, and of all the harsh things that ungodly sinners have spoken against him."

We know the doctrine of the coming of the Lord from heaven is important, because one of the holiest prophets declared it so early in the world's history. The powerful importance of this truth should be crystal clear. The greatest teachers of the Lord's coming were also among the best known for close fellowship with heaven. Enoch "walked with God," Daniel was a "man greatly loved,"[37] and John was that "disciple whom Jesus loved."[38]

Oh Lord, if the excitement of looking for your coming will make us walk with you, then please fill us with that excitement.

---

[33] patriarch - A man regarded as the father or ruler of a family. Bible patriarchs include Abraham, Isaac, Jacob and Jacob's twelve sons.
[34] This quote (translated from Latin) dates to at least the 16th century.
[35] Psalm 19:10
[36] Although the author of the book of Hebrews is uncertain, many believe it is the apostle Paul.
[37] Daniel 10:11
[38] John 13:23

January 12
The End of All Things is At Hand[39]

At first people lived for hundreds of years, but a few generations of long-lived people was enough to make the human race very wicked. When the holy descendants of Seth intermarried with the graceless race of Cain, the people of God changed for the worse. The salt lost its taste and the whole earth became corrupt.

Genesis 6:5-22

5 The LORD saw that the wickedness of man was great in the earth, and that every intention of the thoughts of his heart was only evil continually. *(What a charge against mankind. It is still true of all of us.)*

6 And the LORD was sorry that he had made man on the earth and it grieved him to his heart. **7** So the LORD said, "I will blot out man whom I have created from the face of the land, man and animals and creeping things and birds of the heavens, for I am sorry that I have made them." **8** But Noah found favor in the eyes of the LORD. *(What a blessed "but" that was. In the midst of wrath, the Lord remembered mercy. Even in punishing sin he remembers Christ and all those who are of his family. The distinction was made as a result of grace. It is not said that Noah deserved to be saved, but that Noah found favor, or grace.)*

9 These are the generations of Noah. Noah was a righteous man, blameless in his generation. Noah walked with God. *(In this he was a worthy descendant of Enoch.)* **10** And Noah had three sons, Shem, Ham and Japheth.

11 Now the earth was corrupt in God's sight, and the earth was filled with violence. *(Those who are corrupt toward God are sure to be violent toward others.)* **12** And God saw the earth, and behold, it was corrupt, for all flesh had corrupted their way on the earth. **13** And God said to Noah, "I have determined to make an end of all flesh, for the earth is filled with violence through them. Behold, I will destroy them with the earth.

14 "Make yourself an ark of gopher wood. Make rooms in the ark, and cover it inside and out with pitch. **15** This is how you are to make it: the length of the ark 300 cubits *(about 450 feet)*, its breadth 50 cubits *(about 75 feet)*, and its height 30 cubits *(about 45 feet)*. *(We must follow God's directions in everything we do. If our religious practices do not have, "Thus says the Lord," written over them, they will be worthless.)* **16** Make a roof for the ark, and finish it to a cubit above, and set the door of the ark in its side. Make it with lower, second, and third decks. *(Noah must make the ark according to God's plan. Those who expect to be saved must receive salvation in God's way. God's word must be our guide, not what we may think is right, or "feels" good.)* **17** For behold, I will bring a flood of waters upon the earth to destroy all flesh in which is the breath of life under heaven. Everything that is on the earth shall die.

18 "But I will establish my covenant with you, and you shall come into the ark, you, your sons, your wife, and sons' wives with you. **19** And of every living thing of all flesh, you shall bring two of every sort into the ark to keep them alive with you. They shall be male and female. **20** Of the birds according to their kinds, and of the animals according to their kinds, of every creeping thing of the ground, according to its kind, two of every sort shall come in to you to keep them alive. *(Noah was the saver of lives. So is Jesus. Noah became the new head of the saved race. Our Lord is the Head of his church, who are those he saved out of the world.)*

21 "Also take with you every sort of food that is eaten, and store it up. It shall serve as food for you and for them." **22** Noah did this; he did all that God commanded him. *(Noah's faith caused him to obey. If we are to be saved from the destruction that is coming on the world, we must submit ourselves without question to the commands of our Lord Jesus. We will not be saved by keeping the commands of God, but if we have true faith we shall prove it by following the Lord's directions.)*

---

[39] I Peter 4:7

JANUARY 13
I Give My Sheep Eternal Life[40]
Genesis 7:1-5

¹ Now the LORD said to Noah, "[Come][41] into the ark, you and all your household, for I have seen that you are righteous before me in this generation. *(When the Lord said, "Come," it implied that he was already in the ark and indicated he would be there with his servant. It is also suggestive of the gospel invitation, "The Spirit and the bride say, 'Come.'"[42])*

² "Take with you seven pairs of all clean animals, the male and his mate, and a pair of the animals that are not clean, the male and his mate, ³ and seven pairs of the birds of the heavens also, male and female, to keep their offspring alive on the face of all the earth. *(Christ is the ark of our salvation, the unclean shall be sheltered as well as the clean. Noah had the privilege to bring them in. Likewise, every believer has the privilege to work for the saving of souls.)*

⁴ "For in seven days I will send rain on the earth forty days and forty nights, and every living thing that I have made I will blot out from the face of the ground." ⁵ And Noah did all that the LORD had commanded him.

Genesis 7:11-23

¹¹ In the six hundredth year of Noah's life, in the second month, on the seventeenth day of the month, on that day all the fountains of the great deep burst forth, and the windows of the heavens were opened. ¹² And rain fell upon the earth forty days and forty nights. ¹³ On the very same day Noah and his sons, Shem and Ham and Japheth, and Noah's wife and the three wives of his sons with them entered the ark, ¹⁴ they and every beast according to its kind, and all the livestock according to their kinds, and every creeping thing that creeps on the earth, according to its kind, and every bird according to its kind, every winged creature. *(It was wonderful that all these creatures willingly entered the ark. It is even more wonderful that sinners of all kinds should be led by sovereign grace to find safety in the Lord Jesus. They must come when grace calls.)*

¹⁵ They went into the ark with Noah, two and two of all flesh in which there was the breath of life. ¹⁶ And those that entered, male and female of all flesh, went in as God had commanded him. And the LORD shut him in. *(What a blessed thing for Noah. Those whom God brings into Christ, he takes care to shut in so that they shall go out no more. God did not shut Adam in paradise; Adam threw himself out. And every one of us would leave Christ, if the Lord had not in mercy closed the door.)*

¹⁷ The flood continued forty days on the earth. The waters increased and bore up the ark, and it rose high above the earth. ¹⁸ The waters prevailed and increased greatly on the earth, and the ark floated on the face of the waters. ¹⁹ And the waters prevailed so mightily on the earth that all the high mountains under the whole heaven were covered. ²⁰ The waters prevailed above the mountains, covering them fifteen cubits *(or over twenty feet)* deep.

It was then too late to enter the ark. Dear friends, may we never put off faith in Jesus until it is too late. It will be an awful thing to find ourselves lost in a flood of wrath, with no eye to pity us and no arm to save us. Yet that is what will happen "if we neglect such a great salvation."[43]

²¹ And all flesh died that moved on the earth, birds, livestock, beasts, all swarming creatures that swarm on the earth, and all mankind. ²² Everything on the dry land in whose nostril was the breath of life died. ²³ He blotted out every living thing that was on the face of the ground, man and animals and creeping things and birds of the heavens. They were blotted out from the earth. Only Noah was left, and those who were with him in the ark. *(As there was no safety outside of the ark, so there is no salvation outside of Christ. The Lord grant that every member of this family may flee to Jesus at once and be saved by faith in him.)*

---

[40] From John 10:28
[41] New King James & King James read, "Come." ESV reads, "Go". The Hebrew means "*to go in, enter, come, go.*" - *Vine's Complete Expository Dictionary*
[42] Revelation 22:17
[43] Hebrews 2:3

January 14
My God, My Rock, In Whom I Take Refuge[44]

Our last reading showed us Noah saved while the whole world drowned. Let us now think about the special protection the Lord gives to his own people. The psalmist sings about this so sweetly in:

Psalm 91

1 He who dwells in the shelter of the Most High
   will abide in the shadow of the Almighty.

When a soul is brought into sweet fellowship with God, through the blood of Jesus, its real dangers are all over. It is and must be, safe forever. Noah was protected the moment he entered the ark, and we are too, as soon as we are in Christ.

2 I will say to the LORD, "My refuge and my fortress,
   my God, in whom I trust."
3 For he will deliver you from the snare of the fowler
   and from the deadly pestilence.
4 He will cover you with his pinions,
   and under his wings you will find refuge;
   his faithfulness is a shield and buckler.

What a picture of tenderness. Like the little birds, we hide underneath the wings of God.

5 You will not fear the terror of the night,
   nor the arrow that flies by day,
6 nor the pestilence that stalks in darkness,
   nor the destruction that wastes at noonday.

Some dangers are obvious. Other evils are hidden. God's people are protected from both. There are some false religions that would, if it were possible, mislead even the very elect. But the elect shall not be fooled, because the Lord keeps them safe.

7 A thousand may fall at your side,
   ten thousand at your right hand,
   but it will not come near you.
8 You will only look with your eyes
   and see the recompense of the wicked.

Noah saw the ungodly world destroyed. No doubt, this led him to be even more committed to praise God for the grace that had rescued him from the same sin and resulting destruction.

9 Because you have made the LORD your dwelling place—
   the Most High, who is my refuge—
10 no evil shall be allowed to befall you,
    no plague come near your tent.
11 For he will command his angels concerning you
    to guard you in all your ways.
12 On their hands they will bear you up,
    lest you strike your foot against a stone,
13 You will tread on the lion and the adder;
    the young lion and the serpent you will trample underfoot.

Those who want to see us destroyed will be overthrown. Their power and cleverness will not bring about our defeat.

14 "Because he holds fast to me in love, I will deliver him;
    I will protect him, because he knows my name.
15 When he calls to me, I will answer him;
    I will be with him in trouble;
    I will rescue him and honor him."

We will experience trouble in this life. There is no getting away from that. But prayer is the answer every time! It will bring the right assistance for every danger. When we conquer the trials we meet, we honor the Lord who helps us through them. There is also honor given to believers who remain faithful during times of trouble.

16 "With long life I will satisfy him
    and show him my salvation."

God's righteous saints may live many years or few, but how long we live is not what matters. The good we achieve and the fellowship with God we enjoy are what are most important.

As a family, let us thank God for protecting us from serious illness, from sudden death, and from fatal accidents. God has promised to be involved in our lives. The privilege of coming to God in prayer and the promise of being accepted by him when we do are two of the most precious things he has given us.

---
[44] 2 Samuel 22:3

If we are really God's children, then a guard of angels is hovering over us right now. We may rest assured that whatever dangers are near us, we are kept safe under the wings of God. Therefore, as Christians, we should be very calm in difficult times, and show by our holy courage that we have a definite reason for our confidence.

Parents, keep this psalm in your hearts. Children and young people, treasure it in your memories. It is more precious "than gold, even much fine gold."[45]

January 15
Return, O My Soul, To Your Rest[46]
Genesis 8:1-12, 15-22

[1] But God remembered Noah and all the beasts and all the livestock that were with him in the ark. *(The Lord did not forget the ones saved in the ark. First, he remembered Noah, and then those who were with him. The Lord remembers his dear Son, and then us because of him.)* And God made a wind blow over the earth, and the waters subsided. [2] The fountains of the deep and the windows of the heavens were closed, the rain from the heavens was restrained, *(How easily are all things arranged by the Lord's providence.[47] Winds and waters move at his command, whether for the deliverance of his people or for the destruction of his foes.)* [3] and the waters receded from the earth continually. At the end of 150 days the waters had abated, [4] and in the seventh month, on the seventeenth day of the month, the ark came to rest on the mountains of Ararat. [5] And the waters continued to abate until the tenth month; in the tenth month, on the first day of the month, the tops of the mountains were seen.

[6] At the end of forty days Noah opened the window of the ark that he had made [7] and sent forth a raven. It went to and fro until the waters were dried up from the earth. *(This disgusting bird delighted in the decaying flesh of dead animals it found floating in the water, just as wicked men find delight in sin.)* [8] Then he sent forth a dove from him, to see if the waters had subsided from the face of the ground. [9] But the dove found no place to set her foot, and she returned to him to the ark, for the waters were still on the face of the whole earth. So he put out his hand and took her and brought her into the ark with him. *(The dove is like our worn out souls. After being saved by grace, they find no contentment in polluted things, but return to Jesus, who is their peace. He graciously draws us to himself when we are too weak to come on our own.)*

[10] He waited another seven days, and again he sent forth the dove out of the ark. [11] And the dove came back to him in the evening, and behold, in her mouth was a freshly plucked olive leaf. So Noah knew that the waters had subsided from the earth. [12] Then he waited another seven days and sent forth the dove, and she did not return to him anymore. *(Surrounded by the new and restored world the dove could live at liberty. In much the same way, born again souls flourish when they are surrounded by holy things.)*

[15] Then God said to Noah, [16] "Go out from the ark, you and your wife, and your sons and your sons' wives with you. [17] Bring out with you every living thing that is with you of all flesh—birds and animals and every creeping thing that creeps on the earth—that they may swarm on the earth, and be fruitful and multiply on the earth." [18] So Noah went out, and his sons and his wife and his sons' wives with him. *(He did not come out of the ark until he was instructed to do so by the same voice that called him into it. "The steps of a man are established by the LORD, when he delights in his way"[48])* [19] Every beast, every creeping thing, and every bird, everything that moves on the earth, went out by families from the ark.

[20] Then Noah built an altar to the LORD and took some of every clean animal and some of every clean bird and offered burnt offerings on the altar. *(Before he built a house he built*

---

[45] Psalm 19:10
[46] Psalm 116:7
[47] *Providence* - Usually, when used with a capital "P" it refers to God; when used with a lower case "p", it refers to God's will, his divine intervention, and his predetermination (predestination).

[48] Psalm 37:23

an altar. God must be worshiped first in all things.) **21** And when the LORD smelled the pleasing aroma, the LORD said in his heart, "I will never again curse the ground because of man, for the intention of man's heart is evil from his youth. Neither will I ever again strike down every living creature as I have done. **22** While the earth remains, seedtime and harvest, cold and heat, summer and winter, day and night, shall not cease."

Noah's sacrifice was pleasing to the Lord and the beginning of a new covenant.[49] The offering of the Lord Jesus on the cross will always be "a pleasing aroma," and for his sake the covenant of grace is made with all those who are saved. Are all of us a part of the covenant of grace?

January 16
He Remembers His Covenant Forever[50]

In this passage we have more details about the gracious promise God made to Noah and his descendants.

Genesis 9:8-17

8 Then God said to Noah and to his sons with him, **9** "Behold, I establish my covenant with you and your offspring after you, **10** and with every living creature that is with you, the birds, the livestock, and every beast of the earth with you, as many as came out of the ark; it is for every beast of the earth. **11** I establish my covenant with you that never again shall all flesh be cut off by the waters of the flood, and never again shall there be a flood to destroy the earth."

To those who have been saved in Christ no future destruction is possible. They are forever safe from the floods of wrath.

12 And God said, "This is the sign of the covenant that I make between me and you and every living creature that is with you, for all future generations. **13** I have set my bow in the cloud, and it shall be a sign of the covenant between me and the earth. **14** When I bring clouds over the earth and the bow is seen in the clouds, *(The sign of the promise is seen in cloudy times when faith needs a reminder of the Lord's faithfulness the most. If there is no cloud, there is no rainbow. It is worth having a cloud to have God paint a rainbow on it.)* **15** I will remember my covenant that is between me and you and every living creature of all flesh. And the waters shall never again become a flood to destroy all flesh. **16** When the bow is in the clouds, I will see it," *(This is better than seeing it ourselves, because God will never see it with forgetful eyes.)* "and remember the everlasting covenant between God and every living creature of all flesh that is on the earth." **17** God said to Noah, "This is the sign of the covenant that I have established between me and all flesh that is on the earth."

God made the rainbow to be a lovely symbol of his truthfulness. It is a bow unstrung, because war is over. It is a bow without a string, because it will never be used against us. It is a bow turned upward, so that we may direct our thoughts and prayers to heaven. It is a rainbow of bright colors, because joy and peace are revealed by it. Blessed arch of beauty, always be the Lord's preacher to us.

We will now turn to a passage in the prophets where the promise of God's grace is linked with this rainbow.

Isaiah 54:4-10

4 "Fear not, for you will not be ashamed,
    be not confounded, for you will not be disgraced;
  for you will forget the shame of your youth,
    and the reproach of your widowhood you will remember no more.
5 For your Maker is your husband,
    the LORD of hosts is his name;
  and the Holy One of Israel is your Redeemer,
    the God of the whole earth he is called.
6 For the LORD has called you
    like a wife deserted and grieved in spirit,
  like a wife of youth when she is cast off,
    says your God.
7 For a brief moment I deserted you,
    but with great compassion I will gather you.

---
[49] *covenant* - A promise, guarantee, pledge
[50] Psalm 111:5

⁸ In overflowing anger for a moment
  I hid my face from you,
 but with everlasting love I will have
  compassion on you,"
  says the LORD, your Redeemer.
⁹ "This is like the days of Noah to me;
  as I swore that the waters of Noah
   should no more go over the earth,
 so I have sworn that I will not be angry
  with you,
  and will not rebuke you.
¹⁰ For the mountains may depart
  and the hills be removed,
 but my steadfast love shall not depart
  from you,
  and my covenant of peace shall not be
   removed,"
  says the LORD, who has compassion on
   you.

From this time on, let us be ashamed to doubt the Lord. These trustworthy signs should give us an overwhelming confidence in the faithfulness of our unchangeable God. Only let us make sure that we are exercising true faith in Him.

January 17
The LORD Reigns[51]

Genesis 11:1-9

¹ Now the whole earth had one language and the same words. ² And as people migrated from the east, they found a plain in the land of Shinar and settled there. ³ And they said to one another, "Come, let us make bricks, and burn them thoroughly." And they had brick for stone, and bitumen[52] for mortar. ⁴ Then they said, "Come, let us build ourselves a city and a tower with its top in the heavens, and let us make a name for ourselves, lest we be dispersed over the face of the whole earth." *(They wanted to establish one huge government and make this tower the center of it. Their intention was that the tower would keep the people from being scattered abroad. They had forgotten the command to, "be fruitful and multiply and fill the earth."[53] Ambition was at the heart of the plan. They hoped to build up an empire by centralizing all mankind that, like their tower, would defy heaven itself.)*

⁵ And the LORD came down to see the city and the tower, which the children of man had built.

To God their huge tower was a mere nothing. He is said (to use the language of man) to come down from heaven in order to see such a trifle.

⁶ And the LORD said, "Behold, they are one people, and they have all one language, and this is only the beginning of what they will do. And nothing that they propose to do will now be impossible for them. ⁷ Come, let us go down and there confuse their language, so that they may not understand one another's speech." ⁸ So the LORD dispersed them from there over the face of all the earth, and they left off building the city.

How easy it is for to God frustrate our plans and bring about his own purposes, despite any opposition. What happened the moment God "confused their language"? The scene has been very graphically sketched by Bishop Hall.[54] "One calls for brick, the other looks him in the face, and wonders what he commands, and how and why he speaks such words as were never before heard. Instead of brick he brings him mortar with a reply to him as little understood. Each scolds the other, expressing his anger in words only he can understand. From argument they fall to quiet requests, but still with the same success. At first every man thinks his fellow mocks him; but now aware of this serious confusion, their only answer was silence, and ceasing. They could not come together, for no man could call them to be understood; and if they had assembled, nothing could be determined, because one could never understand the other's purpose."

⁹ Therefore its name was called Babel,[55] because there the LORD confused the language of all the earth. And from there the LORD dispersed them over the face of all the earth.

---

[51] Psalm 99:1
[52] A black, sticky tar-like substance.
[53] Genesis 1:28

[54] Probably Anglican Bishop Joseph Hall (circa 1600).
[55] Babel sounds like the Hebrew word for confused

An appropriate comment on the events at Babel can be found in part of Psalm 33.

Psalm 33:10-22

10 The LORD brings the counsel of the nations to nothing;
  he frustrates the plans of the peoples.
11 The counsel of the LORD stands forever,
  the plans of his heart to all generations.
12 Blessed is the nation whose God is the LORD,
  the people whom he has chosen as his heritage!
13 The LORD looks down from heaven;
  he sees all the children of man;
14 from where he sits enthroned he looks out
  on all the inhabitants of the earth,
15 he who fashions the hearts of them all
  and observes all their deeds.
16 The king is not saved by his great army;
  a warrior is not delivered by his great strength.
17 The war horse is a false hope for salvation,
  and by its great might it cannot rescue.
18 Behold, the eye of the LORD is on those who fear him,
  on those who hope in his steadfast love,
19 that he may deliver their soul from death
  and keep them alive in famine.
20 Our soul waits for the LORD;
  he is our help and our shield.
21 For our heart is glad in him,
  because we trust in his holy name.
22 Let your steadfast love, O LORD, be upon us,
  even as we hope in you.

Our hope should not be in a tower of Babel or in ourselves. Let us depend on the Lord our God who is our tower of protection.

January 18
I Am a Sojourner with You[56]

Genesis 12:1-8

1 Now the LORD said to Abram, "Go from your country and your kindred and your father's house to the land that I will show you. 2 And I will make of you a great nation, and I will bless you and make your name great, so that you will be a blessing. 3 I will bless those who bless you, and him who dishonors you I will curse, and in you all the families of the earth shall be blessed."

God elected Abram. Therefore in due time he called him and separated him to himself. All of God's chosen must also be like their spiritual father Abram and be separated from the world and dedicated to the Lord.[57] All of his chosen spiritual descendants must follow in the same path as the father of the faithful.

4 So Abram went, as the LORD had told him, and Lot went with him. Abram was seventy-five years old when he departed from Haran. *(The same grace that chose him made him obedient. There was only one way for Abram to inherit this blessing. He followed the divine command and left everything. He turned his back on his past life and cheerfully followed his Lord.)* 5 And Abram took Sarai his wife, and Lot his brother's son, and all their possessions that they had gathered, and the people that they had acquired in Haran, and they set out to go to the land of Canaan. *(It is not enough to begin the journey, we must continue to the end.)*

6 Abram passed through the land to the place at Shechem, to the oak of Moreh. At that time the Canaanites were in the land. *(The Lord promised to give the land to the patriarch,[58] but Abram did not actually own a single foot of it. Unbelief would have thought this inheritance was more shadow than real; but "faith is the assurance of things hoped for,"[59] and makes us content to wait. The Canaanite is still in the land, yet we are correct to believe that all things are ours.)*

7 Then the LORD appeared to Abram and said, "To your offspring I will give this land." So he built there an altar to the LORD, who had appeared to him. 8 From there he

---

[56] Psalm 39:12
[57] 2 Corinthians 6:16a, 17a, "What agreement has the temple of God with idols? For we are the temple of the living God. ... 'Therefore go out from their midst, and be separate from them, says the Lord.'"
[58] *patriarch* - A man regarded as the father or ruler of a family. Bible patriarchs include Abraham, Isaac, Jacob and Jacob's twelve sons.
[59] Hebrews 11:1

moved to the hill country on the east of Bethel and pitched his tent, with Bethel on the west and Ai on the east. And there he built an altar to the LORD and called upon the name of the LORD. *(Abram was careful to continue the worship of God wherever he might be placed. Go where we may, let us not forget to give devotion and obedience to God.)*

Abram acted without delay. His reason is found in:

Hebrews 11:8-10

⁸ By faith Abraham obeyed when he was called to go out to a place that he was to receive as an inheritance. And he went out, not knowing where he was going. ⁹ By faith he went to live in the land of promise, as in a foreign land, living in tents with Isaac and Jacob, heirs with him of the same promise. ¹⁰ For he was looking forward to the city that has foundations, whose designer and builder is God.

Abraham had to leave idolatrous Chaldea. We must also separate ourselves from a world that is controlled by the wicked one. He understood he was like an outsider in this temporary life and we must too. This world is not our home where we can relax. Ours is the life of a traveler until we reach "the city that has foundations."[60] *Abraham pitched his tent and wandered up and down in the land as a stranger, not as a citizen of Canaan. We do not have a permanent city here, but we look for one in the future. Those who find a place to rest here do not have one in heaven.*

2 Corinthians 6:14-18

¹⁴ Do not be unequally yoked with unbelievers. For what partnership has righteousness with lawlessness? Or what fellowship has light with darkness? ¹⁵ What accord has Christ with Belial? Or what portion does a believer share with an unbeliever? ¹⁶ What agreement has the temple of God with idols? For we are the temple of the living God; as God said,

> "I will make my dwelling among them
> and walk among them,
> and I will be their God,
> and they shall be my people.

¹⁷ Therefore go out from their midst,
and be separate from them, says the Lord,
and touch no unclean thing;
then I will welcome you,
¹⁸ and I will be a father to you,
and you shall be sons and daughters to me,
says the Lord Almighty."

Oh, that the Lord would make us, as a family, separated to himself.

January 19
Do Not Lie To One Another[61]

Genesis 12:10-20

¹⁰ Now there was a famine in the land. So Abram went down to Egypt to sojourn there, for the famine was severe in the land. ¹¹ When he was about to enter Egypt, he said to Sarai his wife, "I know that you are a woman beautiful in appearance, ¹² and when the Egyptians see you, they will say, 'This is his wife.' Then they will kill me, but they will let you live. ¹³ Say you are my sister, that it may go well with me because of you, and that my life may be spared for your sake." *(To say that she was his sister was part of the truth, but the intention was to deceive. Whether what we say is true or not, if our purpose is to mislead others, we are guilty of falsehood. Let us pray for grace to be entirely truthful.)*

¹⁴ When Abram entered Egypt, the Egyptians saw that the woman was very beautiful. ¹⁵ And when the princes of Pharaoh saw her, they praised her to Pharaoh. And the woman was taken into Pharaoh's house. ¹⁶ And for her sake he dealt well with Abram; and he had sheep, oxen, male donkeys, male servants, female servants, female donkeys, and camels. *(These gifts must have given Abram very little pleasure. He must have felt selfish in spirit and sick at heart.)*

¹⁷ But the LORD afflicted Pharaoh and his house with great plagues because of Sarai, Abram's wife. ¹⁸ So Pharaoh called Abram and said, "What is this you have done to me? Why did you not tell me that she was your

---

[60] Hebrews 11:10

[61] Colossians 3:9

wife? ¹⁹ Why did you say, 'She is my sister,' so that I took her for my wife? Now then, here is your wife, take her, and go." *(It must have been very humbling to the man of God to be rebuked by a heathen. It is sad indeed when the worldling shames the believer; yet it is too often the case.)* ²⁰ And Pharaoh gave men orders concerning him, and they sent him away with his wife and all that he had.

From this Scripture we learn that the best of men, even when they are following the Lord's leading, will still have trials. This is Abram. He is obeying God's command. Nevertheless, he suffers in the famine that falls on the land in which he is living. Trials show the weak places in good men. Even the holy patriarch[62] had his faults. He went into Egypt, into a land where he had no right to be. He was out of the path of duty and therefore out of the place of safety. He stepped into the devil's land and found the way was slippery. It was difficult to continue to follow the Lord. He changed the truth a little in order to save himself and Sarai. He deceived Pharaoh by telling him only half the truth and he exposed his wife to great danger. All this happened because of the unbelief that crippled even the mighty faith of the father of the faithful. The best of men are but men at best. This is enough to show us that even the chief of the patriarchs was "a man with a nature like ours."[63] Like Abram, we are born with Adam's nature, but we can be born again with Abram's faith. The same Holy Spirit that developed Abram's great faith can do the same in our lives and give us victory over the power of our sinful nature.

Genesis 13:1-4

¹ So Abram went up from Egypt, he and his wife and all that he had, and Lot with him, into the Negeb. *(He did not feel safe until he returned to his life of separation in the promised land. Friendship with the world is not good for the believer's soul. The closer he is to God and more set apart from sinners, the better.)*

² Now Abram was very rich in livestock, in silver, and in gold. ³ And he journeyed on from the Negeb as far as Bethel to the place where his tent had been at the beginning between Bethel and Ai, ⁴ to the place where he had made an altar at the first. And there Abram called upon the name of the LORD. *(No doubt he confessed his sinful weakness and renewed the commitment of his faith in God. If we have blundered or backslidden, let us also return to our first love, to the Bethel where we first set up an altar to the Lord.)*

January 20
All Things Are Yours[64]
Genesis 13:5-18

⁵ And Lot, who went with Abram, also had flocks and herds and tents, ⁶ so that the land could not support both of them dwelling together; for their possessions were so great that they could not dwell together, ⁷ and there was strife between the herdsmen of Abram's livestock and the herdsmen of Lot's livestock. *(Rich men may be godly and godly men may be rich, but riches are certainly a cause of problems. In this case wealth did not bring peace. It brought discontent. Good men can control their own tempers, but not the tempers of those who live with them. When relatives live together, they must be very careful. Disagreements may be caused by others in the household. It is a rare thing for relatives to live in the same house without conflict. Everyone who lives in such a situation must guard against being suspicious, envious or quarrelsome.)*

At that time the Canaanites and the Perizzites were dwelling in the land. *(The presence of such powerful enemies should have made these good men cautious about the way they handled their problems. The eyes of the world are watching us. We must be careful how we act. Do not allow our family disagreements to be a reason for those of the world to make fun of us.)*

⁸ Then Abram said to Lot, "Let there be no strife between you and me, and between your herdsmen and my herdsmen, for we are

---

[62] *patriarch* - A man regarded as the father or ruler of a family. Bible patriarchs include Abraham, Isaac, Jacob and Jacob's twelve sons.
[63] James 5:17
[64] 1 Corinthians 3:21

kinsmen. ⁹ Is not the whole land before you? Separate yourself from me. If you take the left hand, then I will go to the right, or if you take the right hand, then I will go to the left." *(Abram was the older, the greater, the richer, and the better man, but he gave his nephew the first choice. In all disagreements, it is good for the more powerful person to be the first to give in. Doing so will prove his high character. Abram's faith had produced a spirit in him that was gentle, generous and willing to bend. All true faith produces this kind of person.)*

¹⁰ And Lot lifted up his eyes and saw that the Jordan Valley was well watered everywhere like the garden of the LORD, like the land of Egypt, in the direction of Zoar. (This was before the LORD destroyed Sodom and Gomorrah.) ¹¹ So Lot chose for himself all the Jordan Valley, and Lot journeyed east. Thus they separated from each other. ¹² Abram settled in the land of Canaan, while Lot settled among the cities of the valley and moved his tent as far as Sodom. ¹³ Now the men of Sodom were wicked, great sinners against the LORD.

Lot made a serious mistake. He looked only to the richness of the country and not to the character of the people. He walked by sight and not by faith.[65] He looked at the material advantage and did not "seek first the kingdom of God."[66] Lot gave up living a life of separation to live in the city. He was influenced by the residents of Sodom and became worldly. He gave up all claim to the inheritance promised to Abram and his descendants and pierced himself through with many sorrows. In the end, the person who wanted everything the world had to offer lost it and the person who was willing to give up anything to honor God found it.

When friends leave us, we may expect the Lord to visit us with comfort and support. After Lot was gone, the Lord appeared again to Abram.

¹⁴ The LORD said to Abram, after Lot had separated from him, "Lift up your eyes and look from the place where you are, northward and southward and eastward and westward, ¹⁵ for all the land that you see I will give to you and to your offspring forever. ¹⁶ I will make your offspring as the dust of the earth, so that if one can count the dust of the earth, your offspring also can be counted. ¹⁷ Arise, walk through the length and the breadth of the land, for I will give it to you." *(Abram was invited to gaze on his possessions; to walk across the land like he was the owner. Our faith should look on the covenant blessings that are ours in Christ Jesus in the same way. Rejoice in them with "joy that is inexpressible."[67])* ¹⁸ So Abram moved his tent and came and settled by the oaks of Mamre, which are at Hebron, and there he built an altar to the LORD.

January 21
The LORD…Trains My Hands for War[68]
Genesis 14:1-3; 10-12; 14-24

¹ In the days of Amraphel king of Shinar, Arioch king of Ellasar, Chedorlaomer king of Elam, and Tidal king of Goiim, ² these kings made war with Bera king of Sodom, Birsha king of Gomorrah, Shinab king of Admah, Shemeber king of Zeboiim, and the king of Bela (that is, Zoar). ³ And all these joined forces in the Valley of Siddim (that is, the Salt Sea).

¹⁰ Now the Valley of Siddim was full of bitumen pits, and as the kings of Sodom and Gomorrah fled, some fell into them, and the rest fled to the hill country. ¹¹ So the enemy took all the possessions of Sodom and Gomorrah, and all their provisions, and went their way. ¹² They also took Lot, the son of Abram's brother, who was dwelling in Sodom, and his possessions, and went their way. *("All is not gold that glitters."[69] Moving to Sodom turned out to be a poor choice for Lot. Believers who try to follow the ways of the world should not be surprised when they suffer for doing so. Lot went to Sodom in the hope of gaining wealth. Now he*

---

[65] A reference to 2 Corinthians 5:6a-7, "We know that while we are at home in the body we are away from the Lord, for we walk by faith, not by sight."
[66] Matthew 6:33
[67] 1 Peter 1:8
[68] Psalm 144:1
[69] William Shakespeare, *The Merchant of Venice* (1596): "All that glisters is not gold." Not everything that is shiny is valuable.

loses everything in one blow. If we put too much effort into growing rich, the Lord can take everything away in a moment in time.)

14 When Abram heard that his kinsman had been taken captive, he led forth his trained men, born in his house, 318 of them, and went in pursuit as far as Dan. *(If our relatives desert us we must not desert them. Lot left Abram, but Abram did not forget Lot.)* **15** And he divided his forces against them by night, he and his servants, and defeated them and pursued them to Hobah, north of Damascus. **16** Then he brought back all the possessions, and also brought back his kinsman Lot with his possessions, and the women and the people.

Faith made Abram a winner in peace and in war. Sadly, poor Lot's trouble did not cure him from wanting to conform to the world. He went back to Sodom and continued to live there. The sins of Sodom distressed him, but he loved what the city offered him too much to leave it.

17 After his return from the defeat of Chedorlaomer and the kings who were with him, the king of Sodom went out to meet him at the Valley of Shaveh (that is, the King's Valley). **18** And Melchizedek king of Salem brought out bread and wine. (He was priest of God Most High.) *(Melchizedek was a type or picture of Christ. When we are worn out with fighting the Lord's battles, we may expect that Jesus will refresh us.)* **19** And he blessed him and said,

"Blessed be Abram by God Most High,
Possessor of heaven and earth;"

The Lord Jesus never meets his people without blessing them. The words from his lips are like lilies dropping sweet-smelling perfume.

20 and blessed be God Most High,
who has delivered your enemies into
your hand!"

And Abram gave him a tenth of everything. *(And we should cheerfully give our great Melchizedek from what we have received. Melchizedek blessed Abram. It was only right that Abram returned some of those blessings to him.)*

21 And the king of Sodom said to Abram, "Give me the persons, but take the goods for yourself." *(The king did not care about what Abram and Melchizedek were doing. He interrupted them to discuss his concerns.)*

22 But Abram said to the king of Sodom, "I have lifted my hand to the LORD, God Most High, Possessor of heaven and earth, **23** that I would not take a thread or a sandal strap or anything that is yours, lest you should say, 'I have made Abram rich.' **24** I will take nothing but what the young men have eaten, and the share of the men who went with me. Let Aner, Eshcol, and Mamre take their share." *(The king of Sodom offered Abram what was rightfully his by the laws of war, but he refused to take it. Sometimes the right thing to do is give up what is rightfully ours. Abram believed God could give him all he needed without owing the king of Sodom a debt of gratitude. Faith does not look for man to provide. She will not give the world the opportunity to say, "See we provided for you, not God. You should praise us, not the Lord." Jehovah is more than enough for believers. We do not need to depend on anyone else.)*

January 22
He Always Lives to Make Intercession for Them[70]

The story of Melchizedek in the book of Genesis is a picture of the Lord Jesus Christ. This is fully explained in today's reading.

Hebrews 7:1-17; 20-25

1 For this Melchizedek, king of Salem, priest of the Most High God, met Abraham returning from the slaughter of the kings and blessed him, **2** and to him Abraham apportioned a tenth part of everything. He is first, by translation of his name, king of righteousness, and then he is also king of Salem, that is, king of peace. **3** He is without father or mother or genealogy, having neither beginning of days nor end of life, but resembling the Son of God he continues a priest forever. *(The Scripture includes nothing about the ancestors of Melchizedek. There is no mention of a priest before him or*

---
[70] Hebrews 7:25

after him. The apostle finds a meaning of why the Bible is silent about these things. Some refuse to learn from what the Bible plainly says. But the apostle could learn even from what it does not say. Melchizedek was both king and priest combined. He did not receive his priesthood by inheriting it. It was by the direct appointment of God. In these things he is an exceptional picture of our Lord Jesus)

⁴ See how great this man was to whom Abraham the patriarch gave a tenth of the spoils! ⁵ And those descendants of Levi who receive the priestly office have a commandment in the law to take tithes from the people, that is, from their brothers, though these also are descended from Abraham. ⁶ But this man who does not have his descent from them received tithes from Abraham and blessed him who had the promises. ⁷ It is beyond dispute that the inferior is blessed by the superior. ⁸ In the one case tithes are received by mortal men, but in the other case, by one of whom it is testified that he lives. ⁹ One might even say that Levi himself, who receives tithes, paid tithes through Abraham, ¹⁰ for he was still in the loins of his ancestor when Melchizedek met him.

¹¹ Now if perfection had been attainable through the Levitical priesthood (for under it the people received the law), what further need would there have been for another priest to arise after the order of Melchizedek, rather than one named after the order of Aaron? ¹² For when there is a change in the priesthood, there is necessarily a change in the law as well. ¹³ For the one of whom these things are spoken belonged to another tribe, from which no one has ever served at the altar. ¹⁴ For it is evident that our Lord was descended from Judah, and in connection with that tribe Moses said nothing about priests. *(Our Lord did not receive the priesthood because he was a descendent of Aaron, but, like Melchizedek, because he was appointed directly by God.)*

¹⁵ This becomes even more evident when another priest arises in the likeness of Melchizedek, ¹⁶ who has become a priest, not on the basis of a legal requirement concerning bodily descent, but by the power of an indestructible life. ¹⁷ For it is witnessed of him,

"You are a priest forever,
    after the order of Melchizedek."

This is the inspired testimony of Psalm 110, where David speaks of the Lord Jesus as his Lord and acknowledges him as king and priest.)

²⁰ And it was not without an oath. For those who formerly became priests were made such without an oath, ²¹ but this one was made a priest with an oath by the one who said to him:

"The Lord has sworn
    and will not change his mind,
'You are a priest forever.'"

²² This makes Jesus the guarantor of a better covenant. *(The priesthood of Jesus is about things that are certain; things that cannot pass away or change. God established this position for Christ and he guarantees it)*

²³ The former priests were many in number, because they were prevented by death from continuing in office, ²⁴ but he holds his priesthood permanently, because he continues forever. ²⁵ Consequently, he is able to save to the uttermost those who draw near to God through him, since he always lives to make intercession for them.

Jesus resembles Melchizedek because he is both king and priest, because there is no one before him or after him, and because his priesthood is greater than the Levitical Priesthood. He is a priest forever by the oath of God. We who trust in Jesus have this wonderful comfort: We know our Great High Priest lives forever, is always in power, is always accessible, and is always ready to perform his office for our benefit.

January 23
I Am Your Shield[71]
Genesis 15:1-18

¹ After these things the word of the LORD came to Abram in a vision: "Fear not, Abram, I am your shield; your reward shall

---
[71] Genesis 15:1

be very great." *(People should be afraid to harm those whom the Lord blesses. And those who trust in the living God have no reason to be alarmed. Five kings or fifty kings may come against them, but while Jehovah defends them they are safe. Perhaps the Lord saw a fear rising up in Abram's mind and therefore came to him with this word of comfort. God is not willing to have his servants in bondage to fear.)*

2 But Abram said, "O Lord GOD, what will you give me, for I continue childless, and the heir of my house is Eliezer of Damascus?" **3** And Abram said, "Behold, you have given me no offspring, and a member of my household will be my heir." **4** And behold, the word of the LORD came to him: "This man shall not be your heir; your very own son shall be your heir." *(The strongest faith has inner struggles. Abram's heart was set on being the direct ancestor of the Messiah and he believed in the promise of God. But it still seemed impossible to him, because he did not have a son and it did not appear likely that he ever would have one. It is always wise to spread our doubts before the Lord, because he can face them for us.)*

5 And he brought him outside and said, "Look toward heaven, and number the stars, if you are able to number them." Then he said to him, "So shall your offspring be." **6** And he believed the LORD, and he counted it to him as righteousness. *(Abram believed in God. No difficulty or physical impossibility stopped him from believing. Therefore he was accepted by the Lord as being righteous.)*

7 And he said to him, "I am the LORD who brought you out from Ur of the Chaldeans to give you this land to possess." **8** But he said, "O Lord GOD, how am I to know that I shall possess it?" **9** He said to him, "Bring me a heifer three years old, a female goat three years old, a ram three years old, a turtledove, and a young pigeon." **10** And he brought him all these, cut them in half, and laid each half over against the other. But he did not cut the birds in half. **11** And when birds of prey came down on the carcasses, Abram drove them away. *(Abram's question was answered by a command to offer a sacrifice. Abram accepted that as a sign that God would keep his promise. He proved his faith by preparing the sacrifice. We confirm our faith in Jesus when we respond to his promises by acting on them. True, a few questions will sometimes distract our faith. Those doubts are like these hungry birds that must be chased away by faith.)*

As the evening approached and the animals had been killed, the Lord assured Abram in the strongest possible words that the promise was true. The death of Jesus gives us the strongest possible assurance that God's promise of salvation to all who believe in his Son is true.

12 As the sun was going down, a deep sleep fell on Abram. And behold, dreadful and great darkness fell upon him. **13** Then the LORD said to Abram, "Know for certain that your offspring will be sojourners in a land that is not theirs and will be servants there, and they will be afflicted for four hundred years. **14** But I will bring judgment on the nation that they serve, and afterward they shall come out with great possessions. **15** As for you, you shall go to your fathers in peace; you shall be buried in a good old age. **16** And they shall come back here in the fourth generation, for the iniquity of the Amorites is not yet complete."

17 When the sun had gone down and it was dark, behold a smoking fire pot and a flaming torch passed between these pieces. *(This represented the history of God's people. They must often endure the darkening smoke of the furnace of affliction, but the flaming lamp of God's salvation is always with them.)* **18** On that day the LORD made a covenant with Abram, saying, "To your offspring I give this land, from the river of Egypt to the great river, the river Euphrates." *(And so, Abram's fear was chased away by the promise. Let our fears also be chased away by God's promises.)*

January 24

Christ is All[72]

Romans 4:1-25

Paul was moved by the Holy Spirit to explain to us the importance of what took place in the fifteenth chapter of Genesis that we considered in our last reading. Let us read his explanation.

¹ What then shall we say was gained by Abraham, our forefather according to the flesh? ² For if Abraham was justified by works, he has something to boast about, but not before God. ³ For what does the Scripture say? "Abraham believed God, and it was counted to him as righteousness." ⁴ Now to the one who works, his wages are not counted as a gift but as his due. ⁵ And to the one who does not work but believes in him who justifies the ungodly, his faith is counted as righteousness, ⁶ just as David also speaks of the blessing to the one to whom God counts righteousness apart from works:

⁷ "Blessed are those whose lawless deeds are forgiven,
and whose sins are covered;
⁸ blessed is the man against whom the Lord will not count his sin."

⁹ Is this blessing then only for the circumcised, or also for the uncircumcised? We say that faith was counted to Abraham as righteousness. ¹⁰ How then was it counted to him? Was it before or after he had been circumcised? It was not after, but before he was circumcised. ¹¹ He received the sign of circumcision as a seal of the righteousness that he had by faith while he was still uncircumcised. The purpose was to make him the father of all who believe without being circumcised, so that righteousness would be counted to them as well, ¹² and to make him the father of the circumcised who are not merely circumcised but who also walk in the footsteps of the faith that our father Abraham had before he was circumcised.

¹³ For the promise to Abraham and his offspring that he would be heir of the world did not come through the law but through the righteousness of faith. ¹⁴ For if it is the adherents of the law who are to be the heirs, faith is null and the promise is void. ¹⁵ For the law brings wrath, but where there is no law there is no transgression.

¹⁶ That is why it depends on faith, in order that the promise may rest on grace and be guaranteed to all his offspring—not only to the adherent of the law but also to the one who shares the faith of Abraham, who is the father of us all, ¹⁷ as it is written, "I have made you the father of many nations"—in the presence of the God in whom he believed, who gives life to the dead and calls into existence the things that do not exist. ¹⁸ In hope he believed against hope, that he should become the father of many nations, as he had been told, "So shall your offspring be." ¹⁹ He did not weaken in faith when he considered his own body, which was as good as dead (since he was about a hundred years old), or when he considered the barrenness of Sarah's womb. ²⁰ No unbelief made him waver concerning the promise of God, but he grew strong in his faith as he gave glory to God, ²¹ fully convinced that God was able to do what he had promised. ²² That is why his faith was "counted to him as righteousness." ²³ But the words "it was counted to him" were not written for his sake alone, ²⁴ but for ours also. It will be counted to us who believe in him who raised from the dead Jesus our Lord, ²⁵ who was delivered up for our trespasses and raised for our justification.

Paul's argument is very clear and convincing. Abraham was justified by faith and therefore by grace. This justification was not given to him as a circumcised man. He was not circumcised until years later. Therefore the covenant[73] blessings are not given in connection with the law and its work, but in connection with faith and grace. The covenant promise was made to the spiritual descendants of Abraham. That is, not those born after the flesh, but those born again according to promise. All of the nations of the world have an interest in that promise, because Abraham's spiritual children come from all of them. The true

---

[72] Colossians 3:11

[73] covenant - A contract, promise, guarantee, pledge or agreement between two or more persons.

children of Abraham are recognized by their faith, not by their keeping the law. Jesus is the promised descendant. Those who believe in him are Abraham's children. Is everyone in this family a believer in Jesus? Is there any among us who is not saved? Let each of us consider these most serious questions.

January 25
You Are a God Who Sees Me[74]

Genesis 16:1-15

1 Now Sarai, Abram's wife, had borne him no children. She had a female Egyptian servant whose name was Hagar. *(Sarai therefore suggested to Abram that Hagar should become his secondary wife. This was a very usual custom in those days, but it was not a praiseworthy one. It was an act of unbelief for Sarai to suggest it. It is not always easy to wait patiently for the Lord's time. We all tend to be too quick to run to our own methods; as if the Lord needed our help to fulfill his promises.)*

2b And Abram listened to the voice of Sarai. *(Those we love best may be the means of leading us astray. Adam, the father of mankind, sinned by listening to his wife and now the father of the faithful follows his poor example.)* **3** So, after Abram had lived ten years in the land of Canaan, Sarai, Abram's wife, took Hagar the Egyptian, her servant, and gave her to Abram her husband as a wife.

4b And when [Hagar] saw that she had conceived, she looked with contempt on her mistress. **5** And Sarai said to Abram, "May the wrong done to me be on you! I gave my servant to your embrace, and when she saw that she had conceived, she looked on me with contempt. May the LORD judge between you and me!" *(It was Sarai who suggested doing this and now she blames her husband for it. It is no use to blame others for our mistakes. If we turn off the road of correctness, we shall certainly and personally feel the pain for it.)*

6 But Abram said to Sarai, "Behold, your servant is in your power; do to her as you please." Then Sarai dealt harshly with her, and she fled from her. *(First Sarai did not believe God, next she was unkind to her husband, and now she is cruel to her servant. One wrong step leads to others. Unbelief is a sin that causes other sins. Even this holy woman had her weaknesses. "No one is good except God alone."[75])*

7 The angel of the LORD found her by a spring of water in the wilderness, the spring on the way to Shur. **8** And he said, "Hagar, servant of Sarai, where have you come from and where are you going?" She said, "I am fleeing from my mistress Sarai." *(She did not say where she was going, because she did not know. Let each of us ask himself, "Where am I going?")* **9** The angel of the LORD said to her, "Return to your mistress and submit to her." **10** The angel of the LORD also said to her, "I will surely multiply your offspring so that they cannot be numbered for multitude." *(No one could use such language as this but the Angel of the Covenant, the Lord Jesus Christ. By promising to multiply her offspring, he proved the inspired statement, "delighting in the children of man."[76])*

11 And the angel of the LORD said to her,

"Behold, you are pregnant
and shall bear a son.
You shall call his name Ishmael,
because the LORD has listened to your affliction.
12 He shall be a wild donkey of a man,
his hand against everyone
and everyone's hand against him,
and he shall dwell over against all his kinsmen."

13 So she called the name of the LORD who spoke to her, "You are a God of seeing," for she said, "Truly here I have seen him who looks after me." *(First, God sees us; and then, by his gracious visits, he leads us to seek him.)* **14** Therefore the well was called Beer-lahai-roi; *(the well of the living One who sees me;)* it lies between Kadesh and Bered.

15 And Hagar bore Abram a son, and Abram called the name of his son, whom Hagar bore, Ishmael. *(But Ishmael was not,*

---

[74] Genesis 16:13 (alternate reading)
[75] Mark 10:18
[76] Proverbs 8:31

as he had hoped, the promised heir. On the contrary, he became the cause of many trials to the family. When we look to the world to help grace, or reason to assist faith, we fail to reach our goal. Instead, we guarantee sorrow. This whole scene is a painful one. It should warn us that even in good families sin may cause infighting and bring unhappiness and heartache.)

January 26
Search Me, O God[77]

In the desert, Hagar learned that God is omniscient.[78] She declared, "You are a God of seeing."[79] Thinking about this truth will do us good. We see this doctrine in great detail in today's Psalm.

Psalm 139

1 O LORD, you have searched me and known me!
2 You know when I sit down and when I rise up;
   you discern my thoughts from afar.
3 You search out my path and my lying down
   and are acquainted with all my ways.

God watches me all the time. Whether I am awake or asleep, his eye is on me!

4 Even before a word is on my tongue,
   behold, O LORD, you know it altogether.

He knows not only the words on my tongue that I have spoken, but those in my tongue which have not yet been voiced. He knows what I intend to say.

5 You hem me in, behind and before,
   and lay your hand upon me.
6 Such knowledge is too wonderful for me;
   it is high; I cannot attain it.
7 Where shall I go from your Spirit?
   Or where shall I flee from your presence?
8 If I ascend to heaven, you are there!
   If I make my bed in Sheol, you are there!
9 If I take the wings of the morning
   and dwell in the uttermost part of the sea,
10 even there your hand shall lead me,
   and your right hand shall hold me.
11 If I say, "Surely the darkness shall cover me,
   and the light about me be night,"
12 even the darkness is not dark to you
   the night is bright as the day
   for darkness is as light with you.
13 For you formed my inward parts;

The Lord sees every part of my anatomy at a glance and understands all of it.

   you knitted me together in my mother's womb.
14 I praise you, for I am fearfully and wonderfully made.
   Wonderful are your works;
   my soul knows it very well.
15 My frame was not hidden from you,
   when I was being made in secret,
   intricately woven in the depths of the earth.

Our body is like a very skillful piece of embroidery, "intricately woven." Its nerves, veins, and muscles are formed by the divine Creator. At conception, the wisdom of the Lord was there developing every cell. The master watchmaker understands the complexities of his creation and our Creator knows all the secret workings of our souls.

16 Your eyes saw my unformed substance;
   in your book were written, every one of them,
   the days that were formed for me,
   when as yet there were none of them.
17 How precious to me are your thoughts, O God!
   How vast is the sum of them!
18 If I would count them, they are more than the sand.
   I awake, and I am still with you.

The omniscient eye is not that of an enemy, but an eye that watches over us to do us good. The Lord's heart is never away from his people. He thinks about them to bless them.

---

[77] Psalm 139:23
[78] *omniscient* (adjective), *omniscience* (noun) - All knowing or knowing everything; all seeing or seeing everything. The capacity to know everything that there is to know.
[79] Genesis 16:13

19 Oh that you would slay the wicked, O God!
   O men of blood, depart from me!

Since the Lord sees and punishes the wicked, we should not be found in their company, to avoid the risk of sharing in their doom.

20 They speak against you with malicious intent;
   your enemies take your name in vain!

Because the Lord is always everywhere, they insult him to his face when they take his name in vain. How can this not anger the Lord God?

21 Do I not hate those who hate you, O LORD?
   And do I not loathe those who rise up against you?
22 I hate them with complete hatred;
   I count them my enemies.

A faithful servant of God has the same interests, the same friends, and the same enemies as his Master.

23 Search me, O God, and know my heart!
   Try me and know my thoughts!
24 And see if there be any grievous way in me,
   and lead me in the way everlasting!

The omniscience of God should fill the sinner with terror. But it is an attribute[80] of God that greatly benefits the believer. Since the Lord will pardon all the sins of believers in Jesus, we are glad that he should see all of them, so that he may remove them completely.

January 27
Is Anything Too Hard for the LORD?[81]
Genesis 18:1-15

1 And the LORD appeared to [Abraham] by the oaks of Mamre, as he sat at the door of his tent in the heat of the day. 2 He lifted up his eyes and looked, and behold, three men were standing in front of him. When he saw them, he ran from the tent door to meet them and bowed himself to the earth 3 and said, "O Lord, if I have found favor in your sight, do not pass by your servant. 4 Let a little water be brought, and wash your feet, and rest yourselves under the tree, 5 while I bring a morsel of bread, that you may refresh yourselves, and after that you may pass on—since you have come to your servant."

Abraham did "not neglect to show hospitality to strangers" and "entertained angels unawares."[82] He ran to meet the strangers, he greeted them respectfully, and he welcomed them warmly. He even told them they would be doing him a favor if they rested near his tent. Ungenerous persons who never entertain either God's servants or the poor, miss many blessings. May we never be a rude and inconsiderate household.

6 And Abraham went quickly into the tent to Sarah and said, "Quick! Three seahs *(about 27 pounds)* of fine flour! Knead it, and make cakes." 7 And Abraham ran to the herd and took a calf, tender and good, and gave it to a young man, who prepared it quickly. 8 Then he took curds and milk and the calf that he had prepared, and set it before them. And he stood by them under the tree while they ate. *(The wealthy old man was glad to serve these strangers. He spoke of a morsel of bread, but he made a feast. He was all kindness, goodness, and humility; a true gentleman and a believer in God. These are the fruits of true holiness. It would bring glory to God if all those who profess Christ displayed these qualities.)*

9 They said to him, "Where is Sarah your wife?" And he said, "She is in the tent."

She was where she should be. At that moment, she was busy with household duties. She was the ideal wife of her ideal husband and she cheerfully helped him to provide for the guests. When we are on the road of duty, we are on the road to blessings. Abraham must have wondered how the leader of the three strangers knew his wife's name.

10 The LORD said, "I will surely return to you about this time next year, and Sarah your wife shall have a son." And Sarah was listening at the tent door behind him. 11 Now Abraham and Sarah were old, advanced in years. The way of women had ceased to be

---
[80] *attribute* - A quality or characteristic that someone has.
[81] Genesis 18:14

[82] Hebrews 13:2

with Sarah. **12** So Sarah laughed to herself, saying, "After I am worn out, and my lord is old, shall I have pleasure?" **13** The LORD said to Abraham, "Why did Sarah laugh and say, 'Shall I indeed bear a child, now that I am old?' **14** Is anything too hard for the LORD? At the appointed time I will return to you, about this time next year, and Sarah shall have a son." *(What an encouraging question. "Is anything too hard for the Lord?" Our family's troubles, cares, and needs are not beyond the power and wisdom of our heavenly Father. Let us not become hopeless, but in faith cast our worries and problems on him.)* **15** But Sarah denied it, saying, "I did not laugh," for she was afraid. He said, "No, but you did laugh."

He who knows all hearts cannot be deceived. See how honest Holy Scripture is, it records the faults of even the best of the saints. See also how tender the Spirit of God is, because in the New Testament Sarah's fault is not mentioned. It had been forgiven and blotted out, but the fact that she called her husband "lord" is recorded to her honor. We serve a gracious God who, when our hearts are right, commends our good fruit, and leaves the unripe figs to drop out of sight.[83] *Let us be careful not to spoil the joy of his promises and grace by any improper words or actions. It would be a sad thing for us to be surrounded by the memories of divine love and have to admit that we laughed at the promise.*

January 28
Pray Without Ceasing[84]
Genesis 18:16-17, 22-33

16 Then the men set out from there, and they looked down toward Sodom. And Abraham went with them to set them on their way. **17** The LORD said, "Shall I hide from Abraham what I am about to do?" *(One of the three was the Lord himself, who had taken on human form for this meeting.*[85] *Perhaps Jesus, who was one day to be born a man, did this to hint at this future event. Truly, "his goings forth are from long ago, from the days of eternity."*[86] *Is this not amazing? Almighty Jehovah made Abraham his confidential friend! He is willing to do the same with us, for even now "the friendship of the Lord is with them that fear him."*[87]*)*

22 So the men turned from there and went toward Sodom, but Abraham still stood before the LORD.

Two of the angels went to Sodom, but the third, the Lord of angels, stayed to talk with Abraham, his friend.

23 Then Abraham drew near and said, "Will you indeed sweep away the righteous with the wicked? **24** Suppose there are fifty righteous within the city. Will you then sweep away the place and not spare it for the fifty righteous who are in it? **25** Far be it from you to do such a thing, to put the righteous to death with the wicked, so that the righteous fare as the wicked! Far be that from you! Shall not the Judge of all the earth do what is just?" *(When we are favored with close access to God, we should use it to pray for the benefit of others. Notice the arguments the patriarch used. We should also use our strongest reasons when we plead for others. The Lord is moved with pleas like those of Abraham. Undoubtedly he saves wicked nations for the sake of the saints who live among them. Of course, all the saved are forgiven not for their own sakes, but for Jesus's sake.)* **26** And the LORD said, "If I find at Sodom fifty righteous in the city, I will spare the whole place for their sake."

27 And Abraham answered and said, "Behold I have undertaken to speak to the Lord, I who am but dust and ashes." *(In our boldest pleadings we must not forget what unworthy creatures we are and how wonderful it is on the Lord's part to let us plead with him.)* **28** "Suppose five of the fifty righteous are lacking. Will you destroy the whole city for lack of five?" And he said, "I will not destroy it if I find forty-five there." *(The Lord kept pace with his servant, being*

---
[83] A reference to Revelation 6:13.
[84] I Thessalonians 5:17
[85] This refers to the visible appearance of Jesus to people in the Old Testament. Often called a "Theophany" or "Christophany".

[86] Micah 5:2 (NASB)
[87] Psalm 25:14

quite as willing to answer as he was to ask.) ²⁹ Again he spoke to him and said, "Suppose forty are found there." He answered, "For the sake of forty I will not do it." ³⁰ Then he said, "Oh let not the Lord be angry, and I will speak. Suppose thirty are found there." He answered, "I will not do it, if I find thirty there." ³¹ He said, "Behold, I have undertaken to speak to the Lord. Suppose twenty are found there." He answered, "For the sake of twenty I will not destroy it." ³² Then he said, "Oh let not the Lord be angry, and I will speak again but this once. Suppose ten are found there." He answered, "For the sake of ten I will not destroy it."

There is a time to keep silent as well as a time to speak. Abraham had gone as far as the Spirit of the Lord guided him. He did not attempt to go further.

³³ And the LORD went his way, when he had finished speaking to Abraham, and Abraham returned to his place.

If there had been only the small number of ten who were righteous, Sodom and Gomorrah would have escaped. This is how precious the saints are to a nation! They may be unknown or despised, but they are the salt that preserves the whole. May our family be a part of that good salt; parents, and children, all being through divine grace counted with the righteous. But we must first have salt in ourselves by possessing a living faith in the Lord Jesus. Otherwise we cannot benefit others, because we are not even saved ourselves.

January 29
I Have Prayed for You[88]

We must not allow the prayers of Abraham to pass away from our thoughts until they have reminded us of the still more powerful prayers of our Blessed Lord Jesus. We see him pictured in one of his own parables. He describes himself as keeping his own sinful lambs safe by pleadings for them to the Father. This passage is a good sequel to yesterday's reading.

---
[88] Luke 22:32

Luke 13:1-9

¹ There were some present at that very time who told him about the Galileans whose blood Pilate had mingled with their sacrifices. ² And he answered them, "Do you think that these Galileans were worse sinners than all the other Galileans, because they suffered in this way? ³ No, I tell you; but unless you repent, you will all likewise perish." *(See the need of repentance?[89] Philip Henry[90] once said, "Some people do not like to hear much about repentance; but I think it so necessary that if I were to die in the pulpit, I should desire to die preaching repentance, and if I should die out of the pulpit I hope to die practicing it.")*

⁴ "Or those eighteen on whom the tower in Siloam fell and killed them: do you think that they were worse offenders than all the others who lived in Jerusalem? ⁵ No, I tell you; but unless you repent, you will all likewise perish" *(When we hear or read about terrible judgments on sinners, like the ones spoken of here or those who lived in Sodom of old, we should not congratulate ourselves and think this could not happen to us because we are not as bad as they were. Instead, we should understand that these are warnings to us. If we fall into the same sins as they did, sooner or later a doom just as overwhelming will come on us. If any of us wonder why nothing like this has happened already, let them pay special attention to the parable that follows. There has been an intercessor[91] at work. Otherwise, we would have perished long before this.)*

⁶ And he told this parable: "A man had a fig tree planted in his vineyard, and he came seeking fruit on it and found none. *(It was in good soil and under the gardener's care. Therefore it would produce fruit or prove to be good for nothing.)* ⁷ And he said to the vinedresser, 'Look, for three years now I have come seeking fruit on this fig tree, and I

---
[89] *repent, repentance* - The act or feeling of remorse, regret, sorrow or shame that results in a change of heart or purpose.
[90] Philip Henry 1631-1696. A nonconformist Anglican pastor and father of the well-known commentator Matthew Henry.
[91] *intercessor* - one who intervenes or gets involved for the benefit of others, especially by praying.

find none. Cut it down. Why should it use up the ground?'"

Three years was long enough for a test. There might have been two bad seasons to account for the absence of fruit, but when the tree was fruitless a third time the fault must be in the tree itself. God gives us enough time to be tested. God has allowed all of us enough time to prove ourselves. Perhaps this is the moment the Lord is saying, "Cut it down." Some of us are like this barren fig tree. By itself it is of no use. If fills the place where a good tree could be planted. It draws nutrients from the soil and hurts other trees that are near it. In the same way some People live useless lives, and at the same time they are in positions that others could be in who would bring glory to God.

8 "And he answered him, 'Sir, let it alone this year also, until I dig around it and put on manure. *(It is the voice of Jesus the Intercessor. He is not willing to see the axe raised, because he is full of compassion. See how unconverted people owe their lives to Jesus? They are not preserved by their own worth or worthiness. They are alive because God tolerates them and they will die as soon as the voice of Jesus stops pleading for them.)* **9** Then if it should bear fruit next year, well and good; but if not, you can cut it down."

May we who have been without grace until now hear the word of God at this hour and live. This may be our last year of grace. When it is over we may be cast into the fire of hell. Jesus has asked that we may be given one more chance. But there is a limit to his pleadings. Note the two ifs, "Then if," and "but if not." Eternity hangs on these two ifs. The Lord grant that none of us may be cut down and cast into the eternal burnings.

January 30
Remember Lot's Wife[92]
Genesis 19:1-3; 15-26

1 The two angels came to Sodom in the evening, and Lot was sitting in the gate of Sodom. When Lot saw them, he rose to meet them and bowed himself with his face to the earth **2** and said, "My lords, please turn aside to your servant's house and spend the night and wash your feet. Then you may rise up early and go on your way." *(Lot's neighbors were bad, but at least he welcomed the two strangers. Grace does not thrive in bad company, but it still lives.)* They said, "No, we will spend the night in the town square." **3** But he pressed them strongly; so they turned aside to him and entered his house. And he made them a feast and baked unleavened bread, and they ate.

Then, when night fell, the angels saw for themselves what a filthy, cruel, mean and despicable place Sodom was. Those holy beings shut the door on the evil Sodomites and waited until the morning to carry out the sentence of God on the city. It was time to sweep away their crimes. Lot had gone to his sons-in-law and urged them to escape with him, but they thought he was crazy and refused.

15 As morning dawned, the angels urged Lot, saying, "Up! Take your wife and your two daughters who are here, lest you be swept away in the punishment of the city."

It is real kindness to warn men of their danger. We cannot be too serious in urging them to escape.

16 But he lingered. So the men seized him and his wife and his two daughters by the hand, the LORD being merciful to him, and they brought him out and set him outside the city.

We must repeat our warnings and use holy force with sinners. At the same time let us beware of remaining in danger ourselves. We are not safe for a single moment until we have fled to Jesus.

17 And as they brought them out, one said, "Escape for your life. Do not look back or stop anywhere in the valley. Escape to the hills, lest you be swept away." **18** And Lot said to them, "Oh, no my lords. **19** Behold, your servant has found favor in your sight, and you have shown me great kindness in saving my life. But I cannot escape to the hills, lest the disaster overtake me and I die. **20** Behold, this city is near enough to flee to, and it is a little one. Let me escape there—is

---
[92] Luke 17:32

it not a little one?—and my life will be saved!" **21** He said to him, "Behold, I grant you this favor also, that I will not overthrow the city of which you have spoken. **22** Escape there quickly, for I can do nothing till you arrive there." Therefore the name of the city was called Zoar *(or, Little)*.

Lot was not as great a believer as Abraham, but he was a good man and his prayer was heard. At his request a little city was saved. Was this not also an answer to Abraham's prayer?

23 The sun had risen on the earth when Lot came to Zoar. **24** Then the LORD rained on Sodom and Gomorrah sulfur and fire from the LORD out of heaven. **25** And he overthrew those cities, and all the valley and all the inhabitants of the cities, and what grew on the ground. **26** But Lot's wife, behind him, looked back, and she became a pillar of salt.

Lot's prayer saved Zoar, but could not save his wife. A pastor may bring thousands to Jesus and yet his own household may perish. The Scripture says, "Remember Lot's wife." Remember that she was Lot's wife and yet she was destroyed. She was out of Sodom and half way to Zoar, but she did not escape. And all because she could not leave sinners. Her heart was still with them. She started to escape, but she turned aside. Oh for grace to keep going the right way.

Remember Lot's wife. Be afraid of even a desire to return to old sins that might demonstrate we are unworthy of eternal life. This terrible chapter should make us tremble if we have not reached the safety of atoning love. Do not delay, but flee to Jesus now and put your trust in him.

January 31
Your Decrees are Very Trustworthy[93]
Genesis 21:1-21

1 The LORD visited Sarah as he had said, and the LORD did to Sarah as he had promised. **2** And Sarah conceived and bore Abraham a son in his old age at the time of which God had spoken to him. *(The Lord's promises are always kept, right down to the hour.)* **3** Abraham called the name of his son who was born to him, whom Sarah bore him, Isaac. *(Or laughter, because both parents had laughed for joy. The best laughing in the world is that which comes from seeing God's promises fulfilled. Then our mouth is filled with laughter and our tongue with singing.)*

4 And Abraham circumcised his son Isaac when he was eight days old, as God had commanded him. *(Abraham's laughter was not because of worldly merriment. It was a joy that led him to be obedient to the Lord's will. This is true happiness.)* **5** Abraham was a hundred years old when his son Isaac was born to him. **6** And Sarah said, "God has made laughter for me; everyone who hears will laugh [with] me."[94] *(When God's promises are fulfilled for any of us, others should share our joy. Let us tell the saints what the Lord has done for us, so they may rejoice too.)* **7** And she said, "Who would have said to Abraham that Sarah would nurse children? Yet I have borne him a son in his old age."

8 And the child grew and was weaned. And Abraham made a great feast on the day that Isaac was weaned. **9** But Sarah saw the son of Hagar the Egyptian, whom she had borne to Abraham, laughing. *(Children are too likely to do this, but how wrong it is for the older child to tease and hurt the younger. God sees it and is not pleased.)* **10** So she said to Abraham, "Cast out this slave woman with her son, for the son of this slave woman shall not be heir with my son Isaac." **11** And the thing was very displeasing to Abraham on account of his son. **12** But God said to Abraham, "Be not displeased because of the boy and because of your slave woman. Whatever Sarah says to you, do as she tells you, for through Isaac shall your offspring be named. **13** And I will make a nation of the son of the slave woman also, because he is your offspring."

It was hard for Abraham to send his son away from his home, but God directed it for the best, even for Ishmael.

14 So Abraham rose early in the morning and took bread and a skin of water and gave

---

[93] Psalm 93:5

[94] NASB, "will laugh with me." ESV, "will laugh over me."

it to Hagar, putting it on her shoulder, along with the child, and sent her away. And she departed and wandered in the wilderness of Beersheba.

¹⁵ When the water in the skin was gone, she put the child under one of the bushes. ¹⁶ Then she went and sat down opposite him a good way off, about the distance of a bowshot, for she said, "Let me not look on the death of the child." And as she sat opposite him, she lifted up her voice and wept. *(Had she forgotten the Lord who appeared to her before? So it seems. Our forgetfulness of mercy in the past is at the heart of our present hopelessness.)* ¹⁷ And God heard the voice of the boy, and the angel of God called to Hagar from heaven and said to her, "What troubles you, Hagar? Fear not, for God has heard the voice of the boy where he is."

God takes pity on boys and girls and hears their little prayers as well as those of their fathers and mothers. Dear children, do you pray?

¹⁸ "Up! Lift up the boy, and hold him fast with your hand, for I will make him into a great nation." ¹⁹ Then God opened her eyes, and she saw a well of water. And she went and filled the skin with water and gave the boy a drink. ²⁰ And God was with the boy, and he grew up. He lived in the wilderness and became an expert with the bow. ²¹ He lived in the wilderness of Paran, and his mother took a wife for him from the land of Egypt. *(It was God who arranged for Hagar and her son to be sent away and then he took good care of them in the desert. It is the same God who will watch over us if we commit ourselves to his care.)*

February 1
We Are Children of Promise[95]

Paul teaches us how to gain instruction from the ancient story of Ishmael and Isaac. Writing to those who wanted to introduce Jewish ceremonies into the Christian church, he says in,

Galatians 4:21-31

²¹ Tell me, you who desire to be under the law, do you not listen to the law?

Can you not see the real meaning of the law? Will you only learn one part of what it teaches and shut your ears to the rest?

²² For it is written that Abraham had two sons, one by a slave woman and one by a free woman. ²³ But the son of the slave was born according to the flesh, while the son of the free woman was born through promise. ²⁴ Now this may be interpreted allegorically: these women are two covenants. One is from Mount Sinai, bearing children for slavery; she is Hagar. ²⁵ Now Hagar is Mount Sinai in Arabia; she corresponds to the present Jerusalem, for she is in slavery with her children. ²⁶ But the Jerusalem above is free, and she is our mother. ²⁷ For it is written,

"Rejoice, O barren one who does not bear;
 break forth and cry aloud, you who are
  not in labor!
For the children of the desolate one will
  be more
 than those of the one who has a
  husband."

²⁸ Now you, brothers, like Isaac, are children of promise. *(We were not made children of God by natural birth, but by the power of divine grace.)* ²⁹ But just as at that time he who was born according to the flesh persecuted him who was born according to the Spirit, so also it is now. *(Pharisees and self-righteous people show great hostility toward those who depend on the grace of God in Christ Jesus. They call them arrogant. They angrily insult their beliefs and claim they lead to immoral behavior.)* ³⁰ But what does the Scripture say? "Cast out the slave woman and her son, for the son of the slave woman shall not inherit with the son of the free woman."

The system of salvation by works must be thrown out if grace is to reign. You cannot mix the two systems. We can no longer trust in the power and energy of our self if we want to be saved through the promise. Human merit, the child of the flesh, will never agree with faith, the child of the promise.

---
[95] From Galatians 4:28

31 So brothers, we are not children of the slave but of the free woman.

Galatians 5:1-6

1 For freedom Christ has set us free; stand firm therefore, and do not submit again to a yoke of slavery. *(Do not go back to hope in keeping the law and ceremonial observances. You are not born again under the law, but freed from it. Do not submit to the yoke of bondage.)*

2 Look: I, Paul, say to you that if you accept circumcision, Christ will be of no advantage to you. **3** I testify again to every man who accepts circumcision that he is obligated to keep the whole law. **4** You are severed from Christ, you who would be justified by the law; you have fallen away from grace. *(If a person could be justified by the law they could not be saved by grace. Law and grace are complete opposites. Thanks be to God, we do not even dare to hope to be made righteous by keeping the law. Anyone who hopes to be saved by keeping even part of the law is no longer depending on God's grace.)* **5** For through the Spirit, by faith, we ourselves eagerly wait for the hope of righteousness. *(Our confidence is in the promise and grace of God, because we are true children of Isaac. We are born of the promise of God.)* **6** For in Christ Jesus neither circumcision nor uncircumcision counts for anything, but only faith working through love. *(Our outward works are ignored. The inward work of the heart is all-important. The flesh, like Ishmael, is sent away, and the newborn nature stays with the father, and inherits the covenant promises. All believers understand this mystery. Can all of us in the household understand it?)*

February 2
Not as I Will, But as You Will[96]

Genesis 22:1-19

1 After these things God tested Abraham and said to him, "Abraham!" And he said, "Here I am." *(This would be at the same time, the patriarch's greatest trial and grandest victory. It came after he had received the best blessing of his life. Great benefits include great trial.)* **2** He said, "Take your son, your only son Isaac, whom you love, and go to the land of Moriah, and offer him there as a burnt offering on one of the mountains of which I shall tell you." **3** So Abraham rose early in the morning, saddled his donkey, and took two of his young men with him, and his son Isaac. And he cut the wood for the burnt offering and arose and went to the place of which God had told him. *(His obedience was quick, without doubting, and complete. Think about Abraham getting up early and splitting the wood to be used for this sacrifice. Could we obey the Lord like this?)*

4 On the third day Abraham lifted up his eyes and saw the place from afar. *(Abraham had three days to think about what he was about to do. This must have been a very difficult test for him. We can do something in a hurry that we might back away from if we thought about it calmly.)* **5** Then Abraham said to his young men, "Stay here with the donkey; I and the boy will go over there and worship and come again to you." *(Perhaps he was afraid that the servants might interfere and stop him from keeping his command from the Lord.)* **6** And Abraham took the wood of the burnt offering and laid it on Isaac his son. And he took in his hand the fire and the knife. So they went both of them together. **7** And Isaac said to his father Abraham, "My father!" And he said, "Here am I, my son." He said, "Behold, the fire and the wood, but where is the lamb for a burnt offering?"

A moving question, but Abraham would not allow his feelings to rule over his faith.

8 Abraham said, "God will provide for himself the lamb for a burnt offering, my son." *(These were very important prophetic words and have been fulfilled by God.)* So they went both of them together.

9 When they came to the place of which God had told him, Abraham built the altar there and laid the wood in order and bound Isaac his son and laid him on the altar, on the top of the wood. **10** Then Abraham reached out his hand and took the knife to slaughter his son. **11** But the angel of the LORD called to him from heaven and said, "Abraham,

---

[96] Matthew 26:39

Abraham!" And he said, "Here am I." **12** He said, "Do not lay your hand on the boy or do anything to him, for now I know that you fear God, seeing you have not withheld your son, your only son, from me." **13** And Abraham lifted up his eyes and looked, and behold, behind him was a ram, caught in a thicket by his horns. And Abraham went and took the ram and offered it up as a burnt offering instead of his son. **14** So Abraham called the name of that place, "The LORD will provide";[97] as it is said to this day, "On the mount of the LORD it shall be provided."

15 And the angel of the LORD called to Abraham a second time from heaven **16** and said, "By myself I have sworn, declares the LORD, because you have done this and have not withheld your son, your only son, **17** I will surely bless you, and I will surely multiply your offspring as the stars of heaven and as the sand that is on the seashore. And your offspring shall possess the gate of his enemies, **18** and in your offspring shall all the nations of the earth be blessed, because you have obeyed my voice." *(After Abraham proved he would obey the Lord even if it cost him his son, the Lord renewed his promise to him. It is wonderful to see the promise of grace actually carried out in the offering up of Jesus, the Only Son of the Father. Oh for grace to be part of God's family through his Son Christ Jesus.)*

19 So Abraham returned to his young men, and they arose and went together to Beersheba. And Abraham lived at Beersheba.

John Spurgeon (1810-1902)
Pastor in the Independent Congregationalist Church and father of Charles Spurgeon

February 3
Out of the Anguish of His Soul He Shall See and Be Satisfied[98]

The sacrifice of Isaac reminds us of the Divine Father, who did not spare his own Son, but freely delivered him up for us all. Let us read Isaiah's account of the sufferings of the Great Son of God.

Isaiah 53

1 Who has believed what he heard from us?
   And to whom has the arm of the LORD been revealed?

No one believes the gospel, except those who are changed by the power of God.

2 For he grew up before him like a young plant,
   and like a root out of dry ground;
   he had no form or majesty that we should look at him,
   and no beauty that we should desire him.
3 He was despised and rejected by men;
   a man of sorrows and acquainted with grief;

---

[97] KJV *Jehovah-jireh*

[98] Isaiah 53:11

and as one from whom men hide their
faces
he was despised, and we esteemed him
not.

The Eternal Father, out of love to mankind, sent his Son into this world where he would be dishonored and shamefully treated by men. This is love!

4 Surely he has borne our griefs
and carried our sorrows;
yet we esteemed him stricken,
smitten by God, and afflicted.
5 But he was pierced for our transgressions;
he was crushed for our iniquities;
upon him was the chastisement that
brought us peace,
and with his stripes we are healed.

Four words are used to describe the pains of the Lord Jesus: "pierced," "crushed," "chastisement," and "stripes." How many, how wide-ranging, and how awful his pains were none of us can tell.

6 All we like sheep have gone astray;
we have turned—every one—to his own
way;
and the LORD has laid on him
the iniquity of us all.

This is the heart of the gospel: Sin was placed on Jesus and is no longer on his people. Jehovah himself made the transfer. Therefore no one should dare to question the rightness of it.

7 He was oppressed, and he was afflicted,
yet he opened not his mouth;
like a lamb that is led to the slaughter,
and like a sheep that before its shearers
is silent,
so he opened not his mouth.
8 By oppression and judgment he was taken
away;
and as for his generation, who
considered
that he was cut off out of the land of the
living,
stricken for the transgression of my
people?
9 And they made his grave with the wicked
and with a rich man in his death,
although he had done no violence,
and there was no deceit in his mouth.

10 Yet it was the will of the LORD to crush
him;

Jehovah took pleasure in the atoning sacrifice. His love was so great that he crushed the Son of his love to save rebellious sinners.

he has put him to grief;

Yes, Jehovah himself put his own Son to grief. This is the way God proves his love for us. In return, we should give our entire lives to him.

when his soul makes an offering for sin,
he shall see his offspring; he shall
prolong his days;
the will of the LORD shall prosper in his
hand.
11 Out of the anguish of his soul he shall see
and be satisfied;
by his knowledge shall the righteous one,
my servant
make many to be accounted righteous,
and he shall bear their iniquities.
12 Therefore I will divide him a portion with
the many,
and he shall divide the spoil with the
strong,
because he poured out his soul to death
and was numbered with the
transgressors;
yet he bore the sin of many,
and makes intercession for the
transgressors.

Those who genuinely trust in the Lord Jesus may rest assured that their sins have ceased to exist, because Jesus has paid their debt in full! They may also rejoice because the non-stop praying of our King and Intercessor[99] keeps us safe. Let us come near to the cross of Jesus and rest our souls underneath the shadow of the Crucified One. God has provided himself a Lamb for a burnt offering. The victim is put to death, the promise is fulfilled, and believers are safe. Because of this, let us adore the Eternal Father from now to the end of eternity.

---

[99] *intercessor* - one who intervenes or gets involved for the benefit of others, especially by praying.

February 4
The Righteous Shall Live by His Faith[100]

Galatians 3:6-18

In this passage the apostle shows that Abraham's righteousness was a result of his faith; that the promise God made to him was only guaranteed if he had faith; and that we, who are sinners and Gentiles, join in the covenant blessings only by faith.

6 Abraham "believed God, and it was counted to him as righteousness."

7 Know then that it is those of faith who are the sons of Abraham.

Those who trust in works or boast about the rituals they keep are not the true sons of Abraham. Jews may be the natural children of Abraham, but so was Ishmael and he was not a son of promise. Abraham is the father of the faithful. The most important thing is not that Abraham is the father of a rebellious nation, but that he is the father of those who believe.

8 And the Scripture, foreseeing that God would justify the Gentiles by faith, preached the gospel beforehand to Abraham saying, "In you shall all the nations be blessed." **9** So then, those who are of faith are blessed along with Abraham, the man of faith.

This is the only way all nations can share in the blessing. They do not receive it because they are natural children of Abraham, or because they keep the Jewish ceremonial laws, or because they do something to earn it.

10 For all who rely on works of the law are under a curse; for it is written, "Cursed be everyone who does not abide by all things written in the Book of the Law, and do them." *(Let us learn this verse well. May it ring the death knell[101] of all hope of being saved by doing good works. The only thing the law can do for sinners is to judge them, condemn them, and curse them. Let us run away from the useless hope that ignorant and proud men want us to believe in. Let us look to another way to be saved. In fact, it is the only way.)* **11** Now it is evident that no one is justified before God by the law, for "The righteous shall live by faith." *(The only people who can stand innocent before God are people of faith. They are not righteous in God's eyes because they work to keep the law, but because they believe. It is clear that the law has nothing to do with their righteousness.)*

12 But the law is not of faith, rather "The one who does them shall live by them." *(The apostle is saying that we cannot be saved partly by faith and partly by works. The roads are clearly marked. If we hope to be saved by our good works, then we must keep the whole law. Our only hope is in the righteousness of the Lord Jesus Christ that we receive by faith.)* **13** Christ redeemed us from the curse of the law by becoming a curse for us—for it is written, "Cursed is everyone who is hanged on a tree"— **14** so that in Christ Jesus the blessing of Abraham might come to the Gentiles, so that we might receive the promised Spirit through faith. *(The Father placed the curse on Jesus, so we could have the blessing. All blessings come to us through the gate of Substitution; even the best blessing, which is the Holy Spirit.)*

15 To give a human example, brothers; even with a man-made covenant, no one annuls it or adds to it once it has been ratified.[102] *(Once made, a covenant cannot be legally changed by an afterthought or an unforeseen event. This is a great comfort for all believers!)* **16** Now the promises were made to Abraham and to his offspring. It does not say, "And to offsprings," referring to many, but referring to one, "And to your offspring," who is Christ. *(Notice that the apostle believed in verbal inspiration,[103] because he finds a meaning in so small a matter as the use of a singular word instead of a plural.)* **17** This is what I mean: the law, which came 430 years afterward, does not annul a covenant previously ratified by God, so as to make the promise void. *(The law given on Mount Sinai and recorded in the book of Leviticus cannot replace the

---

[100] Habakkuk 2:4 Hebrews 10:38
[101] the ringing of a church bell to announce either the death or funeral of a person
[102] *ratified* - agreed upon and signed by all involved
[103] *verbal inspiration* - Every **word** in the Bible is inspired by God

covenant of grace. Despite the law, the believer is secure in faith.) **18** For if the inheritance comes by the law, it no longer comes by promise; but God gave it to Abraham by a promise. *(We hold the promise tightly by faith. We are included in the promise God made to Abraham, not because of what we do, but by the simple act of trusting in the Lord Jesus Christ.)*

February 5
You Must be Ready[104]

Genesis 23:1-19

1 Sarah lived 127 years; these were the years of the life of Sarah. **2** And Sarah died at Kiriath-arba (that is, Hebron) in the land of Canaan, And Abraham went in to mourn for Sarah and to weep for her. *(Death comes to the holiest and happiest families, but faith learns how to make him welcome.)* **3** And Abraham rose up from before his dead and said to the Hittites, **4** "I am a sojourner and foreigner among you; give me property among you for a burying place, that I may bury my dead out of my sight." *(Dear as our loved ones may be in life, we cannot endure to look upon their dead bodies. Our fondness for them demands that we hide them in the dust. "Property among you for a burying place" is an informative statement. It is often the only property the godly own.*

5 The Hittites answered Abraham, **6** "Hear us, my lord; you are a prince of God among us. Bury your dead in the choicest of our tombs. None of us will withhold from you his tomb to hinder you from burying your dead." *(But this would not be the way Abraham would want it. He would not wish to sleep in the same grave with those from whom he was separated in life. He would remain separated to God even to the end.)*

7 Abraham rose and bowed to the Hittites, the people of the land. *(Courtesy is due even to the ungodly. A believer should be both gracious in heart and gentle in manners.)* **8** And he said to them, "If you are willing that I should bury my dead out of my sight, hear me and entreat for me Ephron the son of Zohar, **9** that he may give me the cave of Machpelah, which he owns; it is at the end of his field. For the full price let him give it to me in your presence as property for a burying place."

10 Now Ephron was sitting among the Hittites, and Ephron the Hittite answered Abraham in the hearing of the Hittites, of all who went in at the gate of his city, **11** "No, my lord hear me: I give you the field, and I give you the cave that is in it. In the sight of the sons of my people I give it to you. Bury your dead." **12** Then Abraham bowed down before the people of the land. *(This is the second time Abraham bowing is mentioned. The truly noble are friendly and courteous. A believer is not a bear.)* **13** And he said to Ephron in the hearing of the people of the land, "But if you will, hear me: I give the price of the field. Accept it from me, that I may bury my dead there."

14 Ephron answered Abraham, **15** "My lord, listen to me: a piece of land worth four hundred shekels *(about 160 ounces)* of silver, what is that between you and me? Bury your dead." **16** Abraham listened to Ephron, and Abraham weighed out for Ephron the silver that he had named in the hearing of the Hittites, four hundred shekels of silver, according to the weights current among the merchants. *(Abraham would not put himself in the debt of idolaters. True faith produces a spirit that is not dependent on others.)*

17 So the field of Ephron in Machpelah, which was to the east of Mamre, the field with the cave that was in it and all the trees that were in the field, throughout its whole area, was made over **18** to Abraham as a possession in the presence of the Hittites, before all who went in at the gate of this city. **19** After this, Abraham buried Sarah his wife in the cave of the field of Machpelah east of Mamre (that is, Hebron) in the land of Canaan. *(Abraham firmly believed that he would one day own all this land. He buried the bones of his beloved wife in the promised soil. In this way, he was actually taking possession of the land until the time when his ancestors would return to it.)*

---

[104] Matthew 24:44

February 6
Your Dead Shall Live[105]

Our last reading brought us to Abraham weeping for Sarah and burying her in the cave he bought from Ephron the Hittite. This may be a suitable time for a "meditation among the tombs."[106]

Job 14:1-15

1 "Man who is born of a woman
   is few of days and full of trouble."

Our life is not short and sweet, but brief and bitter. The one thing certain in life is trouble. Sin is the cause.

2 "He comes out like a flower and withers;
   he flees like a shadow and continues not."

The flower is not always allowed to grow until it withers, but is cut while still in its glory. We, too, are often taken away in the midst of our days.

3 "And do you open your eyes on such a one
   and bring me into judgment with you?"

Job wonders why the Lord would even think about so frail a creature as a mortal human.

4 "Who can bring a clean thing out of an unclean?
   There is not one."

The length of our troubles and the shortness of our lives are both the result of our sin nature. It is what we inherited from Adam. A pure future generation cannot come from our fallen father. A poisonous plant produces poisonous seed. A fallen man becomes the father of fallen children.

5 "Since his days are determined,
   and the number of his months is with you,
   and you have appointed his limits that he cannot pass,
6 look away from him and leave him alone,
   that he may enjoy, like a hired hand, his day."

God has decided how long we have to live and given us work to do. We are immortal until God's appointed time arrives.

7 "For there is hope for a tree,
   if it be cut down, that it will sprout again,
   and that its shoots will not cease.
8 Though its root grow old in the earth,
   and its stump die in the soil,
9 yet at the scent of water it will bud
   and put out branches like a young plant.
10 But a man dies and is laid low;
   man breathes his last, and where is he?"

So far as this visible world is concerned, a person dies and is gone forever. There is no second budding and sprouting into another mortal life for them. The ancients chose the cypress tree as the symbol of death, because once it is cut down it will not grow again, but dies completely. As far as life on this earth is concerned, their choice was wise and instructive. So, we should live while we are alive.

11 "As waters fail from a lake
   and a river wastes away and dries up,
12 so a man lies down and rises not again;
   till the heavens are no more he will not awake
   or be roused out of his sleep."

Job had seen lakes evaporate and rushing riverbeds left dry. He compares them to a dead body decomposing. But as rain from heaven can refill the lakes and cause the once dry rivers to rush with unlimited strength, so will the Lord restore life to the dead. When the heavens are no more, but have passed away with a great noise,[107] the graves will give up their dead,[108] and people shall rise again.

13 "Oh that you would hide me in Sheol,
   that you would conceal me until your wrath be past,
   that you would appoint me a set time,
   and remember me!"

Suffering Job begged for rest, he prayed for pity, he asked the Lord to remember him.

---

[105] Isaiah 26:19
[106] From James Hervey (1714-1758) Meaning, a suitable time to talk about death.
[107] From 2 Peter 3:10, "The heavens will pass away with a roar."
[108] Revelation 21:13, "And the sea gave up the dead who were in it. Death and Hades gave up the dead who were in them."

But, as a matter of fact, the Lord never forgets his servants.

¹⁴ "If a man dies, shall he live again?
   All the days of my service I would wait,
      till my renewal should come.
¹⁵ You would call, and I would answer you;
      you would long for the work of your hands."

When the resurrection day comes, the saints will answer their Creator's resurrection call and rise to eternal life. In order to share in this blessed event we must have personal faith in the risen Savior. Is this the case with everyone in our family? Is there an unsaved one among us? If so, since we may die today, may God move in us in such a way that we may seek salvation right now through faith in the Lord Jesus. He is always ready to save!

FEBRUARY 7
The LORD Will Guide You Continually[109]

Genesis 24:1-4; 10-31

¹ Now Abraham was old, well advanced in years. And the LORD had blessed Abraham in all things. *(This is the heart of his life. The chapters before this include stories of pain and suffering, but, without a doubt, the Lord made these into blessings too.)* ² And Abraham said to his servant, the oldest of his household, who had charge of all that he had, "Put your hand under my thigh, ³ that I may make you swear by the LORD, the God of heaven and God of the earth, that you will not take a wife for my son from the daughters of the Canaanites, among whom I dwell, ⁴ but will go to my country and to my kindred, and take a wife for my son Isaac." *(The godly family must be kept separate. It is not right for believers to be joined in marriage with the unbelievers.)*

¹⁰ Then the servant took ten of his master's camels and departed, taking all sorts of choice gifts from his master; and arose and went to Mesopotamia to the city of Nahor. ¹¹ And he made the camels kneel down outside the city by the well of water at the time of evening, the time when women go out to draw water. ¹² And he said, "O LORD, God of my master Abraham, please grant me success today and show steadfast love to my master Abraham. ¹³ Behold, I am standing by the spring of water, and the daughters of the men of the city are coming out to draw water. ¹⁴ Let the young woman to whom I shall say, 'Please let down your jar that I may drink,' and who shall say, 'Drink, and I will water your camels'—let her be the one whom you have appointed for your servant Isaac. By this I shall know that you have shown steadfast love to my master." *(The mission that is carried on in the spirit of prayer will certainly end well. Everything about marriage should be especially prayed over.)*

¹⁵ Before he had finished speaking, behold, Rebekah, who was born to Bethuel the son of Milcah, the wife of Nahor, Abraham's brother, came out with her water jar on her shoulder. *(Here was the hand of Providence.[110] We should also be able to see it in our own lives.)* ¹⁶ The young woman was very attractive in appearance, a maiden whom no man had known. She went to the spring and filled her jar and came up. ¹⁷ Then the servant ran to meet her and said, "Please give me a little water to drink from your jar." ¹⁸ She said, "Drink, my lord." And she quickly let down her jar upon her hand and gave him a drink. ¹⁹ When she had finished giving him a drink, she said, "I will draw water for your camels also, until they have finished drinking." ²⁰ So she quickly emptied her jar into the trough and ran again to the well to draw water, and she drew for all his camels. ²¹ The man gazed at her in silence to learn whether the LORD had prospered his journey or not.

²² When the camels had finished drinking, the man took a gold ring weighing a half shekel *(about one-fifth of an ounce)*, and two bracelets for her arms weighing ten gold shekels *(about four ounces)*, ²³ and said, "Please tell me whose daughter you are. Is

---
[109] Isaiah 58:11

[110] *Providence* - Usually, when used with a capital "P" it refers to God; when used with a lower case "p", it refers to God's will, his divine intervention, and his predetermination (predestination).

there room in your father's house for us to spend the night?" ²⁴ She said to him, "I am the daughter of Bethuel the son of Milcah, whom she bore to Nahor." ²⁵ She added, "We have plenty of both straw and fodder, and room to spend the night." ²⁶ The man bowed his head and worshiped the LORD ²⁷ and said, "Blessed be the LORD, the God of my master Abraham, who has not forsaken his steadfast love and his faithfulness toward my master. As for me, the LORD has led me in the way to the house of my master's kinsman." *(We should always remember to thank God for answering our prayers.)* ²⁸ Then the young woman ran and told her mother's household about these things.

²⁹ Rebekah had a brother whose name was Laban. Laban ran out toward the man, to the spring. ³⁰ As soon as he saw the ring and the bracelets on his sister's arms, and heard the words of Rebekah his sister, "Thus the man spoke to me," he went to the man. And behold he was standing by the camels at the spring. ³¹ He said, "Come in, O blessed of the LORD. Why do you stand outside? For I have prepared the house and a place for the camels. *(All difficulties vanished. Everything was as good as he could wish for. It may not always be this way with us, but if any plan of action can make it so, it is that which begins and ends with prayer.)*

February 8
You Follow Me![111]

Laban listened to the story of Abraham's servant and saw the jewelry given to Rebekah, that were no doubt very favorable indicators to his greedy mind. He gave his consent for Rebekah to leave and marry Isaac.

Genesis 24:50-67

⁵⁰ Then Laban and Bethuel answered and said, "The thing has come from the LORD; we cannot speak to you bad or good. ⁵¹ Behold, Rebekah is before you; take her and go, and let her be the wife of your master's son, as the LORD has spoken." *(It is always right for young people to seek the approval of parents and mature persons in such an important decision.)*

⁵² When Abraham's servant heard their words, he bowed himself to the earth before the LORD. *(He was too devoted to God to forget to thank him. Too many people only pray when they have a need. They forget to worship in thanksgiving.)* ⁵³ And the servant brought out jewelry of silver and of gold, and garments, and gave them to Rebekah. He also gave to her brother and to her mother costly ornaments. *(He was a wise servant. He knew what to use to persuade Laban.)* ⁵⁴ And he and the men who were with him ate and drank, and they spent the night there. When they arose in the morning, he said, "Send me away to my master." *(God's servants should be like this servant. They should never be loiterers.[112])* ⁵⁵ Her brother and her mother said, "Let the young woman remain with us a while, at least ten days; after that she may go." ⁵⁶ But he said to them, "Do not delay me, since the LORD has prospered my way. Send me away that I may go to my master." *(We should not be easily sidetracked from out duties. To loiter is to disobey. When God sends us we should be on our way.)*

⁵⁷ They said, "Let us call the young woman and ask her." ⁵⁸ And they called Rebekah and said to her, "Will you go with this man?" She said, "I will go." *(How happy would pastors be if all young people could be as easily led to the great Bridegroom, the Lord Jesus. He accepts all who are willing. He asks for the heart. Unfortunately, many refuse to accept his loving request.)* ⁵⁹ So they sent away Rebekah their sister and her nurse, and Abraham's servant and his men. ⁶⁰ And they blessed Rebekah and said to her,

"Our sister, may you become
   thousands of ten thousands,
and may your offspring possess
   the gate of those who hate them!"

The blessing of parents is a precious marriage gift.

⁶¹ Then Rebekah and her young women arose and rode on the camels and followed

---

[111] John 21:22

[112] *loiterers* - someone who stands or waits around idly or without apparent purpose.

the man. Thus the servant took Rebekah and went his way.

⁶² Now Isaac had returned from Beerlahairoi and was dwelling in the Negeb. ⁶³ And Isaac went out to meditate in the field toward evening. *(This good man chose a quiet and private place for one of the most heavenly of occupations. He is an example to every one of us. If we meditated more we would be far more gracious than we are.)* And he lifted up his eyes and saw, and behold there were camels coming. ⁶⁴ And Rebekah lifted up her eyes, and when she saw Isaac, she dismounted from the camel ⁶⁵ and said to the servant, "Who is that man, walking in the field to meet us?" The servant said, "It is my master." So she took her veil and covered herself. ⁶⁶ And the servant told Isaac all the things that he had done. *(Happy is that servant of God who can, without fear or shame, tell his Master in heaven all that he has done. What a sad account some will have to give; for, "Who has believed what they heard from us? And to whom has the arm of the* LORD *been revealed?"¹¹³)* ⁶⁷ Then Isaac brought her into the tent of Sarah his mother and took Rebekah, and she became his wife, and he loved her. So Isaac was comforted after his mother's death.

February 9
Do Not Love the World[114]

The portion of Scripture we will now read gives us a review of our previous reading. It shows us what gave the patriarchs¹¹⁵ strength in their life of separation in this world.

Hebrews 11:8-19

⁸ By faith Abraham obeyed when he was called to go out to a place that he was to receive as an inheritance. And he went out, not knowing where he was going. *(Faith is a better guide than mere reason, if it is faith in God. Our understanding is incomplete and may mislead us, but trust in the omniscient¹¹⁶ Lord gives us a guide who cannot make a mistake.)* ⁹ By faith he went to live in the land of promise, as in a foreign land, living in tents with Isaac and Jacob, heirs with him of the same promise. ¹⁰ For he was looking forward to the city that has foundations, whose designer and builder is God.

His eye saw into the far off future. His hope looked to eternal things. Are we also looking beyond this world for true contentment? If not, a day will come when shame will cover our faces, because everything that we see and trust in will dry up like the mist of the morning.

Heaven has a solid foundation, earth has none. Job tells us concerning the Great Creator, "he…hangs the earth on nothing."¹¹⁷

¹¹ By faith Sarah herself received power to conceive, even when she was past the age, since she considered him faithful who had promised. ¹² Therefore from one man, and him as good as dead, were born descendants as many as the stars of heaven and as many as the innumerable grains of sand by the seashore. *(Abraham was far too old to expect to have children borne through him. In that sense, his body was as good as dead. Yet the father of the faithful was not amazed at the promise of the Almighty God.*

There is no exaggeration in comparing Abraham's descendants to the stars of heaven and the sand by the seashore. That is because all believers are considered as children of Abraham. His spiritual children are as countless as the stars and his natural or earthly children are even more, like the sand by the seashore.)

¹³ These all died in faith, not having received the things promised, but having seen them and greeted them from afar, and having acknowledged that they were strangers and exiles on the earth. ¹⁴ For people who speak thus make it clear that they are seeking a homeland. *(Even in this day,*

---

[113] Isaiah 53:1
[114] 1 John 2:15
[115] *patriarch* - A man regarded as the father or ruler of a family. Bible patriarchs include Abraham, Isaac, Jacob and Jacob's twelve sons.

[116] *omniscient* (adjective), *omniscience* (noun) - All knowing or knowing everything; all seeing or seeing everything. The capacity to know everything that there is to know
[117] Job 26:7

we are to live on this earth like strangers and foreigners, because we look for a city that cannot be seen. "Jerusalem the golden"[118] is the desire of our hearts. We do not have a permanent home in this world. This is what it means to walk by faith.) **15** If they had been thinking of that land from which they had gone out, they would have had opportunity to return.

Keeping in contact with the old country was easy and the temptation to stay in touch with their homeland was a strong one. But they were determined to continue in the pilgrim life[119] and so must we. Opportunities to return to sin are very, very many, but we must continue to walk with God by the power of the Holy Spirit.

16 But as it is, they desire a better country, that is, a heavenly one. Therefore God is not ashamed to be called their God, for he has prepared for them a city.

17 By faith Abraham, when he was tested, offered up Isaac, and he who had received the promises was in the act of offering up his only son, **18** of whom it was said, "Through Isaac shall your offspring be named." **19** He considered that God was able even to raise him from the dead, from which, figuratively speaking, he did receive him back. *(Isaac was really like someone who had been raised from the dead, because Abraham had decided to obey God and assumed his only son would be sacrificed. In this way, Isaac became a picture of the resurrection to new life in Christ.*

The faith of Abraham was tested in many fires and ours will be too. Will it stand the test? Are we resting on the faithfulness and omnipotence[120] of God? Anything less strong than this will fall out from under us. The faith of God's elect, which is the gift of God and the work of the Holy Spirit, will hold up, conquer and land us safely in the promised inheritance. Do we have this faith or not?

May the Lord give us this most precious grace.)

February 10
The LORD Will Answer None of Man's Words[121]

We will leave out some of the minor details of the history found in the book of Genesis and move on to the birth of Isaac's twin sons, Esau and Jacob. Let us see how the New Testament explains the Old Testament. We will read:

Romans 9:1-13

In this chapter the apostle Paul illustrates the doctrine[122] of election by the history of the families of Abraham and Isaac. He shows us that the Lord chose one child over the other without regard to anything they had done. These are very deep waters, but if our wish is to know only what God reveals and no more, then we can safely follow where Scripture leads. Election is not an appropriate subject for idle curiosity, but it is also not a subject to ignore. Whatever is taught in the Word of God is there for a reason and we should pay attention to it.

1 I am speaking the truth in Christ—I am not lying; my conscience bears me witness in the Holy Spirit— **2** that I have great sorrow and unceasing anguish in my heart. **3** For I could wish that I myself were accursed and cut off from Christ for the sake of my brothers, my kinsmen according to the flesh.

Paul did not write the way he did because he hated the nation that he belonged to. Far from it. He would have sacrificed everything for their good. He felt almost ready to be cast out of the kingdom himself, if by doing so he could have rescued the Jewish people. Intense, heartfelt love speaks in words that should not be weighed in the balances of cold logic. Instead, look on his words as the outburst of a loving heart and they are clear enough. Oh that all Christians had the same kind of love for perishing sinners.

4 They are Israelites, and to them belong the adoption, the glory, the covenants, the giving of the law, the worship, and the

---

[118] probably a reference to a 12th century hymn by St. Bernard
[119] living as strangers on this earth, knowing their real home is in heaven
[120] *omnipotent, omnipotence* - all powerful, almighty, absolute and supreme power, having unlimited power.

[121] Job 33:13
[122] *doctrine* - the belief or teaching of a church or group.

promises. ⁵To them belong the patriarchs, and from their race, according to the flesh, is the Christ who is God over all, blessed forever. Amen.

Paul pauses to adore the Lord whom he loved. Let us bow our heads and also worship him.

⁶But it is not as though the word of God has failed. For not all who are descended from Israel belong to Israel, ⁷and not all are children of Abraham because they are his offspring, but "Through Isaac shall your offspring be named."

God made a distinction according to his own will. He has a right to hand out his favors the way he wants to. It is wrong for us to disapprove his actions or demand that he explain himself.

⁸This means that it is not the children of the flesh who are the children of God, but the children of the promise are counted as offspring. ⁹For this is what the promise said: "About this time next year I will return and Sarah shall have a son." ¹⁰And not only so, but also when Rebecca had conceived children by one man, our forefather Isaac, ¹¹though they were not yet born and had done nothing either good or bad—in order that God's purpose of election might continue, not because of works but because of him who calls— ¹²she was told, "The older will serve the younger." ¹³As it is written, "Jacob I loved, but Esau I hated."

God passed over Esau and gave Jacob the covenant blessing. This is a fact to be believed. It is not a subject for debate. Who are we that we should summon Jehovah to our own courtroom? God is righteous in all his ways. We find that Esau despised his birthright and sold it for a bowl of stew.[123] His actions clearly justified his condemnation, as well as fulfilled the purpose of God.

It ought to humble us when we remember that we have no rights that we can demand from God. If God should allow us to continue in sin and perish, we have no right to complain; it is what we deserve. We should sincerely and humbly beg him to look on us in mercy and save us with his great salvation. "Whoever comes to me I will never cast out,"[124] is the voice of Jesus. Whether we understand it or not, it is in complete agreement with the predestination taught in this chapter. The Lord has a chosen people and yet his gospel is to be preached to every creature. Believe, but do not disapprove. When we believe on the Lord Jesus, we are in the way to making our calling and election sure.[125] Only by faith can we be confident that the Lord has called and chosen us.

February 11
Hold Me Up, That I May Be Safe[126]

We have read about God's purpose for Esau and Jacob. We will now read about their lives.

Genesis 25:27-34

²⁷When the boys grew up, Esau was a skillful hunter, a man of the field, while Jacob was a quiet man, dwelling in tents.

Children of the same parents may differ greatly in temperament, in behavior, and in character. The sovereign grace of God creates visible distinctions when it begins to operate. Every year makes the differences more apparent. Esau was wild and Jacob gentle. One was wandering, unsteady, and proud, and the other comfortable at home, thoughtful and calm.

²⁸Isaac loved Esau because he ate of his game, but Rebekah loved Jacob.

This was bad on the part of both parents. Favoritism should be avoided. Nothing but discontent and bad feelings can come of it. Yet if Rebekah loved Jacob because of his quiet, holy temperament, she had good reason for it. That is more than can be said of Isaac's love of the rough huntsman Esau, only because "he ate of his game."

²⁹Once when Jacob was cooking stew, Esau came in from the field, and he was exhausted. ³⁰And Esau said to Jacob, "Let me eat some of that red stew, for I am exhausted!" (Therefore his name was called

---

[123] Genesis 25:34
[124] John 6:37
[125] 2 Peter 1:10
[126] Psalm 119:117

Edom *{which sounds like the Hebrew word for "red"}*.) ³¹ Jacob said, "Sell me your birthright now." *(This was unbrotherly and ungenerous of Jacob. The only good point about it is that he set a high value on the birthright, which showed his spiritual understanding. It is clear from this passage that Jacob's salvation was due to the mercy of God. There was nothing in his natural character that could be seen as honorable. The good points in him were from the Lord. His tendency to bargain for a good deal was inherited from his mother's family.)* ³² Esau said, "I am about to die; of what use is a birthright to me?" ³³ Jacob said, "Swear to me now." So he swore to him and sold his birthright to Jacob. ³⁴ Then Jacob gave Esau bread and lentil stew, and he ate and drank and rose and went his way. Thus Esau despised his birthright.

Esau valued his birthright so little that a sorry bowl of stew was enough to buy it from him. Surely it was the most expensive dish of meat ever bought. Of course, we remember a little fruit that cost us much more. Many people who live for this world trade their souls for the pleasures of an hour. They cry, "Let us eat and drink, for tomorrow we die."[127] *Many have thrown aside all hope of heaven for the hope of being rich, for the enjoyment of having pleasure, or just to have their own way. This is really trading pearls for pebbles, diamonds for fakes, and lasting happiness for short-lived amusement. May those who are still young take this sad act of Esau as a warning and eagerly choose that which will not be taken away from them.*

The apostle takes the story of Esau and teaches us a valuable lesson in:

Hebrews 12:15-17

¹⁵ See to it that no one fails to obtain the grace of God; *(We are to be on guard, so that any of us who profess to be children of God do not fall short of the grace of God and be like an arrow that does not quite reach the target. To not have grace in the heart is fatal.)* that no "root of bitterness" springs up and causes trouble, and by it many become defiled; *(Sin is a plant that has a bitter root. Its only fruit is sorrow and shame.)* ¹⁶ that no one is sexually immoral or unholy like Esau, who sold his birthright for a single meal. *(It is an unholy thing to compare the priceless blessing of God to a mere physical enjoyment. Our actions show that we are against God.)* ¹⁷ For you know that afterward, when he desired to inherit the blessing, he was rejected, for he found no chance to repent, though he sought it with tears.

The deed was done, the blessing had been given to Jacob, and Isaac could not change it. If people sell their hope of heaven for the joys of earth, it will be too late to repent in the next world. Those who are filthy will still be filthy.[128]

February 12
The Righteous Person Hates Falsehood[129]

Genesis 27:1-6; 17-29

¹ When Isaac was old and his eyes were dim so that he could not see, he called Esau his older son and said to him, "My son"; and he answered, "Here I am." ² He said, "Behold, I am old; I do not know the day of my death. ³ Now then, take your weapons, your quiver and your bow, and go out to the field and hunt game for me, ⁴ and prepare for me delicious food, such as I love, and bring it to me so that I may eat, that my soul may bless you before I die."

⁵ Now Rebekah was listening when Isaac spoke to his son Esau. So when Esau went to the field to hunt for game and bring it, ⁶ Rebekah said to her son Jacob, "I heard your father speak to your brother Esau."

When Rebekah heard this she came up with a devious plan to get the blessing for her favorite son Jacob. She prepared two young goats in a delicious way, dressed Jacob in Esau's clothes, put animal skins on his hands and neck so that he would seem to

---

[127] 1 Corinthians 15:32

[128] Revelation 21:10-11, "And he said to me, 'Do not seal up the words of the prophecy of this book, for the time is near. Let the evildoer still do evil, and the filthy still be filthy, and the righteous still do right, and the holy still be holy.'"

[129] Proverbs 13:5

be hairy like his brother, and sent him in to deceive his father.

17 And she put the delicious food and the bread, which she had prepared, into the hand of her son Jacob.

18 So he went in to his father and said, "My father." And he said, "Here I am. Who are you, my son?" **19** Jacob said to his father, "I am Esau your firstborn. I have done as you told me; now sit up and eat of my game, that your soul may bless me." **20** But Isaac said to his son, "How is it that you have found it so quickly, my son?" He answered, "Because the LORD your God granted me success." *(When we begin to sin we go from bad to worse. It was bad enough for Jacob to tell so many lies, but to bring in the Lord God of his father to give them the appearance of truth, was much worse.)*

21 Then Isaac said to Jacob, "Please come near, that I may feel you, my son, to know whether you are really my son Esau or not." **22** So Jacob went near to Isaac his father, who felt him and said, "The voice is Jacob's voice, but the hands are the hands of Esau." **23** And he did not recognize him, because his hands were hairy like his brother Esau's hands. So he blessed him. **24** He said, "Are you really my son Esau?" He answered, "I am." *(Jacob continued to lie to his father. This story shows us the truthfulness of God's word, because it does not hide the faults of its most famous and respected saints. If the Old Testament were a cleverly told fable, it would never have placed the great father of the twelve tribes in such a bad light.)* **25** Then he said, "Bring it near to me, that I may eat of my son's game and bless you." So he brought it near to him, and he ate; and he brought him wine, and he drank. *(Isaac did not ask the Lord to guide him, so the mistake was his fault too. In this way he was punished for making Esau his favorite son. It was very improper for this patriarch to prefer his ungodly son "because he ate of his game."[130])*

26 Then his father Isaac said to him, "Come near and kiss me, my son." **27** So he came near and kissed him. And Isaac smelled the smell of his garments and blessed him and said,

"See, the smell of my son
   is as the smell of a field that the LORD has blessed!
28 May God give you of the dew of heaven
   and of the fatness of the earth
   and plenty of grain and wine.
29 Let peoples serve you,
   and nations bow down to you.
Be lord over your brothers,
   and may your mother's sons bow down to you.
Cursed be everyone who curses you,
   and blessed be everyone who blesses you!"

The prophecy concerning Esau and Jacob was repeated and enlarged. To "the older shall serve the younger"[131] was now added curses and blessings as well as nations bowing down to a son of Jacob. God's purpose was accomplished, but this did not excuse Rebekah and Jacob, or protect them from the chastisements[132] of God, that began almost immediately. We should never do evil so good may come.

February 13
I Will Never Leave You[133]

After Esau found out that Jacob had tricked his father into giving him the blessing, he vowed to kill his brother. Therefore their mother Rebekah felt she needed to send her favorite son away. Little did she think, when she began this crooked path to deceive her husband into blessing Jacob, that she would actually lose her son in the process.

Genesis 28:10-22

10 Jacob left Beersheba and went toward Haran. *(He was alone. Without a servant to attend him, or a donkey or camel to carry him, and with only his staff to lean on, the heir of the promises set out on his long journey of about five hundred miles.)* **11** And

---
[130] Genesis 25:28

[131] Genesis 25:23

[132] *chasten, chastening* or *chastisement* - The act of discipline which may include scolding, criticizing or pain inflicted for the purpose of correction or moral improvement.

[133] Hebrews 13:5

he came to a certain place and stayed there that night, because the sun had set. Taking one of the stones of the place, he put it under his head and lay down in that place to sleep. *(He had a hard bed and a cold pillow, but he had a sweet sleep, and a sweeter dream. Often when the head lies hardest the heart is lightest, meaning our times of great trial are often times of heavenly visitation.)* **12** And he dreamed, and behold, there was a ladder[134] set up on the earth, and the top of it reached to heaven. And behold, the angels of God were ascending and descending on it! *(Notice the "beholds" in the passage. They call for our special attention. The patriarch dreamed of Jesus, the sweetest of all dreams. He saw how heaven and earth are joined by the Messiah, and how open the relationship between God and man is because of the Mediator.[135])*

13 And behold, the LORD stood above it and said, "I am the LORD, the God of Abraham your father and the God of Isaac. The land on which you lie I will give to you and to your offspring. **14** Your offspring shall be like the dust of the earth, and you shall spread abroad to the west and to the east and to the north and to the south, and in you and your offspring shall all the families of the earth be blessed. **15** Behold, I am with you and will keep you wherever you go, and will bring you back to this land. For I will not leave you until I have done what I have promised you." *(Having seen the Messiah as the ladder, he saw the glory of Jehovah the covenant God, and received the covenant blessing.[136] Every syllable must have sounded like the sweetest music in his ears. Notice those choice words: "I will not leave you." God will never leave the person he loves. And, "until I have done what I have promised you." With men, saying and doing are two very different things, but not with God.)*

16 Then Jacob awoke from his sleep and said, "Surely the LORD is in this place, and I did not know it." **17** And he was afraid and said, "How awesome is this place! This is none other than the house of God, and this is the gate of heaven."

He was full of awe, even to the point of trembling. He felt as if he had slept in the temple of Jehovah and, as a sinner, he was moved with amazement. He had not been afraid of wild beasts or heathen men, but now he is filled with holy confidence and equally filled with holy fear.

18 So early in the morning Jacob took the stone that he had put under his head and set it up for a pillar and poured oil on the top of it. *(We must honor God with our possessions. Some set up a stone of remembrance, but they do not pour oil on the top of it, because they offer nothing that is theirs to the Lord.)* **19** He called the name of that place Bethel, *(the house of God)* but the name of the city was Luz at the first. **20** Then Jacob made a vow, saying, "If God will be with me and will keep me in this way that I go, and will give me bread to eat and clothing to wear, **21** so that I come again to my father's house in peace, then the LORD shall be my God, **22** and this stone, which I have set up for a pillar, shall be God's house. And of all that you give me I will give a full tenth to you."

There was a little of the bargaining spirit here, in asking for food to eat and clothes to put on, but still there was genuine faith. Jacob commits himself completely to the Lord and leaves his trust in anything or anyone else behind and then dedicates a tithe to the Lord. God treats each of us so well, that we should never be ungenerous to his cause. Can we not do something even now to honor the Lord with our possessions and with the first fruits[137] of our labor?)

---

[134] *ladder* or *a flight of steps*
[135] 1 Timothy 2:5, "For there is one God, and there is one mediator [middleman, go-between] between God and men, the man Christ Jesus."
[136] *covenant* - A contract, promise, guarantee, pledge or agreement between two or more persons. The covenant God is the God who promises, and the covenant blessing is the blessing God has promised.

[137] *first fruits* - the first agricultural produce of the harvest. In other words, from the top of our pay checks rather than from what is left over after paying bills.

Spurgeon's Birthplace, Kelvedon, Essex.
Where he lived for ten months, 1834-1835

February 14
The Lord is My Helper[138]

Jacob reached the house of Laban and there married his two wives, Leah and Rachel. After years of hard work for Laban, he wanted to return home to see his father again. Besides, he felt that Laban had treated him badly and that it was time to part ways so he could become his own boss. Therefore he snuck away with his family and his possessions, but he was hotly pursued by Laban, who evidently intended him no good. The night before Laban overtook Jacob the Lord visited him in a dream and warned him against harming Jacob or attempting to lure him back to Haran. This was a very gracious way of getting involved. Jacob had a very good reason to bless the Lord, because it kept Laban from doing any mischief. However, Laban still accused Jacob of stealing his idols. Jacob did not know that Rachel had hidden them and when Laban could not find them he scolded him for bringing such a groundless accusation against him.

Genesis 31:36-44

36 Then Jacob became angry and berated Laban. Jacob said to Laban, "What is my offense? What is my sin, that you have hotly pursued me? **37** For you have felt through all my goods; what have you found of all your household goods? Set it here before my kinsmen and your kinsmen, that they may decide between us two. **38** These twenty years I have been with you. Your ewes and your female goats have not miscarried, and I have not eaten the rams of your flocks. **39** What was torn by wild beasts I did not bring to you. I bore the loss of it myself. From my hand you required it, whether stolen by day or stolen by night. **40** There I was: by day the heat consumed me, and the cold by night, and my sleep fled from my eyes. **41** These twenty years I have been in your house. I served you fourteen years for your two daughters, and six years for your flock, and you have changed my wages ten times. **42** If the God of my father, the God of Abraham and the Fear of Isaac, had not been on my side, surely now you would have sent me away empty-handed. God saw my affliction and the labor of my hands and rebuked you last night."

Laban was a great boaster, but a miserable, mean-spirited person. He claimed credit for leaving Jacob unharmed, but Jacob saw through his lies and knew the only reason Laban did not harm him was because the Lord had appeared to him in a dream.

43 Then Laban answered and said to Jacob, "The daughters are my daughters, the children are my children, the flocks are my flocks, and all that you see is mine. But what can I do this day for these my daughters or for their children whom they have borne? **44** Come now, let us make a covenant, you and I. And let it be a witness between you and me." *(Laban made the best of what, to him, was a bad situation; and so, by the good hand of the Lord, what might have been a terrible slaughter ended in a friendly agreement. The Lord can make the wrath of men to praise him and restrain it when he pleases.[139] This event reminds us of one of David's songs of gratitude.)*

Psalm 124

1 If it had not been the LORD who was on our side—
    let Israel now say—
2 if it had not been the LORD who was on our side
    when people rose up against us,

---

[138] Hebrews 13:6

[139] Psalm 76:10, "Surely the wrath of man shall praise you; the remnant of wrath you will put on like a belt."

3 then they would have swallowed us up alive,
    when their anger was kindled against us;
4 then the flood would have swept us away,
    the torrent would have gone over us;
5 then over us would have gone
    the raging waters.
6 Bless be the LORD,
    who has not given us
    as prey to their teeth!
7 We have escaped like a bird
    from the snare of the fowlers;
    the snare is broken,
    and we have escaped!
8 Our help is in the name of the LORD,
    who made heaven and earth.

February 15
I Give Myself to Prayer[140]

No sooner had Jacob escaped from Laban than he was plunged into another trial. He had to face his brother Esau who he had cheated out of his father's blessing. We will see how the Lord protected his servant once again.

Genesis 32:6-13; 21-31

⁶ And the messengers returned to Jacob, saying, "We came to your brother Esau, and he is coming to meet you, and there are four hundred men with him." ⁷ Then Jacob was greatly afraid and distressed. He divided the people who were with him, and the flocks and herds and camels, into two camps, ⁸ thinking, "If Esau comes to the one camp and attacks it, then the camp that is left will escape." *(People of faith are also people of common sense. We are to use our brains as well as our prayers. Grace does not make people stupid.)*

⁹ And Jacob said, "O God of my father Abraham and God of my father Isaac, O LORD who said to me, 'Return to your country and to your kindred, that I may do you good,' ¹⁰ I am not worthy of the least of all the deeds of steadfast love and all the faithfulness that you have shown to your servant, for with only my staff I crossed this Jordan, and now I have become two camps. ¹¹ Please deliver me from the hand of my brother, from the hand of Esau, for I fear him, that he may come and attack me, the mothers with the children. ¹² But you said, 'I will surely do you good, and make your offspring as the sand of the sea, which cannot be numbered for multitude.'" *(This is a master argument, "but you said." It is a real prayer when we plead the promise and hold the Lord to his word.)*

¹³ So he stayed there that night, and from what he had with him he took a present for his brother Esau.

²¹ So the present passed on ahead of him, and he himself stayed that night in the camp. ²² The same night he arose and took his two wives, his two female servants, and his eleven children, and crossed the ford of the Jabbok. ²³ He took them and sent them across the stream, and everything else that he had. ²⁴ And Jacob was left alone. *(Solitude is the good helper of devotion. Company distracts us, but when we are alone we can get right to the heart of our concerns in prayer.)* And a man wrestled with him until the breaking of the day. *(Prayer must become a serious struggle, a wrestling, if we really want to be victorious with God.)* ²⁵ When the man saw that he did not prevail against Jacob, he touched his hip socket, and Jacob's hip was put out of joint as he wrestled with him. *(He injured one ligament but he could just as easily have crushed Jacob's whole body. If we prevail with the Lord in prayer, it is because he lends us strength and allows himself to be conquered.)* ²⁶ Then he said, "Let me go, for the day has broken." But Jacob said, "I will not let you go unless you bless me." *(This was bravely spoken. Those who ask like this win the day.)*

²⁷ And he said to him, "What is your name?" And he said, "Jacob." ²⁸ Then he said, "Your name shall no longer be called Jacob, but Israel *(which means prince of God or one who prevails with God)*, for you have striven with God and with men, and have prevailed." *(One night spent in prayer gave Jacob a royal title. How few of us have ever tried to win the rank of prince in this way. Who can tell how much we might gain if we*

---
[140] Psalm 109:4

would wrestle for it. When Jacob overcame the angel he virtually disarmed Esau. He who has power with God will certainly prevail with people.) ²⁹ Then Jacob asked him, "Please tell me your name." But he said, "Why is it that you ask my name?" And there he blessed him. *(He did not gratify his curiosity, but he did better, he enriched him with a divine blessing.)* ³⁰ So Jacob called the name of the place Peniel *(or the face of God)*, saying, "For I have seen God face to face, and yet my life has been delivered." ³¹ The sun rose upon him as he passed Penuel, limping because of his hip.

And who would not be content to limp if he might win what Israel won?

February 16
In the World You Will Have Tribulation[141]

Joseph was Jacob's best loved and most afflicted son. "The Lord disciplines the one he loves."[142] This chapter opens a long scene of suffering.

Genesis 37:2-14; 18-24; 28; 31-35

² Joseph, being seventeen years old, was pasturing the flock with his brothers. He was a boy with the sons of Bilhah and Zilpah, his father's wives. And Joseph brought a bad report of them to their father. ³ Now Israel loved Joseph more than any other of his sons, because he was the son of his old age. And he made him a robe of many colors. ⁴ But when his brothers saw that their father loved him more than all his brothers, they hated him and could not speak peacefully to him.

His good character led him to speak out against the wrong his brothers were doing. He would not join them in doing evil, or help them by keeping quiet about their evil deeds.

⁵ Now Joseph had a dream, and when he told it to his brothers they hated him even more. ⁶ He said to them, "Hear this dream that I dreamed: ⁷ Behold, we were binding sheaves in the field, and behold, my sheaf arose and stood upright. And behold, your sheaves gathered around it and bowed down to my sheaf." ⁸ His brothers said to him, "Are you indeed to reign over us? Or are you indeed to rule over us?" So they hated him even more for his dreams and for his words.

⁹ Then he dreamed another dream and told it to his brothers and said, "Behold, I have dreamed another dream. Behold, the sun, the moon, and eleven stars were bowing down to me." ¹⁰ But when he told it to his father and to his brothers, his father rebuked him and said to him, "What is this dream that you have dreamed? Shall I and your mother and your brothers indeed come to bow ourselves to the ground before you?" ¹¹ And his brothers were jealous of him, but his father kept the saying in mind. *(Ungodly people are sure to dislike the person that God favors. The evil hate the righteous.)*

¹² Now his brothers went to pasture their father's flock near Shechem. ¹³ And Israel said to Joseph, "Are not your brothers pasturing the flock at Shechem? Come, I will send you to them." And he said to him, "Here I am." ¹⁴ So he said to him, "Go now, see if it is well with your brothers and with the flock, and bring me word." So he sent him from the Valley of Hebron, and he came to Shechem.

¹⁸ They saw him from afar, and before he came near to them they conspired against him to kill him. ¹⁹ They said to one another, "Here comes this dreamer. ²⁰ Come now, let us kill him and throw him into one of the pits. Then we will say that a fierce animal has devoured him, and we will see what will become of his dreams." ²¹ But when Reuben heard it, he rescued him out of their hands, saying, "Let us not take his life." ²² And Reuben said to them, "Shed no blood; throw him into this pit here in the wilderness, but do not lay a hand on him"—that he might rescue him out of their hand to restore him to his father. ²³ So when Joseph came to his brothers, they stripped him of his robe, the robe of many colors that he wore. ²⁴ And they took him and threw him into a pit. The pit was empty; there was no water in it.

²⁸ Then Midianite traders passed by. And they drew Joseph up and lifted him out of the pit, and sold him to the Ishmaelites for

---
[141] John 16:33
[142] Hebrews 12:6

twenty shekels *(eight ounces)* of silver. They took Joseph to Egypt.

31 Then [his brothers] took Joseph's robe and slaughtered a goat and dipped the robe in the blood. **32** And they sent the robe of many colors and brought it to their father and said, "This we have found; please identify whether it is your son's robe or not." **33** And he identified it and said, "It is my son's robe. A fierce animal has devoured him. Joseph is without doubt torn to pieces." **34** Then Jacob tore his garments and put sackcloth on his loins and mourned for his son many days. **35** All his sons and all his daughters rose up to comfort him, but he refused to be comforted and said, "No, I shall go down to Sheol to my son, mourning." Thus his father wept for him.

This was a very painful event, but let us not forget that the Lord was at work in it to bring about a great blessing.

February 17
The LORD Will Keep You from All Evil He Will Keep Your Life[143]
Genesis 39:1-6; 16-23

1 Now Joseph had been brought down to Egypt, and Potiphar, an officer of Pharaoh, the captain of the guard, an Egyptian, had bought him from the Ishmaelites who had brought him down there. **2** The LORD was with Joseph, and he became a successful man, and he was in the house of his Egyptian master.

Grace gave Joseph the ability to make the best of his situation, and to be pleasant, hard working, and useful. This was as it should be. A child of God, even as a slave, should honor his religion. God will bless him if he does.

3 His master saw that the LORD was with him and that the LORD caused all that he did to succeed in his hands.

This shows that Joseph did not fall into Egyptian idolatry. He declared his faith in Jehovah in a way that showed his master that Jehovah was with him.

4 So Joseph found favor in his sight and attended him, and he made him overseer of his house and put him in charge of all that he had. *(The fear of God leads to honesty and faithfulness. This is often the road to promotion even among mankind. Godliness brings blessings even in this life.)* **5** From the time that he made him overseer in his house and over all that he had, the LORD blessed the Egyptian's house for Joseph's sake; the blessing of the LORD was on all that he had, in house and field. **6** So he left all that he had in Joseph's charge, and because of him he had no concern about anything but the food he ate.

Now Joseph was handsome in form and appearance. *(This became a trial to him. Personal beauty is a dangerous gift. We must not be proud of it, but be the more guarded in our conduct if we possess it.)*

Joseph found a tempter in his master's wife. She tried to lead him into great sin. He refused to listen to her disgraceful request and said, "How then can I do this great wickedness and sin against God?"[144] The wicked woman tried again and again to lead him into sin. At last she grabbed him by his clothes and held him. He fled from her, but he had to leave his garment in her hand. Then her wicked heart turned to spite. She charged Joseph with being guilty of that impure action that he had so firmly refused.)

16 Then she laid up his garment by her until his master came home, **17** and she told him the same story *(she had already told the men of Potiphar's household)*, saying, "The Hebrew servant, whom you have brought among us, came in to me to laugh at me. **18** But as soon as I lifted up my voice and cried, he left his garment beside me and fled out of the house."

She convinced her husband by telling this story and showing the garment that, if it could have spoken, would have declared his innocence. A great deal of evidence may be brought against a perfectly innocent person. Therefore, let us be slow to condemn people of untarnished character.

---

[143] Psalm 121:7

[144] Genesis 39:9b

¹⁹ As soon as his master heard the words that his wife spoke to him, "This is the way your servant treated me," his anger was kindled. ²⁰ And Joseph's master took him and put him in the prison, the place where the king's prisoners were confined, and he was there in prison.

His feet were put in painful iron chains and weighed down his very soul.

²¹ But the LORD was with Joseph and showed him steadfast love and gave him favor in the sight of the keeper of the prison. *(God is with his servants in a prison as much as in a palace. He does not desert us no matter how low we may be brought.)* ²² And the keeper of the prison put Joseph in charge of all the prisoners who were in the prison. Whatever was done there, he was the one who did it.

When a good person is thrown down they are soon up again. Truth always floats to the surface while sin drowns.

²³ The keeper of the prison paid no attention to anything that was in Joseph's charge, because the LORD was with him. And whatever he did, the LORD made it succeed.

May each young child of godly parents be kept by God's grace and may the Lord always be with them. Keep God's approval, and nothing is lost. Lose that, and all is gone.

February 18
God is For Me[145]
Geneses 40:1; 3-23

¹ Some time after [Joseph was imprisoned], the cupbearer of the king of Egypt and his baker committed an offense against their lord the king of Egypt… ³ and he put them in custody in the house of the captain of the guard, in the prison where Joseph was confined. ⁴ The captain of the guard appointed Joseph to be with them, and he attended them. They continued for some time in custody. *(God controlled what went on in Pharaoh's household with Joseph in mind. Even in prison, Joseph was favored by the Lord.)*

⁵ And one night they both dreamed—the cupbearer and the baker of the king of Egypt, who were confined in the prison—each his own dream, and each dream with its own interpretation.

Men are made to serve Joseph's interest when they are awake and even when they are asleep.

⁶ When Joseph came to them in the morning, he saw that they were troubled. ⁷ So he asked Pharaoh's officers who were with him in custody in his master's house, "Why are your faces downcast today?" *(In the same way, we should show friendly concern for others and their well being. What was right in a prison is even more proper in a family.)* ⁸ They said to him, "We have had dreams, and there is no one to interpret them." And Joseph said to them, "Do not interpretations belong to God? Please tell them to me."*(Joseph bravely honored the living God. Every believer should.)*

⁹ So the chief cupbearer told his dream to Joseph and said to him, "In my dream there was a vine before me, ¹⁰ and on the vine there were three branches. As soon as it budded, its blossoms shot forth, and the clusters ripened into grapes. ¹¹ Pharaoh's cup was in my hand, and I took the grapes and pressed them into Pharaoh's cup and placed the cup in Pharaoh's hand." ¹² Then Joseph said to him, "This is its interpretation: the three branches are three days. ¹³ In three days Pharaoh will lift up your head and restore you to your office, and you shall place Pharaoh's cup in his hand as formerly, when you were his cupbearer. ¹⁴ Only remember me, when it is well with you, and please do me the kindness to mention me to Pharaoh, and so get me out of this house. ¹⁵ For I was indeed stolen out of the land of the Hebrews, and here also I have done nothing that they should put me into the pit."*(How lovingly does Joseph hide his brothers' fault. He does not speak about being sold but only of being "stolen." He was stolen, because the Ishmaelites bought what the sellers had no right to sell. Let us use the gentlest words*

---
[145] Psalm 56:9

when we have a reason to talk about wrong actions of others.)

¹⁶ When the chief baker saw that the interpretation was favorable, he said to Joseph, "I also had a dream: there were three cake baskets on my head, ¹⁷ and in the uppermost basket there were all sorts of baked food for Pharaoh, but the birds were eating it out of the basket on my head." ¹⁸ And Joseph answered and said, "This is its interpretation: the three baskets are three days. ¹⁹ In three days Pharaoh will lift up your head—from you!—and hang you on a tree. And the birds will eat the flesh from you."

²⁰ On the third day, which was Pharaoh's birthday, he made a feast for all his servants and lifted up the head of the chief cupbearer and the head of the chief baker among his servants. ²¹ He restored the chief cupbearer to his position, and he placed the cup in Pharaoh's hand. ²² But he hanged the chief baker, as Joseph had interpreted to them. *(Whether for good or evil the word of the Lord will be fulfilled. It is our duty to hold the Word of God in the highest respect and not doubt it.)* ²³ Yet the chief cupbearer did not remember Joseph, but forgot him. *(It would have been sad for Joseph if he had put his trust in humans. The butler forgot him, but his God did not. The Lord was reserving Joseph for a far greater deliverance. He was to come out of prison and straight to a throne and that was best achieved by his waiting a little longer. It is good for a person to have hope and then quietly wait for God to save them from their troubles.)*

FEBRUARY 19

The Friendship of the LORD Is for Those Who Fear Him[146]

Two years rolled by and Joseph was still in prison. The right time had not yet come. If the fulfillment of God's promise seems to be delayed, let us continue to wait for it.

Genesis 41:1; 8-16; 25-36

¹ᵃ After two whole years, Pharaoh dreamed.

⁸ So in the morning his spirit was troubled, and he sent and called for all the magicians of Egypt and all its wise men. Pharaoh told them his dreams, but there was none who could interpret them to Pharaoh.

⁹ Then the chief cupbearer said to Pharaoh, "I remember my offenses today. ¹⁰ When Pharaoh was angry with his servants and put me and the chief baker in custody in the house of the captain of the guard, ¹¹ we dreamed on the same night, he and I, each having a dream with its own interpretation. ¹² A young Hebrew was there with us, a servant of the captain of the guard. When we told him, he interpreted our dreams to us, giving an interpretation to each man according to his dream. ¹³ And as he interpreted to us, so it came about. I was restored to my office, and the baker was hanged."

¹⁴ Then Pharaoh sent and called Joseph, and they quickly brought him out of the pit. And when he had shaved himself and changed his clothes, he came in before Pharaoh. *(Joseph was not released because he promised anyone favors, if they would let him out. He was taken out of prison because the king needed him. Like his ancestor Abraham, he did not owe any man so much as a thread or a sandal strap.[147] God can promote any of his people just as easily. The king of Egypt could not say, "I have made Joseph rich." The Lord will lift up his servants in the best time and in the best way.)*

¹⁵ And Pharaoh said to Joseph, "I have had a dream, and there is no one who can interpret it. I have heard it said of you that when you hear a dream you can interpret it." ¹⁶ Joseph answered Pharaoh, "It is not in me; God will give Pharaoh a favorable answer." *(Then the king described his two dreams to Joseph. In the first, seven plump cows were eaten by seven ugly, thin cows. In the second, seven plump and good ears of grain were swallowed up by seven thin and blighted ears. They were immediately interpreted by*

---

[146] Psalm 25:14

[147] Genesis 14:22-23, "But Abram said to the king of Sodom, 'I have lifted my hand to the LORD, God Most High, Possessor of heaven and earth, that I would not take a thread or a sandal strap or anything that is yours, lest you should say, "I have made Abram rich."'"

divine guidance. Joseph humbly and clearly gave credit for all his knowledge to the true God. Pharaoh had complimented him, but he was not conceited. Therefore he refused to accept any honor for himself.)

25 Then Joseph said to Pharaoh, "The dreams of Pharaoh are one; God has revealed to Pharaoh what he is about to do. 26 The seven good cows are seven years, and the seven good ears are seven years; the dreams are one. 27 The seven lean and ugly cows that came up after them are seven years, and the seven empty ears blighted by the east wind are also seven years of famine. 28 It is as I told Pharaoh; God has shown to Pharaoh what he is about to do.

29 "There will come seven years of great plenty throughout all the land of Egypt, 30 but after them there will arise seven years of famine, and all the plenty will be forgotten in the land of Egypt. The famine will consume the land, 31 and the plenty will be unknown in the land by reason of the famine that will follow, for it will be very severe 32 And the doubling of Pharaoh's dream means that the thing is fixed by God, and God will shortly bring it about. 33 Now therefore let Pharaoh select a discerning and wise man, and set him over the land of Egypt. 34 Let Pharaoh proceed to appoint overseers over the land and take one-fifth of the produce of the land of Egypt during the seven plentiful years. 35 And let them gather all the food of these good years that are coming and store up grain under the authority of Pharaoh for food in the cities, and let them keep it. 36 That food shall be a reserve for the land against the seven years of famine that are to occur in the land of Egypt, so that the land may not perish through the famine."

This was practical wisdom. We should ask God for the same. Knowledge is of little value unless it is used in a practical way. To be constantly worrying about the future is wrong, but to wisely prepare for it is such an obvious virtue that we wonder why anyone would question it.

FEBRUARY 20

All Things Work Together for Good[148]

We left Joseph standing before the king of Egypt. He had interpreted Pharaoh's dream and given him wise advice.

Genesis 41: 37-43; 46-57

37 This proposal pleased Pharaoh and all his servants. 38 And Pharaoh said to his servants, "Can we find a man like this, in whom is the Spirit of God?" *(Joseph's words about the Lord had a real impact on the idolatrous leader of Egypt. His words show great respect for this Hebrew man who had been in prison only hours before. We never need to be ashamed to declare our faith. Good will come when we honor the Lord with our words.)* 39 Then Pharaoh said to Joseph, "Since God has shown you all this, there is none so discerning and wise as you are. 40 You shall be over my house, and all my people shall order themselves as you command. Only as regards the throne will I be greater than you." 41 And Pharaoh said to Joseph, "See, I have set you over all the land of Egypt." 42 Then Pharaoh took his signet ring from his hand and put it on Joseph's hand, and clothed him in garments of fine linen and put a gold chain about his neck. 43 And he made him ride in his second chariot. And they called out before him, "Bow the knee!" Thus he set him over all the land of Egypt.

What a change from the prison to the chariot. In much the same way, the Lord Jesus was lifted up from the grave, so that "at the name of Jesus every knee should bow."[149] Similar honors will be shared by all persecuted saints either in this life or the next.

46 Joseph was thirty years old when he entered the service of Pharaoh king of Egypt. And Joseph went out from the presence of Pharaoh and went through all the land of Egypt.

Prosperity did not spoil him. He went about his business and carried out the duties of his office with great diligence.

---

[148] Romans 8:28
[149] Philippians 2:10

⁴⁷ During the seven plentiful years the earth produced abundantly, ⁴⁸ and he gathered up all the food of these seven years, which occurred in the land of Egypt, and put the food in the cities. He put in every city the food from the fields around it. ⁴⁹ And Joseph stored up grain in great abundance, like the sand of the sea, until he ceased to measure it, for it could not be measured.

⁵⁰ Before the year of famine came, two sons were born to Joseph. Asenath, the daughter of Potiphera priest of On, bore them to him. ⁵¹ Joseph called the name of the firstborn Manasseh. "For," he said, "God has made me forget all my hardship and all my father's house."

Our afflictions leave no sting behind. The Lord's love rinses out our cup of sorrow so that no bitterness remains. Such forgetfulness is very sweet.

⁵² The name of the second he called Ephraim, "For God has made me fruitful in the land of my affliction." *(He credits his God for his happiness and blessings. To forget the past and be productive in the present is a precious blessing.)*

⁵³ The seven years of plenty that occurred in the land of Egypt came to an end, ⁵⁴ and the seven years of famine began to come, as Joseph had said. There was famine in all lands, but in all the land of Egypt there was bread. ⁵⁵ When all the land of Egypt was famished, the people cried to Pharaoh for bread. Pharaoh said to all the Egyptians, "Go to Joseph. What he says to you, do."

This can be seen as a picture of the gospel. Poor hungry sinners are now directed to go to Jesus and, "do whatever he tells you."[150] *May every one of us be led by the Spirit of God to go to Jesus, who is the only one who can open the overflowing storehouses of grace.*

⁵⁶ So when the famine had spread over all the land, Joseph opened all the storehouses and sold to the Egyptians, for the famine was severe in the land of Egypt. ⁵⁷ Moreover, all the earth came to Egypt to Joseph to buy grain, because the famine was severe over all the earth. *(Joseph was a type of Christ.*[151] *He was the only savior who could save people from over all the earth from their hunger. Jesus is the only Savior who can save people from over the whole earth from their sin. Has everyone who reads this gone to the Redeemer for heavenly bread? If not; why not?)*

FEBRUARY 21

The LORD Tests the Righteous[152]

Genesis 42:1-4; 6-10; 13-24b

¹ When Jacob learned that there was grain for sale in Egypt, he said to his sons, "Why do you look at one another?" ² And he said, "Behold, I have heard that there is grain for sale in Egypt. Go down and buy grain for us there, that we may live and not die." *(It is wise to look for assistance instead of losing heart and giving in to hopelessness. If we need heavenly bread we must make an effort and go to Jesus for it.)* ³ So ten of Joseph's brothers went down to buy grain in Egypt. ⁴ But Jacob did not send Benjamin, Joseph's brother, with his brothers, for he feared that harm might happen to him.

⁶ Now Joseph was governor over the land. He was the one who sold to all the people of the land. And Joseph's brothers came and bowed themselves before him with their faces to the ground. *(Here was the fulfillment of his dream. Twenty-two years had gone by during which Joseph was either a slave or in prison, but "the Lord is not slow to fulfill his promise as some count slowness."*[153]*)* ⁷ Joseph saw his brothers and recognized them, but he treated them like strangers and spoke roughly to them. "Where do you come from? he said. They said, "From the land of Canaan, to buy food." ⁸ And Joseph recognized his brothers, but they did not recognize him. ⁹ And Joseph remembered the dreams that he had dreamed of them. And he said to them. "You are spies; you have come to see the nakedness of the land." ¹⁰ They said to him, "No my lord, your servants have come to buy food.

---

[150] John 2:5
[151] *type* - something or someone that represents something or someone else, usually in the future.
[152] Psalm 11:5
[153] 2 Peter 3:9

¹³ And they said, "We, your servants, are twelve brothers, the sons of one man in the land of Canaan, and behold, the youngest is this day with our father, and one is no more." ¹⁴ But Joseph said to them, "It is as I said to you. You are spies. ¹⁵ By this you shall be tested: by the life of Pharaoh, you shall not go from this place unless your youngest brother comes here. ¹⁶ Send one of you, and let him bring your brother, while you remain confined, that your words may be tested, whether there is truth in you. Or else, by the life of Pharaoh, surely you are spies." *(Joseph swears by the life of Pharaoh, He did it to hide his true identity, thinking his brothers would certainly not suspect a spiritual child of Israel of using that kind of language. Joseph was not a stranger in a foreign land intentionally, but even in his case we find, "bad company ruins good morals."[154])* ¹⁷ And he put them all together in custody for three days. *(He stirred up their fears to jar their memories of their sin against their brother. In the same way, the Lord stirs up the fears of sinners with whom he intends to make peace.)*

¹⁸ On the third day Joseph said to them, "Do this and you will live, for I fear God:" *(This assurance must have been both surprising and comforting to them. The person who fears God will not wrong others.* ¹⁹ "if you are honest men, let one of your brothers remain confined where you are in custody, and let the rest go and carry grain for the famine of your households, ²⁰ and bring your youngest brother to me. So your words will be verified, and you shall not die." And they did so. ²¹ Then they said to one another, "In truth we are guilty concerning our brother, in that we saw the distress of his soul, when he begged us and we did not listen. That is why this distress has come upon us." *(Their sin found them out,[155] like ours will sooner or later. When we sow wild oats we ought to remember that we will have to reap them.[156])* ²² And Reuben answered them, "Did I not tell you not to sin against the boy? But you did not listen. So now there comes a reckoning for his blood." *(Reuben was the only one who had the comfort of a clear conscience.)*

²³ They did not know that Joseph understood them, for there was an interpreter between them. ²⁴ᵃ Then he turned away from them and wept. *(This is a touching scene. Joseph in his great wisdom felt obligated not to reveal himself yet, but his love was so great that he could not hold back his tears. When the Lord deals roughly with sinners to make them more deeply aware of sin, he loves them regardless of what they have done. Jesus has an eye of sympathy for those who are so sorry for their sins that they cry over them.)*

FEBRUARY 22
Fear Not, For I Am With You[157]

Joseph's brothers returned to their father with plenty of food, but before long it was running low and Jacob's family was again in distress. Bread is soon gone, but the living bread of heaven lasts forever.[158]

Genesis 43:1-14

¹ Now the famine was severe in the land. ² And when they had eaten the grain that they had brought from Egypt, their father said to them, "Go again, buy us a little food." ³ But Judah said to him, "The man solemnly warned us, saying, 'You shall not see my face unless your brother is with you.' ⁴ If you will send our brother with us we will go down and buy you food. ⁵ But if you will not send him, we will not go down, for the man said to us, 'You shall not see my face, unless your brother is with you.'"

Israel had clearly said, "My son shall not go down with you,"[159] but it was necessary that he should. We had better not be too sure of ourselves or we may have to eat our words.

---

[154] 1 Corinthians 15:33
[155] A reference to Numbers 32:23, "You have sinned against the LORD, and be sure your sin will find you out."
[156] Wild oats are useless weeds. The expression refers to people (especially young men) who spend their time in useless activities and ultimately pay the price for wasting their lives.
[157] Isaiah 41:10
[158] John 6:51, Jesus said, "I am the living bread that came down from heaven. If anyone eats of this bread, he will live forever."
[159] Genesis 42:38

6 Israel said, "Why did you treat me so badly, as to tell the man that you had another brother?" *(Poor Jacob. Out of fear for his darling son, he thinks his sons are unkind. We should not act unfairly to others because we favor someone else more than them, but that is what we tend to do.)* **7** They replied, "The man questioned us carefully about ourselves and our kindred, saying, 'Is your father still alive? Do you have another brother?' What we told him was in answer to these questions. Could we in any way know that he would say, 'Bring your brother down'?" **8** And Judah said to Israel his father, "Send the boy with me, and we will arise and go, that we may live and not die, both we and you and also our little ones. **9** I will be a pledge of his safety. From my hand you shall require him. If I do not bring him back to you and set him before you, then let me bear the blame forever. **10** If we had not delayed, we would now have returned twice."

In volunteering to become surety[160] for Benjamin, Judah became a delightful picture of our Lord Jesus, who is the surety or guarantee of the New Covenant. Jesus will absolutely fulfill his promises and say at the last, "Of those whom you gave me I have lost not one."[161]

11 Then their father Israel said to them, "If it must be so, then do this: take some of the choice fruits of the land in your bags, and carry a present down to the man, a little balm and a little honey, gum, myrrh, pistachio nuts, and almonds. *(This was good judgment. Faith in God is not an excuse for not being practical. It was wise to win over those on whom they were so dependent.)* **12** Take double the money with you. Carry back with you the money that was returned in the mouth of your sacks. Perhaps it was an oversight."

Before they left Egypt, "Joseph gave orders to fill their sacks with grain, and to replace every man's money in his sacks."[162] His brothers did not know how the money got there and were therefore under obligation to return it. This was the right and honest thing to do. We are not permitted to take advantage of the mistakes of others. Every honest person will do what they can to correct mistakes that cause someone a loss, even though the error was not theirs. Notice how Jacob thought ahead. He knew that the grain would rise in price, "Take double the money," says he. Men of faith are not fools.

13 "Take also your brother, and arise, go again to the man. **14** May God Almighty grant you mercy before the man, and may he send back your other brother and Benjamin. And as for me, if I am bereaved of my children, I am bereaved."

Jacob's faith now came to the front. He left what would happen in the hands of Almighty God. If the Lord willed to place this trial on him, he was fully committed to accepting it. When we willingly give up what God has given us, we are most likely to receive it back again. Abraham was allowed to keep Isaac because he was willing to part with him when God commanded it.

Israel received Benjamin again because, after some struggling, he at last accepted it as the Lord's will. When we are at the end of having our own way, we are not far away from the end of our trials.

The home and meeting house in Stambourne where Spurgeon's grandfather, James Spurgeon, was pastor for more than 50 years. Charles lived here with his grandparents from age one until he was about five.

---

[160] *surety* - a person who assumes the responsibility or obligation of someone else
[161] John 18:9
[162] Genesis 42:25

FEBRUARY 23

His Banner Over Me Was Love[163]

This story of Joseph is so deeply interesting, that we must stay with it. The Holy Spirit gives us many details. We may be sure that he intends for us to learn from them.

Genesis 43:15-16; 18-23; 26-34

15 So the men took this present, and they took double the money with them, and Benjamin. They arose and went down to Egypt and stood before Joseph.

16 When Joseph saw Benjamin with them, he said to the steward of his house, "Bring the men into the house, and slaughter an animal and make ready, for the men are to dine with me at noon."

Joseph's love for his brothers caused him to look for an opportunity to talk to them privately.

18 And the men were afraid because they were brought to Joseph's house, and they said, "It is because of the money, which was replaced in our sacks the first time, that we are brought in, so that he may assault us and fall upon us to make us servants and seize our donkeys." *(Joseph's love intended happiness, but their fear turned it into dread. Be on your guard against doubting and not trusting the Lord Jesus or even his goodness may make us afraid.)* 19 So they went up to the steward of Joseph's house and spoke with him at the door of the house, 20 and said, "Oh, my lord, we came down the first time to buy food. 21 And when we came to the lodging place we opened our sacks, and there was each man's money in the mouth of his sack, our money in full weight. So we have brought it again with us, 22 and we have brought other money down with us to buy food. We do not know who put our money in our sacks."

They were afraid, but they wisely decided to tell the truth and hope for peace. Complete honesty and open confession is also the way to peace with God.

23 He replied, "Peace to you, do not be afraid. Your God and the God of your father has put treasure in your sacks for you. I received your money." Then he brought Simeon out to them. *(The prisoner was returned and they were encouraged that all was well. The Lord Jesus returned from death and believers are encouraged because all is well.)*

26 When Joseph came home, they brought into the house to him the present that they had with them and bowed down to him to the ground. 27 And he inquired about their welfare and said, "Is your father well, the old man of whom you spoke? Is he still alive?" 28 They said, "Your servant our father is well; he is still alive." And they bowed their heads and prostrated themselves. *(By calling their father "your servant," and bowing down for themselves and him, they fulfilled Joseph's second dream. The sun and the moon and the eleven stars were bowing down to him.)* 29 And he lifted up his eyes and saw his brother Benjamin, his mother's son, and said, "Is this your youngest brother, of whom you spoke to me? God be gracious to you, my son!" 30 Then Joseph hurried out, for his compassion grew warm for his brother, and he sought a place to weep. And he entered his chamber and wept there. *(Love desires to express itself, but there is a time for everything. Jesus always loves his spiritual siblings, but sometimes he wisely conceals himself for their good.)*

31 Then he washed his face and came out. And controlling himself he said, "Serve the food." 32 They served him by himself, and them by themselves, and the Egyptians who ate with him by themselves, because the Egyptians could not eat with the Hebrews, for that is an abomination to the Egyptians. 33 And they sat before him, the firstborn according to his birthright and the youngest according to his youth. And the men looked at one another in amazement. 34 Portions were taken to them from Joseph's table, but Benjamin's portion was five times as much as any of theirs. And they drank and were merry with him.

How they must have wondered while they feasted to see the order that he placed them in and the favor shown to Benjamin. How plainly everything said, "I am Joseph," but

---
[163] Song of Solomon 2:4

they still did not recognize him. Even when people see all the loving acts of Jesus, no one ever recognizes him until he reveals himself by his Spirit.

FEBRUARY 24
You Have Taken Up My Cause, O Lord[164]

Joseph ordered a silver cup to be secretly placed in Benjamin's sack. When his brothers had set out on their journey he sent his steward after them. His steward accused them of stealing the cup and used this as an excuse to bring them back. This is the way Joseph put his brothers to the test and brought them to the point when they would discover who he really was. Our reading begins with the scene when the brothers had been brought back to Joseph.

Genesis 44:14-34

14 When Judah and his brothers came to Joseph's house, he was still there. They fell before him to the ground. **15** Joseph said to them, "What deed is this that you have done? Do you not know that a man like me can indeed practice divination?" *(He said this because he was still acting the part of an Egyptian. It was still not quite time to reveal his true identity.)* **16** And Judah said, "What shall we say to my lord? What shall we speak? Or how can we clear ourselves? God has found out the guilt of your servants; behold, we are my lord's servants, both we and he also in whose hand the cup has been found." *(Though they were innocent of the present charge, Judah confesses that this present difficult situation was the well deserved reward of other sins.)* **17** But he said, "Far be it from me that I should do so! Only the man in whose hand the cup was found shall be my servant. But as for you, go up in peace to your father." *(To this Judah, who had guaranteed Benjamin's safe return, could not agree. He pleaded in a marvelously touching manner. Notice how fluent and persuasive Judah was. The Lord Jesus is our Judah and his pleadings are mighty.)*

18 Then Judah went up to him and said, "O my lord, please let your servant speak a word in my lord's ears, and let not your anger burn against your servant, for you are like Pharaoh himself. **19** My lord asked his servants, saying, 'Have you a father, or a brother?' **20** And we said to my lord, 'We have a father, an old man, and a young brother, the child of his old age. His brother is dead, and he alone is left of his mother's children, and his father loves him.' **21** Then you said to your servants, 'Bring him down to me, that I may set my eyes on him.' **22** We said to my lord, 'The boy cannot leave his father, for if he should leave his father, his father would die.' **23** Then you said to your servants, 'Unless your youngest brother comes down with you, you shall not see my face again.'

24 "When we went back to your servant my father, we told him the words of my lord. **25** And when our father said, 'Go again, buy us a little food.' **26** we said, 'We cannot go down. If our youngest brother goes with us, then we will go down. For we cannot see the man's face unless our youngest brother is with us.' **27** Then your servant my father said to us, 'You know that my wife bore me two sons. **28** One left me, and I said, "Surely he has been torn to pieces," and I have never seen him since. **29** If you take this one also from me, and harm happens to him, you will bring down my gray hairs in evil to Sheol.'

30 "Now therefore, as soon as I come to your servant my father, and the boy is not with us, then, as his life is bound up in the boy's life, **31** as soon as he sees that the boy is not with us, he will die, and your servants will bring down the gray hairs of your servant our father with sorrow to Sheol. **32** For your servant became a pledge of safety for the boy to my father, saying, 'If I do not bring him back to you, then I shall bear the blame before my father all my life.' **33** Now therefore, please let your servant remain instead of the boy as a servant to my lord, and let the boy go back with his brothers. **34** For how can I go back to my father if the boy is not with me? I fear to see the evil that would find my father."

Much of the power of Judah's pleading was because it was the truth. It is a simple,

---
[164] Lamentations 3:58

straightforward telling of facts. But its master weapon is found in the proposed substitution of himself for Benjamin. He is ready to suffer for his brother. Do we not remember how Judah's great antitype[165] not only offered to be our substitute but actually was so? This is the most powerful part of his intercession.[166]

FEBRUARY 25
The Son of God Loves Me[167]

After Judah's thrilling speech there was a quiet pause. Emotion filled their hearts, but everyone was speechless.

Genesis 45:1-15

1 Then Joseph could not control himself before all those who stood by him. He cried, "Make everyone go out from me." So no one stayed with him when Joseph made himself known to his brothers.

It was not proper for strangers to witness that tender scene. When Jesus reveals himself to his chosen, it is "not to the world."[168]

2 And he wept aloud, so that the Egyptians heard it, and the household of Pharaoh heard it. *(Until this point, Joseph had held back his true feelings, but now they gushed out uncontrollably.)* **3** And Joseph said to his brothers, "I am Joseph! Is my father still alive?" *(How amazed they must have been to see before them the brother they had sold as a slave, knowing they were now in his complete control. What a discovery the soul makes when it becomes aware that Jesus whom it crucified is Lord and God.)* But his brothers could not answer him, for they were dismayed at his presence.

4 So Joseph said to his Brothers, "Come near to me, Please." And they came near. *(Tenderness attracts fellowship and looks for ways to make fear go away. The words before us are such as Jesus used to his troubled companions. Let us not be slow to come near to our tender Lord.)* And he said, "I am your brother Joseph, whom you sold into Egypt. **5** And now do not be distressed or angry with yourselves because you sold me here, for God sent me before you to preserve life. **6** For the famine has been in the land these two years, and there are yet five years in which there will be neither plowing nor harvest. **7** And God sent me before you to preserve for you a remnant on earth, and to keep alive for you many survivors. **8** So it was not you who sent me here, but God. He has made me a father to Pharaoh, and lord of all his house and ruler over all the land of Egypt.

Joseph has so completely pardoned them, that he does not speak of forgiving them himself, but urges them to forgive themselves. He works hard to convince them not to be overcome with the fear that he would now get even with them. He did not want their natural fear to overpower and push away godly sorrow.

9 "Hurry and go up to my father and say to him, 'Thus says your son Joseph, God has made me lord of all Egypt. Come down to me; do not tarry. **10** You shall dwell in the land of Goshen, and you shall be near me, you and your children and your children's children, and your flocks, your herds, and all that you have. *(Being near to Joseph would bring the most joy to Jacob. Living close to Jesus brings the most joy to believers.)* **11** There I will provide for you, for there are yet five years of famine to come, so that you and your household, and all that you have, do not come to poverty.' *(The person who forgives is generous toward those he pardons. Those who Jesus cleanses from sin will have all their needs provided.)*

12 "And now your eyes see, and the eyes of my brother Benjamin see, that it is my mouth that speaks to you. **13** You must tell my father of all my honor in Egypt, and of all that you have seen. Hurry and bring my father down here." **14** Then he fell upon his brother Benjamin's neck and wept, and Benjamin wept upon his neck. *(The love of Jesus for his followers and his followers' love for him*

---

[165] *antytype* - In the Bible, especially in the Old Testament, events or persons are seen as a type or symbol that is fulfilled, usually in the New Testament. The fulfillment of the type is called the antitype. In this case, Judah pleading for his brother is a type of Christ and Christ pleading for us is the antitype.
[166] *intercession* - a prayer or intervention for the benefit of others.
[167] Galatians 2:20
[168] John 14:22

are mutual. What one feels the other feels.) ¹⁵ And he kissed all of his brothers and wept upon them. After that his brothers talked with him. *(These kisses were expressions of love. They were very much like the actions of the Holy Spirit in those who believe. They reassure of us of Jesus' love to us and his holy fellowship with us. The spouse in Solomon's song says, "Let him kiss me with the kisses of his mouth,"[169] Amen. May the Lord do so to each one of us.)*

FEBRUARY 26
The LORD Will Provide[170]

Joseph's meeting with his family could not be kept quiet for long. The happy news got out and the king himself soon heard about it.

Genesis 45:16-28

¹⁶ When the report was heard in Pharaoh's house, "Joseph's brothers have come." it pleased Pharaoh and his servants. *(They were glad because such a great helper of their nation was made happy.)* ¹⁷ And Pharaoh said to Joseph, "Say to your brothers, 'Do this: load your beasts and go back to the land of Canaan, ¹⁸ and take your father and your households, and come to me, and I will give you the best of the land of Egypt, and you shall eat the fat of the land.' ¹⁹ And you, Joseph, are commanded to say, 'Do this: take wagons from the land of Egypt for your little ones and for your wives, and bring your father, and come. ²⁰ Have no concern for your goods, for the best of all the land of Egypt is yours.'"

Pharaoh kindly and with lordly generosity, spared Joseph any second thoughts about inviting his family to live in the land. They were to come into the country as the king's own guests. Observe how he instructs them to leave all their "goods" because they would be better off even if they did not bring their tents or their furniture with them. Certainly, when we come to Jesus, and receive his treasures of grace, all earthly things become just stuff we really do not need.

²¹ The sons of Israel did so: and Joseph gave them wagons, according to the command of Pharaoh, and gave them provisions for the journey. ²² To each and all of them he gave a change of clothes, but to Benjamin he gave three hundred shekels of silver and five changes of clothes. *(Compare Joseph's goodness with his brothers' former cruelty. "They sent him naked to strangers, he sends them in new and rich clothing. They took a small sum of money for him, he give them large treasures. They sent his torn coat to his father, he sends a variety of costly garments. They sold him to be carried away by camels, he sends them home in chariots."[171] Far greater still is the comparison between our selfish behavior toward the Lord Jesus and his generous giving of grace to us.)*

²³ To his father he sent as follows: ten donkeys loaded with the good things of Egypt, and ten female donkeys loaded with grain, bread, and provision for his father on the journey. ²⁴ Then he sent his brothers away, and as they departed, he said to them, "Do not quarrel on the way." *(Joseph knew his brothers well. He was afraid they might begin accusing each other, or might even become jealous of Benjamin, as they had once been of him.)*

²⁵ So they went up out of Egypt and came to the land of Canaan to their father Jacob. ²⁶ And they told him, "Joseph is still alive, and he is ruler over all the land of Egypt." And his heart became numb, for he did not believe them. *(A sad heart is far more ready to believe a sad falsehood than a joyful truth. When his sons wickedly showed him Joseph's coat he said, "Joseph is without doubt torn in pieces," but when they told him a true story, he did not believe them. It is a pity when discouragement makes our judgment lose its balance.)* ²⁷ But when they told him all the words of Joseph, which he had said to them, and when he saw the wagons that Joseph had sent to carry him, the spirit of their father Jacob revived. ²⁸ And Israel said, "It is enough; Joseph my son is still alive. I will go and see him before I die."

---

[169] Song of Solomon 1:2
[170] Genesis 22:14

[171] Quote appears to be from Church of England Bishop Joseph Hall (1574-1656).

First the words and then the wagons helped Jacob to believe, even as the words of Jesus and the gifts of Jesus help us to believe in him. The admired patriarch[172] was more glad to hear that his son was "alive,' than to hear he was "ruler over all the land of Egypt." This was enough for Jacob. He was determined to see his beloved one. Where there is true love there will be a desire for togetherness. Those who love the Son of God will not be willing to live without heavenly fellowship. Oh, may all gathered here in family worship, see Jesus by faith before they die, when they die, and then for ever.

FEBRUARY 27
We Shall See Him As He Is[173]

Genesis 46:1, 2-3; 26; 29-34

1a So Israel took his journey with all that he had.

2 And God spoke to Israel in visions of the night and said, "Jacob, Jacob." And he said, "Here I am." **3** Then he said, "I am God, the God of your father. Do not be afraid to go down to Egypt, for there I will make you into a great nation."

26 All the persons belonging to Jacob who came into Egypt, who were his own descendants, not including Jacob's sons' wives, were sixty-six persons in all.

29 Then Joseph prepared his chariot and went up to meet Israel his father in Goshen. He presented himself to him and fell on his neck and wept on his neck a good while. **30** Israel said to Joseph, "Now let me die, since I have seen your face and know that you are still alive." *(God had granted Israel his final desire and he is now content to lie down and sleep the sleep of death. Bishop Hall says, "And if the meeting of earthly friends is so unspeakably comfortable, how happy will we be in the light of the glorious face of God our Father! of that of our blessed Redeemer, who we sold to death for our sins, and who now, after his noble triumph, has all power given him in heaven and earth."[174])*

31 Joseph said to his brothers and to his father's household, "I will go up and tell Pharaoh and will say to him, 'My brothers and my father's household, who were in the land of Canaan, have come to me. **32** And the men are shepherds, for they have been keepers of livestock, and they have brought their flocks and their herds and all that they have.' **33** When Pharaoh calls you and says, 'What is your occupation?' **34** you shall say, 'Your servants have been keepers of livestock from our youth even until now, both we and our fathers,' in order that you may dwell in the land of Goshen, for every shepherd is an abomination to the Egyptians." *(To speak the honest truth is always the best policy and to continue in honest employment is the best situation. Joseph might have encouraged them to ask to be made high ranking officials, but he knew that they would succeed better as shepherds. "Do you seek great things for yourself? Seek them not."[175])*

Genesis 47:2-10; 12

2 And from among his brothers he took five men and presented them to Pharaoh. **3** Pharaoh said to his brothers, "What is your occupation?" And they said to Pharaoh, "Your servants are shepherds, as our fathers were." **4** They said to Pharaoh, "We have come to sojourn in the land, for there is no pasture for your servants' flocks, for the famine is severe in the land of Canaan. And now please let your servants dwell in the land of Goshen." **5** Then Pharaoh said to Joseph, "Your father and your brothers have come to you. **6** The land of Egypt is before you. Settle your father and your brothers in the best of the land. Let them settle in the land of Goshen, and if you know any able men among them, put them in charge of my livestock."

7 Then Joseph brought in Jacob his father and stood him before Pharaoh, and Jacob blessed Pharaoh. **8** And Pharaoh said to Jacob, "How many are the days of the years

---

[172] *patriarch* - A man regarded as the father or ruler of a family. Bible patriarchs include Abraham, Isaac, Jacob and Jacob's twelve sons.
[173] 1 John 3:2

[174] Church of England Bishop Joseph Hall (1574-1656). The scripture he quotes is from Jeremiah 45:5.
[175] Jeremiah 45:5

of your life?" ⁹ And Jacob said to Pharaoh, "The days of the years of my sojourning are 130 years. Few and evil have been the days of the years of my life, and they have not attained to the days of the years of the life of my fathers in the days of their sojourning."

Jacob told Pharaoh he was simply traveling through this life and perhaps hinted at the hope that kept him going. He gave Pharaoh a gloomier picture of the pilgrim life than Abraham or Isaac would have done. However, because this man of many trials still reached the promised rest, every afflicted believer will also reach heaven.

¹⁰ And Jacob blessed Pharaoh and went out from the presence of Pharaoh. *(The respectful age of Jacob gave him liberty to bless even the king of the land. An old man's blessing is precious. Let us behave toward the elderly in such a way that they will pray blessings on us.)*

¹² And Joseph provided his father, his brothers, and all his father's household with food, according to the number of their dependents. *(In the same way, our older brother Jesus, who is Lord over the whole earth for the good of his church, takes care to provide for all his Father's household. Be pleased, oh Jesus, to let this family share in your great love.)*

FEBRUARY 28
Oh Give Thanks To the LORD [176]

The Psalmist celebrates the Lord's care of the chosen family of Jacob in the delightful verses of:

Psalm 105:1-23

¹ Oh give thanks to the LORD; call upon his name;
  make known his deeds among the peoples!

Thankfulness to God should sweeten our spirit and worshiping him should be our delight. Making his goodness known should be our full time job.

² Sing to him, sing praises to him;
  tell of all his wondrous works!

Our singing and talking should to be dedicated to the Lord's honor. Unfortunately, much that comes from our mouths is actually dishonoring to him.

³ Glory in his holy name;
  let the hearts of those who seek the LORD rejoice!

We are very likely to glory in something. Those who glory only in the Lord are wise.

⁴ Seek the LORD and his strength;
  seek his presence continually!

Even after we have found the Lord and know his love, we should continue to move forward and seek him more and more.

⁵ Remember the wondrous works that he has done,
  his miracles, and the judgments he uttered,
⁶ O offspring of Abraham, his servant,
  children of Jacob, his chosen ones!

Those who receive special favors from God should consider themselves under special obligation to glorify him by making his goodness and power known everywhere.

⁷ He is the LORD our God;
  his judgments are in all the earth.
⁸ He remembers his covenant forever,
  the word that he commanded, for a thousand generations,

To God be the glory, because he has never stopped being faithful to the covenant[177] of grace. It is certain in all things. Not one word of his promise has ever fallen to the ground. His promises stand strong forever, as firm as the throne of the I AM.

⁹ the covenant that he made with Abraham,
  his sworn promise to Isaac,
¹⁰ which he confirmed to Jacob as a statute,
  to Israel as an everlasting covenant,
¹¹ saying, "To you I will give the land of Canaan
  as your portion for an inheritance."
¹² When they were few in number,
  of little account, and sojourners in it,
¹³ wandering from nation to nation,
  from one kingdom to another people,
¹⁴ he allowed no one to oppress them;

---

[176] Psalm 105:1

[177] *covenant* - A contract, promise, guarantee, pledge or agreement between two or more persons.

he rebuked kings on their account,
15 saying, "Touch not my anointed ones,
 do my prophets no harm!"

The surrounding kings and rulers could have crushed the chosen family of Israel when they were so few in number that they could all live in one tent, but the Preserver of people mysteriously guarded them. In the same way, God always looks after the little flock of his people. The saints are sacred and set apart to God. They cannot be touched without those who harm them suffering the consequences.

16 When he summoned a famine on the land
 and broke all supply of bread,

Before the famine came, arrangements had been made for the housing of Jacob and his family. Before our trials come upon us, the way out of them has been prepared. There was a Joseph before there was a famine.

17 he had sent a man ahead of them,
 Joseph, who was sold as a slave.
18 His feet were hurt with fetters;
 his neck was put in a collar of iron;
19 until what he had said came to pass,
 the word of the LORD tested him.

God's word caused Joseph's trial and the same word ended it. God is just as involved in our daily trials as he was in the creation of the world. One word from God can bring us down, but, bless his name, another can raise us up.

20 The king sent and released him;
 the ruler of the peoples set him free;
21 he made him lord of his house
 and ruler of all his possessions,
22 to bind his princes at his pleasure
 and to teach his elders wisdom.
23 Then Israel came to Egypt;
 Jacob sojourned in the land of Ham.

Even favored Israel must go into Egypt where trouble awaited his household. But it was necessary for the preservation of the race of Israel and therefore a matter for praise. Let us also bless God when we go down to Egypt, because the hand of the Lord is in it.

FEBRUARY 29

God Will Be With You[178]

Genesis 48:1-5; 8-21

1 After this, Joseph was told, "Behold, your father is ill." So he took with him his two sons, Manasseh and Ephraim. 2 And it was told to Jacob, "Your son Joseph has come to you." Then Israel summoned his strength and sat up in bed. 3 And Jacob said to Joseph, "God Almighty appeared to me at Luz in the Land of Canaan and blessed me, 4 and said to me, 'Behold, I will make you fruitful and multiply you, and I will make of you a company of peoples and will give this land to your offspring after you for an everlasting possession.'" *(Jacob did not want Joseph to set his heart on Egypt, but rather to keep a believing eye toward the Promised Land of Canaan. That is why he speaks to him about it. We must always guard against loving the world in an attempt to keep things going smoothly for us.)* 5 And now your two sons, who were born to you in the land of Egypt before I came to you in Egypt, are mine; Ephraim and Manasseh shall be mine, as Reuben and Simeon are. *(Jacob calls them his sons rather than grandsons. From this point on Ephraim and Manasseh are included among the tribes of Israel.)*

8 When Israel saw Joseph's sons, he said, "Who are these?" 9 Joseph said to his father, "They are my sons, whom God has given me here." And he said, "Bring them to me, please, that I may bless them." 10 Now the eyes of Israel were dim with age, so that he could not see. So Joseph brought them near him, and he kissed them and embraced them. 11 And Israel said to Joseph, "I never expected to see your face; and behold, God has let me see your offspring also." *(God is much better to us than what we fear might happen. Yes, he is far better than what we even hope might happen.)*

12 Then Joseph removed them from his knees, and he bowed himself with his face to the earth. 13 And Joseph took them both, Ephraim in his right hand toward Israel's left hand, and Manasseh in his left hand toward Israel's right hand, and brought them near

---

[178] Genesis 48:21

him. ¹⁴ And Israel stretched out his right hand and laid it on the head of Ephraim, who was the younger, and his left hand on the head of Manasseh, crossing his hands (for Manasseh was the firstborn). ¹⁵ And he blessed Joseph and said,

> "The God before whom my fathers
>   Abraham and Isaac walked,
>   the God who has been my shepherd all
>   my life long to this day,
> ¹⁶ the angel who has redeemed me from all
>   evil, bless the boys;
>   and in them let my name be carried on,
>   and the name of my fathers
>   Abraham and Isaac;
>   and let them grow into a multitude in the
>   midst of the earth."

¹⁷ When Joseph saw that his father laid his right hand on the head of Ephraim, it displeased him, and he took his father's hand to move it from Ephraim's head to Manasseh's head. ¹⁸ And Joseph said to his father, "Not this way, my father; since this one is the firstborn, put your right hand on his head." ¹⁹ But his father refused and said, "I know, my son, I know. He also shall become a people, and he also shall be great. Nevertheless, his younger brother shall be greater than he, and his offspring shall become a multitude of nations."

The order of nature is not the order of grace. Jacob knew this well. In his case it was written, "the older shall serve the younger."[179] What the Lord intends is what will be.

²⁰ So he blessed them that day, saying,

> "By you Israel will pronounce blessings,
>   saying,
> 'God make you as Ephraim and as
>   Manasseh.'"

Thus he put Ephraim before Manasseh. ²¹ Then Israel said to Joseph, "Behold, I am about to die, but God will be with you and will bring you again to the land of your fathers.

Whoever dies, the Lord remains with his people. Let us not lose hope, even if the best of our friends or the most capable of our pastors are taken from us.

March 1
The Lord Bless You and Keep You[180]

Genesis 49:1-15

¹ Then Jacob called his sons and said, "Gather yourselves together, that I may tell you what shall happen to you in days to come.

> ² "Assemble and listen, O sons of Jacob,
>   listen to Israel your father."

Jacob was about to speak by inspiration. The blessing of a parent whose tongue is taught by God is more precious than can be imagined.

> ³ "Reuben, you are my firstborn,
>   my might, and the firstfruits of my
>   strength,
>   preeminent in dignity and preeminent in
>   power.
> ⁴ Unstable as water, you shall not have
>   preeminence,
>   because you went up to your father's
>   bed;
>   then you defiled it—he went up to my
>   couch!"

Though he was the firstborn Reuben missed the birthright, because he was immoral and not serious. Whatever good points may be in a person, if they are not levelheaded, steady, and true, they will come to nothing. To be unstable like the waves of the sea is one of the worst faults and spoils the whole character.

> ⁵ "Simeon and Levi are brothers;
>   weapons of violence are their swords.
> ⁶ Let my soul come not into their council;
>   O my glory, be not joined to their
>   company.
> For in their anger they killed men,
>   and in their willfulness they hamstrung
>   oxen.
> ⁷ Cursed be their anger, for it is fierce,
>   and their wrath, for it is cruel!
> I will divide them in Jacob
>   and scatter them in Israel."

---

[179] Genesis 25:23

[180] Numbers 6:24

Jacob washes his hands of a great wrong committed by two of his sons. He could not prevent it, because they acted quickly in self will and he did not know about it until after the murderous deed was done. He takes care to give his witness against it in the most serious way. The foolishness of youth will come home to people in their mature years. It is a great mercy from God when we have a good moral compass from our childhood.

8 "Judah, your brothers shall praise you;
>your hand shall be on the neck of your enemies;
>your father's sons shall bow down before you."

When Jacob came to Judah, (Judah being a type[181] of Christ), the dying patriarch rose to a higher level. He had no more faults to mention, only blessings.

9 "Judah is a lion's cub;
>from the prey, my son, you have gone up.
>He stooped down; he crouched as a lion
>and as a lioness; who dares rouse him?"

Who would dare to defy the Lion of the tribe of Judah? Jesus the Lord is terrifying to his enemies.

10 "The scepter shall not depart from Judah,
>nor the ruler's staff from between his feet,
>until tribute comes to him;[182]
>and to him shall be the obedience of the peoples."

When our Lord came to earth as man, his enemies said, "Look, the world has gone after him."[183] To this day, he is the greatest of magnets to attract the hearts of people. He came just when the kingdom had departed from Judah and now he reigns as the Prince of Peace.

11 "Binding his foal to the vine
>and his donkey's colt to the choice vine,
>he has washed his garments in wine
>and his vesture in the blood of grapes.
12 His eyes are darker than wine,
>and his teeth whiter than milk."

Truly in our Immanuel's land the wine and milk flow in rivers. "Come, buy wine and milk without money and without price."[184]

13 "Zebulun shall dwell at the shore of the sea;
>he shall become a haven for ships,
>and his border shall be at Sidon."

May the people who make their living at sea be favored by the Lord and never live in darkness as Zebulun came to do.

14 "Issachar is a strong donkey,
>crouching between the sheepfolds.
15 He saw that a resting place was good,
>and that the land was pleasant,
>so he bowed his shoulder to bear,
>and became a servant at forced labor."

Quiet and industrious, Issachar may have been somewhat lacking in courage and energy. There are no perfect people; but we wish that some of our brothers, who seem so satisfied with themselves, were more energetic in their work for God. Yet as Issachar was a true son of Jacob, we trust our more methodical brothers are too. It is good to be serious in the service of our God, because we serve a serious God.

We will leave the rest of the Jacob's blessing for our next reading.

MARCH 2
I Wait for Your Salvation, O LORD[185]

We will now read the rest of the blessings given by Jacob to his sons.

Genesis 49:16-33

16 "Dan shall judge his people
>as one of the tribes of Israel."

Dan means judge. Dan was the first child born to Jacob by a concubine (a woman with lower status than his wives Leah and Rachel). This blessing indicated that all of these sons who might be considered to be of a lower rank would also be self-governing.

17 "Dan shall be a serpent in the way,
>a viper by the path,

---

[181] type - something or someone that represents something or someone else, usually in the future. As man, Jesus descended from the tribe of Judah. Revelation 5:5 speaks of the Lord Jesus and includes, "Weep no more; behold, the Lion of the tribe of Judah, the Root of David."
[182] ESV footnote: "until Shiloh comes" or "until he comes to Shiloh"
[183] John 12:19

[184] Isaiah 55:1
[185] Genesis 49:18

      that bites the horse's heels
          so that his rider falls backward.
18 I wait for your salvation, O LORD."

Jacob pauses in verse eighteen. His words express his inability to save himself or his family. He is not annoyed by this or complaining about it. He is expressing a hope that grew out of the Lord's faithfulness to him over many years. He was old and knew he was about to die. He was confident that he would soon enjoy the fullness of salvation in the very presence of the Lord.

19 "Raiders shall raid Gad,
          but he shall raid at their heels."

This is often proved in the believer's life. Many trials push him down, but he rises up again.

20 "Asher's food shall be rich,
          and he shall yield royal delicacies.
21 "Naphtali is a doe let loose
          he gives beautiful words."[186]

A lively spirit and the ability to speak and be easily understood; this is a good combination for a minister of the gospel.

22 "Joseph is a fruitful bough,
      a fruitful bough by a spring;
          his branches run over the wall.
23 The archers bitterly attacked him,
          shot at him, and harassed him severely,
24 yet his bow remained unmoved;
      his arms were made agile
      by the hands of the Mighty One of Jacob
        (from there is the Shepherd, the Stone
          of Israel),
25 by the God of your father who will help
      you,
      by the Almighty who will bless you
      with blessings of heaven above,
      blessings of the deep that crouches
        beneath,
      blessings of the breasts and of the
        womb.
26 The blessings of your father
      are mighty beyond the blessings of my
        parents,
      up to the bounties of the everlasting
        hills."

      May they be on the head of Joseph,
      and on the brow of him who was set
        apart from his brothers.

Jacob's heart swelled when he got to Joseph. Evidently, he thought he could not pour out a blessing that was generous enough. Jesus is the greater Joseph. When we truly turn our thoughts to Jesus, no words can lift him up enough. Watts has said it nicely:

> *"Blessings more than we can give,*
> *Be, Lord, for ever thine."*[187]

27 "Benjamin is a ravenous wolf,
      in the morning devouring the prey
      and at evening dividing the spoil."

Benjamin would become a quarrelsome tribe. Even though Benjamin was greatly loved by his father, he did not dare use that as a reason to invent a blessing for him. He speaks only the words the Lord gave him—nothing less, nothing more. To be fighting from morning to night is a shameful business, unless it is against sin.

28 All these are the twelve tribes of Israel. This is what their father said to them as he blessed them, blessing each with the blessing suitable to him. **29** Then he commanded them and said to them, "I am to be gathered to my people; bury me with my fathers in the cave that is in the field of Ephron the Hittite, **30** in the cave that is in the field at Machpelah, to the east of Mamre, in the land of Canaan, which Abraham bought with the field from Ephron the Hittite to possess as a burying place. **31** There they buried Abraham and Sarah his wife. There they buried Isaac and Rebekah his wife, and there I buried Leah— **32** the field and the cave that is in it were bought from the Hittites." **33** When Jacob finished commanding his sons, he drew up his feet into the bed and breathed his last and was gathered to his people.

Jacob was not left among the Egyptians even after death, but slept in the family tomb of his fathers, to awake with them at the resurrection. In all things he kept going as one who was on a journey with God to a city that would only be reached at death.

---

[186] This is the ESV alternate reading. The text reads, "that bears beautiful fawns."

[187] Composer Isaac Watts (1674-1748)

MARCH 3
We Are Not Ignorant of Satan's Designs[188]

It is the general opinion that Job lived at some time between the age of Abraham and the time of Moses. It is probable that Moses wrote this holy poem that records the discussion between Job and his friends. Therefore, at this time, we will consider his history and gather a few gems from the remarkable book that bears his name.

Job 1:1-12

1 There was a man in the land of Uz whose name was Job, *(He was just an ordinary "man." He was not a prince or a king. Yet he was nobler than any of the nobles of his time.)* and that man was blameless and upright, one who feared God and turned away from evil. *(This description of his character is given him by God's perfect inspiration. No one could hope for a higher honor. His life was well balanced and showed that he was righteous, toward both God and man.)* **2** There were born to him seven sons and three daughters. **3** He possessed 7,000 sheep, 3,000 camels, 500 yoke of oxen, and 500 female donkeys, and very many servants, so that this man was the greatest of all the people of the east.

We see here that a rich man may be a good man even though "gold and the gospel seldom do agree."[189] It may be rare, but a man of riches may also have riches in heaven. Job was gracious in prosperity and therefore was supported in hardship.

4 His sons used to go and hold a feast in the house of each one on his day, and they would send and invite their three sisters to eat and drink with them. *(They probably celebrated their birthdays in this happy and united way. It is a great happiness to see brothers and sisters knit together in love.)* **5** And when the days of the feast had run their course, Job would send and consecrate them, and he would rise early in the morning and offer burnt offerings according to the number of them all. For Job said, "It may be that my children have sinned, and cursed God in their hearts." Thus Job did continually. *(He did not forbid their parties, because they were not in themselves sinful. But he knew how likely people are to forget their God and even themselves during a party. He was eager to remove any spot of sin that might result. It is to be feared that few parents are as careful as Job was in this matter.)*

6 Now there was a day when the sons of God came to present themselves before the LORD, and Satan also came among them.

This meeting did not need to take place in heaven. God's assembly room includes all of space. What nerve Satan had to come before God! What equal impudence when hypocrites pretend to worship the Most High.

7 The LORD said to Satan, "From where have you come?" Satan answered the LORD and said, "From going to and fro on the earth, and from walking up and down on it."

Satan is a busy traveler. He is never idle.

8 And the LORD said to Satan, "Have you considered my servant Job, that there is none like him on the earth, a blameless and upright man, who fears God and turns away from evil?"

Satan had "considered" Job and watched him closely. He thinks carefully before giving his clever answer.

9 Then Satan answered the LORD and said, "Does Job fear God for no reason? **10** Have you not put a hedge around him and his house and all that he has, on every side? You have blessed the work of his hands, and his possessions have increased in the land. *(Why should God not treat his servant well? If Job had been poor and miserable, Satan would have said that the Lord paid his servants lousy wages.)* **11** But stretch out your hand and touch all that he has and he will curse you to your face." *(A cruel suggestion, but Satan was measuring Job's corn with his own bushel.[190])* **12** And the LORD said to Satan, "Behold, all that he has is in your hand. Only against him do not stretch out your hand." So Satan went out from the presence of the LORD.

---

[188] 2 Corinthians 2:11
[189] Attributed to John Bunyan
[190] An old country saying meaning "to measure others by oneself"

The Lord intended to glorify himself, to further perfect the character of Job, and to furnish his church with a grand example. This is why he challenged the archenemy. Satan went off on his errand willingly enough, but little did he dream of the defeat that awaited him.

On January 6, 1850, Spurgeon turned in to the Artillery Street Methodist Chapel when snow prevented him from attending his intended chapel. The pastor of the church was not there; the preacher was probably a deacon. The Lord used him to bring Spurgeon into the family of God that morning.

March 4
Many Are the Afflictions of the Righteous[191]
Job 1:13-22

13 Now there was a day when [Job's] sons and daughters were eating and drinking wine in their oldest brother's house,

Satan's timing was crafty. When troubles come on us when we are celebrating, they have a double bitterness. The brightness of that unforgettable day's morning made the darkness of the night all the darker.

14 and there came a messenger to Job and said, "The oxen were plowing and the donkeys feeding beside them, **15** and the Sabeans fell upon them and took them and struck down the servants with the edge of the sword, and I alone have escaped to tell you."

Job did not lose his property because he was being neglectful. The oxen were plowing and the donkeys were watched over. This proves that all of our care and diligence cannot protect our property unless the Lord is the true protector of it. To lose the oxen that plowed his fields and the donkeys that carried his burdens was a huge disaster, but we do not find the man of God making one word of complaint. Some people would have been in a bad mood if only one ox had died.

16 While he was yet speaking, there came another and said, "The fire of God fell from heaven and burned up the sheep and the servants and consumed them, and I alone have escaped to tell you."

Job's trial increased. The first came from man. The second came directly from heaven. The hand of God was seen more clearly and the sting of the loss would have been all the more painful to the holy soul of Job. Furthermore, in that culture a man's wealth was in his flocks and Job went from rich to poor with no warning. But he did not complain. Some who profess to be Christians would have been terribly upset if only one lamb had died.

17 While he was yet speaking, there came another and said, "The Chaldeans formed three groups and made a raid on the camels and took them and struck down the servants with the edge of the sword, and I alone have escaped to tell you."

Each messenger finishes his report with the sad words, "And I alone have escaped to tell you." Satan knows how to beat up a person with terrible news and sadden their heart by repeating the blows. Three companies of servants had been destroyed along with all of his livestock, yet he did not say a word. Job's heart was so focused on God, that he was not afraid of evil news. What an example he is for us!

18 While he was yet speaking, there came another and said, "Your sons and daughters were eating and drinking wine in their oldest brother's house, **19** and behold, a great wind came across the wilderness and struck the four corners of the house, and it fell upon the young people, and they are dead, and I alone have escaped to tell you." *(This last attack was the greatest and most direct against Job. If anything could break a man, this would. Great debaters work from the weakest*

---
[191] Psalm 34:19

arguments to the greatest. In the same way, the archenemy weakens Job with smaller afflictions and saves his heaviest assault for the last. Even through the heartbreak of losing his whole family at the same time, Job's faith did not break down.)

20 Then Job arose and tore his robe and shaved his head and fell on the ground and worshiped. **21** And he said, "Naked I came from my mother's womb, and naked shall I return. The LORD gave, and the LORD has taken away; blessed be the name of the LORD." *(The greatness of Job's faith is clearly visible. Certainly no one, besides the Son of Man in Gethsemane, ever rose to a greater height of accepting the Lord's will for themselves. Instead of cursing God, like Satan said he would, he blesses the Lord with all his heart. How thoroughly beaten the evil spirit must have felt. May the Holy Spirit help each one of us to be victorious over the evil one in the same way. Job did not offend God in either his heart or his words. He understood the holy wisdom of accepting whatever the Lord had in store for him. He did not become upset with his God.)*

22 In all this Job did not sin or charge God with wrong. *(Grace made him more than a conqueror over Satan.)*

MARCH 5
Blessed Is the Man Who Remains Steadfast Under Trial[192]

Job 2:1-13

1 Again there was a day when the sons of God came to present themselves before the LORD, and Satan also came among them to present himself before the LORD.

Even the devil will attend worship services to serve his own ends. Those who hope to be saved because they attend church services regularly are hoping in the wrong thing. We should also "watch and pray" when we attend Christian services. Satan is there and is busy with his temptations.[193]

2 And the LORD said to Satan, "From where have you come?" Satan answered the LORD and said, "From going to and fro on the earth, and from walking up and down on it."

Satan is full of evil, but he is not idle. A lazy person commits one more sin than the devil himself.

3 And the LORD said to Satan, "Have you considered my servant Job, that there is none like him on the earth, a blameless and upright man, who fears God and turns away from evil? He still holds fast his integrity, although you incited me against him to destroy him without reason." *(Job was a good, honest, and sincere man. These qualities were like a strong fortress that resisted the attacks of hell. The prince of darkness himself personally attacked him. God gave Satan permission to take away everything Job had.)*

4 Then Satan answered the LORD and said, "Skin for skin! All that a man has he will give for his life. **5** But stretch out your hand and touch his bone and his flesh, and he will curse you to your face." *(Satan suggested that bodily pain would be the weapon to wound Job's faith and even turn that faith into rebellion. The evil one showed his great skill in this plan. Many people have been able to endure every other trial, but were defeated by the suffering of physical pain. Nevertheless, the Lord can make his people more than conquerors even there.)* **6** And the LORD said to Satan, "Behold, he is in your hand; only spare his life."

7 So Satan went out from the presence of the LORD and struck Job with loathsome sores from the sole of his foot to the crown of his head. **8** And he took a piece of broken pottery with which to scrape himself while he sat in the ashes.

Job did not have a soft bed while in this terrible condition, but sat on the hard ashes. He probably did not have a doctor or nurse to help ease his pain. There he sat, the prince of misery; but there was worse to come.

9 Then his wife said to him, "Do you still hold fast your integrity? Curse God and die." **10** But he said to her, "You speak as one of

---
[192] James 1:12
[193] Matthew 26:41, Jesus said, "Watch and pray that you may not enter into temptation. the spirit indeed is willing, but the flesh is weak."

the foolish women would speak. Shall we receive good from God, and shall we not receive evil?" In all this Job did not sin with his lips. *(Satan tried to ruin Job by using the person who should have been his best comforter, but the evil one was defeated. The words of his wife only led Job to proclaim another of those remarkable speeches that are now the treasures of the church.)*

¹¹ Now when Job's three friends heard of all this evil that had come upon him, they came each from his own place, Eliphaz the Temanite, Bildad the Shuhite, and Zophar the Naamathite. They made an appointment together to come to show him sympathy and comfort him. ¹² And when they saw him from a distance, they did not recognize him. And they raised their voices and wept, and they tore their robes and sprinkled dust on their heads toward heaven. ¹³ And they sat with him on the ground seven days and seven nights, and no one spoke a word to him, for they saw that his suffering was very great.

They showed sympathy, but even this was not allowed to continue. Satan would not let them comfort the afflicted one. Eventually, these three friends became judges of Job's condition. They decided that such unusual suffering could only have been brought about by unusual sin. Under this impression, they added the last drop of bitterness to Job's cup by accusing him of hypocrisy and secret sin.

MARCH 6
He Will Deliver You from Six Troubles[194]

Eliphaz, the Temanite, brought wrong and cruel accusations against Job. Nevertheless, he did touch on some important things. We will read two passages of his first speech. In the first, he shows that weak and guilty man must not question the wisdom and justice of God's actions.

Job 4:12-21

¹² "Now a word was brought to me stealthily;
  my ear received the whisper of it,
¹³ Amid thoughts from visions of the night,
  when deep sleep falls on men,
¹⁴ dread came upon me, and trembling,
  which made all my bones shake.
¹⁵ A spirit glided past my face;
  the hair of my flesh stood up.
¹⁶ It stood still,
  but I could not discern its appearance.
  A form was before my eyes;
  there was silence, then I heard a voice:
¹⁷ 'Can mortal man be in the right before God?
  Can a man be pure before his Maker?
¹⁸ Even in his servants he puts no trust,
  and his angels he charges with error;
¹⁹ how much more those who dwell in houses of clay,
  whose foundation is in the dust,
  who are crushed like the moth.
²⁰ Between morning and evening they are beaten to pieces;
  they perish forever without anyone regarding it.
²¹ Is not their tent-cord plucked up within them,
  do they not die, and that without wisdom?'"

Compared to God what are humans or even angels? The wisdom of angels is limited and where their wisdom ends foolishness begins. Theirs is not sinful folly, but when compared to the All-Wise God, even angels know very little. How then can we think highly of weak human beings who we know will soon die and turn to dust, and be forgotten? How then can a mere insect like ourselves, who is not only foolish, but also sinful, dare to question what the Eternal God does?

Job 5:17-27

In our second selection Eliphaz teaches us not to become discouraged when we receive divine chastisements,[195] because they are intended for our highest good.

¹⁷ "Behold, blessed is the one whom God reproves;
  therefore despise not the discipline of the Almighty."

---

[194] Job 5:19

[195] *chasten, chastening* or *chastisement* - The act of discipline which may include scolding, criticizing or pain inflicted for the purpose of correction or moral improvement

Do not have a strong dislike for God's discipline. Do not rebel against it or think God is acting out of anger. And do not disregard it as if it were not important.

18 "For he wounds, but he binds up;
 he shatters, but his hands heal."

The same Lord is in both our afflictions and our relief. He arranges that the one will surely be followed by the other.

19 "He will deliver you from six troubles;
 in seven no evil shall touch you."

Trouble may roar at us like a lion, but it cannot devour us. It may irritate us, but it will not do us real harm. If we suffer a large number of trials we will have an even larger supply of grace.

20 "In famine he will redeem you from death,
 and in war from the power of the sword.
21 You shall be hidden from the lash of the tongue* (a mercy indeed),
 *and shall not fear destruction when it comes.
22 At destruction and famine you shall laugh,
 and shall not fear the beasts of the earth.
23 For you shall be in league with the stones of the field,
 and the beast of the field shall be at peace with you."

The Great Master's dogs will not bite his friends.

24 "You shall know that your tent is at peace,
 and you shall inspect your fold and miss nothing.
25 You shall know also that your offspring shall be many,
 and your descendants as the grass of the earth."

The Lord is our Friend and he will also be gracious to our children.

26 "You shall come to your grave in ripe old age,
 like a sheaf gathered up in its season.
27 Behold, this we have searched out; it is true.
 Hear, and know it for your good."

Not only have we been told this, we have seen that it is true. "We know that for those who love God all things work together for good."[196]

MARCH 7
For I the LORD Do Not Change[197]

Our space will not allow us to include much of this wonderful book of Job, but the following is an example of the patriarch's expressions of distress.

Job 23
1 Then Job answered and said:
2 "Today also my complaint is bitter;
 my hand is heavy on account of my groaning."

Most people cry before they are hurt, or more than they are hurt; but this was not Job's case. He had good reason for every groan and when he groaned most he fell short of expressing what he really felt.

3 "Oh, that I knew where I might find him,
 that I might come even to his seat!"

Even at his very lowest point the good man knows his true safety is in the Lord. Sinners turn from God in anger. The saints fly to him with hope. Yet sometimes the Lord is a God that hides himself. When he does this, he has wise results to accomplish. He will continue it no longer than is absolutely necessary.

4 "I would lay my case before him
 and fill my mouth with arguments.
5 I would know what he would answer me
 and understand what he would say to me."

Job wished to have the question that his three friends had raised given a fair hearing in the very highest court. He felt that he could freely bring his case before so righteous a judge. It is only the pure heart that can invite such a thorough investigation. Those who know that they are guiltless through Jesus' blood are not afraid to appear in the courts of heaven.

6 "Would he contend with me in the greatness of his power?
 No; he would pay attention to me."

Innocence does not fear power, but like Una rides on the lion.[198] The Lord never

---
[196] Romans 8:28
[197] Malachi 3:6

crushes a person because they are down. Rather, he delights to lift up those who have been cast down.

7 "There an upright man could argue with him,
    and I would be acquitted forever by my judge.
8 "Behold, I go forward, but he is not there,
    and backward, but I do not perceive him;
9 on the left hand when he is working, I do not behold him;
    he turns to the right hand, but I do not see him.
10 But he knows the way that I take;
    when he has tried me, I shall come out as gold."

He comforts himself with the assurance that if he could not find the Lord, and speak in his own defense, yet the case was already known to him, and would in due time be decided in his favor. His faith kept him wonderfully secure during his heavy trial; like a sure anchor in a terribly raging storm.

11 "My foot has held fast to his steps;
    I have kept his way and have not turned aside.
12 I have not departed from the commandment of his lips;
    I have treasured the words of his mouth more than my portion of food."

Job again answers the accusations of his three unfriendly friends. He strongly declares that he is innocent of their charges. He rejects the idea that he is suffering for some secret sin.

13 "But he is unchangeable, and who can turn him back?
    What he desires, that he does.
14 For he will complete what he appoints for me,
    and many such things are in his mind."

Job explains his trials by pointing out that God's ways are both unchanging and unknowable. He suggests that many more troubles might yet visit him; and for which he might also be unable to find a reason.

15 "Therefore I am terrified at his presence;
    when I consider, I am in dread of him."

Great suffering could not kill his faith, but it reduced his joy. He understood that an absolute God could do whatever he wanted. It is no wonder that he trembled at this thought. Only when we see Jesus do we see that God is love.

16 "God has made my heart faint;
    the Almighty has terrified me;
17 yet I am not silenced because of the darkness,
    nor because thick darkness covers my face."

He wished he could have died before these sufferings came on him, but all such wishes have no result. We cannot change what has already happened. Therefore let us by faith move forward.

MARCH 8

The Fear Of the LORD Is the Beginning of Wisdom[199]

Let us read Job's famous passage about the search for wisdom.

Job 28

1 "Surely there is a mine for silver,
    and a place for gold that they refine.
2 Iron is taken out of the earth,
    and copper is smelted from the ore."

The following verses describe mining operations and the dangers to the miner.

3 "Man puts an end to darkness
    and searches out to the farthest limit
    the ore in gloom and deep darkness.
4 He opens shafts in a valley away from where anyone lives;
    they are forgotten by travelers;
    they hang in the air, far away from mankind; they swing to and fro."

That is to say, as the miners are lowered down the mineshaft, their feet dangle and swing to and fro.

5 "As for the earth, out of it comes bread,
    but underneath it is turned up as by fire.

---

[198] A reference to an English fairy tale written in the 1590's by Edmund Spenser. Lady Una is searching for her lost knight when a lion appears, ready to devour her. Una shows no fear, but only remorse for her lost knight. The lion takes pity on Una and allows her to ride on his back as they search together for the lost Knight of the Red Cross.

[199] Psalm 111:10 Proverbs 9:10

6 Its stones are the place of sapphires,
   and it has dust of gold.
7 "That path no bird of prey knows,
   and the falcon's eye has not seen it.
8 The proud beasts have not trodden it;
   the lion has not passed over it.
9 "Man puts his hand to the flinty rock
   and overturns mountains by the roots."

The solid rock is broken and those who search for precious metals dig out the hills. Their tunnels go into the center of the mountains and tear out the insides of the hills.

10 "He cuts out channels in the rocks,
    and his eye sees every precious thing.
11 He dams up the streams so that they do not trickle,
    and the thing that is hidden he brings out to light."

Miners take great care to prevent the water from breaking through and flooding the mines. By taking these precautions they are able to penetrate deep into the earth and reveal her secrets.

12 "But where shall wisdom be found?
    And where is the place of understanding?
13 Man does not know its worth,
    and it is not found in the land of the living.
14 The deep says, 'It is not in me,'
    and the sea says, 'It is not with me.'
15 It cannot be bought for gold,
    and silver cannot be weighed as its price.
16 It cannot be valued in the gold of Ophir,
    in precious onyx or sapphire.
17 Gold and glass cannot equal it,
    nor can it be exchanged for jewels of fine gold."

In ancient times glass was a costly item used only for splendor and luxury. However precious glass might be, wisdom far surpasses it.

18 "No mention shall be made of coral or of crystal;
    the price of wisdom is above pearls.
19 The topaz of Ethiopia cannot equal it,
    nor can it be valued in pure gold.
20 "From where, then, does wisdom come?
    And where is the place of understanding?
21 It is hidden from the eyes of all living
    and concealed from the birds of the air.
22 Abaddon and Death say,
    'We have heard a rumor of it with our ears.'
23 "God understands the way to it,
    and he knows its place.
24 For he looks to the ends of the earth
    and sees everything under the heavens.
25 When he gave to the wind its weight
    and apportioned the waters by measure,
26 when he made a decree for the rain
    and a way for the lightning of the thunder,
27 then he saw it and declared it;
    he established it, and searched it out.
28 And he said to man,
    'Behold, the fear of the Lord, that is wisdom,
    and to turn away from evil is understanding.'"

Job comes to the same conclusion as Solomon, who said, "The fear of the Lord is the beginning of wisdom." True religion is priceless beyond all the treasures of earth. Children and young men! Seek wisdom first, for then you will be truly rich.

Jesus is the Captain of the mine of wisdom and he will show you the treasures of precious knowledge.

MARCH 9

I Work, and Who Can Turn It Back?[200]

When Job's three accusers were silent, when Elihu had finished his eloquent speech, and Job had no more to say, the Lord himself came between them. As if with a long series of thunderclaps, the Lord hushed every heart and voice into fear, wonder and respect.

Job 38:1-11; 16-17; 22-23; 31-41

¹ Then the LORD answered Job out of the whirlwind and said:

2 "Who is this that darkens counsel by
    words without knowledge?

How majestic are those words, "Who is this?" Is it a poor, weak, foolish man? Is it

---
[200] Isaiah 43:13

Job? My servant Job! Does he speak of that which he cannot understand and dare to complain about his God? Our wisdom is only wisdom when it admits its own foolishness.

3 "Dress for action like a man;
   I will question you, and you make it known to me.

4 "Where were you when I laid the foundation of the earth?
   Tell me, if you have understanding.

5 Who determined its measurements—surely you know!
   Or who stretched the line upon it?

6 On what were its bases sunk,
   or who laid its cornerstone,

7 when the morning stars sang together
   and all the sons of God shouted for joy?"

We know nothing about the ways of God. How foolish we are to think that we can pry into his mysteries and explain his difficult secrets. We are far better off singing with angels, than doubting with devils. The angels all sang, sang together, and sang with one common joy. Oh for such unanimous joyful praise among men.

8 "Or who shut in the sea with doors
   when it burst out from the womb,

9 when I made clouds its garment
   and thick darkness its swaddling band,

10 and prescribed limits for it
    and set bars and doors,

11 and said, 'Thus far shall you come, and no farther,
    and here shall your proud waves be stayed'?"

16 "Have you entered into the springs of the sea,
    or walked in the recesses of the deep?

17 Have the gates of death been revealed to you,
    or have you seen the gates of deep darkness?"

The secrets of earth are too deep for us. The mysteries of eternity are even more so. One thing, however, is comforting; if we do not see the gates of death open, we do know who it is that has opened the door of heaven for us.

22 "Have you entered the storehouses of the snow,
    or have you seen the storehouses of the hail,

23 which I have reserved for the time of trouble,
    for the day of battle and war?"

31 "Can you bind the chains of the Pleiades
    or loose the cords of Orion?

32 Can you lead forth the Mazzaroth in their season,
    or can you guide the Bear with its children?"

Pleiades, Orion, Mazzaroth and Bear refer to constellations in the stars. Who among us can control the stars or change the seasons?

33 "Do you know the ordinances of the heavens?
    Can you establish their rule on the earth?

34 "Can you lift up your voice to the clouds,
    that a flood of waters may cover you?

35 Can you send forth lightnings, that they may go
    and say to you, 'Here we are'?

36 Who has put wisdom in the inward parts
    or given understanding to the mind?

37 Who can number the clouds by wisdom?
    Or who can tilt the waterskins of the heavens,

38 when the dust runs into a mass
    and the clods stick fast together?

39 "Can you hunt the prey for the lion,
    or satisfy the appetite of the young lions,

40 when they crouch in their dens
    or lie in wait in their thicket?

41 Who provides for the raven its prey,
    when its young ones cry to God for help,
    and wander about for lack of food?"

In all these things the greatness of the Lord and the nothingness of humanity are obvious. May God keep even one thought of pride from poisoning our spirit.

MARCH 10
You Alone Are God[201]

The majestic language of Jehovah in his speech to Job is far above all human eloquence. Let us read a second lesson from that divine sermon. We begin with the unequalled description of a warhorse.

Job 39:19-30

19 "Do you give the horse his might?
  Do you clothe his neck with a mane?
20 Do you make him leap like the locust?
  His majestic snorting is terrifying.
21 He paws in the valley and exults in his strength;
  he goes out to meet the weapons.
22 He laughs at fear and is not dismayed;
  he does not turn back from the sword.
23 Upon him rattle the quiver,
  the flashing spear and the javelin.
24 With fierceness and rage he swallows the ground;
  he cannot stand still at the sound of the trumpet.
25 When the trumpet sounds, he says 'Aha!'
  He smells the battle from afar,
  the thunder of the captains, and the shouting."

He who created a creature so noble, powerful, and courageous, is not to be summoned to our courtroom or questioned about what he does.

26 "Is it by your understanding that the hawk soars
  and spreads his wings toward the south?"

We often talk about instinct. What is instinct? It is God teaching his creation! He who has given so much wisdom to birds and beasts is full of wisdom himself. Let us bow before him and rest assured that what he does is always best.

27 "Is it at your command that the eagle mounts up
  and makes his nest on high?
28 On the rock he dwells and makes his home,
  on the rocky crag and stronghold.
29 From there he spies out the prey;
  his eyes behold it afar off.
30 His young ones suck up blood,
  and where the slain are, there is he."

The noble eagle sees afar and inspires terror. It does not belong to the kings of the earth even though they adorn their flags and shields with its image. The eagle is another example of the wonderful mind of God and another illustration of his greatness.

Job 40:1-14

1 And the LORD said to Job:
2 "Shall a faultfinder contend with the Almighty?
  He who argues with God, let him answer it."

3 Then Job answered the LORD and said:
4 "Behold, I am of small account; what shall I answer you?
  I lay my hand on my mouth.
5 I have spoken once, and I will not answer;
  twice, but I will proceed no further."

6 Then the LORD answered Job out of the whirlwind and said:
7 "Dress for action like a man;
  I will question you, and you make it known to me.
8 Will you even put me in the wrong?
  Will you condemn me that you may be in the right?
9 Have you an arm like God,
  and can you thunder with a voice like his?"

If we think that we can compete with God about who is the most righteous, then God challenges us to first compete with him over who is the most powerful. All the attributes[202] of God are equally great. If we cannot match him in one, then it will not be wise to call another one into question.

10 "Adorn yourself with majesty and dignity;
  clothe yourself with glory and splendor."

Come you poor little glowworm, show us your light. What are you compared to the sun?

11 "Pour out the overflowings of your anger,

---
[201] Psalm 86:10

[202] *attribute* - A quality or characteristic that someone has.

and look on everyone who is proud and abase him.

¹² Look on everyone who is proud and bring him low
and tread down the wicked where they stand.

¹³ Hide them all in the dust together;
bind their faces in the world below.

¹⁴ Then will I also acknowledge to you
that your own right hand can save you."

The Lord can bring down tyrants and deliver the oppressed. Until we can control the world as he has, we should learn to submit to his divine will and stop our rebellious questioning.

MARCH 11
I Know That You Can Do All Things[203]
Job 42:1-13

¹ Then Job answered the LORD and said:

² "I know that you can do all things,
and that no purpose of yours can be thwarted."

The patriarch made an unconditional acknowledgment. He felt that the very idea of judging the actions of the Almighty was preposterous. Omnipotence[204] and Omniscience[205] make the thought of calling the Eternal God into question absolutely ridiculous.

³ "'Who is this that hides counsel without knowledge?'
Therefore I have uttered what I did not understand,
things too wonderful for me, which I did not know."

The Lord's first question, "Who is this that darkens counsel by words without knowledge?,"[206] lives in Job's memory. In humble wonder at his own boldness he asks himself this question. It is the same as the apostle Paul's question, "But who are you, O man, to answer back to God?"[207] The patriarch now sees his foolishness in a new light and humbly confesses it before the Lord. A very great part of our religious conversation is made up of saying things that we do not understand. Like Job, all of our complaining is the result of our ignorance.

⁴ "'Hear, and I will speak;
I will question you, and you make it known to me.'"

Job desired to enroll in God's school and to be taught by him. He will no longer argue his case, but will be a humble student.

⁵ "I had heard of you by the hearing of the ear,
but now my eye sees you;

⁶ therefore I despise myself,
and repent in dust and ashes."

Hearing does not mean much until the Lord's arm is revealed[208] in a man's heart. Caryl well observes "No man knows what a nothing he is in knowledge, grace, and goodness until the Lord is pleased to reveal himself to him."[209] When we compare ourselves with ourselves, or with others we think are below us, we imagine that we are important persons; but when the Lord reveals himself we become as nothing in our own eyes. The more we see of God the less we will think of ourselves. True knowledge is the death of conceit.

⁷ After the LORD had spoken these words to Job, the LORD said to Eliphaz the Temanite: "My anger burns against you and against your two friends, for you have not spoken of me what is right, as my servant Job has." *(Out of their zeal to defend the way God had dealt with Job, his friends were unfair in their arguments. We have no business defending truth with lies or half-truths. God will have honest defenders or none. He is not pleased with untruthful supporters even though they imagine they are on the Lord's side, or at any rate they want to be.)*

⁸ "Now therefore take seven bulls and seven rams and go to my servant Job and

---

[203] Job 42:2
[204] *omnipotent, omnipotence* - all powerful, almighty, absolute and supreme power, having unlimited power.
[205] *omniscient, omniscience* - All knowing or knowing everything; all seeing or seeing everything. The capacity to know everything that there is to know.
[206] Job 38:2
[207] Romans 9:20

[208] "The Lord's arm revealed" is a reference to Isaiah 53:1 and quoted in John 12:38. It represents the strength and power of God.
[209] Joseph Caryl (1602-1673) Almost certainly from his 12 volume Commentary on Job.

offer up a burnt offering for yourselves. And my servant Job shall pray for you, for I will accept his prayer not to deal with you according to your folly. For you have not spoken of me what is right, as my servant Job has." *(Let us never judge others, because there may come a time we will want their help. We may want them to pray for us in the future, so we should not judge them harshly in the present.)* ⁹ So Eliphaz the Temanite and Bildad the Shuhite and Zophar the Naamathite went and did what the LORD had told them, and the LORD accepted Job's prayer. *(The Lord accepted Job and blessed his friends for his sake. How much more does he accept the Lord Jesus Christ who offered himself a sacrifice for sin? And how much safer are we, his poor offending friends, who are in him?*

¹⁰ And the LORD restored the fortunes of Job, when he had prayed for his friends. And the LORD gave Job twice as much as he had before.

When we pray in a forgiving spirit for those who have been harsh to us, the Lord will bless us.

¹¹ Then came to him all his brothers and sisters and all who had known him before, and ate bread with him in his house. And they showed him sympathy and comforted him for all the evil that the LORD had brought upon him. And each of them gave him a piece of money and a ring of gold.

¹² And the LORD blessed the latter days of Job more than his beginning. And he had 14,000 sheep, 6,000 camels, 1,000 yoke of oxen, and 1,000 female donkeys. ¹³ He had also seven sons and three daughters.

The Lord's way will prove to be the right way. His people will not be the losers because of their hardships.

MARCH 12
The Lord Is Not Slow To Fulfill His Promise[210]

Our reading will now take us back from Job in the land of Uz to the land of Egypt, where we left the chosen family in Goshen.

Exodus 1:1-14; 22

¹ These are the names of the sons of Israel who came to Egypt with Jacob, each with his household: *("The Lord knows those who are his."[211] The names of the godly family are precious to his heart.)* ² Reuben, Simeon, Levi, and Judah, ³ Issachar, Zebulun, and Benjamin, ⁴ Dan and Naphtali, Gad and Asher. ⁵ All the descendants of Jacob were seventy persons; Joseph was already in Egypt. ⁶ Then Joseph died, and all his brothers and all that generation. ⁷ But the people of Israel were fruitful and increased greatly; they multiplied and grew exceedingly strong, so that the land was filled with them. *(The ancient promise that Abraham's family would be many received its first fulfillment. God does not forget any of his promises.)*

⁸ Now there arose a new king over Egypt, who did not know Joseph. *(Out of sight, out of mind. A man may give a nation permanent advantages, but he cannot hope for permanent appreciation. Like Joseph, those who serve mankind are generally rewarded with forgetfulness.)* ⁹ And he said to his people, "Behold, the people of Israel are too many and too mighty for us. ¹⁰ Come, let us deal shrewdly with them, lest they multiply, and, if war breaks out, they join our enemies and fight against us and escape from the land."

The ungodly always try to describe God's people as a dangerous threat. However, if they would treat them kindly they would discover they are the best of neighbors. It is only when they deliberately trip on this stone that it injures them. The Egyptians tried to stop the population of Israel from growing. The attempt was hopeless. Pharaoh might as well have tried to hold back the ocean or stop the Nile River from flooding. Jehovah had decided that the people of Israel would multiply and no policy of kings or politicians could prevent it. The king was an expert in worldly wisdom. His plan had both the craftiness and cruelty of Satan. But he was a fool and every point of his strategy failed.

---

[210] 2 Peter 3:9

[211] 2 Timothy 2:19

¹¹ Therefore they set taskmasters over them to afflict them with heavy burdens. They built for Pharaoh store cities, Pithom and Raamses. ¹² But the more they were oppressed, the more they multiplied and the more they spread abroad. And the Egyptians were in dread of the people of Israel.

The enemies of God's people have been both determined and shameless. Even so, they have been unable to achieve their goal. The church must expand, even expand by the very means that were thought would destroy her. There are herbs²¹² that grow faster when they are walked on and true religion is one of them.

¹³ So they ruthlessly made the people of Israel work as slaves ¹⁴ and made their lives bitter with hard service, in mortar and brick, and in all kinds of work in the field. In all their work they ruthlessly made them work as slaves.

They wanted to humiliate them, crush their spirit and weaken them, but their cruel plan did not succeed. No weapon can win against the Lord's chosen. After all, hard work is less harmful than being inactive and spoiled. It is better to be a slave who is forced to make bricks than to be infected with laziness.

Pharaoh attempted to have all the male children murdered by those who helped at their birth, but this plan failed. The tyrant then passed a monstrous law that is recorded here.

²² Then Pharaoh commanded all his people, "Every son that is born to the Hebrews you shall cast into the Nile, but you shall let every daughter live."

Murder was called and told to make an end of the elect people, but it did not win. The Lord of Israel was greater than the King of Egypt. He proved more than a match for all his plots and plans.

Charles Spurgeon was baptized, at the age of 16, on May 3, 1850, in the river Lark at Isleham Ferry. He walked eight miles to get there.

March 13
Who Is On the Lord's Side?²¹³
Exodus 2:1-10

¹ Now a man from the house of Levi went and took as his wife a Levite woman. ² The woman conceived and bore a son, and when she saw that he was a fine child, she hid him three months. ³ When she could hide him no longer, she took for him a basket made of bulrushes and daubed it with bitumen and pitch. She put the child in it and placed it among the reeds by the river bank. ⁴ And his sister stood at a distance to know what would be done to him. *(Faith watches to see what God will do.)*

⁵ Now the daughter of Pharaoh came down to bathe at the river, while her young women walked beside the river. She saw the basket among the reeds and sent her servant woman, and she took it. *(The hand of God is clear here. How was the basket kept from the crocodiles? Why did the princess come to that particular spot? Why did she look where she would see that little floating treasure chest hidden among the bulrushes? What made her want to look inside it? Surely the Lord's hand was in it all.)* ⁶ When she opened it, she saw the child, and behold, the baby was crying. *(The providence²¹⁴ that*

---

²¹² *herbs* - plants used for flavoring, food, medicine, or perfume

²¹³ Exodus 32:26
²¹⁴ *Providence* - Usually, when used with a capital "P" it refers to God; when used with a lower case "p", it refers to God's will, his divine intervention, and his predetermination (predestination).

brought the princess to the spot brought the tears to the baby's eyes at the very moment when they would be seen, and move the princess with compassion.)* She took pity on him and said, "This is one of the Hebrews' children."

7 Then his sister said to Pharaoh's daughter, "Shall I go and call you a nurse from the Hebrew women to nurse the child for you?" **8** And Pharaoh's daughter said to her, "Go." So the girl went and called the child's mother. *(How graciously the Lord arranges things for our benefit.)* **9** And Pharaoh's daughter said to her, "Take this child away and nurse him for me, and I will give you your wages." *(The Lord speaks to every godly mother in the same way. No service on earth is so well repaid to a parent as the spiritual upbringing of her children.)* So the woman took the child and nursed him. **10** When the child grew older, she brought him to Pharaoh's daughter, and he became her son. She named him Moses, "Because," she said, "I drew him out of the water."

Hebrews 11:24-26

24 By faith Moses, when he was grown up, refused to be called the son of Pharaoh's daughter, *(He had been called "the son of Pharaoh's daughter" when he was young, but as an adult he turned down the highest rank an Egyptian could have and took his place with persecuted Israel.)* **25** choosing rather to be mistreated with the people of God than to enjoy the fleeting pleasures of sin. **26** He considered the reproach of Christ greater wealth than the treasures of Egypt, for he was looking to the reward.

Acts 7:22-29

22 "And Moses was instructed in all the wisdom of the Egyptians, and he was mighty in his words and deeds." *(His education, when sanctified by God's Spirit, helped prepare him for his distinguished position as the leader and lawgiver of the nation of Israel. No other prophet, before our Lord came, was as mighty in both words and deeds.)*

23 "When he was forty years old, it came into his heart to visit his brothers, the children of Israel. *(The life of Moses divides itself into three forties—forty years in the royal household of Pharaoh, forty years with Jethro, and forty years in the wilderness.)* **24** And seeing one of them being wronged, he defended the oppressed man and avenged him by striking down the Egyptian. **25** He supposed that his brothers would understand that God was giving them salvation by his hand, but they did not understand. **26** And on the following day he appeared to them as they were quarreling and tried to reconcile them, saying, 'Men, you are brothers. Why do you wrong each other?' **27** But the man who was wronging his neighbor thrust him aside, saying, 'Who made you a ruler and a judge over us? **28** Do you want to kill me as you killed the Egyptian yesterday?' *(The mission of the greatest and best of men is not always understood immediately.)* **29** At this retort Moses fled and became an exile in the land of Midian, where he became the father of two sons."

MARCH 14

I Have Surely Seen the Affliction Of My People[215]

Exodus 3:1-8; 10-20

1 Now Moses was keeping the flock of his father-in-law, Jethro, the priest of Midian, *(Though a man of deep learning Moses did not think being a shepherd was beneath him. There is no disgrace in work, but there is great shame in idleness)* and he led his flock to the west side of the wilderness and came to Horeb, the mountain of God. **2** And the angel of the LORD appeared to him in a flame of fire out of the midst of a bush. He looked, and behold, the bush was burning, yet it was not consumed. **3** And Moses said, "I will turn aside to see this great sight, why the bush is not burned."

The burning bush is a picture of the church of Christ. It is a wonder that such an uninteresting and powerless thing like a bush can survive the fires that afflict it so fiercely. Moses was puzzled by this marvel and both the friends and enemies of the church are puzzled that the fires of persecution do not consume her.

---

[215] Exodus 3:7

⁴When the LORD saw that he turned aside to see, God called to him out of the bush, "Moses, Moses!" And he said, "Here I am." ⁵Then he said, "Do not come near; take your sandals off your feet, for the place on which you are standing is holy ground." ⁶And he said, "I am the God of your father, the God of Abraham, the God of Isaac, and the God of Jacob." And Moses hid his face, for he was afraid to look at God. *(Like his ancestor Jacob, he felt, "How awesome is this place."[216] Fear proved to be more powerful than joy.)*

⁷Then the LORD said, "I have surely seen the affliction of my people who are in Egypt and have heard their cry because of their taskmasters. I know their sufferings, ⁸and I have come down to deliver them out of the hand of the Egyptians and to bring them up out of that land to a good and broad land, a land flowing with milk and honey, to the place of the Canaanites, the Hittites, the Amorites, the Perizzites, the Hivites, and the Jebusites."

¹⁰"Come, I will send you to Pharaoh that you may bring my people, the children of Israel, out of Egypt." ¹¹But Moses said to God, "Who am I that I should go to Pharaoh and bring the children of Israel out of Egypt?" *(The more capable a person is for God's work, the less likely they are to think they are the best person for the job.)* ¹²He said, "But I will be with you, and this shall be the sign for you, that I have sent you: when you have brought the people out of Egypt, you shall serve God on this mountain." *(The best answer to all our fears are those sweet words, "I will be with you.")*

¹³Then Moses said to God, "If I come to the people of Israel and say to them, 'The God of your fathers has sent me to you,' and they ask me, 'What is his name?' what shall I say to them?" ¹⁴God said to Moses, "I AM WHO I AM." And he said, "Say this to the people of Israel, 'I AM has sent me to you.'" *(God describes himself to Moses. "I AM WHO I AM." "I do not change. I am always the same." And, "I AM." "I have always existed. There has never been a time I did not exist." Our God exists forever and is the same forever.)*

¹⁵God also said to Moses, "Say this to the people of Israel, 'The LORD, the God of your fathers, the God of Abraham, the God of Isaac, and the God of Jacob, has sent me to you.' This is my name forever, and thus I am to be remembered throughout all generations. ¹⁶Go and gather the elders of Israel together and say to them, 'The LORD, the God of your fathers, the God of Abraham, of Isaac, and of Jacob, has appeared to me, saying, "I have observed you and what has been done to you in Egypt, ¹⁷and I promise that I will bring you up out of the affliction of Egypt to…a land flowing with milk and honey."'" *(Sooner or later the Lord will bless his people and deliver them. He may leave them under very harsh conditions for a while, but he will not forget his promises and he will visit them at the proper time.)*

¹⁸"And they will listen to your voice, and you and the elders of Israel shall go to the king of Egypt and say to him, 'The LORD, the God of the Hebrews, has met with us; and now, please let us go a three day's journey into the wilderness, that we may sacrifice to the LORD our God.' ¹⁹But I know that the king of Egypt will not let you go unless compelled by a mighty hand. ²⁰So I will stretch out my hand and strike Egypt with all the wonders that I will do in it; after that he will let you go.

MARCH 15

When I Am Weak, Then I Am Strong[217]

Exodus 4:1-16

¹Then Moses answered, "But behold, they will not believe me or listen to my voice, for they will say, 'The LORD did not appear to you.'" *(Those whom God sends are often slow to go. And people the Lord never sent are often so eager, they push themselves into positions of leadership.)* ²The LORD said to him, "What is that in your hand?" He said, "A staff." ³And he said, "Throw it on the ground." So he threw it on the ground, and it became a serpent, and Moses ran from it. *(This was a sign to him that even though he*

---

[216] Genesis 28:17

[217] 2:Corinthians 12:10

was a humble shepherd now, he would become so powerful that Pharaoh would be terrified of him. Those who do not fear the Lord should find the shepherds of God's people and their message as frightening as a serpent.) ⁴ But the LORD said to Moses, "Put out your hand and catch it by the tail"—so he put out his hand and caught it, and it became a staff in his hand— ⁵ "that they may believe that the LORD, the God of their fathers, the God of Abraham, the God of Isaac, and the God of Jacob, has appeared to you." *(Here he learned that the power given to him would be like a terrible serpent to Egypt, but for himself and for Israel it would be a harmless shepherd's crook. Both of these signs were given to encourage Moses.)*

⁶ Again, the LORD said to him, "Put your hand inside your cloak." And he put his hand inside his cloak, and when he took it out, behold, his hand was leprous like snow. ⁷ Then God said, "Put your hand back inside your cloak." So he put his hand back inside his cloak, and when he took it out, behold it was restored like the rest of his flesh. ⁸ "If they will not believe you," God said, "or listen to the first sign, they may believe the latter sign. *(Here Moses saw that the Lord can both damage and restore. Everyone who works for the Lord should remember this.)* ⁹ If they will not believe even these two signs or listen to your voice, you shall take some water from the Nile and pour it on the dry ground, and the water that you shall take from the Nile will become blood on the dry ground."

¹⁰ But Moses said to the LORD, "Oh, my Lord, I am not eloquent, either in the past or since you have spoken to your servant, but I am slow of speech and of tongue." ¹¹ Then the LORD said to him, "Who has made man's mouth? Who makes him mute, or deaf, or seeing, or blind? Is it not I, the LORD? ¹² Now therefore go, and I will be with your mouth and teach you what you shall speak." ¹³ But he said, "Oh, my Lord, please send someone else."

Moses' unwillingness cost him much honor. His objections ended up giving Aaron the office of high priest and also giving him a helper who proved to be a problem.

¹⁴ Then the anger of the LORD was kindled against Moses and he said, "Is there not Aaron, your brother, the Levite? I know that he can speak well. Behold, he is coming out to meet you, and when he sees you, he will be glad in his heart. ¹⁵ You shall speak to him and put the words in his mouth, and I will be with your mouth and with his mouth and teach you both what to do. ¹⁶ He shall speak for you to the people, and he shall be your mouth, and you shall be as God to him.

It is interesting to note that Moses was not the only famous prophet who was afraid to follow the Lord's instruction at the first. We will now read how Jeremiah also felt unqualified.

Jeremiah 1:6-9

⁶ Then I said, "Ah, Lord GOD! Behold, I do not know how to speak, for I am only a youth." ⁷ But the LORD said to me,

"Do not say, 'I am only a youth';
for to all to whom I send you, you shall go,
and whatever I command you, you shall speak.
⁸ Do not be afraid of them,
for I am with you to deliver you,
declares the LORD."

⁹ Then the LORD put out his hand and touched my mouth. And the LORD said to me,

"Behold, I have put my words in your mouth."

Oh Lord, grant that all your ministers may have their mouths touched in the same way.

MARCH 16

Though He Cause Grief, He Will Have Compassion[218]

Exodus 5:1-4; 6-23

¹ Afterward Moses and Aaron went and said to Pharaoh, "Thus says the LORD, the God of Israel, 'Let my people go, that they may hold a feast to me in the wilderness.'" ² But Pharaoh said, "Who is the LORD, that I should obey his voice and let Israel go? I do not know the LORD, and moreover, I will not let Israel go." *(His proud spirit refused to*

---
[218] Lamentations 3:32

obey Jehovah, but before long he would have a good reason to know who Jehovah was.) ³ Then they said, "The God of the Hebrews has met with us. Please let us go a three days' journey into the wilderness that we may sacrifice to the LORD our God, lest he fall upon us with pestilence or with the sword." *(This was not a big request. No doubt, it was meant to be a test question. He who would not give in to the smaller would be sure to refuse the greater.)* ⁴ But the king of Egypt said to them, "Moses and Aaron, why do you take the people away from their work? Get back to your burdens." *(Pharaoh is arrogant. He defies the Lord's messengers and treats them like slaves who had better go back to work right now.)*

⁶ That same day Pharaoh commanded the taskmasters of the people and their foremen, ⁷ "You shall no longer give the people straw to make bricks, as in the past; let them go and gather straw for themselves. ⁸ But the number of bricks that they made in the past you shall impose on them, you shall by no means reduce it, for they are idle. Therefore they cry, 'Let us go and offer sacrifice to our God.' ⁹ Let heavier work be laid on the men that they may labor at it and pay no regard to lying words." *(The bricks were made of mud mixed with straw. Up until this time, others brought the straw to the Israelites. They were now told they had to gather the straw themselves, which gave them much more work to do.)*

¹⁰ So the taskmasters and the foremen of the people went out and said to the people, "Thus says Pharaoh, 'I will not give you straw. ¹¹ Go and get your straw yourselves wherever you can find it, but your work will not be reduced in the least.'" ¹² So the people were scattered throughout all the land of Egypt to gather stubble for straw. ¹³ The taskmasters were urgent, saying, "Complete your work, your daily task each day, as when there was straw." ¹⁴ And the foremen of the people of Israel, whom Pharaoh's taskmasters had set over them, were beaten and were asked, "Why have you not done all your task of making bricks today and yesterday, as in the past?"

¹⁵ Then the foremen of the people of Israel came and cried to Pharaoh, "Why do you treat your servants like this? ¹⁶ No straw is given to your servants, yet they say to us, 'Make bricks!' And behold, your servants are beaten; but the fault is in your own people." *(These poor Israelite officers thought that the Egyptian taskmasters had decided to keep back the straw on their own. They did not know that they were acting under the King's order.)* ¹⁷ But he said, "You are idle, you are idle; that is why you say, 'Let us go and sacrifice to the LORD.' ¹⁸ Go now and work. No straw will be given you, but you must still deliver the same number of bricks." ¹⁹ The foremen of the people of Israel saw that they were in trouble when they said, "You shall by no means reduce your number of bricks, your daily task each day." ²⁰ They met Moses and Aaron, who were waiting for them, as they came out from Pharaoh; ²¹ and they said to them, "The LORD look on you and judge, because you have made us stink in the sight of Pharaoh and his servants, and have put a sword in their hand to kill us."

Things are always the most unpleasant when they are about to get better. But these people were discouraged and could not see beyond their present circumstances.

²² Then Moses turned to the LORD and said, "O Lord, why have you done evil to this people? Why did you ever send me? ²³ For since I came to Pharaoh to speak in your name, he has done evil to this people, and you have not delivered your people at all."

Moses did the right thing by bringing this problem to the Lord. Let us bring all our troubles to our heavenly Father.

MARCH 17
Pride Goes Before Destruction[219]
Exodus 7:1-5; 10-22

¹ And the LORD said to Moses, "See I have made you like God to Pharaoh, and your brother Aaron shall be your prophet. ² You shall speak all that I command you, and your brother Aaron shall tell Pharaoh to let the

---
[219] Proverbs 16:18

people of Israel go out of his land. **³** But I will harden Pharaoh's heart, and though I multiply my signs and wonders in the land of Egypt, **⁴** Pharaoh will not listen to you. Then I will lay my hand on Egypt and bring my hosts, my people the children of Israel out of the land of Egypt by great acts of judgment. **⁵** The Egyptians shall know that I am the LORD, when I stretch out my hand against Egypt and bring out the people of Israel from among them." *(God's judgments hardened Pharaoh's heart. If they do not soften hearts, they harden them. God's warnings and plagues only made Pharaoh more stubborn.)*

¹⁰ So Moses and Aaron went to Pharaoh and did just as the LORD commanded. Aaron cast down his staff before Pharaoh and his servants, and it became a serpent. *(They had delivered their message, now they show proof that God had sent them.)* **¹¹** Then Pharaoh summoned the wise men and the sorcerers, and they, the magicians of Egypt, also did the same by their secret arts. **¹²** For each man cast down his staff, and they became serpents. But Aaron's staff swallowed up their staffs. **¹³** Still Pharaoh's heart was hardened, and he would not listen to them, as the LORD had said.

Pharaoh assumed that Moses was only a magician, like those on his own payroll. Therefore he defied the power of Jehovah again.

¹⁴ Then the LORD said to Moses, "Pharaoh's heart is hardened; he refuses to let the people go. **¹⁵** Go to Pharaoh in the morning, as he is going out to the water. Stand on the bank of the Nile to meet him, and take in your hand the staff that turned into a serpent. **¹⁶** And you shall say to him, 'The LORD, the God of the Hebrews, sent me to you, saying, "Let my people go, that they may serve me in the wilderness. But so far, you have not obeyed." **¹⁷** Thus says the LORD, "By this you shall know that I am the LORD: behold, with the staff that is in my hand I will strike the water that is in the Nile, and it shall turn into blood. **¹⁸** The fish in the Nile shall die, and the Nile will stink, and the Egyptians will grow weary of drinking water from the Nile."'"

They had contaminated the river with the blood of innocent babies. Now the Nile appears to them in blood-red colors, as if it cried out against their murderous deeds.

¹⁹ And the LORD said to Moses, "Say to Aaron, 'Take your staff and stretch out your hand over the waters of Egypt, over their rivers, their canals, and their ponds, and all their pools of water, so that they may become blood, and there shall be blood throughout all the land of Egypt, even in vessels of wood and in vessels of stone.'"

²⁰ Moses and Aaron did as the LORD commanded. In the sight of Pharaoh and in the sight of his servants he lifted up the staff and struck the water in the Nile, and all the water in the Nile turned into blood. **²¹** And the fish in the Nile died, and the Nile stank, so that the Egyptians could not drink water from the Nile. There was blood throughout all the land of Egypt.

Horrible! An army of horrors! Their drink becomes blood. The river that they called holy pours forth an intolerable stench. The delicious water grows worse than putrid. The fish that were a great part of their diet float dead on the awful stream! This was a plague indeed.

²² But the magicians of Egypt did the same by their secret arts. So Pharaoh's heart remained hardened, and he would not listen to them, as the LORD had said. *(Proud Pharaoh does not care. His magicians cleverly imitate the miracle by sleight of hand and the heartless king cares nothing for the sufferings of his people.)*

MARCH 18

The LORD Tears Down the House of the Proud[220]

Our goal is to gather up the essence of the Scriptures during the reading of two years. Therefore, we are unable to pause over each of the ten great plagues. Each one of us should read them all at another time for our own instruction. For our family reading we have them mentioned in:

---

[220] Proverbs 15:25

Psalm 105:24-38

24 And the LORD made his people very fruitful
   and made them stronger than their foes.

The Lord is just as able to do the same with his church at this time and he will in answer to prayer.

25 He turned their hearts to hate his people
   to deal craftily with his servants.

Persecution generally comes to the church that is truly healthy. Where God blesses, Satan is sure to stir up all his wrath to trouble the church.

26 He sent Moses, his servant,
   and Aaron, whom he had chosen.

When evil days come, the Lord has warriors ready for the battle. They will appear at the exact moment when they are most needed. Let us pray to the Lord to raise up outstanding pastors and evangelists at this time, because they are greatly needed.

27 They performed his signs among them
   and miracles in the land of Ham.

28 He sent darkness, and made the land dark;
   they did not rebel against his words.

This unusual darkness filled all hearts with horror. The Egyptians were so afraid that they gave in for a brief time, but were hardened again when the plague was over.

29 He turned their waters into blood
   and caused their fish to die.

30 Their land swarmed with frogs,
   even in the chambers of their kings.

Fish died, but frogs lived. God can kill our comforts with one hand and multiply our miseries with the other. This time Pharaoh himself had to endure personal irritation, because the army of frogs even invaded the palace.

31 He spoke, and there came swarms of flies,
   and gnats throughout their country.

Filthiness and disease came together in the third and fourth plagues. These little tormentors made the Egyptians feel the power of the great God. Little plagues are often the worst of plagues. Pharaoh's bodyguards could not defend their king from this visitation. Such enemies laughed at both sword and spear.

32 He gave them hail for rain,
   and fiery lightning bolts through their land.

It is a judgment indeed when the fountains of blessing become the spillways of wrath and the very rain is fire. Let the enemies of God beware.

33 He struck down their vines and fig trees,
   and shattered the trees of their country.

God's blows are heavy and they leave no place unbruised. If Egypt will not obey the Lord, then it will not have its pleasant fruits and its wine.

34 He spoke, and the locusts came,
   young locusts without number,
35 which devoured all the vegetation in their land
   and ate up the fruit of their ground.

Locusts literally eat up every green thing. There is no keeping anything from them. God has many ways of punishing people. In this case we wonder at the hardness of heart of those who stood out against such strong judgments. He who can bring up countless hungry locusts with a word is not a God to be trifled with.

36 He struck down all the firstborn in their land,
   the firstfruits of all their strength.

This was the last and heaviest blow. The proud king and nation staggered under it. When one arrow is not enough, the Lord has others in his quiver. One way or another he will hit the mark.

37 Then he brought out Israel with silver and gold,
   and there was none among his tribes who stumbled.

What a miracle that after all their toil and bondage they should all be in good health. They were all called to go on a long journey and therefore the Lord prepared them for it.

38 Egypt was glad when they departed,
   for dread of them had fallen upon it.

God can work in such a way that even the most determined opponents will be only too glad to surrender.

Let us beware of provoking this terrible God. By faith, let us enlist him on our side.

We will then have no reason to be afraid, because all the creatures he has made will be our friends. Fire and water, locusts and flies, darkness and death, were all the friends of Israel. Those who are at peace with God have the whole creation signed up on their side.

March 19
When I See the Blood, I Will Pass Over You[221]

Israel's deliverance from Egypt was a redemption both by blood and by power. In today's chapter we read about the redemption by blood.

Exodus 12:1-15

1 The LORD said to Moses and Aaron in the land of Egypt, **2** "This month shall be for you the beginning of months. It shall be the first month of the year for you. *(To be redeemed is the greatest event in a person's life. The day that we experience redemption must remain the diamond of days to us.)* **3** Tell all the congregation of Israel that on the tenth day of this month every man shall take a lamb according to their fathers' houses, a lamb for a household. **4** And if the household is too small for a lamb, then he and his nearest neighbor shall take according to the number of persons; according to what each can eat you shall make your count for the lamb. **5** Your lamb shall be without blemish, a male a year old. You may take it from the sheep or from the goats, *(Jesus was perfect and in the prime of his life when he became the lamb of our Passover.)* **6** and you shall keep it until the fourteenth day of this month, when the whole assembly of the congregation of Israel shall kill their lambs at twilight." *(It was both in the evening of the day and in the evening of time, when the nation of Israel cried, "Crucify him" and Jesus was put to death.)*

7 "Then they shall take some of the blood and put it on the two doorposts and the lintel of the houses in which they eat it. *(Not on the threshold, for woe to the one who tramples on the blood of Christ.)* **8** They shall eat the flesh that night, roasted on the fire; with unleavened bread and bitter herbs they shall eat it. *(Do these bitter herbs represent our repentance or the Redeemer's great sorrow? Perhaps both.)* **9** Do not eat any of it raw or boiled in water, but roasted, its head with its legs and its inner parts."

Our Lord's sufferings are well pictured by the fire over which the lamb was roasted.

10 "And you shall let none of it remain until the morning; anything that remains until the morning you shall burn. *(Our spiritual nourishment comes from Christ and only from Christ.)* **11** In this manner you shall eat it: with your belt fastened, your sandals on your feet, and your staff in your hand. And you shall eat it in haste. It is the LORD's Passover. **12** For I will pass through the land of Egypt that night, and I will strike all the firstborn in the land of Egypt, both man and beast; and on all the gods of Egypt I will execute judgments: I am the LORD. **13** The blood shall be a sign for you, on the houses where you are. And when I see the blood, I will pass over you and no plague will befall you to destroy you, when I strike the land of Egypt." *(Mark those words, "When I see the blood." Our looking on the atonement brings us comfort, but the Lord's looking on it is the true reason for our salvation.)*

14 "This day shall be for you a memorial day, and you shall keep it as a feast to the LORD; throughout your generations, as a statute forever, you shall keep it as a feast. **15** Seven days you shall eat unleavened bread. On the first day you shall remove leaven out of your houses, for if anyone eats what is leavened, from the first day until the seventh day, that person shall be cut off from Israel."

Sin is that sour leaven that must be removed from the heart where Jesus is the Savior. The apostle Paul describes this more fully in:

1 Corinthians 5:6-8

6b Do you not know that a little leaven leavens the whole lump? *(It is a spreading thing and if any is left it will quickly multiply itself.)* **7** Cleanse out the old leaven that you may be a new lump, as you really are unleavened. For Christ, our Passover lamb, has been sacrificed. **8** Let us therefore celebrate the festival, not with the old leaven,

---
[221] Exodus 12:13

the leaven of malice and evil, but with the unleavened bread of sincerity and truth. *(May the Holy Spirit give us grace to accomplish this cleaning of the house. Where the precious blood is sprinkled, no sin can be tolerated.)*

MARCH 20
The LORD Has Ransomed Jacob[222]

Our last reading described the Lord's orders about the Passover. We will now see them obeyed.

Exodus 12:21-36

21 Then Moses called all the elders of Israel and said to them, "Go and select lambs for yourselves according to your clans, and kill the Passover lamb. **22** Take a bunch of hyssop and dip it in the blood that is in the basin, and touch the lintel and the two doorposts with the blood that is in the basin. None of you shall go out of the door of his house until the morning. *(They must remain under the protection of the blood or perish.)* **23** For the LORD will pass through to strike the Egyptians, and when he sees the blood on the lintel and on the two doorposts, the LORD will pass over the door and will not allow the destroyer to enter your house to strike you. *(Otherwise the firstborn of Israel would have died as well as the firstborn of Egypt. It was not character or position, but the sprinkled blood that made the difference. The sacrifice of Jesus is the true reason of our salvation.)* **24** You shall observe this rite as a statute for you and for your sons forever."

Whatever else we forget we must hold the truth of the substitutionary atonement as long as time endures.

25 "And when you come to the land that the LORD will give you, as he has promised, you shall keep this service. **26** And when your children say to you, 'What do you mean by this service?' **27** you shall say, 'It is the sacrifice of the LORD's Passover, for he passed over the houses of the people of Israel in Egypt, when he struck the Egyptians but spared our houses.'" And the people bowed their heads and worshiped.

Even the children should be taught the doctrine of atonement by blood. It is the most necessary truth of our most holy faith.

28 Then the people of Israel went and did so; as the LORD had commanded Moses and Aaron, so they did.

29 At midnight the LORD struck down all the firstborn in the land of Egypt, from the firstborn of Pharaoh who sat on his throne to the firstborn of the captive who was in the dungeon, and all the firstborn of the livestock. **30** And Pharaoh rose up in the night, he and all his servants and all the Egyptians. And there was a great cry in Egypt, for there was not a house where someone was not dead.

Death reigned where the blood was not sprinkled and so it must be. Are we all marked with the blood of our Great Substitute?

31 Then he summoned Moses and Aaron by night and said, "Up, go out from among my people, both you and the people of Israel; and go, serve the LORD, as you have said. **32** Take your flocks and your herds, as you have said, and be gone, and bless me also!" *(Here was the overthrow of pride. The haughty tyrant surrenders and becomes a beggar. God's sword can reach the heart of even the greatest persecutors of his church. They may think they are indestructible and unbeatable, but they are as nothing to God!)*

33 The Egyptians were urgent with the people to send them out of the land in haste. For they said, "We shall all be dead." **34** So the people took their dough before it was leavened, their kneading bowls being bound up in their cloaks on their shoulders. **35** The people of Israel had also done as Moses told them, for they had asked the Egyptians for silver and gold jewelry and for clothing. *(These were asked for, and freely given, because the people honored the Israelites, and were afraid to stir up their anger.)* **36** And the LORD had given the people favor in the sight of the Egyptians, so that they let them have what they asked. Thus they plundered the Egyptians.

---

[222] Jeremiah 31:11

In this way their long and unpaid services were, in some measure, paid for by the gifts of the Egyptians.

When souls are spiritually set free from sin, the Lord is pleased to give them many precious things. He is generous and loving toward his people.

March 21
Stand Firm and See the Salvation Of the Lord[223]

Exodus 13:17-18; 20-22

17 When Pharaoh let the people go, God did not lead them by the way of the land of the Philistines, although that was near. For God said, "Lest the people change their minds when they see war and return to Egypt." **18** But God led the people around by the way of the wilderness toward the Red Sea. And the people of Israel went up out of the land of Egypt equipped for battle. *(The Lord understands the weaknesses of his people. Their future involved many wars, but at this point they were not ready. Therefore he led them on a longer journey, but one that would have fewer battles to fight. Praise God! Our troubles will not be ready for us until we are ready for them.)*

20 And they moved on from Succoth and encamped at Etham, on the edge of the wilderness. **21** And the Lord went before them by day in a pillar of cloud to lead them along the way, and by night in a pillar of fire to give them light, that they might travel by day and by night. **22** The pillar of cloud by day and the pillar of fire by night did not depart from before the people. *(The pillar was their perfect guide. It also provided shade for them by day and lit up the camp by night. God's mercies are many and varied. We can only do one thing well at a time, but the Lord accomplishes many at one stroke.)*

Exodus 14:1-5; 8-14

1 Then the Lord said to Moses, **2** "Tell the people of Israel to turn back and encamp in front of Pi-hahiroth, between Migdol and the sea, in front of Baal-zephon; you shall encamp facing it, by the sea."

This command seemed strange, but Moses obeyed it without question. Let us go where the Lord directs us even when the way is dangerous.

3 "For Pharaoh will say of the people of Israel, 'They are wandering in the land; the wilderness has shut them in.' **4** And I will harden Pharaoh's heart, and he will pursue them, and I will get glory over Pharaoh and all his host, and the Egyptians shall know that I am the Lord." And they did so.

5 When the King of Egypt was told that the people had fled, the mind of Pharaoh and his servants was changed toward the people, and they said, "What is this we have done, that we have let Israel go from serving us?"

8 And the Lord hardened the heart of Pharaoh king of Egypt, and he pursued the people of Israel while the people of Israel were going out defiantly. *(God's plagues had not changed the King's rebellious nature. When he saw that he had lost his valuable slaves, his greed made him rush after them.)* **9** The Egyptians pursued them, all Pharaoh's horses and chariots and his horsemen and his army, and overtook them encamped at the sea, by Pi-hahiroth, in front of Baal-zephon.

10 When Pharaoh drew near, the people of Israel lifted up their eyes, and behold, the Egyptians were marching after them, and they feared greatly. And the people of Israel cried out to the Lord. **11** They said to Moses, "Is it because there are no graves in Egypt that you have taken us away to die in the wilderness? What have you done to us in bringing us out of Egypt? **12** Is not this what we said to you in Egypt, 'Leave us alone that we may serve the Egyptians'? For it would have been better for us to serve the Egyptians than to die in the wilderness." *(Their unbelief was both unfair and cruel. Had they not seen the Lord's works in the great plagues? Could they not believe that he who had worked such marvels could and would deliver them? They were struck with panic and would rather return to their life of slavery than defend themselves. True freemen never debate about choosing between slavery or death. They will avoid slavery at all costs.)*

---

[223] Exodus 14:13

¹³ And Moses said to the people, "Fear not, stand firm, and see the salvation of the LORD, which he will work for you today. For the Egyptians whom you see today, you shall never see again. ¹⁴ The LORD will fight for you, and you have only to be silent." *(The meekest of men answered the people meekly and with full confidence in Jehovah, because prayer empowered him to conquer his own spirit.)*

Spurgeon's First Sermon • August 1850
"Mr. James Vinter, a friendly, warm hearted person connected with St. Andrews Street Chapel, would send worthy brethren to preach the Gospel in various villages surrounding Cambridge.

"One Saturday, he came to ask me to go over to Teversham, the next evening, for a young man was to preach there who was not much used to services, and very likely would be glad of company. That was a cunningly devised sentence, if I remember it rightly…I have turned it over, and vastly admired its ingenuity. A request to go and preach, would have met with a decided negative."—CHS

MARCH 22
The LORD Will Reign Forever and Ever[224]

Exodus 14:15-31

¹⁵ The LORD said to Moses, "Why do you cry to me? Tell the people of Israel to go forward."

We do not read that Moses had spoken a word; but his heart cried to the Lord. The Lord told him to stop hesitating, but cry, "FORWARD," and advance through the Red Sea.

¹⁶ "Lift up your staff, and stretch out your hand over the sea and divide it, that the people of Israel may go through the sea on dry ground. ¹⁷ And I will harden the hearts of the Egyptians so that they shall go in after them, and I will get glory over Pharaoh and all his host, his chariots, and his horsemen. ¹⁸ And the Egyptians shall know that I am the LORD, when I have gotten glory over Pharaoh, his chariots, and his horsemen."

¹⁹ Then the angel of God who was going before the host of Israel moved and went behind them, and the pillar of cloud moved from before them and stood behind them, *(The glory of the Lord was their rearguard.)* ²⁰ coming between the host of Egypt and the host of Israel. And there was the cloud and the darkness. And it lit up the night without one coming near the other all night. *(God's word and his providence both have two features. They frown on sinners and they smile on saints. The Lord continues to treat spiritual Israel and spiritual Egypt differently.)*

²¹ Then Moses stretched out his hand over the sea, and the LORD drove the sea back by a strong east wind all night and made the sea dry land, and the waters were divided. ²² And the people of Israel went into the midst of the sea on dry ground, the waters being a wall to them on their right hand and on their left. *(The historian records this event calmly, but what a wonder it was! Water standing up like solid ice, and a wet sea bed made dry and ready to be a highway for a marching army.)* ²³ The Egyptians pursued and went in after them into the midst of the sea, all Pharaoh's horses, his chariots, and his horsemen.

What a mindless decision! Were they deceived by the darkness around them or the darkness within them?

²⁴ And in the morning watch the LORD in the pillar of fire and of cloud looked down on the Egyptian forces and threw the Egyptian forces into a panic, ²⁵ clogging their chariot wheels so that they drove heavily. And the Egyptians said, "Let us flee from before Israel, for the LORD fights for them against the Egyptians."

---
[224] Exodus 15:18

One look from Jehovah was enough. One flash from his eye of fire and the entire Egyptian army was struck with panic.

26 Then the LORD said to Moses, "Stretch out your hand over the sea, that the water may come back upon the Egyptians, upon their chariots, and upon their horsemen." 27 So Moses stretched out his hand over the sea, and the sea returned to its normal course when the morning appeared. And as the Egyptians fled into it, the LORD threw the Egyptians into the midst of the sea. 28 The waters returned and covered the chariots and the horsemen; of all the host of Pharaoh that had followed them into the sea, not one of them remained.

Even so, "our overpowering sins are buried and drowned, and though they be looked for they will not be found."[225]

29 But the people of Israel walked on dry ground through the sea, the waters being a wall to them on their right hand and on their left.

30 Thus the LORD saved Israel that day from the Egyptians, and Israel saw the Egyptians dead on the seashore. *(Egypt was crushed so completely, that even though the Israelites were close to the Egyptian borders for the next forty years, their former oppressors never bothered them.)* 31 Israel saw the great power that the LORD used against the Egyptians, so the people feared the LORD, and they believed in the LORD and in his servant Moses.

MARCH 23

He Has Triumphed Gloriously[226]

We will now read the song of Moses. This song also looks ahead to the certain and final victory of the Lord Jesus.

Exodus 15:1-21

1 Then Moses and the people of Israel sang this song to the LORD, saying,

"I will sing to the LORD, for he has triumphed gloriously;
   the horse and his rider he has thrown into the sea.

2 The LORD is my strength and my song,
   and he has become my salvation;
this is my God, and I will praise him,
   my father's God, and I will exalt him.

3 The LORD is a man of war;
   the LORD is his name.

4 "Pharaoh's chariots and his host he cast into the sea,
   and his chosen officers were sunk in the Red Sea.

5 The floods covered them;
   they went down into the depths like a stone.

6 Your right hand, O LORD, glorious in power,
   your right hand, O LORD, shatters the enemy.

7 In the greatness of your majesty you overthrow your adversaries;
   you send out your fury; it consumes them like stubble.

8 At the blast of your nostrils the waters piled up;
   the floods stood up in a heap;
   the deeps congealed in the heart of the sea.

9 The enemy said, 'I will pursue, I will overtake,
   I will divide the spoil, my desire shall have its fill of them.
I will draw my sword; my hand shall destroy them.'

10 You blew with your wind; the sea covered them;
   they sank like lead in the mighty waters.

11 "Who is like you, O LORD, among the gods?
   Who is like you, majestic in holiness,
   awesome in glorious deeds, doing wonders?

12 You stretched out your right hand;
   the earth swallowed them.

13 "You have led in your steadfast love the people whom you have redeemed
   you have guided them by your strength to your holy abode.

14 The peoples have heard; they tremble;
   pangs have seized the inhabitants of Philistia

15 Now are the chiefs of Edom dismayed;
   trembling seizes the leaders of Moab;

---

[225] Probably from "The Poetical Works of John and Charles Wesley.
[226] Exodus 15:21

all the inhabitants of Canaan have melted away.

¹⁶ Terror and dread fall upon them;
    because of the greatness of your arm,
        they are still as a stone,
    till your people, O LORD, pass by,
        till the people pass by whom you have purchased.
¹⁷ You will bring them in and plant them on your own mountain,
    the place, O LORD, which you have made for your abode,
    the sanctuary, O LORD, which your hands have established.
¹⁸ The LORD will reign forever and ever."

¹⁹ For when the horses of Pharaoh with his chariots and his horsemen went into the sea, the LORD brought back the waters of the sea upon them, but the people of Israel walked on dry ground in the midst of the sea. ²⁰ Then Miriam the prophetess, the sister of Aaron, took a tambourine in her hand, and all the women went out after her with tambourines and dancing. ²¹ And Miriam sang to them:

"Sing to the LORD, for he has triumphed gloriously;
    the horse and his rider he has thrown into the sea."

In order to leave the song unbroken, we have reserved our few notes for the end of it.

Observe the beauty and simplicity of the song. Insignificant man glories in his elegant style and big, complicated words, but the Lord has no need to build himself up. Notice how the entire song praises only the Lord. There is no mention of Moses or Aaron; no hint of secondary causes. Jehovah alone is exalted. Notice the noise, hurry, and violence of the enemy in verse nine, the enemy said, 'I will pursue," and the calmness of the Lord in verse ten, "You blew with your wind." It will be good to read theses verses again. Humanity is raving and threatening and the Lord in calm omnipotence[227] defeats its rage. Consider also, how the poet assumes the future from the present. God brought his people through the sea; he will certainly bring them into their promised inheritance.

He, who has worked marvels of grace already, will not leave us until grace is turned into glory.

What a wonderful hallelujah is verse eighteen, "The LORD will reign forever and ever." It is the obvious conclusion after defeating his enemies. Let us rejoice in our reigning God. He has overcome sin, death, and hell for us. Therefore, like Miriam, let us rejoice with all the saints. Let our heart dance, and our hands make music to our Redeemer, who has thrown our enemies into the depths of the sea.

MARCH 24

You Are the God Who Works Wonders[228]

On this occasion we will read:
Psalm 77
This psalm shows us the way that holy people of old found encouragement from the great miracle of the Red Sea. Asaph wrote this psalm. He is almost in despair and then he remembers the Lord's wonderful works of the past and finds comfort.

¹ I cry aloud to God,
    aloud to God, and he will hear me.
² In the day of my trouble I seek the Lord;
    in the night my hand is stretched out without wearying;
    my soul refuses to be comforted.

Asaph's spirits sank so low that he was like a sick man who cannot eat what is good for him. He was unable to believe truths that would cheer him up.

³ When I remember God, I moan;
    when I meditate, my spirit faints.
    Selah

God's people have walked the lonely valleys that trouble the soul. "Selah" is a musical term that means pause, or it may mean "Cheer up the tune." Let us cheer up our hearts.

⁴ You hold my eyelids open;
    I am so troubled that I cannot speak.
⁵ I consider the days of old,
    the years long ago.

---

[227] *omnipotent, omnipotence* - all powerful, almighty, absolute and supreme power, having unlimited power.

[228] Psalm 77:14

6 I said, "Let me remember my song in the night;
    let me meditate in my heart."
    Then my spirit made a diligent search:
7 "Will the Lord spurn forever,
    and never again be favorable?"

Fear brings these questions to mind, but these questions may also be used to drive our fear away. Their answers are obvious and cheering to the heart.

8 "Has his steadfast love forever ceased?
    Are his promises at an end for all time?
9 Has God forgotten to be gracious?
    Has he in anger shut up his compassion?"   Selah
10 Then I said, "I will appeal to this,
    to the years of the right hand of the Most High."

Most of our fears are the result of our weak faith in the Lord. They have no real facts to support them. The problem is in us and not in the God who is always dependable.

11 I will remember the deeds of the LORD;
    yes, I will remember your wonders of old.
12 I will ponder all your work,
    and meditate on your mighty deeds.
13 Your way, O God, is holy.
    What god is great like our God?
14 You are the God who works wonders;
    you have made known your might among the peoples.
15 You with your arm redeemed your people,
    the children of Jacob and Joseph. Selah
16 When the waters saw you, O God,
    when the waters saw you, they were afraid;
    indeed, the deep trembled.

The deep calm waters of the sea were moved with fright and fled as if they were afraid of the Lord.

17 The clouds poured out water;
    the skies gave forth thunder;
    your arrows flashed on every side.

Lightning bolts flew like arrows from the bow of God and the rain came down in torrents.

18 The crash of your thunder was in the whirlwind;
    your lightnings lighted up the world;
    the earth trembled and shook.

According to the first century historian Josephus, there was a terrible storm when the Egyptians were in the midst of the sea. This psalm seems to indicate that there was rain, violent wind and an earthquake. God's power is the friend of Israel and the enemy of the ungodly.

19 Your way was through the sea,
    your path through the great waters;
    yet your footprints were unseen.

Our God has mysterious ways of delivering his people, but deliver them he will.

20 You led your people like a flock
    by the hand of Moses and Aaron.

They did not feel the storm and were not afraid they would be harmed. They were as calm and safe as sheep that are protected by their shepherd. In the same way, all the saints will be safe, while their enemies are totally overwhelmed.

MARCH 25

The LORD Has Heard Your Grumbling[229]

Exodus 15:22-27

22 Then Moses made Israel set out from the Red Sea, and they went into the wilderness of Shur. They went three days in the wilderness and found no water.

Their first trouble was too much water, the second was too little. Our trials are of all kinds.

23 When they came to Marah, they could not drink the water of Marah because it was bitter; therefore it was named Marah. *(Another trial. They had water, but could not drink it.)* 24 And the people grumbled against Moses, saying, "What shall we drink?" 25 And he cried to the LORD, and the LORD showed him a log, and he threw it into the water, and the water became sweet.

There the LORD made for them a statute and a rule, and there he tested them, 26 saying, "If you will diligently listen to the

---
[229] Exodus 16:8

voice of the LORD your God, and do that which is right in his eyes, and give ear to his commandments and keep all his statutes, I will put none of the diseases on you that I put on the Egyptians, for I am the LORD, your healer." *(God provides different solutions for different situations. He gives trees to sweeten bitter waters and the cross to sweeten each of us.)*

27 Then they came to Elim, where there were twelve springs of water and seventy palm trees, and they encamped there by the water. *(It is not always rough work for pilgrims traveling to the Promised Land. There are pleasant times too. Let us thank God for them.)*

Exodus 16:1-10

1a They set out from Elim, and all the congregation of the people of Israel came to the wilderness of Sin. *(It might seem strange that God would lead 2,000,000 people into a desert, but wisdom directed his route. The Lord's pathway may seem strange, but grace, mercy and love are always found on it.)* **2** And the whole congregation of the people of Israel grumbled against Moses and Aaron in the wilderness, **3** and the people of Israel said to them, "Would that we had died by the hand of the LORD in the land of Egypt, when we sat by the meat pots and ate bread to the full, for you have brought us out into this wilderness to kill this whole assembly with hunger."

Their quickness in complaining was shameful. Their lack of confidence in the Lord and his servants was equally so. The meat pots and the bread were all they thought about. They overlooked the brick making and the whips. It is easy to pretend the past was bright when we wish to find fault with the present.

4 Then the LORD said to Moses, "Behold, I am about to rain bread from heaven for you, and the people shall go out and gather a day's portion every day, that I may test them, whether they will walk in my law of not. **5** On the sixth day, when they prepare what they bring in, it will be twice as much as they gather daily." *(God's gifts are often tests. Let us eat and drink to God's glory.[230])* **6** So Moses and Aaron said to all the people of Israel, "At evening you shall know that it was the LORD who brought you out of the land of Egypt, **7** and in the morning you shall see the glory of the LORD, because he has heard your grumbling against the LORD. For what are we, that you grumble against us?" **8** And Moses said, "When the LORD gives you in the evening meat to eat and in the morning bread to the full, because the LORD has heard your grumbling that you grumble against him—what are we? Your grumbling is not against us but against the LORD." *(We think it a small thing to grumble against our parents and friends, but this sheds a new light on the matter. It is clear that a dissatisfied heart really grumbles against God himself.)*

9 Then Moses said to Aaron, "Say to the whole congregation of the people of Israel, 'Come near before the LORD, for he has heard your grumbling.'" *(This is a serious truth. Let those who complain remember that the Lord hears them.)* **10** And as soon as Aaron spoke to the whole congregation of the people of Israel, they looked toward the wilderness, and behold, the glory of the LORD appeared in the cloud.

MARCH 26
I Am the Living Bread[231]

Exodus 16:11-31

11 And the LORD said to Moses, **12** "I have heard the grumbling of the people of Israel. Say to them, 'At twilight you shall eat meat, and in the morning you shall be filled with bread. Then you shall know that I am the LORD your God.'"

One would have expected a more threatening rebuke than this, but the Lord was very compassionate toward them, as he is toward us also. These first grumblings were not dealt with as severely as those later on would be. The Lord is not eager to use his rod.

---

[230] 1 Corinthians 10:31, "So, whether you eat or drink, or whatever you do, do all to the glory of God."
[231] John 6:51

¹³ In the evening quail came up and covered the camp, and in the morning dew lay around the camp. ¹⁴ And when the dew had gone up, there was on the face of the wilderness a fine, flake-like thing, fine as frost on the ground. ¹⁵ When the people of Israel saw it, they said to one another, "What is it?" For they did not know what it was. And Moses said to them, "It is the bread that the LORD has given you to eat." *(They had the best of meat and better than the best of bread. No king and his court ate better than these children of Abraham. If the Lord will feed these grumblers, then we know he will not abandon believers.)*

¹⁶ "This is what the LORD has commanded: 'Gather of it, each one of you, as much as he can eat. You shall each take an omer *(about two quarts)*, according to the number of the persons that each of you has in his tent.'" *(The bread of heaven must be gathered. We must hear the word and keep it in our heart. Otherwise it cannot do us good.)* ¹⁷ And the people of Israel did so. They gathered, some more, some less. ¹⁸ But when they measured it with an omer, whoever gathered much had nothing left over, and whoever gathered little had no lack. Each of them gathered as much as he could eat. ¹⁹ And Moses said to them, "Let no one leave any of it over till the morning." ²⁰ But they did not listen to Moses. Some left part of it till the morning, and it bred worms and stank. And Moses was angry with them.

There were misers in the wilderness. What they hid away stank. There are other misers today, whose worldly possessions are also wormy and spoiled. Coveting is disgusting.

²¹ Morning by morning they gathered it, each as much as he could eat; but when the sun grew hot, it melted. *(And yet it could be cooked! It is unusual that one heat improved it and another destroyed it.)*

²² On the sixth day they gathered twice as much bread, two omers each. And when all the leaders of the congregation came and told Moses, ²³ he said to them, "This is what the LORD has commanded: 'Tomorrow is a day of solemn rest, a holy Sabbath to the LORD; bake what you will bake and boil what you will boil, and all that is left over lay aside to be kept till the morning.'" ²⁴ So they laid it aside till the morning, as Moses commanded them, and it did not stink, and there were no worms in it. ²⁵ Moses said, "Eat it today, for today is a Sabbath to the LORD; today you will not find it in the field. ²⁶ Six days you shall gather it, but on the seventh day, which is a Sabbath, there will be none." *(The seventh day was honored by a double portion the day before and none on the day of rest. However, our first day of the week Sabbath, that we call The Lord's day, has a double portion of spiritual manna. We should gather enough from the preaching, fellowship and worship to provide for the entire week.)*

²⁷ On the seventh day some of the people went out to gather, but they found none. *(This was the certain way to stop this sin, but it was very shocking that a people who were so tremendously favored should be guilty of such an unnecessary and insulting act.)* ²⁸ And the LORD said to Moses, "How long will you refuse to keep my commandments and my laws? ²⁹ See! The LORD has given you the Sabbath; therefore on the sixth day he gives you bread for two days. Remain each of you in his place; let no one go out of his place on the seventh day." ³⁰ So the people rested on the seventh day.

³¹ Now the house of Israel called its name manna. It was like coriander seed, white, and the taste of it was like wafers made with honey. *(God might have made it bitter, but he delights to see his creatures happy. What a wonderful God he is!)*

MARCH 27
Whoever Believes Has Eternal Life[232]
Exodus 16:32-35

³² Moses said, "This is what the LORD has commanded: 'Let an omer *(about two quarts)* of [the manna] be kept throughout your generations, so that they may see the bread with which I fed you in the wilderness, when I brought you out of the land of Egypt.'" *(The education of future generations should be the serious concern of the people of God, because the Lord himself continually provided object lessons for*

---
[232] John 6:47

remembering his works of grace. The Lord knows that the human race tends to forget even his greatest wonders, so he gives us ways to remember them.)

33 And Moses said to Aaron, "Take a jar, and put an omer of manna in it, and place it before the LORD to be kept throughout your generations." **34** As the LORD commanded Moses, so Aaron placed it before the testimony to be kept. *(We should also treasure the memory of the Lord's great goodness to us. The golden jar of God's mercies to us should be kept stored in the holy ark of our memory.)* **35** The people of Israel ate the manna forty years, till they came to a habitable land. They ate the manna till they came to the border of the land of Canaan. *(Jehovah's warehouses are never empty. Whether the Lord's people are in the wilderness for forty years or eighty years, their bread will be provided, their water is guaranteed. Trust in the Lord forever.)*

The manna was a very full and instructive type of our Lord Jesus, who is the spiritual bread of his people. In order to understand this, let us read his own words in

John 6:47-58

47 "Truly, truly, I say to you, whoever believes has eternal life. **48** I am the bread of life. *(To believers, Jesus not only gives them life, he is their life.)* **49** Your fathers ate the manna in the wilderness, and they died. *(Even though the manna came from heaven, it did not give them eternal life. Jesus does! The Jews died, and many of them died very terribly, but those who feed on Jesus live forever.)* **50** This is the bread that comes down from heaven, so that one may eat of it and not die. *(This spiritual bread gives, supports, and protects spiritual life.)* **51** I am the living bread that came down from heaven. If anyone eats of this bread, he will live forever. And the bread that I will give for the life of the world is my flesh."

52 The Jews then disputed among themselves, saying, "How can this man give us his flesh to eat?" *(They heard the words, but did not understand their meaning. So, they asked this very natural question.)* **53** So Jesus said to them, "Truly, truly, I say to you, unless you eat the flesh of the Son of Man and drink his blood, you have no life in you. *(Our Lord would not explain his parable to the Jews and God hid the meaning from them.[233])* **54** Whoever feeds on my flesh and drinks my blood has eternal life, and I will raise him up on the last day. **55** For my flesh is true food, and my blood is true drink."

Some people dream that this applies to the Lord's supper, but that did not even exist at the time. It does not refer to the Lord's supper, to the Roman Catholic mass, or to any other thing or ceremony. It applies to our Lord himself, who must be fed on spiritually. Even now, too many people take these words literally and end up stumbling over this spiritual truth.

56 "Whoever feeds on my flesh and drinks my blood abides in me, and I in him. *(This is the closest possible relationship that exists between Jesus and the believer.)* **57** As the living Father sent me, and I live because of the Father, so whoever feeds on me, he also will live because of me. **58** This is the bread that came down from heaven, not like the bread the fathers ate, and died. Whoever feeds on this bread will live forever." *(Have we all received Jesus in our hearts? Are we trusting in him alone? Do we fellowship with him? This is what it means to feed on him and have a living oneness with him.)*

MARCH 28
Do Not Be Anxious About Anything[234]

The way that the Lord supplied the needs of his people in the desert, suggests today's reading in the Book of Matthew. God cares about the physical needs of his people and he is faithful to provide them. It is our privilege to depend on the Lord for everything in our lives as much as Israel did in the wilderness. It is still true that our God will supply every need we have. That is why our Lord Jesus taught us to steer clear of all worry and walk by faith.

---

[233] Matthew 13:10-11, "Then the disciples came and said to [Jesus], 'Why do you speak to them in parables?' And he answered them, 'To you it has been given to know the secrets of the kingdom of heaven, but to them it has not been given.'"
[234] Philippians 4:6

Matthew 6:25-34

25 "Therefore I tell you, do not be anxious about your life, what you will eat or what you will drink, nor about your body, what you will put on. Is not life more than food, and the body more than clothing? *(Do not stress out and worry about these less important things. God who gives us our life and bodies will give us food and clothing.)* **26** Look at the birds of the air: they neither sow nor reap nor gather into barns, and yet your heavenly Father feeds them. Are you not of more value than they?"

Martin Luther was walking in the fields one day during a difficult time in his life. He had his Bible in his hands, and reading the Sermon on the Mount, he found much comfort when he read Matthew 6:26, "Look at the birds of the air: they neither sow nor reap nor gather into barns, and yet your heavenly Father feeds them." Just then a little bird was hopping from branch to branch, with its sweet chirping music, seeming to say,

> *"Mortal, cease from toil and sorrow,*
> *God provides for tomorrow."*

It then came to the ground to pick up a crumb and rising merrily, again seemed to repeat its simple song—

> *"Mortal, cease from toil and sorrow,*
> *God provides for tomorrow."*

This gave the Reformer's heart great comfort.[235]

27 "And which of you by being anxious can add a single hour to his span of life? **28** And why are you anxious about clothing? Consider the lilies of the field, how they grow: they neither toil nor spin, **29** yet I tell you, even Solomon in all his glory was not arrayed like one of these. **30** But if God so clothes the grass of the field, which today is alive and tomorrow is thrown into the oven, will he not much more clothe you, O you of little faith?" *(This is good reasoning. He who cares for poor fading lilies and dresses them so splendidly, will not let his own immortal children go naked. Surely we can trust our own heavenly Father.)*

31 "Therefore do not be anxious, saying, 'What shall we eat?' or, 'What shall we drink?' or, 'What shall we wear?' **32** For the Gentiles seek after all these things, and your heavenly Father knows that you need them all." *(All anxious worry is forbidden! We have a Father in heaven. Will we worry as if we do not? Do not doubt until you have cause to doubt.)* **33** But seek first the kingdom of God and his righteousness, and all these things will be added to you.

34 "Therefore do not be anxious about tomorrow, for tomorrow will be anxious for itself. Sufficient for the day is its own trouble."

Let us cheer our hearts by reading that delightful song of contentment.

Psalm 23

1   The LORD is my shepherd, I shall not want.
2   He makes me lie down in green pastures.
    He leads me beside still waters.
3   He restores my soul.
    He leads me in paths of righteousness
      for his name's sake.
4   Even though I walk through the valley of
      the shadow of death,
    I will fear no evil,
  for you are with me;
    your rod and your staff,
    they comfort me.
5   You prepare a table before me
    in the presence of my enemies;
  you anoint my head with oil;
    my cup overflows.
6   Surely goodness and mercy shall follow me
    all the days of my life,
  and I shall dwell in the house of the LORD
    forever.

MARCH 29
I Give Water In the Wilderness[236]

Exodus 17:1-7

1 All the congregation of the people of Israel moved on from the wilderness of Sin by stages, according to the commandment of

---

[235] Protestant reformer Martin Luther (1483-1546).

[236] Isaiah 43:20

the LORD, and camped at Rephidim, but there was no water for the people to drink. *(God's people never go long before they are tested.)* ² Therefore the people quarreled with Moses and said, "Give us water to drink." And Moses said to them, "Why do you quarrel with me? Why do you test the LORD?"

Complaining about things that happen to us is really complaining about the Lord, no matter how we may try to hide it. After all, what did Moses have to do with it? The source of this sin of grumbling was unbelief. Could they not trust Jehovah? Would he not be sure to supply their needs? Had he ever forgotten them? In spite of all our experience of God's faithfulness to us, we are also guilty of the sin of not believing our Lord. He who is without fault among us, let him throw the first stone at Israel.

³ But the people thirsted there for water, and the people grumbled against Moses and said, "Why did you bring us up out of Egypt, to kill us and our children and our livestock with thirst?" ⁴ So Moses cried to the LORD, "What shall I do with this people? They are almost ready to stone me." *(Moses took the case into the right court. The people cried against him, but he cried to the Lord. Here is our best plan of action. We may always cry out to God.)* ⁵ And the LORD said to Moses, "Pass on before the people, taking with you some of the elders of Israel, and take in your hand the staff with which you struck the Nile, and go. ⁶ Behold, I will stand before you there on the rock at Horeb, and you shall strike the rock, and water shall come out of it, and the people will drink." *(See how the Lord answers their grumblings. He could let their complaints come true and leave them to die of thirst; but he does not respond to their bitter speeches and give them what they deserved. Instead, he gives them living streams from a rock. Surely the Lord, who repays good for evil like this, deserves our heart's constant trust from this day forward. It is a wicked insult to doubt one who is so overflowing with kindness. Do not repay evil for good.)*

⁷ And he called the name of the place Massah and Meribah, because of the quarreling of the people of Israel, and because they tested the LORD by saying, "Is the LORD among us or not?" *(Massah means testing and Meribah means quarreling. The Lord takes note of his people's disapproval and remembers them. We must not think a grumbling spirit is a small evil. The Lord has marked this occasion with a brand of disgrace.)*

The God who supplied Israel with natural water is ready to grant us the living water of his grace. Hear his words in:

Isaiah 41:17-18

¹⁷ When the poor and needy seek water,
  and there is none,
  and their tongue is parched with thirst,
 I the LORD will answer them,
  I the God of Israel will not forsake
   them.
¹⁸ I will open rivers on the bare heights,
  and fountains in the midst of the
   valleys.
 I will make the wilderness a pool of
   water,
  and the dry land springs of water.

To strengthen our faith in this promise we are told to look back on the Lord's wonders of old and to expect even greater things. God has not changed. The supply of his power and grace never runs out.

Isaiah 43:18-21

¹⁸ "Remember not the former things,
  nor consider the things of old.
¹⁹ Behold, I am doing a new thing;
  now it springs forth, do you not
   perceive it?
 I will make a way in the wilderness
  and rivers in the desert.
²⁰ The wild beasts will honor me,
  the jackals and the ostriches,
 for I give water in the wilderness,
  rivers in the desert,
 to give drink to my chosen people,
²¹ the people whom I formed for myself
  that they might declare my praise."

Glorify the Lord! We receive fresh supplies of grace from him every day and even every hour. He has not kept back any good thing from us. His praise will always be in our mouths.

MARCH 30

Watch and Pray[237]

Exodus 17:8-16

8 Then Amalek came and fought with Israel at Rephidim. *(These violent nomads attacked Israel without warning. It was a cowardly and unprovoked act and came when the Israelites were least able to defend themselves. They seem to have been the most cruel and mean of all Israel's enemies. As such, they are examples that teach us about sin and Satan.)* **9** So Moses said to Joshua, "Choose for us men, and go out and fight with Amalek. Tomorrow I will stand on the top of the hill with the staff of God in my hand." *(We must fight as well as pray. Though effort without prayer would be pride, prayer without effort shows disrespect for God. Joshua must go to battle and Moses must go to pray. Jesus said, "Watch and pray.")*

10 So Joshua did as Moses told him, and fought with Amalek, while Moses, Aaron, and Hur went up to the top of the hill. **11** Whenever Moses held up his hand, Israel prevailed, and whenever he lowered his hand, Amalek prevailed. **12** But Moses' hands grew weary, so they took a stone and put it under him, and he sat on it, while Aaron and Hur held up his hands, one on one side, and the other on the other side. So his hands were steady until the going down of the sun. *(Let all of us make great effort to support the prayerfulness of the church, because if that becomes weak everything becomes weak. "Therefore lift your drooping hands and strengthen your weak knees."[238] Spiritual evil can only be conquered by the life of prayer. When we fail to pray, the enemy easily defeats us.)* **13** And Joshua overwhelmed Amalek and his people with the sword.

14 Then the LORD said to Moses, "Write this as a memorial in a book and recite it in the ears of Joshua, that I will utterly blot out the memory of Amalek from under heaven."

It has been suggested by an old writer, that the Lord's reason for this special command to record this event is so his people will follow the example. We are to fight against sin and to expect victory over it by the help God gives us in answer to our prayers. Our Lord Jesus is both our Joshua who puts our sins to death and our Moses who prays for us to overcome them. His hands never need holding up. "He will not grow faint or be discouraged."[239] Amalek will be totally destroyed and we will be freed from sin forever.

15 And Moses built an altar and called the name of it, The LORD is my banner, *(because when Moses raised his staff, it was like a holy banner to Israel. Whenever we win victories we should bring thank offerings to the Lord and give glory to God alone.)* **16** saying, "A hand upon the throne of the LORD! The LORD will have war with Amalek from generation to generation." *(This war was still going on when King Saul reigned and he was instructed to remove that nation completely.)*

Because of the sinfulness of Amalek, as well as its unprovoked hostility against the tribes of Israel, the nation was doomed by divine justice to complete destruction. In the same way, our sins are doomed by divine grace to be crucified with Christ, so that we should not serve sin any longer. Let us read:

Deuteronomy 25:17-19

17 "Remember what Amalek did to you on the way as you came out of Egypt, **18** how he attacked you on the way when you were faint and weary, and cut off your tail, those who were lagging behind you, and he did not fear God. *(God will not tolerate attacks on his people. Injuries to them are seen as injuries to him.)* **19** Therefore when the LORD your God has given you rest from all your enemies around you, in the land that the LORD your God is giving you for an inheritance to possess, you shall blot out the memory of Amalek from under heaven; you shall not forget.

With the help of the Eternal Holy Spirit let us carry on war against all sin to complete victory, whether it is in ourselves or others. All sins are our deadly enemies. No

---

[237] Matthew 26:41
[238] Hebrews 12:12
[239] Isaiah 42:4

ceasefires or coming to terms of peace are allowed. Death to them all, because they all aim at our death. Our sins were what crucified our Lord Jesus.

Spurgeon's First Pastorate
August 1851 - December 1853
The church meeting at Waterbeach Baptist Chapel asked Spurgeon to become their pastor. He preached to packed audiences including many outside listening through open windows.

MARCH 31

With God All Things Are Possible[240]

Today we will read a part of Israel's history found in

Psalm 78:13-32

13 He divided the sea and let them pass through it,
   and made the waters stand like a heap.

The story of the Israelites freedom from slavery begins at the Red Sea and the drowning of the Egyptian army. Our spiritual liberty begins at the drowning of all our sins in Jesus' blood.

14 In the daytime he led them with a cloud,
   and all the night with a fiery light.

Thanks be to God for his guiding hand. We are not wanderers who have lost their way in a barren desert without roads. We follow where the perfect wisdom of Jehovah leads.

15 He split rocks in the wilderness
   and gave them drink abundantly as from the deep.
16 He made streams come out of the rock
   and caused waters to flow down like rivers.

God gave the Israelites generous and amazing supplies. These are excellent pictures of the streams of grace that flow to us from the great depths of his electing love and covenant faithfulness.

17 Yet they sinned still more against him,
   rebelling against the Most High in the desert.

What a change! They receive grace, but then they sinned. It is enough to make us weep to see how good God is and how badly people respond to that goodness. It would seem as if the more the Lord blesses people the less people bless their God.

18 They tested God in their heart
   by demanding the food they craved.

To wish God would help us to satisfy our unholy feelings is to tempt the Lord. But his holiness will not give in to our desires, because God cannot be tempted.

19 They spoke against God, saying,
   "Can God spread a table in the wilderness?
20 He struck the rock so that water gushed out,
   and streams overflowed.
   Can he also give bread
   or provide meat for his people?"

To question the Lord's power is to speak against him. Unbelief is actually trying to damage the reputation of the all powerful and gracious God.

21 Therefore, when the LORD heard, he was full of wrath;
   a fire was kindled against Jacob;
   his anger rose against Israel,
22 because they did not believe in God
   and did not trust his saving power.

Nothing angers God as much as unbelief. Oh for grace to keep us from not believing the Holy One.

23 Yet he commanded the skies above
   and opened the doors of heaven,
24 and he rained down on them manna to eat
   and gave them the grain of heaven.

This made their unbelief all the worse. To not trust God is a crime. To not trust God when he has been so merciful to us is a

---
[240] Matthew 19:26

greater crime. It is much worse to doubt when we have already received such great favors from our gracious Father.

²⁵ Man ate of the bread of the angels;
    he sent them food in abundance.
²⁶ He caused the east wind to blow in the heavens,
    and by his power he led out the south wind;
²⁷ he rained meat on them like dust,
    winged birds like the sand of the seas;
²⁸ he let them fall in the midst of their camp,
    all around their dwellings.

When God gives, he gives generously.

²⁹ And they ate and were well filled,
    for he gave them what they craved.
³⁰ But before they had satisfied their craving,

Satisfying a desire does not kill it. A person can be satisfied with evil, but they are not sickened by it. They may change the kind of the sin, but they continue to sin. Notice that, in this case, God's generosity was not a sign of his love, but actually a sign of his anger.

    while the food was still in their mouths,
³¹ the anger of God rose against them,
    and he killed the strongest of them
    and laid low the young men of Israel.

God often strikes the mighty while he has pity on the poor and the weak.

³² In spite of all this, they still sinned;
    despite his wonders, they did not believe.

Mercy did not soften them. Punishment did not humble them.

April 1

Let Us Then With Confidence Draw Near To the Throne Of Grace[241]

Exodus 19:1-6; 10-11; 16-18; 20-23

¹ On the third new moon after the people of Israel had gone out of the land of Egypt, on that day they came into the wilderness of Sinai. ² They set out from Rephidim and came into the wilderness of Sinai, and they encamped in the wilderness. There Israel encamped before the mountain, ³ while Moses went up to God. The Lord called to him out of the mountain, saying, "Thus you shall say to the house of Jacob, and tell the people of Israel: ⁴ You yourselves have seen what I did to the Egyptians, and how I bore you on eagles' wings and brought you to myself. ⁵ Now therefore, if you will indeed obey my voice and keep my covenant, you shall be my treasured possession among all peoples, for all the earth is mine; ⁶ᵃ and you shall be to me a kingdom of priests and a holy nation."

What a loving introduction to the law! If anything could have prepared rebellious people to obey God, this would have done it. The Lord has provided for his children and raised them up, but, sadly, they have rebelled against him.

¹⁰ The Lord said to Moses, "Go to the people and consecrate them today and tomorrow, and let them wash their garments ¹¹ and be ready for the third day. For on the third day the Lord will come down on Mount Sinai in the sight of all the people."

Their clothes smell of Egypt and must be washed, to show them that people and everything they touch is unholy. When God meets a person in love, they must be completely cleansed from the filth of sin by being washed in the blood of Jesus Christ.

¹⁶ On the morning of the third day there were thunders and lightnings and a thick cloud on the mountain and a very loud trumpet blast, so that all the people in the camp trembled. *(Those who have ears to hear the law must tremble, because it condemns all who are under it.)* ¹⁷ Then Moses brought the people out of the camp to meet God, and they took their stand at the foot of the mountain. ¹⁸ Now Mount Sinai was wrapped in smoke because the Lord had descended on it in fire. The smoke of it went up like the smoke of a kiln, and the whole mountain trembled greatly.

²⁰ The Lord came down on Mount Sinai, to the top of the mountain. And the Lord called Moses to the top of the mountain, and Moses went up.

²¹ And the Lord said to Moses, "Go down and warn the people, lest they break through

---

[241] Hebrews 4:16

to the LORD to look and many of them perish. **22** Also let the priests who come near to the LORD consecrate themselves, lest the LORD break out against them." **23** And Moses said to the LORD, "The people cannot come up to Mount Sinai, for you yourself warned us, saying, 'Set limits around the mountain and consecrate it.'"

This is the spirit of the law. It shows us our sinfulness. It sets us at a distance from God, but the gospel removes our sin and brings us near to God. Hear how the Holy Spirit speaks concerning the law, by his servant Paul,[242] in

Hebrews 12:18-26

18 For you have not come to what may be touched, a blazing fire and darkness and gloom and a tempest **19** and the sound of a trumpet and a voice whose words made the hearers beg that no further messages be spoken to them. **20** For they could not endure the order that was given, "If even a beast touches the mountain, it shall be stoned." **21** Indeed, so terrifying was the sight that Moses said, "I tremble with fear." **22** But you have come to Mount Zion and to the city of the living God, the heavenly Jerusalem, and to innumerable angels in festal gathering, **23** and to the assembly of the firstborn, who are enrolled in heaven, and to God, the judge of all, and to the spirits of the righteous made perfect, **24** and to Jesus, the mediator of a new covenant, and to the sprinkled blood that speaks a better word than the blood of Abel.

25 See that you do not refuse him who is speaking. For if they did not escape when they refused him who warned them on the earth, much less will we escape if we reject him who warns from heaven. **26** At that time his voice shook the earth, but now he has promised, "Yet once more I will shake not only the earth but also the heavens."

Dear members of this family, let these solemn words sink deep into your souls. Do not despise the Lord Jesus, but believe in him now.

APRIL 2
God, Be Merciful To Me, a Sinner[243]

We are now about to read the awe-inspiring heart of the law of God, that is contained in

Exodus 20:1-17

but, before we read a line, let us sincerely ask the Lord to forgive our offenses against his holy name and to accept us in the Son of his love. God's law has been honored and kept perfectly by the Lord Jesus. There is nothing left out and nothing repeated in the Ten Commandments. It is the only perfect law in the universe. None of us have kept it and therefore it would be foolish to hope for salvation by keeping it, because nothing but perfect obedience can be accepted by the justice of God.

1 And God spoke all these words, saying,

2 "I am the LORD your God, who brought you out of the land of Egypt, out of the house of slavery.

3 "You shall have no other gods before me."

There is only one true God. We must not dare to worship or obey any other. Beware of making gold, or yourself, or your dearest relation into a god. "Little children, keep yourselves from idols."[244]

4 "You shall not make for yourself a carved image, or any likeness of anything that is in heaven above, or that is in the earth beneath, or that is in the water under the earth. **5** You shall not bow down to them or serve them, for I the LORD your God am a jealous God, visiting the iniquity of the fathers on the children to the third and the fourth generation of those who hate me, **6** but showing steadfast love to thousands of those who love me and keep my commandments."

In the second commandment we are forbidden to worship God by bowing down to any image or worshiping him in any way he has not commanded. How great are the crimes of those who worship crosses, pictures, and bread; and even connect the idea of holiness to places and buildings.

---

[242] Many believe the apostle Paul wrote the book of Hebrews.

[243] Luke 18:13
[244] 1 John 5:21

⁷"You shall not take the name of the LORD your God in vain, for the LORD will not hold him guiltless who takes his name in vain."

Any unholy use of the divine name is exceedingly sinful. Beware of flippantly saying, "Oh My God," and other disrespectful expressions.

⁸"Remember the Sabbath day, to keep it holy. ⁹Six days you shall labor, and do all your work, ¹⁰but the seventh day is a Sabbath to the LORD your God. On it you shall not do any work, you, or your son, or your daughter, your male servant, or your female servant, or your livestock, or the sojourner who is within your gates. ¹¹For in six days the LORD made heaven and earth, the sea, and all that is in them, and rested the seventh day. Therefore the LORD blessed the Sabbath day and made it holy."

One day in seven is the Lord's. To rob him of it is to injure ourselves as well as to disobey our Maker. Rest and worship are two of our sweetest blessings. The day should be set aside especially for them.

¹²"Honor your father and your mother, that your days may be long in the land that the LORD your God is giving you."

We owe our parents respect, love, and obedience. This is the first commandment that comes with a promise.

¹³"You shall not murder."

Anger and doing anything that would injure the health of ourselves or others are forbidden.

¹⁴"You shall not commit adultery."

This forbids lust of heart, thought, and look, as well as actual actions.

¹⁵"You shall not steal."

This forbids even taking things of little value as well as cheating and every kind of wrong.

¹⁶"You shall not bear false witness against your neighbor."

All lying is condemned.

¹⁷"You shall not covet your neighbor's house; you shall not covet your neighbor's wife, or his male servant, or his female servant, or his ox, or his donkey, or anything that is your neighbor's"

This deals with sins of the heart. It shows that the command is very far reaching and involves even our thoughts and imaginations. Who can read it and then hope to be saved by their own activities and good deeds? Lord have mercy on us and forgive us for breaking your holy law.

APRIL 3

Whoever Believes and Is Baptized Will Be Saved[245]

We have selected for our present reading a portion that illustrates the difference between the law and the gospel.

Romans 10:1-21

¹Brothers, my heart's desire and prayer to God for them is that they may be saved.

The true spirit of Christianity is that of love and sympathy. It leads to prayer even for persecutors and to hope for the most stubborn of people. Paul prayed for the Jews.

²I bear them witness that they have a zeal for God, but not according to knowledge.

Do not deny the good points in others, even if they are not all we could wish them to be.

³For being ignorant of the righteousness of God, and seeking to establish their own, they did not submit to God's righteousness. ⁴For Christ is the end of the law for righteousness to everyone who believes.

Christ fulfills the law's purpose for us. When we have HIM we have all the law requires.

⁵For Moses writes about the righteousness that is based on the law, that the person who does the commandments shall live by them. ⁶But the righteousness based on faith says, "Do not say in your heart, 'Who will ascend into heaven?'" (that is, to bring Christ down) ⁷or, "'Who will descend into the abyss?'" (that is, to bring Christ up from the dead). ⁸But what does it say? "The word is near you, in your mouth and in your heart" (that is, the word of faith that we proclaim); ⁹because, if you confess with your mouth that Jesus is Lord and believe in your heart

---
[245] Mark 16:16

that God raised him from the dead, you will be saved. *(Precious gospel. Not doing, but believing, saves us. We do not have to do or feel great things but simply to trust.)*

10 For with the heart one believes and is justified, and with the mouth one confesses and is saved. **11** For the Scripture says, "Everyone who believes in him will not be put to shame." **12** For there is no distinction between Jew and Greek; for the same Lord is Lord of all, bestowing his riches on all who call on him. **13** For "everyone who calls on the name of the Lord will be saved."[246] *(Think about this verse. It should comfort even the most depressed seeker. Real prayer will be heard sooner or later.)*

14 How then will they call on him in whom they have not believed? And how are they to believe in him of whom they have never heard? And how are they to hear without someone preaching? **15** And how are they to preach unless they are sent? As it is written, "How beautiful are the feet of those who preach the good news!"[247] **16** But they have not all obeyed the gospel. For Isaiah says, "Lord, who has believed what he has heard from us?"[248] **17** So faith comes from hearing, and hearing through the word of Christ. *(Be determined to continue attending the gospel ministry and be committed to listen carefully, because it is the way that faith comes.)*

18 But I ask, have they not heard? Indeed they have, for

"Their voice has gone out to all the earth,
and their words to the ends of the world."[249]

Sadly, not all hearers become believers. Most hear with deaf ears and do not obey the truth.

19 But I ask, did Israel not understand? First Moses says,

"I will make you jealous of those who are not a nation;
with a foolish nation I will make you angry."[250]

---

[246] Joel 2:32
[247] Isaiah 52:7
[248] Isaiah 53:1
[249] Psalm 19:4
[250] Deuteronomy 32:21

20 Then Isaiah is so bold as to say,

"I have been found by those who did not seek me;
I have shown myself to those who did not ask for me."[251]

Sovereign grace sometimes saves the most unlikely people. At the same time those who sit under a gospel ministry may harden their hearts and perish. Beware of thinking outward advantages are enough. You must have real faith in Jesus.

21 But of Israel he says, "All day long I have held out my hands to a disobedient and contrary people."[252] *(They were sincerely warned and lovingly invited. Yet it was all for nothing. Will this be the case with any of this household? God forbid.)*

APRIL 4

We Have Also Obtained Access By Faith[253]

After being given the law on Mount Sinai, Moses received instructions about public worship and sacrifices. All of these things pointed to spiritual matters. Therefore, we will read the New Testament summary of it found in

Hebrews 9:1-14

1 Now even the first covenant had regulations for worship and an earthly place of holiness. **2** For a tent was prepared, the first section, in which were the lampstand and the table and the bread of the Presence. It is called the Holy Place. **3** Behind the second curtain was a second section called the Most Holy Place *(or Holy of Holies),* **4** having the golden altar of incense and the ark of the covenant covered on all sides with gold, in which was a golden urn holding the manna, and Aaron's staff that budded, and the tablets of the covenant. **5** Above it were the cherubim of glory overshadowing the mercy seat. Of these things we cannot now speak in detail.

6 These preparations having thus been made, the priests go regularly into the first section, performing their ritual duties, **7** but

---

[251] Isaiah 65:1
[252] Isaiah 65:2
[253] Romans 5:2

into the second only the high priest goes, and he but once a year, and not without taking blood, which he offers for himself and for the unintentional sins of the people. *(The greatest of the Jewish high priests had to admit that they were sinners themselves and they had to present sin-offerings for themselves as well as for the people. But our Lord Jesus has no sin of his own; which is part of the reason he was able to bear our sin.)*

8 By this the Holy Spirit indicates that the way into the holy places is not yet opened as long as the first section is still standing **9** (which is symbolic for the present age). *(The Most Holy Place was not open to all everyone, but only to Jews; and not to all Jews, but only to priests; and not to all priests, but only to the high priest; and not even to him at all times, or indeed at any time, but only on one solitary day in the year.)* According to this arrangement, gifts and sacrifices are offered that cannot perfect the conscience of the worshiper *(That is, they could not atone for sin. Therefore these gifts and sacrifices could not give peace to the conscience),* **10** but deal only with food and drink and various washings, regulations for the body imposed until the time of reformation.

These washings and regulations were a shadow of the Lord Jesus Christ. When the Light of the World appeared, the reason for these dim images was over. The time of reformation is now. Jesus is the completion and fulfillment of the ceremonial law. Is it not amazing that anyone would wish to undo this reformation and go back to the uselessness of trying to keep the law? Even worse, many professing Christians want us to practice the follies of the Roman Catholic Church in our own places of worship.

11 But when Christ appeared as a high priest of the good things that have come, then through the greater and more perfect tent (not made with hands, that is, not of this creation) **12** he entered once for all into the holy places, not by means of the blood of goats and calves but by means of his own blood, thus securing an eternal redemption. *(Our Lord's offering is never to be repeated. It has been presented once and the result has been the absolute eternal redemption of all for whom he bled as a substitute. Oh what joy to see Jesus behind the second curtain, in the Most Holy Place, with a perfect offering, and to know that the one sacrifice has saved us.)*

13 For if the blood of goats and bulls, and the sprinkling of defiled persons with the ashes of a heifer sanctify for the purification of the flesh, **14** how much more will the blood of Christ, who through the eternal Spirit offered himself without blemish to God, purify our conscience from dead works to serve the living God.

Who can answer this question, "How much more?" It is a glorious declaration. Jesus can most certainly remove our sins. Beloved, has he removed yours? Answer as if you were answering before the living God!

APRIL 5

Our Fellowship Is With the Father[254]

Exodus 24:1-15; 18

1 Then he said to Moses, "Come up to the LORD, you and Aaron, Nadab, and Abihu, and seventy of the elders of Israel, and worship from afar. **2** Moses alone shall come near to the LORD, but the others shall not come near, and the people shall not come up with him."

Under the law, even those who were favored the most were not allowed to come very near to God. Even when he said, "Come near to Jehovah," it was added, "but the others shall not come near." How different the gospel, is! "But now in Christ Jesus, you who once were far off have been brought near by the blood of Christ."[255]

3 Moses came and told the people all the words of the LORD and all the rules. And all the people answered with one voice and said, "All the words that the LORD has spoken we will do." *(Their tongues went faster than their lives. People are swift at promising, but limping in performing.)* **4** And Moses wrote down all the words of the LORD. He rose early in the morning and built an altar at the

---
[254] 1 John 1:3
[255] Ephesians 2:13

foot of the mountain, and twelve pillars, according to the twelve tribes of Israel. **5** And he sent young men of the people of Israel, who offered burnt offerings and sacrificed peace offerings of oxen to the LORD. **6** And Moses took half of the blood and put it in basins, and half of the blood he threw *(or sprinkled)* against the altar. **7** Then he took the Book of the Covenant and read it in the hearing of the people. And they said, "All that the LORD has spoken we will do, and we will be obedient." **8** And Moses took the blood and threw it on the people and said, "Behold the blood of the covenant that the LORD has made with you in accordance with all these words."

The blood is the main thing in all fellowship with God. No road is open to us but the crimson one. Peace comes where the blood of Jesus falls, but without that we are unclean and unable to have fellowship with God. Dear friends, has the blood of Jesus ever been sprinkled on you? Faith applies the blood. Do you have that faith?

9 Then Moses and Aaron, Nadab, and Abihu, and seventy of the elders of Israel went up, **10** and they saw the God of Israel. There was under his feet as it were a pavement of sapphire stone, like the very heaven for clearness. **11** And he did not lay his hand on the chief men of the people of Israel; they beheld God, and ate and drank. *(When the blood was on them, they could come near, and enjoy quiet fellowship that even included eating and drinking. What they saw is not explained to us except for one detail; they saw the bright blue pavement beneath the sacred feet. All of our knowledge falls below the glory of our God. "For now we see in a mirror dimly," but the day is coming when we will see him "face to face."[256])*

12 The LORD said to Moses, "Come up to me on the mountain and wait there, that I may give you the tablets of stone, with the law and the commandment, which I have written for their instruction." **13** So Moses rose with his assistant Joshua, and Moses went up into the mountain of God. *(Moses enjoyed a higher degree of fellowship than any other man. He went up alone into the cloud. There are elect ones out of the elect who the Master brings very close to Himself, to "walk in the light as he is in the light."[257] To be highly favored in this way is the best honor and the greatest joy.)* **14** And he said to the elders, "Wait here for us until we return to you. And behold, Aaron and Hur are with you. Whoever has a dispute, let him go to them."

15 Then Moses went up on the mountain, and the cloud covered the mountain. *(This was a delightful retreat for Moses, who would now, for a while, forget his responsibility for the people.)*

18 Moses entered the cloud and went up on the mountain. And Moses was on the mountain forty days and forty nights. *(Oh sweet time of fellowship with heaven. Six weeks with God! What a rest! Sadly, Moses needed it, because the people were rebelling down below and making trouble for their leader's heart.)*

APRIL 6

You Shall Be Holy, For I Am Holy[258]
Exodus 30:11-16

11 The LORD said to Moses, **12** "When you take the census of the people of Israel, then each shall give a ransom for his life to the LORD when you number them, that there be no plague among them when you number them. *(Every census included a purchase price for each person counted. Every one of the Lord's people was to be redeemed as a reminder to all generations that redemption is absolutely necessary for God to accept us. If we had not been bought with a price, the fierce plagues of divine judgment would have followed us even to the lowest hell.)* **13** Each one who is numbered in the census shall give this: half a shekel[259] according to the shekel of the sanctuary (the shekel is twenty gerahs), half a shekel as an offering to the LORD."

---

[256] 1 Corinthians 13:12

[257] 1 John 1:7
[258] 1 Peter 1:16
[259] *shekel* - about 2/5 ounce

God places his own value on people, because he knows their worth best. How much we owe is not left for us to decide based on what we think it should be. The Lord's own will is what determines what our debt is. What we owe is what we owe, because HE requires it.

14 Everyone who is numbered in the census, from twenty years old and upward, shall give the LORD's offering. **15** "The rich shall not give more, and the poor shall not give less, than the half shekel, when you give the LORD's offering to make atonement for your lives."

Believers differ in knowledge, gifts and graces, but they are all redeemed with the same price. The lowest believer was bought with the same blood as the foremost of the apostles. The poor, the unknown, the disabled, the illiterate, are as dear to the heart of Jesus as the richest and most gifted saint. What a sweet thought! Here is the true equality. "His righteousness is unto all and upon all them that believe, for there is no difference."[260] Let us all equally bless and love the Lord by whose blood we are equally redeemed.

16 "You shall take the atonement money from the people of Israel and shall give it for the service of the tent of meeting, that it may bring the people of Israel to remembrance before the LORD, so as to make atonement for your lives." *(The atonement money was both a reminder of their relationship with the Lord as well as a reminder of their great obligation to serve their Redeemer.)*

The apostle Peter explains that, when the Lord Jesus purchased our salvation with his precious blood, we became obligated to live a life pleasing to God.

1 Peter 1:15-21

15 As he who called you is holy, you also be holy in all your conduct, **16** since it is written, "You shall be holy, for I am holy." *(The heart of true religion is living our lives in a way that reflects the Lord we worship.)* **17** And if you call on him as Father who judges impartially according to each one's deeds, conduct yourselves with fear throughout the time of your exile, *(Let a childlike fear of offending your Great Father always hold you back from sin. "Blessed is the man who fears always."[261])* **18** knowing that you were ransomed from the futile ways inherited from your forefathers, not with perishable things such as silver or gold, **19** but with the precious blood of Christ, like that of a lamb without blemish or spot.

The same price that redeems us from destruction also redeems us from our pointless way of life. This price is no less than the heart's blood of the Son of God. Until the world can offer us something more precious than the blood of Jesus, we will feel ourselves obligated by bonds of love to walk in holiness, and see Jesus praised.

20 He was foreknown before the foundation of the world but was made manifest in the last times for the sake of you **21** who through him are believers in God, who raised him from the dead and gave him glory, so that your faith and hope are in God.

Jesus' love to us is not something new. He was appointed to redeem us before worlds began. Do not let this world charm you with its constant claim of new and exciting things. It was a real love of concern that brought Jesus to earth to be our suffering substitute. Let our love be real too; not in word only, but in deed and in truth. Oh to be a redeemed family and to live like it. The Lord grant it for Jesus' sake. Amen.

APRIL 7
Keep Yourselves From Idols[262]
Exodus 32:1-14

1 When the people saw that Moses delayed to come down from the mountain, the people gathered themselves together to Aaron and said to him, "Up, make us gods who shall go before us. As for this Moses, the man who brought us up out of the land of Egypt, we do not know what has become of him."

They were so undependable that they could not be trusted alone. Worse than that, they were terribly ungrateful. They forgot their

---

[260] Quoted from *The English Preacher* circa 1831

[261] *Commentary of the Book of Proverbs* by Moses Stuart 1852

[262] 1 John 5:21

God and gave Moses the credit for delivering them and even to him they were disgustingly thankless. They called him "this Moses," as if they despised him and did so to the face of his own brother. They must have been in a state of wild rebellion, to insult both their great leader and his brother in this way. The fact was, they were so utterly unspiritual that they could not live in peace unless they had something they could see to call their god. They lacked the faith that sees him who is invisible.

2 So Aaron said to them, "Take off the rings of gold that are in the ears of your wives, your sons, and your daughters, and bring them to me." 3 So all the people took off the rings of gold that were in their ears and brought them to Aaron. 4 And he received the gold from their hand and fashioned it with a graving tool and made a golden calf. And they said, "These are your gods, O Israel, who brought you up out of the land of Egypt!"

Shame on Aaron for giving in to them! What idolatry to think that the infinite Jehovah looks like a young bull that has horns and hoofs. They went back to old Egyptian idolatry and set up an ox as the symbol of the God of power.

5 When Aaron saw this, he built an altar before it. And Aaron made proclamation and said, "Tomorrow shall be a feast to the LORD." *(That is, a feast to Jehovah. They still claimed to worship Jehovah, but broke the second commandment by making an idol in the form of an ox.)* 6 And they rose up early the next day and offered burnt offerings and brought peace offerings. And the people sat down to eat and drink and rose up to play.

7 And the LORD said to Moses, "Go down, for your people, whom you brought up out of the land of Egypt, have corrupted themselves. 8 They have turned aside quickly out of the way that I commanded them. They have made for themselves a golden calf and have worshiped it and sacrificed to it and said, 'These are your gods, O Israel, who brought you up out of the land of Egypt!'" *(Who wonders that the Lord resented the insult offered to him by the people who owed him so much?)* 9 And the LORD said to Moses, "I have seen this people, and behold, it is a stiff-necked people. 10 Now therefore let me alone, that my wrath may burn hot against them and I may consume them, in order that I may make a great nation of you." *(If Moses had been an ambitious or selfish man, this was a great opportunity for him; but he loved the people better than himself.)*

11 But Moses implored the LORD his God and said, "O LORD, why does your wrath burn hot against your people, whom you have brought out of the land of Egypt with great power and with a mighty hand? *(Notice the heart of his plea: God had called them Moses' people {verse 7}, but he will not have it so, he calls them, "your people," and begs the Lord to not be angry with them.)* 12 Why should the Egyptians say, 'With evil intent did he bring them out, to kill them in the mountains and to consume them from the face of the earth'? Turn from your burning anger and relent from this disaster against your people. *(Moses appeals here to the name and honor of God. This is pleading with force!)* 13 "Remember Abraham, Isaac, and Israel, your servants, to whom you swore by your own self, and said to them, 'I will multiply your offspring as the stars of heaven, and all this land that I have promised I will give to your offspring, and they shall inherit it forever,'" *(His third master plea is "the promise" confirmed by oath. He who can plead the promises of God will succeed.)* 14 And the LORD relented from the disaster that he had spoken of bringing on his people. *(If Moses succeeded as Mediator,[263] how much more will the Lord Jesus, who prays for guilty sinners.)*

APRIL 8

If Anyone Does Sin, We Have an Advocate[264]

Exodus 32:15-20; 30-35

15 Then Moses turned and went down from the mountain with the two tablets of the

---

[263] *mediator* - a person who attempts to make people involved in a conflict come to an agreement; a go-between. As used in the Bible, Jesus Christ intercedes between God the Father and Christians; that is, he prays for them.
[264] 1 John 2:1

testimony in his hand, tablets that were written on both sides; on the front and on the back they were written. **16** The tablets were the work of God, and the writing was the writing of God, engraved on the tablets. *(It is no small difficulty to leave fellowship with God to battle with other people's sins. This can happen to us even today. May the Lord prepare us for it.)* **17** When Joshua heard the noise of the people as they shouted, he said to Moses, "There is a noise of war in the camp."

Joshua was a soldier and therefore, his thoughts ran that way, but Moses knew better. It would be far better to hear the noise of war with spiritual enemies, than the sound of rebellion against the Lord.

18 But he said, "It is not the sound of shouting for victory, or the sound of the cry of defeat, but the sound of singing that I hear." **19** And as soon as he came near the camp and saw the calf and the dancing, Moses' anger burned hot, and he threw the tablets out of his hands and broke them at the foot of the mountain.

Moses is never blamed for this. His action represented his great hatred of sin and his zeal for the Lord of hosts. He felt that the tablets, which were written with God's finger, would be polluted by being brought among such a people.

20 He took the calf that they had made and burned it with fire and ground it to powder and scattered it on the water and made the people of Israel drink it.

Moses shows the greatest contempt for their idol by making them drink it. Is it not strange beyond belief that followers of the Roman Catholic Church of our day actually worship the wafer and then eat it? They imagine that it is great religious respect to eat something they claim is divine.

This is a wonderful example of the influence of one man. In the midst of thousands of idolaters, Moses was able to tear down their idol, deface it, grind it to powder, mix it with water, and force the people to drink it. God was with him or the stubborn and pigheaded mob would have resisted him. He was very clear in his action.

He did not tolerate idol worship for a moment. This decision, no doubt, gave him great influence for good among the people.

30 The next day Moses said to the people, "You have sinned a great sin. And now I will go up to the LORD; perhaps I can make atonement for your sin." *(His one thought was to do them good. He was like our Lord Jesus, a faithful Intercessor.)*

31 So Moses returned to the LORD and said, "Alas, this people has sinned a great sin. They have made for themselves gods of gold. **32** But now, if you will forgive their sin—but if not, please blot me out of your book that you have written." *(This was splendid self-sacrifice, of which we find a similar case in the apostle Paul. Moses meant what he said, but we must not judge his expressions by cold-blooded logic. They were the warm overflow of a tender heart.)* **33** But the LORD said to Moses, "Whoever has sinned against me, I will blot out of my book." *(This is the voice of the law threatening to blot out the sinner, but the gospel freely blots out the sin.)* **34** "But now go, lead the people to the place about which I have spoken to you; behold, my angel shall go before you. Nevertheless, in the day when I visit, I will visit their sin upon them." *(The Lord refused to be personally present with the tribes of Israel, but graciously promised to assign an angel to direct them. This was sad news for Moses, who knew the value of the divine presence; and to the people themselves it was dreadful news, especially the part that the Lord would visit them for sin.)*

35 Then the LORD sent a plague on the people, because they made the calf, the one that Aaron made.

The people were the real makers of the idol. Aaron was only the person they used to create the idol. Neither the people nor Aaron are excused. The guilt of each is clearly stated. It was sad to see such a man as Aaron go so far off the correct path. Lord, keep each one of us by your Holy Spirit.

Spurgeon at About Age 20
People were required to hold a pose for almost 10 seconds in those early days of photography. Photographers seemed to like Spurgeon in poses like this one.

APRIL 9

My Presence Will Go With You[265]

Exodus 33:1-7; 12-23

¹ The LORD said to Moses, "Depart; go up from here, you and the people whom you have brought up out of the land of Egypt, to the land of which I swore to Abraham, Isaac, and Jacob, saying, 'To your offspring I will give it.' ² I will send an angel before you, and I will drive out the Canaanites, the Amorites, the Hittites, the Perizzites, the Hivites, and the Jebusites. ³ Go up to a land flowing with milk and honey; but I will not go up among you, lest I consume you on the way, for you are a stiff-necked people."

⁴ When the people heard this disastrous word, they mourned, and no one put on his ornaments. *(The people still had some conscience left. When Moses spoke to them it was evident, but, like the morning dew, it only lasted a short time.)* ⁵ For the LORD had said to Moses, "Say to the people of Israel, 'You are a stiff-necked people; if for a single moment I should go up among you, I would consume you. So now take off your ornaments, that I may know what to do with you.'" *(As if the Lord did not know how to show mercy to unrepentant sinners.)* ⁶ Therefore the people of Israel stripped themselves of their ornaments, from Mount Horeb onward.

This must always happen before mercy. Pride must remove her disguise, self-righteousness must throw off her cloak and self-importance must take off its jingling jewelry.

⁷ Now Moses used to take the tent and pitch it outside the camp, far off from the camp, and he called it the tent of meeting. And everyone who sought the LORD would go out to the tent of meeting, which was outside the camp.

They were not worthy to have the Lord stay in the center of their community. The Lord did not leave them completely, but he went into the outer circle. All who would seek the Lord must go outside the camp. The lesson is clear and it is still true today.

¹² Moses said to the LORD, "See, you say to me, 'Bring up this people,' but you have not let me know whom you will send with me. Yet you have said, 'I know you by name, and you have also found favor in my sight.' ¹³ Now therefore, if I have found favor in your sight, please show me now your ways, that I may know you in order to find favor in your sight. Consider too that this nation is your people." ¹⁴ And he said, "My presence will go with you, and I will give your rest." *(The Lord gives us his presence now and rest at the end of life's journey. What a precious promise!)* ¹⁵ And he said to him, "If your presence will not go with me, do not bring us up from here. ¹⁶ For how shall it be known that I have found favor in your sight, I and your people? Is it not in your going with us, so that we are distinct, I and your people, from every other people on the face of the earth?"

¹⁷ And the LORD said to Moses, "This very thing that you have spoken I will do, for you have found favor in my sight, and I know you by name." *(We have received grace and that grace is what guarantees answers to our prayers.)* ¹⁸ Moses said, "Please show me your glory." ¹⁹ And he said, "I will make all my goodness pass before you and will

---

[265] Exodus 33:14

proclaim before you my name 'The LORD.' And I will be gracious to whom I will be gracious, and will show mercy on whom I will show mercy. *(We see that the sovereignty of his grace is the very glory of God. Why do people quarrel with it?)* ²⁰ But," he said, "you cannot see my face, for man shall not see me and live." ²¹ And the LORD said, "Behold, there is a place by me where you shall stand on the rock, ²² and while my glory passes by I will put you in a cleft of the rock, and I will cover you with my hand until I have passed by. ²³ Then I will take away my hand, and you shall see my back, but my face shall not be seen."

Nowhere else can God be spiritually seen, except from the Rock of ages cleft for us.[266] *We now see only the edge his garments, but even this glimpse delights us. How sweet to know that however little we see of God, yet it is God, our Father.*

APRIL 10
The LORD Looks On the Heart[267]
1 Corinthians 10:1-12

¹ For I do not want you to be unaware, brothers, that our fathers were all under the cloud, and all passed through the sea, ² and all were baptized into Moses in the cloud and in the sea, *(A great deal of spiritual guidance is lost if we allow ourselves to remain ignorant about Old Testament history. God intended us to learn many practical lessons from the Israelites. They had the law and the special privilege of being the chosen people of Jehovah and yet they perished. We should pay attention, to prevent the same thing from happening to us. Were we baptized with water when we began our religious life? So were they. At the Red Sea, with the cloud above them and the sea on either side, they were buried in baptism with their leader.)* ³ and all ate the same spiritual food, ⁴ and all drank the same spiritual drink. For they drank from the spiritual Rock that followed them, and the Rock was Christ.

This resembles the Lord's Supper. They ate manna and drank from the rock that was split open. The bread and wine of the Communion Service also represent him whose flesh is true food and whose blood is true drink.[268]

⁵ Nevertheless, with most of them God was not pleased, for they were overthrown in the wilderness. *(They died, even though they took part in the sacrifices and other things that God told them to do. We will also fall unless, by faith, we steer clear of their fault of unbelief.)*

⁶ Now these things took place as examples for us, that we might not desire evil as they did. ⁷ Do not be idolaters as some of them were; as it is written, "The people sat down to eat and drink and rose up to play." ⁸ We must not indulge in sexual immorality as some of them did, and twenty-three thousand fell in a single day. ⁹ We must not put Christ to the test, as some of them did and were destroyed by serpents, ¹⁰ nor grumble, as some of them did and were destroyed by the Destroyer. ¹¹ Now these things happened to them as an example, but they were written down for our instruction, on whom the end of the ages has come. ¹² Therefore let anyone who thinks that he stands take heed lest he fall. *(Our baptism, our taking part in the Lord's Supper, and other benefits of being church members, may make us think we are safe from God's anger, but we must take heed, because far more is needed.)*

In the Psalms we find the same lesson set to music.

Psalm 95
1. Oh come, let us sing to the LORD;
   let us make a joyful noise to the rock of our salvation!
2. Let us come into his presence with thanksgiving;
   let us make a joyful noise to him with songs of praise!
3. For the LORD is a great God,
   and a great King above all gods.

---

[266] A reference to the hymn *Rock of Ages, Cleft for Me* written by Augustus Toplady in 1776. A cleft is a hollow place in a rock. The story is told that, one day Toplady was overtaken by a thunderstorm and ran to a limestone rock formation where he took shelter in a "cleft" and wrote his now famous hymn.
[267] 1 Samuel 16:7

[268] John 6:55 - Jesus said, "For my flesh is true food, and my blood is true drink."

4 In his hand are the depths of the earth;
    the heights of the mountains are his also.
5 The sea is his, for he made it,
    and his hands formed the dry land.
6 Oh come, let us worship and bow down;
    let us kneel before the LORD, our Maker!
7 For he is our God,
    and we are the people of his pasture,
    and the sheep of his hand.
  Today, if you hear his voice
8   do not harden your hearts, as at Meribah,
    as on the day at Massah in the wilderness,
9 when your fathers put me to the test
    and put me to the proof, though they had seen my work.
10 For forty years I loathed that generation
    and said, "They are a people who go astray in their heart,
    and they have not known my ways."
11 Therefore I swore in my wrath,
    "They shall not enter my rest."

They were his people on the outside. They were given every advantage to make them worthy to be called God's chosen people. But they never became a spiritual people. Their privileges were of no use and they died in the wilderness. Let us beware of depending on anything short of saving faith and a real change of heart. "You must be born again."[269]

APRIL 11

Make Your Face Shine Upon Your Servant[270]

In our present reading we will see how the Lord reopened his communications with Israel, even though their sin had quickly broken all their agreements almost before they had agreed to them.

Exodus 34:1-5; 28-35

¹ The LORD said to Moses, "Cut for yourself two tablets of stone like the first, and I will write on the tablets the words that were on the first tablets, which you broke."

Let us learn here, that although people have broken the law of God, yet the Lord in infinite mercy to his people visits them again. First, he causes their hearts to be broken and prepared by the preaching of his prophets and ministers. Then, he writes the law on those "tablets of human hearts."[271] Having the law in the heart is better than the law on stone.

² "Be ready by the morning, and come up in the morning to Mount Sinai, and present yourself there to me on the top of the mountain."

Moses must go up a second time and be with the Lord. The people must be tested a second time to see if they will serve God when their leader is absent.

³ "No one shall come up with you, and let no one be seen throughout all the mountain. Let no flocks or herds graze opposite that mountain." *(Distance was always the rule of the law. Moses went up to God alone, but Jesus takes all his people with him.)* ⁴ So Moses cut two tablets of stone like the first. And he rose early in the morning and went up on Mount Sinai, as the LORD had commanded him, and took in his hand two tablets of stone. *(Notice, that Moses, like other good men, was up early in the morning. Matthew Henry says, "the morning is perhaps as good a friend to Christians to grow in grace as it is to thoughtful and creative people to develop their natural skills."[272] God loves servants who are prompt and on time.)* ⁵ The LORD descended in the cloud and stood with him there, and proclaimed the name of the LORD. *(He declared the character and the excellence of Jehovah.)*

²⁸ So he was there with the LORD forty days and forty nights. He neither ate bread nor drank water. And he wrote on the tablets the words of the covenant, the Ten Commandments. *(In being miraculously supported for forty days without food, Moses represents the law, followed by Elijah the*

---

[269] John 3:7
[270] Psalm 119:135
[271] 2 Corinthians 3:3
[272] From Matthew Henry's Commentary on Exodus 34:4. Updated. -ed

chief of the prophets, and finally our Lord Jesus, in whom the gospel is made known.)

29 When Moses came down from Mount Sinai, with the two tablets of the testimony in his hand as he came down from the mountain, Moses did not know that the skin of his face shone because he had been talking with God.

After such long closeness with God Moses came down enriched with the best treasure and adorned with the best beauty. What he had seen was unconsciously reflected from him, as it always is from those who have had fellowship with God.

30 Aaron and all the people of Israel saw Moses, and behold, the skin of his face shone, and they were afraid to come near him.

Everybody could see the brightness of Moses' face except himself; and the same may be said of the person who lives as in the presence of God.

31 But Moses called to them, and Aaron and all the leaders of the congregation returned to him, and Moses talked with them. **32** Afterward all the people of Israel came near, and he commanded them all that the LORD had spoken with him in Mount Sinai. **33** And when Moses had finished speaking with them, he put a veil over his face. *(In this he was unlike most men, who are usually far too ready to show their brightness to everybody, wishing for admiration. True excellence does not try to draw attention to itself.)*

34 Whenever Moses went in before the LORD to speak with him, he would remove the veil, until he came out. *(Before God we must all be unveiled. All things are open before him.)* And when he came out and told the people of Israel what he was commanded, *(The only proper subject for the life and message of the Lord's ministers is what comes from the Word of God.)* **35** the people of Israel would see the face of Moses, that the skin of Moses' face was shining. And Moses would put the veil over his face again, until he went in to speak with him.

APRIL 12
He Is Altogether Desirable[273]

The apostle Paul gathers lessons from the veiled face of Moses and presents them to us in:

2 Corinthians 3:7-18

7 Now if the ministry of death, carved in letters on stone, came with such glory that the Israelites could not gaze at Moses' face because of its glory, which was being brought to an end, **8** will not the ministry of the Spirit have even more glory? *(Moses taught the letter of the law—the outward signs and details of rule and order. The gospel reveals the inner secret of the law—the heart and the spirit of truth. This is certainly more glorious than religious ceremony. Babies in understanding may be most impressed with the shallow glory that dazzles the eye, but mature adults respect most that inner light of spiritual beauty that lights up the soul.)*

9 For if there was glory in the ministry of condemnation, the ministry of righteousness must far exceed it in glory. *(The law only gives condemnation and death. How much more glorious is the gospel, that gives righteousness and life? If the judgments and decisions of a judge are viewed with respect when they sit in court, how much more admiration is there for the chariots of love and the banners of grace that adorn the procession of a beloved Prince?)* **10** Indeed, in this case, what once had glory has come to have no glory at all, because of the glory that surpasses it. *(As the moon's light fades away when the sun appears, so Moses is outshone by our Lord.)* **11** For if what was being brought to an end came with glory, much more will what is permanent have glory.

To the eyes of wisdom, things that are temporary can never shine with the same brightness as facts that are real and eternal. Sparks can never compete with stars. It is the crowning excellence of the gospel that it will never pass away. It is "an eternal gospel."[274] Bless God for this.

---

[273] Song of Solomon 5:16
[274] Revelation 14:6, "Then I saw another angel flying directly overhead, with an eternal gospel to proclaim to

Our Lord's transfiguration[275] was a visible expression of the superior glory of the gospel. Not only our Lord's face, but also his whole body glowed with an overwhelming light, that overpowered the three disciples. The glory of the gospel of grace amazes the angels, delights the perfect spirits in heaven and deserves to be the continual subject of our admiring wonder. In the gospel, God has shown us more of the glory of his nature and character than in all the rest of the world.

12 Since we have such a hope, we are very bold, **13** not like Moses, who would put a veil over his face so that the Israelites might not gaze at the outcome of what was being brought to an end. **14** But their minds were hardened. For to this day, when they read the old covenant, that same veil remains unlifted, because only through Christ is it taken away. *(The glory of the gospel, as shown by types[276] in the Old Testament, was too great for the Jews. A veil was needed to hide much of it. Now, unfortunately, the glory of the fully revealed truth has baffled them; but it is not so with us. We delight in a plain, unveiled gospel.)*

15 Yes, to this day whenever Moses is read a veil lies over their hearts. *(Or else they would clearly see Jesus revealed in their law and would accept Him as Messiah at once. A veil over the brain is bad, but a veil over the heart is worst of all.)* **16** But when one turns to the Lord, the veil is removed. *(Poor Israel will see her Messiah eventually. The veil over the heart will be removed by the Holy Spirit.)* **17** Now the Lord is the Spirit, and where the Spirit of the Lord is, there is freedom. *(The Spirit of God forbids us from standing a long way away from the Lord, because of his awesome appearance. Instead, he gives us freedom to come near to our heavenly Father in the sweet awareness of his deep love for us.)*

18 And we all, with unveiled face, beholding the glory of the Lord, are being transformed into the same image from one degree of glory to another. For this comes from the Lord who is the Spirit. *(We have been given a spiritual faith that looks into the inner truth. The truth about Jesus shines too brightly for the eyes of unbelievers and, like the sun, they cannot look at it. The Spirit of the Lord has brought us close to God, opened our defective eyes, and allowed us to see the character of the Invisible God and to share in it.)*

APRIL 13
You Are Christ's[277]
Exodus 35:4-5b; 20-29

4 Moses said to all the congregation of the people of Israel, "This is the thing that the LORD has commanded. **5a** Take from among you a contribution to the LORD. Whoever is of a generous heart, let him bring the LORD's contribution."

The Lord loves a cheerful giver.[278] He would be right to demand money from us because it really is his, but he would rather we gave because we want to give. Every Israelite indeed[279] should be a giver, because they are first a receiver.

20 Then all the congregation of the people of Israel departed from the presence of Moses.

They went off at once to get their offering. Promptness is an indication of willingness.

21 And they came, everyone whose heart stirred him, and everyone whose spirit moved him, and brought the LORD's contribution to be used for the tent of meeting, and for all its service, and for the holy garments. *(There were some who loved their gold better than their God, but the majority was generous. They gave with joy, not because they were forced to.)* **22** So they came, both men and women. All who were of a willing heart brought brooches and

---

those who dwell on earth, to every nation and tribe and language and people."
[275] *transfigure, transfiguration* - to change into another form. When the Lord was on a high mountain with Peter, James and John, "he was transfigured before them, and his face shone like the sun, and his clothes became white as light." This event is found in Matthew 17:1-8; Mark 9:2-9; and Luke 9:28-36.
[276] *type* - something or someone that represents something or someone else, usually in the future.

[277] 1 Corinthians 3:23
[278] 2 Corinthians 9:7
[279] John 1:47, "Jesus saw Nathanael coming toward him and said of him, 'Behold, an Israelite indeed, in whom there is no deceit!'" In other words, an "Israelite indeed" is a true follower of the true God.

earrings and signet rings and armlets, all sorts of gold objects, every man dedicating an offering of gold to the LORD.

This is a good example of contributing to God's work. If Christian women would throw their jewelry into God's treasury, and if godly men would present their excess of gold, there would be enough and more than enough.

23 And every one who possessed blue or purple or scarlet yarns or fine linen or goats' hair or tanned rams' skins or goatskins brought them. *(The gifts varied in value, but all were accepted alike. They were given voluntarily and accepted graciously.)* **24** Everyone who could make a contribution of silver or bronze brought it as the LORD's contribution. And every one who possessed acacia wood of any use in the work brought it. **25** And every skillful woman spun with her hands, and they all brought what they had spun in blue and purple and scarlet yarns and fine twined linen. **26** All the women whose hearts stirred them to use their skill spun the goats' hair. *(Giving labor is as good as giving money or things. The women worked with their best skill. When the needle is used for the Lord it should be the best needlework in the world.)*

27 And the leaders brought onyx stones and stones to be set, for the ephod and for the breastpiece, **28** and spices and oil for the light, and for the anointing oil, and for the fragrant incense. **29** All the men and women, the people of Israel, whose heart moved them to bring anything for the work that the LORD had commanded by Moses to be done brought it as a freewill offering to the LORD. *(Should we allow those who were under the law to give more than we who are under the gospel? No! We should far exceed them in giving to the Lord our God.)*

Paul gives inspired directions for giving to the work of God in:

2 Corinthians 9:6-8

6 The point is this: whoever sows sparingly will also reap sparingly, and whoever sows bountifully will also reap bountifully. **7** Each one must give as he has decided in his heart, not reluctantly or under compulsion, for God loves a cheerful giver. **8** And God is able to make all grace abound to you, so that having all sufficiency in all things at all times, you may abound in every good work. *(Notice the many "alls" here. Let us aim to have them all and then overflow in giving.)*

1 Corinthians 16:2

2 On the first day of every week, each of you is to put something aside and store it up, as he may prosper, so that there will be no collecting when I come. *(This is the true Christian practice: Set aside the Lord's portion each payday and then give from the Lord's money to the various works that need our help. From the oldest to the youngest, let us all be cheerful givers.)*

APRIL 14

He Has Finished Transgression

The laws the Lord gave to Moses about sacrifices are very instructive. Every detail should be given serious study. We have chosen the law about the sin offering for this reading.

Leviticus 4:1-12

1 And the LORD spoke to Moses, saying, **2** "Speak to the people of Israel, saying, If anyone sins unintentionally in any of the LORD's commandments about things not to be done, and does any one of them, **3** if it is the anointed priest who sins, thus bringing guilt on the people, then he shall offer for the sin that he has committed a bull from the herd without blemish to the LORD for a sin offering. *(The command begins with an "if;" if anyone sins or if the priest sins. Of course, it is all too certain that they do sin. It is most gracious on the Lord's part to appoint a sacrifice to deal with the situation. The victim must be without blemish or it cannot be an acceptable substitute. How well the Lord Jesus fills this requirement.)*

4 "He shall bring the bull to the entrance of the tent of meeting before the LORD and lay his hand on the head of the bull and kill the bull before the LORD. *(By faith we must acknowledge that the sacrifice is the payment for our sin. The victim must die and pour out its blood, because the blood is what satisfies God's justice.)* **5** And the anointed priest shall take some of the blood of the bull and bring it into the tent of meeting, *(The blood was clearly visible everywhere, because it is the very heart of atonement.[280])* ⁶and the priest shall dip his finger in the blood and sprinkle part of the blood seven times before the LORD in front of the veil of the sanctuary.

⁷"And the priest shall put some of the blood on the horns of the altar of fragrant incense before the LORD that is in the tent of meeting, and all the rest of the blood of the bull he shall pour out at the base of the altar of burnt offering that is at the entrance of the tent of meeting. ⁸And all the fat of the bull of the sin offering he shall remove from it the fat that covers the entrails and all the fat that is on the entrails ⁹and the two kidneys with the fat that is on them at the loins and the long lobe of the liver that he shall remove with the kidneys ¹⁰(just as these are taken from the ox of the sacrifice of the peace offerings); and the priest shall burn them on the altar of burnt offering. *(When our Lord Jesus was made sin for us, he was forsaken by God.[281] Nevertheless, he was still dear to God and therefore part of the sin offering was placed on the altar of burnt offering, where offerings of thanksgiving were placed, but not offerings for sin.)*

¹¹"But the skin of the bull and all its flesh, with its head, its legs, its entrails, and its dung— ¹²all the rest of the bull—he shall carry outside the camp to a clean place, to the ash heap, and shall burn it up on a fire of wood. On the ash heap it shall be burned up. *(The sin offering was considered unclean and must be taken "outside the camp." Even so, when Jesus was made sin for us,[282] he was made to suffer outside Jerusalem.)*

Hebrews 13:10-14

¹⁰We have an altar from which those who serve the tent *(that is, those Jews who continue to sacrifice animals)* have no right to eat. ¹¹For the bodies of those animals whose blood is brought into the holy places by the high priest as a sacrifice for sin are burned outside the camp. ¹²So Jesus also suffered outside the gate in order to sanctify the people through his own blood. *(Calvary was outside Jerusalem)* ¹³Therefore let us go to him outside the camp and bear the reproach he endured. ¹⁴For here we have no lasting city, but we seek the city that is to come. *(Our Lord, in who we trust, was set apart and covered with disgrace for our benefit. Even so, our holy faith makes us a people separated from the world. Leaving our friends and relatives behind means little. Going "outside the camp" to Jesus is what really counts. With joy we follow him "outside the camp" to the place of separation, in anticipation of living with him forever.)*

APRIL 15

The LORD Your God…Is a Jealous God[283]

Leviticus 10:1-11

¹Now Nadab and Abihu, the sons of Aaron, each took his censer and put fire in it and laid incense on it and offered unauthorized fire before the LORD, which he had not commanded them. *(These young men were self-willed and they also may have been drunk. They dared to violate the Lord's commands in his own immediate presence. They followed their own wills about the time, place and way of offering the incense. No doubt they thought these were small details, but indeed nothing is small in the service of God. He will be worshiped in his own way and not in ours. In our day some change the ordinances[284] of the Church without considering that there may be more sin involved than they think. Besides, there is one fire in the church and that is the Holy Spirit; and one incense and that is the work of Jesus. It is daring disrespect to look for other excitement or offer any other righteousness to God.)*

---

[280] *atonement* - A payment made to satisfy someone who has been wronged. An animal sacrificed as an offering to restore a relationship. Jesus is the Lamb of God and offered himself as a sacrifice to restore the relationship between God and man that was broken when Adam sinned in the Garden of Eden.
[281] Matthew 27:46, "My God, my God, why have you forsaken me?"
[282] 2 Corinthians 5:21, "For our sake [God] made [Christ] to be sin who knew no sin, so that in him we might become the righteousness of God."

[283] Deuteronomy 6:15
[284] *ordinance* - Religious rite or ceremony specified by God. Spurgeon would mean *Baptism* and *Communion*.

2 And fire came out from before the LORD and consumed them, and they died before the LORD. *(The devouring flame flashed right across the the ark of the covenant and killed them. Think about that, and remember that they were a minister's sons and ministers themselves. "The Lord your God is a consuming fire, a jealous God."[285] Nadab and Abihu died when they worshiped God their way and made offerings the way they wanted to. We fear that thousands will perish the same way. Let us be careful and prayerful and walk respectfully before the jealous God; looking only to worship him as his own Word directs.)* **3** Then Moses said to Aaron, "This is what the LORD has said, 'Among those who are near me I will be sanctified, and before all the people I will be glorified.' " And Aaron held his peace. *(All godly parents must hold their peace when they see their graceless children perish before the Lord. God is most strict with those closest to him. Let them guard themselves against resenting the Lord's actions.)*

4 And Moses called Mishael and Elzaphan, the sons of Uzziel the uncle of Aaron, and said to them, "Come near; carry your brothers away from the front of the sanctuary and out of the camp." **5** So they came near and carried them in their coats out of the camp, as Moses had said.

Everyone saw what happened and were warned. It is very sad when those who should teach holiness by their lives, only teach it when they become examples of God's anger in their deaths.

6 And Moses said to Aaron and to Eleazar and Ithamar his sons, "Do not let the hair of your heads hang loose, and do not tear your clothes, lest you die, and wrath come upon all the congregation; but let your brothers, the whole house of Israel, bewail the burning that the LORD has kindled. **7** And do not go outside the entrance of the tent of meeting, lest you die, for the anointing oil of the LORD is upon you." And they did according to the word of Moses.

The offenders' closest friends were called on to demonstrate their approval of the divine justice. Others might mourn the sin and doom of the offenders, but their family members were told to show no sign of mourning.

8 And the LORD spoke to Aaron, saying, **9** "Drink no wine or strong drink, you or your sons with you, when you go into the tent of meeting, lest you die. It shall be a statute forever throughout your generations. **10** You are to distinguish between the holy and the common, and between the unclean and the clean, **11** and you are to teach the people of Israel all the statutes that the LORD has spoken to them by Moses."

Probably because Nadab and Abihu had been drinking, all priests were forbidden from now on to drink wine during their times of service. It is a disgusting sin when a Christian minister hopes to stimulate his effectiveness by drinking wine. It is an unauthorized offering of strange fire before the Lord and will certainly be dealt with accordingly. He who serves God must be calm, sober, and not excited with any passions of the flesh. Oh for a baptism of the Holy Spirit, to free the Lord's ministers from every false excitement and make them wait on the Lord in quiet holiness.

April 16
We Have All Become Like One Who Is Unclean[286]

The dreadful disease of leprosy was so common among the Israelites that laws were made for controlling it. Rules were put in place so that those who had been cleansed of their leprosy could return to the society of Israel from which they had been excluded. Among the laws was one notable one that we will read because it is full of teaching.

Leviticus 13:12-17; 45-46

12 And if the leprous disease breaks out in the skin, so that the leprous disease covers all the skin of the diseased person from head to foot, so far as the priest can see, **13** then the priest shall look, and if the leprous disease has covered all his body, he shall pronounce him clean of the disease; it has all turned white, and he is clean.

---

[285] Deuteronomy 4:24

[286] Isaiah 64:6

This seems very strange and we cannot use space here to attempt to explain it. But we can confidently assert that when a person sees nothing else but sin in himself he is very close to salvation. The sin we do not recognize within us is far more dangerous than the sin we see and mourn over. When the sinner's wickedness is properly understood, they will come quickly to the Lord Jesus for cleansing. As long as we think there is some goodness in us, we proudly boast about it and we are in a sorry case. However, when we see that, from the sole of our foot even to our head, we are only wounds and bruises and rotting sores, then we are humbled and our cure begins.

14 But when raw flesh appears on him, he shall be unclean. **15** And the priest shall examine the raw flesh and pronounce him unclean. Raw flesh is unclean, for it is a leprous disease.

What we ignorantly value the most about our self is just what the Lord considers to be our deadliest quality.

16 But if the raw flesh recovers and turns white again, then he shall come to the priest, **17** and the priest shall examine him, and if the disease has turned white, then the priest shall pronounce the diseased person clean; he is clean. *(When they thought their disease was the worst they were really better. "The Lord sees not as man sees."[287] When the disease covered the entire body and his case seemed hopeless, he was clean. When self-righteousness is gone, when we realize there is nothing good in us,[288] then our hour of grace has arrived. If the priest found the person to be unclean, the law shut them out from the camp.)*

45 "The leprous person who has the disease shall wear torn clothes and let the hair of his head hang loose, and he shall cover his upper lip and cry out, 'Unclean, unclean.' "

He was required to wear the torn garments of sorrow. His head was uncovered as if in mourning for himself as dead. His mouth was covered as if to show he could never more have contact with others. To prevent others from coming near him and catching the dreadful disease, he had to sound the warning cry, "Unclean, unclean."

46 "He shall remain unclean as long as he has the disease. He is unclean. He shall live alone. His dwelling shall be outside the camp." *(He must live outside the camp. No one would dare approach him. He was not allowed to come near anyone. His disease was repulsive, painful, harmful, and deadly. So are sin and the sinner's condition before the Lord. They are not allowed to be in God's presence and are dead in trespasses and sins.[289] Spiritual power and holiness do not exist in them. Streams of impurity flow in their soul and make them completely abhorrent to God. The shadow of death has fallen on them. No human hand can heal them. There is no balm in Gilead.[290] There is no doctor for them. The sinner is sick to the point of death. They are far beyond all earthly help. Yet there is one who can heal with a word. He is present here, saying to each one of us, "Turn to me and be saved. For I am God, and there is no other."[291] The person who refuses this Physician deserves to die and die they must. Will it be so with any of us? Rather let each one of us put our trust in Jesus from this very hour.)*

APRIL 17

Purge Me With Hyssop, and I Shall Be Clean[292]

Leviticus 14:1-7

1 The LORD spoke to Moses, saying, **2** "This shall be the law of the leprous person for the day of his cleansing. He shall be brought to the priest, **3** and the priest shall go out of the camp, *(If the priest was busy with other duties, the leper had to wait until the priest could leave the camp and come to him, but Jesus is always ready to hear the sinner's cry. Besides, all that the priest could do was to pronounce a person ceremonially clean who was already healed, but Jesus actually*

---

[287] 1 Samuel 16:7
[288] Romans 7:18, "For I know that nothing good dwells in me, that is, in my flesh."
[289] Ephesians 2:1-2b, "You were dead in the trespasses and sins in which you once walked."
[290] A reference to Jeremiah 8:22
[291] Isaiah 45:22
[292] Psalm 51:7

heals the soul that is sick with sin.) and the priest shall look. Then, if the case of leprous disease is healed in the leprous person, ⁴ the priest shall command them to take for him who is to be cleansed two live clean birds and cedarwood and scarlet yarn and hyssop. ⁵ And the priest shall command them to kill one of the birds in an earthenware vessel over fresh water. ⁶ He shall take the live bird with the cedarwood and the scarlet yarn and the hyssop, and dip them and the live bird in the blood of the bird that was killed over the fresh water. ⁷ And he shall sprinkle it seven times on him who is to be cleansed of the leprous disease. Then he shall pronounce him clean and shall let the living bird go into the open field.

Blood and water come together as one bird is sacrificed and the other lives and is pronounced clean. This picture is completed more fully in Jesus. Blood and water flowed from his side when he was slain for us to remove our guilt and he also lives for us and becomes our righteousness. "[He] was delivered up for our trespasses, and raised for our justification."[293] *He came not by water only, but by water and blood. And we are now born of water and of the Spirit. Like the living bird, we also fly in the open field and a new song is in our mouth, even praise to our God.*

In the Gospels we meet with the cure of a leper by our Lord, in which the Jewish practice and ceremonies are referred to.

Mark 1:40-45

⁴⁰ And a leper came to him, imploring him, and kneeling said to him, "If you will, you can make me clean."

Here was enough faith to believe that Jesus could remove an incurable disease, but there was still a sad "if" in his faith, like a dead fly in the jar of lotion. In spite of that, the Lord Jesus accepted the imperfect faith and gave a perfect cure in return.

⁴¹ Moved with pity, he stretched out his hand and touched him and said to him, "I will; be clean." *(What a blessed "I will."* *Christ's will is omnipotent.*[294] *He can save us even with his wish. He can save us at this very moment.)* ⁴² And immediately the leprosy left him, and he was made clean. *(Salvation is immediate. The moment we believe in Jesus we have eternal life.)* ⁴³ And Jesus sternly charged him and sent him away at once, ⁴⁴ and said to him, "See that you say nothing to anyone, but go show yourself to the priest and offer for your cleansing what Moses commanded, for a proof to them." *(While the law was in force our Lord kept it. How much more should we obey the gospel in every point of principle and command?)*

⁴⁵ But he went out and began to talk freely about it, and to spread the news, so that Jesus could no longer openly enter a town, but was out in desolate places, and people were coming to him from every quarter. *(Jesus was humble and did not seek honor from others. But the man's gratefulness would not let him be quiet. He told his story and the news ran along like fire over a prairie. It blazed in every direction, to the praise of the Good Physician.)*

New Park Street Chapel, London
Spurgeon first preached in London on December 18, 1853, at the age of 19. The church called him as their pastor and he accepted the position on April 28, 1854, and remained the pastor until his death in 1892.

---

[293] Romans 4:25

[294] *omnipotent, omnipotence* - all powerful, almighty, absolute and supreme power, having unlimited power.

APRIL 18
Christ Bore the Sins Of Many[295]
Leviticus 16:1-10; 15-22

1 The LORD spoke to Moses after the death of the two sons of Aaron, when they drew near before the LORD and died, **2** and the LORD said to Moses, "Tell Aaron your brother not to come at any time into the Holy Place inside the veil, before the mercy seat that is on the ark, so that he may not die. For I will appear in the cloud over the mercy seat."

The death of Nadab and Abihu became the time of more instruction to Israel. We should always learn from the Lord's judgments on others. Aaron was taught that even he could only come to God as the Lord showed him the correct way to enter the Holy Place.

3 "But in this way Aaron shall come into the Holy Place: with a bull from the herd for a sin offering and a ram for a burnt offering. **4** He shall put on the holy linen coat and shall have the linen undergarment on his body, and he shall tie the linen sash around his waist, and wear the linen turban; these are the holy garments. He shall bathe his body in water and then put them on. *(He was to wear only the ordinary linen garments worn by all the priests and not the glorious robes of the high priest. His washing was meant to show his cleanness from sin. This pictures our Lord Jesus who, in making atonement for us, laid aside his glory and became like his brothers, except without sin.)* **5** And he shall take from the congregation of the people of Israel two male goats for a sin offering, and one ram for a burnt offering.

6 "Aaron shall offer the bull as a sin offering for himself and shall make atonement for himself and for his house."

See how superior our Lord is? He had no need to make an offering for himself.

7 "Then he shall take the two goats and set them before the LORD at the entrance of the tent of meeting. **8** And Aaron shall cast lots over the two goats, one lot for the LORD and the other lot for [the scapegoat].[296] **9** And Aaron shall present the goat on which the lot fell for the LORD and use it as a sin offering, **10** but the goat on which the lot fell for [the scapegoat][297] shall be presented alive before the LORD to make atonement over it, that it may be sent away into the wilderness to Azazel."[298]

The Lord Jesus, our great substitute, takes the sins of his people away into the wilderness of nonexistence.

15 "Then he shall kill the goat of the sin offering that is for the people and bring its blood inside the veil and do with its blood as he did with the blood of the bull, sprinkling it over the mercy seat and in front of the mercy seat. **16** Thus he shall make atonement for the Holy Place, because of the uncleannesses of the people of Israel and because of their transgressions, all their sins. And so he shall do for the tent of meeting, which dwells with them in the midst of their uncleannesses. **17** No one may be in the tent of meeting from the time he enters to make atonement in the Holy Place until he comes out and has made atonement for himself and for his house and for all the assembly of Israel. **18** Then he shall go out to the altar that is before the LORD and make atonement for it, and shall take some of the blood of the bull and some of the blood of the goat, and put it on the horns of the altar all around. **19** And he shall sprinkle some of the blood on it with his finger seven times, and cleanse it and consecrate it from the uncleannesses of the people of Israel. *(Do we not see here our Great High Priest, alone, without a helper, making atonement for us?)*

20 "And when he has made an end of atoning for the Holy Place and the tent of meeting and the altar, he shall present the live goat. **21** And Aaron shall lay both his hands on the head of the live goat, and confess over it all the iniquities of the people of Israel, and all their transgressions, all their sins. And he shall put them on the head of the goat and send it away into the wilderness by the hand of a man who is in readiness.

---

[295] See *Hebrews 9:28*
[296] ESV *Azazel* meaning *scapegoat* or the one to bear the blame for others and suffer in their place.
[297] ESV *Azazel (see preceding footnote)*
[298] *Azazel* can mean either the scapegoat itself or, in this case, the place in the wilderness to which the scapegoat is released.

22 The goat shall bear all their iniquities on itself to a remote area, and he shall let the goat go free in the wilderness."

The first goat showed the Savior suffering. The second goat represented the effect of that suffering in the complete removal of Israel's sin. For the one who rests in Jesus sin is gone. Gone forever.

APRIL 19

Let...Us Celebrate the Festival[299]

Today let us consider two of the holy seasons God commanded his people to observe. First, The Day of Atonement and then The Feast of Tabernacles.

Leviticus 23:26-32; 37-43

26 And the LORD spoke to Moses, saying, 27 "Now on the tenth day of this seventh month is the Day of Atonement. It shall be for you a time of holy convocation,[300] and you shall afflict yourselves and present a food offering to the LORD. *(Sorrow for sin is a blessed thing. Being sorry for sin cannot make a person righteous, but it is always part of receiving the atonement. If sin is sweet to us it will destroy us, but when our soul is distressed about it, the day of atonement has arrived.)* 28 And you shall not do any work on that very day, for it is a Day of Atonement, to make atonement for you before the LORD your God."

If sin could be removed by doing good works, the Lord would not have commanded "you shall not do any work" on the Day of Atonement. There is no thought here of working for salvation.

29 "For whoever is not afflicted on that very day shall be cut off from his people. *(There is no more certain sign of destruction, than to not have any internal pain for sin. True sorrow for sin is intense. The Jews said, "a man had never seen sorrow who had not seen the sorrow of the Day of Atonement.")* 30 And whoever does any work on that very day, that person I will destroy from among his people. 31 You shall not do any work. It is a statute forever throughout your generations in all your dwelling places. 32 It shall be to you a Sabbath of solemn rest, and you shall afflict yourselves. On the ninth day of the month beginning at evening, from evening to evening shall you keep your Sabbath."

This day of expressing sadness for sin was followed by the joyous Feast of Tabernacles. Sacred sorrow prepares the heart for holy joy. We must receive the atonement before we can enter into the joy of the Lord.

37 "These are the appointed feasts of the LORD, which you shall proclaim as times of holy convocation, for presenting to the LORD food offerings, burnt offerings and grain offerings, sacrifices and drink offerings, each on its proper day, 38 besides the LORD's Sabbaths and besides your gifts and besides all your vow offerings and besides all your freewill offerings, which you give to the LORD. *(The Spirit of God places great importance on the joy of our faith. He continues to focus our attention on it. The fruit of the Spirit is joy.)*

39 "On the fifteenth day of the seventh month, when you have gathered in the produce of the land, you shall celebrate the feast of the LORD seven days. On the first day shall be a solemn rest, and on the eighth day shall be a solemn rest."

This was a very happy time. The Jews said, "he who never saw the rejoicing of the Feast of Tabernacles, had never seen rejoicing in his life."

40 "And you shall take on the first day the fruit of splendid trees, branches of palm trees and boughs of leafy trees and willows of the brook, and you shall rejoice before the LORD your God seven days." *(Andrew Bonar says, "Imagine the scene presented to us; earth in its luxuriance during the reign of righteousness and peace and joy. 'Every splendid tree' furnishes its branches for the occasion. The palm is mentioned first because it was the tree that had most often provided them shelter in the wilderness, as at Elim."[301] Being reminded of what divine love had done for them, the people spent a happy*

---

[299] 1 Corinthians 5:8
[300] *convocation* - A large formal assembly of people, a large group gathered together.

[301] Andrew Bonar (1810-1892). A minister of the Free Church of Scotland and youngest brother of hymn writer Horatius Bonar.

week in the shade of the tree branches. They no doubt felt and said, "it is good to be here.")

⁴¹ "You shall celebrate it as a feast to the LORD for seven days in the year. It is a statute forever throughout your generations; you shall celebrate it in the seventh month. ⁴² You shall dwell in booths for seven days. All native Israelites shall dwell in booths, ⁴³ that your generations may know that I made the people of Israel dwell in booths when I brought them out of the land of Egypt: I am the LORD your God." *(Such delightful celebrations refreshed people's hearts with sunny memories. The Day of Atonement and the Feast of Tabernacles picture the loving kindness of the Lord. When the Lord's people sorrow for sin, they have their sorrow turned into joy.)*

APRIL 20
Hallowed Be Your Name³⁰²

We shall now read a short story that is very horrifying to think about. However, it is full of serious teaching for all of us. May the Holy Spirit give us grace to learn from it.

Leviticus 24:10-16; 23

¹⁰ Now an Israelite woman's son, whose father was an Egyptian, went out among the people of Israel. And the Israelite woman's son and a man of Israel fought in the camp, *(Among the people of God there are some who are not actually Christians. In their heart they are Egyptians, that is, lovers of sin, even though they act very much like true believers and freely socialize in their meetings.)* ¹¹ and the Israelite woman's son blasphemed the Name, and cursed. *(He blasphemed THE NAME. There is a name given among us that is above every name, a name at which every knee will bow,³⁰³ and misery shall be on the person who hardly even respects the name of Jesus.)* Then they brought him to Moses. His mother's name was Shelomith, the daughter of Dibri, of the tribe of Dan. *(Bad people bring shame to their mothers. May we never do that.)* ¹² And they put him in custody, till the will of the LORD should be clear to them.

It is not for us to judge unbelievers unless we have the Lord's authority from the Bible. However, statements against the name and glory of the Lord Jesus should fill us with horror and make us consider what the doom of those who speak them will be.

¹³ Then the LORD spoke to Moses, saying, ¹⁴ "Bring out of the camp the one who cursed, and let all who heard him lay their hands on his head, and let all the congregation stone him. *(No ordinary punishment could satisfy such contempt for God. The person must die. There is no other name under heaven given among men by which we must be saved,³⁰⁴ and because the offender had caused injury to the blessed name, he must be destroyed immediately. There is no other way. We would be untrue if we held out even the slightest hope of eternal life to those who despise the name of Jesus. Instead, the faithful must all lay their hands on the unbeliever's head, to show their agreement and approval of his just punishment. There is mercy in Jesus, but those who want the Lord Jesus out of their lives bring down their blood on their own heads.)* ¹⁵ And speak to the people of Israel, saying, ¹⁶ Whoever blasphemes the name of the LORD shall surely be put to death. All the congregation shall stone him. The sojourner as well as the native, when he blasphemes the Name, shall be put to death.

²³ So Moses spoke to the people of Israel, and they brought out of the camp the one who had cursed and stoned him with stones. Thus the people of Israel did as the LORD commanded Moses. *(No other end is proclaimed for a blasphemer of "the Name" except a swift and terrible death. Those awful words of the apostle that we will now quote, should sink down into every heart and move us to devoted obedience to the name of Jesus.)*

Hebrews 10:28-31

²⁸ Anyone who has set aside the law of Moses dies without mercy on the evidence of

---

³⁰² Matthew 6:9
³⁰³ Philippians 2:10-11, "At the name of Jesus every knee should bow, in heaven and on earth and under the earth, and every tongue confess that Jesus Christ is Lord, to the glory of God the Father."

³⁰⁴ Acts 4:12

two or three witnesses. ²⁹ How much worse punishment, do you think, will be deserved by the one who has trampled underfoot the Son of God, and has profaned the blood of the covenant by which he was sanctified, and has outraged the Spirit of grace? ³⁰ For we know him who said, "Vengeance is mine; I will repay." And again, "The Lord will judge his people." ³¹ It is a fearful thing to fall into the hands of the living God.

APRIL 21
The Year Of My Redeemed Has Come[305]

Leviticus 25:8-17; 25-28; 39-42

⁸ "You shall count seven weeks of years, seven times seven years, so that the time of seven weeks of years shall give you forty-nine years. ⁹ Then you shall sound the loud trumpet on the tenth day of the seventh month. On the Day of Atonement you shall sound the trumpet throughout all your land. ¹⁰ And you shall consecrate the fiftieth year, and proclaim liberty throughout the land to all its inhabitants. It shall be a jubilee for you, when each of you shall return to his property and each of you shall return to his clan. *(The preaching of the gospel is declaring a spiritual jubilee. Jesus our great High Priest has proclaimed "liberty to the captives and the opening of the prison to those who are bound."[306] Our Lord's atoning work is the true source of our holy joy. This is the time of every believer's jubilee, because every believer has been set free by Christ!)* ¹¹ "That fiftieth year shall be a jubilee for you; in it you shall neither sow nor reap what grows of itself nor gather the grapes from the undressed vine. ¹² For it is a jubilee. It shall be holy to you. You may eat the produce of the field.

¹³ "In this year of jubilee each of you shall return to his property. ¹⁴ And if you make a sale to your neighbor or buy from your neighbor, you shall not wrong one another. ¹⁵ You shall pay your neighbor according to the number of years after jubilee, and he shall sell to you according to the number of years for crops. ¹⁶ If the years are many, you shall increase the price, and if the years are few, you shall reduce the price, for it is the number of the crops that he is selling to you. ¹⁷ You shall not wrong one another, but you shall fear your God, for I am the LORD your God." *(The Jews were not to purchase property from one another. Instead, their "buying" was leasing or renting the land for however many of the forty-nine years were left until the year of jubilee. The Lord declared that the land should rest every seventh year. Therefore every seventh year was not a "years for crops," but a Sabbath year and therefore did not count in estimating the value of the property. In our buying and selling we should take great care to be fair, so we do not cause the Lord to become angry with us.)*

²⁵ "If your brother becomes poor and sells part of his property, then his nearest redeemer shall come and redeem what his brother has sold. *(Praise God. Our Lord Jesus is our closest brother who has redeemed our lost inheritance for us.)* ²⁶ If a man has no one to redeem it and then himself becomes prosperous and finds sufficient means to redeem it, ²⁷ let him calculate the years since he sold it and pay back the balance to the man to whom he sold it, and then return to his property. ²⁸ But if he has not sufficient means to recover it, then what he sold shall remain in the hand of the buyer until the year of jubilee. In the jubilee it shall be released, and he shall return to his property." *(Our lost possession is now restored to us. In fact, we have received back even more than Adam lost.)*

³⁹ "If your brother becomes poor beside you and sells himself to you, you shall not make him serve as a slave: ⁴⁰ he shall be with you as a hired servant and as a sojourner. He shall serve with you until the year of the jubilee. ⁴¹ Then he shall go out from you, he and his children with him, and go back to his own clan and return to the possession of his fathers. ⁴² For they are my servants, whom I brought out of the land of Egypt; they shall not be sold as slaves." *(The gospel jubilee has set us free and given us true liberty. Now we know the meaning of the Lord's words,*

---

[305] Isaiah 63:4 *alternate reading*
[306] Isaiah 61:1 and quoted by Jesus in Luke 4:18

"My year of redemption has come."[307] Has everyone in this house celebrated this jubilee? If not, may the Holy Spirit bring us to the point where we will.)

APRIL 22
The Righteous Shall Be Glad[308]

Numbers 10:29-36

29 And Moses said to Hobab, the son of Reuel the Midianite, Moses' father-in-law, "We are setting out for the place of which the LORD said, 'I will give it to you.' Come with us, and we will do good to you, for the LORD has promised good to Israel." *(We should talk to our friends and relatives about the advantages that can come from being associated with the people of God. It may be they will be led to join with us.)* **30** But he said to him, "I will not go. I will depart to my own land and to my kindred." **31** And he said, "Please do not leave us, for you know where we should camp in the wilderness, and you will serve as eyes for us. *(Those who are converted to the faith often become of great service to the church. This should encourage us all the more to want to see them trust in Christ.)* **32** And if you do go with us, whatever good the LORD will do to us, the same will we do to you."

The agreement was made to share and share alike. This was true friendship. Believers know that the Lord involves himself with all his servants. All who fear the name of the Lord are one family. God feeds them with the same bread of life, clothes them with the same righteousness, protects them with the same fatherly care, and brings them by the same grace to the same glory. Those who truly join with us in Christ's church will enjoy all the advantages that benefit us.

33 So they set out from the mount of the LORD three days' journey. And the ark of the covenant of the LORD went before them three days' journey, to seek out a resting place for them. **34** And the cloud of the LORD was over them by day, whenever they set out from the camp.

35 And whenever the ark set out, Moses said, "Arise, O LORD, and let your enemies be scattered, and let those who hate you flee before you." *(This is the Rising Prayer. It acknowledges that Israel's journey is troubled by enemies and it looks away from all human help to the Lord alone. The Lord has only to rise up and his enemies and ours are gone. Oh Lord, now arise!)* **36** And when it rested, he said, "Return, O LORD, to the ten thousand thousands of Israel."

This was the Resting Prayer. It pleads for God's presence. Fearing that the Lord may have been offended during the day, it begs him to return and abide with his people.[309]

Let us read a few verses of David's psalm, in which he sings of the Lord's glorious marching through the wilderness.

Psalm 68:1-8

1   God shall arise, his enemies shall be scattered;
    and those who hate him shall flee before him!
2   As smoke is driven away, so you shall drive them away;
    as wax melts before fire,
    so the wicked shall perish before God!
3   But the righteous shall be glad;
    they shall exult before God;
    they shall be jubilant with joy!

Such a God is not to be worshiped with sadness or half-heartedness. Let our joy in him be full.[310]

4   Sing to God, sing praises to his name;
    lift up a song to him who rides through the deserts;
    his name is the LORD;
    exult before him!

God is as much with us as he was with the Jews. Let us sing his praises as much as they did.

5   Father of the fatherless and protector of widows,
    is God in his holy habitation.

---

[307] Isaiah 63:4 *NASB*
[308] Psalm 68:3
[309] John 15:5b - Jesus said, "Whoever abides in me and I in him, it is that bears much fruit, for apart from me you can do nothing."
[310] John 15:11 - Jesus said, "These things I have spoken to you, that my joy may be in you, and that your joy may be full."

Therefore let his people remember the orphan and help those organizations whose mission is to benefit them. Let them also have pity for poor widows who are in God's very special care.

6 God settles the solitary in a home;
      he leads out the prisoners to prosperity,
      but the rebellious dwell in a parched land.

Gracious as God is, he cannot bless those who continue in rebellion. Sin is a source of misery and always will be.

7 O God, when you went out before your people,
      when you marched through the wilderness,   Selah
8 the earth quaked, the heavens poured down rain,
      before God, the One of Sinai,
      before God, the God of Israel.

May the God of Israel be honored forever. His presence is still our support and comfort. Our inmost hearts adore him. Lord throughout this day go before us and bless us with your presence.

APRIL 23

I Am the LORD Your God[311]

Numbers 11:4-5; 10-23

4 Now the rabble[312] that was among them had a strong craving. And the people of Israel also wept again and said, "Oh that we had meat to eat! *(Trouble in the camp usually started with the rabble. It is the same with the church of God now. Those professing Christians in the church who are Christian in name only are the kindling for Satan's matches. It is sad, however, to see that the Israelites were ready enough to follow the bad example of the mixed multitude. Their murmuring was groundless. They lacked neither bread nor water, but they wanted luxuries. Such complaining is sure to be punished.)* 5 We remember the fish we ate in Egypt that cost nothing, the cucumbers, the melons, the leeks, the onions, and the garlic."

10 Moses heard the people weeping throughout their clans, everyone at the door of his tent. And the anger of the LORD blazed hotly, and Moses was displeased. 11 Moses said to the LORD, "Why have you dealt ill with your servant? And why have I not found favor in your sight, that you lay the burden of all this people on me? 12 Did I conceive all this people? Did I give them birth, that you should say to me, 'Carry them in your bosom, as a nurse carries a nursing child,' to the land that you swore to give their fathers? 13 Where am I to get meat to give to all this people? For they weep before me and say, 'Give us meat, that we may eat.' 14 I am not able to carry all this people alone; the burden is too heavy for me. 15 If you will treat me like this, kill me at once, if I find favor in your sight, that I may not see my wretchedness."

The meekest man[313] failed in his meekness. He was so angered by the senseless demands of the people that he spoke unwisely to God. The best of men still have weaknesses. In Moses' case the Lord showed great compassion to his servant by sending him help to assist with such a great responsibility.

16 Then the LORD said to Moses, "Gather for me seventy men of the elders of Israel, whom you know to be the elders of the people and officers over them, and bring them to the tent of meeting, and let them take their stand there with you. 17 And I will come down and talk with you there. And I will take some of the Spirit that is on you and put it on them, and they shall bear the burden of the people with you, so that you may not bear it yourself alone."

The Lord overlooked Moses' childish language and met the real burden of his case. The seventy men would have been of no use without the Spirit, but with it they became valuable helpers. Oh Lord, give your Spirit to all the elders and deacons of our

---

[311] Exodus 20:2
[312] *rabble* - "a multitude consisting of Egyptians or other people, which being affected with God's miraculous works in Egypt … joined themselves to the Israelites". —*Matthew Poole*

[313] Numbers 12:3, "Now the man Moses was very meek, more than all people who were on the face of the earth."

churches, as well as to all pastors and evangelists.

18 "And say to the people, 'Consecrate yourselves for tomorrow, and you shall eat meat, for you have wept in the hearing of the LORD, saying, "Who will give us meat to eat? For it was better for us in Egypt." Therefore the LORD will give you meat, and you shall eat. 19 You shall not eat just one day, or two days, or five days, or ten days, or twenty days, 20 but a whole month, until it comes out at your nostrils and becomes loathsome to you, because you have rejected the LORD who is among you and have wept before him, saying, "Why did we come out of Egypt?"'"

Too much becomes nauseous. In God's wisdom, he gave them so much of what they wrongly desired that they became disgusted with it. In this way, the Lord often makes people sick of their darling sins.

21 But Moses said, "The people among whom I am number six hundred thousand on foot, and you have said, 'I will give them meat, that they may eat a whole month!' 22 Shall flocks and herds be slaughtered for them, and be enough for them? Or shall all the fish of the sea be gathered together for them, and be enough for them?" *(Moses began looking at second causes instead of almighty God. That led to doubting, and he even forgot another possible source for meat. He forgot the birds of heaven from which the Lord provided meat for the people.)* 23 And the LORD said to Moses, "Is the Lord's hand shortened? Now you shall see whether my word will come true for you or not." *(Our Lord is grieved when we do not believe him. Perhaps some of us are also guilty of it. Is it so? Then let us humbly bow before the rebuke of this verse, and then hopefully expect to see every promise of the Lord fulfilled, for so it shall be.)*

APRIL 24
Do Not Quench the Spirit[314]

Numbers 11:24-34

24 So Moses went out and told the people the words of the LORD. And he gathered seventy men of the elders of the people and placed them around the tent. 25 Then the LORD came down in the cloud and spoke to him, and took some of the Spirit that was on him and put it on the seventy elders. And as soon as the Spirit rested on them they prophesied. But they did not continue doing it.

See what the Lord can do! Let it encourage us to "pray earnestly to the Lord of the harvest to send out laborers into his harvest."[315] Many a Moses is overwhelmed because of a lack of helpers, but the Lord can send them all the assistance they need.

26 Now two men remained in the camp, one named Eldad, and the other named Medad, and the Spirit rested on them. They were among those registered, but they had not gone out to the tent, and so they prophesied in the camp. *(Maybe Moses and the people had not expected prophetic gifts to follow the gift of the Spirit, but only the power to govern the people. This was probably the reason for the excitement when two of the elders began to preach in parts of the camp where they had not yet heard about the prophesying at the tabernacle.)* 27 And a young man ran and told Moses, "Eldad and Medad are prophesying in the camp." 28 And Joshua the son of Nun, the assistant of Moses from his youth, said, "My lord Moses, stop them."

Jealousy for his master's honor moved Joshua to try stopping the unusual ministry of Eldad and Medad. There are still many today who are zealous to stop those who "dare" to preach, but have not attended the "right" school or been ordained by the "right" church.

29 But Moses said to him, "Are you jealous for my sake? Would that all the LORD's people were prophets, that the LORD would put his Spirit on them!" *(Moses did not have a selfish spirit. If the men were really moved by the Spirit of God, he had no desire to stop their unusual method. Far from it; he wished that all the Lord's servants had the same gifts and graces. Irregular ministries have been the means of the salvation of thousands,*

---

[314] 1 Thessalonians 5:19

[315] Matthew 9:38

and therefore we rejoice, and will continue to rejoice when they bear fruit.) ³⁰ And Moses and the elders of Israel returned to the camp.

³¹ Then a wind from the LORD sprang up, and it brought quail from the sea and let them fall beside the camp, about a day's journey on this side and a day's journey on the other side, around the camp, and about two cubits *(or three feet)* above the ground. ³² And the people rose all that day and all night and all the next day, and gathered the quail. Those who gathered least gathered ten homers *(or almost 600 gallons)*. And they spread them out for themselves all around the camp.

They feasted without fear even though they had been told that evil would come of it. They no doubt stuffed themselves and then worked hard to come up with a way to preserve what remained; as if they thought they would never have such a great supply again. Greediness is its own plague and brings other evils with it.

³³ While the meat was yet between their teeth, before it was consumed, the anger of the LORD was kindled against the people, and the LORD struck down the people with a very great plague.

These gluttons dug their grave with their teeth. Many die by eating or drinking too much. The sins of drunkenness and gluttony devour their thousands. God punished one sin by another. Those who complained because they wanted meat, received, as a penalty, death while eating the meat they had longed for.

³⁴ Therefore the name of that place was called Kibroth-hattaavah *(or, graves of craving)*, because there they buried the people who had the craving. *(Shocking sins can be reminders for us. They serve to warn us not to become resentful and greedy. May the Lord make us thankful for His mercies and save us from fleshly lusts.)*

APRIL 25

Love Does Not Envy[316]

Numbers 12:1-15

¹ Miriam and Aaron spoke against Moses because of the Cushite woman whom he had married, for he had married a Cushite woman. *(They complained because they were jealous of Moses' power. Moses was a good man; so good that even those who knew him best could find no fault with him. The only complaint they could come up with was that he had married a woman who was not an Israelite. And the only thing they could accuse her of was that she was a foreigner, an Ethiopian.)* ² And they said, "Has the LORD indeed spoken only through Moses? Has he not spoken through us also?" And the LORD heard it. *(Moses must have been hurt by the jealousy of his brother and sister, but he did not fight his own battle. He left the matter to God, who disapproved of the cruel bitterness of Moses' ungrateful siblings.)*

³ Now the man Moses was very meek, more than all people who were on the face of the earth. *(Some other writer has inserted this verse under divine direction. Moses would not have said it of himself, but the Lord took care that somebody else would record it. God honors those who honor him. Moses was meek and so he did not fight to protect his own reputation. Therefore the Lord fought for him.)*

⁴ And suddenly the LORD said to Moses and to Aaron and Miriam, "Come out, you three, to the tent of meeting." And the three of them came out. *(The suddenness of the Lord's action shows the importance of the matter, as well as the Lord's anger about it.)* ⁵ And the LORD came down in a pillar of cloud and stood at the entrance of the tent and called Aaron and Miriam, and they both came forward. ⁶ And he said, "Hear my words: If there is a prophet among you, I the LORD make myself known to him in a vision; I speak with him in a dream. ⁷ Not so with my servant Moses. He is faithful in all my house. ⁸ With him I speak mouth to mouth, clearly, and not in riddles, and he beholds the form of the LORD. Why then were you not

---

[316] 1 Corinthians 13:4

afraid to speak against my servant Moses?" (*Aaron had been wrong about the golden calf; therefore he ought to have been very quiet. As a woman Miriam would be expected to keep her opinion to herself. Yet, envy pushed both of these good people into a bad spirit and then into a wrong and sinful position. Above all things, let us avoid envy, for "jealousy is fierce as the grave."[317] If God chooses to make others greater and more honored than ourselves, what right do we have to question his right to do so?*) ⁹ And the anger of the LORD was kindled against them, and he departed. (*This was the surest sign of his anger. God's presence is heaven to his children and his absence is misery.*)

¹⁰ When the cloud removed from over the tent, behold, Miriam was leprous, like snow. And Aaron turned toward Miriam, and behold, she was leprous.

If Aaron had been made a leper he could not have performed his office of high priest. Miriam's disease was a punishment for both of them and possibly she had also been the leading offender.

¹¹ And Aaron said to Moses, "Oh, my lord, do not punish us because we have done foolishly and have sinned. ¹² Let her not be as one dead, whose flesh is half eaten away when he comes out of his mother's womb." ¹³ And Moses cried to the LORD, "O God, please heal her—please."

Miriam wounded Moses with her tongue and now Moses uses his tongue to cry, "O God, please heal her." This is the true way to heap coals of fire on the heads of those who injure us.[318] We must pray for those who abuse us.[319]

¹⁴ But the LORD said to Moses, "If her father had but spit in her face, should she not be shamed seven days? Let her be shut outside the camp seven days, and after that she may be brought in again." (*In ancient eastern culture, when a child provoked their father, the father would spit in his child's face and then the child was forbidden to be in the father's presence for seven days. How much more then should Miriam be shut out of the camp for a while when she had so grossly offended the Lord. Miriam's leprosy was a terrible mark of God's displeasure.*) ¹⁵ So Miriam was shut outside the camp seven days, and the people did not set out on the march till Miriam was brought in again. (*This showed their respect for her and their grief for her disease.*)

APRIL 26
We Walk By Faith, Not By Sight[320]
Numbers 13:1-2; 17-21; 23-33

¹ The LORD spoke to Moses, saying, ² "Send men to spy out the land of Canaan, which I am giving to the people of Israel. (*The Lord permitted Moses to send spies because of the hardness of the people's hearts. It would have been far better for them to have believed the Word of the Lord and followed the pillar of cloud. How foolish of them to want to spy out the land that the Lord had already spied out for them a long time ago.*) From each tribe of their fathers you shall send a man, every one a chief among them."

¹⁷ Moses sent them to spy out the land of Canaan and said to them, "Go up into the Negeb and go up into the hill country, ¹⁸ and see what the land is, and whether the people who dwell in it are strong or weak, whether they are few or many, ¹⁹ and whether the land that they dwell in is good or bad, and whether the cities that they dwell in are camps or strongholds, ²⁰ and whether the land is rich or poor, and whether there are trees in it or not. Be of good courage and bring some of the fruit of the land." Now the time was the season of the first ripe grapes.

²¹ So they went up and spied out the land from the wilderness of Zin to Rehob, near Lebo-hamath.

---

[317] Song of Solomon 8:6. "Jealousy…swallows up and devours all." —*Matthew Henry*
[318] A reference to Proverbs 25:22 and quoted by Paul in Romans 12:20. Some believe "heaping coals of fire" on an enemy's head was a figure of speech for taking vengeance. Others think it refers to the ancient kindness of giving live coals to your enemy which he carried home in a jar on his head to start a fire in his home for cooking and warmth. Spurgeon evidently intends the second meaning. See his comments on Romans 12:20 (Year Two, October 4).
[319] Luke 6:28
[320] 2 Corinthians 5:7

23 And they came to the Valley of Eshcol (Eshcol means cluster) and cut down from there a branch with a single cluster of grapes, and they carried it on a pole between two of them; they also brought some pomegranates and figs.

They brought back positive proof that the country was excellent for producing wonderful crops. This huge cluster of grapes is like the holy comforts that Christians enjoy even in this world. They are also promises of the joys of heaven.

24 That place was called the Valley of Eshcol, because of the cluster that the people of Israel cut down from there.

25 At the end of forty days they returned from spying out the land. *(Every day of spying cost Israel a year of wandering in the wilderness. The apostle Paul says "we walk by faith, not by sight." Walking by sight is expensive work.)* **26** And they came to Moses and Aaron and to all the congregation of the people of Israel in the wilderness of Paran, at Kadesh. They brought back word to them and to all the congregation, and showed them the fruit of the land. **27** And they told him, "We came to the land to which you sent us. It flows with milk and honey, and this is its fruit. **28** However, the people who dwell in the land are strong, and the cities are fortified and very large. And besides, we saw the descendants of Anak there. **29** The Amalekites dwell in the land of Negeb. The Hittites, the Jebusites, and Amorites dwell in the hill country. And the Canaanites dwell by the sea, and along the Jordan." *(The report of sight was completely discouraging. How much better it would have been for Israel if they had walked by faith! These spies took careful note of everything that could discourage their hearts, but they either left out, or misunderstood many things that should have made them hopeful. If we decide to leave the road of faith, we are sure to have a hard time of it.)*

30 But Caleb quieted the people before Moses and said, "Let us go up at once and occupy it, for we are well able to overcome it." **31** Then the men who had gone up with him said, "We are not able to go up against the people, for they are stronger than we are." **32** So they brought to the people of Israel a bad report of the land that they had spied out, saying, "The land, through which we have gone to spy it out, is a land that devours its inhabitants, and all the people that we saw in it are of great height. **33** And there we saw the Nephilim (the sons of Anak, who come from the Nephilim,), and we seemed to ourselves like grasshoppers, and so we seemed to them." *(If they had only believed their God, these things would not have made any difference! Had he not struck down the Egyptians? Caleb and Joshua had faith and therefore they had courage. But unbelief is cowardly. Oh, for grace to trust in the Lord. If we place our trust in God instead of people, our lives will grow great and good before the Lord.)*

This is a depiction of Exeter Hall in the Strand (reproduced on a 1905 postcard). "The main auditorium could hold more than 4,000 people." Spurgeon often preached here on Sunday evenings during 1855 and 1856.

APRIL 27

Have Faith In God[321]

Numbers 14:1-21

1 Then all the congregation raised a loud cry, and the people wept that night. *(When children cry for no reason, they soon have a good reason for crying. And that was what happened in this case. Have we not also sinned in very much the same way?)* **2** And all the people of Israel grumbled against Moses and Aaron. The whole congregation said to them, "Would that we had died in the land of Egypt! Or would that we had died in this

---
[321] Mark 11:22

wilderness! ³ Why is the LORD bringing us into this land, to fall by the sword? Our wives and our little ones will become a prey. Would it not be better for us to go back to Egypt?"

They asked whether God had brought them out of Egypt to kill them. They should have been ashamed to insult Jehovah like that! Truly we are just as guilty if we think that God has led us so far on the road to heaven only to allow our enemies to be victorious over us.

⁴ And they said to one another, "Let us choose a leader and go back to Egypt."

To avoid one evil they talk about rushing into a worse one. They chatter about going back to Egypt, but they would not have the cloud to guide them or the manna to feed them. Unbelief is insanity.

⁵ Then Moses and Aaron fell on their faces before all the assembly of the congregation of the people of Israel.

The people should have been the ones falling on their faces before Moses and Aaron. The best of people are very often the ones talked about as being the worst.

⁶ And Joshua the son of Nun and Caleb the son of Jephunneh, who were among those who had spied out the land, tore their clothes ⁷ and said to all the congregation of the people of Israel, "The land, which we passed through to spy it out, is an exceeding good land. ⁸ If the LORD delights in us, he will bring us into this land and give it to us, a land that flows with milk and honey. ⁹ Only do not rebel against the LORD. And do not fear the people of the land, for they are bread for us. Their protection is removed from them, and the LORD is with us; do not fear them." ¹⁰ Then all the congregation said to stone them with stones. *(Joshua and Caleb argued their case very well, but the people were about to reward their faithfulness by stoning them to death.)* But the glory of the LORD appeared at the tent of meeting to all the people of Israel. *(God appeared for the defense of his servants. Anyone who touches them, touches the apple of God's eye.[322])*

¹¹ And the LORD said to Moses, "How long will this people despise me? And how long will they not believe in me, in spite of all the signs that I have done among them? ¹² I will strike them with pestilence and disinherit them, and I will make of you a nation greater and mightier than they." *(This was a great offer, but how lovingly Moses turned it down. He was thinking more of Israel's good and of God's glory than of his own honor.)*

¹³ But Moses said to the LORD, "Then the Egyptians will hear of it, for you brought up this people in your might from among them, ¹⁴ and they will tell the inhabitants of this land. They have heard that you, O LORD, are in the midst of this people. For you, O LORD, are seen face to face, and your cloud stands over them and you go before them, in a pillar of cloud by day and in a pillar of fire by night. ¹⁵ Now if you kill this people as one man, then the nations who have heard your fame will say, ¹⁶ 'It is because the LORD was not able to bring this people into the land that he swore to give to them that he has killed them in the wilderness.' ¹⁷ And now, please let the power of the Lord be great as you have promised, saying, ¹⁸ 'The LORD is slow to anger and abounding in steadfast love, forgiving iniquity and transgression, but he will by no means clear the guilty, visiting the iniquity of the fathers on the children, to the third and fourth generation.' ¹⁹ Please pardon the iniquity of this people according to the greatness of your steadfast love, just as you have forgiven this people, from Egypt until now."

²⁰ Then the LORD said, "I have pardoned, according to your word. ²¹ But indeed, as I live, all the earth will be filled with the glory of the LORD.[323] *(Do you see the value of having someone standing between you and the anger of God? Praise God; if anyone*

---

[322] *apple of his eye* is used in Psalm 17:8 and Deuteronomy 32:10. It means *something or someone very precious or dear.*
[323] Verse 21 is taken from the New American Standard Version. The ESV reads, "But truly, as I live, and as all the earth shall be filled with the glory of the LORD,"

does sin, we have an advocate with the Father, Jesus Christ the righteous.[324])

APRIL 28

The Lord Knows Those Who are His[325]

Let us read a passage in the book of Revelation, that will keep us thinking about the twelve tribes whose story we have been considering for so long.

Revelation 7:1-10

¹ After this I saw four angels standing at the four corners of the earth, holding back the four winds of the earth, that no wind might blow on earth or sea or against any tree. *(The most unpredictable powers of nature are under God's control. God's angels have even the most powerful and destructive forces on earth thoroughly under control, as though they were horses controlled by bit and bridle. God has many servants. Therefore no part of the universe will suffer because there are no agents to protect it. No matter where we are, God's holy bodyguard is with us.)*

² Then I saw another angel ascending from the rising of the sun, with the seal of the living God, and he called with a loud voice to the four angels who had been given power to harm earth and sea, ³ saying, "Do not harm the earth or the sea or the trees, until we have sealed the servants of our God on their foreheads." *(Not a ripple disturbed the waters, not a leaf moved on the trees, until God allowed the winds to blow. Evils have no power until the Lord lets them loose. No child of God needs to be afraid of the terrible years to come. No destruction can come until all the Lord's Noahs are safely in his ark.)* ⁴ And I heard the number of the sealed, 144,000, sealed from every tribe of the sons of Israel: *(It is a large number to indicate a great multitude. It is an exact and complete number to represent everyone that God placed in his Church.)*

⁵ 12,000 from the tribe of Judah were sealed,

The royal tribe of Judah takes its place at the front. Otherwise its royalty would mean nothing.

12,000 from the tribe of Reuben,

Unsteady, but yet kept by God. It is not our faithfulness to God, but his faithfulness to us that saves us.

12,000 from the tribe of Gad,

Even though defeated by many trials, they overcome in the end.

⁶ 12,000 from the tribe of Asher,

He was given some of the richest soil in Israel in this life and glory in eternity.

12,000 from the tribe of Naphtali,

He gave generous words,[326] *and now enjoys a generous inheritance.*

12,000 from the tribe of Manasseh,

Manasseh was given a double portion on earth and yet he still has his portion in heaven.

⁷ 12,000 from the tribe of Simeon,

Levi and Simeon were cursed by their father for their sin, yet the tribes contain some of the elect.

12,000 from the tribe of Levi,

Levi was the tribe of priests. Now all believers are priests before God.

12,000 from the tribe of Issachar,

He was too fond of ease, but still redeemed.

⁸ 12,000 from the tribe of Zebulun,

The sea-dwelling people. Thank God for converted sailors.

12,000 from the tribe of Joseph,

Archers shot at him,[327] *but his full number is saved.*

12,000 from the tribe of Benjamin were sealed.

Last and least in Israel, yet not forgotten by electing love.

These make up the Jewish believers. The elect among the Gentiles are mentioned next.

⁹ After this I looked, and behold, a great multitude that no one could number, from

---

[324] 1 John 2:1
[325] 2 Timothy 2:19

[326] Genesis 49:21, "Naphtali is a doe let loose. He gives beautiful [or generous] words." NASB
[327] A reference to Genesis 49:23

every nation, from all tribes and people and languages, standing before the throne and before the Lamb, clothed in white robes, with palm branches in their hands, **10** and crying out with a loud voice, "Salvation belongs to our God who sits on the throne, and to the Lamb!" *(We join this heavenly song with heart and voice. All glory be to Jesus our Lord. Happy was John to hear the eternal unity of the saints in heaven singing their praise to the Lamb of God. We will hear them in heaven in the future, but even now we send up our joyful praise to increase their volume.)*

APRIL 29

Sin When It Is Fully Grown Brings Forth Death[328]

Numbers 14:26-32; 36-45

26 And the LORD spoke to Moses and to Aaron, saying, **27** "How long shall this wicked congregation grumble against me? I have heard the grumblings of the people of Israel, which they grumble against me. **28** Say to them, 'As I live, declares the LORD, what you have said in my hearing I will do to you: *(It is a horrible thing when the Lord takes people at their word and says, "so be it" to their wicked talking. They said that they were brought out to die in the wilderness and the Lord tells them that they will die. It was at this time that the Lord swore in his anger that they would not enter into his rest.[329])* **29** your dead bodies shall fall in this wilderness, and of all your number, listed in the census from twenty years old and upward, who have grumbled against me, **30** not one shall come into the land where I swore that I would make you dwell, except Caleb the son Jephunneh and Joshua the son of Nun. *(God will not forget the innocent. Even if there are only two who are not guilty, God will not include them in his act of judgment.)* **31** "But your little ones, who you said would become a prey, I will bring in, and they shall know the land that you have rejected. **32** But as for you, your dead bodies shall fall in this wilderness." *(God uses words of contempt when speaking of these grumbling people. Again and again their bodies are called "dead bodies," as if they were no better than animals. Sin makes people disgusting.)*

36 And the men whom Moses sent to spy out the land, who returned and made all the congregation grumble against him by bringing up a bad report about the land— **37** the men who brought up a bad report of the land—died by plague before the LORD. **38** Of those men who went to spy out the land, only Joshua the son of Nun and Caleb the son of Jephunneh remained alive. *(The ten spies had been the cause of all this evil and they were rightly brought to an end immediately. It was also proof that the Lord would be as good as his word to the rest of that evil generation.)*

39 When Moses told these words to all the people of Israel, the people mourned greatly. **40** And they rose early in the morning and went up to the heights of the hill country, saying, "Here we are. We will go up to the place that the LORD has promised, for we have sinned." *(Like the pendulum of a grandfather clock that swings from one side to the other, they went from one form of sin to its opposite.)* **41** But Moses said, "Why now are you transgressing the command of the LORD, when that will not succeed? **42** Do not go up, for the Lord is not among you, lest you be struck down before your enemies. **43** For there the Amalekites and the Canaanites are facing you, and you shall fall by the sword. Because you have turned back from following the LORD, the LORD will not be with you."

It is dangerous, even deadly, to go where God will not go with us.

44 But they presumed to go up to the heights of the hill country, although neither the ark of the covenant of the LORD nor Moses departed out of the camp. **45** Then the Amalekites and the Canaanites who lived in that hill country came down and defeated them and pursued them, even to Hormah.

Nothing is difficult when the Lord's power is with us, but to enter into any service without the help of God is foolishness. It can

---

[328] James 1:15
[329] Psalm 95:11, "Therefore I swore in my wrath, 'They shall not enter my rest.'"

only end in defeat. Those who try to fight their own way to heaven, will, like these Jews, find that the enemies of their souls are too many for them. Acting as if something is true when it is not is just as dangerous as no action when something is true. Action and inaction are often companions. They seem to go back and forth in the souls of unbelievers like the heat of summer and the cold of winter. May the Lord deliver us from both.

APRIL 30

He Remembers That We Are Dust[330]

This psalm is the record of Moses' emotions when he saw the people dying in the wilderness. It should not be read as an entirely accurate picture of the feelings of godly people. The death of godly people is not a judgment of God's wrath, but a falling asleep in God's arms. They leave this present evil world to be where Jesus is.

Psalm 90

A Prayer of Moses, the Man of God.

1 Lord, you have been our dwelling place
in all generations.

In every age God is the home of his people. Keep this sweet thought in mind. Moses and the Israelites lived in tents like their fathers before them, but God was still their real home.

2 Before the mountains were brought forth,
or ever you had formed the earth and
the world,
from everlasting to everlasting you are
God.

Men die, but God lives forever. Even if nature itself should die, God does not change.

3 You return man to dust
and say, "Return, O children of man!"

One word from God is enough. When he gives the order, the spirits of people return to him.

4 For a thousand years in your sight
are but as yesterday when it is past,
or as a watch in the night.

What are the centuries compared to eternity? Comparing a drop of water to the ocean makes more sense than comparing time to the life of the Eternal One.

5 You sweep them away as with a flood;
they are like a dream,
like grass that is renewed in the
morning:
6 in the morning it flourishes and is
renewed;
in the evening it fades and withers.

People live and thrive and die and decay. They are as weak as the grass in the field. Where are all the people who lived before us? You cannot find them any more than you can find people who have not even been born yet! Like the grass that grew when Jacob fed his flocks, the people of the past have disappeared.

7 For we are brought to an end by your
anger;
by your wrath we are dismayed.

Remember that Moses was speaking about this group of Israelites in the wilderness; not about us today. We enjoy Jehovah's love, but Israel in the wilderness melted away before the Lord's hot displeasure.

8 You have set our iniquities before you,
our secret sins in the light of your
presence.

Glory to God. As believers, our sins are pardoned and put behind the Lord's back. But it was not so with that generation. This verse can only be applied to the ungodly now. Are there any such in this household?

9 For all our days pass away under your
wrath;
we bring our years to an end like a sigh.

Our days are passed in peace, because the Lord has given us rest. But as for Israel in the desert it was sadly the very opposite. The curse of God rested on them like it does with the ungodly today.

10 The years of our life are seventy,
or even by reason of strength eighty;
yet their span is but toil and trouble;
they are soon gone, and we fly away.

Old age brings sorrow and pain. Do not have your heart set on living to an extreme old age. However, if it does come, remember that God has given it to you. Otherwise, growing older will be a burden to you.

---

[330] Psalm 103:14

ⁱ¹ Who considers the power of your anger,
　　and your wrath according to the fear of you?

May we never know the power of God's anger. The fear of it is awful, but the reality of God's anger is more than we can imagine.

¹² So teach us to number our days
　　that we may get a heart of wisdom.
¹³ Return, O LORD! How long?
　　Have pity on your servants!

That is, be merciful to us whose days are numbered.

¹⁴ Satisfy us in the morning with your steadfast love,
　　that we may rejoice and be glad all our days.
¹⁵ Make us glad for as many days as you have afflicted us,
　　and for as many years as we have seen evil.

Lord, give us mercy equal to our sorrows. Give a joy for every sadness.

¹⁶ Let your work be shown to your servants,
　　and your glorious power to their children.

They should cheerfully accept the hard job of living in the wilderness, because their children would have the joys of the promised land. In the same way, we gladly accept the burden and heat of the day, and are even ready to die, as long as God's church continues in the world.

¹⁷ Let the favor of the Lord our God be upon us,
　　and establish the work of our hands upon us;
　　yes, establish the work of our hands!

Moses spent most of his lifetime working long and hard to build up the nation of Israel. He is prayerfully concerned that his work might be for nothing. His prayers were answered. A great nation was established, and its mission has been accomplished, even to this day. Servants of God, do not be afraid. Even though you fear that your life's work may be swept away by your death, true service for the Lord will outlast the pyramids.

MAY 1
Abstain From Every Form of Evil[331]
Deuteronomy 14:1-21

¹ "You are the sons of the LORD your God. You shall not cut yourselves or make any baldness on your foreheads for the dead. ² For you are a people holy to the LORD your God, and the LORD has chosen you to be a people for his treasured possession, out of all the peoples who are on the face of the earth."

See how the Lord honored Israel. He spoke of their election, "The LORD has chosen you;" of their adoption, "you are a people holy to the LORD your God;" and of their sanctification, "the LORD has chosen you to be a people for his treasured possession." These honors involved responsibilities. They were to continue to be different than other people who did not worship the true God. They were not to imitate the superstition of their neighbors by disfiguring themselves or by any act that showed uncontrolled grief.

³ "You shall not eat any abomination. *(Anything that is obviously disgusting and repulsive.)*

⁴ "These are the animals you may eat: the ox, the sheep, the goat, ⁵ the deer, the gazelle, the roebuck, the wild goat, the ibex,[332] the antelope, and the mountain sheep. ⁶ Every animal that parts the hoof and has the hoof cloven in two and chews the cud, among the animals, you may eat. ⁷ Yet of those that chew the cud or have the hoof cloven you shall not eat these: the camel, the hare, and the rock badger, because they chew the cud but do not part the hoof, are unclean for you."

These may seem like tiny little differences, but God takes note of littles.

⁸ "And the pig, because it parts the hoof but does not chew the cud, is unclean for you. Their flesh you shall not eat, and their carcasses you shall not touch. *(God gave these rules to keep the Jews a separate and special people. They could not join in the feasts of the heathen because one or more of these unclean creatures would be brought to*

---

[331] 1 Thessalonians 5:22
[332] *ibex* - a wild goat with very long horns that curve backwards

the table. Also, the thoughtful Israelite would see these unclean animals around him every day and be reminded of sin. No matter whether he was working or traveling or resting, the watchful Jew would see these animals that represented uncleanness and would be reminded of his need to watch against sin.)

9 "Of all that are in the waters you may eat these: whatever has fins and scales you may eat. **10** And whatever does not have fins and scales you shall not eat; it is unclean for you."

Even when they relaxed by the river or sailed on the sea, the Lord gave them reminders that sin was in the world. No matter where we are, our faith will be tested and God requires us to obey him.

11 "You may eat all clean birds. **12** But these are the ones that you shall not eat: the eagle, the bearded vulture, the black vulture, **13** the kite, the falcon of any kind; **14** every raven of any kind; **15** the ostrich, the nighthawk, the sea gull, the hawk of any kind; **16** the little owl and the short-eared owl, the barn owl **17** and the tawny owl, the carrion vulture and the cormorant, **18** the stork, the heron of any kind; the hoopoe and the bat.[333] **19** And all winged insects are unclean for you; they shall not be eaten. **20** All clean winged things you may eat."

Like the water, the air also had its warnings; its things to stay away from. The danger of being trapped by sin is everywhere. On the land, on the sea, and in the air, there are evils all around. There are snares everywhere.

> *Snares tuck your bed, and snares sit in your home;*
> *Snares watch your thoughts, and snares stick to your words;*
> *Snares in your quiet, snares in your commotion;*
> *Snares in your diet, snares in your devotion.*[334]

21 "You shall not eat anything that has died naturally. You may give it to the sojourner who is within your towns, that he may eat it, or you may sell it to a foreigner. For you are a people holy to the LORD your God. *(An animal that died naturally was ceremonially unclean because the blood had not been properly drained. They might, however, sell it if foreigners cared to eat it. God requires his people to be stricter than others. Entertainment and practices that might be accepted by most people would be out of place for Christians.)*

"You shall not boil a young goat in its mother's milk." *(It is unnatural to make the mother give her milk for the cooking of her own young. God's people are to do nothing that would spoil the quality and tenderness of their sensitive feelings. We are to be overly careful in not doing anything rough, savage or insensitive. Young people— please keep this in mind.)*

MAY 2
Let Us Not Become Conceited[335]
Numbers 16:1-4; 16-24; 26-34

1 Now Korah the son of Izhar, son of Kohath, son of Levi, and Dathan and Abiram the sons of Eliab, and On the son of Peleth, sons of Reuben, took men. **2** And they rose up before Moses, with a number of the people of Israel, 250 chiefs of the congregation, chosen from the assembly, well-known men. **3** They assembled themselves together against Moses and against Aaron and said to them, "You have gone too far! For all in the congregation are holy, every one of them, and the LORD is among them. Why then do you exalt yourselves above the assembly of the LORD?" *(The only thing Moses gained from being the leader of Israel was hardship and trouble. And now there were traitors in the camp who wanted to create a rebellion against him.)* **4** When Moses heard it, he fell on his face.

16 And Moses said to Korah, "Be present, you and all your company, before the LORD, you and they, and Aaron, tomorrow. **17** And

---
[333] ESV translators note: The identity of many of these birds is uncertain.
[334] Philip Quarles (a poet/theologian who lived during the 1600's).
[335] Galatians 5:26

let every one of you take his censer[336] and put incense[337] on it, and every one of you bring before the LORD his censer, 250 censers; you also, and Aaron, each his censer." *(In this way, Moses informs the rebels that God himself will decide who the authorized priests and leaders really are.)* ¹⁸ So every man took his censer and put fire in them and laid incense on them and stood at the entrance of the tent of meeting with Moses and Aaron. ¹⁹ Then Korah assembled all the congregation against them at the entrance of the tent of meeting. And the glory of the LORD appeared to all the congregation.

²⁰ And the LORD spoke to Moses and to Aaron, saying, ²¹ "Separate yourselves from among this congregation, that I may consume them in a moment." ²² And they fell on their faces and said, "O God, the God of the spirits of all flesh, shall one man sin, and will you be angry with all the congregation?" *(They were instantly ready to plead for the congregation! They did not hold a grudge or seek revenge!)* ²³ And the LORD spoke to Moses, saying, ²⁴ "Say to the congregation, Get away from the dwelling of Korah, Dathan, and Abiram." *(If we want to escape from the doom of the wicked, we must flee from their company.)*

²⁶ And he spoke to the congregation, saying, "Depart, please, from the tents of these wicked men, and touch nothing of theirs, lest you be swept away with all their sins." ²⁷ So they got away from the dwelling of Korah, Dathan, and Abiram. And Dathan and Abiram came out and stood at the door of their tents, together with their wives, their sons, and their little ones. ²⁸ And Moses said, "Hereby you shall know that the LORD has sent me to do all these works, and that it has not been of my own accord. ²⁹ If these men die as all men die, or if they are visited by the fate of all mankind, then the LORD has not sent me. ³⁰ But if the LORD creates something new, and the ground opens its mouth and swallows them up with all that belongs to them, and they go down alive into Sheol, then you shall know that these men have despised the LORD."

³¹ And as soon as he had finished speaking all these words, the ground under them split apart. ³² And the earth opened its mouth and swallowed them up, with their households and all the people who belonged to Korah and all their goods. ³³ So they and all that belonged to them went down alive into Sheol, and the earth closed over them, and they perished from the midst of the assembly. ³⁴ And all Israel who were around them fled at their cry, for they said, "Lest the earth swallow us up!"

The Lord showed his approval of his servants in a very terrible but righteous way. How much more will he uphold the throne of his Son? "Kiss the Son, lest he be angry, and you perish in the way, for his wrath is quickly kindled."[338]

MAY 3
Oh, Guard My Soul, and Deliver Me![339]
Numbers 16:41-50

⁴¹ But on the next day all the congregation of the people of Israel grumbled against Moses and against Aaron, saying, "You have killed the people of the LORD."

What amazing boldness! Yesterday they fled in fear when they saw the earth open and swallow up those who had defied the Lord. And now they, themselves, rise up in revolt, and charge Moses with murdering those whom the Lord himself had so justly executed. Is there any limit to human sin? Lions and tigers may be tamed, but humans refuse to be controlled. They follow their own plans, despite every warning and direction from God.

⁴² And when the congregation had assembled against Moses and against Aaron, they turned toward the tent of meeting. And behold, the cloud covered it, and the glory of the LORD appeared. ⁴³ And Moses and Aaron came to the front of the tent of meeting, ⁴⁴ and the LORD spoke to Moses, saying, ⁴⁵ "Get away from the midst of this congregation, that I may consume them in a

---

[336] a *censer* is a container for burning incense
[337] *incense* - something that is burned for the sweet smell it produces

[338] Psalm 2:12
[339] Psalm 25:20

moment." And they fell on their faces. *(This was the second time that the Lord had spoken this way to his servants. And for a second time they fall on their faces in reverent but heartfelt prayer. Moses and Aaron pleaded for those very people who were up in arms against then. This is the true love of God's ministers. They will never give up on sinners while they have breath in their bodies.)*

46 And Moses said to Aaron, "Take your censer, and put fire on it from off the altar and lay incense on it and carry it quickly to the congregation and make atonement for them, for wrath has gone out from the LORD; the plague has begun." *(Moses' spiritual soul could see what others could not. He was aware that danger was near. Those who have close fellowship with God are sensitive to what he will do in a way that others cannot know. Moses told Aaron to hurry. When people are dying, we must not delay our efforts to save them. Lord, help us to fly on the wings of love.)*

47 So Aaron took it as Moses said and ran into the midst of the assembly. And behold, the plague had already begun among the people. And he put on the incense and made atonement for the people. **48** And he stood between the dead and the living, and the plague was stopped. *(Aaron stood as a champion, blocking the pathway of the destroyer. He came to the front of the danger, as though he would either die with the people, or else if he lived, they should live. Was it not both brave and kind of Aaron to do this for his enemies? What an excellent picture he was of the Lord Jesus, who stood between us and the God who would destroy us for our sin!)* **49** Now those who died in the plague were 14,700, besides those who died in the affair of Korah.

Who killed all these grumblers? Or rather, what killed them? Was it not sin that is a murderer from the beginning? Sin will kill us also unless we keep behind our great High Priest who protects us.

50 And Aaron returned to Moses at the entrance of the tent of meeting, when the plague was stopped. *(There was a terrible plague of judgment. Then there was a wonderful miracle of mercy. Both were connected with Aaron's priesthood. After this, one would think that no one would ever argue that Aaron was the right person to hold the holy office of high priest. Yet that was not the case. Sinners are determined to be troublemakers. Sin is deeply rooted in our very nature. Alas! alas!)*

We should, by faith, see our Lord Jesus standing between his living people and dead souls, waving his censer, and keeping off death from all his believing ones. He is our shield from the destroying plague of sin and from all the powers of evil. His sacred person blocks the way. God's anger cannot attack those who are protected by the Lord's Anointed. Happy are those who have Jesus to stand in front of them. On one side all is ruin. On the other all is safety. On which side of Jesus are we at this hour? Are we with those who live in him, or are we with those who are outside of Christ and are therefore condemned already?[340] *Lord save us, or we perish.*

MAY 4

I Have Exalted One Chosen From the People[341]

The question about who should be priests did not stop with the plague we read about in the sixteenth chapter of Numbers. Therefore the Lord ordered a grand solution to end the debate once and for all. It would be a final test that no one could object to.

Numbers 17:1-13

1 And the LORD spoke to Moses, saying, **2** "Speak to the people of Israel, and get from them staffs, one for each fathers' house, from all their chiefs according to their fathers' houses, twelve staffs. Write each man's name on his staff, *(Staffs were the symbol of authority; much like a king with his scepter. To surrender the staff of each tribe to the Lord was a ceremony that acknowledged that the Lord had the right to choose the priestly family. All the staffs were dead and dry, and*

---

[340] John 3:18, "Whoever believes in [the Son] is not condemned, but whoever does not believe is condemned already, because he has not believed in the name of the only Son of God."
[341] Psalm 89:19

it was up to the Lord to choose which one he pleased and give it new life.) ³ and write Aaron's name on the staff of Levi. For there shall be one staff for the head of each fathers' house."

The Levites had not forgotten the destruction of Korah. Therefore they all agreed that Aaron should represent their tribe in this test.

⁴ "Then you shall deposit them in the tent of meeting before the testimony, where I meet with you. ⁵ And the staff of the man whom I choose shall sprout. Thus I will make to cease from me the grumblings of the people of Israel, which they grumble against you." *(God has a right to choose his own servants and he will do so whether we will agree with his decision or not. He gives life and fruitfulness to his chosen servants. God also has a right to deal with those who find fault or are jealous about his decisions. He will visit the murmurers one way or another for their offense.)* ⁶ Moses spoke to the people of Israel. And all their chiefs gave him staffs, one for each chief, according to their fathers' houses, twelve staffs. And the staff of Aaron was among their staffs. ⁷ And Moses deposited the staffs before the LORD in the tent of the testimony.

⁸ On the next day Moses went into the tent of the testimony, and behold, the staff of Aaron for the house of Levi had sprouted and put forth buds and produced blossoms, and it bore ripe almonds. *(A miracle indeed! Here was not only life, but it was instant and had perfect fruitfulness. This was not caused by the seasons of springtime and harvest, but happened suddenly by the divine power! Surely this is the best proof of a divine call to the Lord's work. The natural person is dead regarding the things of God, but the grace of God makes his servants fruitful before God because they spend time in his secret presence. In this way they are known among the Lord's people as his chosen servants.)*

⁹ Then Moses brought out all the staffs from before the LORD to all the people of Israel. And they looked, and each man took his staff. ¹⁰ And the Lord said to Moses, "Put back the staff of Aaron before the testimony, to be kept as a sign for the rebels, that you may make an end of their grumblings against me, lest they die." *(This miraculous proof was meant to stop future quarreling. Otherwise they might not stop until they caused God to deal with them even more severely.)* ¹¹ Thus did Moses; as the LORD commanded him, so he did. *(Moses was a wise man, but he did not allow his own opinions to influence him. His wisdom was in his complete obedience to God.)*

¹² And the people of Israel said to Moses, "Behold, we perish, we are undone, we are all undone. ¹³ Everyone who comes near, who comes near to the tabernacle of the LORD, shall die. Are we all to perish?" *(They could not go very long without some wicked complaint or another. This time they make light of their sin. They behaved very rudely and complained because God commanded them to control themselves and stop grumbling. They should have known that they were the problem and not God. It is very hard to bring Israel, or actually any of us, to true repentance.)*

From this passage of scripture, let us learn that Jesus is our great High Priest. True life comes from him and our souls are saved from that life. That is why Jesus is the true priest of God. If we want true life, we must be joined together with him. If we want our lives to be fruitful and truly useful, we must be joined together with him. If Jesus Christ and his life are not in us, our lives are like dried up branches that are worth nothing more than to be thrown into the fire.

MAY 5

I the LORD Your God Am a Jealous God[342]

Numbers 20:1-13

¹ And the people of Israel, the whole congregation, came into the wilderness of Zin in the first month, and the people stayed in Kadesh. And Miriam died there and was buried there. *(This was a time of great sadness for Moses. Miriam was a virtuous woman, a true princess and prophetess. Her only fault recorded in the Bible was when she and her brother Aaron were jealous of*

---
[342] Exodus 20:5

their brother Moses. No doubt Moses sorrowed greatly under this loss.)

² Now there was no water for the congregation. And they assembled themselves together against Moses and against Aaron. ³ And the people quarreled with Moses and said, "Would that we had perished when our brothers perished before the LORD!"

They should have been in fear and awe of that terrible judgment. But instead, they evidently blamed the destruction of Korah and his companions on Moses. Even while the two holy brothers were sorrowing over their departed sister, the unfeeling crowd raises an uproar against them. They blame the lack of water on them, as if they could be expected to dig rivers in the desert.

⁴ "Why have you brought the assembly of the LORD into this wilderness, that we should die here, both we and our cattle? ⁵ And why have you made us come up out of Egypt to bring us to this evil place? It is no place for grain or figs or vines or pomegranates, and there is no water to drink." *(They tormented Moses with the old, worn out claim that he brought them out to die in the wilderness. They also added a new sting. They accused him of not bringing them into the good land of promise, even though it was only their own sin that kept them out of it. People who want to grumble never go very long before they find another hook on which to hang their complaints.)*

⁶ Then Moses and Aaron went from the presence of the assembly to the entrance of the tent of meeting and fell on their faces. And the glory of the LORD appeared to them, *(These holy men knew where their great strength was. They fell down in prayer and adoration, leaving the matter with the Lord, who was not slow in appearing for them.)* ⁷ and the LORD spoke to Moses, saying, ⁸ "Take the staff, and assemble the congregation, you and Aaron your brother, and tell the rock before their eyes to yield its water. So you shall bring water out of the rock for them and give drink to the congregation and their cattle." *(To show that the Lord is not limited to any one way of doing something, the rock is not to be struck this time, but only spoken to.)* ⁹ And Moses took the staff from before the LORD, as he commanded him.

¹⁰ Then Moses and Aaron gathered the assembly together before the rock, and he said to them, "Hear now, you rebels: shall we bring water for you out of this rock?" ¹¹ And Moses lifted up his hand and struck the rock with his staff twice, and water came out abundantly, and the congregation drank, and their livestock.

Were they not wrong in calling the people rebels and in saying, "Shall we bring water for you?" Certainly Moses was wrong in striking the rock, because he was only told to speak to it. The best of men are men at best.

¹² And the LORD said to Moses and Aaron, "Because you did not believe in me, to uphold me as holy in the eyes of the people of Israel, therefore you shall not bring this assembly into the land that I have given them."

See how much the Lord wants those he loves the most to be those who follow him most closely? He wants them to obey him in every single thing. If they do not, he will let them know how sharply he disapproves. A whole life of serving God will not be an excuse for us to do one big thing wrong. "What sort of people ought you to be?"[343] We should be careful in thought, and word, and deed. That goes double for being careful about the sin of not believing God!

¹³ These are the waters of Meribah *(or quarreling)*, where the people of Israel quarreled with the LORD, and through them he showed himself holy.

This was one of the most unforgettable of Israel's sins, because they repeated an old crime, even after experiencing the Lord's mercies and judgments. May the Lord save us from repeating our sins. Otherwise he may show us his displeasure in a very painful way. Keep us, dear Savior, so that we will not rebel against you.

---

[343] 2 Peter 3:11

Susannah Thompson first heard Spurgeon preach at the New Park Street Chapel very soon after he came to London. Spurgeon baptized her on February 1, 1855. They were married on January 8, 1856.

MAY 6

Sing Aloud To God Our Strength[344]

Psalm 81

This song encourages people to praise the Lord. It tells of his goodness to Israel and cries over the sins and the sorrow that resulted from their misbehavior.

1   Sing aloud to God our strength;
      shout for joy to the God of Jacob!

Singing should be lively and joyful. We should all take our part in thanking God together.

2   Raise a song; sound the tambourine,
      the sweet lyre with the harp.
3   Blow the trumpet at the new moon,
      at the full moon, on our feast day.

This "feast day" was The Passover.

4   For it is a statute for Israel,
      a rule of the God of Jacob.
5   He made it a decree in Joseph
      when he went out over the land of
        Egypt.
    I hear a language I had not known:

The Egyptian language was unknown to the Lord in the sense that Egypt had no fellowship with the true God. In much the same way, we read in the New Testament that the Lord will say to the hypocrite, "I never knew you."[345] The first Passover was kept in Egypt to celebrate Israel's redemption from slavery. The sons of Israel delighted to continue celebrating that freedom.

6   "I relieved your shoulder of the burden;
      your hands were freed from the basket.

That is, from the baskets in which they carried the bricks. God set his people free from the slavish business of brick making, as he has also redeemed all his people from the accursed slavery of their sins.

7   "In distress you called, and I delivered
        you;
      I answered you in the secret place of
        thunder;
      I tested you at the waters of Meribah."
    Selah

They did poorly in that test. Their murmurings were both extreme and loud, and their going back and forth from worshiping God to defying him was obvious. Yet see how, when the Lord was tested by the people, he proved ready to hear them and quick to bless them.

8   "Hear, O my people, while I admonish
        you!
      O Israel, if you would but listen to me!
9   There shall be no strange god among you;
      you shall not bow down to a foreign
        god.
10 I am the LORD your God,
      who brought you up out of the land of
        Egypt.
      Open your mouth wide, and I will fill
        it."

We are told here to expect great things from God and offer great prayers to him. We will be pleased with the large answers God gives to our large prayers. Who would not ask largely if they believed that God would grant their large requests? God has not set a limit on his promise to hear our prayers. If our answers to our prayers are little, it is

---

[344] Psalm 81:1

[345] Matthew 7:23

because our prayers are little. Come then, let those of us who are believers, beg God for the salvation of the whole family, our relatives and our neighbors. Let our prayers today be very great. People sin hugely. Let us pray hugely.

11 "But my people did not listen to my voice;
  Israel would not submit to me.
12 So I gave them over to their stubborn hearts,
  to follow their own counsels.
13 Oh, that my people would listen to me,
  that Israel would walk in my ways!"

See the loving tenderness of the Lord. He grieves over our sins because he sees what they cost us. He knows what we lose by our foolishness and he is sorry for us. He does not condemn us with the cold tearless eye of a judge, but as a father who scolds with a loving sadness in his heart.

14 "I would soon subdue their enemies
  and turn my hand against their foes."

When God sees his people walking carefully in the "way of obedience," he either changes the hearts of our enemies or makes them turn their angry steps away from us. "When a man's ways please the LORD, he makes even his enemies to be at peace with him."[346]

15 "Those who hate the LORD would cringe toward him,
  and their fate would last forever.
16 But he would feed you with the finest of the wheat,
  and with honey from the rock I would satisfy you."

May our family walk continually in obedience to the Lord. By doing so, we will feed on the precious promises that are "the finest of the wheat." May we enjoy a close fellowship with Jesus that gives a sweet peace. Holiness is happiness. Therefore, obeying God is true wisdom. We shall have no enemies to fear if we live close to our friend Jesus.

MAY 7
Turn To Me and Be Saved[347]
Numbers 21:4-8

4 From Mount Hor they set out by the way to the Red Sea, to go around the land of Edom. And the people became impatient on the way.

At mount Hor, Moses had seen his brother Aaron die, and now, all alone, he has to again deal with the quarreling people. Yet he was not alone. His God was with him. The people were getting tired of living in tents and of the bother of always moving, but they forgot their many mercies. They forgot the great deliverances that the Lord had made for them. Being anxious, bellyaching, and complaining are very easy, but they are also ungrateful, unholy, and useless habits.

5 And the people spoke against God and against Moses, "Why have you brought us up out of Egypt to die in the wilderness? For there is no food and no water, and we loathe this worthless food."

How tiring it is to read these same worn out complaints! It is always the same old and cruel false statements against God. But each time there is more sin in it, because it is committed against a longer experience of the divine faithfulness. Discontent is a very unhappy thing. It protests against the bread of heaven and despises the crystal clear water leaping from the rock.

6 Then the LORD sent fiery serpents among the people, and they bit the people, so that many people of Israel died. *(They acted like serpents in hissing at Moses and now serpents are sent to punish them. God has many ways of scolding sinners. He who made Moses' staff a serpent,[348] can also use a serpent as his rod to strike Israel. He will sting those who sting his servants.)* 7 And the people came to Moses and said, "We have sinned, for we have spoken against the LORD and against you. Pray to the LORD, that he

---
[346] Proverbs 16:7

[347] Isaiah 45:22
[348] Exodus 4:2-3, "The LORD said to [Moses], 'What is that in your hand?' He said, 'A staff.' And he said, 'Throw it on the ground.' So he threw it on the ground, and it became a serpent, and Moses ran from it." See also Exodus 7:10.

take away the serpents from us." So Moses prayed for the people.

See and admire the meekness of Moses. He prays at once for the annoying people who had been so shamefully lying about him. They had only to say, "Pray," and Moses prayed. Oh! for the same holy readiness to return good for evil.

8 And the LORD said to Moses, "Make a fiery serpent and set it on a pole, and everyone who is bitten, when he sees it, shall live."

The cure was like what some would call a homeopathic approach. It was "like curing like." The cure for the disease is found in the very thing causing the ailment. Moses lifted up the serpent that healed the trouble caused by a serpent. Death came by man sinning. The resurrection from the dead came from the man who did not sin. The serpent on the pole was, as it were, executed by hanging on a tree. The living Christ became the Crucified One, who was made a curse for us. A look was demanded of all who were bitten. There was one command for rich and poor alike. They must all look, and look in one direction, for no other remedy was provided. It was the duty of Moses to lift up the serpent, but he could not do more, he had no magic power in his own person to heal the wounded. Even so, ministers are to preach Christ Jesus to us, but they cannot save us. They are as weak as other men in such matters. Our Lord applied this incident to himself. We will read his words in:

John 3:14-17

14 "And as Moses lifted up the serpent in the wilderness, so must the Son of Man be lifted up, **15** that whoever believes in him may have eternal life.

16 "For God so loved the world, that he gave his only Son, that whoever believes in him should not perish but have eternal life. **17** For God did not send his son into the world to condemn the world, but in order that the world might be saved through him."

We have only to look to Jesus. Whoever we are, we will be immediately delivered from all our sins. One glance of faith brings salvation right now. This gospel is for all mankind. No one born of woman should hesitate to trust their soul's eternal interests to the hands of the Son of God. Whoever trusts him is and shall be saved.

MAY 8

We Are More Than Conquerors[349]

The defeat of Sihon and Og took place about this time. Here Moses tells the story of what happened.

Deuteronomy 2:26-37

26 "So I sent messengers from the wilderness of Kedemoth to Sihon the king of Heshbon, with words of peace, saying, **27** 'Let me pass through your land. I will go only by the road; I will turn aside neither to the right nor to the left. **28** You shall sell me food for money, that I may eat, and give me water for money, that I may drink. Only let me pass through on foot, **29** as the sons of Esau who live in Seir and the Moabites who live in Ar did for me, until I go over the Jordan into the land that the LORD our God is giving to us.'"

Nothing could be more fair or friendly than this request. Sihon also had good evidence that Israel would act in good faith. The Edomites and Moabites had granted Moses and the Israelites passage through their land, and even though some were against it, their country and people were not hurt by allowing them to pass through their land. Therefore King Sihon should have been at ease believing that Israel would do him no harm.

30 "But Sihon the king of Heshbon would not let us pass by him, for the LORD your God hardened his spirit and made his heart obstinate, that he might give him into your hand, as he is this day. *(When people are mad with sin they only need to be left to themselves and they become hardened against God. Such hardened hearts become their own executioners.)* **31** And the LORD said to me, 'Behold, I have begun to give Sihon and his land over to you. Begin to take possession, that you may occupy his land.' **32** Then Sihon came out against us, he and all his people, to battle at Jahaz. **33** And the

---

[349] Romans 8:37

LORD our God gave him over to us, and we defeated him and his sons and all his people. ³⁴ And we captured all his cities at that time and devoted to destruction every city, men, women, and children. We left no survivors. ³⁵ Only the livestock we took as spoil for ourselves, with the plunder of the cities that we captured. *(God could no longer tolerate the sins of this guilty nation and swept it away. How gracious is he to our sinful country!)*

³⁶ "From Aroer, which is on the edge of the Valley of the Arnon, and from the city that is in the valley, as far as Gilead, there was not a city too high for us. The LORD our God gave all into our hands. ³⁷ Only to the land of the sons of Ammon you did not draw near, that is, to all the banks of the river Jabbok and the cities of the hill country, whatever the LORD our God had forbidden us." *(If we go only where God directs us, and keep away from where he gives us no permission to be, our journey will be a great success.)*

Deuteronomy 3:1-5

¹ "Then we turned and went up the way to Bashan. And Og the king of Bashan came out against us, he and all his people to battle at Edrei. *(One battle is over and another begins. Blessed be God, the power that defeated Sihon is also quite able to overthrow Og.)* ² But the LORD said to me, 'Do not fear him, for I have given him and all his people and his land into your hand. And you shall do to him as you did to Sihon the king of the Amorites, who lived at Heshbon.' *(God's mercies in the past are assurances of his coming favors. He who helped us yesterday is the same today and forever.)* ³ So the LORD our God gave into our hand Og also, the king of Bashan, and all his people, and we struck him down until he had no survivor left. ⁴ And we took all his cities at that time—there was not a city that we did not take from them—sixty cities, the whole region of Argob, the kingdom of Og in Bashan. ⁵ All these were cities fortified with high walls, gates, and bars, besides very many unwalled villages." *(In this way God's chosen people will go from victory to victory. Sin, death, and hell, will flee before us. No one will be able to resist the divine power that surrounds us in the battle. When the Lord leads the army, the enemy's crushing defeat is certain and complete.)*

MAY 9

No Weapon That is Fashioned Against You Shall Succeed[350]

Numbers 22:1-20

¹ Then the people of Israel set out and camped in the plains of Moab beyond the Jordan at Jericho. ² And Balak the son of Zippor saw all that Israel had done to the Amorites. ³ And Moab was in great dread of the people, because they were many. Moab was overcome with fear of the people of Israel.

The Moabites should have rejoiced because the Amorites had been their great enemies and Israel had defeated them. But men who are determined to oppose God's servants are so irrational that they do not recognize God's obvious mercy to them.

⁴ And Moab said to the elders of Midian, "This horde will now lick up all that is around us, as the ox licks up the grass of the field." So Balak the son of Zippor who was king of Moab at that time, ⁵ sent messengers to Balaam the son of Beor at Pethor, which is near the River in the land of the people of Amaw, to call him, saying, "Behold, a people has come out of Egypt. They cover the face of the earth, and they are dwelling opposite me. ⁶ Come now, curse this people for me, since they are too mighty for me. Perhaps I shall be able to defeat them and drive them from the land, for I know that he whom you bless is blessed, and he whom you curse is cursed."

Moab hated Israel, but did not begin with an open attack. Israel has many dishonest and sneaky enemies, but God will defeat their underhanded plans.

⁷ So the elders of Moab and the elders of Midian departed with fees for divination in their hand. And they came to Balaam and gave him Balak's message. ⁸ And he said to them, "Lodge here tonight, and I will bring back word to you, as the LORD speaks to

---
[350] Isaiah 54:17

me." So the princes of Moab stayed with Balaam. ⁹ And God came to Balaam and said, "Who are these men with you?" *(Balaam was probably surprised beyond measure that God should actually come to him. He had been a mere magician, but now for a while he was filled with the true spirit of prophecy.)*

¹⁰ And Balaam said to God, "Balak the son of Zippor, king of Moab, has sent to me, saying, ¹¹ 'Behold, a people has come out of Egypt, and it covers the face of the earth. Now come, curse them for me. Perhaps I shall be able to fight against them and drive them out.'" ¹² God said to Balaam, "You shall not go with them. You shall not curse the people, for they are blessed." *(What an opportunity for Balaam. The Lord told him about a blessed people. If he had been blessed with grace as well as with the prophetic gift, this was his chance to join with them.)* ¹³ So Balaam rose in the morning and said to the princes of Balak, "Go to your own land, for the LORD has refused to let me go with you." *(So far so good. Balaam is obedient because he was afraid of God, but will he hold on?)* ¹⁴ So the princes of Moab rose and went to Balak and said, "Balaam refuses to come with us."

¹⁵ Once again Balak sent princes, more in number and more honorable than these. ¹⁶ And they came to Balaam and said to him, "Thus says Balak the son Zippor: 'Let nothing hinder you from coming to me, ¹⁷ for I will surely do you great honor and whatever you say to me I will do. Come, curse this people for me.'" *(Balak tempts Balaam with larger bribes. What will the prophet do now?)* ¹⁸ But Balaam answered and said to the servants of Balak, "Though Balak were to give me his house full of silver and gold, I could not go beyond the command of the LORD my God to do less or more. ¹⁹ So you, too, please stay here tonight, that I may know what more the LORD will say to me." ²⁰ And God came to Balaam at night and said to him, "If the men have come to call you, rise, go with them; but only do what I tell you."

Balaam wanted to go with the princes, because he loved the honor and money he would receive by being unrighteous. God gave him permission to go if the princes come again and pressure him, but not permission to curse Israel. We shall see in our next reading how his evil heart broke this friendly relationship he had with God. He was a great man, a well educated man, and for a while even a supernaturally gifted man. But a grain of grace would have been of more value to him than all this, and because he lacked it he perished miserably. Oh Lord, give us grace rather than great wealth and the most exceptional talents.

MAY 10
Guard Against All Covetousness[351]
Numbers 22:21-35

²¹ So Balaam rose in the morning and saddled his donkey and went with the princes of Moab. *(It does not seem that the princes pressured him to go. Rather, it appears they started off before him. They were evidently already on their way before the angel met Balaam. A covetous person does not need tempting. They are ready to go wherever greed will take them.)*

²² But God's anger was kindled because he went, and the angel of the LORD took his stand in the way as his adversary. *(Balaam knew he could not curse Israel, but by going along with the princes he showed he was willing to try. God had good reason to be angry about such an evil purpose.)* Now he was riding on the donkey, and his two servants were with him. ²³ And the donkey saw the angel of the LORD standing in the road, with a drawn sword in his hand. *(Why are people so proud of seeing visions since this poor animal saw an angel and saw it before a prophet did?)* And the donkey turned aside out of the road and went into the field. And Balaam struck the donkey, to turn her into the road. *(Even a dumb donkey shows respect for the angel of God. What does that make those who sneer at anything that is holy?)*

²⁴ Then the angel of the LORD stood in a narrow path between the vineyards, with a wall on either side. ²⁵ And when the donkey

---
[351] Luke 12:15

saw the angel of the LORD, she pushed against the wall and pressed Balaam's foot against the wall. So he struck her again. ²⁶ Then the angel of the LORD went ahead and stood in a narrow place, where there was no way to turn either to the right or to the left. ²⁷ When the donkey saw the angel of the LORD, she lay down under Balaam. And Balaam's anger was kindled, and he struck the donkey with his staff. ²⁸ Then the LORD opened the mouth of the donkey, and she said to Balaam, "What have I done to you, that you have struck me these three times?" ²⁹ And Balaam said to the donkey, "Because you have made a fool of me. I wish I had a sword in my hand, for then I would kill you."

Balaam did not seem to be either surprised or alarmed. He was familiar with supernatural wonders; besides that, he was so involved with the one idea of getting Balak's reward that he did not fear and he did not care. Greed for gold hardens people's hearts beyond all thought of consequences. This passion also created the monster Judas Iscariot and others of his kind.

³⁰ And the donkey said to Balaam, "Am I not your donkey, on which you have ridden all your life long to this day? Is it my habit to treat you this way?" And he said, "No."

The best comment on this is to be found in Peter's Second Epistle; "He was rebuked for his own transgression; a speechless donkey spoke with human voice and restrained the prophet's madness."³⁵² Going with the Moabites, in the hope that he would be rewarded for trying to do what he knew was against God's will, was totally insane. Even a dumb animal had more sense than Balaam did. It was only right that he should be rebuked in this way.

³¹ Then the LORD opened the eyes of Balaam, and he saw the angel of the LORD standing in the way, with his drawn sword in his hand. And he bowed down and fell on his face. ³² And the angel of the LORD said to him, "Why have you struck your donkey these three times? Behold, I have come out to oppose you because your way is perverse (or reckless) before me. ³³ The donkey saw me and turned aside before me these three times. If she had not turned aside from me, surely just now I would have killed you and let her live." *(God takes notice of cruelty to animals. The angel takes issue with Balaam for being cruel to his donkey.)* ³⁴ Then Balaam said to the angel of the LORD, "I have sinned, for I did not know that you stood in the road against me. Now therefore, if it is evil in your sight, I will turn back."

He backs down under pressure, but his hearts goes after profit.

³⁵ And the angel of the LORD said to Balaam, "Go with the men, but speak only the word that I tell you." So Balaam went on with the princes of Balak. *(He knew what was right, but he still desired to win the rewards of doing wrong. He opposed God as much as he dared.)*

MAY 11

There Is No Enchantment Against Jacob³⁵³

Balak was very anxious to have Balaam curse Israel. He took him from place to place and offered one sacrifice after another, but it was all for nothing. The Lord stood between his people and the schemings of their enemies. We will read the inspired record of one of Balaam's prophetic speeches. They are all so much alike that one will be enough to understand what was happening.

Numbers 23:13-24

¹³ And Balak said to him, "Please come with me to another place, from which you may see them. You shall see only a fraction of them and shall not see them all. Then curse them for me from there."

King Balak thought that Israel's great number, or their beauty, or the way their soldiers were positioned might have caused Balaam to be afraid to curse them. Therefore, this time he would let him see only a part of them. Of course his trick did not work, because God does not love his people because there are so many of them. If

---

³⁵² 2 Peter 2:16

³⁵³ Numbers 23:23

there were only two or three he would still be sure to bless them.[354]

14 And he took him to the field of Zophim, to the top of Pisgah, and built seven altars and offered a bull and a ram on each altar. *(Moses and Balaam both stood on the same hill, but for very different reasons. The Lord brought Moses up to see the Promised Land. Balak took Balaam up to curse the nation that was to live in the Promised Land. Where we are does not change who we are.)* **15** Balaam said to Balak, "Stand here beside your burnt offering, while I meet the LORD over there." **16** And the LORD met Balaam and put a word in his mouth and said, "Return to Balak, and thus shall you speak." **17** And he came to him, and behold he was standing beside his burnt offering, and the princes of Moab with him. And Balak said to him, "What has the LORD spoken?" *(This is a question we should all ask and then search the Scriptures to find the answer.)* **18** And Balaam took up his discourse and said,

"Rise, Balak, and hear;
　give ear to me, O son of Zippor:
19 God is not man, that he should lie,
　or a son of man, that he should change his mind.
Has he said, and will he not do it?
　Or has he spoken, and will he not fulfill it?"

God's guidance does not change and that is why the saints know they are safe. Our enemies can ask God to curse us all they want, but they will not move the heart of God. We are his chosen people and we always will be! "For all the promises of God find their Yes in [Christ Jesus]."[355] Not a single word of the Lord will ever fall to the ground. Humans are as unstable as quicksand, but the Lord is as firm as a rock.

20 "Behold, I received a command to bless:
　he has blessed, and I cannot revoke it."

No, nor can all the demons in hell stop God from blessing. The promise is not yes and no, but yes, yes.

21 "He has not beheld misfortune in Jacob,
　nor has he seen trouble in Israel.
The LORD their God is with them,
　and the shout of a king is among them."

With these words, Balaam tells Balak that Israel is pure in the Lord's eyes. He knew nothing but sin could separate God from Israel and he saw that by some means or other the Lord had not seen wickedness in his people. Of course, we know why he did not. A Mediator had come between God and the Israelites. Otherwise, Israel's sins would have destroyed her a long time before this. Compared with the wicked Moabites and especially the filthy Canaanites, the people in the wilderness were no doubt remarkably pure in Balaam's judgment. However, if they had to rely on their own righteousness, it would have gone very badly for them.

22 "God brings them out of Egypt
　and is for them like the horns of the wild ox.
23 For there is no enchantment against Jacob,
　no divination against Israel;"

No evil plan of humans or demons can succeed against the elect of God. We have no reason to be afraid of evil threats. In fact, it would be sinful to do so. It is wrong to fear the superstitions of unsaved people. No magical arts, Satanic devices, or spiteful plans can really injure those whom the Lord loves.

"now it shall be said of Jacob and Israel,
　'What has God wrought!'"

God's work will always overcome human accomplishments. It will cause thoughtful people to praise God long after the evil intentions of those who want to hurt God's elect have been forgotten.

24 "Behold, a people! As a lioness it rises up
　and as a lion it lifts itself;
it does not lie down until it has devoured the prey
　and drunk the blood of the slain."

Balaam predicted the military skill that Israel would have and prophesied the destruction of the Canaanites. Even though he was supposed to curse the Israelites, he actually blessed them.

---

[354] Matthew 18:20, Jesus said, "For where two or three are gathered in my name, there am I among them."
[355] 2 Corinthians 1:20

MAY 12
The LORD Is Slow To Anger[356]

We find a summary of the history of the tribes of Israel up to this time in:

Psalm 106:13-33

13 But they soon forgot his works;
    they did not wait for his counsel.

After seeing the wonders of the Red Sea and other displays of divine power, Israel quickly forgot them all. Sinners have short memories.

14 But they had a wanton craving in the wilderness,
    and put God to the test in the desert;
15 he gave them what they asked,
    but sent a wasting disease among them.
16 When men in the camp were jealous of Moses
    and Aaron, the holy one of the LORD,
17 the earth opened and swallowed up Dathan,
    and covered the company of Abiram.
18 Fire also broke out in their company;
    the flame burned up the wicked.
19 They made a calf in Horeb
    and worshiped a metal image.
20 They exchanged the glory of God
    for the image of an ox that eats grass.
21 They forgot God, their Savior,
    who had done great things in Egypt,
22 wondrous work in the land of Ham,
    and awesome deeds by the Red Sea.
23 Therefore he said he would destroy them—
    had not Moses, his chosen one,
    stood in the breach before him,
        to turn away his wrath from destroying them.
24 Then they despised the pleasant land,
    having no faith in his promise.
25 They murmured in their tents,
    and did not obey the voice of the LORD.

It was a great sin on their part that they spoke of the inheritance that the Lord promised them as though it did not really exist, or was impossible to be won, or was not worth all of the struggles they had to go through to reach it. We must not be careless in thinking about our eternal rest in heaven. Otherwise we become lazy in our efforts to reach our Promised Land.

26 Therefore he raised his hand and swore to them
    that he would make them fall in the wilderness,
27 and would make their offspring fall among the nations,
    scattering them among the lands.
28 Then they yoked themselves to the Baal of Peor,
    and ate sacrifices offered to the dead;

Although Balaam was unable to curse Israel, he did his worst to harm them. He believed that only sin could rob Israel of Jehovah's protection, so he advised Balak to persuade the people to join in the immoral festivals they held in honor of Baal of Peor. Balak followed this advice, which was both clever and horrible. The Moabites became very friendly toward the Israelites. Their women captivated the men of Israel and they joined them in their dances and other wild parties that were part of their worship of the Moabite idol. This fiendish plan of Balaam caused the Israelites to act in very wicked ways and this caused the Lord to become very angry with them.

29 they provoked the LORD to anger with their deeds,
    and a plague broke out among them.

This plague killed 24,000 people. It did not stop until the Lord had finished his judgment against those who had chosen to honor the Moabite idols.

30 Then Phinehas stood up and intervened,
    and the plague was stayed.

Phinehas showed a holy zeal for God. A bold blasphemer was daring enough to pollute the camp of Israel with his sin and Phinehas eliminated him. Zeal for God, and anger against sin are highly acceptable to the Lord. One single individual knew what needed to be done and did it and because of him the plague was withdrawn. This teaches us the great value of holy and committed spirits in the church.

31 And that was counted to him as righteousness

---
[356] Numbers 14:18

from generation to generation forever.
³² They angered him at the waters of Meribah,
and it went ill with Moses on their account,
³³ for they made his spirit bitter,
and he spoke rashly with his lips.

Moses was the meekest man on the earth[357] *and even he spoke in anger. We have no perfect example except the Lord Jesus. He was never provoked and never spoke unadvisedly. May we be of the same mind as he was. "The anger of man does not produce the righteousness that God requires."*[358] *May we be delivered from getting angry, no matter how much we may be annoyed or irritated.*

MAY 13
Keep Your Soul Diligently[359]

Let us pay close attention to a part of Moses' last message to the people he had ruled so lovingly.

Deuteronomy 4:9-20; 23-24

⁹ "Only take care, and keep your soul diligently, lest you forget the things that your eyes have seen, and lest they depart from your heart all the days of your life. Make them known to your children and your children's children— *(If the Lord himself is willing to teach, let us not be forgetful hearers. Neither let us neglect to pass on his teachings to our children.)* ¹⁰ how on the day that you stood before the LORD your God at Horeb, the LORD said to me, 'Gather the people to me, that I may let them hear my words, so that they may learn to fear me all the days that they live on the earth, and that they may teach their children so.' ¹¹ And you came near and stood at the foot of the mountain, while the mountain burned with fire to the heart of heaven, wrapped in darkness, cloud, and gloom.

¹² "Then the LORD spoke to you out of the midst of the fire. You heard the sound of words, but saw no form; there was only a voice. *(Moses spends a lot of time here reminding them that they did not see any image or form of God. People are constantly tempted to create an image to make their worship easier. Worshiping symbols and objects is the crying sin of the present age. For this reason, it would be good if all godly people gave up wearing crosses.)* ¹³ And he declared to you his covenant, which he commanded you to perform, that is, the Ten Commandments, and he wrote them on two tablets of stone. ¹⁴ And the LORD commanded me at that time to teach you statutes and rules, that you might do them in the land that you are going over to possess.

¹⁵ "Therefore watch yourselves very carefully. Since you saw no form on the day that the LORD spoke to you at Horeb out of the midst of the fire, ¹⁶ beware lest you act corruptly by making a carved image for yourselves, in the form of any figure, the likeness of male or female, *(People not only dishonor God by worshiping the likeness of something, but they also dishonor themselves.)* ¹⁷ the likeness of any animal that is on the earth, the likeness of any winged bird that flies in the air, ¹⁸ the likeness of anything that creeps on the ground, the likeness of any fish that is in the water under the earth. ¹⁹ And beware lest you raise your eyes to heaven, and when you see the sun and the moon and the stars, all the host of heaven, you be drawn away and bow down to them and serve them, things that the LORD your God has allotted to all the peoples under the whole heaven."

This is a very complete list. It is intended to include virtually every possible object that people wrongly worship. Whether it is some clumsy object made by an unskilled amateur, or the artistic sculpture of an expert, or the beauty of the worshiper of nature; it is not to be bowed down to. God alone is to be worshiped and because he is pure spirit we should guard the holiness and spirituality of his worship. Get rid of all physical objects no matter how much others may respect them and hold them in esteem. The Lord despises them.

²⁰ "But the LORD has taken you and brought you out of the iron furnace, out of Egypt, to be a people of his own inheritance,

---
[357] Numbers 12:3
[358] James 1:20
[359] Deuteronomy 4:9

as you are this day." *(Special privileges involve special responsibilities. He who has done so much for us must be adored with deep respect.)*

²³ "Take care, lest you forget the covenant of the LORD your God, which he made with you, and make a carved image, the form of anything that the LORD your God has forbidden you. *(The command is repeated again and again. God has forever forbidden any attempt to worship him through any image or likeness.)* ²⁴ For the LORD your God is a consuming fire, a jealous God." *(He cannot tolerate sin. He does not treat it as unimportant. His holy anger rises up when he see hearts going away from him. He will have all our love or none. Does anything in our lives lessen our devotion to him?)*

MAY 14

Man Does Not Live By Bread Alone[360]

We will take another passage from the message Moses gave to the Israelites.

Deuteronomy 8

¹ "The whole commandment that I command you today you shall be careful to do, that you may live and multiply, and go in and possess the land that the LORD swore to give to your fathers. *("The whole commandment" or "All the commandments"[361] of God must be obeyed.)* ² And you shall remember the whole way that the LORD your God has led you these forty years in the wilderness, that he might humble you, testing you to know what was in your heart, whether you would keep his commandments or not. ³ And he humbled you and let you hunger and fed you with manna, which you did not know, nor did your fathers know, that he might make you know that man does not live by bread alone, but man lives by every word that comes from the mouth of the LORD. *(The purpose of the Lord's actions in our lives is to teach us to place our faith in him. We learn this lesson all too slowly. What sweet words from the Holy Spirit — "humbled you and let you hunger and fed you with manna.")* ⁴ Your clothing did not wear out on you and your foot did not swell these forty years."

How much grace have we received in forty years? What wonders have we seen?

⁵ "Know then in your heart that, as a man disciplines his son, the LORD your God disciplines you. ⁶ So you shall keep the commandments of the LORD our God by walking in his ways and by fearing him. ⁷ For the LORD your God is bringing you into a good land, a land of brooks of water, of fountains and springs, flowing out in the valleys and hills, ⁸ a land of wheat and barley, of vines and fig trees and pomegranates, a land of olive trees and honey, ⁹ a land in which you will eat bread without scarcity, in which you will lack nothing, a land whose stones are iron, and out of whose hills you can dig copper. ¹⁰ And you shall eat and be full, and you shall bless the LORD your God for the good land he has given you.

¹¹ "Take care lest you forget the LORD your God by not keeping his commandments and his rules and his statutes, which I command you today, ¹² lest, when you have eaten and are full and have built good houses and live in them, ¹³ and when your herds and flocks multiply and your silver and gold is multiplied and all that you have is multiplied, ¹⁴ then your heart be lifted up, and you forget the LORD your God, who brought you out of the land of Egypt, out of the house of slavery,"

Temptations grow out of success and wealth. Has the Lord been very good to this household? Then let us not be lifted up so as to despise his poor people or stop worshiping him with a humble spirit. Instead, let us love our Lord all the more.

¹⁵ "who led you through the great and terrifying wilderness, with its fiery serpents and scorpions and thirsty ground where there was no water, who brought you water out of the flinty rock, ¹⁶ who fed you in the wilderness with manna that your fathers did not know, that he might humble you and test you, to do you good in the end. ¹⁷ Beware lest you say in your heart, 'My power and the might of my hand have gotten me this wealth.' *(Oh for grace to keep us from*

---
[360] Deuteronomy 8:3
[361] New American Standard Version Updated

bragging. Boasting is hateful to both God and others.) ¹⁸ You shall remember the LORD your God, for it is he who gives you power to get wealth, that he may confirm his covenant that he swore to your fathers, as it is this day. ¹⁹ And if you forget the LORD your God and go after other gods and serve them and worship them, I solemnly warn you today that you shall surely perish. ²⁰ Like the nations that the LORD makes to perish before you, so shall you perish, because you would not obey the voice of the LORD your God." *(Indeed, if the Lord withdrew his grace from us, we would certainly become disobedient and perish in our sins. Keep us, good Lord; keep us always.)*

MAY 15
Be Merciful[362]

From the many laws we select a few of the special ones that the Lord gave to his people. They are each filled with instruction and should be studied carefully.

Deuteronomy 21:22-23

²² "And if a man has committed a crime punishable by death and he is put to death, and you hang him on a tree, ²³ his body shall not remain all night on the tree, but you shall bury him the same day, for a hanged man is cursed by God. You shall not defile your land that the LORD your God is giving you for an inheritance."

Let us pause here and lovingly adore the Lord Jesus. For our sakes, he willingly submitted to the accursed death of the cross. Sin brought a curse on us and our blessed Substitute took that curse that was on us and placed it on himself. Christ became "a curse for us."[363] What a holy miracle of love that Christ would lower himself to our place and die for us!

Deuteronomy 22:1-12

¹ "You shall not see your brother's ox or his sheep going astray and ignore them. You shall take them back to your brother. ² And if he does not live near you and you do not know who he is, you shall bring it home to your house, and it shall stay with you until your brother seeks it. Then you shall restore it to him. ³ And you shall do the same with his donkey or with his garment, or with any lost thing of your brother's, which he loses and you find; you may not ignore it. ⁴ You shall not see your brother's donkey or his ox fallen down by the way and ignore them. You shall help him to lift them up again. *(All of these rules are about loving our neighbor as our self.[364] Our Lord is very kind and very careful to give specific details. We should also be very careful concerning them and act kindly toward others in every way.)*

⁵ "A woman shall not wear a man's garment, nor shall a man put on a woman's cloak, for whoever does these things is an abomination to the LORD your God. *(Wearing clothes made for the opposite sex should be avoided. "We are just having fun" is not an excuse for dressing like someone of the opposite sex.)*

⁶ "If you come across a bird's nest in any tree or on the ground, with young ones or eggs and the mother sitting on the young or on the eggs, you shall not take the mother with the young. ⁷ You shall let the mother go, but the young you may take for yourself, that it may go well with you, and that you may live long. *(We must not lack compassion, but act kindly toward the least of God's creatures.)*

⁸ "When you build a new house, you shall make a parapet *(wall or railing)* for your roof, that you may not bring the guilt of blood upon your house, if anyone should fall from it. *(In ancient times, the roof was often used like another room of the house. Concern for life is a duty. Therefore we should keep our homes clean and in good repair. We must not expose ourselves or others to needless risks.)*

⁹ "You shall not sow your vineyard with two kinds of seed, lest the whole yield be forfeited, the crop that you have sown and the yield of the vineyard. ¹⁰ You shall not plow with an ox and a donkey together. ¹¹ You shall not wear cloth of wool and linen mixed together."

---

[362] Luke 6:36
[363] Galatians 3:13

[364] See Mark 12:31

God calls his people to be separate and recognizable. The rules against mixtures in planting, farming, and clothing served to remind them of this. We must plant only the pure gospel, cultivate relationships with honorable motives, and be clothed only in Christ's righteousness. Mixtures are a disgrace in true religion.

12 "You shall make yourself tassels on the four corners of the garment with which you cover yourself." *(This was one of Israel's distinctive marks. Christians should be recognizable by their holiness.)*

Spurgeon (left) with his friend and publisher Joseph Passmore (right). Passmore was a regular attender at the New Park Street Chapel. The two were good friends. Passmore, with his partner James Alabaster, began publishing Spurgeon's sermons and books in 1855.

MAY 16

All His Ways Are Justice[365]

We will now read some verses of Moses' dying song. Like the swan in the fable, he sang himself away.[366]

Deuteronomy 32:1-20

1 "Give ear, O heavens, and I will speak,
　　and let the earth hear the words of my mouth.
2 May my teaching drop as the rain,
　　my speech distill as the dew,
　like gentle rain upon the tender grass,
　　and like showers upon the herb."

Though the law thunders like a storm, Moses as the mediator was like the soft, refreshing, dew. The Lord Jesus is like the dew was to Israel.

3 "For I will proclaim the name of the LORD;
　　ascribe greatness to our God!
4 "The Rock, his work is perfect,
　　for all his ways are justice.
　A God of faithfulness and without iniquity,
　　just and upright is he.
5 They have dealt corruptly with him;
　　they are no longer his children because they are blemished;
　they are a crooked and twisted generation."

The children of Israel did not have the characteristics of saints. They lacked the secret, holy qualities of inner grace by which the heavenly Father recognizes his own children.

6 "Do you thus repay the LORD,
　　you foolish and senseless people?
　Is not he your father, who created you,
　　who made you and established you?
7 Remember the days of old;
　　consider the years of many generations;
　ask your father, and he will show you,
　　your elders, and they will tell you.
8 When the Most High gave to the nations their inheritance,
　　when he divided mankind,
　he fixed the borders of the peoples
　　according to the number of the sons of God.
9 But the LORD's portion is his people,
　　Jacob his allotted heritage."

---

[365] Deuteronomy 32:4
[366] Spurgeon may be referring to Aesop's fable of The Swan and the Goose. When the swan was facing death, it burst into song. Or, he may be referring to the proverbial "Swan Song" that dates back to 458 BC; where the (mistaken) idea that swans sing one beautiful song before dying first appeared in a Greek play.

God is their portion and they are his portion.

10 "He found him in a desert land,
    and in the howling waste of the wilderness;
he enriched him, he cared for him,
    he kept him as the apple of his eye."

This is where the Lord finds all of us. By nature, we live in a desert land. But notice the wise and tender way he deals with us. He enriches us. He cares for us.

11 "Like an eagle that stirs up its nest,
    that flutters over its young,
spreading out its wings, catching them,
    bearing them on its pinions,
12 the LORD alone guided him,
    no foreign god was with him."

The eagle, when its young are ready to leave the nest, will not let them remain idle. She disturbs them and persuades them to try their wings. She even carries them up to teach them to fly. So does the Lord graciously train his people.

13 "He made him ride on the high places of the land,
    and he ate the produce of the field,
and he suckled him with honey out of the rock,
    and oil out of the flinty rock.
14 Curds from the herd, and milk from the flock,
    with fat of lambs,
rams of Bashan and goats,
    with the very finest of the wheat—
and you drank foaming wine made from the blood of the grape.
15 "But Jeshurun grew fat, and kicked;
    you grew fat, stout, and sleek;
then he forsook God who made him
    and scoffed at the Rock of his salvation."

This is a sad picture of many who pretend to be Christians. They are like malnourished horses that come under the care of a kind master. They grow fat and then they kick and leap away from the pasture. People increase in riches and then forget the God who gave them all they have.

16 "They stirred him to jealousy with strange gods;
    with abominations they provoked him to anger.
17 They sacrificed to demons that were no gods,
    to gods they had never known,
to new gods that had come recently,
    whom your fathers had never dreaded.
18 You were unmindful of the Rock that bore *(or fathered)* you,
    and you forgot the God who gave you birth."

Let us never forget our God. It is from him that we have our very existence. We are like the stream that flows from the rock.

19 "The LORD saw it and spurned them
    because of the provocation of his sons and his daughters."

The sins of God's own children are especially irritating to him. He might bear from strangers what he cannot tolerate in his own beloved.

20 "And he said, 'I will hide my face from them;
    I will see what their end will be,
For they are a perverse generation,
    children in whom is no faithfulness."

They are not firm; they hesitate and are undecided. When God hides his face from us, it is always for a reason. Our Lord does it to show us that we have done some evil thing that grieves him. How can he, as our Father, continue to smile on us if we do the things that he hates? May all of us be very careful to please God in all things.

MAY 17

The Eternal God Is Your Dwelling Place[367]

Numbers 35:9-12; 14-16; 19; 22-28

9 And the LORD spoke to Moses, saying, 10 "Speak to the people of Israel and say to them, When you cross the Jordan into the land of Canaan, 11 then you shall select cities to be cities of refuge for you, that the manslayer who kills any person without intent may flee there."

The Israelites, like many other nations, had a custom of blood-revenge. This meant the

---

[367] Deuteronomy 33:27

nearest relative was required to revenge a man's death by killing the person responsible. To handle the evils connected with this long held practice, places were appointed where the manslayer could flee to and be safe until the time came for a fair trial.

12 "The cities shall be for you a refuge from the avenger, that the manslayer may not die until he stands before the congregation for judgment."

14 "You shall give three cities beyond the Jordan, and three cities in the land of Canaan, to be cities of refuge."

These were chosen on each side of the river so that protection would be available for everyone. In the same way, Jesus is a Savior who is freely available to anyone. The roads were repaired and signs set up to direct those who wished to escape the avenger's wrath. The gospel is made plain, so that he who runs to Jesus will find him.

15 "These six cities shall be for refuge for the people of Israel, and for the stranger and for the sojourner among them, that anyone who kills any person without intent may flee there. (No sooner had the fearful deed been done than the unhappy manslayer raced at full speed to the nearest city of refuge, because the blood-avenger was sure to pursue him and demand life for life. Oh! that sinners would hurry to Jesus. Their life depends on it. He is their only hope and certain salvation.)

16 "But if he struck him down with an iron object, so that he died, he is a murderer. The murderer shall be put to death."

19 "The avenger of blood shall himself put the murderer to death; when he meets him, he shall put him to death." (God provided no safety for real guilt. Murder was not winked at. Otherwise, the land would become both poisoned and unsafe. Mercy to murderers would be cruelty to the innocent. Only those who killed accidentally or without premeditation could find shelter in a city of refuge. The spiritual city of refuge, however, far outshines the type,[368] because in Jesus, the real sinner finds complete pardon and safety.)

22 "But if he pushed him suddenly without enmity, or hurled anything on him without lying in wait 23 or used a stone that could cause death, and without seeing him dropped it on him, so that he died, though he was not his enemy and did not seek his harm, 24 then the congregation shall judge between the manslayer and the avenger of blood, in accordance with these rules. 25 And the congregation shall rescue the manslayer from the hand of the avenger of blood, and the congregation shall restore him to his city of refuge to which he had fled, (He was safe there. No avenging hand could touch him. This is a good picture of the security of those who rest in Jesus, the refuge of guilty souls.) and he shall live in it until the death of the high priest who was anointed with the holy oil."

The death of the high priest brought freedom to the man who had fled for refuge. The lesson here is obvious, because our Great High Priest died on the cross.

26 "But if the manslayer shall at any time go beyond the boundaries of his city of refuge to which he fled, 27 and the avenger of blood finds him outside the boundaries of his city of refuge, and the avenger of blood kills the manslayer, he shall not be guilty of blood. 28 For he must remain in his city of refuge until the death of the high priest, but after the death of the high priest the manslayer may return to the land of his possession." (We are no longer under the restrictions and conditions that were forced on a manslayer in a city of refuge. We have been set free unconditionally. We have no avenger to fear. We may live in peace. However, this is only true of believers. Are we all safe?)

---

[368] *type* - something or someone that represents something or someone else, usually in the future. In this case, the city of refuge, where a manslayer could flee to for protection from the avenger of blood, is a type of the Lord Jesus who protects believers from God's wrath.

MAY 18

All His Holy Ones Were In His Hand[369]

Deuteronomy 33:1-3; 6-17

¹ This is the blessing with which Moses the man of God blessed the people of Israel before his death. *(The people of Israel had troubled Moses, but they had not worn him out. They repaid him with evil, but his love for them remained intense. He died with a blessing on his lips.)* ² He said,

"The LORD came from Sinai
 and dawned from Seir upon us;
he shone forth from Mount Paran;
he came from the ten thousands of holy ones,
 with flaming fire at his right hand.
³ Yes, he loved his people,
 all his holy ones were in his hand;
so they followed in your steps,
 receiving direction from you."

Love made the Lord reveal himself through Moses. But what shall we say of his divine display of love in Christ Jesus? This is perfect love!

⁶ "Let Reuben live, and not die,
 but let his men be few."

May God make our little churches alive and strong.

⁷ And this he said of Judah:

"Hear, O LORD, the voice of Judah,
 and bring him in to his people.
With your hands contend for him,
 and be a help against his adversaries."

May the same blessing be on each believer. We need enough strength to do the Lord's will and that is all we need. Too much strength would not be a blessing.

⁸ And of Levi he said,

"Give to Levi your Thummim,
 and your Urim to your godly one,
 whom you tested at Massah,
  with whom you quarreled at the waters of Meribah;
⁹ who said of his father and mother,
  'I regard them not';
he disowned his brothers
 and ignored his children.
For they observed your word
 and kept your covenant."

This refers back to the loyalty of the tribe of Levi on several difficult occasions. They not only stayed true to the Lord, but also became the executioners of divine vengeance on their own brothers. They were found faithful and they were entrusted with the sacred ministry.

¹⁰ "They shall teach Jacob your rules
 and Israel your law;
they shall put incense before you
 and whole burnt offerings on your altar.
¹¹ Bless, O LORD, his substance,
 and accept the work of his hands;
crush the loins of his adversaries,
 of those who hate him, that they rise not again."

¹² Of Benjamin he said,

"The beloved of the LORD dwells in safety.
The High God surrounds him all day long,
 and dwells between his shoulders."

The Lord was Benjamin's strength. He was with him and gave him power.

¹³ And of Joseph he said,

"Blessed by the LORD be his land,
 with the choicest gifts of heaven above,
 and of the deep that crouches beneath,"

That is, bless the Lord for the fountains and springs of water that come up from below the earth,

¹⁴ "with the choicest fruits of the sun
 and the rich yield of the months,"

The sun brings growth and wealth over time. It takes time to develop spiritual maturity.

¹⁵ "with the finest produce of the ancient mountains
 and the abundance of the everlasting hills,
¹⁶ with the best gifts of the earth and its fullness
 and the favor of him who dwells in the bush."

The finest produce and the best gifts are wonderful, but God's favor is the very best gift. Lord, give us this and we are satisfied.

"May these rest on the head of Joseph,

---

[369] Deuteronomy 33:3

on the pate *(head)* of him who is prince
    among his brothers.
17 A firstborn bull—he has majesty,
    and his horns are the horns of a wild ox;
with them he shall gore the peoples,
    all of them, to the ends of the earth;
they are the ten thousands of Ephraim,
    and they are the thousands of Manasseh."

Joseph was persecuted by his brothers, yet he received the richest blessing. He received a double inheritance as each of his two sons (Ephraim and Manasseh) was blessed by his father Jacob. The more the Lord reserves us for his special work, the more blessing we will receive. Joseph was blessed by the Lord and experienced persecution. But persecution may be endured cheerfully because "this slight momentary affliction is preparing for us an eternal weight of glory beyond all comparison."[370]

MAY 19
Underneath Are the Everlasting Arms[371]

We continue with "the blessing with which Moses the man of God blessed the people of Israel before his death."[372]

Deuteronomy 33:18-29

18 And of Zebulun he said,

"Rejoice, Zebulun, in your going out,
    and Issachar, in your tents."

Here is a blessing for the traveler and a blessing for the person who stays close to home. In both cases the blessing is given to the children of God to rejoice, because the Lord is with them. If we go only where we should and live only where we should, we have the Lord for our companion, and therefore, we may rejoice all of the time.

19 "They shall call peoples to their
    mountain;
    there they offer right sacrifices;
for they draw from the abundance of the
    seas
    and the hidden treasures of the sand."

It is a happy activity to encourage others to worship the Lord. It is good to praise the God who makes even the seas and the sandy deserts supply our needs.

20 And of Gad he said,

"Blessed be he who enlarges Gad!
    Gad crouches like a lion;
    he tears off arm and scalp.
21 He chose the best of the land for himself,
    for there a commander's portion was reserved;
and he came with the heads of the people,
    with Israel he executed the justice of the LORD,
    and his judgments for Israel."

It is a blessing from God to be determined and full of energy in doing the will of the Lord. Too many are uncertain and weak.

22 And of Dan he said,

"Dan is a lion's cub
    that leaps from Bashan."

Strength and courage show themselves in bold ventures. Dan leaped at the opportunity to increase his territory. We ought to be bold for the Lord Jesus and grow the size of his kingdom.

23 And of Naphtali he said,

"O Naphtali, sated with favor,
    and full of the blessing of the LORD,
    possess the lake and the south."[373]

What richer words were ever spoken of mortals? Those who are full with the blessing of Jehovah are filled indeed.

24 And of Asher he said,

"Most blessed of sons be Asher;
    let him be the favorite of his brothers,
    and let him dip his foot in oil."

This is a sweet prayer for our pastor, too. Let him have thousands of spiritual children. Let him provide the saints with very good teaching and guidance. May it be obvious to everyone that his work is greatly blessed of the Lord.

25 "Your bars[374] shall be iron and bronze,

---

[370] 2 Corinthians 4:17
[371] Deuteronomy 33:27
[372] Deuteronomy 33:1
[373] ESV translators alternate reading - *possess the west and the south*
[374] KJV *shoes;* NASB *locks.* Matthew Poole and Matthew Henry see this as possibly a reference to iron ore and bronze; hence, great economic strength.

and as your days, so shall your strength be."

This is a blessed promise from God. Our journey through this life is a rough road. We need strength and plenty of grace during our weary days as we travel this temporary life. God will give us both. He will give us the strength needed for every emergency. The saints of God have proved every promise of our Lord to be true. They do not need to be afraid that he will let them down now.

Moses now turns his thoughts to his God, who he praises in glowing language.

26 "There is none like God, O Jeshurun,
    who rides through the heavens to your help,
    through the skies in his majesty."

No one on earth or heaven is so good, so ready, and so able to bless his people.

27 "The eternal God is your dwelling place,
    and underneath are the everlasting arms.
   And he thrust out the enemy before you
    and said, Destroy."

These are very sweet words, "underneath are the everlasting arms." The arms of God will break our fall or prevent us from falling. They will hold us safely. They will give us peace when life is stormy. And finally, they will lift us up to everlasting glory.

28 "So Israel lived in safety
    Jacob lived alone,"

God's people must stay separate from the world if they wish to be safe.

   "in a land of grain and wine,
    whose heavens drop down dew."

Earth's springs of water and heaven's dew both bless the chosen of God. All things are full of blessing to those whom the Lord has set apart for himself.

29 "Happy are you, O Israel! Who is like you,
    a people saved by the LORD,
   the shield of your help,
    and the sword of your triumph!
   Your enemies shall come fawning to you,
    and you shall tread upon their backs."

As there is none like the Lord, so there are none like his people. They are happy in the present, and secure for the future—since this God is their God forever and ever.

May 20

Your Will Be Done[375]

Moses was not allowed to cross the Jordan River and take possession of the promised land. On this occasion, we will hear from his own lips why he was excluded. It does not appear that he was told about it when the sentence was passed on all those who came out of Egypt; but thirty-eight years later, after Moses struck the rock twice at Meribah.[376]

Deuteronomy 1:34-38

34 "And the LORD heard your words *(Not just the actual words themselves, but the inner thoughts of their hearts that were not spoken. "I the LORD search the heart and test the mind, to give every man according to his way, according to the fruit of his deeds."[377])* and was angered, and he swore, 35 'Not one of these men of this evil generation shall see the good land that I swore to give to your fathers, 36 except Caleb the son of Jephunneh. He shall see it, and to him and to his children I will give the land on which he has trodden, because he has wholly followed the LORD!'"

God's vow was firm. Not one of that generation crossed the Jordan except Caleb and Joshua. The Lord notices and rewards the faithfulness of individuals and protects his faithful ones from many of the judgments that fall on his misbehaving church. Blessed are they who work hard in all things to follow in their Lord's tracks.

37 "Even with me the LORD was angry on your account and said, 'You also shall not go in there. *(This was because Moses struck the rock at Meribah instead of telling the rock "to yield its water."[378] This tended to cause the people to honor the Lord less than they should have. If we are placed in an important and influential position, God will not only judge the fault itself, but he will

---
[375] Matthew 6:10
[376] Numbers 20:10-13
[377] Jeremiah 17:10
[378] Numbers 20:2-13

consider the bad effect it may have on his people.) **38** Joshua the son of Nun, who stands before you, he shall enter. Encourage him, for he shall cause Israel to inherit it.'"

The Lord told Moses to encourage Joshua as his replacement as the leader of Israel. To encourage the person who is to take your place is hard for flesh and blood. It is even more difficult if that person has been our servant for years. Who but a meek and humble man could obey the command?[379]

Deuteronomy 3:23-28

23 "And I pleaded with the LORD at that time, saying, **24** 'O Lord GOD, you have only begun to show your servant your greatness and your mighty hand. For what god is there in heaven or on earth who can do such works and mighty acts as yours? **25** Please let me go over and see the good land beyond the Jordan, that good hill country and Lebanon.' *(Moses prayed humbly for the sentence that kept him from Canaan to be reversed. He may have felt encouraged to do so because the Lord did not swear an oath against him as he did against the people. Moses prayed for others and God answered his prayers. But when he pleaded for himself, it proved fruitless in this case. His prayer was powerful in argument, and was presented in humility, and yet it was denied. It is not everything that a good person asks that God will give. There are some points in which he shows himself supreme and gives us the example to pray, "Not as I will, but as you will"[380])*

26 "But the LORD was angry with me because of you and would not listen to me. *(Only Jesus is guaranteed to always be heard by our heavenly father. If Moses' prayer can be rejected, we should not be surprised if sometimes we are denied.)* And the LORD said to me, 'Enough from you; do not speak to me of this matter again. **27** Go up to the top of Pisgah and lift up your eyes westward and northward and southward and eastward, and look at it with your eyes, for you shall not go over this Jordan. *(The Lord does not always answer our prayers the way we expect him to, but he will always give us his peace. Moses saw Canaan on earth, and as the vision melted away he saw the better land above. He was a great gainer by not having his request granted.)* **28** But charge Joshua, and encourage and strengthen him, for he shall go over at the head of this people, and he shall put them in possession of the land that you shall see.'" *(It is very comforting to know that when one good person dies another is ready to take their place. God is never at a loss. His people will not fail because they lack a leader.)*

MAY 21

Your Eyes…Will See a Land That Stretches Afar[381]

Deuteronomy 34

1 Then Moses went up from the plains of Moab to Mount Nebo, to the top of Pisgah, which is opposite Jericho *(Having finished his work and given his last blessing, the prophet cheerfully climbs toward heaven. Death to the saints is rising to a better place. He followed his upward pathway alone, without an earthly friend, but the Lord was at his side. When our earthly companions say their last goodbyes, we will find the Lord at our right hand.)* And the LORD showed him all the land, Gilead as far as Dan, **2** all Naphtali, the land of Ephraim and Manasseh, all the land of Judah as far as the western sea, **3** the Negev, and the Plain, that is, the Valley of Jericho the city of palm trees, as far as Zoar.

No doubt that keen eye of Moses was strengthened supernaturally for its last earthly sight. In a similar way, we have seen the senses of dying saints greatly strengthened just as they were departing this earth. They have appeared to see and know more than normal minds could have been aware of. Heaven lay open before them, and the land so far away to us, was very near to the eye of their faith.

4 And the LORD said to him, "This is the land of which I swore to Abraham, to Isaac, and to Jacob, 'I will give it to your

---

[379] Numbers 12:3
[380] Matthew 26:39

[381] Isaiah 33:17

offspring.' I have let you see it with your eyes, but you shall not go over there."

And truly there was no reason for Moses to cross into the land, because it was full of Canaanites. It was better for the grand old man to go to the land called heaven where the wicked can no longer trouble him, than to live through the struggles of war in his old age.

⁵ So Moses the servant of the LORD died there in the land of Moab, according to the word of the LORD, (Some say, according 'to the mouth of the Lord.' The Jews say, "with a kiss from the mouth of God.") ⁶ and he buried him in the valley in the land of Moab opposite Beth-peor; but no one knows the place of burial to this day.

Otherwise, the Jews might have idolized his bones. We do not need to worry about having the place we are buried known. Even Moses sleeps in forgotten soil.

⁷ Moses was 120 years old when he died. His eye was undimmed, and his vigor unabated. *(Moses represents the law. When Moses died, he was replaced by Joshua, who represents Jesus. As Moses was sweetly laid aside to make room for Joshua, so the law is sweetly laid aside to make room for Jesus. The law still reveals our sin and the law would still condemn us except it has been laid to rest for those who rest in Jesus.)* ⁸ And the people of Israel wept for Moses in the plains of Moab thirty days. Then the days of weeping and mourning for Moses were ended. *(The mourning was long, because Moses was a great man, but it was not too long, because there was other work for the living to do.)*

⁹ And Joshua the son of Nun was full of the spirit of wisdom, for Moses had laid his hands on him. So the people of Israel obeyed him and did as the LORD had commanded Moses. *(Joshua was fully equipped for the work because God had prepared him for it. People may die, but God's work goes on. When those who seem the most necessary for the church are removed, it still stands.)* ¹⁰ And there has not arisen a prophet since in Israel like Moses, whom the LORD knew face to face, ¹¹ none like him for all the signs and the wonders that the LORD sent him to do in the land of Egypt, to Pharaoh and to all his servants and to all his land, ¹² and for all the mighty power and all the great deeds of terror that Moses did in the sight of all Israel.

All other prophets fall almost as much short of Moses as Jesus goes beyond him. Taking his whole life into consideration, we may pronounce him unequalled. A man beyond compare in whom the grace of God brought human nature as near to perfection as we can expect it to be this side of eternity. He fell asleep after having been faithful until death. In this same way, in our own humble surroundings, may we be enabled to continue faithfully until we lay down our body and our obligations, and immediately stop working and live in heaven.

MAY 22
Consider Jesus, the Apostle and High Priest Of Our Confession[382]
Hebrews 3:1-6

¹ Therefore, holy brothers, you who share in a heavenly calling, consider Jesus, the apostle and high priest of our confession, *(This is the most rewarding subject the mind can think about. Studying the Lord Jesus Christ is profitable for our instruction, our comfort, and our best example in life. Moses was the great apostle of the Old Testament and Aaron the greatest high priest under the law. Both picture our Lord. As Moses and Aaron did everything required as an apostle and the high priest, Jesus fulfills both positions completely.)* ² who was faithful to him who appointed him, just as Moses also was faithful in all God's house.

Jesus became a servant and was as faithful as the best of servants could be. Even more, he excelled them all.

³ For Jesus has been counted worthy of more glory than Moses—as much more glory as the builder of a house has more honor than the house itself. ⁴ (For every house is built by someone, but the builder of all things is God.)

Jesus is the builder of the church; Moses was only a supporting column in it. Jesus is

---
[382] Hebrews 3:1

God; Moses was only a man. Yet the Jews give great reverence to Moses. Should we not honor and reverence our Lord even more than they do Moses?

⁵Now Moses was faithful in all God's house as a servant, to testify to the things that were to be spoken later, ⁶but Christ is faithful over God's house as a son. And we are his house if indeed we hold fast our confidence and our boasting in our hope.

Christ's relationship to God is superior to Moses. He is a Son. Moses was a servant. This also raises the relationship of believers to God far above those who are under the law! We should walk in faith and rejoice in hope. Only by holding tightly to faith and hope can we experience our wonderful position as family members in the household of the Son of God. This is how we can personally realize how much the Lord Jesus outshines Moses.

Stephen, in his sermon given before his enemies, gives us a few more words about Moses. We will finish our study of his history with:

Acts 7:37-41; 44-45

³⁷"This is the Moses who said to the Israelites, 'God will raise up for you a prophet like me from your brothers.'"

Jesus is this prophet like Moses! Both Moses and our Lord introduced a new form of government. Both were a ruler, a liberator, a mediator,³⁸³ and a teacher. Both were mighty in actions and words, which is a combination we find nowhere else. Both were rejected by their own people, but approved by God. Moses led his people through the wilderness toward the promised rest and the Lord Jesus does the same today.

³⁸"This is the one who was in the congregation in the wilderness with the angel who spoke to him at Mount Sinai, and with our fathers. He received living oracles to give to us."

Moses received the law from the living God. It was a living message of hope. Only the sins of mankind have made the law a message of death. *God honored Moses by making him the mediator between himself and his people. God also honored Moses by appointing him to represent the great covenant angel who gave him the law.*

³⁹"Our fathers refused to obey him, but thrust him aside, and in their hearts they turned to Egypt, ⁴⁰saying to Aaron, 'Make for us gods who will go before us. As for this Moses who led us out from the land of Egypt, we do not know what has become of him.' ⁴¹And they made a calf in those days, and offered a sacrifice to the idol and were rejoicing in the works of their hands." *(We have read about this before. Will we treat the Lord Jesus in the same way? Will we rebel against him and set up other gods in his place? May the Lord keep this from happening to us!)*

⁴⁴"Our fathers had the tent of witness in the wilderness, just as he who spoke to Moses directed him to make it, according to the pattern that he had seen. ⁴⁵Our fathers in turn brought it in with Joshua when they dispossessed the nations that God drove out before our fathers. So it was until the days of David." *(But even though the Israelites had all the outward signs, they missed the inward spiritual grace. Again, may the Lord keep this from happening to us!)*

MAY 23

There Will Be a Resurrection Of Both the Just and the Unjust[384]

Having seen the great giver of the law breathe his last, it may be appropriate to look at those passages in the Old Testament that reveal a belief in the resurrection. The first is the important passage from the ancient book of Job.

Job 19:21-27

²¹ "Have mercy on me, have mercy on me,
O you my friends,
for the hand of God has touched me!"

The patriarch³⁸⁵ Job was in a very sad condition. He pleaded with his cruel friends

---

[383] *mediator* - a person who attempts to make people involved in a conflict come to an agreement; a go-between. As used in the Bible, Jesus Christ intercedes between God the Father and Christians; that is, he prays for them.

[384] Acts 24:15

to not add to his misery, because he was already pushed down enough by the hand of God. Let us be very gentle with those on whom God has already brought trouble. Be kind even if they seem to be a little childish and irritable. Let us put up with them, because we know that pain is very hard to endure.

²² "Why do you, like God, pursue me?
　　Why are you not satisfied with my flesh?"

His poor flesh was all a mass of pain and yet his friends put him in a worse mood with their harsh scolding. After talking about his flesh, Job goes on to speak of the better condition that he expected for his body. Here is his famous confession of faith.

²³ "Oh that my words were written!
　　Oh that they were inscribed in a book!
²⁴ Oh that with an iron pen and lead
　　they were engraved in the rock forever!
²⁵ For I know that my Redeemer lives,"

Job knew his Redeemer lived. He was certain of it. He was certain that he had a Redeemer who lived and would rescue his body from its captivity, no matter what might happen to it.

　　"and at the last he will stand upon the earth."

He looked to the future, and the victorious second coming of Christ, and his reign over the entire earth. Job's hope of resurrection was based on Christ's second coming.

²⁶ "And after my skin has been thus destroyed,
　　yet in my flesh I shall see God."

He expected the worms to bore through his skin and eat his flesh, but he believed that his body would rise again and that in his flesh he would see the Lord.

²⁷ "whom I shall see for myself,
　　and my eyes shall behold, and not another.
　　My heart faints within me!"

Job himself, in his own personality, would look on the Lord with his own eyes, even though the most vital parts of his body and all his flesh would long before have rotted in the tomb. Job is as clear as the sun in his testimony.

Let us now look to Isaiah.

Isaiah 26:19-21

¹⁹ Your dead shall live; their bodies shall rise.

We shall rise when Jesus returns.

　　You who dwell in the dust, awake and sing for joy!
　For your dew is a dew of light,
　　and the earth will give birth to the dead.
²⁰ Come, my people, enter your chambers,
　　and shut your doors behind you;
　hide yourselves for a little while
　　until the fury has passed by.

The grave will only be a waiting room for the saints' bodies during the troubles to come.

²¹ For behold, the LORD is coming out from his place
　　to punish the inhabitants of the earth for their iniquity,
　and the earth will disclose the blood shed on it,
　　and will no more cover its slain.

People have experienced great troubles and will continue to have them. God will punish tyrants and evil doers. At the last the dead shall rise from the dust and convict all tyrants of their murderous crimes. Until then the saints, as far as their bodies are concerned, sleep in Jesus.

Let us now hear Daniel.

Daniel 12:2-3; 13

² "And many of those who sleep in the dust of the earth shall awake *(This does not refer to the soul that is in heaven, but only to the body that is in the dust of the earth)*, some to everlasting life, and some to shame and everlasting contempt." *(We see here that both the righteous and the wicked will rise from the grave.)* ³ "And those who are wise shall shine like the brightness of the sky above, and those who turn many to righteousness, like the stars forever and

---

[385] *patriarch* - A man regarded as the father or ruler of a family. Bible patriarchs include Abraham, Isaac, Jacob and Jacob's twelve sons.

ever." *(May every one of us labor to be part of that brilliant assembly.[386])*

13 "But go your way till the end. And you shall rest and shall stand in your allotted place at the end of the days." *(We will go to our tombs cheerfully and rest. Our position with Christ is secure until Jesus comes in his Father's glory.)*

MAY 24
Behold, the Lamb Of God[387]

Having followed the history of the Bible to the death of Moses, we will take a break, and vary our readings for a day or two by choosing a number of passages from various parts of the Holy Scriptures. We begin by reading the solemn story of our Lord's crucifixion. The best commentary on it will be our repentance, faith, and love.

Mark 15:16-38

16 And the soldiers led [Jesus] away inside the palace (that is, the governor's headquarters), and they called together the whole battalion.[388] *(The soldiers called others so that their making fun of our Lord would increase his suffering even more. People were united and wholehearted in mocking their Redeemer. When will his people be as enthusiastic in his praises? Should not the "whole battalion" of believers adore him?)* **17** And they clothed him in a purple cloak, and twisting together a crown of thorns, they put it on him. **18** And they began to salute him, "Hail, King of the Jews!" **19** And they were striking his head with a reed and spitting on him and kneeling down in homage to him. *(Here was Majesty in misery! Our Lord, who is the King of angels, was spit on by abusive people! Oh how we should love him for enduring this shame.)* **20** And when they had mocked him, they stripped him of the purple cloak and put his own clothes on him. And they led him out to crucify him.

21 And they compelled a passerby, Simon of Cyrene, who was coming in from the country, the father of Alexander and Rufus, to carry his cross.

The Holy Spirit has honored this Simon by inspiring Mark to take notice of him. However, we should not envy him, because we will also have a cross to carry.

22 And they brought him to the place called Golgotha (which means Place of a Skull). **23** And they offered him wine mixed with myrrh, but he did not take it.

He did not take it because he did not want to be drugged. He came to suffer in our place, and he intended to go through with it, enduring it to the utmost.

24 And they crucified him and divided his garments among them, casting lots for them, to decide what each should take. **25** And it was the third hour when they crucified him. **26** And the inscription of the charge against him read, "The King of the Jews."

> *"A king my title is, prefix'd on high,*
> *Yet by my subjects I'm condemned to die*
> *A servile death, in servile company*
> *Was ever grief like mine!"[389]*

27 And with him they crucified two robbers, one on his right and one on his left. **28** [And the Scripture was fulfilled that says, "He was numbered with the transgressors"][390] *(He died a criminal's death with criminals and they included his innocent name on their list of lawbreakers.)* **29** And those who passed by derided him, wagging their heads and saying, "Aha! You who would destroy the temple and rebuild it in three days, **30** save yourself, and come down from the cross!" **31** So also the chief priests with the scribes mocked him to one another, saying, "He saved others; he cannot save himself. **32** Let the Christ, the King of Israel, come down now from the cross that we may see and believe." Those who were crucified with him also reviled him. *(Oh!*

---

[386] Hebrews 4:9-11, "There remains a Sabbath rest for the people of God, for whoever has entered God's rest has also rested from his works as God did from his. Let us therefore strive to enter that rest, so that no one may fall by the same sort of disobedience."
[387] John 1:29
[388] *battalion* - A unit of soldiers, probably several hundred in number

[389] From the Works of George Hebert, circa 1853
[390] ESV indicates verse 28 as missing in some manuscripts and is included as a footnote

what patience, the omnipotent[391] patience that willingly suffered all this!)

³³ And when the sixth hour had come, there was darkness over the whole land until the ninth hour. *(From noon until three in the afternoon night covered everything.)* ³⁴ And at the ninth hour Jesus cried with a loud voice, "Eloi, Eloi, lema sabachthani?" which means "My God, my God, why have you forsaken me?" ³⁵ And some of the bystanders hearing it said, "Behold, he is calling Elijah." ³⁶ And someone ran and filled a sponge with sour wine, put it on a reed and gave it to him to drink, saying, "Wait, let us see whether Elijah will come to take him down." ³⁷ And Jesus uttered a loud cry and breathed his last. *(He died in full strength, laying down his life voluntarily for our sakes.)* ³⁸ And the curtain of the temple was torn in two, from top to bottom. *(The mysteries of the inner sanctuary of the temple were exposed for all to see and the ceremonies of the law were ended. All glory to You our Dear Redeemer of souls.)*

MAY 25

This Precious Value…Is For You Who Believe[392]

1 Peter 2:1-10

¹ So put away all malice and all deceit and hypocrisy and envy and all slander. ² Like newborn infants, long for the pure spiritual milk, that by it you may grow up to salvation— ³ if indeed you have tasted that the Lord is good.

That is to say, if we are truly believers, God has entrusted us with a spiritual and everlasting life. Therefore, let us be finished with the evil fruit of the old nature. We are born into a new world. Let us throw aside the contaminated and germ infested clothing of our former life. Anger, cheating, and speaking evil of people, are as ugly in a Christian as the rags of a dead mummy would be for a living person. From now on, it is our job to live and practice the truth. We should rejoice in our gracious God and be gracious ourselves. We want to know the word of God. We want its strengthening power to grow our new life toward perfection.

⁴ As you come to him, a living stone rejected by men but in the sight of God chosen and precious, ⁵ you yourselves like living stones are being built up as a spiritual house, to be a holy priesthood, to offer spiritual sacrifices acceptable to God through Jesus Christ.

Our desire to be holy is because we are so closely related to our Lord Jesus. He is the foundation, and we are the stones of the spiritual building. Others may speak out against us, as they did at him, but God has chosen us, and we are precious in his sight, just as Jesus is. Therefore, we desire to live as holy people, in whom God lives, whose whole business is to present spiritual sacrifices to the Lord. We are a living building that is built on the precious living foundation who is our Lord Jesus. We are the living stones that are used to build his church. Therefore we should be lively and precious and holy people.

⁶ For it stands in Scripture:

"Behold, I am laying in Zion a stone,
a cornerstone chosen and precious,
and whoever believes in him will not be put to shame."[393]

These words should cheer those of us who believe in Jesus. Let us be bold and never for a moment hesitate to confess Christ before others.

⁷ So the honor is for you who believe, *(But he does not say how much honor. This is more than tongue or pen could tell. Truly, the Lord Jesus is all in all and more than all to his people.)* but for those who do not believe,

"The stone that the builders rejected
has become the cornerstone,"[394]

⁸ and

"A stone of stumbling,
and a rock of offense."[395]

---

[391] *omnipotent, omnipotence* - all powerful, almighty, absolute and supreme power, having unlimited power.
[392] 1 Peter 2:7 NASB updated

[393] Isaiah 40:6,8
[394] Psalm 118:22
[395] Isaiah 8:14

They stumble because they disobey the word, as they were destined to do.

Clearly no one can be neutral. We must either feel Jesus is precious or else we will stumble over him. If we are so disobedient as to be offended at the Lord, our unbelief will not harm him, because God has appointed him to be the cornerstone, the beginning of his church. Nothing can stop the plans of God. In his plans there is a dark place for the rebel as well as a bright spot for the believer.

⁹ But you are a chosen race, a royal priesthood, a holy nation, a people for his own possession, that you may proclaim the excellencies of him who called you out of darkness into his marvelous light. *(As a family, let us remember how the Lord has favored us in his grace. Let everyone among us who is saved remember why they are called. We are chosen, royal, priestly, unique, and dearly loved in heaven. How should people like this behave? We should be far better than others, because the Lord has treated us so much better. May God's rich grace rest on us and cause others to see why our God is worthy of praise.)* ¹⁰ Once you were not a people, but now you are God's people; once you had not received mercy, but now you have received mercy.

We were outcast Gentiles who were thought to be little better than dogs. We should be very grateful that we now enjoy the same status as the favored people of old. Lord, cleanse us from all sin and make us a family devoted to your service.

MAY 26

Honor Your Father and Mother[396]

Ephesians 6:1-10

¹ Children, obey your parents in the Lord, for this is right. *(Even nature teaches us that this is right. Many animals would not survive if the children did not "obey" those who feed and care for them. It is also right according to the will of God. It is right for the family, because it would not function properly if the children were disobedient. It is right for the children themselves, who will never be happy until they have learned to obey. However, notice that there is a limit. Children are to obey "in the Lord," that is, as long as the commands of parents are not opposed to the laws of God.)*

² "Honor your father and mother" (this is the first commandment with a promise), ³ "that it may go well with you and that you may live long in the land." *(It has been observed that God frequently prospers those who have been respectful and obedient to their parents. At any rate, such children are doing the right thing and we all know that the way of faithfulness is the way of safety and happiness. On the other hand, unkindness to parents has often been remarkably punished in this life. Nothing shortens life like rebellion against parents. Absalom is a famous example of this general rule.[397] Not honoring parents is also a terrible sign that a child does not have grace in their life. Someone who does not love and honor their father and mother {who they can see}, certainly does not love the Lord {who they cannot see}.)*

⁴ Fathers, do not provoke your children to anger, but bring them up in the discipline and instruction of the Lord. *(Unnecessary harshness and maddening severity are forbidden, while holy discipline and religious training are commanded. Wise fathers will take note of this verse. It is not addressed to mothers, because they rarely, if ever, make the mistake of being too severe. Fathers must not be unpleasant and bad tempered to their sons and daughters. Neither should they expect more from them than they are capable of or withhold basic necessities from them. These would be provoking them to anger.)*

⁵ Bondservants, obey your earthly masters with fear and trembling, *(or with concern and meekness)* with a sincere heart as you would Christ, ⁶ not by the way of eye-service, as people-pleasers, but as bondservants of Christ, doing the will of God from the heart, *(Those who need to be constantly watched are disappointing workers. True Christians are more*

---

[396] Ephesians 6:2

[397] Absalom rebelled against his father, King David, and died. See 2 Samuel, chapters 15-18.

concerned about what God sees than what their boss or supervisor notices. They do their jobs just as well when they are alone as they would when everyone is watching them. It is a shameful thing to be hard working only when one is being watched. It is wicked behavior only fit for slaves.) ⁷ rendering service with a good will as to the Lord and not to man, ⁸ knowing that whatever good anyone does, this he will receive back from the Lord, whether he is a boondservant or is free.

George Herbert puts it beautifully.

> *"All may of thee partake:*
> *Nothing can be so mean,*
> *Which with this tincture (for thy sake),*
> *Will not grow bright and clean.*
>
> *A servant with his cause,*
> *Makes drudgery divine:*
> *Who sweeps a room as for thy laws,*
> *Makes that and the action fine."*

⁹ Masters, do the same to them, and stop your threatening, knowing that he who is both their Master and yours is in heaven, and that there is no partiality with him.

Those in charge are not to be always threatening and finding fault. They should act toward those under them in the same way Jesus, their Master, has acted toward them.

The Apostle does not speak against any particular class of society, but he does tell us to show respect to everyone we meet. May our family always be a happy one, because each one seeks the happiness of the rest and does so by keeping their own place, and behaving toward others in the spirit of love.

¹⁰ Finally, be strong in the Lord and in the strength of his might.

George Herbert (1593-1633)
English poet and Anglican priest.

MAY 27
I Have Stored Up Your Word In My Heart[398]

We will now read a part of Psalm 119, the longest of the Psalms. Martin Luther[399] supposedly claimed to prize this psalm so highly that he would not take the whole world in exchange for one page of it. Bishop Cowper[400] called it "a Holy Alphabet." Philip Henry[401] recommended to his children that they take a verse of it every morning "and meditate upon it, and so go over the Psalm twice in a year, and that will bring you to be in love with all the rest of Scripture." May such an excellent result come from our reading from this Psalm today.

Psalm 119:1-16

1   Blessed are those whose way is blameless,
    who walk in the law of the LORD!

---

[398] Psalm 119:11
[399] Martin Luther (1483-1546). Once a German monk in the Roman Catholic Church and then a key person in the 16th century Protestant Reformation movement that began when he posted his "95 Theses" on the church door in Wittenberg, Germany on October 31, 1517.
[400] William Cowper (1566-1619), author of *A Holy Alphabet for Zion's Scholars. A Commentary upon Psalm 119*. Each verse of Psalm 119 begins with a sequential letter of the Hebrew alphabet.
[401] Father of the famous Bible Commentary author Matthew Henry

People destroy themselves with sin. The only safe path to walk is obedience. Such holy walkers enjoy a peace that is far better than having lots of money or being famous. This psalm, like the Sermon on the Mount, begins with good wishes. Our holy faith is filled with blessings.

2   Blessed are those who keep his testimonies,
      who seek him with their whole heart,
3   who also do no wrong,
      but walk in his ways!

Where the whole heart loves the Word of God, the whole life will be clean, and no evil habits will be allowed. Yet even those who keep his Word need to look for God more and more. Their goal is to be perfect, but absolute perfection is not reached in this life.

4   You have commanded your precepts
      to be kept diligently.
5   Oh that my ways may be steadfast
      in keeping your statutes!

What a mercy when our prayer is to keep God's commandments. These two verses show us that what God wants his people to be is their desire too. "It is God who works in [us], both to will and to work for his good pleasure."[402]

6   Then I shall not be put to shame,
      having my eyes fixed on all your commandments.

True obedience does not pick and choose. It is happy with all the rules of the Lord. If we begin to say, "this rule does not apply to me" and, "that rule does not apply to me," where will we stop? The only way a person can truly live a Christian life is to sincerely obey all the commands of God. Then even those who hate them cannot say anything against them that is actually true. We all need great grace from our great God to live this way.

7   I will praise you with an upright heart,
      when I learn your righteous rules.

The result of all of our learning should be to worship God. Prayer helps us in our study of God's Word. Praise should be the aim of our study and the result of it.

8   I will keep your statutes;
      do not utterly forsake me!

Deciding to keep God's laws is good, but we need to pray and ask God to help us keep them. The last sentence, "do not utterly forsake me" should be on our lips every day. What a disaster it would be if our Lord deserted us!

9   How can a young man keep his way pure?
      By guarding it according to your word.

This verse asks a very big question and then gives a very good answer. All young people should think seriously about both the question and the answer. Grace in the heart is the young person's best life insurance.

10 With my whole heart I seek you;
      let me not wander from your commandments!

Those who are most sincere in their Christian faith are the most afraid of failing in it. Their concern is wise. However good our intentions may be, we cannot protect ourselves from sin. The most eager seeker after God will soon wander into terrible sin unless the grace of God keeps them safe.

11 I have stored up your word in my heart,
      that I might not sin against you.

The best thing (his word) in the best place (our hearts), for the best of reasons. Can everyone in this family say what David says here?

12 Blessed are you, O LORD;
      teach me your statutes!

David gives God glory and asks God to give him grace. Prayers and praises should go together.

13 With my lips I declare
      all the rules of your mouth.

Those who can speak well should speak often for their Lord.

14 In the way of your testimonies I delight
      as much as in all riches.

In the last verse he says that he had guided others in the way of truth. In this he rejoices that he himself has accepted God's word.

15 I will meditate on your precepts
      and fix my eyes on your ways.
16 I will delight in your statutes;
      I will not forget your word.

---

[402] Philippians 2:13

What the heart delights in, the mind remembers. A warm heart does not forget the Lord's word. Is our heart warm?

MAY 28

In Christ Jesus, Who Became to Us Wisdom From God[403]

Proverbs 26:1-16

1 Like snow in summer or rain in harvest,
    so honor is not fitting for a fool.

Giving honor to a fool is out of place and leads to trouble. If we want to be honored, we must pray to God to keep us from being foolish or wicked.

2 Like a sparrow in its flitting, like a swallow in its flying,
    a curse that is causeless does not alight.

When someone tries to hurt us with their words, the words fly about harmlessly and hurt only the person who spoke them. If we are doing what is right and people talk about it like we are doing something that is evil, then we do not need to pay attention to it. It will not harm us any more than a small bird flying over our head.

3 A whip for the horse, a bridle for the donkey,
    and a rod for the back of fools.

Acting without good sense will sting us. If we would be happy, God must make us wise. But if we act foolishly, the rod will be what we get.

4 Answer not a fool according to his folly,
    lest you be like him yourself.

5 Answer a fool according to his folly,
    lest he be wise in his own eyes.

The two texts are for two different occasions and persons. One will be best at one time and one at another. Some people may see their foolishness and change their ways if we point out how foolish they are being. However, others will only get mad at us and it is better to remain silent and not respond to their words. Wisdom will direct us which path to follow.

6 Whoever sends a message by the hand of a fool
    cuts off his own feet and drinks violence.

Nothing but loss comes from trusting conceited persons.

7 Like a lame man's legs, which hang useless,
    is a proverb in the mouth of fools.

Fools show their folly when they try to talk wisely, just as a crippled person would display their handicap if they tried to dance. Their words are not dependable and their speech limps like a cripple walking. May true religion make all of us wise.

8 Like one who binds the stone in the sling
    is one who gives honor to a fool.

Helping a senseless person into a place of honor is helping them to be where they can do great damage and where they are not likely to remain very long. Every sinner is like a rock in a slingshot. His soul will be slung out of the hand of God, far away from his present place of rest and comfort.

9 Like a thorn that goes up into the hand of a drunkard
    is a proverb in the mouth of fools.

A fool is better off not trying to quote wise proverbs. He will only hurt himself, like drunken men playing with thorn bushes. Foolish people are sure to expose their foolishness if they attempt to speak as a wise person. If there is any moral point in their story, they will run into it themselves before long. Their own mouths will condemn them.

10 Like an archer who wounds everyone
    is one who hires a passing fool or drunkard.[404]

An archer who does not pay attention injures everyone in their arrow's path. The person who hires a fool or a drunkard is the archer and the person they hire is the arrow. Lord, save us from such people.

11 Like a dog that returns to his vomit
    is a fool who repeats his folly.

Sin is deeply rooted in human nature. If you pull someone away from it for a time, they will naturally go back to it. The dog

---

[403] 1 Corinthians 1:30

[404] Verse 10 reads very differently in the King James and English Standard versions. We have modified Spurgeon's comments to suit the ESV rendering.
—editor

must be changed into a lamb before it will not return to its former delight. If fools are born again from above, they will no longer love their sin.

12 Do you see a man who is wise in his own eyes?
     There is more hope for a fool than for him.

The fool may learn, but the conceited person will not. There is more hope for a sinful tax collector[405] than for a self-righteous Pharisee.

13 The sluggard says, "There is a lion in the road!
     There is a lion in the streets!"

They make up stories to excuse their idleness. Any falsehood will serve as an excuse for their laziness. How double wicked this is; but a lazy person is capable of anything.

14 As a door turns on its hinges,
     so does a sluggard on his bed.
15 The sluggard buries his hand in the dish;
     it wears him out to bring it back to his mouth.
16 the sluggard is wiser in his own eyes
     than seven men who can answer sensibly.

They do nothing, but consider themselves a great genius. Being always half asleep they dream that they are wise, but it is only a dream. Above all things, let us avoid conceited idleness. Let us work with all our might and always try to have a humble spirit.

MAY 29
Be Wise As Serpents and Innocent As Doves[406]

We will continue to read from the wise sayings of Solomon and finish the chapter we started.

Proverbs 26:17-28

17 Whoever meddles in a quarrel not his own
     is like one who takes a passing dog by the ears.

He may expect to be bitten, because he is not likely holding a friendly dog. He has done a very pointless and ridiculous thing, and no one will thank him for doing it. It is honorable to suffer as a Christian, but disgraceful to be injured for sticking your nose in other people's business. Blessed are the peacemakers, but those who interfere in the affairs of others are very far from blessed.

18 Like a madman who throws firebrands, arrows, and death
19 is the man who deceives his neighbor
     and says, "I am only joking!"

To sin by teasing is often a way to be serious in causing trouble. It will be punished in earnest at the last great day.

20 For lack of wood the fire goes out,
     and where there is no whisperer,
     quarreling ceases.

Do not talk about it and it will die out. No hurt ever comes from holding our tongues. Silly tattling causes much sorrow. If we will not respond to those who slander us, they will tire of their dirty work or will be powerless to cause more trouble. Evil speaking seldom injures those who take no notice of it. Do not give these persons fuel for the fire by responding to them. Let the talebearers alone and their fire will go out for lack of wood.

21 As charcoal to hot embers and wood to fire,
     so is a quarrelsome man for kindling strife.

Wherever this person is, quarreling begins; or if the quarrel has already started, he will fan it into a fiercer flame. He is a person who provides fuel for Satan's fires. Let us never grow to be like him.

22 The words of a whisperer are like delicious morsels;
     they go down into the inner parts of the body.

The words of a gossip are like stabs from a knife. They have sent many to their graves with broken hearts.

23 Like the glaze[407] covering an earthen vessel

---

[405] The Pharisee and the Tax Collector — Luke 18:9-14
[406] Matthew 10:16
[407] A substance fused onto pottery that forms a hard, shiny coating.

are fervent lips with an evil heart.

There is a film of pleasant words like a coating on pottery, but underneath is deceit. They appear to glow with love, but they are really boiling over in their souls. Lord, save us from lying lips and spiteful hearts.

24 Whoever hates disguises himself with his lips
   and harbors deceit in his heart;

In his heart, he is preparing mischief and storing up revenge; but with his mouth he says nice things. He pretends to be an angel on the outside, but the devil lives inside.

25 when he speaks graciously, believe him not,
   for there are seven abominations in his heart;

All kinds of evils are hidden in a liar's soul. A liar's heart is a hell, full of evil spirits, the factory of Satan, the workshop of all mischief. Whenever anyone flatters us, let us flee from them at once, and avoid them in the future. They would not spin so nice a web if they did not wish to catch a fly.

26 though his hatred be covered with deception,
   his wickedness will be exposed in the assembly.

If not in this world, yet certainly in the next, all secrets will be revealed to the shame of those who acted the part of the hypocrite. Even in this life their masks of deception are very likely to fall off and they are exposed for what they are. Clever counterfeiters fail in some point or other and are found out. Hiding true motives is a difficult game and sooner or later the players are sure to be the losers.

27 Whoever digs a pit will fall into it,
   and a stone will come back on him who starts it rolling.

We have often seen this law of divine counterattack at work. If any of us try to injure another, we only hurt ourselves. God will make all our bitter thoughts toward others return to us, like birds that come back to their nest. Oh to have a loving spirit that tries to find the good in everyone.

28 A lying tongue hates its victims,
   and a flattering mouth works ruin.

It is the nature of ill will to hate those it injures. Hurt another and you will dislike him. Help him and you will love him. Above all things despise flattery. The person who uses this detestable technique is surely plotting your overthrow. Young people should learn this lesson early or their ignorance may cost them dearly.

May 30

Seek the LORD While He May Be Found[408]

Isaiah 55

1 "Come, everyone who thirsts
   come to the waters;
   and he who has no money,
   come, buy and eat!
   Come, buy wine and milk
   without money and without price."

The Lord comes down from his royal throne in heaven and invites us to come to him. He pleads with us to take advantage of his mercy. The gospel provides for all our spiritual needs in the most plentiful way and it gives us everything for nothing. All we have do is to receive freely what God gives us without price.

2 "Why do you spend your money for that which is not bread,
   and your labor for that which does not satisfy?
   Listen diligently to me, and eat what is good,
   and delight yourselves in rich food."

Why do people labor so hard to earn their own salvation, when Jesus has finished the work? Why do they try to find a heaven in things below when Christ is everything? They try to collect smoke and hunt after shadows. Why are they so foolish?

3 "Incline your ear, and come to me;
   hear, that your soul may live;
   and I will make with you an everlasting covenant,
   my steadfast, sure love for David."

Faith comes by hearing the gospel and receiving grace. A listening ear leads to a changed mind. Salvation comes by the

---

[408] Isaiah 55:6

promise of God. God enters into an agreement with sinners through Christ Jesus and that covenant is everlasting and certain. What an honor and a privilege to be in covenant with God.

4 "Behold, I made him a witness to the peoples,
 a leader and commander for the peoples."

Jesus is described here as the great proof of God's love and as the one who is able and willing to lead people back to God.

5 "Behold, you shall call a nation that you do not know,
 and a nation that did not know you shall run to you,
 because of the LORD your God, and of the Holy One of Israel,
 for he has glorified you."

This is undoubtedly a promise to Jesus, the Messiah. Tens of thousands will gladly accept him as their Lord.

6 "Seek the LORD while he may be found;
 call upon him while he is near;"

Pray for mercy while it is available.

7 "let the wicked forsake his way,
 and the unrighteous man his thoughts;
 let him return to the LORD, that he may have compassion on him,
 and to our God, for he will abundantly pardon.

8 For my thoughts are not your thoughts,
 neither are your ways my ways, declares the LORD.

9 For as the heavens are higher than the earth,
 so are my ways higher than your ways
 and my thoughts than your thoughts."

What a wonderful and free promise! Can anyone want more than this? Mercy is made available for the guilty, even for the worst and most outrageous of sinners. Do not let us miss the gracious opportunity, but come at once and receive pardon as the free gift of God. He speaks to each one of us as much as he did to Israel of old.

10 "For as the rain and the snow come down from heaven
 and do not return there but water the earth,
 making it bring forth and sprout,
 giving seed to the sower and bread to the eater,

11 so shall my word be that goes out from my mouth;
 it shall not return to me empty,
 but it shall accomplish that which I purpose,
 and shall succeed in the thing for which I sent it."

We are invited to trust in a very real gospel that cannot possibly fail. This is not some skillfully written fairy tale, but the guaranteed truth of the God who cannot lie. All other things may let us down, but the promise of God will be fulfilled as surely as God is God.

12 "For you shall go out in joy
 and be led forth in peace;
 the mountains and the hills before you shall break forth into singing,
 and all the trees of the field shall clap their hands.

13 Instead of the thorn shall come up the cypress;
 instead of the brier shall come up the myrtle;
 and it shall make a name for the LORD,
 an everlasting sign that shall not be cut off."

All joy belongs to the pardoned and all of nature is in harmony with that joy. What we are on the outside is a reflection of what we are in the inside. When the soul is relieved of its burden, and drinks in the joy of divine love, earth seems a paradise of sweets, and a temple of rich music. To the miserable the universe is dark and black, but to the joyous the day is clear and bright, "the marriage of the earth and sky."[409] Who would not want to be forgiven? Who would not want to live by the covenant of grace when they know they will inherit such joyous and peaceful things? The joy is no short-lived emotion. It is based on "everlasting" love and faithfulness and this makes it infinitely precious and desirable.

---

[409] From George Herbert's poem *Virtue* written in 1633. [*marriage* is *bridal* in the original.]

MAY 31

Love One Another As I Have Loved You[410]

John 15:1-15

¹ "I am the true vine, and my Father is the vinedresser. *(See how the question is answered as to which is the true Church and who takes care of it. In Jesus, and all who are joined to him deep down, we find the only true Church, and in our heavenly Father, the great leader and purifier of it.)* ² Every branch of mine that does not bear fruit he takes away, and every branch that does bear fruit he prunes that it may bear more fruit. *(Fruitless branches must be removed. The very sign that a branch is alive is its fruit. The dead wood of only claiming to be a Christian is worthless and unhealthy and must be cut off.)* ³ Already you are clean *(or pure)* because of the word that I have spoken to you. ⁴ Abide in me, and I in you. As the branch cannot bear fruit by itself, unless it abides in the vine, neither can you, unless you abide in me. *(Try as we might, we cannot produce any truly good thing unless we are united with our Lord. Our strength and our fruitfulness and even our very life all depend on HIM.)*

⁵ "I am the vine; you are the branches. Whoever abides in me and I in him, he it is that bears much fruit, for apart from me you can do nothing. *(Nothing! Mark the word. He does not say "only a little," but "nothing.")* ⁶ If anyone does not abide in me he is thrown away like a branch and withers; and the branches are gathered, thrown into the fire, and burned. *(This is the end of the person who is fruitless. They do not bear fruit because they are not truly united to Jesus. They utterly perish. What a change. One day they are counted with the branches of the true vine and the next they are burning in the fire.)* ⁷ If you abide in me, and my words abide in you, ask whatever you wish, and it will be done for you. *(Power in prayer depends on being united with Jesus and obeying his will.)* ⁸ By this my Father is glorified, that you bear much fruit and so prove to be my disciples. ⁹ As the Father has loved me, so have I loved you. Abide in my love."

This is one of the most marvelous verses in Holy Scripture. The Father loves the Son without beginning, without change, without limits, and without end; and Jesus loves us the same way.

¹⁰ "If you keep my commandments, you will abide in my love, just as I have kept my Father's commandments and abide in his love. ¹¹ These things I have spoken to you, that my joy may be in you, and that your joy may be full. *(Think of that. Christ's own joy in us! This is enough to fill us with joy running over.)*

¹² "This is my commandment, that you love one another as I have loved you. *(This is the law of love. This is more than the Golden Rule. This is the Diamond Rule!)* ¹³ Greater love has no one than this, that someone lays down his life for his friends. *(Here is love's brightest example. Note it well.)* ¹⁴ You are my friends if you do what I command you. *(The life of love is obeying Jesus' commands. The reward of love is having him as our friend. Obedience to Jesus leads to an awareness of the love of Jesus. If we walk according to his principles he will walk with us.)* ¹⁵ No longer do I call you servants, for the servant does not know what his master is doing; but I have called you friends, for all that I have heard from my Father I have made known to you." *(We have become friends who always have an open invitation to be with the Lord Jesus. We are always welcome to be with him. There are no secrets between us, because he tells us all that is in his heart. This is love indeed! It lifts poor worms of the dirt into friendship with "the ruler of the kings on the earth."[411])*

> Quicken'd by thee, and kept alive,
>   I flourish and bear fruit;
> My life I from thy sap derive,
>   My vigor from thy root.
>
> I can do nothing without thee;
>   My strength is wholly thine:
> Wither'd and barren should I be,

---

[410] John 15:12

[411] Revelation 1:5

If sever'd from the vine.[412]

JUNE 1
A Servant Is Not Greater Than His Master[413]
John 15:16-27

16 "You did not choose me, but I chose you and appointed you that you should go and bear fruit and that your fruit should abide, so that whatever you ask the Father in my name, he may give it to you."

The great reason for our salvation is not that we chose the Lord Jesus, but that he chose us. The election of his people is through him. He takes the first step toward us. However, he has not chosen us to be lazy, but to bear fruit. He has not chosen us to work for his kingdom only once in a while, but to constantly labor for him. He has also chosen us to be people of real prayer, not just worshipers on the outside, but coming to him frequently with our requests. Does our Lord see us bearing the fruit he desires? How can we know if our election is real except by bearing fruits of holiness and receiving answers to prayer?

17 "These things I command you, so that you will love one another. *(This command comes often, but never too often. We need to hear it again and again.)*

18 "If the world hates you, know that it has hated me before it hated you. *(Therefore there is no reason to be surprised when people slander*[414] *and abuse us. It is their normal way of saluting every ship that flies our great Captain's flag.)* **19** If you were of the world, the world would love you as its own; but because you are not of the world, but I chose you out of the world, therefore the world hates you. *(Election guarantees us human hatred as well as divine love. For the sake of the sweet fellowship with Jesus, we joyfully accept the bitter hatred of most of mankind. In fact, we should be worried if the world smiles on us. Many have desired the world's love and fallen into destruction.)*

20 "Remember the word that I said to you: 'A servant is not greater than his master.' If they persecuted me, they will also persecute you. If they kept my word, they will also keep yours. **21** But all these things they will do to you on account of my name, because they do not know him who sent me. *(Let us not expect easy times. We are servants of a Master who was surrounded by disapproval and died on a cross. How can we expect those who crowned HIM with thorns to crown us with roses?)* **22** If I had not come and spoken to them, they would not have been guilty of sin, but now they have no excuse for their sin. *(When truth is rejected, sin increases. There is no excuse left for a person who knows the truth about the Lord Jesus and refuses to accept it. Those who have had Jesus for their teacher and yet refuse to learn, are guilty of being ignorant on purpose, and they deserve the severest judgment.)* **23** Whoever hates me hates my Father also."

An opponent of Christianity cannot, therefore, be a sincere worshiper of God. People who say they believe in the one true God, but do not accept the Lord Jesus Christ really hate the God they pretend to worship.

24 "If I had not done among them the works that no one else did, they would not be guilty of sin, but now they have seen and hated both me and my Father. *(Our Lord's miracles proved he was who he claimed to be and proved that Israel's rejection of him was a deliberate rebellion against the light. When they sinned against the true Light, they actually added to their sin. Once the conscience is enlightened by the Truth, their sin becomes even greater.)* **25** But the word that is written in their Law must be fulfilled: 'They hated me without a cause.'[415]

26 "But when the Helper comes, whom I will send to you from the Father, the Spirit of truth, who proceeds from the Father, he will bear witness about me. *(This is the Holy Spirit's great work. What a sweet proof he gives in his people's hearts! Do we know the power of that inward experience? Let us think seriously about this matter as if we*

---
[412] From a hymn by Augustus Toplady (1740 - 1778). One of Toplady's best known hymns is *Rock of Ages*
[413] John 15:20
[414] slander - To make false and damaging statements about someone.

[415] Psalm 35:19 and Psalm 69:4

were in the very presence of the God.) **27** And you also will bear witness, because you have been with me from the beginning."

Yes. When the Holy Spirit has witnessed in us, we too may become witnesses to others about the Lord Jesus. But we must be with him to know him and we must know him before we can witness about him.

JUNE 2

I Will Not Leave You or Forsake You[416]

Joshua 1:1-9

1 After the death of Moses the servant of the LORD, the LORD said to Joshua the son of Nun, Moses' assistant, **2** "Moses my servant is dead. (Of course, Joshua knew this, but the Lord mentioned the death of this great leader to impress him with the huge task ahead of him and the need to act quickly as Moses' successor. The deaths of good people are calls to others to awaken them to action.) Now therefore arise, go over this Jordan, you and all this people, into the land that I am giving to them, to the people of Israel."

Crossing the Jordan River without boats or bridges was easier said than done, but Joshua's faith was not astonished by the Lord's command. He knew that the Lord was master of the river just as he had been of the Red Sea.

3 "Every place that the sole of your foot will tread upon I have given to you, just as I promised to Moses. **4** From the wilderness and this Lebanon as far as the great river, the river Euphrates, all the land of the Hittites to the Great Sea toward the going down of the sun shall be your territory. **5** No man shall be able to stand before you all the days of your life. Just as I was with Moses, so I will be with you. I will not leave you or forsake you. (Here are extremely great and precious promises to cheer Joshua. A promise of conquest in war, guidance for overseeing the nation of Israel, and blessing for himself personally. The Lord overflows with tender promises. May he, by the Holy Spirit, also speak some pleasant word to our own hearts.

It would be a joy, indeed, to hear him say, "I will not leave you or forsake you."

6 "Be strong and courageous, for you shall cause this people to inherit the land that I swore to their fathers to give them. (The solemn promise and covenant of God are central to faith. That is why the Lord mentions them to his servants. There is no better rock of confidence than the unchangeable promise of a faithful God.) **7** Only be strong and very courageous, being careful to do according to all the law that Moses my servant commanded you. Do not turn from it to the right hand or to the left, that you may have good success wherever you go. (We see here that it needs strength and courage to be obedient to God. Some people think Christians are cowards, but the Holy Spirit does not think so. It is a brave person who is afraid to sin and it is a hero who flees youthful lusts that battle against the soul. Notice that Joshua was to avoid a turn to the right hand as much as a turn to the left. We are not allowed to disobey God by hoping to do good any more than we are permitted to offend him by doing harm.)

8 "This Book of the Law shall not depart from your mouth, (talk about it) but you shall meditate on it day and night, (think about it) so that you may be careful to do according to all that is written in it (practice it). For then you will make your way prosperous, and then you will have good success (rejoice in it). **9** Have I not commanded you? Be strong and courageous. Do not be frightened, and do not be dismayed, for the LORD your God is with you wherever you go."

Where God's command is our authority we can afford to be bold. Who shall contradict us when the Lord of hosts gives us clear direction? To be afraid, in such a case, is to dishonor our Invincible Commander. When the Lord is on his side, the believer has every reason to be confident.

> By faith I on your strength lay hold,
>   And walk in Christ my way,
> Divinely confident and bold
>   Your precepts to obey.
>
> I would perform your utmost will,
>   With heart most fixed and true;

---

[416] Joshua 1:5

And dare to follow onward still
   Where Jesus bids me go.[417]

JUNE 3

For by Grace You Have Been Saved Through Faith[418]

This section is best told in one sitting and therefore, on this occasion, we will take a little extra time for our reading.

Joshua 2:1-21

1 And Joshua the son of Nun sent two men secretly from Shittim as spies, saying, "Go view the land, especially Jericho." And they went and came into the house of a prostitute, whose name was Rahab and lodged there. *(There is no reason for believing that Rahab was anything else than what our Bible says. She had been a sinful woman, but God's grace had appeared to her and empowered her to believe in Jehovah, the only living and true God. Perhaps, because of this, she began to practice hospitality, and therefore, when the two men came to the city gates she was waiting to give them shelter. At any rate, God's directing and God's grace brought Rahab into contact with those who could bring her safety. On her part, it was a work of faith to receive the spies.)* **2** And it was told to the king of Jericho, "Behold, men of Israel have come here tonight to search out the land."

Israel's enemies do not sleep, but are constantly on the lookout. We also may rest assured that Satan and his legions will soon find us out if we go to war against his kingdom.

3 Then the king of Jericho sent to Rahab, saying, "Bring out the men who have come to you, who entered your house, for they have come to search out all the land."

This must have been a trying moment for Rahab. All of a sudden, she found herself in a place where she must immediately decide whether she would give up her country or her God. Whatever error she committed in protecting the spies, her decision to follow the living God had no fault in it.

4 But the woman had taken the two men and hidden them. And she said, "True, the men came to me, but I did not know where they were from. **5** And when the gate was about to be closed at dark, the men went out. I do not know where the men went. Pursue them quickly, for you will overtake them." *(This was a a complete lie and it is not to be looked at in any other way. Her faith was weak and therefore she adopted a wrong plan for achieving a right thing. We may not lie under any circumstances; but Rahab was very imperfectly aware of this. The people of her day did not condemn, but rather admired clever deceit. Therefore her conscience did not condemn her about this. This fact shows that although faith may be imperfect because of our faults, it will save the soul if it is sincere.)*

6 But she had brought them up to the roof and hid them with the stalks of flax that she had laid in order on the roof.

Do we not see evidence of Rahab's new found faith here? Vice is very seldom industrious. Yet here we see a virtuous and hard working woman. She has been diligently gathering linseed to make cloth.

7 So the men pursued after them on the way to the Jordan as far as the fords. And the gate was shut as soon as the pursuers had gone out. *(Rahab had successfully misdirected the pursuers and lulled to sleep all suspicion against herself. Her success does not, however, justify her deceit. Whether it succeeds or fails, falsehood is always wrong.)*

8 Before the men lay down, she came up to them on the roof **9** and said to the men, "I know that the LORD has given you the land, and that the fear of you has fallen upon us, and that all the inhabitants of the land melt away before you. **10** For we have heard how the LORD dried up the water of the Red Sea before you when you came out of Egypt, and what you did to the two kings of the Amorites who were beyond the Jordan, to Sihon and Og, whom you devoted to destruction. **11** And as soon as we heard it, our hearts melted, and there was no spirit left in any man because of you, for the LORD your God, he is God in the heavens above

---

[417] Author unknown.
[418] Ephesians 2:8

and on the earth beneath. *(Rahab declares her faith and gives her reasons for it. Her reasons show that she had diligently gathered all information and carefully studied the facts. In this way, she became fully convinced that Jehovah alone was the true God, ruling both in heaven and earth. She had heard no sermons, and had seen neither Moses nor the prophets, and yet she believed. She will surely rise up in judgment against those, who, even though they live where the grace of God is preached, still remain unbelievers.)*

12 "Now then, please swear to me by the LORD that, as I have dealt kindly with you, you also will deal kindly with my father's house, and give me a sure sign **13** that you will save alive my father and mother, my brothers and sisters, and all who belong to them, and deliver our lives from death." *(She pleaded for her own life, but like a true child of God she did not forget her family. One of the certain results of grace in the heart is a holy concern for others. Grace and selfishness are as opposite as light and darkness. Oh may none of us forget to pray for our fathers, and mothers, and brothers, and sisters. May we live to see the whole family saved in the Lord with an everlasting salvation.)*

14 And the men said to her, "Our life for yours even to death! If you do not tell this business of ours, then when the LORD gives us the land we will deal kindly and faithfully with you."

In this way, she secured a promise of safety at once and it was expressed in the very cheering words "We will deal kindly and faithfully with you." This is the same way in which the Lord Jesus deals with all who put their trust in him.

15 Then she let them down by a rope through the window, for her house was built into the city wall, so that she lived in the wall. **16** And she said to them, "Go into the hills, or the pursuers will encounter you, and hide there three days until the pursuers have returned. Then afterward you may go your way." **17** The men said to her, "We will be guiltless with respect to this oath of yours that you have made us swear. **18** Behold, when we come into the land, you shall tie this scarlet cord in the window through which you let us down, and you shall gather into your house your father and mother, your brothers, and all your father's household. **19** Then if anyone goes out of the doors of your house into the street, his blood shall be on his own head, and we shall be guiltless. But if a hand is laid on anyone who is with you in the house, his blood shall be on our head."

When the men were leaving her they gave her the red rope as a reminder and a symbol of their agreement. An agreement which is full of instruction. The scarlet cord was to her house what the blood over the door was to Israel in Egypt. The blood-red banner is the national flag of believers. Those who want to be part of God's people must enlist under their banner. Therefore, Rahab was instructed to raise the sacred flag. Safety was promised to all beneath the scarlet cord, but to no one else, no matter how near and dear to her they might be. The same advantages belong to Christian households. Those of us who believe in Jesus, and rest in his precious blood, will be saved, but no one else. Oh let us see to it that we do not rest easy until we all live where the blood-red cord is displayed. That house alone will stand when all others fall with a crash. We must live in Jesus, if we hope to escape the great judgment day. The only thing that makes our faith really certain is the blood of the covenant.

20 "But if you tell this business of ours, then we shall be guiltless with respect to your oath that you have made us swear." **21** And she said, "According to your words, so be it." Then she sent them away, and they departed. And she tied the scarlet cord in the window. *(She followed their instructions. We must neglect no gospel command, however unimportant it may seem to those who do not understand it. We must tie the scarlet cord in our window by publicly declaring our faith. Neither Baptism, not the Lord's Supper, nor any other gospel command must be ignored. We must note well that the gospel runs this* way: "Whoever believes and is baptized will be saved."[419]

Faith was very evident in Rahab's case, as Paul reminds us in:

Hebrews 11:31

[31] By faith Rahab the prostitute did not perish with those who were disobedient, because she had given a friendly welcome to the spies.

But at the same time good works were not missing, for we are reminded of the practical nature of her faith in:

James 2:25-26

[25] And in the same way was not also Rahab the prostitute justified by works when she received the messengers and sent them out by another way? [26] For as the body apart from the spirit is dead, so also faith apart from works is dead.

JUNE 4
When You Pass Through the Waters, I Will Be With You[420]

Joshua 3:1-13

[1] Then Joshua rose early in the morning *(He did not serve God and his people in a lazy manner. Those who want to accomplish great things will never do them by lying in bed.)* and they set out from Shittim. And they came to the Jordan, he and all the people of Israel, and lodged there before they passed over.

They had a promise that they would cross over the Jordan River, but they did not know how it would be accomplished. Nevertheless they went forward in faith. If we only know our responsibility up to a certain point, let us continue to that point, even if we cannot see another inch beyond it. Let us follow God's directions as far as we know and leave what happens next to him.

[2] At the end of three days the officers went through the camp [3] and commanded the people, "As soon as you see the ark of the covenant of the LORD your God being carried by the Levitical priests, then you shall set out from your place and follow it. *(During their years in the wilderness, the ark was in the center of all the tribes of Israel, but now it leads the way, as if the Lord defied his enemies and went out in front to battle them alone and without a guard.)*

[4] "Yet there shall be a distance between you and it, about 2,000 cubits *(about 1,000 yards)* in length. Do not come near it, in order that you may know the way you shall go, for you have not passed this way before." *(The distance assigned was intended to allow the people to see the ark and also to show that God met his enemies alone. The Lord kept the armed soldiers behind him and advanced unarmed against his foes. Today we will travel a new road we have never taken before. Let us rejoice that our gracious covenant God goes before us.)*

[5] Then Joshua said to the people, "Consecrate yourselves, for tomorrow the LORD will do wonders among you." *(God always does wonders among a sanctified people. Our sins may limit him, but God will accomplish wonders through a clean heart.)* [6] And Joshua said to the priests, "Take up the ark of the covenant and pass on before the people." So they took up the ark of the covenant and went before the people.

[7] The LORD said to Joshua, "Today I will begin to exalt you in the sight of all Israel, that they may know that, as I was with Moses, so I will be with you."

God works through his ministers and wants his people to honor them.

[8] "And as for you, command the priests who bear the ark of the covenant, 'When you come to the brink of the waters of the Jordan, you shall stand still in the Jordan.'" [9] And Joshua said to the people of Israel, "Come here and listen to the words of the LORD your God." [10] And Joshua said, "Here is how you shall know that the living God is among you and that he will without fail drive out from before you the Canaanites, the Hittites, the Hivites, the Perizzites, the Girgashites, the Amorites, and the Jebusites. [11] Behold, the ark of the covenant of the Lord of all the earth is passing over before you into the Jordan. *(The ark's passing through the Jordan River was both a sign of the Lord's presence and a promise of the conquest of*

---
[419] Mark 16:16
[420] Isaiah 43:2

the land of Canaan. Every time God shows his grace to us, it is a fresh assurance of our ultimate victory over all sin, and our entrance into the promised rest.)

¹² "Now therefore take twelve men from the tribes of Israel, from each tribe a man. ¹³ And when the soles of the feet of the priests bearing the ark of the LORD, the Lord of all the earth, shall rest in the waters of the Jordan, the waters of the Jordan shall be cut off from flowing, and the waters coming down from above shall stand in one heap." *(The Lord who was the Alpha {or beginning} of his people's deliverance at the Red Sea became the Omega {or the end} of it, by repeating the miracle at the Jordan River. Do not be afraid. The Lord will do great things for us at the end of our days, just as he did when he brought us out of the Egyptian bondage of our sins.)*

JUNE 5
The Rivers, They Shall Not Overwhelm You[421]
Joshua 3:14-17

¹⁴ So when the people set out from their tents to pass over the Jordan with the priests bearing the ark of the covenant before the people, ¹⁵ and as soon as those bearing the ark had come as far as the Jordan, and the feet of the priests bearing the ark were dipped in the brink of the water (now the Jordan overflows all its banks throughout the time of harvest), *(The river was overflowing its banks, but this was no difficulty for God. He can dry up an overflowing river as easily as a shallow one.)* ¹⁶ the waters coming down from above stood and rose up in a heap very far away, at Adam, the city that is beside Zarethan, and those flowing down toward the Sea of the Arabah, the Salt Sea, were completely cut off. *(When God parted the Red Sea the waters stood as a wall on both sides, but on this occasion the floods arose on one side only, and on the other side the water quite disappeared, flowing at once into the Dead Sea. The Lord has many ways to bring about the same result. Variety in the way God works is a clear proof that the Lord is never at a loss for ways and means.)*

And the people passed over opposite Jericho. *(The enemies of Israel watched as God worked this miracle and his people passed over to the other side. And in the face of the arch-enemy God will give his people safe passage through death's cold flood.)* ¹⁷ Now the priests bearing the ark of the covenant of the LORD stood firmly on dry ground in the midst of the Jordan, and all Israel was passing over on dry ground until all the nation finished passing over the Jordan. *(The ark of the covenant first led the way and then kept the road open. The priesthood of Jesus and the ark of his redemption give all believers a passage into the better land.)*

Joshua 4:4-11; 18

⁴ Then Joshua called the twelve men from the people of Israel, whom he had appointed, a man from each tribe. ⁵ And Joshua said to them, "Pass on before the ark of the LORD your God into the midst of the Jordan, and take up each of you a stone upon his shoulder, according to the number of the tribes of the people of Israel, ⁶ that this may be a sign among you. When your children ask in time to come, 'What do those stones mean to you?' ⁷ then you shall tell them that the waters of the Jordan were cut off before the ark of the covenant of the LORD. When it passed over the Jordan, the waters of the Jordan were cut off. So these stones shall be to the people of Israel a memorial forever."

In the same way, we should try hard to find ways to remind those who come after us of the wonders of the Lord's grace. This is also an important reason why we baptize new believers and celebrate the Lord's Supper. These two sacred ordinances of our holy faith should be very special to us.

⁸ And the people of Israel did just as Joshua commanded and took up twelve stones out of the midst of the Jordan, according to the number of the tribes of the people of Israel, just as the LORD told Joshua. And they carried them over with them to the place where they lodged and laid them down there. ⁹ And Joshua set up twelve stones in the midst of the Jordan, in the place where

---
[421] Isaiah 43:2

the feet of the priests bearing the ark of the covenant had stood; and they are there to this day. ¹⁰ For the priests bearing the ark stood in the midst of the Jordan until everything was finished that the LORD commanded Joshua to tell the people, according to all that Moses had commanded Joshua.

The people passed over in haste. (Christ will never stop praying for his people until all of his redeemed ones are safely in heaven. Pastors ought to be brave men, the first to risk everything for God's sake, and the last to leave their post. Notice how the Israelites were both trembling and believing. They went "in haste," —here was fear, and "passed over" —here was faith.) ¹¹ And when all the people had finished passing over, the ark of the LORD and the priests passed over before the people.

¹⁸ And when the priests bearing the ark of the covenant of the LORD came up from the midst of the Jordan, and the soles of the priests' feet were lifted up on dry ground, the waters of the Jordan returned to their place and overflowed all its banks, as before. *(This proved that this was truly a miracle. The stopping of an overflowing river cannot be explained away by referring to natural causes. Let the Lord be praised for it.)*

JUNE 6
Do Whatever He Tells You[422]
Joshua 5:1; 10-15

¹ As soon as all the kings of the Amorites who were beyond the Jordan to the west, and all the kings of the Canaanites who were by the sea, heard that the LORD had dried up the waters of the Jordan for the people of Israel until they had crossed over, their hearts melted and there was no longer any spirit in them because of the people of Israel.

Matthew Henry says about this verse, "How dreadful is the case of those who see the wrath of God and his deserved vengeance steadily advancing toward them without any possibility of preventing it or escaping. Such will be the horrible situation of the wicked when summoned to appear before the court of an offended God. Words cannot express the pain of their feelings or the greatness of their terror. Oh, that they would heed the warning now, before it is too late, and flee for safety; that they would take hold of that hope that is set before them in the salvation of the gospel.."[423]

¹⁰ While the people of Israel were encamped at Gilgal, they kept the Passover on the fourteenth day of the month in the evening on the plains of Jericho. *(Before they began the conquest of Canaan the people focused their attention on circumcision and the Passover. We cannot expect God to help us if we are careless about keeping his commands. Before getting involved with any Christian activity it is best to look inwardly. When all is right within ourselves, then we shall be in a fit condition to do battle with the evils around us.)*

¹¹ And the day after the Passover, on the very day, they ate of the produce of the land, unleavened cakes and parched grain. ¹² And the manna ceased the day after they ate of the produce of the land. And there was no longer manna for the people of Israel, but they ate of the fruit of Canaan that year. *(We must not expect miracles when ordinary circumstances will accomplish his will. There is, if we would only see it, as much wisdom and grace in supplying our daily needs by common methods as there would be in the Lord's raining bread from heaven on us. We may also mention here that God will continue to provide what we need until we receive our inheritance above. We must gather the manna of the wilderness until we feast upon the harvests of Immanuel's land. Grace will help us every day until we enter glory.)*

¹³ When Joshua was by Jericho, he lifted up his eyes and looked, and behold, a man was standing before him with his drawn sword in his hand. *(The Lord Jesus usually appears to his people in a way that proves his oneness with them. He shows himself to be like his brothers. To Abraham the pilgrim he appeared as a pilgrim. With Jacob the wrestler he wrestled. To Shadrach, Meshach*

---
[422] John 2:5

[423] Matthew Henry (1662-1714). Spurgeon said of this famous Bible commentator: "First among the mighty for general usefulness." —editor

and Abednego he appeared as one in the furnace. And to Joshua the soldier he showed himself as a warrior. Our Lord is the defender of his chosen and will show himself strong on their behalf.)* And Joshua went to him and said to him, "Are you for us, or for our adversaries?" *(Joshua spoke like the strong and brave friend of Israel that he was. He wanted to know who's side each person was on and would then act toward him accordingly.)*

14 And he said, "No; but I am the commander of the army of the Lord. Now I have come." *(Jesus is the Commander-in-Chief. He is not only, as someone once called him, "our august ally,"[424] but he is the Captain over everything.)* And Joshua fell on his face to the earth and worshiped and said to him, "What does my lord say to his servant?

True adoration bows its heart to hear as well as its knee to worship.

15 And the commander of the Lord's army said to Joshua, "Take off your sandals from your feet, for the place where you are standing is holy." And Joshua did so. *(Joshua must first worship and then he may go to war. God will not honor people who disrespect him. It is not enough to ask the Lord Jesus to instruct us. We must also love him dearly and continue to be faithful to him.)*

Great Captain of the saints and holy angels, we adore you! Give us your commands, and go with us into the battle, and we will not fear those who are against us, however great or many they be.

JUNE 7

My Power Is Made Perfect In Weakness[425]

Joshua 6:1-5; 12-21; 23; 25

1 Now Jericho was shut up inside and outside because of the people of Israel. None went out, and none came in. **2** And the Lord said to Joshua, "See, I have given Jericho into your hand, with its king and mighty men of valor."

God had given the city to them, but they were to take it the way he had already decided on. In the same way God has chosen us before the world began, but he has said we must make a wholehearted effort to come to him.

3 "You shall march around the city, all the men of war going around the city once. Thus shall you do for six days. **4** Seven priests shall bear seven trumpets of rams' horns before the ark. *(What commander would choose such a way to begin a battle? But God works wonders in ways in which we would never even think.)* On the seventh day you shall march around the city seven times, and the priests shall blow the trumpets. **5** And when they make a long blast with the ram's horn, when you hear the sound of the trumpet, then all the people shall shout with a great shout, and the wall of the city will fall down flat, and the people shall go up, everyone straight before him."

There appeared to be virtually no connection between the method used and the desired result; yet it was not for the people to wonder how it could work; it was for them to do what the Lord told them.

12 Then Joshua rose early in the morning, and the priests took up the ark of the Lord. **13** And the seven priests bearing the seven rams' horns before the ark of the Lord walked on, and they blew the trumpets continually. And the armed men were walking before them, and the rear guard was walking after the ark of the Lord, while the trumpets blew continually.

The Israelites did exactly as they were ordered, even though the followers of Belial[426] probably looked on and laughed at them. The citizens of Jericho must have thought this was a very strange way to fight a battle and that God's people had lost their minds.

14 And the second day they marched around the city once, and returned into the camp. So they did for six days.

---

[424] *our august ally* - In other words, *Our strongest military supporter.*
[425] 2 Corinthians 12:9

[426] From 2 Corinthians 6:15 and 16 other Bible passages: Belial is used for Satan, the Wicked One.

15 On the seventh day they rose early, at the dawn of day, and marched around the city in the same manner seven times. It was only on that day that they marched around the city seven times. **16** And at the seventh time, when the priests had blown the trumpets, Joshua said to the people, "Shout, for the LORD has given you the city. *(Up to now they had proved their faith in God by patiently being silent. Now they proved their faith by giving the shout because they believed the victory was theirs.)* **17** And the city and all that is within it shall be devoted to the LORD for destruction. Only Rahab the prostitute and all who are with her in her house shall live, because she hid the messengers whom we sent. **18** But you, keep yourselves from the things devoted to destruction, lest when you have devoted them you take any of the devoted things and make the camp of Israel a thing for destruction and bring trouble upon it. **19** But all the silver and gold, and every vessel of bronze and iron, are holy to the LORD; they shall go into the treasury of the LORD." *(It was only right that the firstfruits of the war against Canaan should be the Lord's.)*

20 So the people shouted, and the trumpets were blown. As soon as the people heard the sound of the trumpet, the people shouted a great shout, and the wall fell down flat, so that the people went up into the city, every man straight before him, and they captured the city. *(This seems like a strange way to break down a wall, and yet when God ordained[427] it, it was as effective as the best made battering ram. How strange Rahab's house must have looked towering above the rubble. Faith destroys strongholds,[428] but faith also builds them up.)* **21** Then they devoted all in the city to destruction, both men and women, young and old, oxen, sheep, and donkeys, with the edge of the sword.

23 So the young men who had been spies went in and brought out Rahab and her father and mother and brothers and all who belonged to her. And they brought all her relatives and put them outside the camp of Israel.

In the day of judgment the house with the scarlet cord in the window is not left to perish in the general destruction. Others may perish, but believers are kept safe by the promise of one who cannot lie, and they have nothing to fear.

25a But Rahab the prostitute and her father's household and all who belonged to her, Joshua saved alive.

JUNE 8
Let the One Who Boasts, Boast In the Lord[429]

The history of the fall of Jericho through the blast of rams' horns reminds us of Paul's words in his letter to the church in Corinth. "The weapons of our warfare are not of the flesh but have divine power to destroy strongholds."[430] Let us read a passage in which the supposed weakness of the gospel is gloried in, because the Lord shows his power by what the world considers weakness.

1 Corinthians 1:18-31

18 For the word of the cross is folly to those who are perishing, but to us who are being saved it is the power of God. *(The same thing is seen differently by different people. One sees folly in the gospel, and another the omnipotence[431] of God. Those who have felt the gracious power of God are positively convinced of what they believe.)* **19** For it is written,

"I will destroy the wisdom of the wise,
    and the discernment of the discerning I will thwart."

20 Where is the one who is wise? Where is the scribe? Where is the debater of this age? Has not God made foolish the wisdom of the world?

Never forget this. It will help cure us of wishing for the world's idea of scholarly and intellectual preaching. Why should we want what God intends to destroy? The plain

---

[427] *ordained* - Ordered, commanded, willed, predetermined.
[428] 2 Corinthians 10:4, "For the weapons of our warfare are not of the flesh but have divine power to destroy strongholds."
[429] 1 Corinthians 1:31
[430] 2 Corinthians 10:4
[431] All powerfulness

gospel of Jesus, simply preached, is infinitely superior to all the "deep thinking" and supposed "scientific reasoning" of modern times.

21 For since, in the wisdom of God, the world did not know God through wisdom, it pleased God through the folly of what we preach to save those who believe. *(Philosophy[432] has left the world in the most disgusting mess of wrong desires and unbelief. At the same time God's servants whom the world considers uneducated have delivered the Lord's message of love just as they received it and millions have been saved.)* **22** For the Jews demand signs and Greeks seek wisdom, **23** but we preach Christ crucified, a stumbling block to Jews and folly to Gentiles, **24** but to those who are called, both Jews and Greeks, Christ the power of God and the wisdom of God. *(Personal tastes must not control the gospel message. What people want is one thing, but what the gospel gives them is another. Instead of signs and wisdom, God's ministers show people the crucified Savior, and nothing else.)*

25 For the foolishness of God is wiser than men, and the weakness of God is stronger than men. *(In the end it will be seen that what people think is foolishness and weakness in God's gospel, will be more than a match for human power and learning.)*

26 For consider your calling, brothers: not many of you were wise according to worldly standards, not many were powerful, not many were of noble birth. **27** But God chose what is foolish in this world to shame the wise; God chose what is weak in the world to shame the strong; **28** God chose what is low and despised in the world, even things that are not, to bring to nothing things that are, **29** so that no human being might boast in the presence of God.

God's election does not take human greatness into account. The preacher must not change his message just to keep from offending people the world thinks are great. He is to proclaim his message to ordinary people and be satisfied if his converts are despised as being the worst humans on earth. If God's election was for the great, then he might have given them a philosophical gospel presented with highly intellectual speeches that most people could not understand. But this is not our Lord's gospel.

As a family, let us hold tightly to the old gospel and love the honest pastors who care more about seeing sinners saved than about being thought of as great public speakers. The gospel that saved the apostles, the martyrs, the reformers, and our godly ancestors, is quite good enough for us. While others want to be wise according to worldly standards, we will follow the teaching of the Lord.

30 And because of him you are in Christ Jesus, who became to us wisdom from God, righteousness and sanctification and redemption, **31** so that, as it is written, "Let the one who boasts, boast in the Lord."

Jesus is everything to us. He deserves all the glory for everything he does through us. Worship the Lord, from the rising of the sun to the going down of the same.

JUNE 9

One Sinner Destroys Much Good[433]

Joshua 7:1-13; 15

1 But the people of Israel broke faith in regard to the devoted things, for Achan the son of Carmi, son of Zabdi, son of Zerah, of the tribe of Judah, took some of the devoted things. And the anger of the LORD burned against the people of Israel.

The chapter opens with a "but," and a very serious "but" it was. One man in Israel had dared to break the express command of Jehovah and had taken for himself from the spoil of Jericho. By doing this Achan defied the curse that had been declared against any who kept any of the plunder for themselves. One sin by one man was like a single drop of a deadly poison. It was enough to harm the whole nation of Israel. Sin is so deadly an evil that the smallest amount of it may do

---

[432] Philosophy is the study of the most basic beliefs and values of mankind without considering what God has to say about it.

[433] Ecclesiastes 9:18

more injury than we can calculate or imagine.

² Joshua sent men from Jericho to Ai, which is near Beth-aven, east of Bethel, and said to them, "Go up and spy out the land." And the men went up and spied out Ai. ³ And they returned to Joshua and said to him, "Do not have all the people go up, but let about two or three thousand men go up and attack Ai. Do not make the whole people toil up there, for they are few." *(Israel had become convinced that victory would not be difficult. Obviously, they were beginning to think they could take life easy. The Lord would fight for them and therefore they could lay down their weapons. In all ages, the grace of God has been abused by people who would rather please themselves than please God.)*

⁴ So about 3,000 men went up there from the people. And they fled before the men of Ai, ⁵ and the men of Ai killed about thirty-six of their men and chased them before the gate as far as Shebarim and struck them at the descent. And the hearts of the people melted and became as water. *(Defeat is the certain result of lazy self-confidence. It is good when such defeats force a believer back to God and leads them to a holy decision to make their best effort. God works in us to make us work ourselves. He never leads us to be lazy.)*

⁶ Then Joshua tore his clothes and fell to the earth on his face before the ark of the LORD until the evening, he and the elders of Israel. And they put dust on their heads. ⁷ And Joshua said, "Alas, O Lord GOD, why have you brought this people over the Jordan at all, to give us into the hands of the Amorites, to destroy us? Would that we had been content to dwell beyond the Jordan! *(Joshua was wrong to think this way. It showed a lack of trust on his part. It was not because Israel had crossed the Jordan River that they had been defeated in battle. It was their sin that had destroyed them!)* ⁸ O Lord, what can I say, when Israel has turned their backs before their enemies!"

The grand old warrior felt his blood boil at the thought of his nation being defeated by Canaanites.

⁹ "For the Canaanites and all the inhabitants of the land will hear of it and will surround us and cut off our name from the earth. And what will you do for your great name?"

This was the master appeal of Moses. When Joshua came to plead that way, he was sure of success. We ought to be more concerned for the honor of God, than for anything else in the world.

¹⁰ The LORD said to Joshua, "Get up! Why have you fallen on your face? ¹¹ Israel has sinned; they have transgressed my covenant that I commanded them, they have taken some of the devoted things; they have stolen and lied and put them among their own belongings. ¹² Therefore the people of Israel cannot stand before their enemies. They turn their backs before their enemies, because they have become devoted for destruction. I will be with you no more, unless you destroy the devoted things from among you. ¹³ Get up! Consecrate the people and say, 'Consecrate yourselves for tomorrow; for thus says the LORD, God of Israel, "There are devoted things in your midst, O Israel. You cannot stand before your enemies until you take away the devoted things from among you."'" *(Sin will take away the power of a church to do good. Though it may be an unknown sin, its effects will soon be visible enough. It really is a blessing when suffering humbles us and, being humbled, we search our hearts. Lord, keep this family from open and hidden sin. Keep us in your will. Make us to always obey you.)*

¹⁵ "'And he who is taken with the devoted things shall be burned with fire, he and all that he has, because he has transgressed the covenant of the LORD, and because he has done an outrageous thing in Israel.'"

Spurgeon (1855)
Very soon after moving to London Spurgeon began tutoring young men who felt called to be pastors. This eventually grew to become The Pastors' College. Over the years hundreds of men were trained and served as pastors and missionaries worldwide.

JUNE 10
Be Sure Your Sin Will Find You Out[434]
Joshua 7:16-26

16 So Joshua rose early in the morning, *(He did not waste time, but acted right away. The sooner sin is found out and put away the better. Nobody would wait around if they knew their house was on fire, but sin is a far worse evil than the raging flame.)* and brought Israel near tribe by tribe, and the tribe of Judah was taken. **17** And he brought near the clans of Judah, and the clan of the Zerahites was taken. And he brought near the clan of the Zerahites man by man, and Zabdi was taken. **18** And he brought near his household man by man, and Achan the son of Carmi, son of Zabdi, son of Zerah, of the tribe of Judah was taken. *(Achan may at first have laughed at the idea of his being detected, but when the tribe of Judah was taken, he must have felt ill at ease; when the Zerahites were taken, fear must have seized him, and his terror must have been extreme when at last the lot fell on his father's family. One way or another sin will be brought home to the guilty person, and what will be their horror when the finger of God points directly at them with a "you are the [one]"?[435])* **19** Then Joshua said to Achan, "My son, give glory to the LORD God of Israel and give praise to him. And tell me now what you have done; do not hide it from me." *(Joshua urged the criminal to confess. Achan had been clearly identified. Joshua gave him the best advice a judge can give to a condemned person. He told Achan to admit his guilt and agree that God was right in punishing him.)* **20** And Achan answered Joshua, "Truly I have sinned against the LORD God of Israel, and this is what I did: **21** when I saw among the spoil a beautiful cloak from Shinar, and 200 shekels *(about 80 ounces)* of silver, and a bar of gold weighing 50 shekels *(about 20 ounces)*, than I coveted them and took them. And see, they are hidden in the earth inside my tent, with the silver underneath." *(He saw, he coveted, he took, he hid, he was detected, convicted, and condemned. This reads like a short version of John Bunyan's book "The Sinner's Progress or the Life and Death of Mr. Badman.")* **22** So Joshua sent messengers, and they ran to the tent; and behold, it was hidden in his tent with the silver underneath. *(What good is it to have treasure and expensive clothes if you need to keep them hidden? Achan was foolish as well as wicked. Stolen goods are not true riches.)* **23** And they took them out of the tent and brought them to Joshua and to all the people of Israel. And they laid them down before the LORD. **24** And Joshua and all Israel with him took Achan the son of Zerah, and the silver and the cloak and the bar of gold, and his sons and daughters and his oxen and donkeys and sheep and his tent and all that he had. And they brought them up to the Valley of Achor. **25** And Joshua said, "Why did you bring trouble on us? The LORD brings trouble on you today." And all Israel stoned him with stones. They burned them with fire and stoned them with stones. *(This terrible punishment may have been all the more necessary, because this happened at*

---
[434] Numbers 32:23

[435] Nathan to King David (2 Samuel 12:7)

the beginning of their new life in Canaan. God wanted them to know right from the start that he was not to be trifled with and that his laws must be respected.)

26 And they raised over him a great heap of stones that remains to this day. Then the LORD turned from his burning anger. Therefore, to this day the name of that place is called the Valley of Achor.[436] *(Let this pile of stones be a awful warning to us. Do we have any hidden sin within our hearts? Are there persons in this family giving in to evil passions or doing wrong things in secret? If so, be sure your sin will find you out. The only way of escape is to make a heartfelt confession to God and a believing cry to the Lord Jesus for pardon.*

*Sins and follies not forsaken,
   All will end in deep despair;
Formal prayers are unavailing,
   Fruitless is the worldling's tear;
Small the number
   Who walk the path of wisdom fair.*[437]

JUNE 11
Speak the Truth To One Another[438]

After the destruction of Achan the conquest of Ai was very swift. And then a remarkable thing happened that is recorded in the following chapter.

Joshua 9:3-21

3 But when the inhabitants of Gibeon heard what Joshua had done to Jericho and to Ai, **4** they on their part acted with cunning and went and made ready provisions and took worn-out sacks for their donkeys, and wineskins, worn-out and torn and mended, **5** with worn-out, patched sandals on their feet, and worn-out clothes. And all their provisions were dry and crumbly. **6** And they went to Joshua in the camp at Gilgal and said to him and to the men of Israel, "We have come from a distant country, so now make a covenant with us." **7** But the men of Israel said to the Hivites, "Perhaps you live among us; then how can we make a covenant with you?" **8** They said to Joshua, "We are your servants." And Joshua said to them, "Who are you? And where do you come from?"

9 They said to him, "From a very distant country your servants have come, because of the name of the LORD your God. For we have heard a report of him, and all that he did in Egypt, **10** and all that he did to the two kings of the Amorites who were beyond the Jordan, to Sihon the king of Heshbon, and to Og king of Bashan, who lived in Ashtaroth. **11** So our elders and all the inhabitants of our country said to us, 'Take provisions in your hand for the journey and go to meet them and say to them, "We are your servants. Come now, make a covenant with us."' **12** Here is our bread. It was still warm when we took it from our houses as our food for the journey on the day we set out to come to you, but now, behold, it is dry and crumbly. **13** These wineskins were new when we filled them, and behold, they have burst. And these garments and sandals of ours are worn out from the very long journey."

Their wish to stay alive was natural. Their submission to Israel was commendable. But their clever deception was inexcusable. When we surrender ourselves to Jesus we need only to speak the truth. There is no need for us to put on old and worn-out clothing. A sinner's spiritual clothing is nothing except honesty.

14 So the men took some of their provisions, but did not ask counsel from the LORD. **15** And Joshua made peace with them and made a covenant with them, to let them live, and the leaders of the congregation swore to them.

Joshua thought the matter was so clear that he did not need to pray and ask for divine direction. It is usually when the right thing to do seems obvious that we make mistakes.

16 At the end of three days after they had made a covenant with them, they heard that they were their neighbors and that they lived among them. **17** And the people of Israel set out and reached their cities on the third day. Now their cities were Gibeon, Chephirah, Beeroth, and Kiriath-jearim. **18** But the people of Israel did not attack them, because the leaders of the congregation had sworn to

---

[436] *Achor* means *trouble*
[437] Isaac Watts (1674-1748).
[438] Zechariah 8:16

them by the LORD, the God of Israel. Then all the congregation murmured against the leaders.

Some probably murmured because they wanted to take the spoil of the Gibeonites, and others because they really believed they should not be spared.

19 But all the leaders said to all the congregation, "We have sworn to them by the LORD, the God of Israel, and now we may not touch them. *(An oath is never to be treated lightly. Neither should any promise. The Christian's word should be their promise and just as unbreakable as an oath.)* **20** This we will do to them: let them live, lest wrath be upon us, because of the oath that we swore to them." **21** And the leaders said to them, "Let them live." So they became cutters of wood and drawers of water for all the congregation, just as the leaders had said of them. *(The poor Gibeonites were glad to escape even on these terms. If the Lord Jesus will only spare us, we will also be only too glad to cut wood or draw water for him, and for his people.)*

The passage shows us that the desire to protect themselves makes people use their wits. And it makes us wonder why so few people appear to use common sense and ordinary care when it comes to the salvation of their souls.

JUNE 12

I Have Chosen the Way Of Truth[439]

The honest way in which Joshua and the leaders of Israel kept their promise to the Gibeonites, even though that promise was the result of lying and deceit, reminds us of that portrait of an honorable man, that was sketched by the master hand of David, in:

Psalm 15

1 O LORD, who shall sojourn in your tent?
 Who shall dwell on your holy hill?.

Who shall be God's special friend? Who shall be an honored guest in his home? Who shall be allowed to always make the Lord's home his home? What kind of person will be allowed to actually live in the presence of the thrice Holy God? Like fire, God's nature burns against all sin. What kind of person can dwell with such a devouring flame?

2 He who walks blamelessly

Here is the first line of the good man's portrait. He must be honest, genuine, sincere, and fair before both God and people. The word, "walks" implies that this is his normal habit.

 and does what is right

His way of life must be right. He not only does not do what is wrong, but does do what is good.

  and speaks truth in his heart;

His words must reflect his soul. He must speak truth, love truth, and live truth. God will not allow liars to stay in his presence. Who can make us righteous like this? Only the Holy Spirit!

3 who does not slander with his tongue
 and does no evil to his neighbor,
  nor takes up a reproach against his
   friend;

The person who lives in the presence of God is too brave to say something behind a person's back that they would not say to their face. They are too good to wish or do their neighbor any harm. God will have no gossips as his guest. He does not keep company with verbal abusers. Those who are quick to express disapproval demonstrate a great lack of love. God is just, and therefore does not listen to hurtful lies, and neither should we. God is love. Therefore if he honors us by making us part of his family, let us not do anything that does not reflect that love.

4 in whose eyes a vile person is despised
 but who honors those who fear the
  LORD;

Honest people do not judge others by their wealth or importance in the world. They honor good people even if they are poor. Wrong and immoral behavior disgust them, even if rich and famous people think it is okay.

 who swears to his own hurt and does not
  change;

---

[439] Psalm 119:30 KJV

This is where Joshua is such a shining example. There is no excuse for not keeping a promise unless we are absolutely unable to keep it or if keeping it would break the law. Even if there are no other people of honor in the world, Christians should be.

  ⁵ who does not put out his money at interest
     and does not take a bribe against the
     innocent.

The true believer does not take advantage of the very poor. They never charge them higher interest rates just because their situation is desperate. And they would never accuse an innocent person unjustly even if someone offered them a lot of money to do it. The very thought of it makes them sick to their stomach.

  He who does these things shall never be moved.

Good people will have troubles just as others do, but they will accept them graciously. God makes Christians to be the most excellent people on earth. Therefore he will protect them because such marvels of his creation are too rare and special to be left unguarded.

As a family, let us aim at a high standard of character. If we are not yet believers in Jesus, may the Lord give us faith, for faith is the first grace he gives us. If we are already believers, let us, by our consistent lives, prove to others the uplifting and purifying power of the religion of the Most Holy God.

    Lord, I would dwell with you,
    On your most holy hill:
  Oh shed your grace abroad in me,
    To mold me to your will.

    Faithful, but meekly kind:
    Gentle, yet boldly true;
  I would possess the perfect mind
    Which in my Lord I view.

    But, Lord, these graces all
    Your Spirit's work must be;
  To you, through Jesus blood I call,
    Create them all in me.

JUNE 13

The LORD, the Most High, Is To Be Feared[440]

Joshua 10:1-6; 8-14

¹ As soon as Adoni-zedek, king of Jerusalem, heard how Joshua had captured Ai and had devoted it to destruction, doing to Ai and its king as he had done to Jericho and its king, and how the inhabitants of Gibeon had made peace with Israel and were among them, *(The name Adoni-zedek means Lord of righteousness, and is very similar to Melchizedek, who was the king of Salem or Jerusalem during the time of Abraham. That's makes Adoni-zedek the successor and perhaps a relative of Melchizedek. How frequently those who come after the best of men, are themselves among the worst of characters. Grace cannot be inherited. Someone may pass on their belongings but not their Christianity.)* ² he feared greatly, because Gibeon was a great city, like one of the royal cities, and because it was greater than Ai, and all its men were warriors.

³ So Adoni-zedek king of Jerusalem sent to Hoham king of Hebron, to Piram king of Jarmuth, to Japhia king of Lachish, and to Debir king of Eglon, saying, ⁴ "Come up to me and help me, and let us strike Gibeon. For it has made peace with Joshua and with the people of Israel." ⁵ Then the five kings of the Amorites, the king of Jerusalem, the king of Hebron, the king of Jarmuth, the king of Lachish, and the king of Eglon, gathered their forces and went up with all their armies and encamped against Gibeon and made war against it.

⁶ And the men of Gibeon sent to Joshua at the camp in Gilgal, saying, "Do not relax your hand from your servants. Come up to us quickly and save us and help us, for all the kings of the Amorites who dwell in the hill country are gathered against us." *(Those who join the Lord's side are sure to have enemies, but they may rest assured that the Lord will come to their rescue.)*

⁸ And the LORD said to Joshua, "Do not fear them, for I have given them into your hands. Not a man of them shall stand before

---

[440] Psalm 47:2

you." **9** So Joshua came upon them suddenly, having marched up all night from Gilgal. *(Joshua made a fast march during the night to rescue the Gibeonites. This showed his commitment to defend all those who were associated with Israel.)* **10** And the LORD threw them into a panic before Israel, who struck them with a great blow at Gibeon and chased them by the way of the ascent of Beth-horon and struck them as far as Azekah and Makkedah. **11** And as they fled before Israel, while they were going down the ascent of Beth-horon, the LORD threw down large stones from heaven on them as far as Azekah, and they died. There were more who died because of the hailstones than the sons of Israel killed with the sword.

The Lord fought for his people, but he gave them the victory only after they fought too. After Joshua and his army showed that they would take part in the battle, then the Lord brought forth his power. God defeated the five kings in such a way, that all the glory for the victory clearly belonged to him. Where we do much, God does more. In fact, he really does it all.

12 At that time Joshua spoke to the LORD in the day when the LORD gave the Amorites over to the sons of Israel, and he said in the sight of Israel,

"Sun, stand still at Gibeon,
   and moon, in the Valley of Aijalon."

13 And the sun stood still, and the moon stopped,
   until the nation took vengeance on their enemies.

Is this not written in the Book of Jashar? The sun stopped in the midst of heaven and did not hurry to set for about a whole day. *(The book of Jashar is lost, but the book of God is not. Not a single line of it! Everything in the Bible is given by divine inspiration and protected by the Holy Spirit. We would never have even heard the name of this book of Jashar if it had not been preserved like a fly in the amber[441] of Scripture.)* **14** There has been no day like it before or since, when the LORD obeyed the voice of a man, for the LORD fought for Israel.

Many people have tried to explain how this wonderful event could have happened, because they want the world to believe it really happened. But there is no need for them to try to protect God's reputation with their theories. The Almighty God can as easily stop the sun and moon as a watchmaker can adjust the timing of a watch. God did do it, and how he did it is no question for us. We may rest assured he extended the daylight by the very wisest means. It is not ours to try and soften down miracles, but to glorify God in them. At the appearing of our greater Joshua,[442] the sun and moon shall be thrown into the background while he will be revealed in flaming fire, taking vengeance on his enemies.

JUNE 14
His Steadfast Love Endures Forever[443]

This is an appropriate place to include this psalm. It celebrates the Lord's relationship with Israel through the time he established them in the land that he had promised to them as their inheritance.

Psalm 136

1 Give thanks to the LORD, for he is good,
   for his steadfast love endures forever.

Praise the Lord for what he naturally is. His own personal goodness deserves our adoration.

2 Give thanks to the God of gods,
   for his steadfast love endures forever.

3 Give thanks to the Lord of lords,
   for his steadfast love endures forever;

His sovereignty over all and his unequalled superiority above everything that exists should command our admiring praise at all times. All his power and majesty are softened with mercy.

4 to him who alone does great wonders
   for his steadfast love endures forever;

---

[441] Amber is fossilized or petrified tree resin (pitch) which has been appreciated for its color and natural beauty since ancient times. It is used as jewelry and sometimes an insect can be found trapped in it.

[442] *Joshua* is an Old Testament type of *Christ*. *Joshua* means "YAHWEY [God] is Salvation". *Jesus* means "God Saves."
[443] Psalm 136

How sweet is this chorus. It comes over and over again, but it never loses its charm by being repeated so often. God is to be praised not only for his nature and lordship, but also for his works.

5 to him who by understanding made the heavens,
      for his steadfast love endures forever;
6 to him who spread out the earth above the waters,
      for his steadfast love endures forever;

Oh Creator of all things, we continue to be amazed by the mercy that shines brightly in all the work of your hands.

7 to him who made the great lights,
      for his steadfast love endures forever;

What would we do without the sun? Could life itself survive? And how gloomy would night be if the moon no longer gave light to the darkness! Light is also a result of God's mercy.

8 the sun to rule over the day,
      for his steadfast love endures forever;
9 the moon and stars to rule over the night,
      for his steadfast love endures forever;

Each and every blessing deserves a verse of praise all to itself.

10 to him who struck down the firstborn of Egypt,
      for his steadfast love endures forever;

From nature, the psalmist turns to God's involvement in the world and sees mercy all around him. Mercy is everywhere around us, like the air we breathe. What was judgment to Egypt was mercy to Israel.

11 and brought Israel out from among them,
      for his steadfast love endures forever;
12 with a strong hand and an outstretched arm,
      for his steadfast love endures forever;
13 to him who divided the Red Sea in two,
      for his steadfast love endures forever;
14 and made Israel pass through the midst of it,
      for his steadfast love endures forever;
15 but overthrew Pharaoh and his host in the Red Sea,
      for his steadfast love endures forever;

For Pharaoh it was destruction, but that destruction was necessary for the escape of the Israelites, as well as for their safety while they were in the wilderness. Therefore mercy was in it all.

16 to him who led his people through the wilderness,
      for his steadfast love endures forever;

Even though the Israelites continually provoked the Lord, he did not stop leading them on their journey. In their case, as in ours, God proved the infinity of his mercy. Time cannot rust it, sin cannot conquer it; throughout eternity it must and will remain.

17 to him who struck down great kings,
      for his steadfast love endures forever;
18 and killed mighty kings,
      for his steadfast love endures forever;
19 Sihon, king of the Amorites,
      for his steadfast love endures forever;
20 and Og, king of Bashan,
      for his steadfast love endures forever;
21 and gave their land as a heritage,
      for his steadfast love endures forever;
22 a heritage to Israel his servant,
      for his steadfast love endures forever.

He makes the well earned punishment of some to contribute to the gain of others. Even God's judgments prove his grace.

23 It is he who remembered us in our low estate,
      for his steadfast love endures forever;
24 and rescued us from our foes,
      for his steadfast love endures forever;

Our personal experience is one of the sweetest notes of the song that celebrates infinite mercy. Our redemption is the joy of all our joy.

25 he who gives food to all flesh,
      for his steadfast love endures forever.

The daily providence that feeds the countless fish of the sea, and the birds of the air, and the creatures of the field, deserves our admiring thankfulness.

26 Give thanks to the God of heaven,
      for his steadfast love endures forever.

The Lord reigns from his heavenly throne of glory. "Our Father in heaven, hallowed be your name."[444]

---

[444] Matthew 6:9

JUNE 15
I Will Run In the Way Of Your Commandments[445]

Joshua 14:6-14

⁶ Then the people of Judah came to Joshua at Gilgal. And Caleb the son of Jephunneh the Kenizzite said to him, "You know what the LORD said to Moses the man of God, in Kadesh-barnea concerning you and me. *(We are glad to meet with this old hero, Joshua's fellow countryman. Notice how he talks about the promise, "You know what the Lord said...concerning you and me." Faithful hearts treasure up the divine word. To them, God's promises are more valuable than gold.)* ⁷ I was forty years old when Moses the servant of the LORD sent me from Kadesh-barnea to spy out the land, and I brought him word again as it was in my heart. *(He was a man of true heart. He spoke as his heart directed him and not as the majority of the spies wanted him to speak. Only a person who is true to their own convictions has the courage to go against the stream and speak the truth in the teeth of a false public opinion. Oh, that we had more people like this today! Old Caleb looks back with gratitude to this event that took place so many years ago. It is well to sow seed in our youth, that we will not be afraid to harvest in our old age.)*

⁸ "But my brothers who went up with me made the heart of the people melt; yet I wholly followed the LORD my God. ⁹ And Moses swore on that day, saying, 'Surely the land on which your foot has trodden shall be an inheritance for you and your children forever, because you have wholly followed the LORD my God.' *(Moses agreed with Caleb that what his own conscience had already told him was true. It is well when our own thinking is the same as the praise that others give to us. Otherwise their praises may embarrass us instead of pleasing us. Caleb now asks for what had been promised him. Things are very sweet when they are the result of a promise made to us.)*

¹⁰ "And now, behold, the LORD has kept me alive, just as he said, these forty-five years since the time that the LORD spoke this word to Moses, while Israel walked in the wilderness. And now, behold, I am this day eighty-five years old. ¹¹ I am still as strong today as I was in the day that Moses sent me; my strength now is as my strength was then, for war and for going and coming.

This was a rare privilege and Caleb was thankful for it. He was ready to use all the strength that God had given him against the enemies of Israel. He could probably have retired and asked for a pension, but instead, he asks for fresh work, with all the eagerness of a young man.

¹² "So now give me this hill country of which the LORD spoke on that day, for you heard on that day how the Anakim were there, with great fortified cities. It may be that the LORD will be with me, and I shall drive them out just as the LORD said."

Perhaps Caleb reminded Joshua of a brave conversation he had with him under the walls of the city of Hebron, when they had seen both the giants and the phenomenal strength of the fortifications. Forty-five years earlier Caleb spoke like a bold believer. Now he wanted to prove that his words were not empty words, but could be backed up by brave actions. It appears that Hebron had once been captured by Israel, but the giants had returned to their strongholds. Caleb felt that with God's help, he would chase them out again, once and for all.

¹³ Then Joshua blessed him, and he gave Hebron to Caleb the son of Jephunneh for an inheritance. ¹⁴ Therefore Hebron became the inheritance of Caleb the son of Jephunneh the Kenizzite to this day, because he wholly followed the LORD, the God of Israel. *(The good old soldier had his wish. In due time he took possession of the territory that was assigned to him. Wholehearted loyalty to the Lord will have its reward. The Lord never allowed a anyone, who trusted in him completely and followed him with all their heart, to be beaten.)*

In this family may there be many Calebs. Indeed, may we all be wholehearted for the Lord.

---
[445] Psalm 119:32

JUNE 16
Open Your Mouth Wide, and I Will Fill It[446]

We shall now see what Caleb did with his inheritance in the land of promise.

Joshua 15:13-19

13 According to the commandment of the LORD to Joshua, he gave to Caleb the son of Jephunneh a portion among the people of Judah, Kiriath-arba, that is, Hebron (Arba was the father of Anak.) **14** And Caleb drove out from there the three sons of Anak, Sheshai and Ahiman and Talmai, the descendants of Anak. *(These were giants, but their gigantic size did not frighten Caleb. He did not hesitate in attacking them. The one who fears God is not someone who will fear anyone else.)* **15** And he went up from there against the inhabitants of Debir. Now the name of Debir formerly was Kiriath-sepher. *(The Israelites appear to have captured Debir once already, but the Canaanites had retaken it. Our sins have a strong tendency to return, and when they do we must drive them out a second time. The ancient name of Debir is used here. The former name, Kiriath-sepher means "the city of the book." Since education was rare in those days, it may be that this place was famous for having a great library that contained ancient documents. In any case, it was a city in the land of Canaan and it was supposed to be captured. Ungodliness is not better because it is connected with education.)* **16** And Caleb said, "Whoever strikes Kiriath-sepher and captures it, to him will I give Achsah my daughter as wife." **17** And Othniel the son of Kenaz, the brother of Caleb, captured it. And he gave him Achsah his daughter as wife. *(This adventure is also recorded in the book of Judges; probably because years later Othniel, the hero of it, was moved by the Spirit of God to become a judge and rescue Israel from the king of Mesopotamia.[447] He was a virtuous nephew of a noble man. The younger members of a family should never allow their elders to have all the enthusiasm and faith. If there is one serious Christian in our family, let us at least try to equal them.)* **18** When she came to him, she urged him to ask her father for a field. And she got off her donkey, and Caleb said to her, "What do you want?" **19** She said to him, "Give me a blessing. Since you have given me the land of the Negeb, give me also springs of water." And he gave her the upper springs and the lower springs. *(If earthly parents give to their children what they desire, how much more will our heavenly Father give us more of his Holy Spirit. We must fight for some blessings, as Othniel fought for Kiriath-sepher. Others may be won by prayer, the way Achsah received the field with springs of water.)*

Caleb obtained his promised inheritance. Then he demonstrates a generous spirit by his willingness to give the city of Hebron to the Levites. He was brave to win it, but not greedy to hold on to it.

Joshua 21:3; 10-13

3 So by command of the LORD the people of Israel gave to the Levites the following cities and pasturelands out of their inheritance.

10 The following cities … went to the descendants of Aaron, one of the clans of the Kohathites who belonged to the people of Levi; since the lot fell to them first. **11** They gave them Kiriath-arba (Arba being the father of Anak), that is Hebron, in the hill country of Judah, along with the pasture lands around it. **12** But the fields of the city and its villages had been given to Caleb the son of Jephunneh as his possession. *(Caleb had the Lord's ministers for closest neighbors and the leader of them lived right next door. It was good for the Lord's ministers to have such a valiant defender so close to them, as well as for Caleb and his family to have such excellent instructors so nearby. God's ministers are our best friends.)*

13 And to the descendants of Aaron the priest they gave Hebron, the city of refuge for the manslayer, with its pasturelands, Libnah with its pasture lands. *(A double honor was thus given to Caleb's city. If the Lord will use our property for his service we*

---
[446] Psalm 81:10
[447] Judges 3:7-11

will cheerfully give him the best that we have.)

JUNE 17

You Shall Rest and Shall Stand In Your Allotted Place At the End Of the Days[448]

Joshua 18:1-10

¹ Then the whole congregation of the people of Israel assembled at Shiloh and set up the tent of meeting there. The land lay subdued before them. *(Shiloh means tranquil or peace; a very fitting name for the tabernacle of the God who is Israel's rest. The tabernacle, the sacrifices and the offerings also picture Jesus, who is our peace. Yet it was in the city of peace that Joshua stirred up the people to war. True peace wages a determined war against all the enemies of the Lord. Even The Great Peacemaker came to make war in the earth; war with evil and war with Satan, because holiness can have no peace until sin is destroyed.)*

² There remained among the people of Israel seven tribes whose inheritance had not yet been apportioned. ³ So Joshua said to the people of Israel, "How long will you put off going in to take possession of the land, which the LORD, the God of your fathers, has given you? *(The people had become wealthy from all the things they had acquired from winning the many battles against the Canaanites. They did not feel like continuing the war to which God had called them. Too often this is the sin of believers. They are satisfied with the progress they have already made in their Christian lives and they no longer feel like waging the daily battle against sin. Self-satisfaction is the end of progress. May the Lord deliver us from it. Joshua rebuked the people for their laziness.)*

⁴ "Provide three men from each tribe, and I will send them out that they may set out and go up and down the land. They shall write a description of it with a view to their inheritances, and then come to me. ⁵ They shall divide it into seven portions. Judah shall continue in his territory on the south, and the house of Joseph shall continue in their territory on the north. ⁶ And you shall describe the land in seven divisions and bring the description here to me. And I will cast lots for you here before the LORD our God. *(They were sent out to survey and inspect the land. With this information they would know what they were fighting for. It is good for us to think about what blessings are available to us, because it will help get us moving forward. Dividing the land among the tribes would also encourage more eager service on the part of each tribe. Dividing the work in the service of God is also a wise thing to do; as long as it does not lead to envy and jealousy. All the land will be conquered when each tribe fights for its own portion. All church work will be done when each of us works diligently to accomplish the job the Lord has given them.)*

⁷ "The Levites have no portion among you, for the priesthood of the LORD is their heritage. *(God's ministers should be cared for by the people. Remember, many of them have sacrificed the profits they might have made in the business world or the rewards of public service. God will take care of those whose lives are freely given to his service.)* And Gad and Reuben and half the tribe of Manasseh have received their inheritance beyond the Jordan eastward, which Moses the servant of the LORD gave them."

⁸ So the men arose and went, and Joshua charged those who went to write the description of the land, saying, "Go up and down in the land and write a description and return to me. And I will cast lots for you here before the LORD in Shiloh." *(Joshua was once a spy himself. Now he sends others to do what he had done before. Those who serve God well in a lower position are the most likely to be promoted to a higher office.)* ⁹ So the men went and passed up and down in the land and wrote in a book a description of it by towns in seven divisions. Then they came to Joshua to the camp at Shiloh, *(The men who performed this service were brave and forceful. The church can always use talented people who will survey and describe the state of the unconverted*

---
[448] Daniel 12:13

world; as well as brave, hard working soldiers, who will go forth to conquer it. We are too slow to go up and possess the land. We need to be fired up to do what we know we should. Oh that we would once again be soldiers in the Lord's holy war against evil.) ¹⁰ and Joshua cast lots[449] for them in Shiloh before the LORD. And there Joshua apportioned the land to the people of Israel, to each his portion.

God chose to reveal his will by the casting of lots. However, this in no way teaches us to follow this superstitious method of making decisions. It is virtually tempting the Lord our God. We have no command from God for casting lots. There is no promise in the Bible connected with it. A Christian who would cast lots to make decisions in our day would be acting like an unbeliever.

JUNE 18

Judge Not, That You Be Not Judged[450]

Joshua 22:1-6; 10-20

¹ At that time Joshua summoned the Reubenites and the Gadites and the half-tribe of Manasseh, ² and said to them, "You have kept all that Moses the servant of the LORD commanded you and have obeyed my voice in all that I have commanded you. ³ You have not forsaken your brothers these many days, down to this day, but have been careful to keep the charge of the LORD your God. *(It is only right to give praise wherever it is deserved. Some people think it is dangerous to give someone a compliment, but wise people of old did not think so. In a world where fault-finding and complaining is all around us, it is refreshing to meet with someone who congratulates others on a job well done. Unfortunately, people do not usually fulfill their commitments wholeheartedly and completely. When it does happen, we should be pleased to praise them for doing so.)*

⁴ "And now the LORD your God has given rest to your brothers, as he promised them. Therefore turn and go to your tents in the land where your possession lies, which Moses the servant of the LORD gave you on the other side of the Jordan. ⁵ Only be very careful to observe the commandment and the law that Moses the servant of the LORD commanded you, to love the LORD your God, and to walk in all his ways and to keep his commandments and to cling to him and to serve him with all your heart and with all your soul."

Having first praised them, Joshua then speaks to them about their other obligations. His words of warning deserve careful notice. They were to observe the commandment; their religion must be active. They were to love the Lord; their service must be cheerful and sincere. They were to walk in all his ways; they must obey the Lord in everything they do. They were to cling to him; it must continue all the time. A believer's obedience to the Lord is made up of many excellent qualities. The lack of any one will seriously scar it. Who but the Spirit of God can produce all these good things in fallen humanity?

⁶ So Joshua blessed them and sent them away, and they went to their tents.

¹⁰ And when they came to the region of the Jordan that is in the land of Canaan, the people of Reuben and the people of Gad and the half-tribe of Manasseh built there an altar of imposing size.

Building an altar was not a wise thing to do. God had not commanded it. Other people would very likely misunderstand why they did it. And those who built it were very likely to misuse it.

¹¹ And the people of Israel heard it said, "Behold, the people of Reuben and the people of Gad and the half-tribe of Manasseh have built the altar at the frontier of the land of Canaan, in the region about the Jordan, on the side that belongs to the people of Israel." ¹² And when the people of Israel heard of it, the whole assembly of the people of Israel gathered at Shiloh to make war against them. *(The Israelites in Canaan thought their relatives who lived across the Jordan River were getting ready to start a false religion.*

---

[449] Casting lots: Throwing pebbles or other objects on the ground and making a decision based on the way they land. Similar to tossing a coin in the air and making a decision based on whether it lands "heads" or "tails."
[450] Matthew 7:1

Their eagerness to nip it in the bud showed their loyalty to the Lord. However, did not their quick decision to go to war with their relatives show they were to also too quick to judge?)

13 Then the people of Israel sent to the people of Reuben and the people of Gad and the half-tribe of Manasseh, in the land of Gilead, Phinehas the son of Eleazar the priest, **14** and with him ten chiefs, one from each of the tribal families of Israel, every one of them the head of a family among the clans of Israel.

We should listen before we judge. Israel did not rush into battle. Instead, they sent wise men to find out what was really going on.

15 And they came to the people of Reuben, the people of Gad, and the half-tribe of Manasseh, in the land of Gilead, and they said to them, **16** "Thus says the whole congregation of the Lord, 'What is this breach of faith that you have committed against the God of Israel in turning away this day from following the Lord by building yourselves an altar this day in rebellion against the Lord? *(They told them why the building of another altar made them angry. If their suspicions were correct, they would have been justified in trying to stop it.)* **17** Have we not had enough of the sin at Peor[451] from which even yet we have not cleansed ourselves, and for which there came a plague upon the congregation of the Lord, **18** that you too must turn away this day from following the Lord? And if you too rebel against the Lord today then tomorrow he will be angry with the whole congregation of Israel. *(They knew that the sin of a few might bring judgment on all of them. Therefore they were determined to stamp out the evil before it spread further.)*

19 "But now, if the land of your possession is unclean, pass over into the Lord's land where the Lord's tabernacle stands, and take for yourselves a possession among us. Only do not rebel against the Lord or make us as rebels by building for yourselves an altar other than the altar of the Lord our God.'"

They very generously invited them to move to their own side of the Jordan and share the land with them rather than sinning by setting up another altar. To find a way for someone to correct an error without it costing them a lot is a great help toward getting them to do the right thing. The pleading of the tribes with their brothers was very sensible, serious, determined, and generous.

20 "'Did not Achan the son of Zerah break faith in the matter of the devoted things, and wrath fell upon all the congregation of Israel? And he did not perish alone for his iniquity.'" *(This judgment was great in their memories and therefore, they finished their argument with it. They were afraid their relatives were about to do something very wrong, something that would cause God to create a lot of trouble for all Israel. Therefore, they spoke to them forcefully. Oh that we all wanted to keep ourselves and our family from sin. God still chastens[452] those he has chosen, and though in this life the wicked may go unpunished, he will not fail to discipline his own children. Let us be humble before the Lord and jealous for the honor of his word.)*

To God the Father, God the Son,
And God the Spirit, three in one,
Be honor, praise, and glory given
By all on earth, and all in heaven.[453]

JUNE 19

A Soft Answer Turns Away Wrath[454]

The tribes on the other side of the Jordan had built an altar of imposing size and the people of Israel were ready to wage war against their brothers because of it. A delegation made up of Phinehas and ten tribal chiefs was sent to the two and one-half tribes. They were received with courtesy and their accusations were received without showing anger.

---

[451] This refers to Balak asking Balaam to curse Israel and the punishment God inflicted on his people for joining the Moabites in their false religion. The story is found in Numbers chapters 22 through 25.

[452] *chasten, chastening* or *chastisement* - The act of discipline which may include scolding, criticizing or pain inflicted for the purpose of correction or moral improvement
[453] Isaac Watts (1674-1748)
[454] Proverbs 15:1

Joshua 22:21-34

21 Then the people of Reuben, the people of Gad, and the half-tribe of Manasseh said in answer to the heads of the families of Israel, **22** "The Mighty One, God, the LORD! He knows; and let Israel itself know! If it was in rebellion or in breach of faith against the LORD, do not spare us today **23** for building an altar to turn away from following the LORD. Or if we did so to offer burnt offerings or grain offerings or peace offerings on it, may the LORD himself take vengeance. *(They appealed to God with sincere hearts. They had no intention of offering sacrifices anywhere but at the one appointed altar before the tabernacle. Too often people say, "So help me God" or, "As God as my witness" or similar statements. Appeals to God must never be made lightly. If we feel we must use such language, it should be only for the most important situations. It is comforting to feel that God knows our motives. However, we must do our best to act in such a way that God's people also understand our reasons for doing something.)*

24 "No, but we did it from fear that in time to come your children might say to our children, 'What have you to do with the LORD, the God of Israel? **25** For the LORD has made the Jordan a boundary between us and you, you people of Reuben and people of Gad. You have no portion in the LORD.' So your children might make our children cease to worship the LORD. **26** Therefore we said, 'Let us now build an altar, not for burnt offering, nor for sacrifice, **27** but to be a witness between us and you, and between our generations after us, that we do perform the service of the LORD in his presence with our burnt offerings and sacrifices and peace offerings, so your children will not say to our children in time to come, "You have no portion in the LORD."'"

They were afraid they would lose access to worshiping at the tabernacle and that the Jordan River might prevent fellowship with their relatives sometime in the future.

28 "And we thought, If this should be said to us or to our descendants in time to come, we should say, 'Behold, the copy of the altar of the LORD, which our fathers made, not for burnt offerings, nor for sacrifice, but to be a witness between us and you.' **29** Far be it from us that we should rebel against the LORD and turn away this day from following the LORD by building an altar for burnt offering, grain offering, or sacrifice, other than the altar of the LORD our God that stands before his tabernacle!" *(Their intention was good, but the action had a very questionable appearance. We should always think the best of others' actions unless there is clear evidence not to.)*

30 When Phinehas the priest and the chiefs of the congregation, the heads of the families of Israel who were with him, heard the words that the people of Reuben and the people of Gad and the people of Manasseh spoke, it was good in their eyes. **31** And Phinehas the son of Eleazar the priest said to the people of Reuben and the people of Gad and the people of Manasseh, "Today we know that the LORD is in our midst, because you have not committed this breach of faith against the LORD. Now you have delivered the people of Israel from the hand of the LORD." *(Religious disagreements are usually very stormy, but in this case true wisdom ended the hostility. When one is ready to explain, and the other willing to receive the explanation, difficulties will soon be overcome. May all differences in this family be handled wisely and tenderly, and peace and love always rule among us.)*

32 Then Phinehas the son of Eleazar the priest, and the chiefs, returned from the people of Reuben and the people of Gad in the land of Gilead to the land of Canaan, to the people of Israel, and brought back word to them. **33** And the report was good in the eyes of the people of Israel. And the people of Israel blessed God and spoke no more of making war against them to destroy the land where the people of Reuben and the people of Gad were settled. *(Love for the truth made Israel prepare for war, but they were not hot-headed like some are in these days. As soon as the reasons for building the altar were explained to them, they were glad to stop talking about war. They thanked God that this questionable situation was cleared* up. It is good to watch over others with holy jealousy, but not to be hateful and bitter.)

34 The people of Reuben and the people of Gad called the altar Witness, "For," they said, "it is a witness between us that the LORD is God." (Everything ended well. The one true religion ruled on both sides of the Jordan. Pray that our country will become one; by knowing the one true Lord, the one true faith, and the one true baptism.)

JUNE 20
Cling To the LORD Your God[455]

Joshua served his nation faithfully. At the close of his life he shared his inmost thoughts to the people, urging them to remember the Lord's goodness to them and encouraging them to continue to follow their God. Believers today need to follow Joshua's advice as much as Israel did in his day.

Joshua 23:1-15

1 A long time afterward, when the LORD had given rest to Israel from all their surrounding enemies, and Joshua was old and well advanced in years, 2 Joshua summoned all Israel, its elders and heads, its judges and officers, and said to them, "I am now old and well advanced in years. 3 And you have seen all that the LORD your God has done to all these nations for your sake, for it is the LORD your God who has fought for you. *(Thinking about the judgments of God on the ungodly should have a serious influence on us. Remembering the Lord's mercy to us should always keep us close to him.)*

4 "Behold, I have allotted to you as an inheritance for your tribes those nations that remain, along with all the nations that I have already cut off, from the Jordan to the Great Sea in the west. 5 The LORD your God will push them back before you and drive them out of your sight. And you shall possess their land, just as the LORD your God promised you. 6 Therefore, be very strong to keep and to do all that is written in the Book of the Law of Moses, turning aside from it neither to the right hand nor to the left, *(Joshua repeats to them what the Lord had said to him after Moses died.[456] The words were still like music to his ears. We hope that the precious promises of God that have had a powerful influence in our hearts will have the same result on others.)* 7 that you may not mix with these nations remaining among you or make mention of the names of their gods or swear by them or serve them or bow down to them, 8 but you shall cling to the LORD your God just as you have done to this day."

He compliments them as well as commands them. A little well deserved praise makes people all the more ready to listen. Joshua's lesson was: Separation from Sinners. It is a lesson that has not gone out of date and needs to be repeated to the church today.

9 "For the LORD has driven out before you great and strong nations. And as for you, no man has been able to stand before you to this day. 10 One man of you puts to flight a thousand, since it is the LORD your God who fights for you, just as he promised you. 11 Be very careful, therefore, to love the LORD your God. *(Sin is weakness. Love to God gives us the strength of God.)* 12 For if you turn back and cling to the remnant of these nations remaining among you and make marriages with them, so that you associate with them and they with you, 13 know for certain that the LORD your God will no longer drive out these nations before you, but they shall be a snare and a trap for you, a whip on your sides and thorns in your eyes, until you perish from off this good ground that the LORD your God has given you." *(Marriage with unbelievers is specifically mentioned, because it is a frequent and deadly trap. It has done more harm in the church of God than tongue can tell. It is the wolf that destroys the lambs.)*

Note from this verse that any sins in our own hearts that we do not resolve to drive out will become a contagious disease in our lives and a whip for our back. Think of "thorns in your eyes." No one can have peace while they are at peace with any sin. Can anyone carry red hot coals in their heart and not be burned?

---

[455] Joshua 23:8
[456] Joshua 1:7

14 "And now I am about to go the way of all the earth, and you know in your hearts and souls, all of you, that not one word has failed of all the good things that the LORD your God promised concerning you. All have come to pass for you; not one of them has failed. 15 But just as all the good things that the LORD your God promised concerning you have been fulfilled for you, so the LORD will bring upon you all the evil things until he has destroyed you from off this good land that the LORD your God has given you."

God is faithful to fulfill all his promises. That should be enough to convince us that he is just as faithful to fulfill all his threats. He is a true God, both in mercy and in justice. We need to be careful to be obedient, because the Lord is committed to fulfill everything in his word.

JUNE 21
Let Me Not Wander From Your Commandments[457]

Joshua was moved by the Holy Spirit to speak in the name of the Lord. He reminded the people of what God had done for them. He reviewed the wonders of Egypt and the wilderness. Now he mentions the Lord's goodness to them in Canaan.

Joshua 24:11-26

11 "'And you went over the Jordan and came to Jericho, and the leaders of Jericho fought against you, and also the Amorites, the Perizzites, the Canaanites, the Hittites, the Girgashites, the Hivites, and the Jebusites. And I gave them into your hand. 12 And I sent the hornet before you, which drove them out before you, the two kings of the Amorites; it was not by your sword or by your bow. *(God can make insects to be more terrible than soldiers with weapons. That is what he did in this case. Israel fought, but her victories were really from a higher force. Our best efforts to win the battle with Satan are not enough. Our salvation comes from the Lord alone.)* 13 I gave you a land on which you had not labored and cities that you had not built, and you dwell in them. You eat the fruit of vineyards and olive orchards that you did not plant.'"

Everything that we call our own has been given to us by God, just as much as Canaan was given to the Israelites.

14 "Now therefore fear the LORD and serve him in sincerity and in faithfulness. Put away the gods that your fathers served beyond the River and in Egypt, and serve the LORD. 15 And if it is evil in your eyes to serve the LORD, choose this day whom you will serve, whether the gods your fathers served in the region beyond the River, or the gods of the Amorites in whose land you dwell. But as for me and my house, we will serve the LORD." *(Everyone has a god. The question is, who will their god be? Joshua declares that Jehovah alone would be his God and the God of his household. We cannot serve two gods and it will be a happy thing if we never attempt it in our home. Let us once and for all choose the Lord alone to be our God. May divine grace show us the way.)*

16 Then the people answered, "Far be it from us that we should forsake the LORD to serve other gods, 17 for it is the LORD our God who brought us and our fathers up from the land of Egypt, out of the house of slavery, and who did those great signs in our sight and preserved us in all the way that we went, and among all the peoples through whom we passed. 18 And the LORD drove out before us all the peoples, the Amorites who lived in the land. Therefore we also will serve the LORD, for he is our God." *(They spoke well, but not well enough. They were much too confident in their decision. They had turned their backs on the Lord many times. They would have been more sensible to pray, "Lord, keep us," than to shout so confidently, "we will" and "we will.")*

19 But Joshua said to the people, "You are not able to serve the LORD, for he is a holy God. He is a jealous God; he will not forgive your transgressions or your sins. 20 If you forsake the LORD and serve foreign gods, then he will turn and do you harm and consume you, after having done you good."

Joshua reminded them that their promise would not be so easy to keep as they imagined. It is one thing to promise, but

---
[457] Psalm 119:10

quite another to perform. How awe-inspiring are the thoughts suggested by the words, "he is a jealous God." He will not put up with a rival, nor tolerate half-hearted service.

21 And the people said to Joshua, "No, but we will serve the LORD." **22** Then Joshua said to the people, "You are witnesses against yourselves that you have chosen the LORD, to serve him." And they said, "We are witnesses." *(Their intentions may have been good, but they were far too over-confident. They made a promise that they soon broke. Beware of trusting yourself even when you are in your best state of mind. Self is as fickle as the wind that constantly changes direction.)*

23 He said, "Then put away the foreign gods that are among you, and incline your heart to the LORD, the God of Israel." **24** And the people said to Joshua, "The LORD our God we will serve, and his voice we will obey." **25** So Joshua made a covenant with the people that day, and put in place statutes and rules for them at Shechem. **26** And Joshua wrote these words in the book of the Law of God. And he took a large stone and set it up there under the terebinth[458] that was by the sanctuary of the LORD.

Oh Lord, we in this family want to serve you forever. Help us by your grace to be your beloved children and your faithful servants.

JUNE 22
Give Me Life According To Your Word[459]

As we have now ended the book of Joshua, we will select a few passages from other portions of the Bible before we continue the history. We will again read a part of David's wonderful speech about the book of God.

Psalm 119:17-32

17 Deal bountifully with your servant,
   that I may live and keep your word.

Our lives are protected by God's generosity. That is why we should dedicate our lives to serving him. True life is the result of the rich grace of God in our lives.

---
[458] *Terebinth:* A small tree.
[459] Psalm 119:25

We may think our obeying God is often done in secret, but if it is real others will see it.

18 Open my eyes, that I may behold
   wondrous things out of your law.

The Scriptures are full of wonders, and especially they call attention to him whose name is "Wonderful." We need to have our eyes opened by the Holy Spirit, or we will not see anything correctly. Our very nature keeps us a long way from being able to keep God's law. We cannot even understand his law unless God teaches us through the Holy Spirit.

19 I am a sojourner on the earth;
   hide not your commandments from me!

Lord, to the world I am a stranger. Do not let me be a stranger to your will. If I use your commandments as my map, I will find the road to heaven, even while traveling in this foreign country we call the world. Without your commandments, I will be like a traveler lost in the desert.

20 My soul is consumed with longing
   for your rules at all times.

David says he wanted to please God "at all times," even if doing so would break his heart. This kind of strong desire to do the Lord's will is a sure sign that the Spirit of God is living within us.

21 You rebuke the insolent, accursed ones,
   who wander from your commandments.

Pride causes sin and sin causes God to inflict the proud with trouble and distress. And that is only the beginning of God's dealing with them.

22 Take away from me scorn and contempt,
   for I have kept your testimonies.

The best of people are slandered with terrible lies said about them. But God is their true judge and a clear conscience before him is their comfort.

23 Even though princes sit plotting against me,
   your servant will meditate on your statutes.

He did not become so troubled or discouraged that he gave up his faith. He found his strength and comfort in the best spiritual food—God's word!

24 Your testimonies are my delight;
  they are my counselors.

As a result of meditating in the word, David was kept from both sadness and confusion. We can only get comfort from the Bible by following its directions and living by its instructions.

25 My soul clings to the dust;
  give me life according to your word!

We always seem to be in danger of dying, both physically and spiritually. Even our new life in Christ has the filth of sin constantly attacking us and trying to keep us from fellowship with God. We need reviving every day. The Lord has promised to refresh our new life and that is all the reason we need to pray for it.

26 When I told of my ways, you answered me;
  teach me your statutes!

Confession to God is good for the soul and divine instruction is life's best protection. While we confess past failure, we can only avoid future sin by seeking heavenly instruction.

27 Make me understand the way of your precepts,
  and I will meditate on your wondrous works.

The more we think about God's wondrous works, the more he gives us understanding as to how we should live. Meditating on God's wonders is like mining for gold. The more we dig, the more we understand. The more we understand the more golden our words will be. When God teaches us, our speaking will be to everyone's benefit. When we ignore God's precepts, we would be better off not talking.

28 My soul melts away for sorrow;
  strengthen me according to your word!

Lord, when sorrow makes us too weak to do anything, make your word to become bread of heaven that gives us strength.

29 Put false ways far from me

Take false ways away from me and me away from false ways. My hearts aches when I am around them.

  and graciously teach me your law!

30 I have chosen the way of faithfulness;
  I set your rules before me.

A young child learns by copying their lesson. An artist learns by copying his model. The Bible is our textbook. We cannot learn unless we open it and use it.

31 I cling to your testimonies, O LORD;
  let me not be put to shame!

32 I will run in the way of your commandments
  when you enlarge my heart!

The more God gives us of comfort and knowledge, the more we will serve him. The weight of his grace will lead us to lay aside "every weight" of sin.[460] May the Lord make more room in our hearts for himself and his love.

JUNE 23
I Trust In Your Word[461]
Psalm 119:33-48

33 Teach me, O LORD, the way of your statutes;
  and I will keep it to the end.

Bernard says, "He who is his own teacher has a fool for his master."[462] We cannot teach ourselves what we do not know. True understanding comes as a result of having God's viewpoint about everything we learn. Those who are taught by the Lord become levelheaded students and continue to follow him no matter what happens. Lessons learned from God are never forgotten.

34 Give me understanding, that I may keep your law
  and observe it with my whole heart.

Where the Spirit of God gives a spiritual understanding of the Word, the whole person is purified and is determined to keep the Lord's commands. This is a good prayer for everyone in the family. Let us stop for a moment and silently pray these words from our hearts.

35 Lead me in the path of your commandments,
  for I delight in it.

---

[460] A reference to Hebrews 12:1, "Let us also lay aside every weight, and sin which clings so closely."
[461] Psalm 119:42
[462] Bernard of Clairvaux (1090-1153)

I am like the poor invalid who had no one to help him.[463] *Lord, command me to walk. Where my heart is, I will do everything in my power to get the rest of me there too.*

36 Incline my heart to your testimonies,
    and not to selfish gain!

Greed is the opponent of true religion. Those who do not love God, often make a god of their money. This sin is certain to destroy anyone who falls into it. It made Judas a traitor, and dragged him down to hell.

37 Turn my eyes from looking at worthless things;
    and give me life in your ways.

Looking brings longing, and longing leads to sin, therefore keep the eye from staring at evil.

38 Confirm to your servant your promise,
    that you may be feared.

Lord, my whole heart wants to honor you. Please make all your promises to me come true.

39 Turn away the reproach that I dread,
    for your rules are good.

Rejoice when people reject you because you are a Christian. But pray that you do not give Christianity a bad name because you seem to honor Christ one day and dishonor him the next.

40 Behold, I long for your precepts;
    in your righteousness give me life!

Those who only claim to be Christians hope God will bless them abundantly. True Christians are more concerned about living a life that pleases their Lord. He who does not desire to be holy will be shut out of heaven. Lord, send us more grace that we may be more holy.

41 Let your steadfast love come to me, O Lord,
    your salvation according to your promise;

We need great mercy. We cannot be saved without God's loving mercy. Our comfort and joy come from knowing he has promised to give us his never ending love. Let us pray with King David, "Let your steadfast love come to me, O Lord."

42 then shall I have an answer for him who taunts me,
    for I trust in your word.

Our faith is a gift from God. It brings us joy and makes us want to live a holy life. When those who make fun of our faith see our joy and a life that puts God first, their mouths are shut.

43 And take not the word of truth utterly out of my mouth,
    for my hope is in your rules.

Lord, when there are times when my joy is missing, do not let me stop praising you. It is better to stumble around with our praise for the Lord, than to be entirely silent.

44 I will keep your law continually,
    forever and ever,

This would be heaven on earth. It is heaven in heaven.

45 and I shall walk in a wide place,
    for I have sought your precepts.

Holiness is what really sets us free.

46 I will also speak of your testimonies before kings
    and shall not be put to shame,

What is there to be ashamed of? May God give us the boldness of true faith no matter whose presence he puts us in.

47 for I find my delight in your commandments,
    which I love.

"I live a life of pleasure," said holy Joseph Alleine; "but it is a life of spiritual delights, such as men of the world do not know and cannot understand."[464]

48 I will lift up my hands toward your commandments, which I love,
    and I will meditate on your statutes.

David wanted to hold God's truth tightly. He held up his hands to receive it with open arms. It was his joy and delight to keep the law of his God. He loved the Lord's Word and meditated on it every day. That encouraged him to keep the Lord's commandments all the more.

---

[463] John 5:2-15

[464] Joseph Alleine (1634-1668) is perhaps best known for his book *An Alarm to the Unconverted*.

It should be our daily habit to read and study the Scriptures. We must not be satisfied with just this family reading. We must feed on the precious Word. Do all understand this?

JUNE 24

[Disciples] Ought Always To Pray[465]

Our time will be well spent if we study one of our Lord's messages about prayer. It consists of two parables.

Luke 18:1-14

[1] And he told them a parable to the effect that they ought always to pray and not lose heart. *(To begin praying is easy, but to continue in it is another thing. Too often we allow ourselves to become weary or distracted and then we lose our focus, and then we lose the blessing.)* [2] He said, "In a certain city there was a judge who neither feared God nor respected man. [3] And there was a widow in that city who kept coming to him and saying, 'Give me justice against my adversary.' [4] For a while he refused, but afterward he said to himself, 'Though I neither fear God nor respect man, [5] yet because this widow keeps bothering me, I will give her justice, so that she will not beat me down by her continual coming.'"

He was a wicked man without feeling. He was more than willing to be dishonest and rule in the wrong person's favor. The person who brought her case to him was a poor woman. Her husband who might have pled her case for her had died. He was hard hearted and did not care about her sad story. Yet her persistence won her case. He was afraid of being tired to death and therefore he paid attention to her cry. Every part of the parable strengthens our case. We deal with a faithful and gracious God, who is ready to hear us. While it is true that we are poor and feeble, it is also true that we have a powerful Advocate[466] in the great Husband of the church. Therefore if we do not receive an answer to our prayer the first time, we should pray again and again, and never stop until our persistence is answered.

[6] And the Lord said, "Hear what the unrighteous judge says. [7] And will not God give justice to his elect, who cry to him day and night? Will he delay long over them? *(They are not strangers, but "his elect." God will certainly listen to them.)* [8] I tell you, he will give justice to them speedily. *(The prayers of the suffering church will not have long to wait. God's time does arrive.)* Nevertheless, when the Son of Man comes, will he find faith on earth?" *(Faith is so rare that even Jesus will hardly find any of it when he returns to earth. Shame on our unbelief.)*

[9] He also told this parable to some who trusted in themselves that they were righteous, and treated others with contempt: [10] "Two men went up into the temple to pray, one a Pharisee and the other a tax collector. [11] The Pharisee, standing by himself, prayed thus: *(He stood by himself as if he was too holy to be touched by others. His prayer was not a real prayer, but just his way of showing his presumed superiority.)* 'God, I thank you that I am not like other men, extortioners, unjust, adulterers, or even like this tax collector, [12] I fast twice a week; I give tithes of all that I get.' *(He pretended to be praising God, but he was only praising himself. It is all "I," "I fast," "I give," and so on. As if this was not bad enough, he felt a need to criticize others by making a list of his own "virtues" while insulting his neighbor by pointing out what he considered the tax collector's "faults.")*

[13] "But the tax collector, standing far off, would not even lift up his eyes to heaven, but beat his breast, saying, 'God be merciful to me, a sinner!' *("He confessed his sin. He beat upon his heart as the cause of his sin. He pleaded for mercy, and looked to the atonement as his only hope. His prayer was real! 'Be favorable toward me because of the atonement.'"[467])* [14] I tell you, this man went down to his house justified, rather than the

---

[465] Luke 18:1
[466] *Advocate* - An attorney or lawyer. Also a champion crusader, spokesperson, fighter. Someone who has your best interests at heart and acts on your behalf. See 1 John 2:1: "We have an advocate with the Father, Jesus Christ the righteous."

[467] This is the editor's paraphrase. Spurgeon is quoting from Adam Clarke's Commentary (circa 1817), "Be propitious toward me through sacrifice." (KJV)

other. *(The despised tax collector had a sweet sense of pardon in his heart. The Pharisee did not. In fact, he did not even ask to be pardoned.)* For everyone who exalts himself will be humbled, but the one who humbles himself will be exalted."

From all this let us learn to pray persistently, but not proudly. We must be in earnest, but still humble. We may be bold, but not proud. Lord teach us to pray.

"Be favorable toward me because of the atonement."

JUNE 25
The LORD Weighs the Spirit[468]

Let us learn a little from the wisdom of Solomon, from

Proverbs 16:1-16

1 The plans of the heart belong to man,
   but the answer of the tongue is from the LORD.

We are not able to think or say anything properly without God guiding us. This is especially true when we pray. We need to have our heart prepared and our mouth opened by the Spirit of all grace.

2 All the ways of a man are pure in his own eyes,
   but the LORD weighs the spirit.

We judge by looking on the surface or outward appearance. The Lord uses an infallible test. He puts everything into his perfect balances and arrives at a very different conclusion from ours.

3 Commit your work to the LORD,
   and your plans will be established.

Both our physical and spiritual concerns will be safe when we place them in the Lord's hands. Then the peace that comes from our faith, will give us a steady, calm, determined, and joyful state of mind.

4 The LORD has made everything for its purpose,
   even the wicked for the day of trouble.

Let the wicked oppose God all they want; he will make them serve some part in his plans.

5 Everyone who is arrogant in heart is an abomination to the LORD;
   be assured, he will not go unpunished.

The pride of the wicked makes them despicable, but their power cannot protect them. God will break up all godless nations and associations, however strong they may be.

6 By steadfast love and faithfulness iniquity is atoned for,
   and by the fear of the LORD one turns away from evil.

7 When a man's ways please the LORD,
   he makes even his enemies to be at peace with him.

The Lord often does this, as in the cases of Isaac and Abimelech, Jacob and Esau. But this truth must be qualified by another truth. The Lord's enemies will not always be at peace with us, no matter how kind and pleasant we may be.

8 Better is a little with righteousness
   than great revenues with injustice.

9 The heart of man plans his way,
   but the LORD establishes his steps.

"Man proposes, but God disposes."[469] Napoleon sneered at this saying, and vowed that he would propose and dispose too, but his end was not far off.

10 An oracle is on the lips of a king;
    his mouth does not sin in judgment.

This should be true. In King Solomon's case it was true. But the opposite might be said of many other kings. There is one King, the Lord of all, concerning whom this is absolutely true.

11 A just balance and scales are the LORD's;
    all the weights in the bag are his work.

Justice should rule everywhere including in the courtroom and in everyday life. Let us be very honest in all our relationships, because anything else displeases the Lord.

12 It is an abomination to kings to do evil,
    for the throne is established by righteousness.

---

[468] Proverbs 16:2

[469] From *Of the Imitation of Christ* by Thomas a Kempis *(1379-1471).* An English translation from the Latin meaning: "Human beings can make any plans they want, but it is God who determines whether they succeed or fail."

13 Righteous lips are the delight of a king,
   and he loves him who speaks what is right.
14 A king's wrath is a messenger of death,
   and a wise man will appease it.
15 In the light of a king's face there is life,
   and his favor is like the clouds that bring the spring rain.

This is most true of the King of kings. His anger is death. His love is life. Those who enjoy the awareness of the favor of the Lord, know by experience the refreshing and comforting influence of his presence. To walk in the light of God's acceptance is perfect happiness. To lose fellowship with God, brings bitter sorrow to his chosen.

16 How much better to get wisdom than gold!
   To get understanding is to be chosen rather than silver.

Wisdom from God is better, much better than gold. No one can even imagine how much better. Gold can be earned by anyone, but only God can chose us, by his free grace, to be a part of his holy family. Gold is just a valuable piece of earth, but grace is the very heart of heaven. Gold is soon spent and gone. The more we use grace, the more grace we are given. Gold may be stolen from us, but no one can take grace away from us. Gold and silver cannot comfort us in death, but true wisdom can. The wealth of precious metals will be useless in eternity, but grace will make us glorious there. Lord, always give us understanding through your Holy Spirit!

Proverbs 16:11, "A just balance."

JUNE 26
Blessed Is He Who Trusts In the LORD[470]

Proverbs 16:17-33

17 The highway of the upright turns aside from evil;
   whoever guards his way preserves his life.

Keep on the right road and God will keep you safe. The right road is the King's highway, the ancient, well-used way. It is the road traveled by the saints before us and walked by the Prince of pilgrims himself.

18 Pride goes before destruction,
   and a haughty spirit before a fall.

Pride will cause a fall. As the needle in the barometer forecasts the weather, so does pride warn us that a humbling time is near.

19 It is better to be of a lowly spirit with the poor
   than to divide the spoil with the proud.

This may not seem like good advice, and few would choose to follow it, but the Word of God knows best. The person dividing up the loot is afraid that he may lose it again, and is probably already unhappy with his share and greedy for more. But the humble mind is satisfied, and therefore possesses happiness.

20 Whoever gives thought to the word will discover good,
   and blessed is he who trusts in the LORD.

---
[470] Proverbs 16:20

To trust God in all our matters is the wise way of handling them. Let us trust him in all things today.

²¹ The wise of heart is called discerning,
    and sweetness of speech increases persuasiveness.

The really wise person will eventually be discovered and will receive the credit they deserve. Those who can speak in an interesting and pleasing way can increase the knowledge of others if their own hearts are taught correctly.

²² Good sense is a fountain of life to him who has it,
    but the instruction of fools is folly.

The wisdom of a fool is ridiculous. Even his best advice is foolishness.

²³ The heart of the wise makes his speech judicious
    and adds persuasiveness to his lips.

²⁴ Gracious words are like a honeycomb,
    sweetness to the soul and health to the body.

Since pleasant words are both sweet and healthful, let us use many of them. Use words out of God's Word, kind words, words that give pleasure to others. Let us use them from morning to night, and even though we are not beekeepers, we will never be without honeycombs.

²⁵ There is a way that seems right to a man,
    but its end is the way to death.

²⁶ A worker's appetite works for him;
    his mouth urges him on.

We need food to eat everyday and therefore we must work for it. We need spiritual food everyday and our Savior has told us we must work for that too.

²⁷ A worthless man plots evil,

He searches for evil like a miner for gold. He searches for places where it is hidden. He digs hard to find it. People will work hard for Satan.

    and his speech is like a scorching fire.

He is always ready to speak hurtfully and do untold harm.

²⁸ A dishonest man spreads strife,
    and a whisperer separates close friends.

If you have anything to say that you would be embarrassed to say to the person you are talking about, then never say it at all. Whispering against people is extremely mean and those who listen to it are mean too.

²⁹ A man of violence entices his neighbor
    and leads him in a way that is not good.

³⁰ Whoever winks his eyes plans dishonest things;
    he who purses his lips brings evil to pass.

Some shut their eyes and move their lips in prayer, but hateful people spend their time thinking about cruel things they can do. They are always thinking of it and muttering about it to themselves.

³¹ Gray hair is a crown of glory;
    it is gained in a righteous life.

Honor older Christians. Think of their gray hair as crowns on their heads, and treat them with double respect. Old age is honorable by itself, but when godliness goes along with it, it is even more honorable.

³² Whoever is slow to anger is better than the mighty,
    and he who rules his spirit than he who takes a city.

People with self-control have conquered themselves. They have crushed a rebellion that comes from within. These are wonderful and unselfish achievements. May the Lord make each one of us gentle and patient. Are we of a hot and angry spirit? Then let us pray for the waters of grace to quench the flames of nature.

³³ The lot is cast into the lap,
    but its every decision is from the LORD.

The Lord controls even what seems like unimportant matters or what may appear to be accidents. This is a sweet comfort.

JUNE 27

Love Never Ends[471]

In today's reading the apostle Paul tells us what holy love is. This excellent grace is an absolutely essential ingredient in the Christian's witness to the world.

---

[471] 1 Corinthians 13:8

1 Corinthians 13

¹ If I speak in the tongues of men and of angels, but have not love, I am a noisy gong or a clanging cymbal.

The greatest speaker's words are only so much sound, unless there is love in their heart to give power to their words. Better to have a loving heart than to speak twenty languages.

² And if I have prophetic powers, and understand all mysteries and all knowledge, and if I have all faith, so as to remove mountains, but have not love, I am nothing. (We may be blessed with extraordinary talent and abilities and yet still perish in our sins. Grace in the heart is the only sure evidence of salvation. A man may prophesy and be a Balaam.[472] He may understand mysteries and be a Simon the Magician.[473] He may have all knowledge and perish like Ahithophel.[474] He may have a faith that can move mountains, and be a son of destruction like Judas. If we do not love both God and people, then we have nothing good in us.) ³ If I give away all I have, and if I deliver up my body to be burned, but have not love, I gain nothing. (People may give all their money for the poor just to show off. They may die as martyrs because they are simply down right stubborn. But if they have no love to God their suffering is actually pointless. Love is an essential grace. It is the heart of godliness. Without love true religion is just a dead body.)

⁴ Love is patient and kind; love does not envy (It rejoices when good things happen to others.) or boast; (It never glorifies itself.) it is not arrogant (It hates flattery.) ⁵ or rude. (Christian love behaves itself. Love to others will not allow us to act in ways that are improper for Christians or that society thinks are in bad taste.) It does not insist on its own way; it is not irritable or resentful; (It is not suspicious and always finding fault with others.) ⁶ it does not rejoice at wrongdoing, but rejoices with the truth. ⁷ Love bears all things, (Love tolerates the faults of others. As Old Master Trapp says, love "swallows down whole many pills which would be very bitter in her mouth if she were so foolish as to chew them."[475]) believes all things, (That is to say, love believes all things that would make us have a good opinion of our neighbors, even when it takes great faith to be able to do so.) hopes all things, endures all things.

⁸ Love never ends. (It is like a beautiful flower that never withers.) As for prophecies, they will pass away; as for tongues, they will cease; as for knowledge, it will pass away. ⁹ For we know in part and we prophesy in part. (Our greatest knowledge is to know that we know nothing. We are only beginner students in Christ's College.) ¹⁰ but when the perfect comes, the partial will pass away. ¹¹ When I was a child, I spoke like a child, I thought like a child, I reasoned like a child. When I became a man, I gave up childish ways. ¹² For now we see in a mirror dimly, but then face to face. Now I know in part; then I shall know fully, even as I have been fully known.

Paul shows us that our best intellectual accomplishments here below, even in heavenly things, are temporary. He teaches us to place the greatest value on those superior graces of the heart that will outlast time and be made perfect in eternity.

¹³ So now faith, hope, and love abide, these three; but the greatest of these is love.

It is not true that faith and hope will come to an end any more than love will. The three divine sisters are each immortal. We will trust the Lord all the more when we meet him face to face and we will hope all the more enthusiastically for the continued enjoyment of his glory when we enter into it.

---

[472] Balaam was a prophet in Moab who was hired to curse Israel, but instead prophesied as the Lord directed him. His story begins in Number 22. He later gave advice to the king of Moab that, "caused the people of Israel to act treacherously against the LORD" (Number 31:16).
[473] Or in Latin, *Simon Magus*. His story in found in Acts 8:9-24.
[474] Ahithophel advised David's son Absalom when he tried to overthrow his father's throne. His story is found in 2 Samuel 15:12 - 17:23.
[475] John Trapp (1601-1669) We swallow pills whole because they taste terrible if we chew them. Love thinks the best of others' words and actions and does not spend time (chewing on them) trying to figure out whether their intentions were good or bad.

Still love is the best. May we become perfect in love.

JUNE 28

Fear God. Honor the Emperor[476]

1 Peter 2:13-25

¹³ Be subject for the Lord's sake to every human institution, *(True religion is always the friend of peace and liberty. The gospel does not encourage lawlessness and the Christian does not start fights.)* whether it be to the emperor[477] as supreme, ¹⁴ or to governors as sent by him to punish those who do evil and to praise those who do good. *(Civil government is necessary for the well-being of mankind, and those who delight in the law of the Lord are among the last to wish to see its power weakened, or its police officers hated. We would rather suffer because of a few bad laws, than see our country terrorized by lawless mobs.)*

¹⁵ For this is the will of God, that by doing good you should put to silence the ignorance of foolish people. *(Others are quick to speak against our holy faith. In Peter's day Christians were accused of being opposed to the government. The constant obedience of Christians to the laws of the countries they lived in was the most convincing answer to the people who thought they wanted to overthrow the government.)* ¹⁶ Live as people who are free, not using your freedom as a cover-up for evil, but living as servants of God. *(Believers are the freest of people, but they know the difference between liberty and ignoring the law. As servants of the Lord, they agree to obey laws made to keep the peace in their country. The reason they do is because their Great Lawgiver commands them to.)* ¹⁷ Honor everyone. Love the brotherhood. Fear God. Honor the emperor. *(Four general principles that are intended to balance one another. There should be a blending of all of them in our lives. We are to honor not only our country's leaders, but everyone. Every human being should be treated with respect. Not just rich people or those who always wear the latest style, or who are admired by the world, but poor people and those who wear secondhand clothing and do not seem to have friends. We are all created in the image of God and we should treat everyone in the best way we can.)*

¹⁸ Servants, be subject to your masters with all respect, not only to the good and gentle but also to the unjust. ¹⁹ For this is a gracious thing, when, mindful of God, one endures sorrows while suffering unjustly. ²⁰ For what credit is it if, when you sin and are beaten for it, you endure? *(Ordinary people can do that, but Christians are extraordinary people and must rise to the highest point of goodness.)* But if when you do good and suffer for it you endure, this is a gracious thing in the sight of God. *(Many will say, "If I deserve to be punished, then I will live through it without complaining." That is obviously the right thing to do. If we are wise, we can put up with suffering patiently even when we see no reason for deserving such treatment. We thank God for the grace he gives us that helps us rejoice in the middle of our suffering even when we are in the right.)*

²¹ For to this you have been called, because Christ also suffered for you, leaving you an example, so that you might follow in his steps. ²² He committed no sin, neither was deceit found in his mouth. ²³ When he was reviled, he did not revile in return; when he suffered, he did not threaten, but continued entrusting himself to him who judges justly. *(What an example! May the Holy Spirit work in us to imitate it. The Lord Jesus was the perfect example of patience and the perfect picture of tolerance. He was absolutely perfect. He endured suffering all the time for no reason except that he was hated. But he never complained, or resented being treated so wrongly. Master of Patience, teach your followers.)*

²⁴ He himself bore our sins in his body on the tree, that we might die to sin and live to righteousness. By his wounds you have been healed. ²⁵ For you were straying like sheep, but have now returned to the Shepherd and Overseer of your souls. *(Let us then follow our Shepherd wherever he leads. Let us walk closely with Jesus especially in the paths of sacred patience and self-control.)*

---

[476] 1 Peter 2:17
[477] Or *king;* also verse 17

Oh Spirit of love, we need your grace to do this!

JUNE 29

We Will Always Be With the Lord[478]

1 Thessalonians 4:13-18

13 But we do not want you to be uninformed, brothers, about those who are asleep, that you may not grieve as others do who have no hope. *(We may sorrow, but not as much and not for as long as those who have no hope. We know that the souls of believers who have died are safe and that their bodies will rise from the grave when Jesus comes back. Therefore what reason do we have to weep and complain the way the godless and unbelieving do?)* **14** For since we believe that Jesus died and rose again, even so, through Jesus, God will bring with him those who have fallen asleep. *(Note the words, "fallen asleep." Fallen asleep in Jesus! Death does not break the relationship between Jesus and his saints. We are one with him eternally; and therefore just as surely as Jesus rose from the grave, all the members of his mystical body[479] must also rise.)*

15 For this we declare to you by a word from the Lord, that we who are alive, who are left until the coming of the Lord, will not precede those who have fallen asleep. *(We who are alive are not in a better position than those who have died in the Lord. At the same time, those who have gone before us are not in line ahead of us. The dead in Christ and the alive in Christ are equal. There is no reason to be anxious to be alive when our Lord returns. What is important is that we are confident that the Lord will return. Whether we are alive or dead when he comes is not a big deal. There is no special award given just because we happen to be alive when he comes again.)*

16 For the Lord himself will descend from heaven with a cry of command, with the voice of an archangel, and with the sound of the trumpet of God. And the dead in Christ will rise first. *(Those who have died in Christ will be the first to receive new glorified bodies.)* **17** Then we who are alive, who are left, will be caught up together with them in the air, and so we will always be with the Lord. *(The resurrection of the dead comes first, then the rapture when both living and dead rise up in the air together to live with Jesus for forever. Jesus is our best and only hope. Does he belong to us and we to him?)* **18** Therefore encourage one another with these words.

1 Thessalonians 5:1-10

1 Now concerning the times and the seasons, brothers, you have no need to have anything written to you. **2** For you yourselves are fully aware that the day of the Lord will come like a thief in the night. *(Those who reject the warning of this prophecy will be caught off guard when Jesus comes back.)* **3** While people are saying, "There is peace and security," then sudden destruction will come upon them as labor pains come upon a pregnant woman, and they will not escape. *(Certainly, suddenly, unstoppably. No matter which way they turn they will find no safe way to escape; they will not be rescued.)* **4** But you are not in darkness, brothers, for that day to surprise you like a thief.

Even though you do not know when it will happen, your faith stands on guard, and you are prepared.

5 For you are all children of light, children of the day. We are not of the night or of the darkness. **6** So then let us not sleep, as others do, but let us keep awake and be sober.

Are we all children of the light? If we are God's special people, we should be responsible people. We need to stay awake and be alert. The children of darkness may have an excuse for being caught sleeping, but we do not. A "sleeping Christian" is a contradiction in terms.

7 For those who sleep, sleep at night, and those who get drunk, are drunk at night.

---

[478] 1 Thessalonians 4:17
[479] The Mystical Body of Christ refers to all Christians in all times in all places as being part of Jesus Christ and one another. Paul refers to this in Romans 12:4-5. Verse 5: "So we, though many, are one body in Christ, and individually members one of another." See also, 1 Corinthians 10:17 Ephesians 4:11-13.

In those days, drunkenness had not grown as bold as it is now. People who were in the habit of becoming intoxicated waited for the cover of darkness to have their drunken parties. It would be completely out of place for someone who has heavenly light to fall into the wicked activities of nature's midnight.

⁸ But since we belong to the day, let us be sober, having put on the breastplate of faith and love, and for a helmet the hope of salvation. ⁹ For God has not destined us for wrath, but to obtain salvation through our Lord Jesus Christ, ¹⁰ who died for us so that whether we are awake or asleep we might live with him.

The great love of Jesus is understood best when his redeemed ones show it in their lives, at all times and in all places.

Spirit of holiness, work in us to be in fellowship with Jesus and to be like him. Amen.

JUNE 30
Bear Fruit In Keeping With Repentance[480]

We will now return to the Bible history.

Judges 2:6-16

⁶ When Joshua dismissed the people, the people of Israel went each to his inheritance to take possession of the land. *(Joshua dismissed the people after the angel of the Lord had finished speaking to them. The right thing to do after a good sermon is to put it into practice.)* ⁷ And the people served the Lord all the days of Joshua, and all the days of the elders who outlived Joshua, who had seen all the great work that the Lord had done for Israel.

Good men have a very strong influence. Pray that God will always provide the church with helpful pastors and holy men. They act as anchors to the church, which otherwise might drift into error. What brings us the most comfort is knowing that our great Joshua, the Lord Jesus Christ, will never die.

⁸ And Joshua the son of Nun, the servant of the Lord, died at the age of 110 years. ⁹ And they buried him within the boundaries of his inheritance in Timnath-heres, in the hill country of Ephraim, north of the mountain of Gaash.

The best of people will eventually die. Even those who live longest die at last, and so must we.

¹⁰ And all that generation also were gathered to their fathers. And there arose another generation after them who did not know the Lord or the work that he had done for Israel.

¹¹ And the people of Israel did what was evil in the sight of the Lord and served the Baals. ¹² And they abandoned the Lord, the God of their fathers, who had brought them out of the land of Egypt. They went after other gods, from among the gods of the peoples who were around them, and bowed down to them. And they provoked the Lord to anger. ¹³ They abandoned the Lord and served the Baals and the Ashtaroth. *(They were carried away from the true God by their love of the false gods of Canaan. They worshiped idols that are nothing more than the work of people's hands.)*

¹⁴ So the anger of the Lord was kindled against Israel, and he gave them over to plunderers, who plundered them. And he sold them into the hand of their surrounding enemies, so that they could no longer withstand their enemies. ¹⁵ Whenever they marched out, the hand of the Lord was against them for harm, as the Lord had warned, and as the Lord had sworn to them. And they were in terrible distress.

When God's people sin, God steps in to correct their behavior. Even though others who disobey God seem to get away with it, the Lord's chosen will not. What misery comes as a result of trying to run away from the Lord.

¹⁶ Then the Lord raised up judges, who saved them out of the hand of those who plundered them. *(He was far more ready to rescue them than to strike them. The Lord delights in mercy.)*

Judges 2:1-5

¹ Now the angel of the Lord went up from Gilgal to Bochim. And he said, "I brought

---

[480] Matthew 3:8

you up from Egypt and brought you into the land that I swore to give to your fathers. I said, 'I will never break my covenant with you, *(Could this "angel of the Lord" be anyone else than the Lord Jesus? Who could use such language but one who is equal with God?)* ² and you shall make no covenant with the inhabitants of this land; you shall break down their altars.' But you have not obeyed my voice. What is this you have done? ³ So now I say, I will not drive them out before you, but they shall become thorns in your sides, and their gods shall be a snare to you." *(Their sin was to be their punishment. If we will not fight against our sins, our sins will fight against us.)*

⁴ As soon as the angel of the LORD spoke these words to all the people of Israel, the people lifted up their voices and wept. ⁵ And they called the name of that place Bochim *(or the place of weeping).* And they sacrificed there to the LORD. *(Tears will not be enough, there must also be sacrifice. Blessed are they who, with broken hearts, surround the altar of the Lord. May the Holy Spirit work in each of us a holy sorrow for all sin. Amen.)*

JULY 1

I Chose You Out Of the World[481]

Judges 3:1-15; 31

¹ Now these are the nations that the LORD left, to test Israel by them, that is, all in Israel who had not experienced all the wars in Canaan. ² It was only in order that the generations of the people of Israel might know war, to teach war to those who had not known it before.

Israel was surrounded by hostile nations. The Lord intended to keep his people expert in war. Therefore he allowed certain of the neighboring nations to cause them trouble. In this way Israel's army would always be on the alert and ready to go into battle. The church is also intended to be an army on active duty because the Lord will not allow everything around us to be peaceful.

³ These are the nations: the five lords of the Philistines and all the Canaanites and the Sidonians and the Hivites who lived on Mount Lebanon, from Mount Baal-hermon as far as Lebohamath. ⁴ They were for the testing of Israel, to know whether Israel would obey the commandments of the LORD, which he commanded their fathers by the hand of Moses. ⁵ So the people of Israel lived among the Canaanites, the Hittites, the Amorites, the Perizzites, the Hivites, and the Jebusites. ⁶ And their daughters they took to themselves for wives, and their own daughters they gave to their sons, and they served their gods. *(Ungodly marriages are the source of unceasing evil. We must maintain the separated condition of the people of God or else we will fall into sin and pierce ourselves through with many sorrows. We are not of the world and we must not act as if we are.)*

⁷ And the people of Israel did what was evil in the sight of the LORD. They forgot the LORD their God and served the Baals and the Asheroth.

They got used to hearing talk about Baal and the Asheroth (the groves of trees where Baal was worshiped). They eventually developed a deep respect for the religious beliefs of their idolatrous neighbors. And then their deceiving memories forgot their God. Beware of sin's slippery slide.

⁸ Therefore the anger of the LORD was kindled against Israel, and he sold them into the hand of Cushan-rishathaim king of Mesopotamia. And the people of Israel served Cushan-rishathaim eight years.

This king ruled from a great distance. God will find a rod[482] for rebels, even if he goes hundreds of miles to find it.

⁹ But when the people of Israel cried out to the LORD, the LORD raised up a deliverer for the people of Israel, who saved them, Othniel the son of Kenaz, Caleb's younger brother. ¹⁰ The Spirit of the LORD was upon him, and he judged Israel. He went out to war, and the LORD gave Cushan-rishathaim king of Mesopotamia into his hand. And his hand prevailed over Cushan-rishathaim. ¹¹ So the land had rest forty years. Then Othniel the

---

[481] John 15:19

[482] Proverbs 13:24, "Whoever spares the rod hates his son, but he who loves him is diligent to discipline him."

son of Kenaz died. *(Othniel had been brave in his youth and it is pleasant to hear of him in his old age. If we serve God well in the morning of life, we may be sure that he will honor us before the day is over.)*

12 And the people of Israel again did what was evil in the sight of the LORD, and the LORD strengthened Eglon the king of Moab against Israel, because they had done what was evil in the sight of the LORD. *(This time the oppressor was closer to home and the punishment was more severe.)* **13** He gathered to himself the Ammonites and the Amalekites, and went and defeated Israel. And they took possession of the city of palms. **14** And the people of Israel served Eglon the king of Moab eighteen years.

15a Then the people of Israel cried out to the LORD, and the LORD raised up for them a deliverer, Ehud, the son of Gera, the Benjaminite, a left-handed man. *(This man struck King Eglon a deadly blow and saved his country from the rule of the Moabites. God hears the cries of his suffering people and at some point, he will raise up just the right person to rescue them.*

31 After him was Shamgar the son of Anath, who killed 600 of the Philistines with an oxgoad,[483] and he also saved Israel. *(Rough as he was, God honored Shamgar. His simple weapon is a famous treasure in the Lord's arsenal. God can use us for great purposes and he will, if we have real faith in him and are fully submitted to his will.)*

Oxgoad

---

[483] *oxgoad* - A tool somewhat like a spear that farmers used to prod or goad oxen to guide them.

JULY 2
Does Not the LORD Go Out Before You?[484]

Judges 4:1-23

1 And the people of Israel again did what was evil in the sight of the LORD after Ehud died. *(That sentence, "The people of Israel again did what was evil in the sight of the Lord," comes over and over again; so often that it seems to be the only thing in their history that never changes. If our biographies were written without leaving anything out, would words like these be said about us?)* **2** And the LORD sold them into the hand of Jabin king of Canaan, who reigned in Hazor. The commander of his army was Sisera, who lived in Harosheth-hagoyim. **3** Then the people of Israel cried out to the LORD for help, for he had 900 chariots of iron and he oppressed the people of Israel cruelly for twenty years. *(When we read of Israel crying, we know that victory will come. Prayer has mercy running close behind it.)*

4 Now Deborah, a prophetess, the wife of Lappidoth, was judging Israel at that time.

God uses all kinds of people for his work, including both males and females. In this case a man plays a very secondary part and two women share the honor for defeating Sisera and his army. One strikes the first blow, and the other last. Although women are not called to go out into public preaching,[485] or to fight in the open field like Barak, they can do much at home with the tent peg of one-on-one conversation, and outside of the home by encouraging the soldiers of the Lord.

5 She used to sit under the palm of Deborah between Raman and Bethel in the hill country of Ephriam, and the people of Israel came up to her for judgement. **6** She sent and summoned Barak the son of Abinoam from Kedesh-naphtali and said to him, "Has not

---

[484] Judges 4:14
[485] Spurgeon is speaking here of the Bible's instruction that only qualified men should be preachers of the gospel. He encouraged women to be active in ministry including one Mrs. Bartlett who taught a weekly class of over 600 women at the Metropolitan Tabernacle. "Spurgeon used often to say that his best deacon was a woman—alluding to Mrs. Bartlett." (*The Full Harvest*, page 79) —editor

the Lord, the God of Israel, commanded you, 'Go, gather your men at Mount Tabor, taking 10,000 from the people of Naphtali and the people of Zebulun. **7** And I will draw out Sisera, the general of Jabin's army, to meet you by the river Kishon with his chariots and his troops, and I will give him into your hand'?"

The Lord leads his people with lightweight, easily broken strings. But he has deadly cords to pull his enemies wherever he wants to take them.

8 "Barak said to her, "If you will go with me, I will go, but if you will not go with me, I will not go." **9** And she said, "I will surely go with you. Nevertheless, the road on which you are going will not lead to your glory, for the Lord will sell Sisera into the hand of a woman." Then Deborah arose and went with Barak to Kedesh. *(He did not have enough faith to lead the battle by himself. Therefore, even though he won the battle, Barak did not get the credit for the victory. We lose a lot when we depend on other people to help us. At the same time he showed he had a humble spirit by battling against General Sisera even after the prophetess told him most of the honor would go to someone else.)*

10 And Barak called out Zebulun and Naphtali to Kedesh. And 10,000 men went up at his heels, and Deborah went up with him. *(Many good people need only a call from some brave leader and they will join forces with them. God still has his ten thousands in our Israel. Oh for the right person at the right time! Or, more correctly speaking, Oh for the Lord's own Spirit to call us to the combat!)*

11 Now Heber the Kenite had separated from the Kenites, the descendants of Hobab the father-in-law of Moses, and had pitched his tent as far away as the oak in Zaanannim, which is near Kedesh.

12 When Sisera was told that Barak the son of Abinoam had gone up to Mount Tabor, **13** Sisera called out all his chariots, 900 chariots of iron, and all the men who were with him, from Harosheth-hagoyim to the river Kishon.

Little did he dream, when he rode out in his egotistical pride, that he was being pulled to his own destruction. Some trust in horses, and some in chariots,[486] but such weapons are useless against the Lord of hosts.

14 And Deborah said to Barak, "Up! For this is the day in which the Lord has given Sisera into your hand. Does not the Lord go out before you?" So Barak went down from Mount Tabor with 10,000 men following him.

The words of Deborah sharpened the sword of Barak. Holy women often encourage the Lord's ministers.

15a And the Lord routed Sisera and all his chariots and all his army before Barak by the edge of the sword. *(The Lord won the battle. Barak was just the sword in his hand.)* **16** And Barak pursued the chariots and the army to Harosheth-hagoyim, and all the army of Sisera fell by the edge of the sword; not a man was left.

God's sword never misses one who he intends to strike. This is fatal news for the unrepentant.

17 But Sisera fled away on foot to the tent of Jael, the wife of Heber the Kenite, for there was peace between Jabin the king of Hazor and the house of Heber the Kenite. **18** And Jael came out to meet Sisera and said to him, "Turn aside, my lord; turn aside to me; do not be afraid." So he turned aside to her into the tent, and she covered him with a rug. **19** And he said to her, "Please give me a little water to drink, for I am thirsty." So she opened a skin of milk and gave him a drink and covered him. **20** And he said to her, "Stand at the opening of the tent, and if any man comes and asks you, 'Is anyone here?' say, 'No' "

Sisera's instructions sound all too much like many in our time. People say, "Tell him I'm not home," when they really are. Christians should not borrow lying habits from unbelievers.

21 But Jael the wife of Heber took a tent peg, and took a hammer in her hand. Then she went softly to him and drove the peg into his temple until it went down into the ground

---

[486] A reference to Psalm 20:7

while he was lying fast asleep from weariness. So he died.

This would have been a very wicked thing to do if her motive was to get wealthy or famous. However, in this case, she acted as the executioner of a man God had already condemned. Sisera was the great enemy of her adopted country and her actions should be praised. Jael understood that this man who had fled to her tent was the enemy of her God and of his people. She carried out her patriotic duty and had no pity on him.

22 And behold, as Barak was pursuing Sisera, Jael went out to meet him and said to him, "Come, and I will show you the man whom you are seeking." So he went in to her tent, and there lay Sisera dead, with the tent peg in his temple. *(So the proud tyrant was disgraced as well as killed. Somewhere or other God has unknown agents he will use to crush error. He will give them the wisdom to drive a nail through the head of false teaching. Oh Lord, rise up and fight for your kingdom.)*

23 So on that day God subdued Jabin the king of Canaan before the people of Israel.

JULY 3

Lead Away Your Captives[487]

We will now hear Deborah sing her wonderful poem of victory. She was both prophetess and poetess. All powers of poetry should be dedicated to the glory of the God who gives them.

Judges 5:1-18

1 Then sang Deborah and Barak the son of Abinoam on that day:

2 "That the leaders took the lead in Israel,
　　that the people offered themselves willingly,
　　　bless the LORD!"

All the praise is given to God. The people were willing, but it is God who made their great bravery successful.

3 "Hear, O kings; give ear, O princes;
　　to the LORD I will sing;
　　　I will make melody to the LORD, the God of Israel."

Kings and mighty leaders would be wise to listen and learn from a woman like Deborah. She encourages them to praise the Lord.

4 "LORD, when you went out from Seir,
　　when you marched from the region of Edom,
　the earth trembled
　　and the heaven dropped,
　　　yes, the clouds dropped water.

5 The mountains quaked before the LORD,
　　even Sinai before the LORD, the God of Israel."

All the kings around are reminded to remember the glorious advance of Jehovah, when he led his people from Egypt to Canaan. His glory and majesty are shown even on the battlefield.

6 "In the days of Shamgar, son of Anath,
　　in the days of Jael, the highways were abandoned,
　　and travelers kept to the byways."

We read about Shamgar in Judges chapter three and Jael in chapter four. In their days traveling for pleasure or business was unsafe. People stayed off the main roads.

7 "The villagers ceased in Israel;
　　they ceased to be until I arose;
　　　I, Deborah, arose as a mother in Israel."

Farming could not be carried on. The people fled to the walled towns because they were afraid to live in unprotected places.

8 "When new gods were chosen,
　　then war was in the gates.
　Was shield or spear to be seen
　　among forty thousand in Israel?"

When Israel began to worship gods made by humans, God quit protecting them. They were too weak to stop other kings from completely disarming them. They no longer had weapons of war.

9 "My heart goes out to the commanders of Israel
　　who offered themselves willingly
　　　among the people.
　Bless the LORD."

It is indeed a blessing when those in charge set a good example for others to follow.

---

[487] Judges 5:12

10 "Tell of it, you who ride on white donkeys,
   you who sit on rich carpets
   and you who walk by the way.

Laws could not be enforced. The wheels of business had fallen off. No one was safe. But Deborah and Barak changed all that.

11 "To the sound of musicians[488] at the watering places,
   there they repeat the righteous triumphs of the L<small>ORD</small>,
   the righteous triumphs of his villagers in Israel.

   "Then down to the gates marched the people of the L<small>ORD</small>."

In times of peace, people were not in fear of robbers when they went to the well to get water. They would sing this song of thanksgiving, and the Lord would be praised.

12 "Awake, awake, Deborah!
   Awake, awake, break out in a song!
   Arise, Barak, lead away your captives,
   O son of Abinoam."

Notice how excited the poet becomes.

13 "Then down marched the remnant of the noble;
   the people of the L<small>ORD</small> marched down for me against the mighty."

God placed Deborah in the position of ruler, but that did not stop her from praising the others who shared in the fight. It also did not stop her from later scolding those who wanted nothing to do with helping in the fight.

14 "From Ephraim their root they marched down into the valley
   following you, Benjamin, with your kinsmen;
   from Machir marched down the commanders,
   and from Zebulun those who bear the lieutenant's staff;
15 the princes of Issachar came with Deborah,
   and Issachar faithful to Barak;
   into the valley they rushed at his heels.
   Among the clans of Reuben
   there were great searchings of heart.
16 Why did you sit still among the sheepfolds,
   to hear the whistling for the flocks?
   Among the clans of Reuben,
   there were great searchings of heart."

The tribe of Reuben debated whether to help, but they were lazy in spirit. They did not support their brothers. This was a sad business.

17 "Gilead stayed beyond the Jordan;
   and Dan, why did he stay with the ships?
   Asher sat still at the coast of the sea,
   staying by his landings."

Some gave no excuse. Others made up bad excuses. They were not patriotic. They would not fight in the war and missed the glories of victory. How disgraceful that they would not willingly help in such a great cause. Lord, save us from cowardice and laziness. Instead, let us be like the bold, self-sacrificing spirits the poet sings about in the next verse.

18 "Zebulun is a people who risked their lives to the death;
   Naphtali, too, on the heights of the field."

We must stop here until our next reading.

J<small>ULY</small> 4

The Right Hand Of the L<small>ORD</small> Does Valiantly[489]

Let us now consider the rest of Deborah's magnificent song from:

Judges 5:19-31

19 "The kings came, they fought;
   then fought the kings of Canaan,
   at Taanach, by the waters of Megiddo;
   they got no spoils of silver."

The enemies of Israel were willing volunteers. They hated Israel so much they were eager for the battle. They did not care if they were paid. They just wanted to persecute and abuse the nation of Israel. Satan has his volunteers to serve him. Why should any of us need forcing to serve the Lord?

---

[488] Or *archers*; the meaning of the Hebrew word is uncertain.

[489] Psalm 118:16

20 "From heaven the stars fought,
    from their courses they fought against Sisera."

The heavenly hosts joined forces with Israel. Even the weather was on their side. The rain from the sky was in their favor. The clouds blazed with lightning and tremendous floods poured from them.

21 "The torrent Kishon swept them away,
    the ancient torrent, the torrent Kishon."

The Kishon River suddenly swelled to overflowing and flash floods washed away whole armies of men.

    "March on, my soul, with might!

22 "Then loud beat the horses' hoofs
    with the galloping, galloping of his steeds."

The frighted horses pranced until their legs failed them. Sisera's boasted cavalry became useless. His chariots of iron created only problems for his army.

23 "Curse Meroz, says the angel of the LORD,
    curse its inhabitants thoroughly,
  because they did not come to the help of the LORD,
    to the help of the LORD against the mighty."

The people of Meroz dragged their feet. They are cursed not for what they did, but for what they failed to do. Fear made them neutral. Those who will not fight in a patriotic war are a disgrace. "Would that you were either cold or hot!"[490] Those who love the Lord the most, are the most disappointed with those who drag their feet and do not seem to care when the kingdom God is attacked.

24 "Most blessed of women be Jael,
    the wife of Heber the Kenite,
    of tent-dwelling women most blessed.
25 He asked for water and she gave him milk;
    she brought him curds in a noble's bowl.

Sisera saw the milk, but not the nail. Many who are tempted do not see the danger they are in.

26 "She sent her hand to the tent peg
    and her right hand to the workmen's mallet;
  she struck Sisera;
    she crushed his head;
    she shattered and pierced his temple.
27 Between her feet
    he sank, he fell, he lay still;
  between her feet
    he sank, he fell;
  where he sank,
    there he fell—dead."

Jael's life may not have seemed important to others, but she did her very best for Israel. Therefore she received as much praise as Barak who led thousands into battle.

28 "Out of the window she peered,
    the mother of Sisera wailed through the lattice:
  'Why is his chariot so long in coming?
    Why tarry the hoofbeats of his chariots?'"

This is a beautiful picture of the disappointment of the women at home when their warriors do not return in triumph. They did not think about what God might do in the battle and therefore their expectation failed them. The next two verses are almost comical.

29 "Her wisest princesses answer,
    indeed, she answers herself,
30 'Have they not found and divided the spoil?—
    A womb or two for every man;
  spoil of dyed materials for Sisera,
    spoil of dyed materials embroidered,
    two pieces of dyed work embroidered for the neck as spoil?'"

They imagined out loud, thinking her son and the other soldiers were busy dividing the spoils of war, when they had really lost. The enemies of the church have often thought they have been victorious, only to find their rejoicing was premature. Up until now, the Lord has always helped us and he always will.

31 "So may all your enemies perish, O LORD!
    But your friends be like the sun as he rises in his might."

Amen! Amen! Under the gospel we dare to say Amen. But our fight is against spiritual

---

[490] Revelation 3:15

powers, not humans. It is against error, sin, Satan, and unbelief. Oh for the brave hands of men and women to strike our real enemies.

July 5

Arise, O God, Defend Your Cause[491]

Many years after the times of the Judges, Israel was again in serious trouble. Her holy men and women remembered the Lord's overthrow of Jabin and Sisera and used those victories as part of their prayer. We must never doubt that the Lord will answer our prayers today, just as he did for his people in the distant past. He may use different methods, but he will achieve the same result.

Psalm 83
A Song. A Psalm Of Asaph

1 O God, do not keep silence;
   do not hold your peace or be still, O God!
2 For behold, your enemies make an uproar;
   those who hate you have raised their heads.

Oh Lord, your enemies are in a rage. Do not be deaf and silent. Hear their furious threats and rebuke them. They are very proud. Lord, humiliate them.

3 They lay crafty plans against your people;
   they consult together against your treasured ones.

God's people are his finest treasure. He protects them like others protect gold. Their lives are as precious as jewels to him. To the wicked, however, God's people are puzzling and worthless. They plot against them. They are dishonest and cruel. But we can still learn from them. Believers sometimes act without thinking things through, but their enemies almost never do that.

4 They say, "Come, let us wipe them out as a nation;
   let the name of Israel be remembered no more!"

They will only be satisfied with destroying us completely. If they had their way, the powers of evil would not leave a single believer on earth. Remember the massacre of St. Bartholomew,[492] and be assured that the spirit of antichrist has not changed.

5 For they conspire with one accord;
   against you they make a covenant—
6 the tents of Edom and the Ishmaelites,
   Moab and the Hagrites,
7 Gebal and Ammon and Amalek,
   Philistia with the inhabitant of Tyre;
8 Asshur also has joined them;
   they are the strong arm of the children of Lot. *Selah*

Relatives and neighbors. Old enemies and new. They came together against the favored nation. The wicked will come together for evil, but Christians often refuse to come together for good. This is very shameful.

9 Do to them as you did to Midian,
   as to Sisera and Jabin at the river Kishon,
10 Who were destroyed at En-dor,
   who became dung for the ground.
11 Make their nobles like Oreb and Zeeb,
   all their princes like Zebah and Zalmunna,
12 who said, "Let us take possession for ourselves
   of the pastures of God."

The "pastures of God" refers to the tabernacle. These evil men wanted to attack it and take over the Most Holy Place itself. Their total destruction was a well deserved reward for such vicious disrespect.

13 O my God, make them like whirling dust,
   like chaff before the wind.

Oh Lord. Let them have no peace. Let them have no power to fight against you.

14 As fire consumes the forest,
   as the flame sets the mountains ablaze,
15 so may you pursue them with your tempest
   and terrify them with your hurricane!

We must love our own enemies, but when we think of people as the enemies of God and his glorious cause, we cannot love them nor is it our duty to do so. May all those who

---

[491] Psalm 74:22

[492] The slaughter of thousands Huguenots (Christians) by Roman Catholic supporters in Paris, France in August, 1572.

fight against God; his truth, his love, and his holiness, be totally defeated.

¹⁶ Fill their faces with shame,
    that they may seek your name, O Lord.

A sweet prayer. It is a very proper one for Christian lips, because it asks for the salvation of those who are now the Lord's enemies.

¹⁷ Let them be put to shame and dismayed forever;
    let them perish in disgrace,

If wicked people will not bend, then let them break. All the rights of people and all the laws of God should not be set aside just so unholy people have the freedom to sin as they please. If truth and holiness cannot exist unless bad people are crushed, then let them be crushed.

¹⁸ that they may know that you alone,
    whose name is the Lord,
    are the Most High over all the earth.

"Your kingdom come."[493] *This is God's magnificent plan. All events in history move toward it. As a household and as individuals, let us always be found on the Lord's side.*

JULY 6
My Grace Is Sufficient For You[494]
Judges 6:1-16

¹ The people of Israel did what was evil in the sight of the Lord, *("A burnt child dreads the fire," is a common saying, but Israel, after being burned again and again as the result of her sin, returned to it the moment the chastisement*[495] *stopped or the judge was dead. Such is the strange fascination people have for sin.)* and the Lord gave them into the hand of Midian seven years. *(This nation was but a puny enemy, and yet they were too much for sinful Israel. Israel had once brought the Midianites to a very weak condition and now they are unable to stand before them. See how sin weakens people.)*

² And the hand of Midian overpowered Israel, and because of Midian the people of Israel made for themselves the dens that are in the mountains and the caves and the strongholds. ³ For whenever the Israelites planted crops, the Midianites and the Amalekites and the people of the East would come up against them. ⁴ They would encamp against them and devour the produce of the land, as far as Gaza, and leave no sustenance in Israel and no sheep or ox or donkey. ⁵ For they would come up with their livestock and their tents; they would come like locusts in number—both they and their camels could not be counted—so that they laid waste the land as they came in. ⁶ And Israel was brought very low because of Midian. And the people of Israel cried out for help to the Lord. *(These wandering looters were hard to stop. They were a terrible problem for Israel.)*

⁷ When the people of Israel cried out to the Lord on account of the Midianites, ⁸ the Lord sent a prophet to the people of Israel. And he said to them, "Thus says the Lord, the God of Israel: I led you up from Egypt and brought you out of the house of slavery. *(It seems that when the Lord sends his faithful ministers, their main job is to condemn. But when we look more closely we see that they also bring encouragement. First the scolding, then the comfort.)* ⁹ And I delivered you from the hand of the Egyptians and from the hand of all who oppressed you, and drove them out before you and gave you their land. ¹⁰ And I said to you, 'I am the Lord your God; you shall not fear the gods of the Amorites in whose land you dwell.' But you have not obeyed my voice." *("Faithful are the wounds of a friend."*[496] *God had a good reason to complain. By bringing up Israel's great sin, the Lord's servant was taking them on the most direct route to peace with God. Peace with God comes only by admitting we are sinners and pleading for mercy through the blood of Jesus.)*

¹¹ Now the angel of the Lord came and sat under the terebinth at Ophrah, which

---

[493] Matthew 6:10
[494] 2 Corinthians 12:9
[495] *chasten, chastening* or *chastisement* - The act of discipline which may include scolding, criticizing or pain inflicted for the purpose of correction or moral improvement.

[496] Proverbs 27:6

belonged to Joash the Abiezrite, while his son Gideon was beating out wheat in the winepress to hide it from the Midianites. ¹² And the angel of the LORD appeared to him and said to him, "The LORD is with you, O mighty man of valor." *(The angel of the Lord found Gideon hiding from his enemy, working hard with little to show for it, and miserable. He had very little wheat, because he had no oxen to thresh it. He was in great fear of the enemy, so he threshed in the winepress instead of a regular threshing floor. And yet in his poverty, he received rich grace. "God shows no partiality."[497])*

¹³ And Gideon said to him, "Please, sir, if the LORD is with us, why then has all this happened to us? And where are all his wonderful deeds that our fathers recounted to us, saying, 'Did not the LORD bring us up from Egypt?' But now the LORD has forsaken us and given us into the hand of Midian." *(These were sensible questions, and proved that Gideon had really thought about it.)* ¹⁴ And the LORD turned to him and said, "Go in this might of yours and save Israel from the hand of Midian; do not I send you?" *(It is clear that the angel was the Lord himself. What power there is in that question, "Do not I send you?" And how inspired must Gideon have been when "the Lord turned to him" and spoke to him.)*

¹⁵ And he said to him, "Please, Lord, how can I save Israel? Behold, my clan is the weakest in Manasseh, and I am the least in my father's house." ¹⁶ And the LORD said to him, "But I will be with you, and you shall strike the Midianites as one man." *(God told Gideon to "go in this might of yours" and made him mighty. He sent him on his mission and went with him. He taught him faith and then honored his faith. How will the Lord glorify himself in each of us?)*

JULY 7
Peace Be To You. Do Not Fear.[498]
Judges 6:17-32

¹⁷ And [Gideon] said to the [angel of the LORD], "If now I have found favor in your eyes, then show me a sign that it is you who speaks with me. ¹⁸ Please do not depart from here until I come to you and bring out my present and set it before you." And he said, "I will stay till you return." *(To one person God refuses to give a sign, and to another he does give one. God works one way with one person and another way with someone else. This demonstrates not only God's wisdom, but also his sovereignty or absolute power to do as he pleases. In this case, Gideon asked for and was given many signs and was not rebuked for needing them.)*

¹⁹ So Gideon went into his house and prepared a young goat and unleavened cakes from an ephah *(or about three gallons)* of flour. The meat he put in a basket, and the broth he put in a pot, and brought them to him under the terebinth and presented them. ²⁰ And the angel of God said to him, "Take the meat and the unleavened cakes, and put them on this rock, and pour the broth over them." And he did so. *(What Gideon intended for a feast was turned into a sacrifice. It did not matter what the Lord did with Gideon's gift. What really matters is that the Lord accepted both the gift and the giver.)*

²¹ Then the angel of the LORD reached out the tip of the staff that was in his hand and touched the meat and the unleavened cakes. And fire sprang up from the rock and consumed the meat and the unleavened cakes. And the angel of the LORD vanished from his sight. *(Gideon is given both a sign that God was with him and a hint of the power God could use. God could bring fiery courage out of Gideon's heart, as well as fire out of a rock. And he could consume Midian as easily as he burned up the unleavened cakes.)*

²² Then Gideon perceived that he was the angel of the LORD. And Gideon said, "Alas, O Lord GOD! For now I have seen the angel of the LORD face to face." ²³ But the LORD said to him, "Peace be to you. Do not fear; you shall not die. ²⁴ Then Gideon built an altar there to the LORD and called it, The LORD is Peace. To this day it still stands at Ophrah, which belongs to the Abiezrites.

---
[497] Acts 10:34
[498] Judges 6:23

²⁵ That night the LORD said to him, "Take your father's bull, and the second bull seven years old, and pull down the altar of Baal that your father has, and cut down the Asherah that is beside it ²⁶ and build an altar to the LORD your God on the top of the stronghold here, with stones laid in due order. Then take the second bull and offer it as a burnt offering with the wood of the Asherah that you shall cut down." *(Gideon is told to start right away and get rid of everything in his house that is used to worship the false god. Those who want to serve God in a foreign country should begin by serving God at home. He was not commanded to dedicate Baal's temple to God, but to destroy it. He was not ordered to sacrifice to God on the idol's altar, but to destroy it. We cannot overdo it when it comes to cleaning out the things that tempt us. The filthy birds of sin will return if we do not destroy their dirty nests. God gave Gideon a wonderful job to do. We should rejoice if he gives us a special assignment.)*

²⁷ So Gideon took ten men of his servants and did as the LORD had told him. But because he was too afraid of his family and the men of the town to do it by day, he did it by night. *(If we cannot do our duty exactly as we should, we must do it as we can. One way or another, it should be done. Gideon did a glorious night's work.)*

²⁸ When the men of the town rose early in the morning, behold, the altar of Baal was broken down, and the Asherah beside it was cut down, and the second bull was offered on the altar that had been built. ²⁹ And they said to one another, "Who has done this thing?" And after they had searched and inquired, they said, "Gideon the son of Joash has done this thing." ³⁰ Then the men of the town said to Joash, "Bring out your son, that he may die, for he has broken down the altar of Baal and cut down the Asherah beside it."

The penalty for idolatry was death. Very often, the people who are the most guilty of a sin are the loudest in accusing others of doing it. They demand that the innocent get the punishment they themselves deserve.

³¹ But Joash said to all who stood against him, "Will you contend for Baal? Or will you save him? Whoever contends for him shall be put to death by morning. If he is a god, let him contend for himself, because his altar has been broken down." *(He reasoned with them. If Baal is really a god, then he can take care of himself. If Baal is not a god, then those who claim he is should be put to death. That was the penalty God commanded for those who worshiped false gods.)* ³² Therefore on that day Gideon was called Jerubbaal, that is to say, "Let Baal contend against him," because he broke down his altar.

JULY 8

Blessed Are Those Who Have Not Seen and Yet Have Believed[499]

Judges 6:33-40

³³ Now all the Midianites and the Amalekites and the people of the East came together, and they crossed the Jordan and encamped in the Valley of Jezreel. ³⁴ But the Spirit of the LORD clothed Gideon, and he sounded the trumpet, and the Abiezrites were called out to follow him. *(When the enemy crossed over the Jordan River, the Lord moved his chosen servant to meet them. At the sound of Gideon's trumpet, many of the downtrodden people gained courage and came out of their hiding places to face the enemy.)* ³⁵ And he sent messengers throughout all Manasseh, and they too were called out to follow him. And he sent messengers to Asher, Zebulun, and Naphtali, and they went up to meet them. *(The Lord's people will offer themselves freely on the day of his power.[500])*

³⁶ Then Gideon said to God, "If you will save Israel by my hand, as you have said, ³⁷ behold, I am laying a fleece[501] of wool on the threshing floor. If there is dew on the fleece alone, and it is dry on all the ground, then I shall know that you will save Israel by my hand, as you have said." ³⁸ And it was so. When he rose early next morning and squeezed the fleece, he wrung enough dew

---
[499] John 20:29
[500] A reference to Psalm 110: 3a, "Your people will offer themselves freely on the day of your power."
[501] *Fleece*, a soft cloth or coat made from sheep's wool or the wool obtained from a sheep at one shearing.

from the fleece to fill a bowl with water. **39** Then Gideon said to God, "Let not your anger burn against me; let me speak just once more. Please let me test just once more with the fleece. Please let it be dry on the fleece only, and on all the ground let there be dew." **40** And God did so that night; and it was dry on the fleece only, and on all the ground there was dew. *(See how tenderly the Lord looks on the weakness of his servant's faith and gives a double miracle to strengthen his confidence. The Lord also gives assurance of his presence to strengthen our faith. Sometimes during the Communion Service he will give us a special awareness of his grace, even though others do not experience it. On another occasion others rejoice in the abundance of the Lord's grace and we do not. If our religion was a lifeless machine, we could adjust it to always act the same way. If it were merely rituals and ceremonies, we could always keep it from changing. But because it is from the Lord, he is the one who decides when and where his almighty power will be made evident.)*

Judges 7:1-8

1a Then Jerubbaal (that is, Gideon) and all the people who were with him rose early and encamped beside the spring of Harod.

2 The LORD said to Gideon, "The people with you are too many for me to give the Midianites into their hand, lest Israel boast over me, saying, 'My own hand has saved me.' *(God's helpers are never too few, but we learn from this passage that they may be too many. This is a blow for those who boast in their numbers, and an encouragement for the few and the weak.)* **3** Now therefore proclaim in the ears of the people, saying, 'Whoever is fearful and trembling, let him return home and hurry away from Mount Gilead.'" Then 22,000 of the people returned, and 10,000 remained.

4 And the LORD said to Gideon, "The people are still too many. Take them down to the water, and I will test them for you there, and anyone of whom I say to you, 'This one shall go with you,' shall go with you, and anyone of whom I say to you, 'This one shall not go with you,' shall not go." *(This was a great test for Gideon's faith. He may have been weak in some points, but he was mighty in others.)* **5** So he brought the people down to the water. And the LORD said to Gideon, "Every one who laps the water with his tongue, as a dog laps, you shall set by himself. Likewise, every one who kneels down to drink." *(Those who reached down with their hand and drank only a little water at a time were the men who would respond quickly to the enemy. They were ready for war. They were not about to relax until their cruel oppressors had been driven out of the land. These are the kind of people the Lord will use.)*

6 And the number of those who lapped, putting their hands to their mouth, was 300 men, but all the rest of the people knelt down to drink water. **7** And the LORD said to Gideon, "With the 300 men who lapped I will save you and give the Midianites into your hand, and let all the others go every man to his home." **8** So the people took provisions in their hands, and their trumpets. And he sent all the rest of Israel every man to his tent, but retained the 300 men. *(The armed soldiers melted away, and only a few trumpeters remained. Now everything was prepared for the fight. Now they were ready for victory. When we are weak, then are we strong.[502] When we have no strength that can be seen, we rely on the Power that is invisible.)* And the camp of Midian was below him in the valley.

JULY 9

Show Me a Sign Of Your Favor[503]

Judges 7:9-21; 23-25

9 That same night the LORD said to [Gideon], "Arise, go down against the camp, for I have given it into your hand. **10** But if you are afraid to go down, go down to the camp with Purah your servant. *(See how gently the Lord deals with his servant. He tells Gideon there is no reason to be afraid and gives him a way to overcome what fear still remains.)* **11** And you shall hear what they say, and afterward your hands shall be strengthened to go down against the camp."

---

[502] See 2 Corinthians 12:10
[503] Psalm 86:17

(God does give signs and assurances to certain sincere people. However, for others it might be sinful to even hope for them. Just because Gideon was given so many signs, does not mean we should expect them. Instead, we should remember our Lord's words in John 20:29: "Blessed are those who have not seen and yet have believed.") Then he went down with Purah his servant to the outposts of the armed men who were in the camp.

12 And the Midianites and the Amalekites and all the people of the East lay along the valley like locusts in abundance, and their camels were without number, as the sand that is on the seashore in abundance. **13** When Gideon came, behold, a man was telling a dream to his comrade. And he said, "Behold, I dreamed a dream, and behold, a cake of barley bread tumbled into the camp of Midian and came to the tent and struck it so that it fell and turned it upside down, so that the tent lay flat." **14** And his comrade answered, "This is no other than the sword of Gideon the son of Joash, a man of Israel; God has given into his hand Midian and all the camp." *(God brings about a remarkable combination of circumstances. One soldier has a particular dream, another gives it a fearful interpretation, and Gideon is listening in on their conversation. The wonders of Providence[504] deserve the careful and adoring eye of the observer. The dream was just what Gideon needed. He was the poor barley cake that would turn the Midianites upside down and flatten them.)*

15 As soon as Gideon heard the telling of the dream and its interpretation, he worshiped. And he returned to the camp of Israel and said, "Arise, for the LORD has given the host of Midian into your hand." *(Notice that Gideon takes time to worship even before he returns to the camp. Devotion does not wait for a convenient time.)* **16** And he divided the 300 men into three companies and put trumpets into the hands of all of them and empty jars, with torches inside the jars. **17** And he said to them, "Look at me, and do likewise. When I come to the outskirts of the camp, do as I do. **18** When I blow the trumpet, I and all who are with me, then blow the trumpets also on every side of all the camp and shout, 'For the LORD and for Gideon.'"

19 So Gideon and the hundred men who were with him came to the outskirts of the camp at the beginning of the middle watch, when they had just set the watch. And they blew the trumpets and smashed the jars that were in their hands. **20** Then the three companies blew the trumpets and broke the jars. They held in their left hands the torches, and in their right hands the trumpets to blow. And they cried out, "A sword for the LORD and for Gideon!" **21** Every man stood in his place around the camp, and all the army ran. They cried out and fled. *(Seeing so many torchbearers, and hearing so many trumpeters, they assumed that the army itself must be immense. They panicked and ran for their lives.)*

23 And the men of Israel were called out from Naphtali and from Asher and from all Manasseh, and they pursued after Midian. *(Those who cannot go first, may still be a great help if they will come in later and aid the good cause.)*

24 Gideon sent messengers throughout all the hill country of Ephraim, saying, "Come down against the Midianites and capture the waters against them, as far as Beth-barah, and also the Jordan." So all the men of Ephraim were called out, and they captured the waters as far as Beth-barah, and also the Jordan. *(A wise leader is anxious to obtain all the success he can from a victory. When we have overcome evil of any kind we must work hard to make the success a permanent one.)* **25a** And they captured the two princes of Midian, Oreb and Zeeb. They killed Oreb at the rock of Oreb, and Zeeb they killed at the winepress of Zeeb. *(Faith wins the day against unnumbered foes. Let us only believe and we shall be victorious. The Lord Jesus is our Captain. We shall be more than conquerors.)*

---

[504] Usually, when used with a capital "P", *Providence* refers to God; when with a lower case "p", it refers to God's will, his divine intervention, and his predetermination (predestination).

JULY 10

A Soft Answer Turns Away Wrath[505]

Judges 8:1-3; 22-27; 32-35

¹ Then the men of Ephraim said to him, "What is this that you have done to us, not to call us when you went to fight with Midian?" And they accused [Gideon] fiercely. *(When there is a success, everybody thinks that he should have been in on it. They are quick to blame somebody else if they were not included. If Gideon had invited them to join him, would they have accepted? Those who grow angry because they cannot share the honor, are usually the very persons who would have been the least likely to share in the work.)* ² And he said to them, "What have I done now in comparison with you? Is not the gleaning of the grapes of Ephraim better than the grape harvest of Abiezer? ³ God has given into your hands the princes of Midian, Oreb and Zeeb. What have I been able to do in comparison with you?" Then their anger against him subsided when he said this. *(A soft answer turns away wrath. This shows Gideon's gentle spirit. He obviously had a right to claim the victory all to himself. But rather than coveting all the praise, he gives credit to others; even to the point of overemphasizing the credit they did deserve. Sometimes it is better to give way to people who are being ridiculous, rather than allow their anger to start fights among brothers and sisters in the Lord.)*

²² Then the men of Israel said to Gideon, "Rule over us, you and your son and your grandson also, for you have saved us from the hand of Midian." ²³ Gideon said to them, "I will not rule over you, and my son will not rule over you; the Lord will rule over you."

Gideon shines again. He had no desire to become their ruler. He believed the Lord should be their ruler. At the same time, it is natural that our deliverer should be our ruler. If the Lord Jesus has set us free from sin and Satan, then it is not only natural, but also right that he should rule over us.

²⁴ And Gideon said to them, "Let me make a request of you: every one of you give me the earrings from his spoil." (For they had golden earrings, because they were Ishmaelites.) ²⁵ And they answered, "We will willingly give them." And they spread a cloak, and every man threw in it the earrings of the spoil. ²⁶ And the weight of the golden earrings that he requested was 1,700 shekels *(about 40 pounds)* of gold, besides the crescent ornaments and the pendants and the purple garments worn by the kings of Midian, and besides the collars that were around the necks of their camels. ²⁷ And Gideon made an ephod of it and put it in his city, in Ophrah. And all Israel whored after it there, and it became a snare to Gideon and to his family.

What a pity that so good a man, with so good a motive, should do so wrong a thing. What good reason did Gideon have to make an article of clothing that only the high priest was commanded to wear? A huge amount of evil has come into the world because religious leaders try to dress like a high priest. There is One High Priest above and his ephod is the glory of God. How foolish and how wicked to dream of making priestly costumes for mortal men.

³² And Gideon the son of Joash died in a good old age and was buried in the tomb of Joash his father, at Ophrah of the Abiezrites.

³³ As soon as Gideon died, the people of Israel turned again and whored after the Baals and made Baal-berith their god. *(From worshiping God in a wrong way, to the worshiping a wrong god, is an easy step. Sadly! Gideon, what evil you did.)* ³⁴ And the people of Israel did not remember the Lord their God, who had delivered them from the hand of all their enemies on every side, ³⁵ and they did not show steadfast love to the family of Jerubbaal (that is, Gideon) in return for all the good that he had done to Israel. *(It is no wonder if those who forget God, also forget all others to whom they owe their freedom.)*

This chapter warns us to keep close to God's rules of worship as we find them in the Bible. Even the smallest change may lead to deadly error and terrible evils.

---

[505] Proverbs 15:1

JULY 11

My People Are Bent On Turning Away From Me[506]

Judges 10:6, 7; 9-18

⁶ The people of Israel again did what was evil in the sight of the LORD *(Clearly, the suffering the Lord brings on Israel does little to change their hearts. The good effect lasts only for a short time. As soon as God withdraws his afflicting hand, people return to their old sinful ways.)* and served the Baals and the Ashtaroth, the gods of Syria, the gods of Sidon, the gods of Moab, the gods of the Ammonites, and the gods of the Philistines. And they forsook the LORD and did not serve him.

These idols should have been despicable in the eyes of those who knew the only living and true God. One sin leads to another, like one drink leads to another. The Israelites became drunk with worshiping the images of false gods. The ceremonies used in the worship of all these false gods were as shameful as shameful can be. This made Israel's sin all the more disgusting. They abandoned Jehovah completely when they became devoted to these idols. People cannot serve God and Satan. Where falsehood enters, truth leaves in disgust.

⁷ So the anger of the LORD was kindled against Israel, and he sold them into the hand of the Philistines and into the hand of the Ammonites. *(As they idolized on all sides, so were they tyrannized on all sides. On the west by Philistines and on the east by Ammonites.)*

⁹ And the Ammonites crossed the Jordan to fight also against Judah and against Benjamin and against the house of Ephraim, so that Israel was severely distressed.

Israel was being crushed under the heavy hand of these idolators. Eventually, their cry for help went up to heaven with great intensity.

¹⁰ And the people of Israel cried out to the LORD, saying, "We have sinned against you, because we have forsaken our God and have served the Baals." ¹¹ And the LORD said to the people of Israel, "Did I not save you from the Egyptians and from the Amorites, from the Ammonites and from the Philistines? ¹² The Sidonians also, and the Amalekites and the Maonites oppressed you, and you cried out to me, and I saved you out of their hand. ¹³ Yet you have forsaken me and served other gods; therefore I will save you no more. *(God's goodness to them in the past only made this current rebellion worse. If God had been rough with them and hard on them, then they might have had some excuse for forsaking him. But they turned against a God who had been kind and gentle and generous to them. How often might the Lord have said to us, "I will save you no more"?)*

¹⁴ "Go and cry out to the gods whom you have chosen; let them save you in the time of your distress." *(This made real sense if they really believed in their false gods, but these words must have been a dreadful sound in Israel's ears. What would happen if the Lord said this to us? How would it turn out for us if God told us to rely on the sinful pleasures and false gods we have trusted in the past? Imagine what would happen if he said, "Go to your self-righteousness for security; turn to your merrymaking or your money for comfort." What would you say to such hopeless words?)*

¹⁵ And the people of Israel said to the LORD, "We have sinned; do to us whatever seems good to you. Only please deliver us this day." *(Confessing their sin and surrendering to God's will was the wisest thing to do. Everyone who is truly sorry for their sins should do the same thing.)* ¹⁶ So they put away the foreign gods from among them and served the LORD, and he became impatient over the misery of Israel.

They did more than just say they were sorry, they did something about it. They threw away the idols they had worshiped. True repentance is not only for sin, but from sin. They turned to worshiping the true God before he rescued them from the mess they had gotten themselves into. This showed their repentance was real. The Lord would not stay angry with them very long after he saw his people had a genuine change of heart. He loves them too well to do that.

---

[506] Hosea 11:7

17 Then the Ammonites were called to arms, and they encamped in Gilead. And the people of Israel came together, and they encamped at Mizpah. **18** And the people, the leaders of Gilead, said one to another, "Who is the man who will begin to fight against the Ammonites? He shall be head over all the inhabitants of Gilead." *(Once again, Israel was invaded by enemies. They assembled to defend themselves, but they did not have someone to lead them against the Ammonites. They agreed to submit to the rule of any man who would be bold enough to begin the battle against their cruel enemy. At this point the Lord raised up Jephthah as his answer to their prayers.)*

JULY 12
I Have Made Him a…Leader and Commander For the Peoples[507]

Judges 11:5-7; 9-10; 12-21; 23-28

5 And when the Ammonites made war against Israel, the elders of Gilead went to bring Jephthah from the land of Tob. **6** And they said to Jephthah, "Come and be our leader, that we may fight with the Ammonites." **7** But Jephthah said to the elders of Gilead, "Did you not hate me and drive me out of my father's house? Why have you come to me now when you are in distress?"

We should be careful who we insult. We may need their help some day. Jephthah was a mighty warrior, but his relatives had forced him to move from Gilead because they did not approve of his father's marriage to a prostitute.

9 Jephthah said to the elders of Gilead, "If you bring me home again to fight with the Ammonites, and the LORD gives them over to me, I will be your head." **10** And the elders of Gilead said to Jephthah, "The LORD will be witness between us, if we do not do as you say."

Jephthah asked no more than had been publicly promised. It was his reasonable reward. So when the Lord Jesus saves us from our sins, it is only reasonable that he should reign over us.

12 Then Jephthah sent messengers to the king of the Ammonites and said, "What do you have against me, that you have come to me to fight against my land?"

Rather than just getting into a fight with the Ammonites, Jephthah first tries to reason with them. Let us make every effort to live in peace with everyone.[508]

13 And the king of the Ammonites answered the messengers of Jephthah, "Because Israel on coming up from Egypt took away my land, from the Arnon to the Jabbok and to the Jordan; now therefore restore it peaceably." *(This was just the excuse they used for attacking Israel. Diplomacy*[509] *abounds with falsehoods. The Ammonites had lost the territory in war with the Amorites, and when Israel captured it from the Amorites, it became theirs.)* **14** Jephthah again sent messengers to the king of the Ammonites *(He tried one more time to reason with them, by reminding them what really happened.)* **15** and said to him, "Thus says Jephthah: Israel did not take away the land of Moab or the land of the Ammonites, **16** but when they came up from Egypt, Israel went through the wilderness to the Red Sea and came to Kadesh. **17** Israel then sent messengers to the king of Edom, saying, 'Please let us pass through your land,' but the king of Edom would not listen. And they sent also to the king of Moab, but he would not consent. So Israel remained at Kadesh.

18 "Then they journeyed through the wilderness and went around the land of Edom and the land of Moab and arrived on the east side of the land of Moab and camped on the other side of the Arnon. But they did not enter the territory of Moab, for the Arnon was the boundary of Moab. **19** Israel then sent messengers to Sihon king of the Amorites, king of Heshbon, and Israel said to him, 'Please let us pass through your land to our country,' **20** but Sihon did not trust Israel to pass through his territory, so Sihon gathered

---
[507] Isaiah 55:4

[508] A reference to Hebrews 12:14a, "Strive for peace with everyone."
[509] *Diplomacy* is the work of maintaining good relations between the governments of different countries.

all his people together and encamped at Jahaz and fought with Israel. ²¹ And the LORD, the God of Israel, gave Sihon and all his people into the hand of Israel, and they defeated them. So Israel took possession of all the land of the Amorites, who inhabited that country.

²³ "So then the LORD, the God of Israel, dispossessed the Amorites from before his people Israel; and are you to take possession of them? ²⁴ Will you not possess what Chemosh your god gives you to possess? And all that the LORD our God has dispossessed before us, we will possess. *(Jephthah used their own arguments against them. If they really wanted justice, this would have convinced them.)* ²⁵ Now are you any better than Balak the son of Zippor, king of Moab? Did he ever contend against Israel, or did he ever go to war with them? ²⁶ While Israel lived in Heshbon and its villages, and in Aroer and its villages, and in all the cities that are on the banks of the Arnon, 300 years, why did you not deliver them within that time? *(Undisputed possession for three hundred years was certainly a good reason to not give the land back. It was rather late to use that argument.)*

²⁷ "I therefore have not sinned against you, and you do me wrong by making war on me. The LORD, the Judge, decide this day between the people of Israel and the people of Ammon." *(He did well to say the Lord would be the final judge in the matter. When right is on our side, we may fearlessly leave results with God. If we have done all we can to make peace, and men will not act fairly, they are the ones who sin.)* ²⁸ But the king of the Ammonites did not listen to the words of Jephthah that he sent to him.

JULY 13

Be Not Rash With Your Mouth, Nor Let Your Heart Be Hasty To Utter a Word Before God[510]

Judges 11:29-40

²⁹ Then the Spirit of the LORD was upon Jephthah, and he passed through Gilead and Manasseh and passed on to Mizpah of Gilead, and from Mizpah of Gilead he passed on to the Ammonites.

Jephthah was a brave man, but he still needed the Lord to prepare him for his work. When the Spirit of the Lord comes on someone, it makes them far more than they were before. The Holy Spirit lifts up, guides, inspires, and strengthens. The one who has the Spirit will find whatever strength they need for the job God gives them to do, even the task that seems impossible. May this same Spirit rest upon us even more than he did on Jephthah.

³⁰ And Jephthah made a vow to the LORD and said, "If you will give the Ammonites into my hand, ³¹ then whatever comes out from the doors of my house to meet me when I return in peace from the Ammonites shall be the LORD's, and I will offer it up for a burnt offering." *(Jephthah was very careless when he made this promise. It was undoubtedly done in the heat of the moment. He was not thinking clearly. If we make a solemn promise to God, we should think long and hard about it. A vow to God is very serious and we should be extremely careful how we express it. It is very unwise for a Christian to obligate themselves with promises that are made rashly and in words that are not well thought through. Jephthah's case should be a warning to us.)*

³² So Jephthah crossed over to the Ammonites to fight against them, and the LORD gave them into his hand. ³³ And he struck them from Aroer to the neighborhood of Minnith, twenty cities, and as far as Abel-keramim, with a great blow. So the Ammonites were subdued before the people of Israel.

Our hero returned home in great joy, but his triumph quickly crashed into his promise. The vow he had made without thinking had now become a trap for him.

³⁴ Then Jephthah came to his home at Mizpah. And behold, his daughter came out to meet him with tambourines and with dances. She was his only child; beside her he had neither son nor daughter. ³⁵ And as soon as he saw her, he tore his clothes and said, "Alas, my daughter! You have brought me very low, and you have become the cause of

---

[510] Ecclesiastes 5:2

great trouble to me. For I have opened my mouth to the Lord, and I cannot take back my vow." *(In this case, it would have been far better to break a wrong promise than to keep it. His mistake was that he even made such a promise in the first place. He had not considered the possible terrible consequences. He had sworn that he would use whatever came through the door for a burnt offering. His knowledge of God was limited. Perhaps he thought such a bold promise was needed to satisfy Jehovah. But now he seems to fear the true God like the heathen fear their false gods and is afraid not to keep his foolish promise.)*

³⁶ And she said to him, "My father, you have opened your mouth to the Lord; do to me according to what has gone out of your mouth, now that the Lord has avenged you on your enemies, on the Ammonites." *(Now it was his daughter who showed bravery. She was willing to die or remain unmarried, so long as her country was free.)* ³⁷ So she said to her father, "Let this thing be done for me: leave me alone two months, that I may go up and down on the mountains and weep for my virginity, I and my companions."

³⁸ So he said, "Go." Then he sent her away for two months, and she departed, she and her companions, and wept for her virginity on the mountains. ³⁹ And at the end of two months, she returned to her father, who did with her according to his vow that he had made. She had never known a man, *(Let us hope that Jephthah did not actually sacrifice his daughter. If he did, it was a most horrible action in the sight of God. Her willingness to accept whatever happened to her was beautiful. Let us hope that the vow was somehow fulfilled without her death, and that she lived a long time as an unmarried woman fully committed to the Lord. Many things said in this chapter encourage us to hope this is what happened. At the same time, there is enough doubt about the outcome of this vow to cause us to repeat our warning against every rash promise. Stop, hot spirit! Look at what you are about to do! Think about all the possible consequences before you open your mouth and make a promise to the Lord. Make sure your vow is really for his glory and will not make you do anything that you should not.)* and it became a custom in Israel ⁴⁰ that the daughters of Israel went year by year to lament the daughter of Jephthah the Gileadite four days in the year.

July 14

He Will Send Them a Savior and Defender[511]

Israel sinned again. This time they fell under the control of the Philistines. But God did not forget his people. He raised up another champion to defend them. An angel appeared to Manoah and his wife, telling them they would have a son who would deliver Israel. In due time, his promise was fulfilled by the birth of Samson. We include some of the events of his life beginning with

Judges 14

¹ Samson went down to Timnah, and at Timnah he saw one of the daughters of the Philistines. ² Then he came up and told his father and mother, "I saw one of the daughters of the Philistines at Timnah. Now get her for me as my wife."

The history of this strongest of men begins with an act of weakness. His whole life is damaged by the same fault rising up over and over. His unusually developed physical nature made him the easy victim of his passions. If any of us are as athletic as he was, we are probably enticed by the same temptations that captured him. His faith in God was clearly his strong point, but his physical strength carried an unguarded spot in his character, and that turned out to be his downfall.

³ But his father and mother said to him, "Is there not a woman among the daughters of your relatives, or among all our people, that you must go to take a wife from the uncircumcised Philistines?" *(It must always grieve parents who have high spiritual standards to see their children marrying ungodly persons. No good can possibly come of it. It is very damaging to the soul, and usually leads to heart breaking experiences.*

---

[511] Isaiah 19:20

Surely there are enough good people in the church of God without our looking to the synagogue of Satan for a spouse.) But Samson said to his father, "Get her for me, for she is right in my eyes." *(Too often, this is the only reason people will give or can give for the path they follow. It is the worst reason in the world. What pleases our flesh, usually hurts our spirit. Let us never be slaves to our physical nature. Instead, let us be controlled by clear thinking and spiritual understanding.)*

4 His father and mother did not know that it was from the LORD, for he was seeking an opportunity against the Philistines. At the time the Philistines ruled over Israel.

They were not aware that God intended to use this incident to force Samson into a quarrel with the tormentors of his country.

5 Then Samson went down with his father and mother to Timnah, and they came to the vineyards of Timnah. And behold, a young lion came toward him roaring. **6** Then the Spirit of the LORD rushed upon him, and although he had nothing in his hand, he tore the lion in pieces as one tears a young goat. But he did not tell his father or his mother what he had done. *(A supernatural power was given to Samson. The strong lion was no match for his unarmed strength. But he did not brag about it. He seems to have understood that his great strength was a gift from God and not for his own glory. This was a warm-up exercise for him. It was a good test of his strength before his great battles with the enemy. Like David, he learned to fight Philistines by first fighting animals.)* **7** Then he went down and talked with the woman, and she was right in Samson's eyes.

8 After some days he returned to take her. And he turned aside to see the carcass of the lion, and behold, there was a swarm of bees in the body of the lion, and honey. *(Samson remembered the spot where he killed the lion and stopped to look at it and thank the Lord for delivering him. His memory brought about a reward, because that's where he found the honey. It is good for us to look back on times when we have been in trouble and God has been merciful to us. It helps us learn how easily the Lord can turn our terrors into pleasures.*

"Thus the lion yields us honey;
From the eater food is given."[512])

9 He scraped it out into his hands and went on, eating as he went. And he came to his father and mother and gave some to them, and they ate. But he did not tell them that he had scraped the honey from the carcass of the lion. *(He did not say anything about what happened. Great doers are very often little talkers. Dr. Kitto very properly remarks:[513]*

"The whole story of the lion is mentioned in the sacred history, not merely as an event, but because of the circumstances that grew out of it. Samson, doubtless, performed many mighty feats which are not recorded; the only ones mentioned are the ones that directly influenced the course of his history and brought him more of less into collision with Philistines. No one would have thought that out of this slaughter of the lion, and finding a swarm of bees in the carcass—occurring, as it did, while the hero was engaged in forming friendly relations with the Philistines—would result in the act of his destroying energies being used against the oppressors of Israel. But so it came to pass. The most unlikely agents—lions, bees, honeycombs—may become the instruments of accomplishing the purposes of God, and of leading or driving someone to their appointed task, when they are not even thinking about it.")

10 His father went down to the woman, and Samson prepared a feast there, for so the young men used to do. **11** As soon as the people saw him, they brought thirty companions to be with him. *(These thirty men, who acted like they were his good friends, were probably spies sent to keep an eye on Samson. The friendship of Philistines should always be mistrusted.)* **12** And Samson said to them, "Let me now put a riddle to you. If you can tell me what it is,

---

[512] Author unknown. This poem appears in an article titled *The Honeycomb* dated 1866 by Rev. Cornelius Elven.
[513] Dr. John Kitto (1801-1900) in *Daily Bible Illustrations, Volume 2*

within the seven days of the feast, and find it out, then I will give you thirty linen garments and thirty changes of clothes, **13** but if you cannot tell me what it is, then you shall give me thirty linen garments and thirty changes of clothes." And they said to him, "Put your riddle, that we may hear it." **14** And he said to them,

"Out of the eater came something to eat.
Out of the strong came something sweet."

And in three days they could not solve the riddle.

15 On the fourth[514] day they said to Samson's wife, "Entice your husband to tell us what the riddle is, lest we burn you and your father's house with fire. Have you invited us here to impoverish us." *(The wedding festivities stirred up bitterness. How can we hope things will go well if we join the unregenerate[515] on their level? Samson was acting very wrongly in all this, but God was intentionally using it to make him the opponent of the Philistines, and the champion of the Israelites.)*

16 And Samson's wife wept over him and said, "You only hate me; you do not love me. You have put a riddle to my people, and you have not told me what it is." And he said to her, "Behold, I have not told my father nor my mother, and shall I tell you?"

17 She wept before him the seven days that their feast lasted, and on the seventh day he told her, because she pressed him hard. Then she told the riddle to her people. **18** And the men of the city said to him on the seventh day before the sun went down,

"What is sweeter than honey?
What is stronger than a lion?"

And he said to them,

"If you had not plowed with my heifer,
    you would not have found out my
        riddle."

Here he began to learn that an unbelieving wife was not to be trusted. How could he expect that someone who worshiped a false god, would be true to him! How sad it was that he did not benefit from this experience.)

19 And the Spirit of the LORD rushed upon him, and he went down to Ashkelon and struck down thirty men of the town and took their spoil and gave the garments to those who had told the riddle. *(These garments were the kind only wealthy people would have. Samson must have dealt the Philistines a heavy blow. The loss of thirty men of such high standing and influence would be great.)* In hot anger he went back to his father's house. **20** And Samson's wife was given to his companion, who had been his best man.

God used Samson as his executioner of Philistines, but he himself was stung sharply for his thoughtless actions that led up to it. His foolish love affair brought him no happiness. He looked for love, but found deceit and desertion. It is very unsafe for anyone to let their weaker passions guide them. Sooner or later sinful joys will sour into miseries. Let us never take the risks that Samson did. Let his shipwrecked life be a warning signal to us.

John Kitto (1801-1900)
The compiler and illustrator of the best Bible encyclopedias of his day, including *The Cyclopedia of Biblical Literature*. He lost his hearing at the age of twelve.

---

[514] Septuagint, Syriac; Hebrew *seventh*. Also *seventh* in King James Version
[515] *unregenerate* - Unbelievers. Persons who are not born again.

JULY 15
He Gives Power To the Faint[516]

Samson's marriage led to a complicated argument. He ended up burning wheat fields belonging to the Philistines by tying flaming torches on the tails of foxes and also killing many of his enemies. He then left and camped at the top of a rock called Etam. But God gave him only a little rest, because there were many more Philistines for Samson to conquer.

Judges 15:9-20

9 Then the Philistines came up and encamped in Judah and made a raid on Lehi. *(This was probably the valley below the stronghold Samson used to protect himself. It was later named Lehi, or the place of the jawbone.)* 10 And the men of Judah said, "Why have you come up against us?" They said, "We have come up to bind Samson, to do to him as he did to us. *(The men of Judah had become almost like slaves. They cringed with fear before their harsh masters. Sin makes people cowards.)*

11 Then 3,000 men of Judah went down to the cleft of the rock of Etam, and said to Samson, "Do you not know that the Philistines are rulers over us? What then is this that you have done to us?" *(What a depressing sight! These cowards act like friends of their persecutors and the enemy of their best friend. Could things be any worse than to talk this way to this great champion?)* And he said to them, "As they did to me, so have I done to them." 12 And they said to him, "We have come down to bind you, that we may give you into the hands of the Philistines." *(False brothers are our worst enemies. They will ruin us when our enemies cannot. Beware of hypocrites.)* And Samson said to them, "Swear to me that you will not attack me yourselves." 13 They said to him, "No; we will only bind you and give you into their hands. We will surely not kill you." So they bound him with two new ropes and brought him up from the rock. *(Does this not remind us of our Lord who was bound by those whom he came to save and then turned over to his enemies?)*

14 When he came to Lehi, the Philistines came shouting to meet him. *(This shout came a little too soon. It was quickly turned into a shriek of horror and then into the silence of death.)* Then the Spirit of the LORD rushed upon him, and the ropes that were on his arms became as flax that has caught fire, and his bonds melted off his hands. 15 And he found a fresh jawbone of a donkey, and put out his hand and took it, and with it he struck 1,000 men. *(The weapon used did not matter much. The power was in the arm. The Lord can use the weakest to overcome the strongest.)* 16 And Samson said,

"With the jawbone of a donkey,
   heaps upon heaps,
with the jawbone of a donkey
   have I struck down a thousand men."

Like our greater Champion, who exclaimed, "I have trodden the winepress alone, and from the peoples no one was with me."[517]

17 As soon as he had finished speaking, he threw away the jawbone out of his hand. And that place was called Ramath-lehi. *(Which means either the throwing away of the jawbone or the hill of the jawbone.)*

18 And he was very thirsty, and he called upon the LORD and said, "You have granted this great salvation by the hand of your servant, and shall I now die of thirst and fall into the hands of the uncircumcised?" *(Samson knew how to pray and to pray in faith too. This was the saving point in his character.)* 19 And God split open the hollow place that is at Lehi, and water came out from it. And when he drank, his spirit returned, and he revived. Therefore the name of it was called En-hakkore (the fountain of him who prayed); it is at Lehi (or the place called Jawbone), to this day. *(God helps his servants in big situations, but sometimes he strengthens their faith by bringing smaller tests into their lives. But he will not leave them alone even in their minor difficulties. He quenched Samson's thirst by bringing a refreshing spring of water right where the jawbone fell from the hero's hand. God never runs low on power. We have only to*

---

[516] Isaiah 40:29

[517] Isaiah 63:3

trust him, and we shall do great things, and receive great things.) **20** And he judged Israel in the days of the Philistines twenty years. *(He used his skill and bravery to defeat Israel's enemies and bring peace to the land. God used Samson to show Israel that he could make one man chase a thousand and two to make ten thousand run away.)*

JULY 16

Take Care That You Are Not Carried Away With the Error Of Lawless People[518]

We do not have space to include Samson's famous triumph at Gaza, where he pulled up the heavy gates to the city and carried them to the top of a hill. Instead, we must come to the unhappy story in which this great man became a victim of his own foolishness; that is, the event that took away his power to judge and protect his countrymen. Delilah was paid to seduce Samson and persuade him to reveal the secret of his great strength.

Judges 16:6-20

6 So Delilah said to Samson, "Please tell me where your great strength lies, and how you might be bound, that one could subdue you."

7 Samson said to her, "If they bind me with seven fresh bowstrings that have not been dried, then I shall become weak and be like any other man." **8** Then the lords of the Philistines brought up to her seven fresh bowstrings that had not been dried, and she bound him with them. **9** Now she had men lying in ambush in an inner chamber. And she said to him, "The Philistines are upon you, Samson!" But he snapped the bowstrings, as a thread of flax snaps when it touches the fire. So the secret of his strength was not known. *(After this narrow escape, Samson had no excuse to hang around this double-crossing woman. "For in vain is a net spread in the sight of any bird."[519] But this man was so infatuated[520] with Delilah that he plunged right back into the trap he had just escaped from. Sin is madness.)*

10 Then Delilah said to Samson, "Behold, you have mocked me and told me lies. Please tell me how you might be bound." **11** And he said to her, "If they bind me with new ropes that have not been used, then I shall become weak and be like any other man." **12** So Delilah took new ropes and bound him with them and said to him, "The Philistines are upon you, Samson!" And the men lying in ambush were in an inner chamber. But he snapped the ropes off his arms like a thread.

A second time betrayed! A second time delivered! Is this not enough to make him run away from the deceiver's house? Sadly, no. It would be easier to teach a moth to stay away from the flame than to convince someone who is under the influence of sin to stay away from its sparkle and glitter.

13 Then Delilah said to Samson, "Until now you have mocked me and told me lies. Tell me how you might be bound." And he said to her, "If you weave the seven locks of my head with the web and fasten it tight with the pin, then I shall become weak and be like any other man." **14** So while he slept, Delilah took the seven locks of his head and wove them into the web. And she made them tight with the pin and said to him, "The Philistines are upon you, Samson!" But he awoke from his sleep and pulled away the pin, the loom, and the web.

This time he came dangerously near his secret. The whirlpool in which he was surging was sucking him down. Poor Samson! Who could save you when you were determined to destroy yourself?

15 And she said to him, "How can you say, 'I love you,' when your heart is not with me? You have mocked me these three times, and you have not told me where your great strength lies." **16** And when she pressed him hard with her words day after day, and urged him, his soul was vexed to death. **17** And he told her all his heart, and said to her, "A razor has never come upon my head, for I have been a Nazirite to God from my mother's womb. If my head is shaved, then my strength will leave me, and I shall become weak and be like any other man." *(Samson's dedication to the instructions the angel of the Lord gave his parents was his*

---

[518] 2 Peter 3:17
[519] Proverbs 1:17
[520] *infatuated* - Head over heels in love with, lovesick for, attracted to, smitten with, crazy about, enchanted by.

real strength. His uncut hair was the symbol of that dedication. When he gave up his secret, the Lord left him and he received the just reward of his sinful pleasures. He sinned deliberately, and therefore God allowed him to suffer the harm that naturally comes with it.)*

18 When Delilah saw that he had told her all his heart, she sent and called the lords of the Philistines, saying, "Come up again, for he has told me all his heart." Then the lords of the Philistines came up to her and brought the money in their hands. *(Bad men and women are always ready sell out the very persons they loudly claim to love. They are never to be trusted.)* **19** She made him sleep on her knees. And she called a man and had him shave off the seven locks of his head. Then she began to torment him, and his strength left him. **20** And she said, "The Philistines are upon you, Samson!" And he awoke from his sleep and said, "I will go out as at other times and shake myself free." But he did not know that the LORD had left him. *(We cannot hope to succeed if God is not with us. We may have been brave and powerful in the past, but if the Lord leaves us we will fail and the devil will have the victory. What a warning this unhappy story presents to us. May the infinite mercy of God allow us to truly learn from it.)*

JULY 17
But I Will Not Remove From Him My Steadfast Love[521]

Judges 16:21-31

21 And the Philistines seized [Sampson] and gouged out his eyes *(according to the eighth century Bible translation into the Arabic language, they used fire to blind Samson),* and brought him down to Gaza and bound him with bronze shackles. *(The strongest they could find, and the most painful to the wearer).* And he ground at the mill in the prison. *(The great champion became a slave and was forced to do a job even slaves thought was beneath them. Milton[522] describes the fallen hero as saying:*

> *"Made of my enemies the scorn and gaze;*
> *To grind in brazen fetters under task*
> *With this Heaven-gifted strength. O glorious strength,*
> *Put to the labor of a beast, debased*
> *Lower than bond slave! Promise was that I*
> *Should Israel from Philistine yoke deliver;*
> *Ask for this great deliverer now, and find him*
> *Eyeless in Gaza at the mill with slaves.")*

22 But the hair of his head began to grow again after it had been shaved. *(Our gracious God does not throw away his servants. His grace is like the receding tide of the ocean. Just like Samson's hair, it returns as strong as ever. It is one of the wonders of God that he will not stop loving someone even when that person proves they do not deserve to be loved.)*

23 Now the lords of the Philistines gathered to offer a great sacrifice to Dagon their god and to rejoice, and they said, "Our god has given Samson our enemy into our hand." **24** And when the people saw him, they praised their god. For they said, "Our god has given our enemy into our hand, the ravager of our country, who has killed many of us." *(They blasphemed Jehovah by magnifying Baal. They do, however, teach us a lesson we often forget. That is, to give all the credit for our victories to God.)*

25 And when their hearts were merry, they said, "Call Samson, that he may entertain us." So they called Samson out of the prison, and he entertained them. They made him stand between the pillars. **26** And Samson said to the young man who held him by the hand, "Let me feel the pillars on which the house rests, that I may lean against them." *(The poor blind prisoner was now just someone for the lords of the Philistines to laugh at and mock. Eventually, they let him rest a bit, while they refilled their cups and thought about fresh insults to throw at him.)* **27** Now the house was full of men and

---

[521] Psalm 89:33

[522] John Milton (1608 - 1674). Probably best know for his poem *Paradise Lost*. Some spelling updated. -ed

women. All the lords of the Philistines were there, and on the roof there were about 3,000 men and women, who looked on while Samson entertained.

²⁸ Then Samson called to the LORD and said, "O Lord GOD, please remember me and please strengthen me only this once, O God, that I may be avenged on the Philistines for my two eyes." (*How touching is that sweetest of prayers, "Remember me." Whether it be Samson or the dying thief who uses it, the Lord did remember him.*) ²⁹ And Samson grasped the two middle pillars on which the house rested, and he leaned his weight against them, his right hand on the one and his left hand on the other. ³⁰ And Samson said, "Let me die with the Philistines." Then he bowed with all his strength, and the house fell upon the lords and upon all the people who were in it. So the dead whom he killed at his death were more than those whom he had killed during his life.

Milton will again comment for us:

"Those two massive pillars
With horrible convulsion to and fro
He tugged, he shook, till down they came
    and drew
The whole roof after them, with burst of
    thunder,
Upon the heads of all who sat beneath,
Lords, ladies, captains, counselors, or
    priests,
Their choice nobility and flower, not only
Of this but each Philistine city round.

O dearly-bought revenge, yet glorious!
Living or dying you have fulfilled
The work for which you were foretold
To Israel, and now you lie victorious
Among the slain, self-killed
Not willingly, but tangled in the fold
Of dire necessity, whose law in death now
    joined
You with your slaughtered foes."

So the Lord God of Israel silenced the boastings of his enemies, as he will do in the last great day.

³¹ Then his brothers and all his family came down and took him and brought him up and buried him between Zorah and Eshtaol in the tomb of Manoah his father. He had judged Israel twenty years.

John Milton (1608-1674)
English poet best known for his 1667 poem *Paradise Lost*.

JULY 18
Flee Youthful Passions[523]

The sad case of Samson reminds us of the warnings in the book of Proverbs against that treacherous form of sin. Evil company is always dangerous, but keeping company with people whose lives are impure is deadly. May the young men of the household take today's lesson to heart. It has been hard to write, but a sense of duty has forced it on us.

Proverbs 7:1-18; 21-27

1   My son, keep my words
        and treasure up my commandments
            with you;

Treasure up this warning as a precious thing. It may keep you from becoming miserable and heartbroken in your old age.

2   keep my commandments and live;
        keep my teaching as the apple of your
            eye;
3   bind them on your fingers;
        write them on the tablet of your heart.

---
[523] 2 Timothy 2:22

Keep the commandments of the Bible at your finger tips and in the center of your heart.

4 Say to wisdom, "You are my sister,"
   and call insight your intimate friend,
5 to keep you from the forbidden woman,
   from the adulteress with her smooth words,

As good women are our greatest blessings, so bad women are among the worst curses in the world. Flee immoral women. Do not listen to their words. To show us how wicked they are, Solomon tells us a true story. Let us read it with the sincere prayer that none of us will ever act like this foolish young man.

6 For at the window of my house
   I have looked out through my lattice,
7 and I have seen among the simple,
   I have perceived among the youths,
   a young man lacking sense,

The young man does not have grace in his heart or common sense in his head.

8 passing along the street near her corner
   taking the road to her house

He would have been much better off taking a long detour rather than going past her house.

9 in the twilight, in the evening,
   at the time of night and darkness.

Being out late leads to no good.

10 And behold, the woman meets him,
    dressed as a prostitute, wily of heart.
11 She is loud and wayward;
    her feet do not stay at home;
12 now in the street, now in the market,
    and at every corner she lies in wait.

If she was someone who was okay to be with, she would have been at home at this hour of the night.

13 She seizes him and kisses him
    and with bold face she says to him,
14 "I had to offer sacrifices,
    and today I have paid my vows;

Oh the wickedness of those who combine religion with their filthiness. It was only part of the bait she used to trap the foolish young man.

15 so now I have come out to meet you,
    to seek you eagerly, and I have found you.

This was another lie. She only pretended he was special to her. Beware of these deceivers.

16 I have spread my couch with coverings,
    colored linens from Egyptian linen;
17 I have perfumed my bed with myrrh,
    aloes, and cinnamon.
18 Come, let us take our fill of love till morning;
    let us delight ourselves with love.
21 With much seductive speech she persuades him;
    with her smooth talk she compels him.

What a servant of Satan was she! There are many like her, who trap fools in their nets.

22 All at once he follows her,
    as an ox goes to the slaughter,

The ox has no idea of what is coming, or he would never enter the slaughterhouse. Wicked young men do not realize their sin is leading them to a terrible slaughterhouse.

   or as a stag is caught fast

A deer, thinking it has found a meal, goes to the bait only to be caught in the trap the hunter has set. A foolish man, thinking he has found pleasure, goes to this wicked woman only to be ensnared in the trap she has prepared. What he thinks is rare fun, soon turns to disaster.

23 till an arrow pierces its liver;

The deer soon feels the pain of the hunter's arrow. The foolish man's pleasures will soon be followed by the suffering his folly brings.

   as a bird rushes into a snare;
      he does not know that it will cost him his life.

The life of both his body and his soul will be ruined by his wicked acts.

24 And now, O sons, listen to me,
    and be attentive to the words of my mouth.
25 Let not your heart turn aside to her ways;
    do not stray into her paths,
26 for many a victim has she laid low,
    and all her slain are a mighty throng,

Samson and Solomon paid dearly because they did not steer clear from these types of women.

²⁷ Her house is the way to Sheol,
  going down to the chambers of death.

Strong language, but not too strong. If young people knew what would finally happen as a result of their unclean actions, they would rather burn their flesh with fire, or sleep with venomous snakes, than have any close friendship with sexually impure persons. Young women, should detest those vulgar fellows whose actions should not even be talked about. Everyone, whether they are young or old, male or female, should be disgusted by any lewd thoughts, words, or actions in what they read, watch, or take part in.

JULY 19

Flee From Idolatry[524]

Judges 17

¹ There was a man of the hill country of Ephraim, whose name was Micah. ² And he said to his mother, "The 1,100 pieces of silver that were taken from you, about which you uttered a curse, and also spoke it in my ears, behold, the silver is with me; I took it." And his mother said, "Blessed be my son by the LORD." *(Her blessing was not worth much. She was just as ready to curse as bless. Her silver was her god while it was in the form of coins and remained so when it was changed into a metal image. The fact that she cursed when she lost it proves that. We will read that Micah had some appearance of religion, but what was that worth when he was a thief to begin with? Some unknown fear caused him to return the money even though his conscience had not stopped him from stealing it in the first place. His personality was the type that can easily be attracted to the religious practices we find him involved in.)*

³ And he restored the 1,100 pieces of silver to his mother. And his mother said, "I dedicate the silver to the LORD from my hand for my son, to make a carved image and a metal image. Now therefore I will restore it to you."

They had an image made even though it was against God's law. To make matters worse, they dedicated the image to Jehovah. Good intentions are no excuse for disobedience. Today, churches that have images tell us they do not worship the images, but worship the god they represent. If we accept this excuse, then idolatry no longer exists in the world. God does not accept that kind of thinking.

⁴ So when he restored the money to his mother, his mother took 200 pieces of silver and gave it to the silversmith, who made it into a carved image and a metal image. And it was in the house of Micah. ⁵ And the man Micah had a shrine, and he made an ephod and household gods, and ordained one of his sons, who became his priest.

Children imitate their parents. The mother makes one image, the son has a house full of gods, and the grandson becomes a priest. "God is spirit, and those who worship him must worship in spirit and truth."[525] Once we leave the spiritual worship of God, there is no telling how far we will stray.

⁶ In those days there was no king in Israel. Everyone did what was right in his own eyes. *(Which meant that everyone did whatever evil they liked.)*

⁷ Now there was a young man of Bethlehem in Judah, of the family of Judah, who was a Levite, and he sojourned there. ⁸ And the man departed from the town of Bethlehem in Judah to sojourn where he could find a place. And as he journeyed, he came to the hill country of Ephraim to the house of Micah. ⁹ And Micah said to him, "Where do you come from?" And he said to him, "I am a Levite of Bethlehem in Judah, and I am going to sojourn where I may find a place." ¹⁰ And Micah said to him, "Stay with me, and be to me a father and a priest, and I will give you ten pieces of silver a year and a suit of clothes, and your living." And the Levite went in. *(It was poor pay. 200 shekels had been spent on the carved image and ten is thought to be enough for the priest. They*

---

[524] 1 Corinthians 10:14

[525] John 4:24

preferred an expensive idol, even though the priest is kept in poverty. His pay was even worse when we consider that the priest was selling his soul for such a tiny amount. How shameful for a Levite, the servant of the living God, to be serving lifeless idols.)

11 And the Levite was content to dwell with the man, and the young man became to him like one of his sons. **12** And Micah ordained the Levite, and the young man became his priest, and was in the house of Micah. **13** Then Micah said, "Now I know that the LORD will prosper me, because I have a Levite as priest." *(This is the way superstitious people talk. They have a real priest with the proper background, therefore they think blessings are virtually guaranteed. The images were forbidden. The ephods were forbidden. Their whole worship was in direct violation to the Lord's true worship at Jerusalem. But that did not matter to this family! Their priest was a Levite and that was all they cared about. They assumed they would be blessed in spite of all the rules they had broken. Not much has changed in our times. Today people set up crosses, hang pictures and build altars and expect special favors from God even though all their misguided worship is really imaginary and an insult to the Lord Jesus. Outward ceremonies and performances that are not commanded in Scripture should not be part of our worship. If we attend these kinds of services, we will eventually be caught up in the sin of them.)*

JULY 20

The LORD, He Is God![526]

Judges 18:1-6; 14-20; 22-26

1 In those days there was no king in Israel. And in those days the tribe of the people of Dan was seeking for itself an inheritance to dwell in, for until then no inheritance among the tribes of Israel had fallen to them. **2** So the people of Dan sent five able men from the whole number of their tribe, from Zorah and from Eshtaol, to spy out the land and to explore it. And they said to them, "Go and explore the land." And they came to the hill country of Ephraim, to the house of Micah, and lodged there. **3** When they were by the house of Micah, they recognized the voice of the young Levite. And they turned aside and said to him, "Who brought you here? What are you doing in this place? What is your business here?" *("What are you doing in this place?" is the kind of question people who are concerned with the cares of this world would ask. And in this case it was actually a good one to ask this priest who had accepted such a shameful job.)*

4 And he said to them, "This is how Micah dealt with me: he has hired me, and I have become his priest." **5** And they said to him, "Inquire of God, please, that we may know whether the journey on which we are setting out will succeed."

They were not concerned whether he was a true servant of God or not. Like many people today, they thought one religion was as good as another. They saw the metal idol, the ephod, and a priest, and that was good enough for them. One would think that if they cared about religion at all, they would have been anxious to have the right one. But no, the very people who are careful about what they eat, what they wear, and what medicine they take, will welcome anyone else's religious beliefs without examining them first.

6 And the priest said to them, "Go in peace. The journey on which you go is under the eye of the LORD."

False priests always seem to have lots of nice things to say.

The spies finished their job and returned to the tribe of Dan with their report. Then the men of war marched toward the city of Laish. On their way they stopped near or at Micah's house for the night, like the five spies had done earlier. But instead of being grateful for Micah's hospitality, they returned his kindness by robbing him!

14 Then the five men who had gone to scout out the country of Laish said to their brothers, "Do you know that in these houses there are an ephod, household gods, a carved image, and a metal image? Now therefore consider what you will do." *(This was a hint*

---

[526] Psalm 100:3

that perhaps the gods would be worth stealing.) ¹⁵ And they turned aside there and came to the house of the young Levite, at the home of Micah, and asked him about his welfare. ¹⁶ Now the 600 men of the Danites, armed with their weapons of war, stood by the entrance of the gate. ¹⁷ And the five men who had gone to scout out the land went up and entered and took the carved image, the ephod, the household gods, and the metal image, while the priest stood by the entrance of the gate with the 600 men armed with weapons of war.

They kept the priest in conversation while they stole the pathetic gods that could not protect themselves. It is almost funny. What a crazy thing to do. They steal what they had already worshiped and then they worship what they had stolen.

¹⁸ And when these went into Micah's house and took the carved image, the ephod, the household gods, and the metal image, the priest said to them, "What are you doing?" ¹⁹ And they said to him, "Keep quiet; put your hand on your mouth and come with us and be to us a father and a priest. Is it better for you to be priest to the house of one man, or to be priest to a tribe and clan in Israel?" *(They knew the most powerful arguments to keep him quiet. They asked him if he would make more money being the priest of an entire community or just one man. The person who has already sold themselves is easily bought.)*

²⁰ And the priest's heart was glad. He took the ephod and the household god and the carved image and went along with the people. *(Bishop Hall says, "He that was won with ten shekels, may be lost with eleven. The Levite had too many gods to bother his conscience over which one to worship. There is nothing more inconsistent than a Levite who seeks nothing but himself."*[527]*)*

²² When they had gone a distance from the home of Micah, the men who were in the houses near Micah's house were called out, and they overtook the people of Dan. ²³ And they shouted to the people of Dan, who turned around and said to Micah, "What is the matter with you, that you come with such a company?" ²⁴ And he said, "You take my gods that I made and the priest, and go away, and what have I left? How then do you ask me, 'What is the matter with you?' " *(What a pile of superstition and absurdity! You have stolen my gods that are all I have. They are my own gods. I made them myself. The are very precious and dear to my heart. Nothing can cheer me up if I lose them. He was foolish enough to trust in gods that could not take care of themselves and just as foolish to grieve for their loss. If we lose the smile of the true and living God, then we would have a reason to say, "What have I left?" To lose the presence of God is to lose everything.)*

²⁵ And the people of Dan said to him, "Do not let your voice be heard among us, lest angry fellows fall upon you, and you lose your life with the lives of your household." *(They who have power on their side are rarely at a loss for words. They have very little reason to conceal the lion's claw beneath the lion's pad.)* ²⁶ Then the people of Dan went their way. And when Micah saw that they were too strong for him, he turned and went back to his home.

If Micah became a wise man from this incident, he was a great winner by his loss. If those who rely on rituals and ceremonies had their altars and images broken in pieces and their cathedrals torn down, it would be a cheap cure of their foolishness. Oh that the Lord would take his great broom and sweep out the priests and their idols. Let us also pray that he will clean the temples of our hearts.

JULY 21
Our God Is In the Heavens[528]

The sad and foolish history of idol worship given in our last two readings makes us want to turn to another subject. Let us adore and worship the only true and living God, who has revealed himself to us as Father, Son, and Holy Spirit. He is the God of promise, who alone should have our worship. Let us read the holy song of the Jewish church in

---

[527] Bishop Joseph Hall (1574-1656)

[528] Psalm 115:3

Psalm 115

1 Not to us, O Lord, not to us, but to your
   name give glory,
     for the sake of your steadfast love and
     your faithfulness!

When we find ourselves in trouble, the answer to our problem is not in us. We must be humble and realize the best solution is to pray to our merciful and faithful God.

2 Why should the nations say,
     "Where is their God?"

The enemies of God complain about him and blame him for their troubles. The saints of God mention these blasphemies in their prayers and ask the Lord to shut the mouths of these bitter people.

3 Our God is in the heavens;
     he does all that he pleases.

No matter how much the ungodly may rage, God sits on the throne. They cannot overthrow him from his position of control over them. The most violent efforts to defeat God will not stop him from accomplishing everything he intends to do. Every plan of the Lord will be completed, right down to the smallest detail. This is sweet comfort for his saints.

4 Their idols are silver and gold,
     the work of human hands.

The very best idols are really just lumps of metal. What contempt the psalmist pours on these sacred images! They deserve to be made fun of. The next sentences are harsh, but deserved. Idols are not to be respected but despised.

5 They have mouths, but do not speak;
     eyes, but do not see.
6 They have ears, but do not hear;
     noses, but do not smell.
7 They have hands, but do not feel;
     feet, but do not walk;
     and they do not make a sound in their
     throat.

These idols are designed to represent various features of physical ability, but they are just so many lies. An eye that cannot see, cannot acquire insight. A mouth that cannot speak, cannot convince anyone. Hands that cannot move, cannot accomplish anything.

8 Those who make them become like them;
     so do all who trust in them.

They are as disgusting and ridiculous as the images they adore.

9 O Israel, trust in the Lord!
     He is their help and their shield.
10 O house of Aaron, trust in the Lord!
     He is their help and their shield.
11 You who fear the Lord, trust in the Lord!
     He is their help and their shield.

Trusting in God is the duty and privilege of all saints, at all times, in all places.

12 The Lord has remembered us; he will
     bless us;

Past blessings guarantee the future, because our God does not change.

     he will bless the house of Israel;
     he will bless the house of Aaron;
13 he will bless those who fear the Lord,
     both the small and the great.

These are precious promises for those who are very young, for those who live in poverty, for those who have little ability, and for those who are rejected by the world. They are not and will not be forgotten when God blesses his chosen.

14 May the Lord give you increase,
     you and your children!

Believers will become more numerous. The chosen race shall increase.

15 May you be blessed by the Lord,
     who made heaven and earth!

And this is true, whatever people may say, or whatever the Lord may bring. You who are righteous before God, rejoice!

16 The heavens are the Lord's heavens,
     but the earth he has given to the
     children of man.
17 The dead do not praise the Lord,
     nor do any who go down into silence.

So far as this world is concerned, death ends human praise. Therefore, let us make up our mind to bless the Lord as long as we live, according to the commitment made in the next verse.

18 But we will bless the Lord
     from this time forth and forevermore.
   Praise the Lord!

JULY 22

Can Man Make For Himself Gods?[529]

One of the most revealing satires[530] about the worship of idols is found in the book of the prophet Isaiah.

Isaiah 44:9-20

9 All who fashion idols are nothing, and the things they delight in do not profit. Their witnesses neither see nor know, *(If these people had any sense they would understand how useless their idols are. They will not allow themselves to be corrected. If they did, they would be admitting they had been deceived.)* that they may be put to shame. **10** Who fashions a god or casts an idol that is profitable for nothing? *(These mighty good-for-nothing gods, when do they actually become gods? When do they become worthy of adoration?)* **11** Behold, all his companions shall be put to shame, and the craftsmen are only human. *(The stupid idol and its senseless worshipers will all be laughed to scorn. Let both makers and worshipers, and everyone who has anything to do with idol worship, come forward and answer a few questions which will expose the shame of their false worship.)* Let them all assemble, let them stand forth. They shall be terrified; they shall be put to shame together.

12 The ironsmith takes a cutting tool and works it over the coals. He fashions it with hammers and works it with his strong arm. He becomes hungry, and his strength fails; he drinks no water and is faint. *(The prophet begins with the last person who worked on the idol. He takes us to the blacksmith's shop where the wooden idol is coated with precious metal. But this maker of gods has human weaknesses. He is thirsty and faints because he has no water. What a mighty god-maker is he! The god does not come to life in the blacksmith's shop.)* **13** The carpenter sketches a line; he marks it out with a pencil. He shapes it with planes and marks it with a compass. He shapes it into the figure of a man, with the beauty of a man, to dwell in a house. *(Isaiah goes back a little further in the process, to the place where the design of the idol takes place. He shows us the carpenter working with his tools. He marks the block of wood with his pencil and carves it with his plane and chisel, but no sign of a god is visible here either.)*

14 He cuts down cedars, or he chooses a cypress tree or an oak and lets it grow strong among the trees of the forest. He plants a cedar and the rain nourishes it.

Perhaps there was something holy about the tree the wood came from. No. Isaiah takes us back another step before the wood came to the carpenter's shop. It was just a common tree that was planted in the forest. The rain watered it and it grew the same as the others.

15 Then it becomes fuel for a man. He takes a part of it and warms himself; he kindles a fire and bakes bread. Also he makes a god and worships it; he makes it an idol and falls down before it.

The tree is chopped down and behold, it serves a double purpose. Part of the wood is used for the fire to bake bread and part is used to make a god.

16 Half of it he burns in the fire. Over the half he eats meat; he roasts it and is satisfied. Also he warms himself and says, "Aha, I am warm, I have seen the fire!" **17** And the rest of it he makes into a god, his idol, and falls down to it and worships it. He prays to it and says, "Deliver me, for you are my god!"

One part of the tree cooks meals and blazes on the hearth to keep people warm and happy. The rest they talk to in a pleading voice, "Deliver me, for you are my god." What drunken-like stupidity!

18 They know not, nor do they discern, for he has shut their eyes, so that they cannot see, and their hearts, so that they cannot understand. *(The minds of idolaters are blinded and they deserve to be. If people were reasonable, and not lovers of sin, they would put an end to such foolish behavior.)* **19** No one considers, nor is there knowledge or discernment to say, "Half of it I burned in the fire; I also baked bread on its coals; I roasted meat and have eaten. And shall I

---

[529] Jeremiah 16:20
[530] *satire;* a parody, spoof, mockery, caricature. A method to show scorn, derision and ridicule.

make the rest of it an abomination? Shall I fall down before a block of wood?" ²⁰ He feeds on ashes; a deluded heart has led him astray, and he cannot deliver himself or say, "Is there not a lie in my right hand?" *(People have fallen so low through sin that their thinking is illogical. They cook their food with the same wood they make their idol from and the wind blows away the ashes. All that remains is the idol they hold in their right hand and they are so blind they cannot see how obvious their foolishness is.)*

Oh Lord, have pity on human madness and save people from themselves. Amen.

JULY 23
You Shall Be Clean From All Your Uncleannesses and From All Your Idols[531]

We find the whole history of the book of Judges briefly retold in

Psalm 106:34-48

³⁴ They did not destroy the peoples,
    as the LORD commanded them,

This was the Jews main sin. All of their other faults were a result of not obeying this command. They were brought to Canaan to destroy the criminal nations that lived there. Israel was either too afraid or too rebellious to finish the job. As a result, more sin and sorrow followed their first sin. No one can fully understand how much evil may follow one act of disobedience. If we allow just one sin to be out of control, it will become a terrible plague in our life. Oh for grace to make careful work of removing such sin. Only the Holy Spirit can help us in doing this.

³⁵ but they mixed with the nations
    and learned to do as they did.

Close friendship leads to imitation. We cannot live with the wicked without being influenced by them. The blazing wood that does not burn us may still blacken us.

³⁶ They served their idols,
    which became a snare to them.

Sometimes heathen worship was pleasing and attractive. Often it was immoral and tempting to the flesh. God's own people were trapped by their natural urges and desires.

³⁷ They sacrificed their sons
    and their daughters to the demons;
³⁸ they poured out innocent blood,
    the blood of their sons and daughters,
    whom they sacrificed to the idols of Canaan,
    and the land was polluted with blood.

These sacrifices were the high point in idolatrous worship. They were also the most horrible of crimes. What a miserable fact, that a people who had known the Lord should fall so low as to murder their innocent babies at the altars of demons! Human nature is capable of the worst crimes imaginable! Can even devils perform worse wickedness than this?

³⁹ Thus they became unclean by their acts,
    and played the whore in their deeds.
⁴⁰ Then the anger of the LORD was kindled against his people,
    and he abhorred his heritage;

The Lord looked on their disgusting acts and was disgusted with them. He decided he would make them understand that he would not put up with his own people doing these things. Sin was worse in God's people than in others, because they knew better. They had made a most holy promise to act better than this.

⁴¹ he gave them into the hand of the nations,
    so that those who hated them ruled over them.
⁴² Their enemies oppressed them,
    and they were brought into subjection under their power.
⁴³ Many times he delivered them,
    but they were rebellious in their purposes
    and were brought low through their iniquity.

See how patient God was. He delivered them many times, even though they kept returning to their wickedness. Have we experienced the same great mercy?

⁴⁴ Nevertheless, he looked upon their distress,
    when he heard their cry.

---
[531] Ezekiel 36:25

⁴⁵ For their sake he remembered his covenant,
  and relented according to the abundance of his steadfast love.

How beautiful and wonderful these words are! They describe the tender heart of God! Oh God, who can pardon like you do? Who besides you would keep his promise to this kind of people? What huge amounts of mercies were used to cover such huge amounts of sins? To read Israel's story is like looking into a mirror. It is enough to bring tears to our eyes. Our shame is mixed with our thankfulness as we think how wonderful God has been to us too.

⁴⁶ He caused them to be pitied
  by all those who held them captive.

The Lord who brought water out of rock, made even their tormentors feel sorry for them and before long he brought about the means to deliver them.

⁴⁷ Save us, O Lord our God,
  and gather us from among the nations,
  that we may give thanks to your holy name
  and glory in your praise.

Later generations learned from this history. We should do the same. Let us join in the words of praise that bring this psalm to its conclusion.

⁴⁸ Blessed be the Lord, the God of Israel,
  from everlasting to everlasting!
  And let all the people say, "Amen!"
  Praise the Lord!

July 24

Will You Not Revive Us Again?[532]

Israel slid back into the sin of idolatry repeatedly. And each time they did they experienced more pain and suffering. We can imagine the feelings of the nation's godly during these times. Their prayer may have been much like the psalmist Asaph in

  Psalm 80
¹ Give ear, O Shepherd of Israel,
  you who lead Joseph like a flock!
  You who are enthroned upon the cherubim, shine forth.

Lord, in ancient times you were Israel's leader. Even now, you live above the ark of the covenant in the tabernacle of Shiloh. Therefore, find it in your heart to show your power for the benefit of your people.

² Before Ephraim and Benjamin and Manasseh,
  stir up your might
  and come to save us!

The prayer mentions the names of the tribes of Israel; just as the High Priest had them written on the ephod when he came into the presence of the Lord. May God save and bless every part of his one church and not just our own tribe.

³ Restore us, O God;
  let your face shine, that we may be saved!

Everything will turn out properly if we are first saved. A change of character is better than a change of circumstances. Change us, oh Lord, and then change our situation.

⁴ O Lord God of hosts,
  how long will you be angry with your people's prayers?
⁵ You have fed them with the bread of tears
  and given them tears to drink in full measure.

Sorrow was both their food and drink. Would the Lord never bring an end of their miseries? This is mighty pleading.

⁶ You make us an object of contention for our neighbors,
  and our enemies laugh among themselves.

When the wicked are happy because we are miserable and laugh because we seem confused, then the Lord will hear and rescue us.

⁷ Restore us, O God of hosts;
  let your face shine, that we may be saved!

This is a repetition, but not a useless one, because it was the most important blessing asked for.

⁸ You brought a vine out of Egypt;
  you drove out the nations and planted it.
⁹ You cleared the ground for it;
  it took deep root and filled the land.

---

[532] Psalm 85:6

10 The mountains were covered with its shade,
   the mighty cedars with its branches.
11 It sent out its branches to the sea
   and its shoots to the River.

Asaph's poetry is filled with emotion as he describes Israel being brought into Canaan. God's goodness to us in the past makes our present sorrows very bitter, when we know the change in our circumstances is caused by our sin.

12 Why then have you broken down its walls,
   so that all who pass along the way pluck its fruit?
13 The boar from the forest ravages it,
   and all that move in the field feed on it.

Israel's living conditions were very bad. They could no longer defend their borders. Ferocious enemies were destroying the land. Their distress had reached the breaking point. Only those who know what it is to see invaders in their country and homes can even imagine the conditions Israel endured.

14 Turn again, O God of hosts!
   Look down from heaven, and see;
   have regard for this vine,
15   the stock that your right hand planted,
   and for the son whom you made strong for yourself.

What was needed was a visit from God. What was needed was power given to the judges God had raised up to deliver Israel. Barak, and Gideon, and Jephthah were nothing without God, but if the Lord appeared they would become branches of the vine that produce fruit and display God's power.

All that was needed was a visit from God and his anointing on the judge he appointed to deliver Israel.

16 They have burned it with fire; they have cut it down;
   may they perish at the rebuke of your face!
17 But let your hand be on the man of your right hand,
   the son of man whom you have made strong for yourself!

Israel's great need was a bold and brave leader. One appointed by the Lord to save them. Jesus is our great Leader and he has the power of Jehovah within him. In a small way, the judges were given power from God to save their people. People sin alone, but they must have help to escape from the trouble their sin brings. We are helpless to save ourselves. We must have power from heaven. Only Jesus can save us.

18 Then we shall not turn back from you;
   give us life, and we will call upon your name!

If God would rescue them, they thought they would be so thankful that they would never sin against the Lord again.

19 Restore us, O LORD God of hosts!
   let your face shine, that we may be saved!

Even though their situation was extremely bad, they were confident that the Lord would change them and their circumstances. They believed he would show his grace by bringing about events that would save them. Let us keep this closing prayer on our heart and lips for many days to come.

JULY 25

Who Shall Separate Us From the Love Of Christ?[533]

We have reached the shortest of the historical books, which contains the sweet story of Ruth. Her story is told in the Bible because she was one of the ancestors of our Lord Jesus. He came to save Gentiles as well as Jews and he was pleased to include a foreigner from a heathen land in the family tree of his ancestors.

Ruth 1:1-11; 13b-18

1 In the days when the judges ruled there was a famine in the land, and a man of Bethlehem in Judah went to sojourn in the country of Moab, he and his wife and his two sons. 2 The name of the man was Elimelech and the name of his wife Naomi, and the names of his two sons were Mahlon and Chilion. They were Ephrathites from Bethlehem in Judah. They went into the

---

[533] Romans 8:35

country of Moab and remained there. ³ But Elimelech, the husband of Naomi, died, and she was left with her two sons. *(They had escaped the famine, but other troubles visited them. No matter where we live, trials will be a part of our lives.)*

⁴ These took Moabite wives; the name of the one was Orpah and the name of the other Ruth. They lived there about ten years, ⁵ and both Mahlon and Chilion died, so that the woman was left without her two sons and her husband. *(Alas, poor soul! The arrows of death wounded her terribly! Yet the Lord did not leave her alone in her widowhood. He prepared the loving heart of a young woman to comfort her.)*

⁶ Then she arose with her daughters-in-law to return from the country of Moab, for she had heard in the fields of Moab that the LORD had visited his people and given them food. *(This was welcome news, and was easy to believe, because empty gossip would not have given the Lord credit for ending the famine. Or, perhaps this was just what Naomi wanted to believe. We should try to believe the best whenever possible. And, we should always give credit for good gifts to the giver. Our food, whether it is physical or spiritual, comes from the Lord.)* ⁷ So she set out from the place where she was with her two daughters-in-law, and they went on the way to return to the land of Judah.

⁸ But Naomi said to her two daughters-in-law, "Go, return each of you to her mother's house. May the LORD deal kindly with you, as you have dealt with the dead and with me. ⁹ The LORD grant that you may find rest, each of you in the house of her husband!" Then she kissed them, and they lifted up their voices and wept. ¹⁰ And they said to her, "No, we will return with you to your people." ¹¹ But Naomi said, "Turn back, my daughters; why will you go with me? Have I yet sons in my womb that they may become your husbands?"

She reminded them that she had no more sons to become their husbands and urged them to go back to their own nation. Then she added,

¹³ᵇ "For it is exceedingly bitter to me for your sake that the hand of the LORD has gone out against me." *(The mature widow acted wisely in testing the young women. Many say they will join the Lord's people who have not thought about the trials of true religion. They should count the cost.)* ¹⁴ Then they lifted up their voices and wept again. And Orpah kissed her mother-in-law, but Ruth clung to her. *(These two women were opposites. We have known both types. One, like Orpah, is delighted with religion and happy to follow the Lord Jesus until some difficulty or trial comes. Then she gives it all up. The other, like Ruth, is really converted and holds onto Jesus through fair and stormy conditions. She continues to the end.)*

¹⁵ And she said, "See, your sister-in-law has gone back to her people and to her gods; return after your sister-in-law." ¹⁶ But Ruth said, "Do not urge me to leave you or to return from following you. For where you go I will go, and where you lodge I will lodge. Your people shall be my people and your God my God. ¹⁷ Where you die I will die, and there will I be buried. May the LORD do so to me and more also if anything but death parts me from you."

Ruth joined herself to the Lord's people and never lived to regret it. Those who choose to walk with Jesus may have it rough for a while, but better times are ahead.

¹⁸ And when Naomi saw that she was determined to go with her, she said no more. *(She was only too glad to have Ruth for a lifetime companion. The people of God are glad to welcome sincere souls into their fellowship.)*

JULY 26

May the God Of Peace Be With You All[534]

Ruth 1:19-22

¹⁹ So the two of them went on until they came to Bethlehem. And when they came to Bethlehem, the whole town was stirred because of them. And the women said, "Is this Naomi?" *(She had been gone ten years, but her good character was still held in high*

---

[534] Romans 15:33

respect with the people. Therefore they were glad to see her return, though they were surprised by her poverty. Her many bereavements may have changed her looks, because even her former acquaintances asked, "Is this Naomi?" We may experience similar changes in our lives. May faith and patience prepare us for them.)

20 She said to them, "Do not call me Naomi *(pleasant or sweet)*; call me Mara *(or bitter)*, for the Almighty has dealt very bitterly with me. *(God can soon change our sweets into bitters, therefore let us be humble. But he can just as easily transform our bitters into sweets. Therefore let us be hopeful. It is very usual for Naomi and Mara, sweet and bitter, to meet in the same person. He who was called Benjamin, or "the son of his father's right hand," was first called Benoni, or "the son of sorrow." The comforts of God's grace are all the sweeter when they follow the troubles of life.)* **21** I went away full, and the LORD has brought me back empty. *(When she had her husband, and sons, and property, she was full, and went her way to a foreign land, perhaps wrongly. But now that she was deprived of everything, she felt that God was with her in her emptiness, and that he had brought her back.)* Why call me Naomi, when the LORD has testified against me and the Almighty has brought calamity upon me?"

It is wise to know and appreciate that everything that happens to us is part of God's will for us. Naomi submitted to her Master even though she suffered from what seemed like harsh treatment. This is the proper kind of attitude for a believer to have who has been disciplined by God. Our Lord is the great example of it, for he said, "Shall I not drink the cup that the Father has given me?"

22 So Naomi returned, and Ruth the Moabite her daughter-in-law with her, who returned from the country of Moab. And they came to Bethlehem at the beginning of barley harvest.

Ruth 2:1-7

1 Now Naomi had a relative of her husband's, a worthy man of the clan of Elimelech, whose name was Boaz.

If it was good for Naomi to have a wealthy relative, then how blessed it is for poor sinners to have a rich relative in the person of the Lord Jesus.

2 And Ruth the Moabite said to Naomi, "Let me go to the field and glean among the ears of grain after him in whose sight I shall find favor." And she said to her, "Go, my daughter."

These good women were not ashamed of honest and humble work. They did not take to begging, or doing nothing. They desired to support themselves through honest labor. Ruth had been a wealthy woman, but she was not above working to support her mother-in-law and herself.

3 So she set out and went and gleaned in the field after the reapers, and she happened to come to the part of the field belonging to Boaz, who was of the clan of Elimelech.

To Ruth, it seemed she chose this field by chance, but the hand of the Lord was in it. It was he who directed her to the very best place that would move her toward her future prosperity.

4 And behold, Boaz came from Bethlehem. and he said to the reapers, "The LORD be with you!" And they answered, "The LORD bless you." *(What a blessing when employer and employees work together in such a holy way. It is a shame that this kind of godly fellowship is so rare!)* **5** Then Boaz said to his young man who was in charge of the reapers, "Whose young woman is this?" **6** And the servant who was in charge of the reapers answered, "She is the young Moabite woman, who came back with Naomi from the country of Moab. **7** She said, 'Please let me glean and gather among the sheaves after the reapers.' So she came, and she has continued from early morning until now, except for a short rest."

Boaz was a good master to his servants, and he was also kind to the poor. Those who excel in one direction are generally excellent in others. Ruth must have been happy to glean under the care of a man like Boaz. She had given up everything for God and the Lord took care of her. She was busy doing the right thing and God's love was watching over her.

JULY 27

The Lord Give You a Full Reward For What You Have Done[535]

Ruth 2:8-23

Boaz asked his servant about the new gleaner in his field. Then he approached Ruth and spoke very kindly to her.

8 Then Boaz said to Ruth, "Now, listen, my daughter, do not go to glean in another field or leave this one, but keep close to my young women. **9** Let your eyes be on the field that they are reaping, and go after them. Have I not charged the young men not to touch you? And when you are thirsty, go to the vessels and drink what the young men have drawn." **10** Then she fell on her face, bowing to the ground, and said to him, "Why have I found favor in your eyes, that you should take notice of me, since I am a foreigner?" **11** But Boaz answered her, "All that you have done for your mother-in-law since the death of your husband has been fully told to me, and how you left your father and mother and your native land and came to a people that you did not know before. **12** The LORD repay you for what you have done, and a full reward be given you by the LORD, the God of Israel, under whose wings you have come to take refuge!" **13** Then she said, "I have found favor in your eyes, my lord, for you have comforted me and spoken kindly to your servant, though I am not one of your servants."

14 And at mealtime Boaz said to her, "Come here and eat some bread and dip your morsel in the wine." So she sat beside the reapers, and he passed to her roasted grain. And she ate until she was satisfied, and she had some left over. **15** When she rose to glean, Boaz instructed his young men, saying, "Let her glean even among the sheaves, and do not reproach her. **16** And also pull out some from the bundles for her and leave it for her to glean, and do not rebuke her."

17 So she gleaned in the field until evening. Then she beat out what she had gleaned, and it was about an ephah *(or about five gallons)* of barley.

The main reason Boaz was so kind to Ruth was that she was a guest in Israel, a dove nestling beneath Jehovah's wings. His religion was most important to him, and therefore he rejoiced that this woman had left everything to follow the living God. Meanwhile Ruth acted in the most modest and humble way. She was simply being herself. She was glad to work all day in the field to help support Naomi and herself. She considered it a pleasure to work for the benefit of someone who loved her so much. When children are kind to their parents, they are on the road to blessings. Little did Ruth imagine that she would one day be married to the owner of the fields in which she gleaned. There are good things in store for those who live correctly before God.

18 And she took it up and went into the city. Her mother-in-law saw what she had gleaned. She also brought out and gave her what food she had left over after being satisfied. **19** And her mother-in-law said to her, "Where did you glean today? And where have you worked? Blessed be the man who took notice of you." So she told her mother-in-law with whom she had worked and said, "The man's name with whom I worked today is Boaz." **20** And Naomi said to her daughter-in-law, "May he be blessed by the LORD, whose kindness has not forsaken the living or the dead!" Naomi also said to her, "The man is a close relative of ours, one of our redeemers." **21** And Ruth, the Moabite said, "Besides, he said to me, 'You shall keep close by my young men until they have finished all my harvest.'" **22** And Naomi said to Ruth, her daughter-in-law, "It is good, my daughter, that you go out with his young women, lest in another field you be assaulted." **23** So she kept close to the young women of Boaz, gleaning until the end of the barley and wheat harvests. And she lived with her mother-in-law.

Matthew Henry gives us the following lessons from this passage:

---

[535] From Ruth 2:12

"Ruth finished her day's work, (verse 17). She took care not to lose time, for she gleaned until evening. We must not grow weary of doing good, because in due season we shall reap. She did not make an excuse to sit still or go home before the evening. Let us 'work the works of him who sent us while it is day.' She barely used, much less did she abuse the kindness of Boaz, for though he ordered his servants to leave handfuls for her, she continued to glean the scattered ears. She took care not to lose what she had gathered, but threshed it herself, that she might the easier carry it home, and might have it ready for use. 'Whoever is slothful will not roast his game,' and so loses the benefit of it; 'but the diligent man will get precious wealth.' Ruth had gathered it ear by ear; but when she had put it all together, it was an ephah of barley, or about four pecks. Many a little makes a great deal. It is encouraging to industry, that 'in all toil,' even that of gleaning, 'there is profit, but mere talk tends only to poverty.' When she had got her barley into as little space as she could, she took it up herself, and carried it into the city, though had she asked them, it is likely some of Boaz's servants would have done that for her. We should study to be as little trouble as possible to those who are kind to us. She did not think it either too hard or too lowly a service, to carry her barley herself into the city; but was pleased with what she had got by her own industry, and was careful to secure it. And let us thus take care that we 'may not lose what we have worked for,' or which we have gained."

JULY 28
Fear Not, For I Have Redeemed You[536]

Jewish law allowed for a close relative of Ruth's deceased husband to buy his estate and marry his widow. Naomi advised Ruth to take advantage of this law because it would make Boaz her redeemer and place Ruth under his protection. Boaz's immediate response was to propose to Ruth. However, the law gave an even closer relative the opportunity to buy the property of Mahlon instead of Boaz. Only if he refused could Boaz buy it and marry Ruth. Boaz wasted no time in tactfully approaching this closer relative. He arranged to do this at a public gathering so that everything was done properly and in the open.

Ruth 4:1-17

1 Now Boaz had gone up to the gate *(where these types of transactions usually took place)*, and sat down there. And behold, the redeemer, of whom Boaz had spoken, came by. So Boaz said, "Turn aside, friend; sit down here." And he turned aside and sat down. **2** And he took ten men of the elders of the city and said, "Sit down here." So they sat down. *(Boaz did this to make sure everything was done according to the law.)*

3 Then he said to the redeemer, "Naomi, who has come back from the country of Moab, is selling the parcel of land that belonged to our relative Elimelech. **4** So I thought I would tell you of it and say, 'Buy it in the presence of those sitting here and in the presence of the elders of my people.' but if you will not, tell me, that I may know, for there is no one besides you to redeem it, and I come after you." And he said, "I will redeem it. *(He was ready to buy the land, but he did not know yet that marrying Ruth was part of the agreement.)*

5 Then Boaz said, "The day you buy the field from the hand of Naomi, you also acquire Ruth the Moabite, the widow of the dead, in order to perpetuate the name of the dead in his inheritance." *(You cannot have the land unless you marry the wife of the deceased, and then any children which you may have will be regarded as the children of Mahlon, your deceased relative.)* **6** Then the redeemer said, "I cannot redeem it for myself, lest I impair my own inheritance. Take my right of redemption yourself, for I cannot redeem it." *(This was exactly what Boaz wanted him to say.)*

7 Now this was the custom in former times in Israel concerning redeeming and exchanging: to confirm a transaction, the one drew off his sandal and gave it to the other, and this was the manner of attesting in Israel. *(This law is found in Deuteronomy 25:5-10. It was given so that no family in Israel would*

---
[536] Isaiah 43:1

die out. May God grant that this household will always have the Lord's people in it.) ⁸ So when the redeemer said to Boaz, "Buy it for yourself," he drew off his sandal. ⁹ Then Boaz said to the elders and all the people, "You are witnesses this day that I have bought from the hand of Naomi all that belonged to Elimelech and all that belonged to Chilion and to Mahlon. ¹⁰ Also Ruth the Moabite, the widow of Mahlon, I have bought to be my wife, to perpetuate the name of the dead in his inheritance, that the name of the dead may not be cut off from among his brothers and from the gate of his native place. You are witnesses this day." ¹¹ Then all the people who were at the gate and the elders said, "We are witnesses. May the LORD make the woman, who is coming into your house, like Rachel and Leah, who together built up the house of Israel. May you act worthily in Ephrathah and be renowned in Bethlehem, ¹² and may your house be like the house of Perez, whom Tamar bore to Judah, because of the offspring that the LORD will give you by this young woman."

¹³ So Boaz took Ruth, and she became his wife…and she bore a son. *(Here we see her self-denying faith rewarded. She left behind her relatives, her country, and her hope for the future, to be with Naomi and the Lord's people. And the Lord not only blessed her, but blessed generations far into the future through her. Those who follow the Lord no matter what, will not be losers in the long run. To increase Ruth's joy and crown her happiness, the Lord gave her a son who was also a joy to Naomi.)*

¹⁴ Then the women said to Naomi, "Blessed be the LORD, who has not left you this day without a redeemer, and may his name be renowned in Israel! ¹⁵ He shall be to you a restorer of life and a nourisher of your old age, for your daughter-in-law who loves you, who is more to you than seven sons, has given birth to him." ¹⁶ Then Naomi took the child and laid him on her lap and became his nurse. ¹⁷ And the women of the neighborhood gave him a name, saying, "A son has been born to Naomi." They named him Obed. He was the father of Jesse, the father of David. *(Here we find the reason the book of Ruth is included in the Bible. Ruth was the great-grandmother of King David, whose family line leads all the way to the birth of the Lord Jesus. All the Scriptures are intended to lead us in faith to the great Redeemer. May God grant that this purpose is or will be true in our case.)*

JULY 29
Your Promise Gives Me Life[537]

Before beginning the book of Samuel we will take another portion from David's Holy Alphabet—the hundred and nineteenth Psalm. Martin Luther prized this psalm so much that he declared he would not take the whole world in exchange for a single page of it. May the Holy Spirit impact our hearts while we read it.

Psalm 119:49-64

⁴⁹ Remember your word to your servant,
     in which you have made me hope.

The Christian's assurance of eternal life comes from the Lord himself through his perfect word. It is a certain hope, because the Lord will remember his promises. Believers will never be embarrassed, because God will fulfill his promises. But he keeps his promises in answer to our prayers. Therefore our praying must include the promises of God.

⁵⁰ This is my comfort in my affliction,
     that your promise gives me life.

Good people will have times of suffering. Their best comfort at these times is the shining grace of God. Instead of praying, "Lord, remove the trouble," we should cry, "Lord, give the grace promised in your word."

⁵¹ The insolent utterly deride me,
     but I do not turn away from your law.

He refused to be laughed out of his religion. People's scorn is hardly felt when the Lord Jesus smiles on us. If we reject holiness because bad people laugh, we will make good people weep.

⁵² When I think of your rules from of old,
     I take comfort, O LORD.

---
[537] Psalm 119:50

⁵³ Hot indignation seizes me because of the wicked,
　　who forsake your law.

A holy heart is horrified at sin, at sinners, and at the sinner's doom. Those who think lightly of other people's sins will soon think lightly of their own sin.

⁵⁴ Your statutes have been my songs
　　in the house of my sojourning.

The Bible is the believer's songbook. The songs and hymns found in it are sweet to their ear. Let us all sing more and complain less.

⁵⁵ I remember your name in the night, O Lord,
　　and keep your law.

Singing is for the day, and remembering is for the sleepless hours of the night. This is the way godly people make all twenty-four hours of the day holy to the Lord.

⁵⁶ This blessing has fallen to me,
　　that I have kept your precepts.

Godly songs and holy memories are the result of obedience. And many other comforts come to us as rewards when we stay on the right road.

⁵⁷ The Lord is my portion;
　　I promise to keep your words.

The Lord gives himself to us. It is only right that we should be determined to give ourselves to him.

⁵⁸ I entreat your favor with all my heart;
　　be gracious to me according to your promise.
⁵⁹ When I think on my ways,
　　I turn my feet to your testimonies;
⁶⁰ I hasten and do not delay
　　to keep your commandments.

Have we done the same? Is there anything we have neglected? When it comes to obeying God quickly, we cannot be too quick.

⁶¹ Though the cords of the wicked ensnare me,
　　I do not forget your law.
⁶² At midnight I rise to praise you,
　　because of your righteous rules.
⁶³ I am a companion of all who fear you,
　　of those who keep your precepts.

Those who love good company have some good things in their own hearts. The friends we choose ought to be those with whom we are willing to live with forever and ever. An elderly woman once said, "I cannot believe that the Lord will shut me up with the ungodly, for I have never loved such company. His people have been my friends on earth and I expect to dwell with them forever in heaven."

⁶⁴ The earth, O Lord, is full of your steadfast love;
　　teach me your statutes!

We are full of wants, and sins, and sorrow. That is why it is such a tremendous comfort to learn that the Lord has filled the whole earth with his mercy. Let us ask for mercy in the most sensible way. Ask the Lord to teach us how to live in his fear. "The fear of the Lord is the beginning of wisdom."[538]

July 30

Your Testimonies Are My Delight[539]

We will take another drink from the overflowing well of David's ever fresh and sparkling Psalm. May the Holy Spirit make it really refreshing to us.

　　　　Psalm 119:65-80

⁶⁵ You have dealt well with your servant,
　　O Lord, according to your word.

This is most joyfully true. Blessed be the name of God, our Father. Some of us can say, "Amen, Amen." Every promise has been fulfilled in its proper time. We have served a good Master and loved a faithful God. Sadly, we have not lived for him as well as we should have.

⁶⁶ Teach me good judgment and knowledge,
　　for I believe in your commandments.

One of the Reformers,[540] in a public debate, was seen writing on a piece of paper in front of him. His friend wished to see the notes that had helped him so much, and was surprised to find that they consisted simply of these brief prayers, "More light, Lord; more

---
[538] Psalm 111:10
[539] Psalm 119:24
[540] Protestant Reformation: A 16th century movement to reform the Roman Catholic Church.

light, more light." This is just what David asked for. Let us pray for the same.

⁶⁷ Before I was afflicted I went astray,
    but now I keep your word.

The use of affliction is sweet. It keeps us safe, like sheep kept in pens so that they cannot wander away as before.

⁶⁸ You are good and do good;
    teach me your statutes.

Goodness tends to rub off on others. Therefore the psalmist asks the Lord to show him how to be good.

⁶⁹ The insolent smear me with lies,
    but with my whole heart I keep your precepts;

He would answer their slander in the most effective manner, by living in such a way that their lies would be obvious to everyone.

⁷⁰ their heart is unfeeling like fat,
    but I delight in your law.

They suffered spiritually from fatty failing hearts. Their lives were monotonous, gluttonous, and lifeless. David used them as a warning to himself, to delight in the law of the Lord all the more.

⁷¹ It is good for me that I was afflicted,
    that I might learn your statutes.

⁷² The law of your mouth is better to me
    than thousands of gold and silver pieces.

⁷³ Your hands have made and fashioned me;
    give me understanding that I may learn your commandments.

You have made me Lord, be pleased to make me again. I am your work, complete me. I am your harp, tune me. I am your child, teach me.

⁷⁴ Those who fear you shall see me and rejoice,
    because I have hoped in your word.

The grace experienced by one believer cheers others. In fact, a good man is always a "son of encouragement"[541] to his fellow Christians. The delight experienced by someone who enjoys spending lots of time in God's word is contagious and gives delight to those around him.

⁷⁵ I know, O LORD, that your rules are righteous,
    and that in faithfulness you have afflicted me.

We may be quite sure of this, but we often forget it when we are on the gloomy side of the hill.

⁷⁶ Let your steadfast love comfort me
    according to your promise to your servant.

The phrase, "according to your promise," shows us that we should use the very words of God when we pray. We should keep his promises at our finger tips, and by the power of the Holy Spirit, we should ask the Lord to be as good as his own promises. Rest assured he will never deny himself. God is not "a son of man, that he should change his mind."[542]

⁷⁷ Let your mercy come to me, that I may live;
    for your law is my delight.

⁷⁸ Let the insolent be put to shame,
    because they have wronged me with falsehood;
    as for me, I will meditate on your precepts.

The psalmist was persecuted and his immediate response was to run to God's Word. When those on earth do you wrong, never begin to argue, or grow angry, but run to your Father in heaven.

⁷⁹ Let those who fear you turn to me,
    that they may know your testimonies.

Lord, make your children willing to help me and to be helped by me. Let me be a magnet to gather good company, not a broom to sweep them away. May I show love and encourage unity; yet not at the expense of truth. Let my prayer be,

⁸⁰ May my heart be blameless in your statutes,
    that I may not be put to shame!

---

[541] Acts 4:36

[542] Numbers 23:19

July 31
O People; Pour Out Your Heart Before Him[543]

1 Samuel 1:1-3; 9-18

1 There was a certain man of Ramathaim-zophim of the hill country of Ephraim whose name was Elkanah the son of Jeroham, son of Elihu, son of Tohu, son of Zuph, an Ephrathite. **2** He had two wives. The name of the one was Hannah, and the name of the other, Peninnah. And Peninnah had children, but Hannah had no children.

It is a sad thing to find a Levite stained with the error of double marriage. In Elkanah's case, as in every other, it caused much misery in the family, especially to that wife who was the best and holiest. Poor Hannah. She was a woman of great gifts as well as great grace, even though denied the blessing of children. Yet she was so tormented by Peninnah, that her life was made bitter. How great a mercy it is that Christianity forbids polygamy; which the old dispensation barely tolerated, and did so only because of the hardness of men's hearts.

3 Now this man used to go up year by year from his city to worship and to sacrifice to the Lord of hosts at Shiloh, where the two sons of Eli, Hophni and Phinehas, were priests of the Lord.

9 After they had eaten and drunk in Shiloh, Hannah rose. Now Eli the priest was sitting on the seat beside the doorpost of the temple of the Lord. **10** She was deeply distressed and prayed to the Lord and wept bitterly.

Hannah's husband loved her, but she needed more comfort than he could give her. She sought it in diligent prayer. This is the sure source of comfort.

11 And she vowed a vow and said, "O Lord of hosts, if you will indeed look on the affliction of your servant and remember me and not forget your servant, but will give to your servant a son, then I will give him to the Lord all the days of his life, and no razor shall touch his head."

Bishop Hall[544] well remarks that, "The way to obtain any benefit is to devote it, in our hearts, and to the glory of that God of whom we ask it. In this way God will both please his servant and honor himself. However, if the hope of our desires is simply to satisfy ourselves, then we may be sure that either our request will be denied or no blessing will come of it."

12 As she continued praying before the Lord, Eli observed her mouth. *(With all his faults, Eli did not neglect his duty, but sat at his post and watched the worshipers. The very presence of the priest helped to keep order in God's house.)* **13** Hannah was speaking in her heart; only her lips moved, and her voice was not heard. Therefore Eli took her to be a drunken woman. *(Good men may make mistakes. Eli was too permissive where he should have been stern, and too critical where he should have been charitable. We should not allow ourselves to be overly influenced by what others think of us.)*

14 And Eli said to her, "How long will you go on being drunk? Put away your wine from you." **15** But Hannah answered, "No, my lord, I am a woman troubled in spirit. I have drunk neither wine nor strong drink, but I have been pouring out my soul before the Lord. **16** Do not regard your servant as a worthless woman, for all along I have been speaking out of my great anxiety and vexation."

How gently she replied! Some would have flown into a passion. Meekness is a lovely part of godliness.

17 Then Eli answered, "Go in peace, and the God of Israel grant your petition that you have made to him."

Eli was not above confessing his error and quickly correcting himself. Let us never be ashamed to acknowledge when we are wrong, nor slow to correct everything in our power.

18 And she said, "Let your servant find favor in your eyes." Then the woman went her way and ate, and her face was no longer sad. *(Hannah's faith in the word of God that was spoken by his servant was so strong that she immediately began to rejoice in the*

---

[543] Psalm 62:8

[544] Church of England Bishop Joseph Hall (1574-1656).

blessing promised to her. We should have the same confidence in the divine promises. Rather than being sad, we should look for the blessing, and welcome it with a smile on our face.)

Susannah & Charles Spurgeon

August 1
May the Lord Establish His Word[545]
1 Samuel 1:19-28

The sacrifice was over, but god-fearing Elkanah and his family did not think of leaving Shiloh without bowing before the Lord one more time. They were not tired of worship, but having begun well they would finish well. There was one heart in the family which adored the Lord with a special joy. Hannah had come to the tabernacle "a woman troubled in spirit," but that is not how she felt on her way home. How wonderful it is to leave our burdens behind us after we have joined in worship with the people of God. Is anyone among us troubled? May this time of devotion have the same calming effect on them that Hannah experienced.

19 They rose early in the morning and worshiped before the Lord; then they went back to their house at Ramah. And Elkanah knew Hannah his wife, and the Lord remembered her. **20** And in due time Hannah conceived and bore a son, and she called his name Samuel, for she said, "I have asked for him from the Lord."

How doubly precious a blessing is when it comes in answer to prayer. Have we nothing to ask for? Have we not also received special favors that were even sweeter because we "asked them from the Lord."?

21 The man Elkanah and all his house went up to offer to the Lord the yearly sacrifice and to pay his vow.

Parents must not neglect church services because of their children. When mothers must stay home with a child, the rest of the household must not make empty excuses for staying away too.

22 But Hannah did not go up, for she said to her husband, "As soon as the child is weaned, I will bring him, so that he may appear in the presence of the Lord and dwell there forever." **23** Elkanah her husband said to her, "Do what seems best to you; wait until you have weaned him; only, may the Lord establish his word." *(What a choice saying, "Only may the Lord establish his word." Everything else must be less important than this. If God will just treat us according to his promise, other things do not matter much.)* So the woman remained and nursed her son until she weaned him.

24 And when she had weaned him, she took him up with her, along with a three-year-old bull, an ephah[546] of flour, and a skin of wine, and she brought him to the house of the Lord at Shiloh, And the child was young.

It was natural that the mother should be sorry to part with her dear boy. Yet grace had the victory over nature and she went to Shiloh with a glad heart even though she knew Samuel would not be returning home with her. She expressed her thankfulness for her son with an offering to the God who had answered her prayer. She returned the child which God had loaned to her without a second thought. Oh, that all our dear children may be the Lord's. It is better to part with them to be God's servants, than to

---

[545] 1 Samuel 1:23

[546] An *ephah* was about 3/5 bushel or 5 1/2 gallons.

keep them with us, and see them grow up graceless.

25 Then they slaughtered the bull, and they brought the child to Eli. **26** And she said, "Oh, my lord! As you live, my lord, I am the woman who was standing here in your presence, praying to the LORD. **27** For this child I prayed, and the LORD has granted me my petition that I made to him. **28** Therefore I have lent him to the LORD. As long as he lives, he is lent to the LORD." *(She gave up this one child, and before long, the Lord sent her five others. The Lord takes care to be in no one's debt. He generously rewards those who cheerfully make sacrifices for his cause.)*

And he worshiped the LORD there. *(Eli rejoiced in the good woman's piety.*[547] *All tender hearts are glad to see dedicated love to God in others. Perhaps, however, the text means that Samuel also worshiped the Lord there. How wonderful it is to see young children truly pray. Is there a little Samuel in this house who will worship the Lord now? Let us all aim to do so with our whole hearts.)*

AUGUST 2

My Heart Exults In the LORD[548]

1 Samuel 2:1-11

1 And Hannah prayed *(Her prayer for a son was answered, but she did not stop praying. Rather, she prayed all the more. However, now her prayers were no longer salted with sorrow, but were sweetened with the spices of thankfulness. She ascended from prayer to praise.)* and said,

"My heart exults in the LORD;"

Not in my child so much as in my God. God must always be our greatest joy.

"my strength is exalted in the LORD."

Her reputation and her energy were raised, but she gave the Lord the glory for it.

"My mouth derides my enemies,
because I rejoice in your salvation."

She understood her need of salvation and her faith found all that she wanted in the Lord her God.

2 "There is none holy like the LORD;
there is none besides you;
there is no rock like our God."

Her joy was all in God; in his salvation, in his matchless holiness, and in his eternal strength. Her Samuel did not become her idol, she loved her God better than her boy. Woe to that mother who permits son or daughter to rival the Lord. God's people must learn to feel and say, "There is none besides you, O Lord."

3 "Talk no more so very proudly,
let not arrogance come from your mouth;
for the LORD is a God of knowledge,
and by him actions are weighed."

God does not judge by appearances. His judgments call for a sincere heart and he will not be content without it.

4 "The bows of the mighty are broken,
but the feeble bind on strength.
5 Those who were full have hired
themselves out for bread,
but those who were hungry have ceased to hunger.
The barren has borne seven,
but she who has many children is forlorn."

It is the Lord's way to pull down the arrogant and lift up the humble. Those who are great and full of themselves he regards with scorn; but the poor and the empty he looks on with pity.

6 "The LORD kills and brings to life;
he brings down to Sheol and raises up.
7 The LORD makes poor and makes rich;
he brings low and he exalts."

It is the Lord's method to show his grace by humbling those whom he intends to exalt. None will ever be rich in Christ until they are made to feel that they are bankrupt in themselves.

8 "He raises up the poor from the dust,
he lifts the needy from the ash heap
to make them sit with princes
and inherit a seat of honor.
For the pillars of the earth are the LORD's,

---

[547] *piety* - devotion, religion, holiness, godliness, reverence, faith, spirituality, religious zeal.
[548] 1 Samuel 2:1

and on them he has set the world."

The Lord alone is the Creator and he does as he wills with his creation. Who shall question his absolute right to do whatever he wishes?

9 "He will guard the feet of his faithful ones,
  but the wicked shall be cut off in darkness,
  for not by might shall a man prevail.
10 The adversaries of the LORD shall be broken to pieces;
  against them he will thunder in heaven.
  The LORD will judge the ends of the earth;
  he will give strength to his king
  and exalt the power of his anointed."

This is a powerful song. It breathes not only warm devotion, but the true spirit of poetry. Hannah was a great original poetess and even the Virgin Mary's sweet hymn of gratitude followed Hannah's example. Even though no psalms had been written which Hannah could use as a model, her song is exquisitely composed, and has a delightful suggestion of spiritual religion about it. She is the first who sings of the "anointed" king, and as there was no king over Israel in her day, the words would seem to have a prophetic reference to Christ. He is the crown of all the saints' joys, and their songs reach their highest notes when they sing of "the anointed."

11 Then Elkanah went home to Ramah. And the boy was ministering to the LORD in the presence of Eli the priest.

AUGUST 3

Discipline Your Son, and He Will Give You Rest[549]

1 Samuel 2:12-21; 23-26

12 Now the sons of Eli were worthless men. They did not know the LORD.

This is a sad thing to say about those who teach others. And it is sad for the people to have such ministers. Let our hearts go up to God in thankfulness for the great blessing of holy teachers who practice what they preach. Eli's sons were worse than the worst, when they ought to have been better than the best of ordinary men.

13 The custom of the priests with the people was that when any man offered sacrifice, the priest's servant would come, while the meat was boiling, with a three-pronged fork in his hand, 14 and he would thrust it into the pan or kettle or cauldron or pot. All that the fork brought up the priest would take for himself. This is what they did at Shiloh to all the Israelites who came there.

The divine law said that the thigh and the breast of the sacrifice were to be given to the priests[550] and the remaining meat was for the person who made the offering. But these greedy priests took whatever they wanted and took it before the Lord's portion had been burned on the altar.

15 Moreover, before the fat was burned, the priest's servant would come and say to the man who was sacrificing, "Give meat for the priest to roast, for he will not accept boiled meat from you but only raw." 16 And if the man said to him, "Let them burn the fat first, and then take as much as you wish," he would say, "No, you must give it now, and if not, I will take it by force." 17 Thus the sin of the young men was very great in the sight of the LORD, for the men treated the offering of the LORD with contempt.

Godly people were shocked by such irreverent greediness. And they were grieved by the rudeness of those who should have acted with holy courtesy. If ministers become proud, domineering, and self-seeking, the people will soon despise the worship. This was great sin on the part of Eli's sons.

18 Samuel was ministering before the LORD, a boy clothed with a linen ephod.

It must have been a lovely sight to see the young boy actively engaged in the service of God and wearing the style of clothing that our Great King would wear when he was on this earth.

19 And his mother used to make for him a little robe and take it to him each year when she went up with her husband to offer the yearly sacrifice. *(Hannah understood that*

---

[549] Proverbs 29:17

[550] Leviticus 10:15

young Samuel would only be able to give limited help in maintaining the tabernacle. So she assumed the expense for the clothes he needed. In doing this, she showed her concern for the Lord's house and her love for her dear boy.) ²⁰ Then Eli would bless Elkanah and his wife, and say, "May the LORD give you children by this woman for the petition she asked of the LORD." So then they would return to their home.

²¹ Indeed the LORD visited Hannah, and she conceived and bore three sons and two daughters. And the young man Samuel grew in the presence of the LORD. *(But while this holy child was living near to God, Eli's sons went from bad to worse, until at last Eli spoke to them about their great sins.)*

²³ And he said to them, "Why do you do such things? For I hear of your evil dealings from all these people. ²⁴ No, my sons; it is no good report that I hear the people of the LORD spreading abroad. ²⁵ If someone sins against a man, God will mediate for him, but if someone sins against the LORD, who can intercede for him?" But they would not listen to the voice of their father, for it was the will of the LORD to put them to death.

They had gone so far that the Lord decided to destroy them and therefore would not give them grace to repent. Eli should have put an end to their wickedness much sooner by using stronger actions. His mild rebuke, which came so late in the day, was of no use whatever. If he had chastened[551] his sons earlier, he might have saved their characters and their lives. Children should be thankful for parents who will not let their sins go unpunished. It would be a terrible thing for a curse to come upon a family because the sons and daughters were not kept from sin. A dear little girl who died believing in Jesus, affectionately thanked her mother on her deathbed for all her tender love and then added, "But dear mother, I thank you most of all for having conquered my self-will." Children sometimes think their parents are too strict, but when they grow up they will bless them for not allowing them to sin.

²⁶ Now the young man Samuel continued to grow both in stature and in favor with the LORD and also with man. *(A sweet way of growing, but to do this a child must be gracious, obedient, and kind.)*

AUGUST 4

Those Whom He Predestined He Also Called[552]

1 Samuel 3:1-18

¹ Now the boy Samuel was ministering to the LORD in the presence of Eli. *(Josephus[553] claimed that Samuel was about twelve years of age at this time, and so he was like our blessed Lord Jesus, who at that age said, "Did you not know that I must be in my Father's house?"[554] How charming a sight it is to see a young child serving the Lord.)* And the word of the LORD was rare in those days; there was no frequent vision. *(The sin of the priests and the people had made prophetic visions very rare.)*

² At that time Eli, whose eyesight had begun to grow dim so that he could not see, was lying down in his own place. ³ The lamp of God had not yet gone out, and Samuel was lying down in the temple of the LORD, where the ark of God was.

⁴ Then the LORD called Samuel, and he said, "Here I am!" *(God calls his servants when he pleases, and it is well for them to be able to reply, "Here I am." Whether it is for duty or suffering, the true child of God says, "Here I am.")* ⁵ and ran to Eli and said, "Here I am, for you called me." But he said, "I did not call; lie down again." So he went and lay down.

⁶ And the LORD called again, "Samuel!" and Samuel arose and went to Eli and said, "Here I am, for you called me." But he said, "I did not call, my son; lie down again." ⁷ Now Samuel did not yet know the LORD, and the word of the LORD had not yet been revealed to him. *(That is, Samuel was not a prophet yet and did not know the Lord with the clarity he would later receive. But without doubt, he was already a godly child.)*

---

[551] *chastening* or *chastisement* - The act of discipline which may include scolding, criticizing or pain inflicted for the purpose of correction or moral improvement.

[552] Romans 8:30
[553] Flavius Josephus was a first century Jewish historian.
[554] Luke 2:49

⁸ And the LORD called Samuel again the third time. And he arose and went to Eli and said, "Here I am, for you called me." *(Samuel's behavior was lovely, honest and obedient. Do we not wish that all children were like this?)* Then Eli perceived that the LORD was calling the boy. ⁹ Therefore Eli said to Samuel, "Go, lie down, and if he calls you, you shall say, 'Speak, LORD, for your servant hears.' " So Samuel went and lay down in his place.

¹⁰ And the LORD came and stood, calling as at other times, "Samuel! Samuel!" And Samuel said, "Speak, for your servant hears."

When God speaks to us, it is a great mercy to have a listening ear. But a deaf ear is a sad judgment against us.

¹¹ Then the LORD said to Samuel, "Behold, I am about to do a thing in Israel at which the two ears of everyone who hears it will tingle. ¹² On that day I will fulfill against Eli all that I have spoken concerning his house, from beginning to end. ¹³ And I declare to him that I am about to punish his house forever, for the iniquity that he knew, because his sons were blaspheming God, and he did not restrain them. ¹⁴ Therefore I swear to the house of Eli that the iniquity of Eli's house shall not be atoned for by sacrifice or offering forever." *(Their day of grace was over and their doom was sealed. What a warning to those who do not respect holy things. These men used the grace of God as an excuse to act wickedly.)*

¹⁵ Samuel lay until morning; then he opened the doors of the house of the LORD. *(He did not become arrogant because he had seen a vision. He went about his daily work, even as our Lord did when he returned from Jerusalem with Mary and Joseph, and was submissive to them. Holy children are always humble children.)* And Samuel was afraid to tell the vision to Eli. ¹⁶ But Eli called Samuel and said, "Samuel, my son." And he said, "Here I am." ¹⁷ And Eli said, "What was it that he told you? Do not hide it from me. May God do so to you and more also if you hide anything from me of all that he told you." *(Eli's conscience convicted him. The Lord had spoken and he was afraid that something terrible was going to happen.)*

¹⁸ So Samuel told him everything and hid nothing from him. *(This was a difficult order for Samuel, but grace made him do his duty.)* And he said, "It is the LORD. Let him do what seems good to him." *(Eli was wrong with his sons, but he was right with God. We must admire the old man's holy submission and imitate it.)*

AUGUST 5
Act Like Men, Be Strong[555]

1 Samuel 3:19-21

¹⁹ And Samuel grew, and the LORD was with him and let none of his words fall to the ground. ²⁰ And all Israel from Dan to Beersheba knew that Samuel was established as a prophet of the LORD. ²¹ And the LORD appeared again at Shiloh, for the LORD revealed himself to Samuel at Shiloh by the word of the LORD. *(Samuel was faithful when God spoke to him the first time and therefore the Lord honored him again. May all young Christians be unwavering and true from the start and God will bless them. Meanwhile God was preparing terrible judgment for the wicked sons of Eli.)*

1 Samuel 4:1-11

¹ᵇ Now Israel went out to battle against the Philistines. They encamped at Ebenezer, and the Philistines encamped at Aphek. ² The Philistines drew up in line against Israel, and when the battle spread, Israel was defeated by the Philistines, who killed about four thousand men on the field of battle. ³ And when the troops came to the camp, the elders of Israel said, "Why has the LORD defeated us today before the Philistines? Let us bring the ark of the covenant of the LORD here from Shiloh, that it may come among us and save us from the power of our enemies." *(The Israelites trusted in the ark instead of the God it represented. They forgot that the most holy symbols will not bring blessings to ungodly hearts. God shows us here that religion on the outside is worthless unless holiness is on the inside. It is pointless to trust in words and ceremonies. They cannot help us if the Lord is not with us. A cross*

---

[555] 1 Corinthians 16:13

hanging from our neck is worthless, but Christ in the heart is precious.)

4 So the people sent to Shiloh and brought from there the ark of the covenant of the Lord of hosts, who is enthroned on the cherubim. And the two sons of Eli, Hophni and Phinehas, were there with the ark of the covenant of God. *(God had his own way to bring Eli's sons to the battlefield where they were doomed to lose their guilty lives. God knows how to reach wicked people and deliver justice to them.)*

5 As soon as the ark of the covenant of the Lord came into the camp, all Israel gave a mighty shout, so that the earth resounded.

Overconfident people are always ready to shout, but before long they will have reason to weep and wail, just as these noisy boasters did. The law was in the ark, but what help could the law they had broken bring to them. Its very presence condemned them. Those who trust in the law face certain judgment.

6 And when the Philistines heard the noise of the shouting, they said, "What does this great shouting in the camp of the Hebrews mean?" And when they learned that the ark of the Lord had come to the camp, **7** the Philistines were afraid, for they said, "A god has come into the camp." And they said, "Woe to us! For nothing like this has happened before. **8** Woe to us! Who can deliver us from the power of these mighty gods? These are the gods who struck the Egyptians with every sort of plague in the wilderness. **9** Take courage, and be men, O Philistines, lest you become slaves to the Hebrews as they have been to you; be men and fight."

The Philistines were heathens and thought the ark was God himself. However, they were correct in thinking that if God was on Israel's side, it would not go well with them. If they had understood that God is Almighty, they would not have attempted to fight against him. But they thought Jehovah was like their own god, Dagon, who had only limited powers. Therefore they showed their bravery by deciding to fight like true soldiers. If these Philistines could be so bold in what appeared to be a hopeless situation, how brave should we be who have the assurance of victory, because the Lord of hosts is with us? Our Lord says to us, "Take courage, and be men." To be cowardly in the cause of Jesus would be disgraceful! Never let the fear of man have the slightest power over you. Do not doubt the reality of the power of your Lord.

10 So the Philistines fought, and Israel was defeated, and they fled, every man to his home. And there was a very great slaughter, for thirty thousand foot soldiers of Israel fell. **11** And the ark of God was captured, *(The ark was never captured until it was defended with physical weapons. True religion will always suffer when people try to defend it with force.)* and the two sons of Eli, Hophni and Phinehas, died.

The Lord kept his word. He will be just as faithful to keep his threats as to he is to keep his promises. Woe to us if we continue in sin; because the Lord will certainly punish us. Are we all saved in Christ Jesus?

August 6

For You Are the Glory Of Their Strength[556]

1 Samuel 4:12-18; 20-22

12 A man of Benjamin ran from the battle line and came to Shiloh the same day, with his clothes torn and with dirt on his head. *(Bad news is sure to find a messenger and a swift one. Sadly, the good news of the gospel often remains untold.)* **13** When he arrived, Eli was sitting on his seat by the road watching, for his heart trembled for the ark of God. And when the man came into the city and told the news, all the city cried out. *(In this way, the prophecy that the judgments of the Lord on Eli's sons was fulfilled and the two ears of everyone who heard of it tingled.[557] Shiloh had been contaminated with sin, and as a result, the city was infected with sorrow.)* **14** When Eli heard the sound of the outcry, he said, "What is this uproar?" Then the man hurried and came and told Eli.

15 Now Eli was ninety-eight years old and his eyes were set so that he could not see. **16** And the man said to Eli, "I am he who has

---
[556] Psalm 89:17
[557] 1 Samuel 3:11

come from the battle; I fled from the battle today." And he said, "How did it go, my son?" **17** He who brought the news answered and said, "Israel has fled before the Philistines, and there has also been a great defeat among the people. Your two sons also, Hophni and Phinehas, are dead, and the ark of God has been captured."

The distinguished old priest, within two years of a century old, endured all the sad news patiently until the messenger came to the last item.

18 As soon as he mentioned the ark of God, Eli fell over backward from his seat by the side of the gate, and his neck was broken and he died, for the man was old and heavy. He had judged Israel forty years. *(First his heart was broken and then his neck. Eli fainted from grief and the fall caused his death. No sword of the Philistines could have killed him any more effectively than this terrible news that God's ark was captured. Nothing affects good people as much as injury to the Church or dishonor brought upon the name of the Lord.)*

The sad news that the ark was taken, and that her husband had been killed, caused the pregnant wife of Phinehas to go into labor and die right after the child was born.

20 And about the time of her death the women attending her said to her, "Do not be afraid, for you have borne a son." But she did not answer or pay attention. **21** And she named the child Ichabod, saying, "The glory has departed from Israel!" because the ark of God had been captured and because of her father-in-law and her husband. **22** And she said, "The glory has departed from Israel, for the ark of God has been captured." *(She seems to have been a God-fearing woman, though her husband was a wicked man. Her faith led her to forget her own miseries, because the miseries of the Church of God were even greater. She named her child Ichabod, which means, "without honor" or, "where is the glory?" because honor and glory had been taken away from Israel. Her death was another strike against Eli's house, but it was sent in love to her, because she was spared from seeing Israel's sorrow.)*

The sad story of the destruction of Eli's family is a special warning to all parents to not allow sin to go unpunished in their households. Lack of discipline is lack of love. Let us see what Solomon says about it.

Proverbs 23:13-18

13 Do not withhold discipline from a child.
  if you strike him with a rod, he will not die.
14 If you strike him with the rod,
  you will save his soul from Sheol.

Charles Bridges[558] in his "Exposition on the Book of Proverbs," says, "Eli tried gentler means and the sad result is written for our instruction. Is it not cruel love that turns away from painful duty? To tolerate sin in a child is tantamount to hating him in our heart. Is it not better that the flesh should smart than that the soul should die? What if your child should rebuke you throughout eternity, for the neglect of that timely correction that might have saved their soul from hell."

15 My son, if your heart is wise,
  my heart too will be glad.
16 My inmost being will exult
  when your lips speak what is right.

It is a father's greatest happiness to have a son who is not only good himself, but the bold champion of goodness, speaking out bravely for right and truth and God.

17 Let not your heart envy sinners,
  but continue in the fear of the Lord all the day.
18 Surely there is a future,
  and your hope will not be cut off.

The trouble in this life will soon be over and then the godly will begin their best life. Their hope is a certain hope. May the Lord teach us as a family to serve him faithfully, so that we may be blessed both here and hereafter.

---

[558] Charles Bridges (1794-1869). An evangelical pastor and theologian in the Church of England..

AUGUST 7

For the LORD Is a...Great King Above All Gods[559]

1 Samuel 5:1-4; 6-12

¹ When the Philistines captured the ark of God, they brought it from Ebenezer to Ashdod. ² Then the Philistines took the ark of God and brought it into the house of Dagon and set it up beside Dagon. ³ And when the people of Ashdod rose early the next day, behold, Dagon had fallen face downward on the ground before the ark of the LORD. *(The true God would not tolerate having an idol standing upright in the same temple with his ark. Therefore, down it must go. The ark was brought into the house as a captive, but immediately became a conqueror. If the Lord, by his Spirit, comes into the human heart, sin soon falls before him.)* So they took Dagon and put him back in his place. *(It was a worthless god that needed help putting itself back in place. Idolatry makes people foolish. If it did not, they would see how irrational their behavior is.)*

⁴ But when they rose early on the next morning, behold, Dagon had fallen face downward on the ground before the ark of the LORD, and the head of Dagon and both his hands were lying cut off on the threshold. Only the trunk of Dagon was left to him. *(The second fall was greater than the first, for the fish god was broken, and only his scaly tail remained. The head and hands which symbolized wisdom and power, were dashed to atoms. The ark in the pagan temple resulted in the destruction of Dagon. Grace in the heart destroys the power and energy of sin.)*

⁶ The hand of the LORD was heavy against the people of Ashdod, and he terrified and afflicted them with tumors, both Ashdod and its territory. ⁷ And when the men of Ashdod saw how things were, they said, "The ark of the God of Israel must not remain with us, for his hand is hard against us and against Dagon our god." ⁸ So they sent and gathered together all the lords of the Philistines and said, "What shall we do with the ark of the God of Israel?" They answered, "Let the ark of the God of Israel be brought around to Gath." So they brought the ark of the God of Israel there. ⁹ But after they had brought it around, the hand of the LORD was against the city, causing a very great panic, and he afflicted the men of the city, both young and old, so that tumors broke out on them.

¹⁰ So they sent the ark of God to Ekron. But as soon as the ark of God came to Ekron, the people of Ekron cried out, "They have brought around to us the ark of the God of Israel to kill us and our people. ¹¹ They sent therefore and gathered together all the lords of the Philistines and said, "Send away the ark of the God of Israel, and let it return to its own place, that it may not kill us and our people." For there was a deathly panic throughout the whole city. The hand of God was very heavy there. ¹² The men who did not die were struck with tumors, and the cry of the city went up to heaven. *(This disease was not only extremely painful but was intended to embarrass the Philistines, because they dared to seize the ark of God and held it in contempt. How glad they would have been to get rid of their captive, who even in captivity achieved victory over them.)*

We have a summary of this part of Israel's history in the Psalms. Let us read it.

Psalm 78:58-66

⁵⁸ For they provoked him to anger with their high places;
   they moved him to jealousy with their idols.
⁵⁹ When God heard, he was full of wrath,
   and he utterly rejected Israel.
⁶⁰ He forsook his dwelling at Shiloh,
   the tent where he dwelt among mankind,

Shiloh was abandoned. The ark never returned to it. The place became a desert and no buildings remained standing. The lampstand of the Lord went out in Shiloh.

⁶¹ and *(the Lord)* delivered his power to captivity,
   his glory to the hand of the foe.
⁶² He gave his people over to the sword
   and vented his wrath on his heritage.
⁶³ Fire devoured their young men,

---

[559] Psalm 95:3

and their young women had no marriage song.

⁶⁴ Their priests fell by the sword,
and their widows made no lamentation.

The wife of Phinehas was so overcome with sorrow because the ark had been captured by the Philistines, that she was unable to grieve over the death of her husband.

⁶⁵ Then the Lord awoke as from sleep,
like a strong man shouting because of wine.

⁶⁶ And he put his adversaries to rout;
he put them to everlasting shame.

Wickedness will not win for long. God will always be victorious.

AUGUST 8

Nations Will Fear the Name Of the LORD[560]

1 Samuel 6:1-10; 12-15; 19-21

¹ The ark of the LORD was in the country of the Philistines seven months. ² And the Philistines called for the priests and the diviners and said, "What shall we do with the ark of the LORD? Tell us with what we shall send it to its place." ³ They said, "If you send away the ark of the God of Israel, do not send it empty, but by all means return him a guilt offering. Then you will be healed, and it will be known to you why his hand does not turn away from you." *(They were correct in believing that some acknowledgement of their fault must go with the ark when they returned it. If people want to be forgiven, they must use every possible way to right the wrongs they have committed. Even unbelievers understand this.)*

⁴ And they said, "What is the guilt offering that we shall return to him?" They answered, "Five golden tumors and five golden mice, according to the number of the lords of the Philistines, for the same plague was on all of you and on your lords. ⁵ So you must make images of your tumors and images of your mice that ravage the land, and give glory to the God of Israel. Perhaps he will lighten his hand from off you and your gods and your land. ⁶ Why should you harden your hearts as the Egyptians and Pharaoh hardened their hearts? After he had dealt severely with them, did they not send the people away, and they departed? *(It is likely that a plague of mice had been destroying their crops at the same time the tumors were tormenting their bodies. Therefore, they recognized that both judgments came from Jehovah.)*

⁷ "Now then, take and prepare a new cart and two milk cows on which there has never come a yoke, and yoke the cows to the cart, but take their calves home, away from them. ⁸ And take the ark of the LORD and place it on the cart and put in a box at its side the figures of gold, which you are returning to him as a guilt offering. Then send it off and let it go its way ⁹ and watch. If it goes up on the way to its own land, to Beth-shemesh, then it is he who has done us this great harm, but if not, then we shall know that it is not his hand that struck us; it happened to us by coincidence."

¹⁰ The men did so, and took two milk cows and yoked them to the cart and shut up the calves at home.

¹² And the cows went straight in the direction of Beth-shemesh along one highway, lowing as they went. They turned neither to the right nor to the left, and the lords of the Philistines went after them as far as the border of Beth-shemesh. *(How wonderfully God guided these animals. Of their own accord they wandered away from their calves, lamenting them as they went along. Without a driver they chose the nearest road to the city of the Levites. God led the cows every step of the way.)*

¹³ Now the people of Beth-shemesh were reaping their wheat harvest in the valley. And when they lifted up their eyes and saw the ark, they rejoiced to see it. *(They must have been shocked to see the ark returning to them without any human assistance. God wanted them to understand that this was completely his doing.)* ¹⁴ The cart came into the field of Joshua of Beth-shemesh and stopped there. A great stone was there. And they split up the wood of the cart and offered the cows as a burnt offering to the LORD. ¹⁵ And the Levites took down the ark of the

---

[560] Psalm 102:15

Lord and the box that was beside it, in which were the golden figures, and set them upon the great stone. And the men of Beth-shemesh offered burnt offerings and sacrificed sacrifices on that day to the Lord.

19 And he struck some of the men of Beth-shemesh, because they looked upon the ark of the Lord. He struck seventy men of them, and the people mourned because the Lord had struck the people with a great blow. *(The God who judged his enemies for their blasphemy, also judges his own people for not obeying his law. He demands the deep respect of all who come near him. Let us never treat holy things lightly.)* **20** Then the men of Beth-shemesh said, "Who is able to stand before the Lord, this holy God? And to whom shall he go up away from us?" *(Instead of confessing their own sin, they laid the blame at the door of God's incomparable holiness. People have not changed. They still complain that God is too strict.)*

21 So they sent messengers to the inhabitants of Kiriath-jearim, saying, "The Philistines have returned the ark of the Lord. Come down and take it up to you."

AUGUST 9

Till Now the Lord Has Helped Us[561]

1 Samuel 7:1-13; 15-17

1 And the men of Kiriath-jearim came and took up the ark of the Lord and brought it to the house of Abinadab on the hill. And they consecrated his son Eleazar to have charge of the ark of the Lord. *(The ark of God was moved from Shiloh, but the light of God that it represented*[562] *was even brighter than before.)* **2** From the day that the ark was lodged at Kiriath-jearim, a long time passed, some twenty years, and all the house of Israel lamented after the Lord. *(This was a happy sorrow. They were full of regret because the Lord had left them. Whenever people seek God and mourn over their sin, he will soon make his presence known to them. Anyone who has not yet found Jesus, should sigh and cry after him. It will not be long before he looks on us in love. God had already come back to Israel when the people lamented after him. When a soul sighs for the Lord, the Lord is already with it.)*

3 And Samuel said to all the house of Israel, "If you are returning to the Lord with all your heart, then put away the foreign gods and the Ashtaroth from among you and direct your heart to the Lord and serve him only, and he will deliver you out of the hand of the Philistines." **4** So the people of Israel put away the Baals and the Ashtaroth, and they served the Lord only. *(Their repentance would not have been real if it did not change the way they lived. People cannot keep their sins and have their God. No one can serve two masters.)*

5 Then Samuel said, "Gather all Israel at Mizpah, and I will pray to the Lord for you. **6** So they gathered at Mizpah and drew water and poured it out before the Lord and fasted on that day and said there, "We have sinned against the Lord." And Samuel judged the people of Israel at Mizpah. **7** Now when the Philistines heard that the people of Israel had gathered at Mizpah, the lords of the Philistines went up against Israel. And when the people of Israel heard of it, they were afraid of the Philistines. *(Yet they had no cause for fear, because they were now reunited with God. The person who is at peace with God should be fearless.)*

8 And the people of Israel said to Samuel, "Do not cease to cry out to the Lord our God for us, that he may save us from the hand of the Philistines." *(They spoke wisely, and showed that they had faith as well as fear. Faith in God gave them faith in the power of prayer.)* **9** So Samuel took a nursing lamb and offered it as a whole burnt offering to the Lord. And Samuel cried out to the Lord for Israel, and the Lord answered him.

True repentance, true prayer, and faith in the true Lamb of God, will win the day.

10 As Samuel was offering up the burnt offering, the Philistines drew near to attack Israel. But the Lord thundered with a mighty sound that day against the Philistines and threw them into confusion, and they were defeated before Israel. **11** And the men of Israel went out from Mizpah and pursued the

---

[561] 1 Samuel 7:12
[562] 1 John 1:5, "God is Light."

Philistines and struck them, as far as below Beth-car.

¹² Then Samuel took a stone and set it up between Mizpah and Shen and called its name Ebenezer *(or, stone of help),* for he said, "Till now the LORD has helped us." *(Samuel won that battle on his knees. Then he placed a stone as a reminder to praise the Lord for answering prayer. Praying people are thankful people.)* ¹³ So the Philistines were subdued and did not again enter the territory of Israel. And the hand of the LORD was against the Philistines all the days of Samuel.

¹⁵ Samuel judged Israel all the days of his life. *(God does not abandon his faithful servants when they grow old. And they do not ask their Lord for permission to retire and stop serving him. To serve God from our childhood to our old age is an honor. May such grace be given to the young members of our family.)* ¹⁶ And he went on a circuit year by year to Bethel, Gilgal, and Mizpah. And he judged Israel in all these places. ¹⁷ Then he would return to Ramah, for his home was there, and there also he judged Israel. And he built there an altar to the LORD.

AUGUST 10
Put Not Your Trust In Princes[563]

1 Samuel 8:1; 3-22

¹ When Samuel became old, he made his sons judges over Israel.

³ Yet his sons did not walk in his ways but turned aside after gain. They took bribes and perverted justice. *(Grace cannot be passed down from generation to generation. An honored father may have disgraceful children. Perhaps Samuel was wrong in making his sons judges. We do not read that the Lord instructed him to appoint them. Great people should not injure the church or the state by putting their children into offices that they are not qualified to fill.*

⁴ Then all the elders of Israel gathered together and came to Samuel at Ramah, ⁵ and said to him, "Behold, you are old and your sons do not walk in your ways. Now appoint for us a king to judge us like all the nations." ⁶ But the thing displeased Samuel when they said, "Give us a king to judge us." And Samuel prayed to the LORD. *(This little sentence is most instructive. When we are perplexed or displeased, we should turn immediately to prayer. We continually read of the prayers of the Lord Jesus. We ought to imitate him in this. As the fish loves the stream, and the bird the branch, so the believer loves prayer.)*

⁷ And the LORD said to Samuel, "Obey the voice of the people in all that they say to you, for they have not rejected you, but they have rejected me from being king over them. ⁸ According to all the deeds that they have done, from the day I brought them up out of Egypt even to this day, forsaking me and serving other gods, so they are also doing to you. ⁹ Now then, obey their voice; only you shall solemnly warn them and show them the ways of the king who shall reign over them." *(They wanted to do things their way and the Lord finally allowed them to have it. But they were to be warned of the consequences, so they would not be ignorant about the decision they were making. Many things that people's hearts lust after will be their curse. God may allow them to have their heart's desire, but he does it in anger and he knows it will bring them only limited satisfaction.)*

¹⁰ So Samuel told all the words of the LORD to the people who were asking for a king from him. ¹¹ He said, "These will be the ways of the king who will reign over you: he will take your sons and appoint them to his chariots and to be his horsemen and to run before his chariots. ¹² And he will appoint for himself commanders of thousands and commanders of fifties, and some to plow his ground and to reap his harvest, and to make his implements of war and the equipment of his chariots. ¹³ He will take your daughters to be perfumers and cooks and bakers. ¹⁴ He will take the best of your fields and vineyards and olive orchards and give them to his servants. ¹⁵ He will take the tenth of your grain and of your vineyards and give it to his officers and to his servants. ¹⁶ He will take your male servants and female servants and the best of your young men and your

---
[563] Psalm 146:3

donkeys, and put them to his work. **17** He will take the tenth of your flocks, and you shall be his slaves. **18** And in that day you will cry out because of your king, whom you have chosen for yourselves, but the LORD will not answer you in that day."

Under the government of God they had been free from taxes and demands of service. But if they chose to put their necks under the yoke of a king, they would have to keep them there. When Christians are free from the cares and worries of a complicated and strict form of church government, they are better off not changing things. Let us not run into spiritual bondage willingly. It is delightful to serve King Jesus, but it is hard to serve others, or live for self-promotion, wealth, or tradition.

19 But the people refused to obey the voice of Samuel. And they said, "No! But there shall be a king over us, **20** that we also may be like all the nations, and that our king may judge us and go out before us and fight our battles." **21** And when Samuel had heard all the words of the people, he repeated them in the ears of the LORD. **22** And the LORD said to Samuel, "Obey their voice and make them a king." Samuel then said to the men of Israel, "Go every man to his city." *(May God save us from having our prayers answered like theirs were! Oh Lord, if we ask anything that is not according to your will, please have mercy on us and refuse our request.)*

AUGUST 11
He Knows the Way That I Take[564]

1 Samuel 9:1-6; 14-21; 26, 27

1 There was a man of Benjamin whose name was Kish ... a man of wealth. **2** And he had a son whose name was Saul, a handsome young man. *(It would have been better if he had been godly as well as handsome.)* There was not a man among the people of Israel more handsome than he. From his shoulders upward he was taller than any of the people.

3 Now the donkeys of Kish, Saul's father, were lost. So Kish said to Saul his son, "Take one of the young men with you, and arise, go and look for the donkeys." *(A quaint writer[565] says, "Saul's obedience was a proper way to begin his reign as king. The job was not all that important for the son of a great man, yet, he does not refuse to go with his father's servant on such a humble errand. The disobedient and scornful are good for nothing. They are not ready to be subjects or governors. Kish was a great man in his country, yet he was not above sending his son Saul on a simple errand; neither does Saul plead that it would disgrace him. Pride and love of pleasure have marred our times. Great parents count it a dishonor to employ their sons in honest labor, and their pampered children think it is shameful to do anything, and so they behave as if they considered it a glory to be idle or wicked.")*

4 And he passed through the hill country of Ephraim and passed through the land of Shalishah, but they did not find them. And they passed through the land of Shaalim, but they were not there. Then they passed through the land of Benjamin, but did not find them.

5 When they came to the land of Zuph, Saul said to his servant who was with him, "Come, let us go back, lest my father cease to care about the donkeys and become anxious about us." **6** But he said to him, "Behold, there is a man of God in this city, and he is a man who is held in honor; all that he says comes true. So now let us go there. Perhaps he can tell us the way we should go." *(They came to the man of God about donkeys, and learned something about a kingdom. Many go to hear preachers out of idle curiosity, but God leads them into the kingdom of his dear Son.)*

14 So they went up to the city. As they were entering the city, they saw Samuel coming out toward them on his way up to the high place.

15 Now the day before Saul came, the LORD had revealed to Samuel: **16** "Tomorrow about this time I will send to you a man from the land of Benjamin, and you shall anoint him to be prince over my people Israel. He shall save my people from the hand of the

---

[564] Job 23:10

[565] The original quote is found in a volume by Joseph Hall (circa 1650).

Philistines. For I have seen my people, because their cry has come to me." **17** When Samuel saw Saul, the LORD told him, "Here is the man of whom I spoke to you! He it is who shall restrain my people." **18** Then Saul approached Samuel in the gate and said, "Tell me where is the house of the seer?" **19** Samuel answered Saul, "I am the seer. Go up before me to the high place, for today you shall eat with me, and in the morning I will let you go and will tell you all that is on your mind. *(That he did, and very much more. God's ministers are enabled by his Spirit to expose the secrets of people's hearts, and then they tell them about the kingdom of heaven.)*

20 As for your donkeys that were lost three days ago, do not set your mind on them, for they have been found. And for whom is all that is desirable in Israel? Is it not for you and for all your father's house?" *(Who cares about finding donkeys when a kingdom is on the horizon? Who cares about earthly joys when heaven is nearby? How foolish are those who spend all their thoughts on this world's stray donkeys, and lose the unfading crown of glory.)* **21** Saul answered, "Am I not a Benjaminite, from the least of the tribes of Israel? And is not my clan the humblest of all the clans of the tribe of Benjamin? Why then have you spoken to me in this way?"

26 Then at the break of dawn Samuel called to Saul on the roof, "Up, that I may send you on your way." So Saul arose, and both he and Samuel went out into the street.

27 As they were going down to the outskirts of the city, Samuel said to Saul, "Tell the servant to pass on before us, and when he has passed on, stop here yourself for a while, that I may make known to you the word of God. *(Today, let each of us do our best to have a little time for thought and prayer; while we keep these words in our hearts, "Stop here yourself for a while, that I may make known to you the word of God.")*

AUGUST 12
They Have Forsaken Me, the Fountain Of Living Waters[566]

1 Samuel 10:1; 17-27

1a Then Samuel took a flask of oil and poured it on his head and kissed [Saul] and said, "Has not the LORD anointed you to be prince over his people Israel? *(It has been remarked that only a small bottle of oil was used and not a ram's horn as in the case of David. This seemed to be a sign that Saul's reign as king would be a short one and that the abundant grace of God was lacking in his life.)*

17 Now Samuel called the people together to the LORD at Mizpah. **18** And he said to the people of Israel, "Thus says the LORD, the God of Israel, 'I brought up Israel out of Egypt, and I delivered you from the hand of the Egyptians and from the hand of all the kingdoms that were oppressing you.' **19** But today you have rejected your God, who saves you from all your calamities and your distresses, and you have said to him, 'Set a king over us.' Now therefore present yourselves before the LORD by your tribes and by your thousands."

The Lord's people often refuse to walk by faith. This is just one example of an evil that is all too common among them. They are not spiritual enough to trust only in the invisible God. They want to depend on something they can see. They are not satisfied with the unseen hand of God helping them. They demand visible assistance. They cry out for help the same way the world does. The Lord often gives these people just what they ask for. However, it soon becomes more of a curse than a blessing—just as it was for Saul and Israel. When we pray we should always say, "Not as I will, but as you will."[567] If we pray thinking we know more about what is good for us than God does, he may answer our prayer in anger and the result will not be one that brings real happiness.

20 Then Samuel brought all the tribes of Israel near, and the tribe of Benjamin was taken by lot. **21** He brought the tribe of

---
[566] Jeremiah 2:13
[567] Matthew 26:39

Benjamin near by its clans, and the clan of the Matrites was taken by lot; and Saul the son of Kish was taken by lot. But when they sought him, he could not be found. *(He knew the lot must fall on him because Samuel had already anointed him king. He may have thought the job was too big for him and was afraid he would be a failure. Crowns are heavy things and often give those who wear them headaches. Saul should not be blamed for hiding from such a difficult honor. If people understood the trials of the great, they would stop wanting to trade places with them.)*

²² So they inquired again of the LORD, "Is there a man still to come?" and the LORD said, "Behold, he has hidden himself among the baggage." *(God knows where we are. Let us never dream of hiding from him. We are like bees in a glass hive. He sees everything we do.)* ²³ Then they ran and took him from there. And when he stood among the people, he was taller than any of the people from his shoulders upward. *(Saul was the kind of man that most people would be impressed by and give their respect to. They looked up to him in more ways than one.)* ²⁴ And Samuel said to all the people, "Do you see him whom the LORD has chosen? There is none like him among all the people." And all the people shouted, "Long live the king!"

²⁵ Then Samuel told the people the rights and duties of the kingship, and he wrote them in a book and laid it up before the LORD. *(The book was the nation's law explaining how the king was to rule over his subjects. Saul was to be a king under God's authority and to govern according to principles God had given to Israel.)* Then Samuel sent all the people away, each one to his home. ²⁶ Saul also went to his home at Gibeah, and with him went men of valor whose hearts God had touched. *(They saw God's hand in choosing Saul and joined him.)*

²⁷ But some worthless fellows said, "How can this man save us?" *(No one can hope to please everybody. Even the man God himself selects is not approved by people who are never satisfied. Saul was from a good family, he had good character, he was humble, and he was pleasant. But these things did not count for anything with these troublemakers. May none of us ever belong to that evil class of people, who are always in opposition, always faultfinding, and never willing to work with anybody. This is not the mind of Christ, nor is it the fruit of the Spirit, which is always peaceable.)* And they despised him and brought him no present. But he held his peace. *(This was a very sensible thing to do. Those who can be quiet will defeat their enemies. Do not be quick to defend yourself, or answer those who lie about you. "Fear not, stand firm, and see the salvation of the Lord."[568])*

AUGUST 13

The LORD Will Not Forsake His People[569]

1 Samuel 12

Saul proved his courage and bravery by defeating Nahash, king of the Ammonites when he and his army surrounded the city of Jabesh and made demands of their citizens. After his victory, the people of Israel gathered to show their complete support for Saul as their king. Samuel took advantage of this occasion by announcing that the time of his life as their judge was at an end and to warn the people one more time.

¹ And Samuel said to all Israel, "Behold, I have obeyed your voice in all that you have said to me and have made a king over you. ² And now, behold, the king walks before you, and I am old and gray, and behold, my sons are with you. I have walked before you from my youth until this day. ³ Here I am; testify against me before the LORD and before his anointed. Whose ox have I taken? Or whose donkey have I taken? Or whom have I defrauded? Whom have I oppressed? Or from whose hand have I taken a bribe to blind my eyes with it? Testify against me and I will restore it to you."

⁴ They said, "You have not defrauded us or oppressed us or taken anything from any man's hand." ⁵ And he said to them, "The LORD is witness against you, and his anointed

---

[568] Exodus 14:13
[569] Psalm 94:14

is witness this day, that you have not found anything in my hand." And they said, "He is witness."

⁶And Samuel said to the people, "The LORD is witness, who appointed Moses and Aaron and brought your fathers up out of the land of Egypt. ⁷Now therefore stand still that I may plead with you before the LORD concerning all the righteous deeds of the LORD that he performed for you and for your fathers. ⁸When Jacob went into Egypt, and the Egyptians oppressed them, then your fathers cried out to the LORD and the LORD sent Moses and Aaron, who brought your fathers out of Egypt and made them dwell in this place. ⁹But they forgot the LORD their God. And he sold them into the hand of Sisera, commander of the army of Hazor, and into the hand of the Philistines, and into the hand of the king of Moab. And they fought against them. ¹⁰And they cried out to the LORD and said, 'We have sinned, because we have forsaken the LORD and have served the Baals and the Ashtaroth. But now deliver us out of the hand of our enemies, that we may serve you.' ¹¹And the LORD sent Jerubbaal and Barak and Jephthah and Samuel and delivered you out of the hand of your enemies on every side, and you lived in safety.

¹²"And when you saw that Nahash the king of the Ammonites came against you, you said to me, 'No, but a king shall reign over us,' when the LORD your God was your king. ¹³And now behold the king whom you have chosen, for whom you have asked; behold, the LORD has set a king over you. ¹⁴If you will fear the LORD and serve him and obey his voice and not rebel against the commandment of the LORD, and if both you and the king who reigns over you will follow the LORD your God, it will be well. ¹⁵But if you will not obey the voice of the LORD, but rebel against the commandment of the LORD, then the hand of the LORD will be against you and your king. ¹⁶Now therefore stand still and see this great thing that the LORD will do before your eyes. ¹⁷Is it not wheat harvest today? I will call upon the LORD, that he may send thunder and rain. And you shall know and see that your wickedness is great, which you have done in the sight of the LORD, in asking for yourselves a king." ¹⁸So Samuel called upon the LORD, and the LORD sent thunder and rain that day, and all the people greatly feared the LORD and Samuel. *(It seldom or never rains at that time of year in Palestine. Samuel's prayers were as mighty as those of Elijah.)*

¹⁹And all the people said to Samuel, "Pray for your servants to the LORD your God, that we may not die, for we have added to all our sins this evil, to ask for ourselves a king." ²⁰And Samuel said to the people, "Do not be afraid; you have done all this evil. Yet do not turn aside from following the LORD, but serve the LORD with all your heart. ²¹And do not turn aside after empty things that cannot profit or deliver, for they are empty. ²²For the LORD will not forsake his people, for his great name's sake, because it has pleased the LORD to make you a people for himself."

These are very precious verses. God guarantees his unchanging love to those he elects, but no one can give a reason why he elects them.

²³"Moreover, as for me, far be it from me that I should sin against the LORD by ceasing to pray for you, and I will instruct you in the good and the right way. ²⁴Only fear the LORD and serve him faithfully with all your heart. For consider what great things he has done for you. ²⁵But if you still do wickedly, you shall be swept away, both you and your king."

AUGUST 14

To Obey is Better Than Sacrifice[570]

1 Samuel 13:1-14

¹Saul reigned one year *(No one found fault with Saul during his first year as king. However, he was like the short winded runner who starts well, but cannot finish the race.)* and when he had reigned two years over Israel,[571] ²Saul chose three thousand

---

[570] 1 Samuel 15:22
[571] We have used verse one from the *New King James Version*. According to some, the number "one" is missing in the Hebrew and many translators believe another number (perhaps thirty or forty) precedes the number "two". Matthew Henry understands the text to

men of Israel. Two thousand were with Saul in Michmash and the hill country of Bethel, and a thousand were with Jonathan in Gibeah of Benjamin. The rest of the people he sent home, every man to his tent. ³ Jonathan defeated the garrison of the Philistines that was at Geba, and the Philistines heard of it. *(After the Philistines had defeated Israel, they placed soldiers in the region's forts to keep the people under their control. Saul's son, Jonathan, began Israel's march to victory by destroying one of these groups of soldiers.)* And Saul blew the trumpet throughout all the land, saying, "Let the Hebrews hear." *(This was the normal Hebrew call to war. The blast of the trumpet was followed by fires lit from hill to hill and the country immediately banded together to fight against the Philistines.)*

⁴ And all Israel heard it said that Saul had defeated the garrison of the Philistines, and also that Israel had become a stench to the Philistines. And the people were called out to join Saul at Gilgal.

⁵ And the Philistines mustered to fight with Israel, thirty thousand chariots and six thousand horsemen and troops like the sand on the seashore in multitude. They came up and encamped in Michmash, to the east of Beth-aven. *(The Philistines were determined to put down Israel's revolt as quickly as possible. They called on other nations to join them against Israel. The huge army terrified Israel and many people deserted Saul. Even his regular army of 3,000 was reduced to 700 men.)* ⁶ When the men of Israel saw that they were in trouble (for the people were hard pressed), the people hid themselves in caves and in holes and in rocks and in tombs and in cisterns, ⁷ and some Hebrews crossed the fords of the Jordan to the land of Gad and Gilead. Saul was still at Gilgal, and all the people followed him trembling. *(Those who did stay with Saul were losing hope. They did not think there was much chance they could succeed against the huge army the Philistines had brought together.)*

⁸ He waited seven days, the time appointed by Samuel. But Samuel did not come to Gilgal, and the people were scattering from him. ⁹ So Saul said, "Bring the burnt offering here to me, and the peace offerings." And he offered the burnt offering. *(King Saul had no right to do this. Only the priests were permitted to make the burnt offering. Saul was supposed to be a king who was under the authority of the Lord. He should have waited for instructions from the Lord through Samuel. Instead, in his self-will, he acted as though God's rules did not apply to him. His impatience cost him his kingdom.)*

¹⁰ As soon as he had finished offering the burnt offering, behold, Samuel came. And Saul went out to meet him and greet him. ¹¹ Samuel said, "What have you done?" And Saul said, "When I saw that the people were scattering from me, and that you did not come within the days appointed, and that the Philistines had mustered at Michmash, ¹² I said, 'Now the Philistines will come down against me at Gilgal, and I have not sought the favor of the Lord.' So I forced myself, and offered the burnt offering."

He was a hypocrite.[572] He tried to cover his rebellious act by pretending to be very eager to keep the outward form of religion.

¹³ And Samuel said to Saul, "You have done foolishly. You have not kept the command of the Lord your God, with which he commanded you. For then the Lord would have established your kingdom over Israel forever. ¹⁴ But now your kingdom shall not continue. The Lord has sought out a man after his own heart, and the Lord has commanded him to be prince over his people, because you have not kept what the Lord commanded you."

At first sight Saul's wrongdoing appears small, but no sin is little, because there is no little God to sin against. He had rejected Jehovah's supremacy, and therefore the Lord would no longer allow his family to rule over Israel.

---

read, "Saul was the son of one year," which he understood to mean, "Saul reigned one year."

[572] *hypocrite* - a pretender, deceiver, phony, fraud, fake. It is from a Latin word which means "a stage actor."

Hypocrite Is Latin for *a Stage Actor*
Actors pretend to be something they are not. They can pretend to be happy or sad, whatever is called for.

AUGUST 15

If You Love Me, You Will Keep My Commandments[573]

1 Samuel 15:1-3; 9-11; 13-23

1 And Samuel said to Saul, "The LORD sent me to anoint you king over his people Israel; now therefore listen to the words of the LORD. **2** Thus says the LORD of hosts, 'I have noted what Amalek did to Israel in opposing them on the way when they came up out of Egypt. **3** Now go and strike Amalek and devote to destruction all that they have. Do not spare them, but kill both man and woman, child and infant, ox and sheep, camel and donkey.'"

The Amalekites were a nomadic people who traveled from place to place to find food for their livestock. They had violently attacked the Israelites in the desert. It was a cowardly attack. It was a sin committed by all of them and God had kept a record against them for a long time. They were a cruel and violent race of thieves who presented an extreme danger to their neighbors and any cities close to where they took their flocks and herds. The time had come for divine justice; their punishment was well deserved. Therefore, God sent Saul to be the executioner and commanded him to do his work thoroughly.

9 But Saul and the people spared Agag and the best of the sheep and of the oxen and of the fattened calves and the lambs, and all that was good, and would not utterly destroy them. All that was despised and worthless they devoted to destruction. *(This was half-obedience, which is whole rebellion. Many are ready to give up sins that might give them a bad reputation, but not the ones that the world views as popular and acceptable.)*

10 The word of the LORD came to Samuel: **11** "I regret that I have made Saul king, for he has turned back from following me and has not performed my commandments." And Samuel was angry, and he cried to the LORD all night. *(The rejection of sinners is a great grief to saints. The word translated "anger" can also mean "grieve." We can see from 1 Samuel 16:1 that Samuel's anger included grief over Saul's actions.[574] God has no pleasure in the death of sinners, nor do his people.)*

13 And Samuel came to Saul, and Saul said to him, "Blessed be you to the LORD. I have performed the commandment of the LORD."

The person who brags the most, usually has the most to be ashamed of.

14 And Samuel said, "What then is this bleating of the sheep in my ears and the lowing of the oxen that I hear?" **15** Saul said, "They have brought them from the Amalekites, for the people spared the best of the sheep and of the oxen to sacrifice to the LORD your God, and the rest we have devoted to destruction." *(First he blamed others and then claims they did it with good intentions. Neither one was an acceptable excuse.)* **16** Then Samuel said to Saul, "Stop! I will tell you what the LORD said to me this night." And he said to him, "Speak."

17 And Samuel said, "Though you are little in your own eyes, are you not the head of the tribes of Israel? The LORD anointed you king over Israel. **18** And the LORD sent you on a mission and said, 'Go, devote to destruction the sinners, the Amalekites, and fight against them until they are consumed.' **19** Why then did you not obey the voice of the LORD? Why did you pounce on the spoil and do what was

---

[573] John 14:15

[574] 1 Samuel 16:1, "The LORD said to Samuel, 'How long will you grieve over Saul, since I have rejected him from being king over Israel?'"

evil in the sight of the LORD?" ²⁰ And Saul said to Samuel, "I have obeyed the voice of the LORD. I have gone on the mission on which the LORD sent me. I have brought Agag the king of Amalek, and I have devoted the Amalekites to destruction. ²¹ But the people took of the spoil, sheep and oxen, the best of the things devoted to destruction, to sacrifice to the LORD your God in Gilgal." ²² And Samuel said,

"Has the LORD as great delight in burnt offerings and sacrifices,
　as in obeying the voice of the LORD?
Behold, to obey is better than sacrifice,
　and to listen than the fat of rams.
²³ For rebellion is as the sin of divination,
　and presumption is as iniquity and idolatry.
Because you have rejected the word of the LORD,
　he has also rejected you from being king."

Nothing can make up for disobeying God's will. We may pretend to be very zealous for God's glory, but intentionally disobeying his commands will condemn us. Being religious on the outside is not a substitute for holiness. Saul put to death those who practiced witchcraft, but as long as he would not obey the Lord, he was as guilty as the fake witches he had executed. Idolatry was an obvious sin against Jehovah, but stubbornly disobeying his law was just as much a form of evil rebellion. May the Holy Spirit cause us to be obedient down to the last detail. Nothing short of this will prove that we are the true servants of the Lord.

AUGUST 16
Rend Your Hearts and Not Your Garments[575]

Saul claimed that he had kept the best of the livestock to sacrifice to the Lord, but the Lord had clearly told him to destroy all of them. This reminds us of the thoughtlessness of those who imagine that true religion is made up of outward ceremonies and rituals, and forget that it is really a matter of the heart. This is the kind of person the Lord spoke to by the mouth of his servant Isaiah, who said:

Isaiah 1:10-20

¹⁰ Hear the word of the LORD,
　you rulers of Sodom!
Give ear to the teaching of our God,
　you people of Gomorrah!

Sodom and Gomorrah are mentioned to warn them of the certain punishment of their crimes. They assumed that their ceremonies and style of worship would make them the favorites of heaven, but because of their hypocrisy they were compared to the despicable people of those accursed cities.

¹¹ "What to me is the multitude of your sacrifices?
　says the LORD;
I have had enough of burnt offerings of rams
　and the fat of well-fed beasts;
I do not delight in the blood of bulls,
　or of lambs, or of goats."

They stopped at the outward shell of religion and never got to the kernel of real love to God. That is why their religion was useless.

¹² "When you come to appear before me,
　who has required of you
　this trampling of my courts?"

God does not want superstitious people to adore him. He has never invited them to worship him. He looks for those who worship him in spirit and in truth, not those who think true religion means only keeping traditions.

¹³ "Bring no more vain offerings;
　incense is an abomination to me.
New moon and Sabbath and the calling of convocations—
　I cannot endure iniquity and solemn assembly.
¹⁴ Your new moons and your appointed feasts
　my soul hates;
they have become a burden to me;
　I am weary of bearing them.
¹⁵ When you spread out your hands,
　I will hide my eyes from you;
even though you make many prayers,
　I will not listen;
your hands are full of blood."

---
[575] Joel 2:13

As long as they were cruel and brutal, it was useless for them to offer complicated ceremonies, holy looking poses, holy days and many prayers, because God is disgusted with heartless worship. People who do not really believe in the Lord Jesus and obey the Lord's will might just as well save themselves the trouble of attending these kinds of church services. They only make their case worse, and add to their sins.

16 "Wash yourselves; make yourselves clean;
　remove the evil of your deeds from before my eyes;
cease to do evil,
17 　learn to do good;
seek justice,
　correct oppression;
bring justice to the fatherless,
　plead the widow's cause."

Our great gospel requires real and complete repentance. A grain of it is better than a ton of ceremonies.

18 "Come now, let us reason together, says the Lord:
　though your sins are like scarlet,
　　they shall be as white as snow;
　though they are red like crimson,
　　they shall become like wool.
19 If you are willing and obedient,
　you shall eat the good of the land;
20 but if you refuse and rebel,
　you shall be eaten by the sword;
　　for the mouth of the Lord has spoken."

Stop bragging about your empty religious practices. Instead, worship the Lord with your heart and spirit. Come to the Lord with a humble heart and ask for his mercy. He is ready to give it. The most appalling and shocking sins can be put away by the blood of Jesus, but mere ceremonies count for nothing.

The same lesson is taught in that wonderful passage in the book of Micah.

Micah 6:6-8

6 "With what shall I come before the Lord,
　and bow myself before God on high?
Shall I come before him with burnt offerings,
　with calves a year old?
7 Will the Lord be pleased with thousands of rams,
　with ten thousands of rivers of oil?
Shall I give my firstborn for my transgression,
　the fruit of my body for the sin of my soul?"
8 He has told you, O man, what is good;
　and what does the Lord require of you
but to do justice, and to love kindness
　and to walk humbly with your God?

The true proof of godliness is not expensive rituals, but wholehearted obedience; not a showy profession of faith, but holy living; not in giving large amounts of money, but a surrendering of the heart. Do we have this all important godliness? Has the Holy Spirit made a change in our hearts?

AUGUST 17

The Lord Looks On the Heart[576]

1 Samuel 16:1; 4-14; 22-23

1 The Lord said to Samuel, "How long will you grieve over Saul, since I have rejected him from being king over Israel? Fill your horn with oil, and go. I will send you to Jesse the Bethlehemite, for I have provided for myself a king among his sons." *(It was both natural and right for the prophet to mourn over Saul's sin, but he must not be upset because the Lord punished him. Instead, he must continue with the work God has for him. In this case that meant a journey to anoint a better king who would one day prove to be a great blessing to Israel. We should grieve for any who sin in such a way that God becomes angry against them. But we must not rebel because of his judgments on them. "Shall not the Judge of all the earth do what is just?"[577] When the wicked are thrown into hell, the saints in heaven do not complain to God because they feel sorry for the convicted sinners. They respect and support the wisdom of the most Holy God and worship him with admiration and awe.)*

4a Samuel did what the Lord commanded and came to Bethlehem.

---

[576] 1 Samuel 16:7
[577] Genesis 18:25

5b And he consecrated Jesse and his sons and invited them to the sacrifice.

6 When they came, he looked on Eliab and thought, "Surely the Lord's anointed is before him." *(Even prophets make mistakes when they judge by appearances. People are not to be valued by their looks but by their hearts.)* **7** But the Lord said to Samuel, "Do not look on his appearance or on the height of his stature, because I have rejected him. For the Lord sees not as man sees: man looks on the outward appearance, but the Lord looks on the heart." **8** Then Jesse called Abinadab and made him pass before Samuel. And he said, "Neither has the Lord chosen this one." **9** Then Jesse made Shammah pass by. And he said, "Neither has the Lord chosen this one." **10** And Jesse made seven of his sons pass before Samuel. And Samuel said to Jesse, "The Lord has not chosen these."

11 Then Samuel said to Jesse, "Are all your sons here?" And he said, "There remains yet the youngest, but behold, he is keeping the sheep." And Samuel said to Jesse, "Send and get him, for we will not sit down till he comes here." *(He who was humble and God-fearing was not appreciated very much by his family. Parents make great mistakes when they undervalue good children who are not brilliant or self-assertive. Those who are looked down on by others should remember that the Lord knows all about them and take comfort. He will bring them forward at the proper time. Many are last who will be first.[578])* **12** And he sent and brought him in. Now he was ruddy and had beautiful eyes and was handsome. And the Lord said, "Arise, anoint him, for this is he." **13** Then Samuel took the horn of oil and anointed him in the midst of his brothers. And the Spirit of the Lord rushed upon David from that day forward. *(The horn of oil was a sign of great grace. We all need the power of the Holy Spirit. May he live in us fully and then we shall be kings and priests for God.)* And Samuel rose up and went to Ramah.

14 Now the Spirit of the Lord departed from Saul, and a harmful spirit from the Lord tormented him. *(We have seen what divine love did for David. We now learn what divine anger did for Saul. The one thing needed above all others, is the favor of the Lord. Have that, and we are blessed; be without it, and we are miserable.)*

22 And Saul sent to Jesse, saying, "Let David remain in my service, for he has found favor in my sight." **23** And whenever the harmful spirit from God was upon Saul, David took the lyre and played it with his hand. So Saul was refreshed and was well, and the evil spirit departed from him. *(Saul was probably overcome with a guilty conscience and needed music to calm his mind. Even in this life, sinful behavior is the cause of countless problems. How much happier was the shepherd youth who had music in his heart and was filled with the good Spirit. God grant that we may live in the fear of God and thereby enjoy lasting peace.)*

A Lyre is a musical instrument similar to a harp.

August 18
He Must Reign[579]

In the Psalms, the Holy Spirit has spoken about the election of David more than once. One of these in found in

Psalm 78:67-72

67 He rejected the tent of Joseph;
  he did not choose the tribe of Ephraim,

---

[578] A reference to Matthew 20:16

[579] 1 Corinthians 15:25

The ark of the covenant had been at Shiloh for a long time. But the tribe of Ephraim was no longer qualified to lead Israel and therefore the symbol of God's presence was moved.

68 but he chose the tribe of Judah,
 Mount Zion, which he loves.
69 He built his sanctuary like the high heavens,
 like the earth, which he has founded forever.
70 He chose David his servant
 and took him from the sheepfolds;
71 from following the nursing ewes he brought him
 to shepherd Jacob his people,
 Israel his inheritance.

Part of David's job as a shepherd was to follow the ewes as they wandered about and watch for and care for the young lambs that were born. The tenderness and patience he learned from doing this would help to build the characteristics a king should have. God was preparing David to shepherd people. When the time was right, the Lord made him king and the skills he learned as a shepherd proved very helpful. It is delightful to see how God, in his wisdom, often uses the early and hidden parts of a life as a school for preparing for a more active and useful future.

72 With upright heart he shepherded them
 and guided them with his skillful hand.

During David's reign the people were peaceful and prosperous. No better king ever sat on the throne of Israel.

We will now read a passage in which our Lord Jesus is spoken of as Israel's king and his reign is described.

Isaiah 11:1-10

1 There shall come forth a shoot from the stump of Jesse,
 and a branch from his roots shall bear fruit.
2 And the Spirit of the Lord shall rest upon him,
 the Spirit of wisdom and understanding,
 the Spirit of counsel and might,
 the Spirit of knowledge and the fear of the Lord.
3 And his delight shall be in the fear of the Lord.

Our Lord knows those who really have a holy fear of him. He is very quick to recognize their heart's desire and the inward pain they feel when they fall short in trying to please him. He delights in those who seek after God, even though their efforts may seem weak.

 He shall not judge by what his eyes see,
 or decide disputes by what his ears hear,
4 but with righteousness he shall judge the poor,
 and decide with equity for the meek of the earth;
 and he shall strike the earth with the rod of his mouth,
 and with the breath of his lips he shall kill the wicked.

His gospel destroys evil and his last judgment will send the wicked to eternal death.

5 Righteousness shall be the belt of his waist,
 and faithfulness the belt of his loins.
6 The wolf shall dwell with the lamb,
 and the leopard shall lie down with the young goat,
 and the calf and the lion and the fattened calf together;
 and a little child shall lead them.
7 The cow and the bear shall graze;
 their young shall lie down together;
 and the lion shall eat straw like the ox.
8 The nursing child shall play over the hole of the cobra,
 and the weaned child shall put his hand on the adder's den.

In his own good time, Jesus will deliver this earth from the curse of the fall and restore it to the purity and peace of the garden of Eden. By his power, even the animals will be raised to a new level. The "creation itself will be set free from its bondage to decay and obtain the freedom of the glory of the children of God."[580]

9 They shall not hurt or destroy
 in all my holy mountain;

---

[580] Romans 8:21

for the earth shall be full of the
knowledge of the LORD
as the waters cover the sea.

¹⁰ In that day the root of Jesse, who shall stand as a signal for the peoples—of him shall the nations inquire, and his resting place shall be glorious. *(Christ is the rallying point for mankind. He draws all people to himself. All people will offer him their loyalty. The place where he lives will be glorious. What can this place be except his church, of which he said, "This is my resting place forever."⁵⁸¹)*

AUGUST 19
Salvation Belongs To the LORD⁵⁸²
1 Samuel 17:1-12; 14-18

¹ᵃ Now the Philistines gathered their armies for battle. And they were gathered at Socoh, which belongs to Judah.

Israel had sinned and king Saul was no longer loyal to Jehovah. The Lord's severe rebuke is coming. God has the hearts of the wicked Philistines in his hands and can use them to be a source of great suffering to his offending people.

² And Saul and the men of Israel were gathered, and encamped in the Valley of Elah, and drew up in line of battle against the Philistines. ³ And the Philistines stood on the mountain on the one side, and Israel stood on the mountain on the other side, with a valley between them. *(They had been like this for forty days. If Israel had been faithful to her God, she would have been victorious long before now; because God's promise to them would have been fulfilled: "Five of you shall chase a hundred, and a hundred of you shall chase ten thousand, and your enemies shall fall before you by the sword."⁵⁸³ When God departs, the strongest are as weak as water.)*

⁴ And there came out from the camp of the Philistines a champion named Goliath of Gath, whose height was six cubits and a span *(about 10 feet)*. ⁵ He had a helmet of bronze on his head, and he was armed with a coat of mail, and the weight of the coat was five thousand shekels of bronze *(about 125 pounds)*. ⁶ And he had bronze armor on his legs, and a javelin of bronze slung between his shoulders. ⁷ The shaft of his spear was like a weaver's beam, and his spear's head weighed six hundred shekels of iron *(about 15 pounds)*. And his shield-bearer went before him. ⁸ He stood and shouted to the ranks of Israel, "Why have you come out to draw up for battle? Am I not a Philistine, and are you not servants of Saul? Choose a man for yourselves, and let him come down to me. ⁹ If he is able to fight with me and kill me, then we will be your servants. But if I prevail against him and kill him, then you shall be our servants and serve us." ¹⁰ And the Philistine said, "I defy the ranks of Israel this day. Give me a man, that we may fight together." *(Goliath is called 'the champion," or, in the Hebrew, the middleman or Mediator. He is a picture of our great enemy, Satan. Where could we have found another Mediator to confront him if the Son of David had not taken our place?)*

¹¹ When Saul and all Israel heard these words of the Philistine, they were dismayed and greatly afraid. *(There had been a time when Saul, who was himself gigantic, would have accepted the challenge, but when God departs from someone they become a coward. The words of Jesus, "apart from me you can do nothing,"⁵⁸⁴ are a great truth. Many have learned it the hard way.)*

¹² Now David was the son of an Ephrathite of Bethlehem in Judah, named Jesse, who had eight sons. In the days of Saul the man was already old and advanced in years.

When old age has made us weak, it is a great blessing to have strong and healthy sons to take our place in the Lord's army. Young men! Fill the places of your godly fathers.

¹⁴ David was the youngest. The three eldest followed Saul,¹⁵ but David went back and forth from Saul to feed his father's sheep at Bethlehem.

David had probably left the courts of king Saul long ago and gone back to the quiet pastures he loved so well; just as our Lord

---
⁵⁸¹Psalm 132:14
⁵⁸² Psalm 3:8
⁵⁸³ Leviticus 26:8

⁵⁸⁴ John 15:5

spent time in the temple and then went back to Nazareth with his parents and was submissive to them.[585]

¹⁶ For forty days the Philistine came forward and took his stand, morning and evening.

Even as for forty days Satan tempted our Lord.

¹⁷ And Jesse said to David his son, "Take for your brothers an ephah *(or about five gallons)* of this parched grain, and these ten loaves, and carry them quickly to the camp to your brothers. ¹⁸ Also take these ten cheeses to the commander of their thousand. See if your brothers are well and bring some token from them." *(The greater Son of David visited his brothers here on earth, with heavenly food and messages of love sent by his Father. Sadly, like David, he met with an unfriendly reception, "he came to his own, and his own people did not receive him."*[586] *May the Lord grant that Jesus will always be welcome in our hearts.)*

AUGUST 20
He Has Delivered Us…and He Will Deliver Us[587]

1 Samuel 17:20-37

²⁰ And David rose early in the morning and left the sheep with a keeper and took the provisions and went, as Jesse had commanded him. And he came to the encampment as the host was going out to the battle line, shouting the war cry. *(David was a good shepherd. He did not leave his sheep without someone to watch over them. In this he is a picture of the great Shepherd and Overseer of souls.)* ²¹ And Israel and the Philistines drew up for battle, army against army. ²² And David left the things in charge of the keeper of the baggage and ran to the ranks and went and greeted his brothers. ²³ As he talked with them, behold, the champion, the Philistine of Gath, Goliath by name, came up out of the ranks of the Philistines and spoke the same words as before. And David heard him.

²⁴ All the men of Israel, when they saw the man, fled from him and were much afraid. ²⁵ And the men of Israel said, "Have you seen this man who has come up? Surely he has come up to defy Israel. And the king will enrich the man who kills him with great riches and will give him his daughter and make his father's house free in Israel."

The Church, the bride of Christ, was offered to our champion the Lord Jesus. "All glorious is the princess,"[588] was to be the reward of his battle.

²⁶ And David said to the men who stood by him, "What shall be done for the man who kills this Philistine and takes away the reproach from Israel? For who is this uncircumcised Philistine, that he should defy the armies of the living God?" ²⁷ And the people answered him in the same way, "So shall it be done to the man who kills him."

²⁸ Now Eliab his eldest brother heard when he spoke to the men. And Eliab's anger was kindled against David, and he said, "Why have you come down? And with whom have you left those few sheep in the wilderness? I know your presumption and the evil of your heart, for you have come down to see the battle." ²⁹ And David said, "What have I done now? Was it not but a word?" (Brave people may expect to be misunderstood and charged with self-promotion. It will be to their honor if they bear it patiently and continue on. Our Lord was rejected by his brothers, but he did not stop from his work of love, or answer them roughly. If we can conquer our own spirits we shall be able to conquer others.) ³⁰ And he turned away from him toward another, and spoke in the same way, and the people answered him again as before.

³¹ When the words that David spoke were heard, they repeated them before Saul, and he sent for him. (Saul was at his wit's end and therefore jumped at any opportunity to fix his desperate situation. Sometimes people are driven to Jesus because everything else they have tried has failed to save them.)
³² And David said to Saul, "Let no man's heart fail because of him. Your servant will

---
[585] Luke 2:51
[586] John 1:11
[587] 2 Corinthians 1:10

[588] Psalm 45:13

go and fight with this Philistine." ³³ *And Saul said to David, "You are not able to go against this Philistine to fight with him, for you are but a youth, and he has been a man of war from his youth."* (Saul despised David because he did not believe he could save him. The Jewish nation did not think our Lord could save them and they despised him too. Nevertheless, David won the victory over the enemy Goliath and our Lord won the victory over our fearful enemy Satan.)

³⁴ But David said to Saul, "Your servant used to keep sheep for his father. And when there came a lion, or a bear, and took a lamb from the flock, ³⁵ I went after him and struck him and delivered it out of his mouth. And if he arose against me, I caught him by his beard and struck him and killed him. (Christ also delivers his own sheep out of the power of him who prowls around like a roaring lion.[589] The Psalmist says of Christ: "You will tread on the lion and the adder; the young lion and the serpent you will trample underfoot."[590])

³⁶ Your servant has struck down both lions and bears, and this uncircumcised Philistine shall be like one of them, for he has defied the armies of the living God." ³⁷ And David said, "The LORD who delivered me from the paw of the lion and from the paw of the bear will deliver me from the hand of this Philistine. And Saul said to David, "Go, and the LORD be with you!"

Wisdom teaches us that what God has done for us once, he can and will do again. We have an unchanging helper to depend on and therefore we may depend on his continual help.

AUGUST 21

I Will Go In the Strength Of the Lord God[591]

1 Samuel 17:38-51

³⁸ Then Saul clothed David with his armor. He put a helmet of bronze on his head and clothed him with a coat of mail, ³⁹ and David strapped his sword over his armor. And he tried in vain to go, for he had not tested them. Then David said to Saul, "I cannot go with these, for I have not tested them." So David put them off. (The usual weapons of war were not used by the man who depended on the Lord. Neither did our Lord think they were appropriate. When his disciples offered swords to him, he turned them down.[592] To this day our Lord's battles are not fought with the weapons of human force, but with those of spiritual energy. His warriors do not wear chain-mail armor, but the armor of righteousness.) ⁴⁰ Then he took his staff in his hand and chose five smooth stones from the brook and put them in his shepherd's pouch. His sling was in his hand, and he approached the Philistine.

These were the right weapons for a shepherd, because he was used to them. They were also reasonable and practical weapons. They were not shiny and showy, but just right for a shepherd. Brave and believing men and women act as carefully in the choice of weapons as if everything depended on them, and then trust completely in the Lord, because they know their success depends on him alone.

The scene before us is a wonderful picture of Jesus, the great Shepherd. We see him with the pastoral staff in his hand, going forth to sling the smooth stones of the word of God at the head of the deadly enemy of his people. Glorious hero, we bless you!

⁴¹ And the Philistine moved forward and came near to David, with his shield-bearer in front of him. ⁴² And when the Philistine looked and saw David, he disdained him, for he was but a youth, ruddy and handsome in appearance. ⁴³ And the Philistine said to David, "Am I a dog, that you come to me with sticks?" And the Philistine cursed David by his gods. ⁴⁴ The Philistine said to David, "Come to me, and I will give your flesh to the birds of the air and to the beasts of the field."

Bragging words are worth little.

⁴⁵ Then David said to the Philistine, "You come to me with a sword and with a spear and with a javelin, but I come to you in the name of the LORD of hosts, the God of the

---

[589] 1 Peter 5:8
[590] Psalm 91:1
[591] Psalm 71:16 NKJV

[592] Luke 22:38

armies of Israel, whom you have defied. ⁴⁶ This day the LORD will deliver you into my hand, and I will strike you down and cut off your head. And I will give the dead bodies of the host of the Philistines this day to the birds of the air and to the wild beasts of the earth, that all the earth may know that there is a God in Israel, ⁴⁷ and that all this assembly may know that the LORD saves not with sword and spear. For the battle is the LORD's, and he will give you into our hand." (This was not boasting, but faith speaking firmly and bravely.)

⁴⁸ When the Philistine arose and came and drew near to meet David, David ran quickly toward the battle line to meet the Philistine.

His actions matched his words. He was a doer as well as a speaker. Our Lord was a prophet, mighty in his actions as well as his words.

⁴⁹ And David put his hand in his bag and took out a stone and slung it and struck the Philistine on his forehead. The stone sank into his forehead, and he fell on his face to the ground. (How are the mighty fallen! The giant was struck down by the hand of a despised and ridiculed youth! And by the foolishness of preaching, the Lord wins the battle against Satan.)

⁵⁰ So David prevailed over the Philistine with a sling and with a stone, and struck the Philistine and killed him. There was no sword in the hand of David. (He did not need a sword until now. But faith had led him to face Goliath without one, so it was certain that his God would supply his need now. If we will only trust God, everything will be supplied as we need it.) ⁵¹ Then David ran and stood over the Philistine and took his sword and drew it out of its sheath and killed him and cut off his head with it. (Augustine[593] beautifully says, "Our David has cast down our adversary, and cut off his head with his own sword," because "by death he destroyed him that had the power of death, that is the devil." The crucifixion of our Lord was the execution of sin. God's enemies provide the weapons for their own destruction.) When the Philistines saw that their champion was dead, they fled.

AUGUST 22
My Soul Keeps Your Testimonies[594]

1 Samuel 17:55-58

⁵⁵ As soon as Saul saw David go out against the Philistine, he said to Abner, the commander of the army, "Abner, whose son is this youth?" And Abner said, "As your soul lives, O king, I do not know. ⁵⁶ And the king said, "Inquire whose son the boy is." *(Saul should have recognized the young man who played music to calm his nerves. Great people usually have bad memories when it comes to those who serve them. David's appearance may have changed and the king was almost insane the last time he saw him. Perhaps this is why he did not remember David. To this day the Jews cannot answer that question concerning Christ "Whose son is he?" The blind world looks for an outward glory and does not recognize the Son of the Highest.)*

⁵⁷ And as soon as David returned from the striking down of the Philistine, Abner took him, and brought him before Saul with the head of the Philistine in his hand. ⁵⁸ And Saul said to him, "Whose son are you, young man?" And David answered, "I am the son of your servant Jesse the Bethlehemite." *(It is difficult to be honored for such a victory and still remain humble. David showed his greatness as much after the fight as he did before and during it. Saul was not a man of integrity. If he had been, he would have given the youthful hero his daughter's hand in marriage and every other reward within his power.)*

1 Samuel 18:6-16; 28-30

⁶ As they were coming home, when David returned from striking down the Philistine, the women came out of all the cities of Israel, singing and dancing, to meet King Saul, with tambourines, with songs of joy, and with musical instruments. ⁷ And the women sang to one another as they celebrated,

"Saul has struck down his thousands,

---

[593] Augustine was a theologian and bishop in Africa during the late fourth and early fifth centuries.

[594] Psalm 119:167

and David his ten thousands."

When our Lord returned victorious over death and hell, and leading a host of captives,[595] the heavenly angels praised him in their songs. Do not our hearts also rejoice in the victories of Immanuel our King?

8 And Saul was very angry, and this saying displeased him. He said, "They have ascribed to David ten thousands, and to me they have ascribed thousands, and what more can he have but the kingdom?" **9** And Saul eyed David from that day on. *(Envy, first-born of hell, whom will you not attack? David's modest behavior should have protected him from Saul's bitterness. We should not be surprised that Saul was again struck with his old mental illness. Those who allow an evil temper into their heart, should not be astonished when a gloomy spirit comes along with it to haunt their deepest thoughts.)*

10 The next day a harmful spirit from God rushed upon Saul, and he raved within his house while David was playing the lyre, as he did day by day. Saul had his spear in his hand. **11** And Saul hurled the spear, for he thought, "I will pin David to the wall." But David evaded him twice.

12 Saul was afraid of David because the LORD was with him but had departed from Saul. **13** So Saul removed him from his presence and made him a commander of a thousand. And he went out and came in before the people. **14** And David had success in all his undertakings, for the LORD was with him. **15** And when Saul saw that he had great success, he stood in fearful awe of him.

We might have expected to find David afraid of his powerful enemy, but it was just the opposite. "The wicked flee when no one pursues, but the righteous are bold as a lion."[596]

16 But all Israel and Judah loved David, for he went out and came in before them.

The more they saw him, the better they loved him. He was an active leader and always ready to serve. Persistence and steadfastness earn the respect of the wise.

28 But when Saul saw and knew that the LORD was with David, and that Michal, Saul's daughter, loved him, **29** Saul was even more afraid of David. So Saul was David's enemy continually.

30 Then the commanders of the Philistines came out to battle, and as often as they came out David had more success than all the servants of Saul, so that his name was highly esteemed. *(Good conduct is the great thing in life. May the Lord make us followers of him who was greater than David, of whom it was said, "He has done all things well."[597] Holy Spirit, form us in the image of our Lord, that he may be glorified in us.)*

AUGUST 23
The LORD Preserves the Simple[598]

Saul's fierce hostility was a painful trial for David. But the Lord comforted David even within the king's family, because both his eldest son Jonathan and his daughter Michal—whom Saul had given to David for a wife—loved him.

1 Samuel 18:3-4

3 Then Jonathan made a covenant with David, because he loved him as his own soul.

Jonathan loved him even though he knew David was going to be king and that he himself would never wear the crown. How beautiful to see pure love; love that does not have personal gain as a motive. Our love for Jesus should be the same. A love for our Lord because of who he is, not for what we hope to get from the relationship.

4 And Jonathan stripped himself of the robe that was on him and gave it to David, and his armor, and even his sword and his bow and his belt. *(We should delight to give all we have for Jesus. Let him have everything, because he deserves everything.)*

1 Samuel 19:1; 4-18

1 And Saul spoke to Jonathan his son and to all his servants, that they should kill David. But Jonathan, Saul's son, delighted much in David.

---

[595] A reference to Ephesians 4:8 where Paul quotes Psalm 68:18
[596] Proverbs 28:1

[597] Mark 7:37
[598] Psalm 116:6

Saul was now worse than ever, or else he would not have asked others to help him in a wicked and cruel murder. When God leaves a person, the devil comes to them.

4 And Jonathan spoke well of David to Saul his father and said to him, "Let not the king sin against his servant David, because he has not sinned against you, and because his deeds have brought good to you. **5** For he took his life in his hand and he struck down the Philistine, and the LORD worked a great salvation for all Israel. You saw it, and rejoiced. Why then will you sin against innocent blood by killing David without cause?" *(Here Jonathan proved himself a real friend. We should always be ready to speak up for those who are falsely accused.)*

6 And Saul listened to the voice of Jonathan. Saul swore, "As the LORD lives, he shall not be put to death." *(His oath, however, only lasted a short time. Saul was never in a good state of mind for very long. Envy cannot hold still.)* **7** And Jonathan called David, and Jonathan reported to him all these things. And Jonathan brought David to Saul, and he was in his presence as before.

8 And there was war again. And David went out and fought with the Philistines and struck them with a great blow, so that they fled before him. **9** Then a harmful spirit from the LORD came upon Saul, as he sat in his house with his spear in his hand. And David was playing the lyre. **10** And Saul sought to pin David to the wall with the spear, but he eluded Saul, so that he struck the spear into the wall. And David fled and escaped that night.

> *"Not a single [arrow] can hit,*
> *Till the God of love thinks fits."*[599]

We are safe anywhere while the Lord has work for us to do. If our role in life is to have a harp in our hand, praising God and blessing others, then we will be kept safe from the javelins of our enemies.

11 Saul sent messengers to David's house to watch him, that he might kill him in the morning. But Michal, David's wife, told him, "If you do not escape with your life tonight, tomorrow you will be killed." **12** So Michal let David down through the window, and he fled away and escaped. **13** Michal took an image and laid it on the bed and put a pillow of goats' hair at its head and covered it with the clothes. **14** And when Saul sent messengers to take David, she said, "He is sick." **15** Then Saul sent the messengers to see David, saying, "Bring him up to me in the bed, that I may kill him." **16** And when the messengers came in, behold, the image was in the bed, with the pillow of goats' hair at its head. *(We cannot admire Michal's deceit or her having idols in her house. She was Saul's daughter and was not raised properly. God will use even Michal's misguided love to arrange for David's escape. He will keep his own safe.)*

17 Saul said to Michal, "Why have you deceived me thus and let my enemy go, so that he has escaped?" And Michal answered Saul, "He said to me, 'Let me go. Why should I kill you?'"

18 Now David fled and escaped, and he came to Samuel at Ramah and told him all that Saul had done to him. And he and Samuel went and lived at Naioth.

AUGUST 24

The LORD Has Become My Stronghold[600]

This Psalm is called A Golden Psalm of David.

WHEN SAUL SENT MEN TO WATCH HIS HOUSE IN ORDER TO KILL HIM.

Psalm 59

1 Deliver me from my enemies, O my God;
   protect me from those who rise up
      against me;

They had the house surrounded, they were armed with orders from the king and they had enough soldiers to capture him. Yet David had enough faith to pray and to not be discouraged and give up. God has ways for his birds of paradise to escape, even when the most expert hunters are trying to catch them.

---

[599] This appears to be from a hymn found in a compilation of hymns published by S. B. Haslam in 1824. - ed

[600] Psalm 94:22

2   deliver me from those who work evil,
        and save me from bloodthirsty men.

When a house is surrounded by thieves, the good man of the house sounds the alarm. We hear it sounded loudly in these verses: "Deliver me," "protect me," "deliver me," "save me." David could not be defeated by Saul while he prayed this way.

3   For behold, they lie in wait for my life;
        fierce men stir up strife against me.
    For no transgression or sin of mine, O
        Lord,
4   for no fault of mine, they run and make
        ready.
    Awake, come to meet me, and see!
5   You, Lord God of hosts, are God of
        Israel.
    Rouse yourself to punish all the nations;
        spare none of those who treacherously
            plot evil.   Selah

Be merciful to them as humans, but not as lawbreakers. Mercy to such criminals would be cruelty to those who do not break the law.

6   Each evening they come back,
        howling like dogs
        and prowling about the city
7   There they are, bellowing with their
        mouths
        with swords in their lips—
        for "Who," they think, "will hear us?"

The most brutal and out of control people are those who think that God has deserted the world and no longer pays attention to what people say or do.

8   But you, O Lord, laugh at them;
        you hold all the nations in derision.
9   O my Strength, I will watch for you,
        for you, O God are my fortress.

Is the person who persecutes me strong? Then for this very reason, my God, I will pray to you and leave the entire situation in your hand. We are wise to realize that the greater our difficulties are, the more reason we have for trusting ourselves to the Lord.

10 My God in his steadfast love will meet
        me;
    God will let me look in triumph on my
        enemies.
11 Kill them not, lest my people forget;
        make them totter by your power and
            bring them down,
        O Lord, our shield!

Enemies help to keep God's servants alert. Therefore let them live, but let them have no power to do the evil they desire.

12 For the sin of their mouths, the words of
        their lips,
        let them be trapped in their pride
    For the cursing and lies that they utter,

Those who curse and swear are usually liars.

13   consume them in wrath;
        consume them till they are no more,
        that they may know that God rules over
            Jacob
        to the ends of the earth.   Selah

14 Each evening they come back,
        howling like dogs
        and prowling about the city.
15 They wander about for food
        and growl if they do not get their fill.

David is speaking here as a prophet and not as an unforgiving spirit seeking revenge. This is not the character of the man who often spared his enemies when he had the power to harm them. His only vengeance was his overwhelming kindness to them. These passages should be read as predictions rather than wishes.

16 But I will sing of your strength;
        I will sing aloud of your steadfast love
            in the morning.
    For you have been to me a fortress
        and a refuge in the day of my distress.
17 O my Strength, I will sing praises to you,
        for you, O God, are my fortress,
        the God who shows me steadfast love.

David felt sure he would escape, because he believed his prayer was approved by God. Then he began to sing to his Deliverer. This was not easy to do. What would we have done if we were in David's place? Furious murderers were in the street around the house, thirsting for the good man's blood, and yet his faith enabled him to sing praises to God. Oh that we could believe in God like David did!

AUGUST 25
Keep Watch Over the Door Of My Lips![601]

1 Samuel 21:1-3; 6-7

1 Then David came to Nob to Ahimelech the priest. *(Saul drove David away from the prophet Samuel, so David escaped to the priests. He loved the servants of God and wanted to be with them.)* And Ahimelech came to meet David trembling and said to him, "Why are you alone, and no one with you?" *(Seeing David alone, and obviously in distress, Ahimelech suspected something was wrong.)* **2** And David said to Ahimelech the priest, "The king has charged me with a matter and said to me, 'Let no one know anything of the matter about which I send you, and with which I have charged you.' I have made an appointment with the young men for such and such a place."

David spoke falsely and his error is not written here to his honor, but for our warning. This sad falsehood led to terrible results. Oh that good people could always trust in the Lord.

3 "Now then, what do you have on hand? Give me five loaves of bread, or whatever is here."

6 So the priest gave him the holy bread, for there was no bread there but the bread of the Presence, which is removed from before the LORD, to be replaced by hot bread on the day it is taken away.

This act was a violation of the ceremonial law, but because it was an emergency, the priest okayed it. The Lord loves mercy better than sacrifice.

7 Now a certain man of the servants of Saul was there that day, detained before the LORD. His name was Doeg the Edomite, the chief of Saul's herdsmen.

Doeg hated the priests and hurried to Saul to accuse them of giving help to a traitor.

1 Samuel 22:9-23

9 Then answered Doeg the Edomite, who stood by the servants of Saul, "I saw the son of Jesse coming to Nob, to Ahimelech the son of Ahitub, **10** and he inquired of the LORD for him and gave him provisions and gave him the sword of Goliath the Philistine."

11 Then the king sent to summon Ahimelech the priest, the son of Ahitub, and all his father's house, the priests who were at Nob, and all of them came to the king. **12** And Saul said, "Hear now, son of Ahitub." And he answered, "Here I am, my lord." **13** And Saul said to him, "Why have you conspired against me, you and the son of Jesse, in that you have given him bread and a sword and have inquired of God for him, so that he has risen against me, to lie in wait, as at this day?"

14 And Ahimelech answered the king, "And who among all your servants is so faithful as David, who is the king's son-in-law, and captain over your bodyguard, and honored in your house? **15** Is today the first time that I have inquired of God for him? No! Let not the king impute anything to his servant or to all the house of my father, for your servant has known nothing of all this, much or little." *(The high priest was blameless, even though he may have lacked good sense. He did not know about the quarrel between Saul and David. David had lied to him and Doeg knew it, but did not mention that to Saul. When we tell about something that has happened, we must be completely truthful. If we hide something, those who are the most innocent may look guilty.)*

16 And the king said, "You shall surely die, Ahimelech, you and all your father's house." **17** And the king said to the guard who stood about him, "Turn and kill the priests of the LORD, because their hand also is with David, and they knew that he fled and did not disclose it to me." But the servants of the king would not put out their hand to strike the priests of the LORD. **18** Then the king said to Doeg, "You turn and strike the priests." And Doeg the Edomite turned and struck down the priests, and he killed on that day eighty-five persons who wore the linen ephod. *(The Israelite guards refused to obey Saul's command, but this foreigner was more than willing to carry out this cruel order. The Lord once again carried out his threat against the house of Eli, for Ahimelech was*

---
[601] Psalm 141:3

his great-grandson.[602] However, that in no way excused that worthless Doeg's one-sided story that caused so many murders or the hateful king who commanded the slaughter.)

19 And Nob, the city of the priests, he put to the sword; both man and woman, child and infant, ox, donkey and sheep, he put to the sword.

20 But one of the sons of Ahimelech the son of Ahitub, named Abiathar, escaped and fled after David. **21** And Abiathar told David that Saul had killed the priests of the LORD. **22** And David said to Abiathar, "I knew on that day, when Doeg the Edomite was there, that he would surely tell Saul. I have occasioned the death of all the persons of your father's house. **23** Stay with me; do not be afraid, for he who seeks my life seeks your life. With me you shall be in safekeeping." (David must have been cut to the heart when he saw the result of his falsehood. The Lord keep each of us true in every word we speak.)

AUGUST 26
I Will Thank You Forever[603]

At this time, David wrote a psalm, which is titled:

TO THE CHOIRMASTER. A MASKIL[604] OF DAVID, WHEN DOEG, THE EDOMITE, CAME AND TOLD SAUL, "DAVID HAS COME TO THE HOUSE OF AHIMELECH."

Psalm 52

1 Why do you boast of evil, O mighty man?

Doeg did not have any reason for bragging. He had killed a group of defenseless people who never drew a sword. This coward should have been ashamed instead of proud. David might be talking about Saul here. If that is the case, his words are just as true. How could a man who had once been a heroic soldier rejoice in the murder of helpless victims?

> The steadfast love of God endures all the day.

Priests may be killed, but their Master lives forever. God's kingdom lives on, even though good people may be hunted down.

2 Your tongue plots destruction,
  like a sharp razor, you worker of deceit.

In eastern countries, barbers are known for using the razor so well that a man barely knows that his hair is being cut. And clever, scheming, evil men injure the servants of God almost before they know what has happened. Doeg's tongue with its soft but sharp speeches, cut off the priests of the Lord. May the Lord save us from those who tell lies to hurt us.

3 You love evil more than good,
  and lying more than speaking what is right.   *Selah*

Some can go so low that they actually love telling lies more than speaking the truth. It is a sign of the most hurtful character when someone prefers dishonesty to justice.

4 You love all words that devour,
  O deceitful tongue.

Some people are so evil that they are never more pleased than when they hurt someone who is better than they are. Stay away from them. Above all, never fall into their sin.

5 But God will break you down forever;
  he will snatch and tear you from your tent;
  he will uproot you from the land of the living.   *Selah*

One day, God will pay back those who hurt other people with their words. He will pull them up like weeds and throw them into the fire. A terrible fate is coming for all liars. They will not let others live, and God will not let them live.

6 The righteous shall see and fear,
  and shall laugh at him, saying,
7 "See the man who would not make God his refuge,
  but trusted in the abundance of his riches
  and sought refuge in his own destruction!"

Good people will look down on schemers and liars with the utmost contempt. The Lord will give them a good reason for doing so, as they see them being caught in their own trap and being destroyed by their own cleverness.

---

[602] 1 Samuel 3:11-14
[603] Psalm 52:9
[604] Probably a musical or liturgical term

Persecutors may be rich, but their wealth will not save them. Justice has ways and methods for bringing the great ones of the earth to its courtroom. God is a judge who cannot be bribed. Those who lie about his servants will be found guilty and quickly sentenced accordingly. Therefore let us patiently endure all types of verbal abuse for Christ's sake.

8   But I am like a green olive tree
    in the house of God.
  I trust in the steadfast love of God
    forever and ever.

David received a great deal of abuse and hate. But he was not captured or destroyed like his enemies were. He was a member of the divine family and found himself in God's household wherever he was. More than that; he was like an evergreen olive plant that is fresh and growing during all the seasons of its life. Some think that Nob, where David fled to Ahimelech, is located on the Mount of Olives. If this is true, we can understand why the psalmist compared himself to "a green olive tree." The olive trees were still alive even though Nob was gone. David continued to live even though Saul hated him and wanted him dead. The psalmist's faith is like an olive tree. Its leaf did not fade nor did it stop bearing fruit. David's faith grew every day and possessed a sacred immortality. He knew that God's mercy was forever and he trusted in that. What a rock to build on! What a fortress to hide in!

9   I will thank you forever,
    because you have done it.
  I will wait for your name, for it is good,
    in the presence of the godly.

David's thankfulness was always there, just like the mercy he rejoiced in. He looked on God's punishment of his enemies as if it had already happened: "You have done it." Therefore he waited patiently until the bright days should dawn for himself and the persecuted church. He believed, as we also should, that he should wait quietly for the Lord to act in his own good time. It is good for the Lord's saints to act this way. It is also a good way to encourage our fellow believers. Patiently waiting on the Lord helps us to keep our souls at peace.

AUGUST 27

When I am Afraid, I Put My Trust in You[605]

After David had obtained food from the priests, he fled from the country in fear.

1 Samuel 21:10-15

10 And David rose and fled that day from Saul and went to Achish the king of Gath. *(There is something very wrong when an Israelite flees to the Philistine. When the man of God associates with heathen,[606] there is bound to be trouble.)* **11** And the servants of Achish said to him, "Is not this David the king of the land? Did they not sing to one another of him in dances,

'Saul has struck down his thousands,
  and David his ten thousands'?"

12 And David took these words to heart and was much afraid of Achish the king of Gath. **13** So he changed his behavior before them and pretended to be insane in their hands and made marks on the doors of the gate and let his spittle run down his beard. **14** Then Achish said to his servants, "Behold, you see the man is mad. Why then have you brought him to me? **15** Do I lack madmen, that you have brought this fellow to behave as a madman in my presence? Shall this fellow come into my house?"

David did escape, but his plan was both embarrassing and unacceptable. When we leave the clear path of faith, there is no telling on what road we will end up. The Holy Spirit is faithful to record the mistakes of the man after God's own heart. We should pay attention to this warning.

In the book of Psalms we find a reminder of the danger David placed himself in and his deliverance.

Psalm 56

TO THE CHOIRMASTER: ACCORDING TO THE DOVE ON FAR-OFF TEREBINTHS *(or the silent doves among strangers)*. A MIKTAM[607] OF DAVID, WHEN THE PHILISTINES SEIZED HIM IN GATH.

---

[605] Psalm 56:3
[606] *heathen* - Means an unbeliever. It is often used as a synonym for pagan, infidel, idolater, heretic, skeptic, agnostic or atheist.
[607] Probably a musical or liturgical term

1 Be gracious to me, O God, for man tramples on me;
    all day long an attacker oppresses me;

Saul was always hunting for David to kill him. David told his Lord about his trouble and distress; which was a far better reaction than running to Achish in Gath. But his narrow escape taught him wisdom.

2 my enemies trample on me all day long,
    for many attack me proudly.
3 When I am afraid,
    I put my trust in you.

Those who trust in God when they are afraid, will soon learn to trust and not be afraid. To trust in God when there is no reason to be afraid is not real faith. True faith is seen in God's elect when there is real danger.

4 In God, whose word I praise,
    in God I trust; I shall not be afraid.
    What can flesh do to me?

A believer's faith may grow dim, but it blazes up again. See how strong David's trust in God became.

5 All day long they injure my cause,
    all their thoughts are against me for evil.
6 They stir up strife, they lurk;
    they watch my steps,
    as they have waited for my life.
7 For their crime will they escape?
    In wrath cast down the peoples, O God!
8 You have kept count of my tossings;
    put my tears in your bottle.
    Are they not in your book?
9 Then my enemies will turn back
    in the day when I call.
    This I know, that God is for me.
10 In God, whose word I praise,
    in the LORD, whose word I praise,
11 in God I trust; I shall not be afraid.
    What can man do to me?

David had been afraid. Therefore he decides to trust in the Lord all the more in the future. Good people see their faults and choose to stay away from them.

12 I must perform my vows to you, O God;
    I will render thank offerings to you.

He had probably made a solemn promise when he was in danger and says he will now make good on that vow. We should be true to any promises we have made to the Lord. His Spirit will help us to do this.

13 For you have delivered my soul from death,
    yes, my feet from falling,
    that I may walk before God
    in the light of life.

David knew he had fallen and this led him to ask God for grace to keep him from falling again. Let us now confess our own failings, and ask the Lord to deliver our feet from falling in the future.

AUGUST 28
Keep Your Tongue from Evil[608]

OF DAVID, WHEN HE CHANGED HIS BEHAVIOR BEFORE ABIMELECH, SO THAT HE DROVE HIM OUT, AND HE WENT AWAY

Psalm 34

1 I will bless the LORD at all times;
    his praise shall continually be in my mouth.
2 My soul makes its boast in the LORD;
    let the humble hear and be glad.

This is the only kind of boasting that humble people can tolerate. We may boast in the Lord as much as we want and never say anything untrue or have anyone hurt by our words. We have good reasons to boast in the Lord. Let us not rob him of glory.

3 Oh, magnify the LORD with me,
    and let us exalt his name together!
4 I sought the LORD, and he answered me
    and delivered me from all my fears.

We too, may seek the Lord and find answers and deliverance. Why do we wallow in our fears when prayer is a certain cure for them? Do we have any troubles at this time? Then let us tell them all to our heavenly Father.

5 Those who look to him are radiant,
    and their faces shall never be ashamed.

David was not the only person full of joy. Anyone who has looked to the Lord has found help.

6 This poor man cried, and the LORD heard him

---
[608] Psalm 34:13

and saved him out of all his troubles.

David describes himself as a poor man, and so he was, because he had been driven from his home and his country. His prayer was only a cry, and yet the Lord answered him, and all his troubles disappeared. Let the poor in spirit, and the poor in pocket, try the psalmist's plan, and they will soon sing as David did.

7 The angel of the Lord encamps
     around those who fear him and delivers them.
8 Oh, taste and see that the Lord is good!
     Blessed is the man who takes refuge in him!

No one knows how sweet honey is until they taste it. True religion is like honey. Its sweetness cannot be learned by only hearing about it. We must try it for ourselves. Oh Lord, help all in this family prove the power of faith in Jesus and the effectiveness of praying to God.

9 Oh, fear the Lord, you his saints,
     for those who fear him have no lack!
10 The young lions suffer want and hunger;
     but those who seek the Lord lack no good thing.

Lions are strong, fierce, and cunning, yet they hunger. Those of the world are also very cunning and full of self confidence; yet, like the lion, they are not satisfied. But believers who are humble and often weak are blessed with every necessary blessing even though the world thinks they are very foolish. Our God is a gracious God.

11 Come, O children, listen to me;
     I will teach you the fear of the Lord.

When David was in the city of Gath, even the children in the streets laughed at him. Therefore, when he came back to his own people, he wanted to do good to the little ones as a way to make up for the mischief he had done when he was there.

12 What man is there who desires life
     and loves many days, that he may see good?
13 Keep your tongue from evil
     and your lips from speaking deceit.
14 Turn away from evil and do good;
     seek peace and pursue it.

Seek after peace. If it flies away from you, chase after it. Be zealous; be eager to recommend love over hate to those around you. The way to be happy in this life is to love and strive for peace.

15 The eyes of the Lord are toward the righteous
     and his ears toward their cry.
16 The face of the Lord is against those who do evil,
     to cut off the memory of them from the earth.
17 When the righteous cry for help, the Lord hears
     and delivers them out of all their troubles.
18 The Lord is near to the brokenhearted
     and saves the crushed in spirit.

What a blessing to have a heartfelt understanding of our sin. We have heard of people dying of a broken heart, but if repentance[609] breaks our hearts we will live eternally.

19 Many are the afflictions of the righteous,
     but the Lord delivers him out of them all.
20 He keeps all his bones;
     not one of them is broken.
21 Affliction will slay the wicked
     and those who hate the righteous will be condemned.
22 The Lord redeems the life of his servants;
     none of those who take refuge in him will be condemned.

Faith is the most important thing. To trust the Lord is more important than anything else. Beloved ones, are we all trusting in the Lord? May the Lord lead us all to do so at this very hour. It would be terrible and dreadful to die in unbelief.

AUGUST 29

This Man Receives Sinners[610]

David realized that living among the Philistines put him in great danger, so he returned to his own country, which he never should have left.

---

[609] *repentance* - The act of feeling remorse, regret, or sorrow for, and being ashamed because of, our sin.
[610] Luke 15:2

1 Samuel 22:1-2

1 David departed from there and escaped to the cave of Adullam. *(These were huge caverns which could be used as shelter and hiding places for several hundred people. David was now back where he belonged and could expect the Lord to bless him. He had separated himself from the world of the Philistines, which is exactly what he should have done.)* And when his brothers and all his father's house heard it, they went down there to him. **2** And everyone who was in distress, and everyone who was in debt, and everyone who was bitter in soul, gathered to him. And he became captain over them. And there were with him about four hundred men.

By doing this, David became a type of our Lord Jesus, of whom it was said, "This man receives sinners and eats with them."[611] The men who followed David had been losing hope because Saul had persecuted them as well. They were bold warriors, but they do not appear to have been evil men. They sympathized with David and may have been the best men in the kingdom. Like their captain, their difficulties were the result of Saul's spiteful actions against them. Those who follow Jesus must expect to be treated like he was. If this drives us into closer fellowship with our despised and rejected Lord, so much the better.

It was at this time that some of his most courageous followers joined him.

1 Chronicles 11:15-19

15 Three of the thirty chief men went down to the rock to David at the cave of Adullam, when the army of Philistines was encamped in the Valley of Rephaim. **16** David was then in the stronghold, and the garrison of the Philistines was then at Bethlehem. **17** And David said longingly, "Oh that someone would give me water to drink from the well of Bethlehem that is by the gate!" **18** Then the three mighty men broke through the camp of the Philistines and drew water out of the well of Bethlehem that was by the gate and took it and brought it to David. But David would not drink it. He poured it out to the Lord **19** and said, "Far be it from me before my God that I should do this. Shall I drink the lifeblood of these men? For at the risk of their lives they brought it." Therefore he would not drink it. These things did the three mighty men. *(This brave act showed the enthusiastic devotion of David's warriors. They were willing to risk their lives to satisfy even his smallest wish. We should serve the Lord Jesus with the same spirit. David showed his tenderness for human life when he refused to drink the water. His refusal also revealed one of the reasons he had so much influence over his men. Our great Captain is even more considerate and compassionate. Oh may we love him even more!)*

1 Chronicles 11:10-14

Several other brave men joined David during this time. Some of their feats have been included in the inspired history.

10 Now these are the chiefs of David's mighty men, who gave him strong support in his kingdom, together with all Israel, to make him king, according to the word of the Lord concerning Israel. **11** This is an account of David's mighty men: Jashobeam, a Hachmonite, was chief of the three. He wielded his spear against 300 whom he killed at one time.

12 And next to him among the three mighty men was Eleazar the son of Dodo, the Ahohite. **13** He was with David at Pasdammim when the Philistines were gathered there for battle. There was a plot of ground full of barley, and the men fled from the Philistines. **14** But he took his stand in the midst of the plot and defended it and killed the Philistines. And the Lord saved them by a great victory.

The honors of Christ's kingdom are for those who can fight and suffer, not for lazy people who only pretend to be Christians. The wonders that these men performed were the result of divine power. That same holy strength is ready to help us in all holy struggles and activities. In the end, the highest of all honors will be being associated with the Lord Jesus in his shame and disgrace. Who will join Christ in this evil generation? Who will "go to him outside the

---

[611] Luke 15:2

camp and bear the reproach he endured?"[612] Whose name shall the recording angel write down on the roll today? Who in this house will be a warrior for Jesus?

AUGUST 30
You Are My Refuge[613]

David has told us about some of his experiences in Gath in his sacred psalms. We will now read two of the psalms he wrote while living in the cave of Adullam. Many life stories are just a list of one complaint and violent act after another. David's gives his history in hymns and prayers.

Psalm 142
A MASKIL[614] OF DAVID, WHEN HE WAS IN THE CAVE. A PRAYER.

1 With my voice I cry out to the LORD;
 with my voice I plead for mercy to the LORD.
2 I pour out my complaint before him;
 I tell my trouble before him.

In his lonely travels he made the forests and caverns echo with his prayers.

"The calm retreat, the silent shade,
 With prayer and praise agree,
And seem by thy kind bounty made
 For those who worship thee."[615]

3 When my spirit faints within me,
 you know my way!
 In the path where I walk
 they have hidden a trap for me.

But God knew his path, so he was not captured in their traps. We owe eternal praises to the Lord for keeping us out of the hands of our enemies.

4 Look to the right and see:
 there is none who takes notice of me;
 no refuge remains to me;
 no one cares for my soul.
5 I cry to you, O LORD;
 I say, "You are my refuge,
 my portion in the land of the living."
6 Attend to my cry,
 for I am brought very low!
 Deliver me from my persecutors,
 for they are too strong for me!

Even in the worst times, everything is all right if we do not lose our faith in the Lord. No matter how powerful our enemies, we will overcome if we hold the divine arm tightly.

7 Bring me out of prison,
 that I may give thanks to your name!
 The righteous will surround me,
 for you will deal bountifully with me.

Within a short time, good and honest men came in great numbers and placed themselves under David's authority. He was no longer alone, but became a powerful leader. The Lord can find us friends when we are friendless.

Let us now read:

Psalm 141
A Psalm of David.

1 O LORD, I call upon you; hasten to me!
 Give ear to my voice when I call to you!
2 Let my prayer be counted as incense before you,
 and the lifting up of my hands as the evening sacrifice!

David could not go to the tabernacle to offer sacrifices and burn incense, but he felt that his prayers would be accepted instead. If we are forced to stay at home on the Lord's day we should still worship the Lord in our hearts. God does not accept our prayer and praise depending on where we are. True spiritual worship, even in a cave, is far better than the most wonderful ceremonies offered in a cathedral.

3 Set a guard, O LORD, over my mouth;
 keep watch over the door of my lips!
4 Do not let my heart incline to any evil,
 to busy myself with wicked deeds
 in company with men who work iniquity,
 and let me not eat of their delicacies!

Even at his lowest point, David had no desire to be with wicked men who seemed to enjoy the best things in life.

5 Let a righteous man strike me—it is a kindness;
 let him rebuke me—it is oil for my head;
 let my head not refuse it.

---
[612] Hebrews 13:13
[613] Psalm 142:5
[614] Probably a musical or liturgical term
[615] A verse from the poem *Retirement* by William Cowper (1731-1800)

Yet my prayer is continually against their
evil deeds.

It requires great grace to rebuke someone correctly. It takes even more grace to receive a rebuke with the proper attitude. Wise people are thankful when their errors are pointed out to them. Unfortunately, there are very few wise people.

6 When their judges are thrown over the
cliff,
then they shall hear my words, for they
are pleasant.

When the world resents us, the word of God brings joy. Those who do not like us now, may be glad to have us comfort them when they are suffering.

7 As when one plows and breaks up the
earth,
so shall our bones be scattered at the
mouth of Sheol.

David was like wood cut and split for the fire. He felt that he and his followers were sentenced to die, yet he turned to God with hope.

8 But my eyes are toward you, O GOD, my
Lord;
in you I seek refuge; leave me not
defenseless!
9 Keep me from the trap that they have laid
for me
and from the snares of evildoers!
10 Let the wicked fall into their own nets,
while I pass by safely.

God heard David's prayer and protected him. He protects all believers who trust their souls to his faithfulness. All is well if faith is unmoved.

AUGUST 31

You Guide Me With Your Counsel[616]

In today's passage, we see an example of David's patriotism. Although he was persecuted in his own country, he did not stop loving his nation. He took a deep interest in everything concerning it. When he found out that the Philistines were robbing the grain storehouses of Keilah, he marched against them with his little army.

---

[616] Psalm 73:24

1 Samuel 23:1-13

1 Now they told David, "Behold, the Philistines are fighting against Keilah and are robbing the threshing floors." 2 Therefore David inquired of the LORD, "Shall I go and attack these Philistines?" And the LORD said to David, "Go and attack the Philistines and save Keilah."

Here we see David's deep commitment to the Lord. He would do nothing until he asked God for guidance. Oh for more of this holy caution.

3 But David's men said to him, "Behold, we are afraid here in Judah; how much more then if we go to Keilah against the armies of the Philistines? *(These were brave men, but they still thought fighting in Keilah was a reckless move. They would not only have the Philistines to contend with, but Saul's soldiers, too. David listened to their advice, but did not let them make up his mind for him. He again turned to God for guidance.)* 4 Then David inquired of the LORD again. And the LORD answered him, "Arise, go down to Keilah, for I will give the Philistines into your hand." 5 And David and his men went to Keilah and fought with the Philistines and brought away their livestock and struck them with a great blow. So David saved the inhabitants of Keilah. *(This was a bold action and as their reward they kept the property of the Philistines. But the people David rescued from their enemies betrayed him. This shows how disgraceful and deceitful human nature can be.)*

6 When Abiathar the son of Ahimelech had fled to David to Keilah, he had come down with an ephod in his hand.

David has been banished and was no longer able to worship at the tabernacle. But that did not keep the exiled hero from having spiritual comfort. He had the high priest himself along with the breastplate of righteousness.[617] See how God provides for the faithful!

7 Now it was told Saul that David had come to Keilah. And Saul said, "God has

---

[617] From Ephesians 6:14. The breastplate was attached to the high priest's ephod and may signify the protection of God. The ephod held the Urim and Thummim which were somehow used in determining God's will.

given him into my hand, for he has shut himself in by entering a town that has gates and bars." **8** And Saul summoned all the people to war, to go down to Keilah, to besiege David and his men. *(He should have honored David for the distinguished service he provided to the state of Israel. Instead, Saul's evil intentions were like a hungry wolf craving for the blood of its prey)*

9 David knew that Saul was plotting harm against him. And he said to Abiathar the priest, "Bring the ephod here." **10** Then David said, "O LORD, the God of Israel, your servant has surely heard that Saul seeks to come to Keilah, to destroy the city on my account. *(David was more concerned for the city than for himself. Saul had destroyed the city of Nob for protecting David, and he might do the same to Keilah. Unselfish spirits cannot bear to have a part in bringing evil upon others.)* **11** Will the men of Keilah surrender me into his hand? Will Saul come down, as your servant has heard? O LORD, the God of Israel, please tell your servant." And the LORD said, "He will come down. **12** Then David said, "Will the men of Keilah surrender me and my men into the hand of Saul?" And the LORD said, "They will surrender you."

God knows people so well, that he can not only tell what they will do, but what they will do under certain conditions. He knows us better than we know ourselves. Let us always ask for his wisdom for all occasions. We will not make mistakes when we follow his directions.

13 Then David and his men, who were about six hundred, arose and departed from Keilah, and they went wherever they could go. When Saul was told that David had escaped from Keilah, he gave up the expedition.

SEPTEMBER 1
God Is My Helper[618]

For a while, David hid himself in the well protected forest of Ziph. The people who lived in the city of Ziph wanted to win the approval of Saul, so they betrayed the man God had anointed as their leader.

1 Samuel 23:19-29

19a Then the Ziphites went up to Saul at Gibeah, saying, "Is not David hiding among us in the strongholds at Horesh? **20** Now come down, O king, according to all your heart's desire to come down, and our part shall be to surrender him into the king's hand." **21** And Saul said, "May you be blessed by the LORD, for you have had compassion on me."

Saul had come to the point that he thought David had wronged him and not the other way around. He even dared to use God's name in his hypocritical speech. This shows that he had lost all understanding of right and wrong and was under "a strong delusion, so that [he] may believe what is false."[619] A bad person can travel the road of sin long enough that they convince themselves that they are in the right and even believe God is on their side. May the Lord save us from such a terrible state of mind. Saul instructed the Ziphites what to do in order to capture David.

22 "Go, make yet more sure. Know and see the place where his foot is, and who has seen him there, for it is told me that he is very cunning. **23** See therefore and take note of all the lurking places where he hides, and come back to me with sure information. Then I will go with you. And if he is in the land, I will search him out among all the thousands of Judah." **24** And they arose and went to Ziph ahead of Saul.

Now David and his men were in the wilderness of Maon, in the Arabah to the south of Jeshimon. **25** And Saul and his men went to seek him. And David was told, so he went down to the rock and lived in the wilderness of Maon. And when Saul heard that, he pursued after David in the wilderness of Maon. **26** Saul went on one side of the mountain, and David and his men on the other side of the mountain. And David was hurrying to get away from Saul. As Saul and his men were closing in on David and his men to capture them, *(They hunted David*

---

[618] Psalm 54:4

[619] 2 Thessalonians 2:11

like he was a pheasant on the mountains. Saul and his 3,000 soldiers chased him while the traitors of Ziph beat the bushes for him. It seemed to be all over for the young chieftain, but when he was in the most danger, the Lord stepped in.) **27** a messenger came to Saul, saying, "hurry and come, for the Philistines have made a raid against the land." **28** So Saul returned from pursuing after David and went against the Philistines. Therefore that place was called the Rock of Escape. *(The pursuer and the pursued were within sight of each other, and yet the victim escaped. The memory of this deliverance was preserved by naming the place the Rock of Escape or the Cliff of Divisions, because David was climbing down one side of the cliff while Saul was surrounding the hill on the other side. God caused Saul to suddenly panic by the threat of a Philistine invasion.)*

29 And David went up from there and lived in the strongholds of Engedi.

At this time David wrote
Psalm 54

1. O God, save me by your name,
    and vindicate me by your might.
2. O God, hear my prayer;
    give ear to the words of my mouth.
3. For strangers have risen against me;
    ruthless men seek my life;
    they do not set God before themselves.
        Selah

Perhaps the Ziphites were descendants of the Canaanites, and so David called them "strangers". At any rate they were enemies to David for no reason. If anyone treats us like this, our best response is praying to God.

4. Behold, God is my helper;
    the Lord is the upholder of my life.
5. He will return the evil to my enemies;
    in your faithfulness put an end to them.
6. With a freewill offering I will sacrifice to you;
    I will give thanks to your name, O Lord, for it is good.
7. For he has delivered me from every trouble,
    and my eye has looked in triumph on my enemies.

SEPTEMBER 2
Keep Me as the Apple of Your Eye[620]

A Prayer of David.
Psalm 17

Much of this Psalm could be related to the time David was hiding from Saul in the forests and mountains of Ziph, so it is appropriate to read it at this time.

1. Hear a just cause, O Lord; attend to my cry!

Do not allow might to crush right. Judge my case and do not let King Saul harm me.

   Give ear to my prayer from lips free of deceit!
2. From your presence let my vindication come!
    Let your eyes behold the right!

David believed he was so much in the right that fairness would rule in his favor. We cannot take an unrighteous case before the Lord. That would be blasphemy. But we can leave a just cause in his hands with confidence.

3. You have tried my heart, you have visited me by night,

Like Peter, David uses the argument, "Lord, you know everything; you know that I love you."[621] It is a most assuring thing to be able to appeal immediately to the Lord, and call upon our Judge to be a witness for our defense. "Beloved, if our heart does not condemn us, we have confidence before God."[622] "You have visited me in the night." David said, "Lord you have entered my house at all hours. You have seen me when no one else is around. You have come in when I was not aware of your presence. You have noted what I did in private. You know whether I am guilty of the crimes that I am accused of committing." Happy is the person who can remember that God sees everything, is always present with us and still find comfort in knowing it. We also have had our midnight visits from our Lord and they have been very sweet. So wonderful, in fact, that just thinking about them makes us want more of these visits. Lord, if we really were

---
[620] Psalm 17:8
[621] John 21:17
[622] 1 John 3:21

hypocrites, could we have had such marvelous times of fellowship with you or hungered for more of them?

> you have tested me, and you will find nothing;
> I have purposed that my mouth will not transgress.

4 With regard to the works of man, by the word of your lips
> I have avoided the ways of the violent.

Divine guidance had kept him on a safe path. It will for us too, if that is really our desire.

5 My steps have held fast to your paths;
> my feet have not slipped.

6 I call upon you, for you will answer me, O God;
> incline your ear to me; hear my words.

7 Wondrously show your steadfast love,
> O Savior of those who seek refuge
> from their adversaries at your right hand.

8 Keep me as the apple of your eye;

No part of the body is more precious, more tender, and more carefully guarded than the eye. And no part of the eye is more especially protected than the central apple, or the pupil. The Hebrew calls it, "the daughter of the eye." The All-wise Creator has placed the eye in a well protected position. It is surrounded by protruding bones, like Jerusalem is encircled by mountains. Its great Creator has also surrounded it with many layers of inward covering: The hedge of the eyebrows, the curtain of the eyelids, and the fence of the eyelashes. In addition, God has made us value our eyes so much and protect them from danger so quickly that no part of the body is more cared for than the organ of sight. Lord, protect me because I trust I am one with Jesus and therefore a part of the spiritual body of Christ.

> hide me in the shadow of your wings,

9 from the wicked who do me violence,
> my deadly enemies who surround me.

10 They close their hearts to pity;
> with their mouths they speak arrogantly.

11 They have now surrounded our steps;
> they set their eyes to cast us to the ground.

12 He is like a lion eager to tear,
> as a young lion lurking in ambush.

This is a brilliant picture of Saul pursuing him. David and his men were surrounded. Their enemies chased after them like wild animals eagerly on the hunt.

13 Arise, O Lord! Confront him, subdue him!
> Deliver my soul from the wicked by your sword,

14 from men by your hand, O Lord,
> from men of the world whose portion is in this life.
> You fill their womb with treasure;
> they are satisfied with children,
> and they leave their abundance to their infants.

15 As for me, I shall behold your face in righteousness;
> when I awake, I shall be satisfied with your likeness.

September 3

God Is a Righteous Judge[623]

This psalm was probably written during these dark days when David was still under the fierce displeasure of Saul.

Psalm 7

This Psalm is titled,

A Shiggaion[624] of David, which he sang to the Lord concerning the words of Cush, a Benjaminite.

It appears likely that this Cush had accused David of treason and plotting against Saul's authority or some other crime. The king would be more than willing to believe anything against David, because he was jealous of him. Another reason was because Cush and Saul were both from the same tribe of Benjamin. Allegations from a relative are often easier to believe.

1 O Lord my God, in you do I take refuge;
> save me from all my pursuers and deliver me,

2 lest like a lion they tear my soul apart,
> rending it in pieces, with none to deliver.

---
[623] Psalm 7:11
[624] Probably a musical or liturgical term

3 O Lord my God, if I have done this,
    if there is wrong in my hands,
4 if I have repaid my friend with evil
    or plundered my enemy without cause,
5 let the enemy pursue my soul and overtake it,
    and let him trample my life to the ground
    and lay my glory in the dust.   Selah

We learn from these verses that no matter how innocent we are, the wicked will still tell lies about us. David had been extremely careful to avoid even the appearance of rebelling against Saul. He always called him, "the Lord's Anointed," but even this could not protect him from the lying tongues of those who hated him. As the shadow follows the substance, so envy pursues goodness. It is only the tree filled with fruit at which people throw stones. If we want to live without being lied about, we must wait until we get to heaven. Let us be very careful to not believe the gossip that flies around good people. If there were no Christians to slander, there would not be so many lies told. A person's good reputation is not safe. Ill-will never spoke well. Sinners have always been hostile toward saints. We may be sure they will not speak highly of them.

6 Arise, O Lord, in your anger;
    lift yourself up against the fury of my enemies;
    awake for me; you have appointed a judgment.
7 Let the assembly of the peoples be gathered about you;
    over it return on high.
8 The Lord judges the peoples;
    judge me, O Lord, according to my righteousness
    and according to the integrity that is in me.
9 Oh, let the evil of the wicked come to an end,
    and may you establish the righteous—
    you who test the minds and hearts,
    O righteous God!
10 My shield is with God,
    who saves the upright in heart.
11 God is a righteous judge,
    and a God who feels indignation every day.
12 If a man does not repent, God will whet his sword;
    he has bent and readied his bow;
13 he has prepared for him his deadly weapons,
    making his arrows fiery shafts.
14 Behold, the wicked man conceives evil
    and is pregnant with mischief
    and gives birth to lies.
15 He makes a pit, digging it out,
    and falls into the hole that he has made.
16 His mischief returns upon his own head,
    and on his own skull his violence descends.
17 I will give to the Lord the thanks due to his righteousness,
    and I will sing praise to the name of the Lord, the Most High.

Oh, how wonderful to have an honest and decent heart. Dishonest sinners use their craftiness, but God derails their plans against righteous souls. God defends the right. The mud sinners throw cannot last long on the pure white robes of the saints. God will brush it off and frustrate those whose evil hands have thrown it. Believers should not fear anything that their enemies can do or say against them. The tree that God plants will stand against the strongest winds. God is a righteous judge. He will not give his saints as prey to the teeth of those who are against them.

September 4
Overcome Evil With Good[625]

1 Samuel 24:1-7; 17-19

¹ When Saul returned from following the Philistines, he was told, "Behold, David is in the wilderness of Engedi." *(Everybody was willing to spy on David. The saints of God are always watched by the world, and this should make them all the more careful in their behavior.)* ² Then Saul took three thousand chosen men out of all Israel and went to seek David and his men in front of the Wildgoats' Rocks.

---
[625] Romans 12:21

Saul had been seriously disappointed in his attempts to kill David, but that did not stop the jealous king from returning to his cruel work. No matter where David might hide or how harmless he continued to be to him, Saul would not let him alone. Envy can never be satisfied until it has had its revenge and then some.

3 And he came to the sheepfolds by the way, where there was a cave, and Saul went in to relieve himself.[626] Now David and his men were sitting in the innermost parts of the cave. *(This cave was so large and dark that a huge number of people could be so hidden from view that someone might come into it and leave without ever being aware of their presence.)* **4** And the men of David said to him, "Here is the day of which the Lord said to you, 'Behold, I will give your enemy into your hand, and you shall do to him as it shall seem good to you.'" *(Our best friends will mislead us if we let them. In this case, David's followers had the best of intentions when they urged him to murder Saul. But grace prevented him from doing it.)* Then David arose and stealthily cut off a corner of Saul's robe. **5** And afterward David's heart struck him, because he had cut off a corner of Saul's robe. *(Good people tremble at doing little wrongs, even when others delight in committing great crimes.)*

6 He said to his men, "The Lord forbid that I should do this thing to my lord, the Lord's anointed, to put out my hand against him, seeing he is the Lord's anointed." **7** So David persuaded his men with these words and did not permit them to attack Saul. And Saul rose up and left the cave and went on his way. *(Dr. Kitto, in his Daily Bible Illustrations, effectively describes this scene, and what happened next: "Although Saul was at the mercy of fierce outlaws, God held them back and allowed Saul to escape unharmed from that dangerous cave. David was willing to secure some evidence of the fact that Saul's life had been in his power. He therefore approached him softly as he slept, and cut off the skirt of his robe. No sooner, however, did Saul arise and leave the cavern, that his men begin to laugh at the ridiculous figure the sovereign presented in his skirtless robe. David's heart smote him for the indignity he had been instrumental in inflicting on the royal person. Yielding to the impulse of the moment, which again was correct, and even though it seemed a most dangerous act, he went boldly forth to the entrance of the cave, and called to the king as he descended into the valley. 'My lord, the king!' The king knew that voice well. A thunderclap would not have struck him more. He looked up, and David bowed himself very low, in proper respect to his king. He spoke. In a few rapid and strong words, he told what had happened. He described the temptation he had resisted. He held up the skirt in proof of how completely his life had been in his hand and said, 'I have not sinned against you; even though you hunt me to take my life. The Lord judge between me and you; and the Lord avenge me: but I will not lay a hand on you.' Behold, now that stoney heart is melted. The hard wintry frosts thaw fast before the kindly warmth of his generous nature. Saul weeps. The hot tears, the blessed tears, fall once more from those eyes, dry too long."[627])*

17 He said to David, "You are more righteous than I, for you have repaid me good, whereas I have repaid you evil. **18** And you have declared this day how you have dealt well with me, in that you did not kill me when the Lord put me into your hands. **19** For if a man finds his enemy, will he let him go away safe? So may the Lord reward you with good for what you have done to me this day."

September 5
I Will Sing and Make Melody[628]

David was always ready to express his gratitude, and when he had escaped from Saul, he was careful to praise the Lord with a new song. This is when he wrote

---

[626] Hebrew: "cover his feet"

[627] John Kitto (1804-1854).
[628] Psalm 57:7

Psalm 57

TO THE CHOIRMASTER: ACCORDING TO DO NOT DESTROY. A MIKTAM[629] OF DAVID, WHEN HE FLED FROM SAUL, IN THE CAVE.

"Do not destroy," probably refers to his refusing to destroy Saul.

1. Be merciful to me, O God, be merciful to me,
    for in you my soul takes refuge;
   in the shadow of your wings I will take refuge,
    till the storms of destruction pass by.
2. I cry out to God Most High,
    to God who fulfills his purpose for me.
3. He will send from heaven and save me;
    he will put to shame him who tramples on me. *Selah*
   God will send out his steadfast love and his faithfulness!
4. My soul is in the midst of lions;
    I lie down amid fiery beasts—
   the children of man, whose teeth are spears and arrows,
    whose tongues are sharp swords.
5. Be exalted, O God, above the heavens!
    Let your glory be over all the earth!
6. They set a net for my steps;
    my soul was bowed down.
   They dug a pit in my way,
    but they have fallen into it themselves. *Selah*
7. My heart is steadfast, O God,
    my heart is steadfast!
   I will sing and make melody!

Under the circumstances, one would have thought David would say, "My heart is trembling." But no! He is calm, firm, happy, determined, and aware that he is accepted by God. When the central axle is secure, the wheels works well. When the ship's main anchor holds, the ship cannot drift away. "My heart is steadfast, O God." I am committed to trust you, to serve you, and to praise you. He repeats himself to give glory to the God who comforts the souls of those who serve him. Surely it will be well with each one of us if we take our drifting hearts and anchor them securely on God and proclaim his glory. "I will sing and make melody!" With my voice and with instruments, I will worship and celebrate you, my Lord and God! With my lips and my heart I will give you the credit. Satan shall not stop me; neither will Saul or the Philistines. I will make the town of Adullam ring with music and all its caves will echo in joyful praise.

8. Awake, my glory!
   Awake, O harp and lyre!
    I will awake the dawn!

It is as if he had said, "Let everything in me, wake up! The brain that creates thought, the tongue that puts thoughts into words, the vivid imagination that gives beauty to those words; let them all rise up now that the hour for praise has come. 'Awake, O harp and lyre!' Let all the music of which I am capable be adapted for the sacred service of praise. 'I will awake the dawn!' I will delight the dawn with my joyous music. No sleepy verses and tired notes shall be heard from me. I will be completely awake for this most important assignment."

Even when we are at our best, we fall short of giving the Lord the praise he deserves. Therefore, we should make the best effort of which we are capable. It may be less than perfect, but never let it be cheapened by laziness. Three times the psalmist calls upon himself to awake. Do we need to be motivated for such work? Then let us make the necessary effort. This assignment is too honorable and too important to be left undone, or to be done in a halfhearted manner.

9. I will give thanks to you, O Lord, among the peoples;
    I will sing praises to you among the nations.
10. For your steadfast love is great to the heavens,
     your faithfulness to the clouds.

God's mercy reaches the lowest places on earth and ascends to the highest places in the heavens. Our imagination cannot begin to understand the wonderfulness of heaven and the richness of God's mercy. The psalmist, as he sat at the cave's entrance, and looked up to the heavens, rejoiced that God's goodness

---

[629] Probably a musical or liturgical term

is greater and more majestic than even the vastness of the universe.

11 Be exalted, O God, above the heavens!
    Let your glory be over all the earth!

A magnificent chorus! Let us hold it with all our hearts and lovingly adore the all glorious Lord.

SEPTEMBER 6

O God, You Are My God[630]

Perhaps it was during this time when Saul was pursuing him that David wrote

Psalm 63

A PSALM OF DAVID, WHEN HE WAS IN THE WILDERNESS OF JUDAH

1 O God, you are my God; earnestly I seek you;
    my soul thirsts for you;
    my flesh faints for you,
       as in a dry and weary land where there is no water.
2 So I have looked upon you in the sanctuary,
       beholding your power and glory.
3 Because your steadfast love is better than life,
    my lips will praise you.
4 So I will bless you as long as I live;
    in your name I will lift up my hands.
5 My soul will be satisfied as with fat and rich food,
    and my mouth will praise you with joyful lips,
6 when I remember you upon my bed,
    and meditate on you in the watches of the night;
7 for you have been my help,
    and in the shadow of your wings I will sing for joy.
8 My soul clings to you;
    your right hand upholds me.
9 But those who seek to destroy my life
    shall go down into the depths of the earth;
10 they shall be given over to the power of the sword;
    they shall be a portion for jackals.

In the East, jackals are always ready to devour the dead. Saul and his men fell on the battlefield, and David foresaw it would happen, and that he would then be made king.

11 But the king shall rejoice in God;
    all who swear by him shall exult,
       for the mouths of liars will be stopped.

We have held back from commenting, in order to quote the sweet remarks of our dear friend Andrew Bonar, upon the whole psalm: "It may have been near the Dead Sea, on his way to the ford of Jordan, that the psalmist first sang this song. It is a psalm first heard by David's faithful ones in the wilderness of Judah; but truly a psalm for every godly person who in the dry world-wilderness can sing: "All my springs are in you."[631] — a psalm for the Church in every age — a psalm for every member of the church in the weary land! What assurance, what vehement desire, what soul-filling delight in God, in God alone; in God, the only fountain of living water amid a vast wilderness! Hope, too, has its visions here; for it sees the ungodly perish (verse 9-10), and the King on the throne surrounded by a company who swear allegiance to Jehovah. Hope sees for itself what Isaiah 65:16 describes as, every mouth swearing 'by the God of truth;' and what Revelation 21:27, has foretold, the mouth of liars closed forever. All who sought other gods, and trusted to other saviors, gone forever.

"And when we read all this as spoken of Christ, how much does every verse become enhanced. His thirst for God! His vision of God! His estimate of God's loving-kindness! His soul satisfied! His mouth full of praise! His soul following hard after God! 'O God, you are my God,' my mighty one. You are my omnipotence. It is this God he still seeks. The word translated 'so' in verses 2 and 4, is interesting. In verse 2, the force of it is this: 'No wonder that I so thirst for you; no wonder that my first thoughts in the morning are about you; no wonder that my very soul longs for you! Who would not, who has seen what I have seen? So have I gazed on you in

---

[630] Psalm 63:1

[631] Psalm 87:7

the sanctuary, seeing your power and glory!' The 'so' is like 2 Peter 1:17. 'The voice...[of] Majestic Glory!' And then, if the past has been so extremely blessed, my prospects for the future are not less so. I see limitless bliss coming in like a tide; 'so' will I bless you as long as I live! (verse 4). Yes; in ages to come, as well as in many a happy moment on earth, my soul will be filled as with marrow and fatness! And when verse 7 shows us the soul under the shadow of God's wings, rejoicing, we may say, it is not only like 'the bird, which, sheltered from the heat of the sun amid the rich foliage, sings its merry note,' [632] *but it is the soul peacefully resting there as if entering the cloud of glory, like Moses and Elijah. O world! come and see The Righteous One finding springs of water in God."*

Andrews Alexander Bonar (1810-1892)
A minister of the Free Church of Scotland and youngest brother of Horatius Bonar.

September 7

Beloved, Never Avenge Yourselves[633]

Today's reading gives us another example of David's spirit of restraint.

---

[632] I was unable to find the composer of this poem Bonar is obviously quoting from. —ed
[633] Romans 12:19

1 Samuel 26:1-22; 25

1 Then the Ziphites came to Saul at Gibeah, saying, "Is not David hiding himself on the hill of Hachilah, which is on the east of Jeshimon?" **2** So Saul arose and went down to the wilderness of Ziph with three thousand chosen men of Israel to seek David in the wilderness of Ziph. **3** And Saul encamped on the hill of Hachilah, which is beside the road on the east of Jeshimon. But David remained in the wilderness. When he saw that Saul came after him into the wilderness, **4** David sent out spies and learned that Saul had indeed come. **5** Then David rose and came to the place where Saul had encamped. And David saw the place where Saul lay, with Abner the son of Ner, the commander of his army. Saul was lying within the encampment, while the army was encamped around him.

6 Then David said to Ahimelech the Hittite, and to Joab's brother Abishai the son of Zeruiah, "Who will go down with me into the camp to Saul?" And Abishai said, "I will go down with you." **7** So David and Abishai went to the army by night. And there lay Saul sleeping within the encampment, with his spear stuck in the ground at his head, and Abner and the army lay around him. **8** Then said Abishai to David, "God has given your enemy into your hand this day. Now please let me pin him to the earth with one stroke of the spear, and I will not strike him twice." **9** But David said to Abishai, "Do not destroy him, for who can put out his hand against the LORD's anointed and be guiltless?" **10** And David said, "As the LORD lives, the LORD will strike him, or his day will come to die, or he will go down into battle and perish. **11** The LORD forbid that I should put out my hand against the LORD's anointed. But take now the spear that is at his head and the jar of water, and let us go." **12** So David took the spear and the jar of water from Saul's head, and they went away. No man saw it or knew it, nor did any awake, for they were all asleep, because a deep sleep from the LORD had fallen upon them.

13 Then David went over to the other side and stood far off on the top of the hill, with a great space between them. **14** And David called to the army, and to Abner the son of Ner, saying, "Will you not answer, Abner?" Then Abner answered, "Who are you who calls to the king?" ¹⁵ And David said to Abner, "Are you not a man? Who is like you in Israel? Why then have you not kept watch over your lord the king? For one of the people came in to destroy the king your lord. ¹⁶ This thing that you have done is not good. As the LORD lives, you deserve to die, because you have not kept watch over your lord, the LORD's anointed. And now see where the king's spear is and the jar of water that was at his head."

¹⁷ Saul recognized David's voice and said, "Is this your voice, my son David?" And David said, "It is my voice, my lord, O king." ¹⁸ And he said, "Why does my lord pursue after his servant? For what have I done? What evil is on my hands? ¹⁹ Now therefore let my lord the king hear the words of his servant. If it is the LORD who has stirred you up against me, may he accept an offering, but if it is men, may they be cursed before the LORD, for they have driven me out this day that I should have no share in the heritage of the LORD, saying, 'Go, serve other gods.' ²⁰ Now therefore, let not my blood fall to the earth away from the presence of the LORD, for the king of Israel has come out to seek a single flea like one who hunts a partridge in the mountains."

²¹ Then Saul said, "I have sinned. Return, my son David, for I will no more do you harm, because my life was precious in your eyes this day. Behold, I have acted foolishly, and have made a great mistake." ²² And David answered and said, "Here is the spear, O king! Let one of the young men come over and take it.

²⁵ Then Saul said to David, "Blessed be you, my son David! You will do many things and will succeed in them." So David went his way, and Saul returned to his place.

David conquered by patient self-control. The lesson for us is, "Overcome evil with good."[634]

SEPTEMBER 8
David Strengthened Himself In the LORD His God[635]

Fear got the better of David and he again made the mistake of fleeing to the land of the Philistines to escape Saul's pursuit. He, his family, and his six hundred men and their families were kindly welcomed by King Achish of Gath and lived there for a short time. Then Achish gave them the city of Ziklag to live in. Soon war broke out between the Philistines and Israel and Achish expected David to march into battle with him against his own people. When we walk by sight and not by faith, we are sure to be placed in an embarrassing situation before long. This is what happened to David! The Lord rescued David from this difficulty. The other lords of the Philistines did not trust David and persuaded Achish to send David and his men back to Ziklag. But the Lord, in his love, chastened[636] *him. A sad scene was waiting for him at Ziklag.*

1 Samuel 30:1-13; 15-18

¹ Now when David and his men came to Ziklag on the third day, the Amalekites had made a raid against the Negeb and against Ziklag. They had overcome Ziklag and burned it with fire ² and taken captive the women and all who were in it, both small and great. They killed no one, but carried them off and went their way. ³ And when David and his men came to the city, they found it burned with fire, and their wives and sons and daughters taken captive. ⁴ Then David and the people who were with him raised their voices and wept until they had no more strength to weep. ⁵ David's two wives also had been taken captive, Ahinoam of Jezreel and Abigail the widow of Nabal of Carmel. ⁶ And David was greatly distressed, for the people spoke of stoning him, because all the people were bitter in soul, each for his sons and daughters. But David strengthened himself in the LORD his God.

---

[634] Romans 12:21

[635] 1 Samuel 30:6
[636] *chasten* or *chastise* - An act of discipline which may include pain inflicted for the purpose of correction or moral improvement.

Some time before, David had said, "There is nothing better for me than that I should escape to the land of the Philistines,"[637] but this only proved the foolishness of turning to humans for help. He now turns to the Lord his God. This was very different from Saul, who at this time was looking for Satan's help by asking the witch of Endor for advice.[638]

7 And David said to Abiathar the priest, the son of Ahimelech, "Bring me the ephod." So Abiathar brought the ephod to David. *(It was a good thing David always kept the priest and the ephod close to him. Otherwise, they would have been carried off with those who stayed in Ziklag. Whatever else we lose, let us stay close to Christ and his word.)* **8** And David inquired of the LORD, "Shall I pursue after this band? Shall I overtake them?" He answered him, "Pursue, for you shall surely overtake and shall surely rescue." *(David proved that the God of truth may be trusted, and that the heart that waits on the Lord will be comforted.)*

9a So David set out, and the six hundred men who were with him, and they came to the brook Besor. **10b** Two hundred stayed behind, who were too exhausted to cross the brook Besor. *(They were not equally strong. Neither are all the followers of the Lord Jesus equally full of grace. Yet our great leader is full of tenderness, and does not reject even the weakest believers. They will also have a share from his royal treasury.)*

11 They found an Egyptian in the open country and brought him to David. And they gave him bread and he ate. They gave him water to drink, **12** and they gave him a piece of a cake of figs and two clusters of raisins. And when he had eaten, his spirit revived, for he had not eaten bread or drunk water for three days and three nights. **13** And David said to him, "To whom do you belong? And where are you from?" He said, "I am a young man of Egypt, servant to an Amalekite, and my master left me behind because I fell sick three days ago." *(Only a non-Christian master would turn their back on their servant because of illness. We should not be unconcerned about others just because they can no longer help us.)*

15 And David said to him, "Will you take me down to this band?" And he said, "Swear to me by God that you will not kill me or deliver me into the hands of my master, and I will take you down to this band."

16 And when he had taken him down, behold, they were spread abroad over all the land, eating and drinking and dancing, because of all the great spoil they had taken from the land of the Philistines and from the land of Judah. **17** And David struck them down from twilight until the evening of the next day, and not a man of them escaped, except four hundred young men, who mounted camels and fled. **18** David recovered all that the Amalekites had taken, and David rescued his two wives.

David's faith was honored. The clouds of trouble poured out showers of mercy. Our faith will be given the same honor and blessings.

SEPTEMBER 9

I Am Afraid Of Your Judgments[639]

1 Samuel 31:1-5; 7-13

1 Now the Philistines fought against Israel, and the men of Israel fled before the Philistines and fell slain on Mount Gilboa. **2** And the Philistines overtook Saul and his sons, and the Philistines struck down Jonathan and Abinadab and Malchi-shua, the sons of Saul. **3** The battle pressed hard against Saul, and the archers found him, and he was badly wounded by the archers. **4** Then Saul said to his armor-bearer, "Draw your sword, and thrust me through with it, lest these uncircumcised come and thrust me through, and mistreat me." But his armor-bearer would not, for he feared greatly. Therefore Saul took his own sword and fell upon it.

The unhappy king had turned his back on the Lord and had lost divine protection. He does not appear to have felt the slightest repentance. His hardness of heart continued even to the end. His last thought was not

---

[637] 1 Samuel 27:1
[638] This story is found in 1 Samuel 28

[639] Psalm 119:120

about his sin and his God. His own poor honor and how the world would remember him was still his biggest concern. If he had thought more about his reputation before God and cared less for human praise, then he would never have been driven to such envy in life or such hopelessness in death. With his sons dead around him, and his bravest warriors killed, the miserable king committed self murder. His attempt to escape being dishonored by the Philistines earned him the dishonorable name of suicide.

5 And when his armor-bearer saw that Saul was dead, he also fell upon his sword and died with him. *(While we strongly condemn the self-destruction, we still admire the faithfulness of the armor-bearer to his king. He was "faithful unto death."[640] He refused to outlive his master. This man was so loyal, he lived and died for Saul. Shall we do anything less for our royal master, Jesus the Lord?)*

7 And when the men of Israel who were on the other side of the valley and those beyond the Jordan saw that the men of Israel had fled and that Saul and his sons were dead, they abandoned their cities and fled. And the Philistines came and lived in them.

8 The next day, when the Philistines came to strip the slain, they found Saul and his three sons fallen on Mount Gilboa. **9** So they cut off his head and stripped off his armor and sent messengers throughout the land of the Philistines, to carry the good news to the house of their idols and to the people. **10** They put his armor in the temple of Ashtaroth, and they fastened his body to the wall of Bethshan. *(The disgrace, that the fallen king tried to escape by killing himself, happened anyway. The looting bands of the Philistines came to strip the dead bodies of their clothing. When they came to the mountain side, not far from the corpses of his three sons, they discovered the remains of Saul, swimming in his own blood. Hearts of stone might have softened at the sight, but these barbarians rejoiced at it. They separated the king's head from the torso, and stripped off his armor and weapons. They sent the head from city to city as a trophy of their victory; they displayed the armor in the temple of their goddess, as a token of their gratitude to her; and, they nailed the body to a wall to further humiliate Israel and their fallen king.)*

11 But when the inhabitants of Jabeshgilead heard what the Philistines had done to Saul, **12** all the valiant men arose and went all night and took the body of Saul and the bodies of his sons from the wall of Bethshan, and they came to Jabesh and burned them there. **13** And they took their bones and buried them under the tamarisk tree in Jabesh and fasted seven days. *(This was a good and proper thing to do. Saul had saved their city from the Amorites and their actions showed their honor and respect, even for Saul's mutilated remains. They burned his bones so that his body could never be treated so shamefully again. Then they buried the ashes and paid the last mournful honors to their former ruler and deliverer.)*

1 Chronicles 10:13-14

13 So Saul died for his breach of faith. He broke faith with the LORD in that he did not keep the command of the LORD, and also consulted a medium, seeking guidance. **14** He did not seek guidance from the LORD. Therefore the LORD put him to death and turned the kingdom over to David the son of Jesse. *(We read that no one consulted the ark of God "in the days of Saul."[641] His evil example corrupted the whole nation and therefore his sin was even more injurious. He began well, but his character was based on love of human approval, rather than on the fear of God, and therefore it came to nothing. Let this be a warning to each one of us.)*

SEPTEMBER 10

Affliction Will Slay the Wicked[642]

2 Samuel 1:1-16

1 After the death of Saul, when David had returned from striking down the Amalekites, David remained two days in Ziklag. **2** And on the third day, behold, a man came from

---

[640] Revelation 2:10
[641] 1 Chronicles 13:3
[642] Psalm 34:21

Saul's camp, with his clothes torn and dirt on his head. And when he came to David, he fell to the ground and paid homage. ³ David said to him, "Where do you come from?" And he said to him, "I have escaped from the camp of Israel." ⁴ And David said to him, "How did it go? Tell me." And he answered, "The people fled from the battle, and also many of the people have fallen and are dead, and Saul and his son Jonathan are also dead." ⁵ Then David said to the young man who told him, "How do you know that Saul and his son Jonathan are dead?" ⁶ And the young man who told him said, "By chance I happened to be on Mount Gilboa, and there was Saul leaning on his spear, and behold, the chariots and the horsemen were close upon him. ⁷ And when he looked behind him, he saw me, and called to me. And I answered, 'Here I am.' ⁸ And he said to me, 'Who are you?' I answered him, 'I am an Amalekite.' ⁹ And he said to me, 'Stand beside me and kill me, for anguish has seized me, and yet my life still lingers.' ¹⁰ So I stood beside him and killed him, because I was sure that he could not live after he had fallen. And I took the crown that was on his head and the armlet that was on his arm, and I have brought them here to my lord."

The chances are that this man was really on the battlefield to rob the dead right after the battle was over. Either Saul was already dead or his self-inflicted wound had not yet resulted in his death and the Amalekite finished the job. He hoped that by telling this story to David, he would win his thanks and a reward. The crown and bracelet were worth something, but this adventurer hoped to earn a far bigger prize by bringing them to the rival leader. The Amalekite thought he was being very clever, but little did he realize he was dealing with a man of God and not someone like he was. Instead of winning the new king's favor for the rest of his life, his story condemned him and he met with a speedy doom.

¹¹ Then David took hold of his clothes and tore them, and so did all the men who were with him. ¹² And they mourned and wept and fasted until evening for Saul and for Jonathan his son and for the people of the LORD and for the house of Israel, because they had fallen by the sword. *(This man of God felt no joy in his enemy's death. A gracious heart will never rejoice in the misfortune of others, no matter how cruel they may have been.)*

¹³ And David said to the young man who told him, "Where do you come from?" And he answered, "I am the son of a sojourner, an Amalekite." ¹⁴ David said to him, "How is it you were not afraid to put out your hand to destroy the LORD's anointed?" ¹⁵ Then David called one of the young men and said, "Go, execute him." And he struck him down so that he died. *(Whether he was telling the truth or not, the sentence was just. Because there was now no king in the land, and because David was a military officer, he exercised his office of judge, using the man's own testimony to condemn him).*

¹⁶ And David said to him, "Your blood be on your head, for your own mouth has testified against you, saying, 'I have killed the LORD's anointed.'" *(Those who choose to go down the wrong paths, will be discovered sooner or later and be punished for their actions. The Amalekite thought the crown and armlet would convince David and enrich him. Instead, they became the evidence that convicted him. This clever sinner made only one mistake, but it proved to be a fatal one. Let this be a warning to us, to never leave the path of truth. We should avoid every form of deception, because the Lord will not put up with liars and will definitely overthrow them.)*

SEPTEMBER 11
Tell It Not In Gath[643]

2 Samuel 1:17-27

¹⁷ And David lamented with this lamentation over Saul and Jonathan his son, ¹⁸ and he said it should be taught to the people of Judah; behold, it is written in the Book of Jashar.

The Book of Jashar was probably a collection of national songs and records of heroic acts. It is now lost. It was not inspired and therefore no special act of God

---
[643] 2 Samuel 1:20

protected it. David not only mourned over Saul and Jonathan personally, but he composed a funeral song to be sung by the whole nation, and especially by his own tribe. He called it "The Song of the Bow,"[644] referring to the skill in archery for which Jonathan was famous and which is mentioned in verse 22. David lamenting over the rejected house of Saul, reminds us of Jesus weeping over Jerusalem, which was destroyed because it did not know the time of its visitation.[645]

He said:

19 "Your glory, O Israel, is slain on your high places!
    How the mighty have fallen!
20 Tell it not in Gath,
    publish it not in the streets of Ashkelon,
  lest the daughters of the Philistines rejoice,
    lest the daughters of the uncircumcised exult.
21 "You mountains of Gilboa,
    let there be no dew or rain upon you,
    nor fields of offerings!
  For there the shield of the mighty was defiled,
    the shield of Saul, not anointed with oil.
22 "From the blood of the slain,
    from the fat of the mighty,
  the bow of Jonathan turned not back,
    and the sword of Saul returned not empty.
23 "Saul and Jonathan, beloved and lovely!
    In life and in death they were not divided;
  they were swifter than eagles;
    they were stronger than lions.
24 "You daughters of Israel, weep over Saul,
    who clothed you luxuriously in scarlet,
    who put ornaments of gold on your apparel.
25 "How the mighty have fallen
    in the midst of the battle!
  "Jonathan lies slain on your high places.
26 I am distressed for you, my brother Jonathan;
    very pleasant have you been to me;
    your love to me was extraordinary,
    surpassing the love of women.
27 "How the mighty have fallen,
    and the weapons of war perished!"

Dr. Krummacher, in his "David, the King of Israel," has the following excellent passage, "David did not, in his lamentation, speak too highly in praise of the king. Was not Saul truly a valiant hero? Did not also that which was gentle and tender often find an echo in his soul? Did not Jonathan and his other sons show themselves true and faithful brothers toward David even unto death? All these things hovered before the mind of David at this time. With memories such as these came a deep, sorrowful compassion for the sad fate of the king. And thus it was David's genuine feeling and sentiment to which he gave full honest expression in his lamentations for the dead. These words of the song— 'Tell it not in Gath, publish it not in the streets of Ashkelon.' have, since that time, become a proverb in the circles of the faithful. It is frequently heard when one of their community has failed to take heed to his ways, and, therefore, has given rise to a scandal. Would that the call were more faithfully observed than is usually the case! Would that the honor of the spiritual Zion was always as close to the heart of the children of the kingdom as the earthly Zion was to the heart of David. But how often does it happen that they even try hard to expose the weakness of their brothers before the world? By doing so, they repeat the wickedness of Ham and become traitors to the Church which Christ has purchased with his own blood. They make themselves guilty of bringing dishonor on the gospel, by showing their disapproval to the world through their talebearing, and to their own great injury they disown the love which 'believes all things' and 'hopes all things.'"

---

[644] The "it" in verse 18 is "the bow" or "the song of the bow" in some translations. The ESV uses the Greek Septuagint, "it", but includes a footnote "Hebrew *the bow*"
[645] Luke 19:41-44

Dr. Friedrich Wilhelm (F.W.) Krummacher
(1796-1868)
German Reformed pastor and prolific writer.
Best known for his book, *Elijah the Tishbite*.

SEPTEMBER 12
Wait For the LORD

David waited seven years and more before he came to the throne of Israel. However, during that time he reigned with great wisdom and fairness over that part of the land over which he did have influence. His conduct earned him the general respect of the people. It was far better to be preparing for the crown than to be plotting to take it by force.

2 Samuel 5:1-3

1 Then all the tribes of Israel came to David at Hebron and said, "Behold, we are your bone and flesh. **2** In times past, when Saul was king over us, it was you who led out and brought in Israel. And the LORD said to you, 'You shall be shepherd of my people Israel, and you shall be prince over Israel.'" **3** So all the elders of Israel came to the king at Hebron, and King David made a covenant with them at Hebron before the LORD, and they anointed David king over Israel.

[646] Psalm 27:14

The crown came to David by the popular consent of the Israelites. He never stooped to a violent takeover attempt. When the Lord has ripened a blessing for us, it will drop into our lap like an apple from the tree. We must not reach out an unholy hand to take it before the proper time. David's exemplary past and the fact that he was chosen by the Lord could not be overlooked forever. People have bad memories, but in due time they must and will remember the credit deserved by those who have acted heroically. All the tribes of Israel were pleased to place the crown on the man who had proven himself so worthy to wear it.

1 Chronicles 12:39-40

39 And they were there with David for three days, eating and drinking, for their brothers had made preparation for them. **40** And also their relatives, from as far as Issachar and Zebulun and Naphtali, came bringing food on donkeys and on camels and on mules and on oxen, abundant provisions of flour, cakes of figs, clusters of raisins, and wine and oil, oxen and sheep, for there was joy in Israel. *(Those who lived closest to Hebron provided the feast, because they did not have the cost of the long journey others took. Those who can best afford it should do the most for the honor of our Lord's kingdom.)*

2 Samuel 5:4-9

4 David was thirty years old when he began to reign, and he reigned forty years. **5** At Hebron he reigned over Judah seven years and six months, and at Jerusalem he reigned over all Israel and Judah thirty-three years.

David had already been anointed king. He was now eager to prove he really was a king by getting rid of his country's enemies who still remained in Israel. Therefore he decided to remove the Jebusites from their fortress on Mount Zion.

6 And the king and his men went to Jerusalem against the Jebusites, the inhabitants of the land, who said to David, "You will not come in here, but the blind and the lame will ward you off"— thinking, "David cannot come in here." *(Most likely, this means that David had called their gods both blind and lame, and now they responded by saying that their blind and* lame gods were more than enough to keep him out of their stronghold.) **7** Nevertheless, David took the stronghold of Zion, that is, the city of David. **8** And David said on that day, "Whoever would strike the Jebusites, let him get up the water shaft to attack 'the lame and the blind,' who are hated by David's soul." *(Joab led the troops in this horrific fight. Fort after fort was captured and the gigantic fortifications were attacked. Israel's warriors climbed over the walls and defeated their enemies in hand-to-hand combat.)* Therefore it is said, "The blind and the lame shall not come into the house."

That is to say, it became a proverb that Israel would not depend on lame and blind gods or set them up in their houses as protection, because they had proven to be worthless defenders.

9 And David lived in the stronghold and called it the city of David. And David built the city all around from the Millo inward. *(In this way the sacred mount of Zion was taken out of the hands of enemies and became the site of King David's palace. Likewise, the church has been saved from all her enemies and is the place her King, Jesus, calls home.)*

SEPTEMBER 13
Fight the Good Fight Of the Faith[647]

David soon found that being the king gave him not only advantages, but hard work and wars as well. As it was true of David, it is of all believers. Victory over this wicked world involves struggle.

2 Samuel 5:17-25

17 When the Philistines heard that David had been anointed king over Israel, all the Philistines went up to search for David. But David heard of it and went down to the stronghold. **18** Now the Philistines had come and spread out in the Valley of Rephaim.

Their success against Saul made them bold to attack David. They did not consider the important difference between the two men. Saul had been abandoned by God and was defeated easily. But David was approved and strengthened by the Lord of hosts. He was a very different opponent. It is hopeless to fight against someone who has God for their friend.

19 And David inquired of the L<small>ORD</small>, "Shall I go up against the Philistines? Will you give them into my hand?" And the L<small>ORD</small> said to David, "Go up, for I will certainly give the Philistines into your hand."

David's path seemed obvious, but he wanted God to lead in every step he took. No one ever lost their way by asking for directions too many times. Asking the Lord to direct us is never unnecessary. Every member of our family should follow David's example. If we do, we will walk in the way of peace all our days.

20 And David came to Baal-perazim, and David defeated them there. And he said, "The L<small>ORD</small> has burst through my enemies before me like a bursting flood." *(David did the fighting, but he gave all the glory to the Lord. Grace is active and fights, but it is also humble and gives praise to him who gives the victory.)* Therefore the name of that place is called Baal-perazim. *(Or, "the lord who breaks through," because the Lord had broken the ranks of the enemy, and made a way for David to scatter them.)* **21** And the Philistines left their idols there, and David and his men carried them away.

As the Philistines had once captured the ark, so now the Israelites seized their idols. We read in First Chronicles 14:12 that the idols "were burned." They destroyed them to show their intense hatred of them and to prevent their becoming a snare to Israel.

22 And the Philistines came up yet again and spread out in the Valley of Rephaim. **23** And when David inquired of the L<small>ORD</small>, he said, "You shall not go up; go around to their rear, and come against them opposite the balsam trees. **24** And when you hear the sound of marching in the tops of the balsam trees, then rouse yourself, for then the L<small>ORD</small> has gone out before you to strike down the army of the Philistines." *(When the wind rustled among the leaves of the trees, David was to regard it as a sign for battle. As we wait for God to direct us, he will give us hints to know when to become active. Surely, whenever we hear that the Spirit of God is*

---

[647] 1 Timothy 6:12

moving like the wind through the churches, it should move us to sevenfold activity.) **25** And David did as the LORD commanded him, and struck down the Philistines from Geba to Gezer.

If we do as the Lord commands us, he will command success to be with us.

By successfully defeating the invading foe, David was firmly established as king. In Psalm 101, he tells us how he is determined to act in his exalted position.

Psalm 101

1 I will sing of steadfast love and justice;
    to you, O LORD, I will make music.
2 I will ponder the way that is blameless.
    Oh when will you come to me?
  I will walk with integrity of heart
    within my house;
3 I will not set before my eyes
    anything that is worthless.
  I hate the work of those who fall away;
    it shall not cling to me.
4 A perverse heart shall be far from me;
    I will know nothing of evil.
5 Whoever slanders his neighbor secretly
    I will destroy.
  Whoever has a haughty look and an
    arrogant heart
    I will not endure.
6 I will look with favor on the faithful in the land,
    that they may dwell with me;
  he who walks in the way that is blameless
    shall minister to me.
7 No one who practices deceit
    shall dwell in my house;
  no one who utters lies
    shall continue before my eyes.
8 Morning by morning I will destroy
    all the wicked in the land,
  cutting off all the evildoers
    from the city of the LORD.

SEPTEMBER 14

I Love You, O LORD, My Strength[648]

After David had sent his enemies retreating and his kingdom was firmly established, he sang this sacred song to the Lord.

Psalm 18:1-24

1 I love you, O LORD, my strength.
2 The LORD is my rock and my fortress and
    my deliverer,
  my God, my rock, in whom I take refuge,
  my shield, and the horn of my salvation,
    my stronghold.
3 I call upon the LORD, who is worthy to be praised,
    and I am saved from my enemies.
4 The cords of death encompassed me;
    the torrents of destruction assailed me;
5 the cords of Sheol entangled me;
    the snares of death confronted me.
6 In my distress I called upon the LORD;
    to my God I cried for help.
  From his temple he heard my voice,
    and my cry to him reached his ears.
7 Then the earth reeled and rocked;
    the foundations also of the mountains trembled
  and quaked, because he was angry.

Oh! the power of prayer. It can move heaven and earth. It can climb to heaven and bring the Lord down to earth to help his people. Traps are broken, sorrows are removed, death is defeated, and Satan is frustrated. Who would not pray?

8 Smoke went up from his nostrils,
    and devouring fire from his mouth;
    glowing coals flamed forth from him.

This is an Oriental way of expressing fierce wrath. God came to help his servant, burning with displeasure against his enemies. The following verses describe the Lord as using storm and wind to help his suffering servant.

9 He bowed the heavens and came down;
    thick darkness was under his feet.
10 He rode on a cherub and flew;
    he came swiftly on the wings of the wind.

God helps his people quickly. He will come in time, because the winds carry him.

11 He made darkness his covering, his canopy around him,
    thick clouds dark with water.

---

[648] Psalm 18:1

12 Out of the brightness before him
   hailstones and coals of fire broke
      through his clouds.
13 The Lord also thundered in the heavens,
   and the Most High uttered his voice,
      hailstones and coals of fire.
14 And he sent out his arrows and scattered
      them;
   he flashed forth lightnings and routed
      them.

Who can stand against this frightful God? Who can injure those he protects?

15 Then the channels of the sea were seen,
   and the foundations of the world were
      laid bare
   at your rebuke, O Lord,
      at the blast of the breath of your
         nostrils.
16 He sent from on high, he took me;
   he drew me out of many waters.
17 He rescued me from my strong enemy
   and from those who hated me,
      for they were too mighty for me.
18 They confronted me in the day of my
      calamity,
   but the Lord was my support.

David's enemies were very strong, but God was more than capable of helping him.

19 He brought me out into a broad place;
   he rescued me, because he delighted in
      me.
20 The Lord dealt with me according to my
      righteousness;
   according to the cleanness of my hands
      he rewarded me.
21 For I have kept the ways of the Lord,
   and have not wickedly departed from
      my God.
22 For all his rules were before me,
   and his statutes I did not put away from
      me.
23 I was blameless before him,
   and I kept myself from my guilt.
24 So the Lord has rewarded me according
      to my righteousness,
   according to the cleanness of my hands
      in his sight.

Happy is the one who can bless God from their heart because they have been kept pure and true. They will discover, like David, that the Lord would sooner destroy the heavens and dry up the seas, than leave the godly to their enemies.

This psalm is so long, we must wait until our next worship time to finish it.

SEPTEMBER 15

This God—His Way is Perfect[649]

We will now return to Psalm 18 and read from verse 30 to the end.

Psalm 18:30-50

30 This God—his way is perfect;

The experience of all his people bears witness to this. Perfect wisdom, perfect truth, and perfect love, are to be seen in all that he does. Blessed be his name.

   the word of the Lord proves true;

The word of the Lord has been tried, proved and tested, but it has never failed. Our soul knows this is true.

   he is a shield for all those who take
      refuge in him.

This is true for us too, even though our faith has often been weak.

31 For who is God, but the Lord?
   And who is a rock, except our God?—
32 the God who equipped me with strength
   and made my way blameless.

Believers have been equipped with complete armor, of which the belt of truth is a most important part.

33 He made my feet like the feet of a deer
   and set me secure on the heights.

The apostle Paul refers to a believer's spiritual shoes as "given by the gospel of peace."[650] They are from God, permitting the believer to walk safely where others fall.

34 He trains my hands for war,
   so that my arms can bend a bow of
      bronze.

In spiritual conflict, the believer's hands are made strong so they can break the enemy's weapons by the power of truth.

35 You have given me the shield of your
      salvation,
   and your right hand supported me,

---
[649] Psalm 18:30
[650] Ephesians 6:15

and your gentleness made me great.

Above all, we are to take the shield of faith, which is made in heaven, and extinguishes all the enemy's flaming darts.[651]

36 You gave a wide place for my steps under me,
　　and my feet did not slip.

Never let us forget that unless the Lord protected us, we would have fallen as others have done, to our shame and ruin.

37 I pursued my enemies and overtook them,
　　and did not turn back till they were consumed.
38 I thrust them through, so that they were not able to rise;
　　they fell under my feet.
39 For you equipped me with strength for the battle;
　　you made those who rise against me sink under me.
40 You made my enemies turn their backs to me,
　　and those who hated me I destroyed.
41 They cried for help, but there was none to save;
　　they cried to the Lord, but he did not answer them.
42 I beat them fine as dust before the wind;
　　I cast them out like the mire of the streets.

David gives God the credit for all his victories. Notice how often he repeats the word "you." "You have given." "You equipped." "You made." You, oh Lord, have done it all.

43 You delivered me from strife with the people;
　　you made me the head of the nations;
　　people whom I had not known served me.

The neighboring nations submitted to David's authority. When God is with us, "he makes even his enemies to be at peace with" us,[652] *or else they are powerless to harm us.*

44 As soon as they heard of me they obeyed me;
　　foreigners came cringing to me.
45 Foreigners lost heart
　　and came trembling out of their fortresses.
46 The Lord lives, and blessed be my rock,
　　and exalted be the God of my salvation—
47 the God who gave me vengeance
　　and subdued peoples under me,
48 who rescued me from my enemies;
　　yes, you exalted me above those who rose against me;
　　you delivered me from the man of violence.
49 For this I will praise you, O Lord, among the nations,
　　and sing to your name.
50 Great salvation he brings to his king,
　　and shows steadfast love to his anointed
　　to David and his offspring forever.

As we read this psalm we should try to apply these expressions of praise to ourselves and personally bless the Lord for all the benefits that our own lives have witnessed. Has not the Lord done great things for us also? Shall we not also give thanks to his name? Yes, certainly. We will!

September 16
A God Greatly To Be Feared[653]
1 Chronicles 13

1 David consulted with commanders of thousands and of hundreds, with every leader. 2 And David said to all the assembly of Israel, "If it seems good to you and from the Lord our God, let us send abroad to our brothers who remain in all the lands of Israel, as well as to the priests and Levites in the cities that have pasturelands, that they may be gathered to us. 3 Then let us bring again the ark of our God to us, for we did not seek it in the days of Saul." 4 All the assembly agreed to do so, for the thing was right in the eyes of all the people. *(The son of Jesse loved the Lord too well to forget to honor him. As soon as he became king over all Israel his first thought was to glorify his God. How different this is from many who obtain wealth and honors. Most turn their*

---
[651] An allusion to Ephesians 6:16
[652] Proverbs 16:7

[653] Psalm 89:7

back on the God who has given them so much!)*

⁵ So David assembled all Israel from the Nile of Egypt to Lebo-hamath, to bring the ark of God from Kiriath-jearim. ⁶ And David and all Israel went up to Baalah, that is, to Kiriath-jearim that belongs to Judah, to bring up from there the ark of God, which is called by the name of the Lord who sits enthroned above the cherubim. ⁷ And they carried the ark of God on a new cart, from the house of Abinadab, and Uzzah and Ahio were driving the cart. *(At this point they made a critical mistake. The law commanded the priests to carry the ark using poles on their shoulders. God will be served in his own way and not in ours. Ignoring God in even the smallest detail may lead to serious consequences. The two young men who drove the cart had probably grown so familiar with the ark, that they no longer respected it as they should. A stern lesson was needed to teach all Israel that the Lord is "a God greatly to be feared.")*

⁸ And David and all Israel were rejoicing before God with all their might, with song and lyres and harps and tambourines and cymbals and trumpets.

⁹ And when they came to the threshing floor of Chidon, Uzzah put out his hand to take hold of the ark, for the oxen stumbled. ¹⁰ And the anger of the Lord was kindled against Uzzah, and he struck him down because he put out his hand to the ark, and he died there before God. *(There are very many today who commit the sin of Uzzah. They dream that Christianity will suffer greatly unless they adapt it to the tastes and whims of their generation. They change its teachings. They decorate its worship to satisfy modern desires. They add philosophy to the simple gospel. Plain speaking must give place to eloquence. In their zeal and conceit they attempt to help HIM who does not need such helpers. They insult the true religion their unbelieving fear tries to protect. We must beware of even imagining that our hand is needed to steady God's ark. The thought is blasphemy.)*

¹¹ And David was angry because the Lord had broken out against Uzzah. And that place is called Perez-uzza *(which means "the breaking out against Uzzah")* to this day. ¹² And David was afraid of God that day, and he said, "How can I bring the ark of God home to me?" ¹³ So David did not take the ark home into the city of David, but took it aside to the house of Obed-edom the Gittite.

Israel's joy in the Lord was interrupted that day, because God and his law were not given the holy respect they deserve. This was actually good for David and all Israel. It postponed their rejoicing, but it removed lightheartedness and disrespect from their hearts. It taught them to be not only zealous for, but obedient to, the Lord's word. We all need to be taught these lessons.

¹⁴ And the ark of God remained with the household of Obed-edom in his house three months. And the Lord blessed the household of Obed-edom and all that he had. *(As a family, may we always cheerfully open our house to the Lord's servants. Many households have been blessed because they did.)*

September 17
Serve the Lord With Gladness![654]
2 Samuel 6:12-23

¹² And it was told King David, "The Lord has blessed the household of Obed-edom and all that belongs to him, because of the ark of God." So David went and brought up the ark of God from the house of Obed-edom to the city of David with rejoicing.

Obed-edom's prosperity was a sure sign that the Lord was ready to bless all who would treat his ark with reverence. When God blesses people "with a nature like ours,"[655] we are encouraged to expect that he will bless us also.

This time the ark was carried by the priests and Levites, "Consecrate yourselves, you and your brothers, so that you may bring up the ark of the Lord, the God of Israel, to the place that I have prepared for it. Because you did not carry it the first time, the Lord

---
[654] Psalm 100:2
[655] James 5:17

our God broke out against us, because we did not seek him according to the rule."[656]

13 And when those who bore the ark of the Lord had gone six steps, he sacrificed an ox and a fattened animal. **14** And David danced before the Lord with all his might. And David was wearing a linen ephod. *(He took off his royal robes and exchanged them for the simple outfit of the Levites to show that he, too, was a servant of the Lord. He "danced before the Lord with all his might." Krummacher says, "He gave expression in outward movements, and by a rhythmic action of his body, to the feelings which swelled in his heart. The idea that the world of the present day likes to associate with the word dance is not appropriate here at all. In Israel, dancing was a form of divine worship, in which the highest and holiest inspiration often expressed itself. For example, in the case of Miriam and her companions at the Red Sea. If it had not been so, how would the spirit of prophecy have said by the prophet Jeremiah, 'Again you shall adorn yourself with tambourines and shall go forth in the dance of the merrymakers.'*[657]*"*[658] *And why would the singer of Psalm 150 have encouraged the God-fearing, by saying to them, "Praise him with tambourine and dance"*[659]*!)* **15** So David and all the house of Israel brought up the ark of the Lord with shouting and with the sound of the horn.

16 As the ark of the Lord came into the city of David, Michal the daughter of Saul looked out of the window and saw King David leaping and dancing before the Lord, and she despised him in her heart. **17** And they brought in the ark of the Lord and set it in its place, inside the tent that David had pitched for it. And David offered burnt offerings and peace offerings before the Lord. **18** And when David had finished offering the burnt offerings and the peace offerings, he blessed the people in the name of the Lord of hosts, **19** and distributed among all the people, the whole multitude of Israel, both men and women, a cake of bread, a portion of meat, and a cake of raisins to each one. Then all the people departed each to his house.

20 And David returned to bless his household. But Michal the daughter of Saul came out to meet David and said, "How the king of Israel honored himself today, uncovering himself today before the eyes of his servants' female servants as one of the vulgar fellows shamelessly uncovers himself!" *(She could not share David's enthusiasm. No doubt she thought he was half-crazy. Even today, cold, heartless religious people complain about those who are enthusiastic about the Lord. They call holy excitement hypocrisy and fanaticism.)* **21** And David said to Michal, "It was before the Lord, who chose me above your father and above all his house, to appoint me as prince over Israel, the people of the Lord— and I will celebrate before the Lord. *(He reminded her of God's electing love. Truly, if anything can make a person's heart dance this will.)* **22** I will make myself yet more contemptible than this, and I will be abased in your eyes. But by the female servants of whom you have spoken, by them I shall be held in honor." *(One is reminded here of Paul counting "everything as loss because of the surpassing worth of knowing Christ Jesus my Lord."*[660] *If others think less of us because we glorify God, we should rejoice.)* **23** And Michal the daughter of Saul had no child to the day of her death. *(She acted more as the daughter of Saul than as the wife of David, and therefore like her father she died, leaving no heir to the throne of Israel.)*

September 18

The Most High Does Not Dwell in Houses Made by Hands[661]

2 Samuel 7:1-17

1 Now when the king lived in his house and the Lord had given him rest from all his surrounding enemies, **2** the king said to Nathan the prophet, "See now, I dwell in a house of cedar, but the ark of God dwells in a tent."

---

[656] 1 Chronicles 15:12b-13
[657] Jeremiah 31:4b
[658] F. W. Krummacher (1796-1868).
[659] Psalm 150:4a

[660] Philippians 3:8
[661] Acts 7:48

It was good for David to compare his house to the place where the ark was kept and it is good for us to think along the same lines. If we live in a comfortable house and our place of worship is neglected, then let us not be slow to do what we can to correct the situation.

3 And Nathan said to the king, "Go, do all that is in your heart, for the LORD is with you."

Good people naturally like to encourage good intentions and Nathan spoke from the love in his heart. But he was mistaken. Only the Lord Jesus knew the mind of God perfectly and therefore always spoke it perfectly. Other prophets only spoke the mind of God when the spirit of prophecy rested on them. If they spoke without full knowledge, the Lord quickly corrected them. Nathan did not refuse to correct his own advice when he was better informed and neither should any of us be slow to retract any error we have unknowingly taught.

4 But that same night the word of the LORD came to Nathan, **5** "Go and tell my servant David, 'Thus says the LORD: Would you build me a house to dwell in? **6** I have not lived in a house since the day I brought up the people of Israel from Egypt to this day, but I have been moving about in a tent for my dwelling. **7** In all places where I have moved with all the people of Israel, did I speak a word with any of the judges of Israel, whom I commanded to shepherd my people Israel, saying, "Why have you not built me a house of cedar?" **8** Now, therefore, thus you shall say to my servant David, 'Thus says the LORD of hosts, I took you from the pasture, from following the sheep, that you should be prince over my people Israel. **9** And I have been with you wherever you went and have cut off all your enemies from before you. And I will make for you a great name, like the name of the great ones of the earth. **10** And I will appoint a place for my people Israel and will plant them, so that they may dwell in their own place and be disturbed no more. And violent men shall afflict them no more, as formerly, **11** from the time that I appointed judges over my people Israel. And I will give you rest from all your enemies. Moreover, the LORD declares to you that the LORD will make you a house.'"

The Lord knows the desire of our heart and he rewards the desire as though it has already been accomplished. Because David wanted to build God a house, God built David's house. Truly, we serve a good master.

12 "'When your days are fulfilled and you lie down with your fathers, I will raise up your offspring after you, who shall come from your body, and I will establish his kingdom. **13** He shall build a house for my name, and I will establish the throne of his kingdom forever. **14** I will be to him a father, and he shall be to me a son. When he commits iniquity, I will discipline him with the rod of men, with the stripes of the sons of men, **15** but my steadfast love will not depart from him, as I took it from Saul, whom I put away from before you. **16** And your house and your kingdom shall be made sure forever before me. Your throne shall be established forever.'" *(This was a glorious covenant even as to its surface meaning, but there was a deeper meaning to it. The promise also has a special reference to that greater Son of David building up his church and establishing it forever. Some translate the words, "when he commits iniquity," as "when I make him sin," and believe this entire passage is about, "Him who knew no sin to be sin on our behalf, so that we might become the righteousness of God in Him."[662])*

17 In accordance with all these words, and in accordance with all this vision, Nathan spoke to David. *(In 1 Chronicles 22:7-8, David mentions one of the reasons why he was not allowed to build the temple: "I had it in my heart to build a house to the name of the LORD my God. But the word of the LORD came to me, saying, 'You have shed much blood and have waged great wars. You shall not build a house to my name, because you have shed so much blood before me on the earth.'" It was not right that he who had been the Lord's executioner on so large a scale should build the temple. God is very*

---

[662] 2 Corinthians 5:21 (New American Standard Version)

jealous of his own honor. Even where there may be no real sin, a person's way of life may disqualify them from some positions in the Lord's service.)

SEPTEMBER 19
Bless the House of Your Servant[663]
2 Samuel 7:18-29

18 Then King David went in and sat before the LORD *(After Nathan told David that his "throne shall be established forever," the king was overwhelmed with gratitude. He entered the Lord's tabernacle with great respect, sat down, and worshiped.)* and said, "Who am I, O Lord GOD, and what is my house, that you have brought me thus far? *(This should be the normal feeling of all the Lord's kings and priests.[664] They wonder why they should be chosen, and they adore the sovereign grace[665] that elected them.)* **19** And yet this was a small thing in your eyes, O Lord GOD. You have spoken also of your servant's house for a great while to come, and this is instruction for mankind, O Lord GOD!"

As the heavens are higher than the earth, so are God's ways higher than our ways.[666] The greatest human attempts at compassion cannot begin to compare with divine blessings.

20 "And what more can David say to you? For you know your servant, O Lord GOD!"

God knows our hearts even when we are so full of emotion we cannot find words to express ourselves. He hears our songs and understands our sighs.

21 "Because of your promise, and according to your own heart, you have brought about all this greatness, to make your servant know it."

David does not claim any of the credit for his greatness. He gives all the credit to God and the richness of his grace. He was a free grace man. He placed the crown on the right head and gave the glory to God alone.

22 "Therefore you are great, O LORD God. For there is none like you, and there is no God besides you, according to all that we have heard with our ears. *(There is none like the Lord, and there are no people like his people. Faith is about things that are unique, therefore our gratefulness should motivate us to remarkable service for our Lord. If we receive more than others, we must do more than others.)* **23** And who is like your people Israel, the one nation on earth whom God went to redeem to be his people, making himself a name and doing for them great and awesome things by driving out before your people, whom you redeemed for yourself from Egypt, a nation and its gods? **24** And you established for yourself your people Israel to be your people forever. And you, O LORD, became their God."

This is delightful to think about. God's choice of his people is not temporary, but eternal. He never changes in his relationship to his people.

25 "And now, O LORD God, confirm forever the word that you have spoken concerning your servant and concerning his house, and do as you have spoken. *(These last words explain what true prayer should be: "Do as you have spoken." The only solid foothold for faith is God's word. When a sinner comes before God, they must have nothing else to depend on except, "do as you have spoken." If we cannot plead a promise, then we cannot ask in confidence. We know that God will be true to his word and this gives us boldness before the throne of grace.)* **26** And your name will be magnified forever, saying, 'The LORD of hosts is God over Israel,' and the house of your servant David will be established before you. **27** For you, O LORD of hosts, the God of Israel, have made this revelation to your servant, saying, 'I will build you a house.' Therefore your servant has found courage to pray this prayer to you."

We are on solid ground when our hearts pray for that which we find promised in God's word. Has the Lord said it? Then let us ask for it!

---

[663] 2 Samuel 7:29
[664] A reference to all Christians. "You are a chosen race, a royal priesthood." (1 Peter 29)
[665] *sovereign grace* - A term indicating that salvation is entirely the result of God's mercy and grace. A person is incapable of contributing anything to his own salvation.
[666] See Isaiah 55:9

²⁸ "And now, O Lord GOD, you are God, and your words are true, and you have promised this good thing to your servant. ²⁹ Now therefore may it please you to bless the house of your servant, so that it may continue forever before you. For you, O Lord GOD, have spoken, and with your blessing shall the house of your servant be blessed forever."

Pleading the promises is the sinew and muscle of prayer. When we have a promissory note from someone, we present it to them and ask for payment. We should bring the promises of Holy Scripture before the Lord and request him to make good on his word. Let us continually cry to God, "Do as you have spoken."

SEPTEMBER 20

May the LORD Answer You In the Day Of Trouble![667]

When David became king, his people loved him and were in the habit of praying for him. Psalm Twenty is one of the prayer-hymns they used.

Psalm 20

As we read this psalm, we will see Jesus and use it to our spiritual benefit.

¹ May the LORD answer you in the day of trouble!
   May the name of the God of Jacob protect you!
² May he send you help from the sanctuary and give you support from Zion!

When Jesus was praying at Gethsemane and facing death on the cross, an angel came from heaven and strengthened him.[668] There is no other help like that which God sends and no other rescue like that which comes out of his sanctuary.[669] For us, that sanctuary is the person of our blessed Lord who is pictured as the temple and the place of true protection that God has provided. Let us rush to the Cross for support anytime we have a need. Our God will send us help. The world despises our sanctuary help, but our hearts have learned to prize it more than any human aid. They look to human strength or money, but we turn to the sanctuary that is Jesus.

"And give you support from Zion." Zion was the hill in Jerusalem where David built his palace. The spiritual City of Zion is the home of our great King. The saints of the Church look to Zion for all blessings. When we look to the sanctuary in Zion for help, we are looking to the Father to help us through his Son. We have the greatest confidence that he will send the help he has promised. This verse is suitable for a Sunday morning benediction.[670] It could be given by the pastor for his people or by the Church for its pastor.

³ May he remember all your offerings
   and regard with favor your burnt sacrifices!   Selah

Before going to war, kings offered sacrifices. When their offering was accepted, it was a sign for success in the battle. Our blessed Lord presented himself as a sacrifice that was accepted by the Most High God as a pleasing aroma,[671] after which he attacked and defeated the fortified armies of hell. The sacrifice of Christ still perfumes the courts of heaven and continues to make the offerings and worship of his people acceptable. In our spiritual battles, we should never march forth to war until the Lord has given us a sign to proceed. Our faith should be in our bleeding Lord and his sacrifice for us.

⁴ May he grant you your heart's desire
   and fulfill all your plans!
⁵ May we shout for joy over your salvation,
   and in the name of our God set up our banners!
   May the LORD fulfill all your petitions!
⁶ Now I know that the LORD saves his anointed;
   he will answer him from his holy heaven
   with the saving might of his right hand.

---

[667] Psalm 20:1
[668] Luke 22:43
[669] *sanctuary* - The dwelling place of God. The tabernacle is called a sanctuary and the place where God dwells (Exodus 25:8). Also, a shelter, retreat, or place of safety and protection.

[670] *benediction* - a short prayer for divine help, blessing and guidance, usually at the end of a worship service.
[671] *pleasing aroma* - The Bible speaks of the smell of a sacrifice being pleasing or sweet to God and therefore accepted by him.

⁷ Some trust in chariots and some in horses,
   but we trust in the name of the LORD our God.

Chariots and horses were impressive and awe inspiring. Men took great pride in their modern weapons of war; their enemies were terrified by them. But the sharp eye of faith sees far more power in an invisible God than in even a huge army of chariots and horses. The most dreaded war machine in David's day was the war-chariot, armed with blades that mowed men down like grass. This is what the nations surrounding Israel gloried in and bragged about. But the saints considered the name of Jehovah to be a far better defense. The Lord did not allow the Israelites to keep warhorses, so it was only natural for them to have a great fear of the enemy's cavalry. We should admire the great faith of the bold singer who scorned even the great horses of Egypt when compared with the Lord of hosts. Sadly, there are many in our time who profess to be the Lord's, but are hopelessly depending on other people and act as if they had never known the name of Jehovah at all!

⁸ They collapse and fall,
   but we rise and stand upright.

At first, the enemies of God seem to be winning, but before long they are brought down by either force or their own mistakes. Their position is unsafe, and therefore when the time comes it gives way under them. Their chariots are burned in the fire, and their horses die of disease. Where is their boasted strength now? Those who trust in Jehovah may begin to lose heart as the battle begins, but an Almighty arm lifts them up and they joyfully stand upright. Victory through Jesus is the birthright of his people. The world, death, Satan, and sin, will all be trampled underneath the feet of the champions of faith; while those who trust in human strength shall be ashamed and destroyed forever.

⁹ O LORD, save the king!
   May he answer us when we call

War Chariot

SEPTEMBER 21

His Glory Is Great Through Your Salvation[672]

In this psalm we find King David rejoicing in the mercy of the Lord his God.

Psalm 21

This has been called the Royal Triumphal Ode or the Song of Great Victory. If we can see King Jesus in it, our reading will be rewarded even more.

¹ O LORD, in your strength the king rejoices,
   and in your salvation how greatly he exults!
² You have given him his heart's desire
   and have not withheld the request of his lips.   *Selah*

Souls are saved by Jesus. He enriches his people with all spiritual blessings and this makes King David rejoice greatly.

³ For you meet him with rich blessings;

The word "meet" includes the idea of preceding or going before and Jehovah most certainly preceded his Son with blessings. Before Jesus died, saints were saved by the anticipated merit of his death. The Father is so willing to give blessings through his Son, that instead of waiting to give his grace, his mercy goes ahead of the Mediator on his journey to his death. "The Father himself loves you."[673]

   you set a crown of fine gold upon his head.

Jesus wore the crown of thorns, but now wears the crown of glory. His new crown points to his royal nature, kingly power, well-earned honor, glorious victory and

---
[672] Psalm 21:5
[673] John 16:27

divine authority. The crown is made from the richest, rarest, most brilliant and long lasting metal. Gold! Pure gold. The most valuable gold, to indicate the superiority of his kingdom. The crown is set on his head by Jehovah himself to declare that no one can remove it.

4 He asked life of you; you gave it to him,
 length of days forever and ever.
5 His glory is great through your salvation;
 splendor and majesty you bestow on him.
6 For you make him most blessed forever;
 you make him glad with the joy of your presence.
7 For the king trusts in the LORD,
 and through the steadfast love of the Most High he shall not be moved.
8 Your hand will find out all your enemies;
 your right hand will find out those who hate you.

No one will escape from the Great King when he comes in his righteous anger. We are commanded to accept his love before it is too late.

9 You will make them as a blazing oven when you appear.
 The LORD will swallow them up in his wrath,
 and fire will consume them.
10 You will destroy their descendants from the earth,
 and their offspring from among the children of man.
11 Though they plan evil against you,
 though they devise mischief, they will not succeed.
12 For you will put them to flight;
 you will aim at their faces with your bows.

Opposing Jesus will be useless. He will defeat his enemies with a frightening victory. Do not be found among them in that day.

13 Be exalted, O LORD, in your strength!
 We will sing and praise your power.

This whole psalm is meant to proclaim the praises of the Lord Jesus. Isaac Ambrose writes:[674] "I remember a dying woman who heard some sermon about Jesus Christ; 'Oh,' said she, 'speak more of this, let me hear of this, do not be weary of telling his praise. I want to see him and therefore I love to hear about him!' Surely I cannot say too much of Jesus Christ. On this blessed subject no man can possibly exaggerate. If I had the tongues of men and angels, I could never fully describe Christ. It is impossible for the creature to fully understand his Creator. Suppose all the sands on the seashore, all the flowers, herbs, leaves, twigs of trees in woods and forests, all the stars of heaven, were all rational creatures; and that they had wisdom, and tongues of angels to speak of the loveliness, beauty, glory, and excellency of Christ, as gone to heaven, and sitting at the right-hand of his Father, they would, in all their expressions, stay millions of miles on this side of Jesus Christ. Oh, the loveliness, beauty, and glory of his face! Can I speak, or you hear of such a Christ? And are we not all in a blazing love, in a angelic love, or at least in love like a bride for her husband? Oh my heart, how is it you are not lovesick? Why is it that you have not earnestly asked the daughters of Jerusalem as the spouse did? 'I adjure you, O daughters of Jerusalem, if you find my beloved, that you tell him I am sick with love.'"[675]

---

[674] Isaac Ambrose (1604-1664).

[675] Song of Solomon 5:8

Isaac Ambrose (1604-1664)
An English Puritan and Pastor

September 22
There Is a Friend Who Sticks Closer Than a Brother[676]

2 Samuel 9

¹ And David said, "Is there still anyone left of the house of Saul, that I may show him kindness for Jonathan's sake?"

Good people are thankful people. Jonathan had shown David great kindness, and therefore David looked for a way to be kind to Jonathan's descendants. Someone who is not loyal to their friends is probably someone who is not loyal to the Savior.

² Now there was a servant of the house of Saul whose name was Ziba, and they called him to David. And the king said to him, "Are you Ziba?" And he said, "I am your servant." ³ And the king said, "Is there not still someone of the house of Saul, that I may show the kindness of God to him?" Ziba said to the king, "There is still a son of Jonathan; he is crippled in his feet." ⁴ The king said to him, "Where is he?" And Ziba said to the king, "He is in the house of Machir the son of Ammiel, at Lo-debar." *(He was living far away from the city. He may have been afraid that David wanted to kill him because he was an heir of king Saul. We often fear the very people who will turn out to be our best friends.)*

⁵ Then King David sent and brought him from the house of Machir the son of Ammiel, at Lo-debar. ⁶ And Mephibosheth the son of Jonathan, son of Saul, came to David and fell on his face and paid homage. *(He was both awed by the splendor of the court and nervous because he thought the king might want to injure him. But David was kind to him and quickly put him at ease.)* And David said, "Mephibosheth!" And he answered, "Behold I am your servant." ⁷ And David said to him, "Do not fear, for I will show you kindness for the sake of your father Jonathan, and I will restore to you all the land of Saul your father, and you shall eat at my table always." ⁸ And he paid homage and said, "What is your servant, that you should show regard for a dead dog such as I?"

⁹ Then the king called Ziba, Saul's servant, and said to him, "All that belonged to Saul and to all his house I have given to your master's grandson. ¹⁰ And you and your sons and your servants shall till the land for him and shall bring in the produce, that your master's grandson may have bread to eat. But Mephibosheth your master's grandson shall always eat at my table." Now Ziba had fifteen sons and twenty servants. *(Mephibosheth was the grandson of a king. Ziba, his sons, and his servants made up a good court for a descendant of royalty.)*

¹¹ Then Ziba said to the king, "According to all that my lord the king commands his servant, so will your servant do." So Mephibosheth ate at David's table, like one of the king's sons. ¹² And Mephibosheth had a young son, whose name was Mica. And all who lived in Ziba's house became Mephibosheth's servants. ¹³ So Mephibosheth lived in Jerusalem, for he ate always at the king's table. Now he was lame in both his feet.

---
[676] Proverbs 18:24

From this story, we learn to remember those who have been kind to us. If someone has shared with us when they were prosperous, we should return their kindness if we ever see them or their children in need. Never let it be said that a child of God is ungrateful to others. If we are to show kindness to those who treat us badly, how much more are we obligated to repay the favors of those who have been our friends.

Another lesson may be learned here. David and Jonathan had made a covenant and David kept it. Jonathan's son was not well known, he was poor, and he was deformed. None of these things stopped David from keeping his promise. The Lord is also true to his covenant. He will not abandon those who put their trust in him. Many of God's people are, spiritually, as disabled as Mephibosheth, but he remembers them, and invites them to sit at his table and fellowship with him. The Father is not ashamed of the poor and helpless friends of Jesus. Because he loves their Lord and Master, he accepts them at the king's table, even though both their feet are crippled.

SEPTEMBER 23

Pray That You May Not Enter Into Temptation[677]

2 Samuel 11:1-3; 6-10; 12-17; 26-27

1 In the spring of the year, the time when kings go out to battle, David sent Joab, and his servants with him, and all Israel. And they ravaged the Ammonites and besieged Rabbah. But David remained at Jerusalem.

Perhaps David had begun to give in to a life of ease and decided to allow the battles of his country to be fought by others. If this is the case, then it teaches us that laziness is the helper of wrongdoing.

2 It happened, late one afternoon, when David arose from his couch and was walking on the roof of the king's house, *(Had he been sleeping in until so late in the day? Had he become that self-indulgent? If so, is it any wonder that he fell?)* that he saw from the roof a woman bathing; and the woman was very beautiful. **3** And David sent and inquired about the woman. And one said, "Is not this Bathsheba, the daughter of Eliam, the wife of Uriah the Hittite?" *(David sent for her at once and took her to himself, thus committing the grossest sin. Alas! Alas! how far the mighty have fallen!)*

In a short time David found that his sin would be discovered. So he came up with an excuse to have Uriah return home from the battle in an attempt to hide his shameful sin.

6 So David sent word to Joab, "Send me Uriah the Hittite." And Joab sent Uriah to David. **7** When Uriah came to him, David asked how Joab was doing and how the people were doing and how the war was going. **8** Then David said to Uriah, "Go down to your house and wash your feet." And Uriah went out of the king's house, and there followed him a present from the king. **9** But Uriah slept at the door of the king's house with all the servants of his lord, and did not go down to his house. **10** When they told David, "Uriah did not go down to his house," David said to Uriah, "Have you not come from a journey? Why did you not go down to your house?" *(Uriah answered that he would not go home to sleep in comfort while the ark of the covenant and his fellow soldiers were in tents, or encamped in the open field.)*

Here we find a common soldier being self-disciplined and self-denying, while the famous psalmist had become pleasure seeking and shameless.

12 Then David said to Uriah, "Remain here today also, and tomorrow I will send you back." So Uriah remained in Jerusalem that day and the next. **13** And David invited him, and he ate in his presence and drank, so that he made him drunk. And in the evening he went out to lie on his couch with the servants of his lord, but he did not go down to his house. *(David deliberately got Uriah drunk. This was a very wicked thing to do. But with all of his cleverness, David did not succeed in covering up his crime. This led him to act even more wickedly. Now he would become guilty of murder. "How you are fallen from heaven, O Day Star, son of Dawn!"*[678]

---

[677] Matthew 26:41

[678] Isaiah 14:12

"Therefore let anyone who thinks that he stands take heed lest he fall."[679])

14 In the morning David wrote a letter to Joab and sent it by the hand of Uriah. **15** In the letter he wrote, "Set Uriah in the forefront of the hardest fighting, and then draw back from him, that he may be struck down and die." **16** And as Joab was besieging the city, he assigned Uriah to the place where he knew there were valiant men. **17** And the men of the city came out and fought with Joab, and some of the servants of David among the people fell. Uriah the Hittite also died.

The man after God's own heart had fallen so low that he had become both an adulterer and a murderer! In those days, other kings did these kinds of things repeatedly and their people would not dare to complain about it. But king David was a chosen servant of God and it was a disgustingly evil thing for him to commit such crimes.

26 When the wife of Uriah heard that Uriah her husband was dead, she lamented over her husband. **27** And when the mourning was over, David sent and brought her to his house, and she became his wife and bore him a son. But the thing that David had done displeased the LORD. *(The sinner may have dreamed that he had cleverly hidden his crime, but this last sentence was the signal that announced the death of his secret. If our actions displease the Lord, nothing else in our life will win his approval.)*

SEPTEMBER 24

Have Mercy Upon Us, O LORD [680]

2 Samuel 12:1-10; 13, 14

1 And the LORD sent Nathan to David. *(This kind of sin could not remain unpunished. The Lord sent the same messenger to rebuke David who had previously come to bless him. It was great mercy on God's part to send a faithful preacher to David. If he did not love him, he might have left him to his own hardness of heart. We should be thankful to God when he sends an honest person to deliver his divine message to us, whether that message is sweet or bitter.)* He came to him and said to him, "There were two men in a certain city, the one rich and the other poor. **2** The rich man had very many flocks and herds, **3** but the poor man had nothing but one little ewe lamb, which he had bought. And he brought it up, and it grew up with him and with his children. It used to eat of his morsel and drink from his cup and lie in his arms, and it was like a daughter to him. **4** Now there came a traveler to the rich man, and he was unwilling to take one of his own flock or herd to prepare for the guest who had come to him, but he took the poor man's lamb and prepared it for the man who had come to him."

5 Then David's anger was greatly kindled against the man, and he said to Nathan, "As the LORD lives, the man who has done this deserves to die, **6** and he shall restore the lamb fourfold, because he did this thing, and because he had no pity." *(Little did he realize that he had just judged himself. We are ready enough to condemn others, but, ah! how slow to see sin in ourselves.)*

7 Nathan said to David, "You are the man! *(The parable was full of wisdom and Nathan showed great courage to apply it to the king. How David's color must have changed! How loudly did his conscience say "Amen"[681] to everything the prophet said. Nathan went on to describe David's sin so he could see more of its blackness and be wholeheartedly sincere in his repentance.)* Thus says the LORD, the God of Israel, 'I anointed you king over Israel, and I delivered you out of the hand of Saul. **8** And I gave you your master's house and your master's wives into your arms and gave you the house of Israel and of Judah. And if this were too little, I would add to you as much more. **9** Why have you despised the word of the LORD, to do what is evil in his sight? You have struck down Uriah the Hittite with the sword and have taken his wife to be your wife and have killed him with the sword of the Ammonites. **10** Now therefore the sword shall never depart from your house, because you have despised

---

[679] 1 Corinthians 10:12
[680] Psalm 123:3

[681] *amen* - So be it, it is so, it is true, truly.

me and have taken the wife of Uriah the Hittite to be your wife'"

This was harsh medicine, but it was for a putrid disease. If we sin, we must pay the price for it. The Lord's beloved cannot escape the rod if they disobey his commands. In David's case, as in most others, the punishment matched the sin. He had killed Uriah with the sword and now the sword was to visit his own family.

13 David said to Nathan, "I have sinned against the LORD." *(A child of God may sin, but he cannot continue in it. If there had been no grace in David, he would have been angry with Nathan. But the spiritual life within him caused David to repent immediately and greatly. Many sin, as David did; but never repent, as he did.)* And Nathan said to David, "The LORD also has put away your sin; you shall not die."

How quickly the pardon came! "Confess, and live" is God's word to the guilty. The Lord our God delights in mercy. Let us go to him and acknowledge our transgressions at once, and find immediate pardon.

14 "Nevertheless, because by this deed you have utterly scorned the LORD, the child who is born to you shall die." *(David will live, but he will be struck in a tender place. God forgives his children, but he will not allow them to think lightly of sin. He will strike them heavily, though not to the point of death. Oh Lord, keep us from sin.)*

SEPTEMBER 25
He Will Gather the Lambs In His Arms[682]

2 Samuel 12:15-23

15 Then Nathan went to his house.

And the LORD afflicted the child that Uriah's wife bore to David, and he became sick. *(God is true to his word, whether he threatens or promises.)* **16** David therefore sought God on behalf of the child. And David fasted and went in and lay all night on the ground. *(We are allowed to pray about difficulties that are about to happen. If David was not forbidden to pray for mercy even after the Lord had declared what he was going to do, how much more may we plead to God when his will is still unknown?)* **17** And the elders of his house stood beside him, to raise him from the ground, but he would not, nor did he eat food with them. *(They feared for his health, but he was ready to sacrifice himself for his poor suffering baby. He was a tender father. It pierced him to the heart to see his child suffering because of the father's sin. Perhaps it was during this time that David came to the point of fully repenting and getting back the smile of his heavenly Father)*

18 On the seventh day the child died. And the servants of David were afraid to tell him that the child was dead, for they said, "Behold, while the child was yet alive, we spoke to him, and he did not listen to us. How then can we say to him the child is dead? He may do himself some harm." **19** But when David saw that his servants were whispering together, David understood that the child was dead. And David said to his servants, "Is the child dead?" They said, "He is dead." **20** Then David arose from the earth and washed and anointed himself and changed his clothes. And he went into the house of the LORD and worshiped. He then went to his own house. And when he asked, they set food before him, and he ate.

While the child was still alive David pleaded for its life. But after he died David immediately submitted to the divine will. He also seems to have been aware that God had pardoned him through his faith in the atoning sacrifice. He went again to the house of the Lord to worship in humble appreciation of his God. Some people mourn so long after the loss of a child that they appear to be angry with God and to be carrying on a rebellion against him. This was not the way David acted.

21 Then his servants said to him, "What is this thing that you have done? You fasted and wept for the child while he was alive; but when the child died, you arose and ate food." *(People who have not been taught by God cannot understand why believers act the way they do. Believers do not rejoice the way the world does and do not mourn the way the*

---
[682] Isaiah 40:11

world does. Their feelings have full play, but those feelings understand that God is always in control. Dependable Christians are not overly influenced by outward circumstances and this makes them appear odd and strange.) ²² He said, "While the child was still alive, I fasted and wept, for I said, 'Who knows whether the LORD will be gracious to me, that the child may live?' ²³ But now he is dead. Why should I fast? Can I bring him back again? I shall go to him, but he will not return to me."

A great deal is suggested by the words, "I shall go to him." David could not have thought his child had been annihilated. David's hope was not for annihilation. Even less could David have imagined that the child was suffering in hell. He did not expect to be in hell when he died. David believed that his baby was in heaven and that he would meet him there. We also believe that all the dear little ones who die in infancy are in glory. We say all the little ones, because this child was the offspring of shame, and if it is where David is now, we feel sure that all other departed infants are there also.

"Millions of infant souls compose the family above."[683]

By the death of his baby the first blow of the rod fell on David, and throughout the remainder of his life his trials increased.

SEPTEMBER 26
Cleanse Me From My Sin[684]
Psalm 51

David's conscience experienced great pain as a result of his great sin. Psalm 51 is often called "The Sinner's Guide." It is one of the penitential psalms[685] that David composed.

1 Have mercy on me, O God,
    according to your steadfast love;
    according to your abundant mercy
    blot out my transgressions.

David appealed to God's great tenderness. Penitence has a sharp eye for the loving and merciful qualities of God. Let us also look to them.

2 Wash me thoroughly from my iniquity,
    and cleanse me from my sin!

He could not bear to be contaminated by sin. His heart longed for complete pardon.

3 For I know my transgressions,
    and my sin is ever before me.
4 Against you, you only, have I sinned
    and done what is evil in your sight,
    so that you may be justified in your words
    and blameless in your judgment.

Sin clashes with God. Sin boldly defies God. It wants to be on the throne of our lives and drive God away. David had wronged Bathsheba and Uriah, but his greatest misery was that he had offended his God. Those who do not have the grace of God in their lives do not care if their actions dishonor the Almighty.

5 Behold, I was brought forth in iniquity,
    and in sin did my mother conceive me.
6 Behold, you delight in truth in the inward
        being
    and you teach me wisdom in the secret
        heart.

David's outward act of evil led him to look within and see that his innermost self was disgusting. He was a direct descendant of the first Adam whose fall in the Garden of Eden extends to the entire human race. When our falls lead us to discover and mourn over the sin within us, we are on the sure way to recovery.

7 Purge me with hyssop, and I shall be
        clean;
    wash me, and I shall be whiter than
        snow.

This is the wonderful voice of faith. The humbled soul, while mourning over its sin, yet trusts in the cleansing blood, and believes that it can remove all stain. Bad as I am yet I am not too filthy for the precious blood of atonement! The blood of Jesus can remove every kind of sin and blasphemy.)

8 Let me hear joy and gladness;

---

[683] These words are from a hymn written by Samuel Stennett (1727-1795) that is found in a *Selection of Hymns* compiled by John Rippon in 1787. John Rippon preceded Spurgeon as pastor of his church in London.
[684] Psalm 51:2
[685] penitential psalms - Seven psalms (6, 32, 38, 51, 102, 130 143) attributed to David which express penitence, repentance, regret, sorrow, grief, guilt or pangs of conscience over sin.

let the bones that you have broken
rejoice.
9 Hide your face from my sins,
and blot out all my iniquities.
10 Create in me a clean heart, O God,
and renew a right spirit within me.

Sin destroys! Grace must create a new heart. Penitents who are sincere are not satisfied with only a pardon. Their heart's desire is to be holy in the future.

11 Cast me not away from your presence.
and take not your Holy Spirit from me.
12 Restore to me the joy of your salvation,
and uphold me with a willing spirit.
13 Then I will teach transgressors your ways,
and sinners will return to you.

No one can teach about the power of forgiving love as well as those who have personally experienced it. Pardoned sinners are the best preachers to their rebellious fellow humans.

14 Deliver me from bloodguiltiness, O God,
O God of my salvation,
and my tongue will sing aloud of your
righteousness.
15 O Lord, open my lips,
and my mouth will declare your praise.
16 For you will not delight in sacrifice, or I
would give it;
you will not be pleased with a burnt
offering.
17 The sacrifices of God are a broken spirit;
a broken and contrite heart, O God, you
will not despise.

David's deep experience led him away from the mere practice of religion to the true spirit of the gospel. A real sense of sin will never allow someone to be satisfied with only ceremonies and forms of worship. They want the Lord himself to accept their spiritual worship and to accept their penitent cries for mercy.

18 Do good to Zion in your good pleasure;
build up the walls of Jerusalem;
19 then will you delight in right sacrifices,
in burnt offerings and whole burnt
offerings;
then bulls will be offered on your altar.

David was delighted to be able to reverse the disgrace he had brought to the church and build up the walls of honor he had pulled down by his bad example.

May the Lord be pleased to keep us from being the reason his name or people suffer. Amen.

SEPTEMBER 27

Blessed Is the One Whose Transgression Is Forgiven[686]

After David had received a sense of pardon, he sang that sweet gospel psalm, the thirty-second.

Psalm 32

1 Blessed is the one whose transgression is
forgiven,
whose sin is covered.

Yes, even a great sinner may be blessed. When their sin is effectively hidden by the great propitiation,[687] they are as blessed as if they had never sinned. Have all the members of this family experienced this blessing? Sin has cursed all of us. Has pardon blessed all of us?

2 Blessed is the man against whom the
LORD counts no iniquity,
and in whose spirit there is no deceit.

The person who is released from their guilt is also cleansed from scheming or deceiving. David had been very crafty in his efforts to hide his crime. He felt greatly relieved to escape from the tangled way of living that came from trying to cover up his sin.

3 For when I kept silent, my bones wasted
away
through my groaning all day long.
4 For day and night your hand was heavy
upon me;
my strength was dried up as by the heat
of summer.   Selah

As long as sin remains unconfessed it grows in the heart and is like mental torture. When God adds to this by applying his

---

[686] Psalm 32:1
[687] *propitiation* - The act of satisfying someone's demands and changing that someone from an enemy into a friend. When Jesus Christ died on the cross he satisfied the demand of God the Father that a sacrifice for sin must be made to him. The wrath or anger of God was used up on Christ so that God's justice was satisfied and we who were once the enemies of God became his friends.

pressure from the outside, the sinner's unhappy predicament becomes even worse. These are the feelings, to one degree or another, experienced by everyone who seeks the Lord,.

5 I acknowledged my sin to you,
    and I did not cover my iniquity;
  I said, "I will confess my transgressions to the LORD,"
    and you forgave the iniquity of my sin. *Selah*

Forgiveness followed on the heels of David's confession, because Christ's atonement had already taken place in eternity's future. If anyone admits their sin before the Lord, the blood of Jesus will put it all away immediately and forever.

6 Therefore let everyone who is godly
    offer prayer to you at a time when you may be found;
  surely in the rush of great waters,
    they shall not reach him.
7 You are a hiding place for me;
    you preserve me from trouble;
    you surround me with shouts of deliverance. *Selah*

David was overcome with sighs before he prayed to the Lord. Now he is overcome with songs. If we want to be happy, we must be pardoned. If we want to be pardoned, we must confess our iniquities and look to Jesus who covers all our sin.

8 I will instruct you and teach you in the way you should go;
    I will counsel you with my eye upon you.
9 Be not like a horse or mule, without understanding,
    which must be curbed with bit and bridle,
    or it will not stay near you.

People who have been forgiven should have tender hearts and be afraid to sin again. We should not need to be treated roughly, like a stubborn animal, but should be sensitive to the slightest touch of the Lord's hand.

10 Many are the sorrows of the wicked,
    but steadfast love surrounds the one who trusts in the LORD.
11 Be glad in the LORD, and rejoice, O righteous,
    and shout for joy, all you upright in heart!

Those who begin with holy weeping shall end with holy rejoicing. If there is someone in this family who is unforgiven, let him or her go to the heavenly Father and cry for that gracious forgiveness that is given to all who believe in Jesus. It is not given as a reward for good works. It is not given because of any efforts of our own. It is the free gift of God in Christ Jesus. Paul says that David is describing "the blessing of the one to whom God counts righteousness apart from works."[688] The apostle clearly says that our salvation is not a matter of merit but of grace. The very worst and most horrible sins will be freely and immediately forgiven if we will confess them to the Lord and trust in the infinite worthiness of his dear Son. Do not wait! Rush, right now, to the open fountain of Jesus' blood.

SEPTEMBER 28

A Flattering Mouth Works Ruin[689]

The hand of God fell heavily on David from the time of his great sin until the end of his life. His children became the source of many of his troubles. Ammon committed an awful sin and his brother, Absalom, killed him for it. Absalom was forgiven for murdering his brother and returned to the king's court. Then he began to plot the overthrow of his own father, who loved him far too much. In his attempts to undercut his father's authority Absalom acted very cunningly. He used every method he could to win the approval of the people and make them suspicious of his father.

2 Samuel 15:1-12

1 After this Absalom got himself a chariot and horses, and fifty men to run before him. (*Outward show often catches the attention of ordinary people. Absalom added the attraction of magnificent chariots and running footmen to his own handsome self.*) 2 And Absalom used to rise early and stand

---
[688] Romans 4:6
[689] Proverbs 26:28

beside the way of the gate. And when any man had a dispute to come before the king for judgment, Absalom would call to him and say, "From what city are you?" And when he said, "Your servant is of such and such a tribe in Israel," ³ Absalom would say to him, "See, your claims are good and right, but there is no man designated by the king to hear you." ⁴ Then Absalom would say, "Oh that I were judge in the land! Then every man with a dispute or cause might come to me, and I would give him justice." ⁵ And whenever a man came near to pay homage to him, he would put out his hand and take hold of him and kiss him.

Absalom's ambition prompted him to take great pains to appear very friendly and attentive to everyone. He came to the palace gate early in the morning and spoke to anyone who had a reason to see the king. He flattered them. He convinced them their cause was good. He pretended to regret they were not getting the justice they deserved and that they had to wait so long before their case was heard. He persuaded them that if he were the king, their concerns would have his immediate attention. There would be no delay or injustice for them to complain about. Everybody said, "What a courteous prince! What a just and careful ruler Absalom would be!"

⁶ Thus Absalom did to all of Israel who came to the king for judgment. So Absalom stole the hearts of the men of Israel.

The hearts of the people were not won, but stolen. The vain young prince deceived them. While pretending such zeal for their welfare, he was only advancing his own traitorous schemes.

⁷ And at the end of four years Absalom said to the king, "Please let me go and pay my vow, which I have vowed to the Lord, in Hebron. ⁸ For your servant vowed a vow while I lived at Geshur in Aram, saying, 'If the Lord will indeed bring me back to Jerusalem, then I will offer worship to the Lord.'"

To crown all his other deceit, Absalom pretended to be extremely religious, and claimed that he needed to make a trip to Hebron, in order to keep a holy vow that he had made in the days of his exile. It is a bad person indeed who uses religion to hide their shameful ambition.

⁹ The king said to him, "Go in peace." So he arose and went to Hebron. ¹⁰ But Absalom sent secret messengers throughout all the tribes of Israel, saying, "As soon as you hear the sound of the trumpet, then say, 'Absalom is king at Hebron!'" ¹¹ With Absalom went two hundred men from Jerusalem who were invited guests, and they went in their innocence and knew nothing.

These two hundred men joined Absalom in his devotions out of respect because he was the king's son. They did not know about his plot to overthrow the king. Absalom used their presence for his own ends. The common people believed in these honorable men. The rebellious Absalom convinced them they had left David and had come over to his side.

¹² And while Absalom was offering the sacrifices, he sent for Ahithophel the Gilonite, David's counselor, from his city Giloh. And the conspiracy grew strong, and the people with Absalom kept increasing.

Ahithophel was a very close friend of David as well as his counselor. However, he appears to have been a selfish person who cared more about his own well being than doing what was right. He was convinced that Absalom was stronger than the king and joined his side. David was driven to great distress. His friends were deserting him. His enemy was growing stronger and aiming to dethrone him. Worst of all, that enemy was his favorite son. What dark clouds hung over David after he so sadly turned from the way of holiness.

September 29
The King Crossed the Brook Kidron[690]
2 Samuel 15:13-15; 17-26

¹³ And a messenger came to David, saying, "The hearts of the men of Israel have gone after Absalom." *(This must have sounded like a thunderclap in David's ear. He was rejoicing because he believed his son was paying his vows and making offerings to*

---

[690] 2 Samuel 15:23

God. Then the news of his son's rebellion was suddenly brought to him. David had rebelled against his God and king and now he sees his own son in arms against himself. God had told David that evil would come to him out of his own house. How well God keeps both his promises and his threats!) **14** Then David said to all his servants who were with him at Jerusalem, "Arise, and let us flee, or else there will be no escape for us from Absalom. Go quickly, lest he overtake us quickly and bring down ruin on us and strike the city with the edge of the sword." *(The city could not be defended, because its walls were not built. David had prayed, "Build up the walls of Jerusalem."*[691]*)*

15 And the king's servants said to the king, "Behold, your servants are ready to do whatever my lord the king decides."

17 So the king went out, and all the people after him. And they halted at the last house. *(His wicked son had horses, but David had to leave the city on foot. He took his family with him. He was always a loving father and would not leave them in danger. Who can tell the sorrow that filled poor David's heart? God's rod struck him heavily.)* **18** And all his servants passed by him, and all the Cherethites, and all the Pelethites, and all the six hundred Gittites who had followed him from Gath, passed on before the king.

This was his bodyguard. They remained faithful when others deserted to the popular side. May we always stay close to our Lord Jesus, even if all the world should wander after the beast and the false prophet.[692]

19 Then the king said to Ittai the Gittite, "Why do you also go with us? Go back and stay with the king, for you are a foreigner and also an exile from your home. **20** You came only yesterday, and shall I today make you wander about with us, since I go I know not where? Go back and take your brothers with you, and may the LORD show steadfast love and faithfulness to you."

David was too generous to wish troubles on others. He could have used Ittai's help, but he would not take advantage of his kindness.

21 But Ittai answered the king, "As the LORD lives, and as my lord the king lives, wherever my lord the king shall be, whether for death or for life, there also will your servant be." *(This true and loyal heart shows us how we should follow Jesus.)* **22** And David said to Ittai, "Go then, pass on." So Ittai the Gittite passed on with all his men and all the little ones who were with him. *(The Lord did not leave his servant completely alone. He provided him friends in his time of need.)* **23** And all the land wept aloud as all the people passed by, and the king crossed the brook Kidron, and all the people passed on toward the wilderness. *(The common people mourned with their king, and well they should. There was even a sadder sight when Jesus, "the King, crossed the brook Kidron."*[693] *Oh Lord, we see you represented by David and our hearts adore you.)*

24 And Abiathar came up, and behold, Zadok came also with all the Levites, bearing the ark of the covenant of God. And they set down the ark of God until the people had all passed out of the city. **25** Then the king said to Zadok, "Carry the ark of God back into the city. If I find favor in the eyes of the LORD, he will bring me back and let me see both it and his dwelling place. **26** But if he says, 'I have no pleasure in you,' behold, here I am, let him do to me what seems good to him." *(David was concerned for the safety of the ark and the priests. He would not permit them to be exposed to the same danger he was in. He was also deeply submissive to the Lord's will. This shows the sanctifying influence his trials had on him. It is a blessing when God sends us trials because of our sin and they make us bow before our Master in holy and humble submission.)*

---

[691] Psalm 51:18
[692] The reference is to Revelation 13. The beast and false prophet rise up and deceive those who dwell on the earth. The false prophet is also referred to as "another beast". —ed

[693] John 18:1, "When Jesus had spoken these words, he went out with his disciples across the Kidron Valley, where there was a garden, which he and his disciples entered" (and where Judas betrayed him).

Lord, when you afflict our family, make it always a blessing to each one of us.

September 30
The Lord Disciplines the One He Loves[694]

2 Samuel 15:29-37

29 So Zadok and Abiathar carried the ark of God back to Jerusalem, and they remained there.

30 But David went up the ascent of the Mount of Olives, weeping as he went, barefoot and with his head covered. And all the people who were with him covered their heads, and they went up, weeping as they went. *(This was a sad scene. The good king was fleeing from the rage of his own son. He was old, his heart was heavy, his head was covered, his feet were bare, his eyes were weeping. This much sorrow and distress is rarely seen. It is not at all surprising to see the people so touched and joining the king in his mourning. Little did David think, when he acted so wickedly with Bathsheba, that his sin would cost him so dearly.)* **31** And it was told David, "Ahithophel is among the conspirators with Absalom." And David said, "O Lord, please turn the counsel of Ahithophel into foolishness."

David was grieving, but not to the point where he did not pray. He knew where his strength lay and did not fail to turn to his strong helper.

32 While David was coming to the summit, where God was worshiped, behold, Hushai the Archite came to meet him with coat torn and dirt on his head. *(Perhaps the king stopped at the top of the hill, looked back toward the ark, and fell to the ground in worship. Just as he rose from his knees, he found that God had sent him a valuable helper in the person of Hushai. His tactfulness would lead to the downfall of Ahithophel. When we honor God the most, he will be ready to help the most. David was glad to see Hushai, but thought he would be the most useful to his cause by returning to Jerusalem)* **33** David said to him, "If you go on with me, you will be a burden to me. **34** But if you return to the city and say to Absalom, 'I will be your servant, O King; as I have been your father's servant in time past, so now I will be your servant,' then you will defeat for me the counsel of Ahithophel."

No Christian can approve of this sort of trickery, even though it was highly admired in that society. We are sorry that David should fall into it. In this case, we must look at him as a warning, rather than as an example.

35 "Are not Zadok and Abiathar the priests with you there? So whatever you hear from the king's house, tell it to Zadok and Abiathar the priests. **36** Behold, their two sons are with them there, Ahimaaz, Zadok's son, and Jonathan, Abiathar's son, and by them you shall send to me everything you hear." **37** So Hushai, David's friend, came into the city, just as Absalom was entering Jerusalem.

2 Samuel 17:22; 24; 27-29

David's plan succeeded because, "The Lord had ordained to defeat the good counsel of Ahithophel, so that the Lord might bring harm upon Absalom."[695] Hushai sent his report by the two young priests. He urged the king to get further away from Absalom by crossing the Jordan River and retreating to the far eastern part of the country.

22 Then David arose, and all the people who were with him, and they crossed the Jordan. By daybreak not one was left who had not crossed the Jordan. *(Here was another sad march. It was a discouraging sight to see David and the people crossing the Jordan in the dead of night.)*

24 Then David came to Mahanaim. And Absalom crossed the Jordan with all the men of Israel. *(This wicked young prince hotly pursued his father and could not be content unless he could shed his blood. Yet this was a son of David! What bad sons may come of holy fathers!)*

27 When David came to Mahanaim, Shobi the son of Nahash from Rabbah of the Ammonites, and Machir the son of Ammiel from Lo-debar, and Barzillai the Gileadite

---

[694] Hebrews 12:6

[695] 2 Samuel 17:14

from Rogelim, ²⁸ brought beds, basins, and earthen vessels, wheat, barley, flour, parched grain, beans and lentils, ²⁹ honey and curds and sheep and cheese from the herd, for David and the people with him to eat, for they said, "The people are hungry and weary and thirsty in the wilderness." *(In that way, strangers became the good man's friends. They were like drops of sweetness in his cup of sorrow. The Lord never leaves his people completely. He may strike them, but he is always on their side. Never stop trusting him.)*

October 1

Let Patience Have Its Perfect Work[696]

2 Samuel 16:5-14

⁵ When King David came to Bahurim, there came out a man of the family of the house of Saul, whose name was Shimei, the son of Gera, and as he came he cursed continually. *(At the very moment when grief had made poor David very sensitive, the foul mouth of Shimei was opened to curse him. When a person turns his abuse on a person who really needs pity, it proves he has a very cruel temperament. It is considered very cowardly to strike a man when he is down. Shimei was just such a coward. All the time that David was successful we do not hear about Shimei. Our trials show us who our friends are. They also reveal our enemies.)*

⁶ And he threw stones at David and at all the servants of King David, and all the people and all the mighty men were on his right hand and on his left. *(His stones and his words were meant to not only hurt the king, but to show his utter contempt for him; contempt which he had found convenient to keep secret for many years.)* ⁷ And Shimei said as he cursed, "Get out, get out, you man of blood, you worthless man! ⁸ The Lord has avenged on you all the blood of the house of Saul, in whose place you have reigned, and the Lord has given the kingdom into the hand of your son Absalom. See, your evil is on you, for you are a man of blood."

This was an obvious lie. David had never laid his hand on Saul or any of his family. Did he not execute the Amalekite who said he had killed Saul? Did he not mourn intensely when Saul and Jonathan died? Did he not ask about any of Jonathan's family who still might be alive, so that he could show kindness to him? Had he not entertained Mephibosheth at his own table? Evil tongues will not be quiet. No amount of innocence can prevent their slanderous lies.

⁹ Then Abishai the son of Zeruiah said to the king, "Why should this dead dog curse my lord the king? Let me go over and take off his head." *(No one can be surprised at Abishai's anger. Shimei was barking like a vicious dog. It seemed only fair to repay his stones with iron. But David was not eager to take revenge, so he rebuked his angry bodyguard.)* ¹⁰ But the king said, "What have I to do with you, you sons of Zeruiah? If he is cursing because the Lord has said to him, 'Curse David,' who then shall say, 'Why have you done so?'" ¹¹ And David said to Abishai and to all his servants, "Behold, my own son seeks my life; how much more now may this Benjaminite! Leave him alone, and let him curse, for the Lord has told him to. ¹² It may be that the Lord will look on the wrong done to me, and that the Lord will repay me with good for his cursing today."

How humbly did David submit to the abuse the Lord sent. He refused to take revenge on Shimei for attacking him so furiously, because he understood it was God's way of chastening him for his past sins. Nothing helps us be patient when being taunted or harassed as humbly seeing the hand of God in it as his discipline for our former faults. David has well said in the psalms, "I do not open my mouth, for it is you who have done it."[697] He took comfort because he believed the Lord would not always scold him, but would eventually return and bring him peace. Nothing brings God to his children's rescue like the attacks of their enemies. Fathers cannot bear to hear their dear ones abused.

¹³ So David and his men went on the road, while Shimei went along on the hillside opposite him and cursed as he went and

---

[696] James 1:4 (New King James Version)

[697] Psalm 39:9

threw stones at him and flung dust. *(David's patience only encouraged Shimei's rude behavior. That horrible person went from bad to worse, but he could not provoke the king to take revenge. The tolerance that David showed here makes him look even greater than when he enjoyed everyone's praise. Expensive clothes and gold do not look as good on a king as patience and tolerance. Here, David can be compared to our Redeemer who "endured from sinners such hostility against himself,"[698] and answered those who criticized him with prayers and blessings.)*

¹⁴ And the king, and all the people who were with him, arrived weary at the Jordan. And there he refreshed himself. *(Even when David was at his lowest point, he still had some who followed him. When he and his men were worn out, providence[699] gave them refreshment. In the worst of times, let us hope for better days to come.)*

OCTOBER 2
My Sighing Is Not Hidden From You[700]

David probably wrote this during these sad times when he was fleeing from his son Absalom.

Psalm 38

A PSALM OF DAVID, FOR THE MEMORIAL OFFERING.

¹ O LORD, rebuke me not in your anger,
  nor discipline me in your wrath!

I deserve to be rebuked, but Lord be gentle with me. I richly deserve to be chastened,[701] but do not strike me so heavily that I perish.

² For your arrows have sunk into me,
  and your hand has come down on me.

³ There is no soundness in my flesh
  because of your indignation;
  there is no health in my bones
  because of my sin.

Spiritual distress is extremely painful. However sweet sin may have been in David's mouth, it was bitter enough when it reached his inner being.

⁴ For my iniquities have gone over my head;
  like a heavy burden, they are too heavy for me.

⁵ My wounds stink and fester
  because of my foolishness,

His conscience struck blow after blow until his soul was wounded in a thousand places. And the wounds became repulsive as well as painful. No infected blisters or foul-smelling sores can compare to the extreme suffering that our sin causes us.

⁶ I am utterly bowed down and prostrate;
  all the day I go about mourning.

⁷ For my sides are filled with burning,
  and there is no soundness in my flesh.

⁸ I am feeble and crushed;
  I groan because of the tumult of my heart.

Those who truly regret their sinning feel real pain because of it. Unbelievers feel none of this, but go singing merrily down to hell. Those whom the Lord loves are never allowed to find comfort in sin.

⁹ O Lord, all my longing is before you;
  my sighing is not hidden from you.

The good Physician understands our case without our needing to explain it to him:

"He takes the meaning of our tears,
The language of our groans."[702]

¹⁰ My heart throbs; my strength fails me,
  and the light of my eyes—it also has gone from me.

Here begins another story of sadness. While he was in pain on the inside, he was forsaken and persecuted by those he thought were friends.

¹¹ My friends and companions stand aloof from my plague,
  and my nearest kin stand far off.

¹² Those who seek my life lay their snares;
  those who seek my hurt speak of ruin

---

[698] Hebrews 12:3
[699] *Providence* - Usually, when used with a capital "P" it refers to God; when used with a lower case "p", it refers to God's will, his divine intervention, and his predetermination (predestination).
[700] Psalm 38:9
[701] *chasten, chastening* or *chastisement* - The act of discipline which may include scolding, criticizing or pain inflicted for the purpose of correction or moral improvement.

[702] Taken from Spurgeon's *The Treasury of David*.

and meditate treachery all day long.
13 But I am like a deaf man; I do not hear,
like a mute man who does not open his mouth.

He would not listen to Shimei and punish him for what he said. A deaf ear is often a great blessing.

14 I have become like a man who does not hear,
and in whose mouth are no rebukes.
15 But for you, O Lord, do I wait;
it is you, O Lord my God, who will answer.
16 For I said, "Only let them not rejoice over me,
who boast against me when my foot slips!"
17 For I am ready to fall,
and my pain is ever before me.
18 I confess my iniquity;
I am sorry for my sin.

He would not deny that he was in the wrong, even though he was innocent of the worst charges he was accused of.

19 But my foes are vigorous, they are mighty,
and many are those who hate me wrongfully.
20 Those who render me evil for good
accuse me because I follow after good.
21 Do not forsake me, O Lord!
O my God, be not far from me!
22 Make haste to help me,
O Lord, my salvation!

God is not only our Savior, but our salvation. The one who has the Lord on their side already has salvation. In this last sentence, the eye of faith sees her prayers as being already answered and begins to glorify God for the mercy she expects to receive. Our heavenly Father will never forsake us. His grace will come to the rescue, and before long we will magnify his name for saving us out of all our troubles. Have we all repented of sin? Are we all resting by faith in him?

OCTOBER 3

Cursed Be Anyone Who Dishonors His Father[703]

2 Samuel 18:1; 5-18

Hushai returned to the city and offered his service to Absalom as David asked him to do. "Now in those days the counsel that Ahithophel gave was as if one consulted the word of God; so was all the counsel of Ahithophel esteemed."[704] Absalom listened to the counsel of both Ahithophel and Hushai, but he took Hushai's advice, because "the Lord had ordained to defeat the good counsel of Ahithophel, so that the Lord might bring harm upon Absalom."[705] "When Ahithophel saw that his counsel was not followed, he...hanged himself, and he died."[706] Absalom gathered a great army and pursued his father. The battle that followed decided who would be king in Israel.

¹ Then David mustered the men who were with him and set over them commanders of thousands and commanders of hundreds. *(But when all the troops were counted, David did not have even half as many as his rebellious son.)*

⁵ And the king ordered Joab and Abishai and Ittai, "Deal gently for my sake with the young man Absalom." And all the people heard when the king gave orders to all the commanders about Absalom. *(The order to be gentle with his son showed that David expected to win the battle, but hoped Absalom would not be killed in it. This is a picture of that gracious King, who, even while his persecutors were scorning and killing him, prayed, "Father, forgive them; for they know not what they do."[707])*

⁶ So the army went out into the field against Israel, and the battle was fought in the forest of Ephraim. ⁷ And the men of Israel were defeated there by the servants of David, and the loss there was great on that day, twenty thousand men. ⁸ The battle spread over the face of all the country, and the forest

---
[703] Deuteronomy 27:16
[704] 2 Samuel 16:23
[705] 2 Samuel 17:14
[706] 2 Samuel 17:23
[707] Luke 23:34

devoured more people that day than the sword.

⁹And Absalom happened to meet the servants of David. Absalom was riding on his mule, and the mule went under the thick branches of a great oak, and his head caught fast in the oak, and he was suspended between heaven and earth, while the mule that was under him went on.

The very trees of the forest are lined up against the ungodly. Absalom had made his hair his pride and it became his downfall. People are often defeated by the very things they idolize. What must have been the thoughts of this underhanded young prince when he found himself caught in the forked branch of the oak tree and suspended between heaven and earth to die the death of the accursed? Let children beware of not appreciating their parents. It is a sin that especially earns the anger of the Most High God.

¹⁰And a certain man saw it and told Joab, "Behold, I saw Absalom hanging in an oak." ¹¹Joab said to the man who told him, "What, you saw him! Why then did you not strike him there to the ground? I would have been glad to give you ten pieces of silver and a belt." ¹²But the man said to Joab, "Even if I felt in my hand the weight of a thousand pieces of silver, I would not reach out my hand against the king's son, for in our hearing the king commanded you and Abishai and Ittai, 'For my sake protect the young man Absalom.' ¹³On the other hand, if I had dealt treacherously against his life (and there is nothing hidden from the king), then you yourself would have stood aloof." ¹⁴Joab said, "I will not waste time like this with you." And he took three javelins in his hand and thrust them into the heart of Absalom while he was still alive in the oak. ¹⁵And ten young men, Joab's armor-bearers, surrounded Absalom and struck him and killed him.

¹⁶Then Joab blew the trumpet, and the troops came back from pursuing Israel, for Joab restrained them. ¹⁷And they took Absalom and threw him into a great pit in the forest and raised over him a very great heap of stones. And all Israel fled every one to his own home.

An old writer says, "One death was not enough for Absalom. He was at once hanged, shot, mangled and stoned. Justly was he lifted up by the oak, for he had lifted himself against his father and sovereign. Justly was he pierced with arrows, for he had pierced his father's heart with many sorrows. Justly was he mangled, for he had dismembered and divided all Israel. And, justly was he stoned, for he had not only cursed, but pursued his own parent."[708]

¹⁸Now Absalom in his lifetime had taken and set up for himself the pillar that is in the King's Valley, for he said, "I have no son to keep my name in remembrance." He called the pillar after his own name, and it is called Absalom's monument to this day.

Absalom's pillar is still pointed out to travelers, but its only purpose is to immortalize the shame of this unprincipled son. Children! Love and obey your parents, so you will not fall into Absalom's sin and destruction.

This is probably the monument Spurgeon was referring to as Absalom's Pillar. Like many "historical objects" met with on Holy Land Tours, it is no longer believed to be authentic. This rock-cut monument dates back only to New Testament times.

OCTOBER 4

He Will Sustain You[709]

This psalm most clearly describes David's condition when he had fled far away into the

---

[708] Bishop Joseph Hall (1574-1656)
[709] Psalm 55:22

wilderness to escape from his son. He bitterly describes the treachery of Ahithophel, and prophesies his doom. But his psalm ends with most faithful and cheerful advice. Advice we will all do well to follow.

Psalm 55

1 Give ear to my prayer, O God,
    and hide not yourself from my plea for mercy!
2 Attend to me, and answer me;
    I am restless in my complaint and I moan,
  because of the noise of the enemy,
    because of the oppression of the wicked.
3 For they drop trouble upon me,
    and in anger they bear a grudge against me.
4 My heart is in anguish within me;
    the terrors of death have fallen upon me.
5 Fear and trembling come upon me,
    and horror overwhelms me.
6 And I say, "Oh, that I had wings like a dove!
    I would fly away and be at rest;
7 yes, I would wander far away;
    I would lodge in the wilderness;
        Selah
8 I would hurry to find a shelter
    from the raging wind and tempest."
9 Destroy, O Lord, divide their tongues;
    for I see violence and strife in the city.
10 Day and night they go around it on its walls,
    and iniquity and trouble are within it;
11 ruin is in its midst;
    oppression and fraud
        do not depart from its marketplace.
12 For it is not an enemy who taunts me—
    then I could bear it;
  it is not an adversary who deals insolently with me—
    then I could hide from him.
13 But it is you, a man, my equal,
    my companion, my familiar friend.
14 We used to take sweet counsel together;
    within God's house we walked in the throng.
15 Let death steal over them;
    let them go down to Sheol alive;
  for evil is in their dwelling place and in their heart.
16 But I call to God,
    and the LORD will save me.
17 Evening and morning and at noon
    I utter my complaint and moan,
    and he hears my voice.
18 He redeems my soul in safety
    from the battle that I wage,
    for many are arrayed against me.
19 God will give ear and humble them,
    he who is enthroned from of old,
        Selah
  because they do not change
    and do not fear God.
20 My companion stretched out his hand against his friends;
    he violated his covenant.
21 His speech was smooth as butter,
    yet war was in his heart;
  his words were softer than oil,
    yet they were drawn swords.
22 Cast your burden on the LORD,
    and he will sustain you;
  he will never permit
    the righteous to be moved.
23 But you, O God, will cast them down
    into the pit of destruction;
  men of blood and treachery
    shall not live out half their days.
  But I will trust in you.

Let us dwell a moment on the twenty-second verse, "Your burden." Whatever burden your God lays on you, lay it "on the Lord." In His wisdom, he brought this burden on you. In your wisdom, you should give it right back to him. God will give you your share of suffering. Accept it with cheerful patience and then take it back to him with confident assurance. "He will sustain you." He who placed the burden on you will also give you the strength to endure it. Everything you need, and then some, will be provided for you to live through all your labors and trials. "As your days, so shall your strength be."[710] "He will never permit the righteous to be moved." He may seem to move away from us, like a tree bends away

---

[710] Deuteronomy 33:25

from the windy storm, but he will never be moved like the tree that is torn up by the roots. The person who stands with God stands firm. Many seek to destroy the saints, but God has not allowed them to perish and he never will. The godly stand like pillars, "steadfast, immovable,"[711] *to the glory of the Great Designer.*

OCTOBER 5

See How He Loved Him[712]

While the great battle was raging in the forest, the elderly king was anxiously watching for news.

2 Samuel 18:24-33

24 Now David was sitting between the two gates, and the watchman went up to the roof of the gate by the wall, and when he lifted up his eyes and looked, he saw a man running alone. **25** The watchman called out and told the king. And the king said, "If he is alone, there is news in his mouth." And he drew nearer and nearer. *(If there were many men running from the fight they would probably be deserters, but only one would naturally be a messenger from the camp.)* **26** The watchman saw another man running. And the watchman called to the gate and said, "See another man running alone!" The king said, "He also brings news." **27** The watchman said, "I think the running of the first is like the running of Ahimaaz the son of Zadok." And the king said, "He is a good man and comes with good news." *(It is a great blessing when this can be said of the son of a priest. The children of pastors should always be blessings, but it is not always so.)*

28 Then Ahimaaz cried out to the king, "All is well." And he bowed before the king with his face to the earth and said, "Blessed be the LORD your God, who has delivered up the men who raised their hand against my lord the king." **29** And the king said, "Is it well with the young man Absalom?" *(There was a tender place in David's heart for his son. If we see such love in an earthly father, how much greater is the love of our heavenly Father! He certainly does not delight in the death of any, but prefers that they would turn to him and live.)* Ahimaaz answered, "When Joab sent the king's servant, your servant, I saw a great commotion, but I do not know what it was." *(He had learned to hold his tongue. He was in no hurry to grieve the king.)* **30** And the king said, "Turn aside and stand here." So he turned aside and stood still.

31 And behold, the Cushite came, and the Cushite said, "Good news for my lord the King! For the LORD has delivered you this day from the hand of all who rose up against you." **32** The king said to the Cushite, "Is it well with the young man Absalom?" And the Cushite answered, "May the enemies of my lord the king and all who rise up against you for evil be like that young man." *(The honest Cushite told his devastating news as reasonably as he could, but a dagger went to the father's heart as he heard it.)* **33** And the king was deeply moved and went up to the chamber over the gate and wept. And as he went, he said, "O my son Absalom, my son, my son Absalom! Would I had died instead of you, O Absalom, my son, my son!" *(This was love! Intense, great, passionate love. But the love of Jesus to us was even greater. Jesus did not say, "Would I had died instead of you," but he has actually died that we might live. Oh love, amazing and incomprehensible! David's tears were a display of his love, but Jesus actually dying is an even more incredible expression of love!)*

2 Samuel 19:2; 4-8

2 So the victory that day was turned into mourning for all the people, for the people heard that day, "The king is grieving for his son."

4 The king covered his face, and the king cried with a loud voice, "O my son Absalom, O Absalom, my son, my son!" **5** Then Joab came into the house to the king and said, "You have today covered with shame the faces of all your servants, who have this day saved your life and the lives of your sons and your daughters and the lives of your wives and your concubines, **6** because you love those who hate you and hate those who love you. For you have made it clear today that

---
[711] 1 Corinthians 15:58
[712] John 11:36

commanders and servants are nothing to you, for today I know that if Absalom were alive and all of us were dead today, then you would be pleased. ⁷ Now therefore arise, go out and speak kindly to your servants, for I swear by the Lord, if you do not go, not a man will stay with you this night, and this will be worse for you than all the evil that has come upon you from your youth until now." *(Joab was probably right, but his manner was rough and unfeeling. It is always good to speak gently, even when we are required to be firm.)* ⁸ᵃ Then the king arose and took his seat in the gate. And the people were all told, "Behold, the king is sitting in the gate." And all the people came before the king. *(Joab's harsh intervention produced a good result. Good people follow sound advice, even when it is presented incorrectly. We must not act foolishly just because the person giving the advice is not courteous.)*

October 6

Let Me Fall Into the Hand Of the Lord[713]

After many trials, David again enjoyed a time of peace. But this inactivity again brought him into temptation. He decided to take a measurement of his own greatness so he could glory in it.

2 Samuel 24:1-4; 9-15

¹ Again the anger of the Lord was kindled against Israel, and he incited David against them saying, "Go, number Israel and Judah." *(In the Book of Chronicles, we read that, "Satan stood against Israel and incited David to number Israel."[714] Satan certainly was the one who tempted David and the blame for doing so falls completely on him. But the writer of the Book of Second Samuel saw the hand of the Lord in it. He informs us that the Lord used the sin of David as the way to punish the sins of the people. Both statements are true. There is no reason to try to force them to agree, because one truth must agree with another whether we see it or not.)* ² So the king said to Joab, the commander of the army, who was with him, "Go through all the tribes of Israel, from Dan to Beersheba, and number the people, that I may know the number of the people." ³ But Joab said to the king, "May the Lord your God add to the people a hundred times as many as they are, while the eyes of my lord the king still see it, but why does my lord the king delight in this thing?"

This time, Joab was not only right, but courteous as well. He knew that the people would think the reason for the census was for either new taxes or a military draft. Either way, numbering the people would make them uneasy and rebellious. Therefore he thought David's plan was unwise. According to the law of Moses, "Everyone who is numbered in the census, from twenty years old and upward, shall give the Lord's offering."[715] Even though this law had been ignored, Moses numbered the people because God instructed him to. But David acted as if they were his own people and counted them without asking God. The Lord would not put up with this.

⁴ But the king's word prevailed against Joab and the commanders of the army. So Joab and the commanders of the army went out from the presence of the king to number the people of Israel.

⁹ And Joab gave the sum of the numbering of the people to the king: in Israel there were 800,000 valiant men who drew the sword, and the men of Judah were 500,000.

¹⁰ But David's heart struck him after he had numbered the people. *(David ordered the census to give him something to brag about, but in the end it only gave him something to be ashamed of. His army of over one-and-a-quarter million warriors gave him no joy, because he ended up bringing sorrow to his God.)* And David said to the Lord, "I have sinned greatly in what I have done. But now, O Lord, please take away the iniquity of your servant, for I have done very foolishly." *(God's grace was in David and when it came to the front, he was quite ready to regret his mistake. Oh that we all had a tender conscience like*

---

[713] 1 Chronicles 21:13
[714] 1 Chronicles 21:1
[715] Exodus 30:14

David's!) **11** And when David arose in the morning, the word of the Lord came to the prophet Gad, David's seer, saying, **12** "Go and say to David, *(Just "David". Not "David my servant" as it had been before. If we oppose God, he will oppose us.)* 'Thus says the Lord, Three things I offer you. Choose one of them, that I may do it to you.'"

13 So Gad came to David and told him, and said to him, "Shall three years of famine come to you in your land? Or will you flee three months before your foes while they pursue you? Or shall there be three days' pestilence in your land? Now consider, and decide what answer I shall return to him who sent me." **14** Then David said to Gad, "I am in great distress. Let us fall into the hand of the Lord, for his mercy is great; but let me not fall into the hand of man." *(He had a hard decision, but he chose wisely. David showed that for all his straying from the will of God, he still had a solid and loving trust in the Lord his God. A child of God always feels safest in his Father's hands.)*

15 So the Lord sent a pestilence on Israel from the morning until the appointed time. And there died of the people from Dan to Beersheba 70,000 men.

OCTOBER 7

It Is Enough; Now Stay Your Hand[716]

David's pride tempted him to number the people. Seventy-thousand of those men were swept away by the plague God sent by his angel.

2 Samuel 24:16-25

16 And when the angel stretched out his hand toward Jerusalem to destroy it, the Lord relented from the calamity and said to the angel who was working destruction among the people, "It is enough; now stay your hand." And the angel of the Lord was by the threshing floor of Araunah the Jebusite. *(The angel of pestilence appeared in visible form. Actually being able to see the angel added special terror to the judgment. What frightening thoughts must have entered their minds as they saw the destroyer unsheathe his sword to strike the empire's capital city.)* **17** Then David spoke to the Lord when he saw the angel who was striking the people, and said, "Behold, I have sinned, and I have done wickedly. But these sheep, what have they done? Please let your hand be against me and against my father's house."

These were brave and well spoken words. Like a true patriot, the king is moved by the misery of his subjects. Like the father of his country, he would rather perish himself than see Israel in such great distress. These people had often acted like wolves to him, but he forgets all their injuries and calls them sheep. They had been guilty of a thousand sins, but, in his zeal for their safety, he makes himself out to be a far greater sinner. He would rather have the punishment fall on him and his, than on those who had sinned against him. In the same way, "Our Lord Jesus, the Great Shepherd of the sheep"[717] stands between the destroying angel and his own redeemed. "If you seek me," he says, "let these men go."[718]

18 And Gad *(the prophet)* came that day to David and said to him, "Go up, raise an altar to the Lord on the threshing floor of Araunah the Jebusite." *(God held back the sword of the destroying angel at the very spot where his angel had held back Abraham from killing his son with a knife.)* **19** So David went up at Gad's word, as the Lord commanded. **20** And when Araunah looked down, he saw the king and his servants coming on toward him. And Araunah went out and paid homage to the king with his face to the ground.

21 And Araunah said, "Why has my lord the king come to his servant?" David said, "To buy the threshing floor from you, in order to build an altar to the Lord, that the plague may be averted from the people." **22** Then Araunah said to David, "Let my lord the king take and offer up what seems good to him. Here are the oxen for the burnt offering and the threshing sledges and the yokes of the oxen for the wood. **23** All this, O king, Araunah gives to the king." And

---

[716] 2 Samuel 24:16
[717] Hebrews 13:20
[718] John 18:8

Araunah said to the king, "May the LORD your God accept you." **24** But the king said to Araunah, "No, but I will buy it from you for a price. I will not offer burnt offerings to the LORD my God that cost me nothing." So David bought the threshing floor and the oxen for fifty shekels of silver.

Here we have two generous spirits entering into holy competition. One hardly knows who to admire most. True devotion is never stingy. For godly people, the more costly service to God is, the sweeter it is. When giving to God, nothing is too precious. The cost of the gift is not to be thought about when the gift is for him. Some only give to God what they can collect from other people. Our gifts should be from what we actually possess.

25 And David built there an altar to the LORD and offered burnt offerings and peace offerings. So the LORD responded to the plea for the land, and the plague was averted from Israel.

The hill where this threshing floor was located became known as Mount Zion, where Solomon built the temple of the Lord. The temple is a picture of Zion, the church of God, which was also established on a hill of sacrifice. Spiritual Zion, the church of God, is a living memorial in praise of the mercy of God that spared his people. It is where the sword of justice is forever sheathed. Have we come to Mount Zion? Are we safe in the precious blood of sprinkling? These are extremely serious questions that must be answered. Each one of us will one day be required to answer them before the great heart-searching God of heaven.

OCTOBER 8
The LORD Has Chosen Zion[719]

Psalm 132

This psalm brings us to the close of David's active life. It introduces us to his last thoughts and concerns. He had a strong desire to see the temple built on the holy spot where the Lord stopped the angel that brought the plague against Israel. He repeats the story of his longstanding hope to build a house for the Lord. Then he talks about the covenant[720] that the Lord, in his mercy, made with his servant.

1 Remember, O LORD, in David's favor,
    all the hardships he endured,

David endured many of these hardships for the Lord's sake and because he worshiped the Lord. He talks at length about his desire to build a temple for his God and asks the Lord to remember him.

2 how he swore to the LORD
    and vowed to the Mighty One of Jacob,
3 "I will not enter my house
    or get into my bed,
4 I will not give sleep to my eyes
    or slumber to my eyelids,
5 until I find a place for the LORD,
    a dwelling place for the Mighty One of Jacob."
6 Behold, we heard of it in Ephrathah;
    we found it in the fields of Jaar.

As a boy living in Bethlehem Ephrathah, he had heard about the ark and loved it. At last, he found it in the forest city of Kiriath-jearim. Happy are they who love the cause of God in their youth; who are determined to be with his church and his people, even if they are as hard to find as a small object in a great forest.

7 "Let us go to his dwelling place;
    let us worship at his footstool!"

David wanted to be where God was worshiped. Let us have the same holy desire. Even if the saints are few, poor, and despised, we would rather worship with them than with the great congregations of the worldly rich.

8 Arise, O LORD, and go to your resting place,
    you and the ark of your might.

This was the song of Israel when the ark was moved from place to place. We may use it in these days when we are pleading for the presence and power of the Lord in his church.

9 Let your priests be clothed with righteousness,

---

[719] Psalm 132:13

[720] *covenant* - A contract, promise, guarantee, pledge or agreement between two or more persons.

and let your saints shout for joy.
10 For the sake of your servant David,
do not turn away the face of your
anointed one.

Let this always be our prayer. Pray that the church will move forward and that the Lord will be praised by his people. David, as the anointed king, asked the Lord to not turn away from him. Let us ask the Father, for the sake of our anointed greater king Jesus, to not turn away from us.

11 The LORD swore to David a sure oath
from which he will not turn back:
"One of the sons of your body
I will set on your throne.
12 If your sons keep my covenant
and my testimonies that I shall teach
them,
their sons also forever
shall sit on your throne."
13 For the LORD has chosen Zion;
he has desired it for his dwelling place;
14 "This is my resting place forever;
here I will dwell, for I have desired it."

What God has chosen, let us choose. Where he dwells, let us dwell. Where he rests, let us rest. The church of God should be very dear to our hearts. We should be eager to unite with those who follow the Lord in all things. And when we are joined to their fellowship we should work toward building up the church by our prayers and efforts. What precious promises are these that follow!

15 "I will abundantly bless her provisions;
I will satisfy her poor with bread."

The gospel is our food. May the Lord give us grace to feast on this rich provision and make us poor in spirit so that this heavenly bread will always be sweet to us.

16 "Her priests I will clothe with salvation,
and her saints will shout for joy."

No one is so full of joy or so determined to show it as those who fellowship with God.

17 "There I will make a horn to sprout for
David;
I have prepared a lamp for my
anointed."

The glory of Jesus, the Son of David, is great in his church. He is the light of truth that shines from her among mankind.

18 "His enemies I will clothe with shame,
but on him his crown will shine."

King Jesus shall reign. Oh, to be found among his friends! Who would wish to wear the clothes of shame?

OCTOBER 9

The People Rejoiced Because They Had Given Willingly[721]

David never turned away from his desire to see a glorious temple built to the honor of the Lord his God. Although he was not allowed to build it himself, he worked hard to provide the materials for it and eagerly encouraged Solomon to follow through with the construction. At last the time came to gather the people and turn this great work over to his son.

1 Chronicles 29:1-9; 20-23

1 And David the king said to all the assembly, "Solomon my son, whom alone God has chosen, is young and inexperienced, and the work is great, for the palace will not be for man but for the LORD God. *(God must never be served in a careless manner. We should feel under obligation to do our best in all religious work, because the work is not for us, but for the Lord God.)* 2 So I have provided for the house of my God, so far as I was able, the gold for the things of gold, the silver for the things of silver, and the bronze for the things of bronze, the iron for the things of iron, and wood for the things of wood, besides great quantities of onyx and stones for setting, antimony,[722] colored stones, all sorts of precious stones and marble."

David had given a lot of thought about having the temple built and provided many things of the best quality. He has given us an excellent example of serving God with clear thinking and sacrificial giving.

3 "Moreover, in addition to all that I have provided for the holy house, I have a treasure

---
[721] 1 Chronicles 29:9
[722] *antimony* - A shiny, silvery white metal often mixed with other metals to produce a higher quality metal.

of my own of gold and silver, and because of my devotion to the house of my God I give it to the house of my God: ⁴ 3,000 talents (*about 112 tons*) of gold, of the gold of Ophir, and 7,000 talents (*about 262 tons*) of refined silver, for overlaying the walls of the house, ⁵ and for all the work to be done by craftsmen, gold for the things of gold and silver for the things of silver. Who then will offer willingly, consecrating himself today to the Lord?" *(Those who give freely have a clear conscience to ask others to give. Those who ask others to give but never contribute are inconsistent.)*

⁶ Then the leaders of fathers' houses made their freewill offerings, as did also the leaders of the tribes, the commanders of thousands and of hundreds, and the officers over the king's work. ⁷ They gave for the service of the house of God 5,000 talents (*about 187 tons*) and 10,000 darics (*about 156 pounds*) of gold, 10,000 talents (*about 375 tons*) of silver, 18,000 talents (*about 675 tons*) of bronze and 100,000 talents (*about 3,750 tons*) of iron. ⁸ And whoever had precious stones gave them to the treasury of the house of the Lord, in the care of Jehiel the Gershonite.

David kept a very accurate record of what was given. God's business should be done in a well organized way. Church funds should be very carefully accounted for. This also helps to prevent someone from stealing from the church treasury and bringing disgrace on God's name.

⁹ Then the people rejoiced because they had given willingly, for with a whole heart they had offered freely to the Lord. David the king also rejoiced greatly.

The joy of giving to the Lord is a very great one. Angels might well envy us such happiness.

²⁰ Then David said to all the assembly, "Bless the Lord your God." And all the assembly blessed the Lord, the God of their fathers, and bowed their heads and paid homage to the Lord and to the king. *(They gave worship to God and respectful honor to the king.)* ²¹ And they offered sacrifices to the Lord, and on the next day offered burnt offerings to the Lord, 1,000 bulls, 1,000 rams, and 1,000 lambs, with their drink offerings, and sacrifices in abundance for all Israel. *(The threshing floor of Araunah was saturated with blood. The foundation of the temple was built on the blood of sacrifice. Happy are those who are built on the substitutionary death of Jesus.)* ²² And they ate and drank before the Lord on that day with great gladness. *(Our sacred worship should not be done in sadness. It should be considered a special celebration.)*

And they made Solomon the son of David king the second time, and they anointed him as prince for the Lord, and Zadok as priest.

²³ Then Solomon sat on the throne of the Lord as king in place of David his father, And he prospered, and all Israel obeyed him.

For a while, Solomon acted as his father's representative, then he succeeded him with the approval of the whole nation.

October 10

His Name Shall Endure…As Long As the Sun[723]

Psalm 72

David wrote this psalm about his son Solomon, but it applies even more to our Lord Jesus Christ.

1 Give the king your justice, O God,
  and your righteousness to the royal son!
2 May he judge your people with righteousness,
  and your poor with justice!
3 Let the mountains bear prosperity for the people,
  and the hills, in righteousness!
4 May he defend the cause of the poor of the people,
  give deliverance to the children of the needy,
  and crush the oppressor!
5 May they fear you while the sun endures,
  and as long as the moon, throughout all generations!
6 May he be like rain that falls on the mown grass,
  like showers that water the earth!
7 In his days may the righteous flourish,

---
[723] Psalm 72:17

and peace abound, till the moon be no
more!
8 May he have dominion from sea to sea,
and from the River to the ends of the
earth!
9 May desert tribes bow down before him
and his enemies lick the dust!
10 May the kings of Tarshish and of the
coastlands
render him tribute;
may the kings of Sheba and Seba
bring gifts!
11 May all kings fall down before him,
all nations serve him!
12 For he delivers the needy when he calls,
the poor and him who has no helper.
13 He has pity on the weak and the needy,
and saves the lives of the needy.
14 From oppression and violence he redeems
their life,
and precious is their blood in his sight.
15 Long may he live;
may gold of Sheba be given to him!
May prayer be made for him continually,
and blessings invoked for him all the
day!
16 May there be abundance of grain in the
land;
on the tops of the mountains may it
wave;
may its fruit be like Lebanon;
and may people blossom in the cities
like the grass of the field!
17 May his name endure forever,
his fame continue as long as the sun!
May people be blessed in him,
all nations call him blessed!
18 Blessed be the LORD, the God of Israel,
who alone does wondrous things.
19 Blessed be his glorious name forever;
may the whole earth be filled with his
glory!
Amen and Amen!
20 The prayers of David, the son of Jesse, are
ended.

David's heart was glad to look ahead to the glory his son Solomon would have as king. But he rejoiced even more as his prophetic eye looked to the greater reign of the Messiah. At the second coming of the *Lord Jesus, this psalm will have a grand fulfillment. Until then, our job is to pray and work for the increase of his kingdom. If anything can warm the heart of the Christian, it is knowing the Redeemer will reign over everything and his enemies cannot stop it. The Lord Jehovah has promised to give our Lord Jesus the nations for his inheritance.[724] His almighty power and faithfulness stand behind that promise and therefore, we may rest fully assured that it will be done. Jesus has fought the fight and won the victory. His reward from the Father is great! There is no reason for hopelessness or fear. God is on our side and he has sworn to give the victory. There is no danger that he will be defeated. David's wishes had reached their summit. He had nothing more to ask for.*

He ended his prayers when he prayed for the filling of the whole earth with Messiah's glory. With this prayer on his lips he is content to die. In the presence of his royal Messiah he is no longer King David, but only "the son of Jesse." He is only too happy to become nothing before the ruler of the universe. His believing eyes see Jesus reigning, like the sun, filled all around with light. His heart rejoiced. He felt like that holy man, Simeon, when he said, "Lord, now you are letting your servant depart in peace, for my eyes have seen your salvation."[725] May our one great wish be like David's— that the glorious name of the Lord be blessed forever and the whole earth be filled with his glory.

OCTOBER 11

Bless the LORD, O My Soul[726]

Before we proceed to the reign of Solomon, we must read two or three of David's most familiar psalms. We only regret that we do not have time to read them all in our family worship. However, in our private devotions, we should study every one. They are all more precious than pure gold. Today, we will read one of the sweetest and best known.

---

[724] Psalm 2:8
[725] From Luke 2:29 30
[726] Psalm 103:1

Psalm 103

OF DAVID.

1 Bless the LORD, O my soul,
and all that is within me,
bless his holy name!

Music from the heart is the most precious music. When we praise the Lord it should rise up from deep within us.

2 Bless the LORD, O my soul,
and forget not all his benefits,

We have poor memories when it comes to good things. Still, let us try to remember them when we praise the Lord.

3 who forgives all your iniquity,
who heals all your diseases,
4 who redeems your life from the pit,
who crowns you with steadfast love and mercy,
5 who satisfies you with good
so that your youth is renewed like the eagle's.

The sweet singer threads a few of the best pearls of mercy on the string of memory, then places them around the neck of gratitude, where they sparkle as she sings the joyful praises of her God.

6 The LORD works righteousness
and justice for all who are oppressed.

No person in need will ever plead their case to the Lord and be disappointed. Woe to those who oppress the poor.

7 He made known his ways to Moses,
his acts to the people of Israel.
8 The LORD is merciful and gracious,
slow to anger and abounding in steadfast love.
9 He will not always chide,
nor will he keep his anger forever.

His very love will cause him to chasten[727] us at times, but the hand of discipline is soon withdrawn.

10 He does not deal with us according to our sins,
nor repay us according to our iniquities.
11 For as high as the heavens are above the earth,
so great is his steadfast love toward those who fear him;
12 as far as the east is from the west,
so far does he remove our transgressions from us.

What a glorious fact. The east is infinitely distant from the west and so our sin is removed an infinite distance from us. In fact, it is washed away. It disappears and is forgotten forever.

13 As a father shows compassion to his children,
so the LORD shows compassion to those who fear him.

At their best, children need their father's compassion. At their strongest, they are defective and weak.

14 For he knows our frame;
he remembers that we are dust.

We are not iron, and not even clay, but dust held together by a continuous miracle.

15 As for man, his days are like grass;
he flourishes like a flower of the field;
16 for the wind passes over it, and it is gone,
and its place knows it no more.
17 But the steadfast love of the LORD is from everlasting to everlasting on those who fear him,
and his righteousness to children's children,
18 to those who keep his covenant
and remember to do his commandments.

Children who reject the Lord will not be saved because their parents are. Living unsaved in a Christian home will only increase the judgment against them. Their parents cannot remove their guilt. They must accept the Lord's promise for themselves personally or they will have no place in heaven.

19 The LORD has established his throne in the heavens,
and his kingdom rules over all.
20 Bless the LORD, O you his angels,
you mighty ones who do his word,
obeying the voice of his word!
21 Bless the LORD, all his hosts,
his ministers, who do his will!
22 Bless the LORD, all his works,

---

[727] *chasten, chastening* or *chastisement* - The act of discipline which may include scolding, criticizing or pain inflicted for the purpose of correction or moral improvement.

in all places of his dominion.
Bless the L ORD, O my soul!

The psalmist was so full of praise that he wanted all of creation to join him in glorifying the Lord. But he did not forget that the most important thing is that our own soul adores the Lord. He concludes, as all good composers do, with his main point. Let our motto be today and every day, "Bless the Lord, O my soul."

OCTOBER 12

O LORD My God, You Are Very Great![728]

This is another of David's grandest psalms. Our space forces us to include only a few comments.

Psalm 104

1 Bless the LORD, O my soul!
   O LORD my God, you are very great!
   You are clothed with splendor and majesty,
2 covering yourself with light as with a garment,
   stretching out the heavens like a tent.
3 He lays the beams of his chambers on the waters;
   he makes the clouds his chariot;
   he rides on the wings of the wind;
4 he makes his messengers winds,
   his ministers a flaming fire.
5 He set the earth on its foundations,
   so that it should never be moved.
6 You covered it with the deep as with a garment;
   the waters stood above the mountains.

He is probably referring to the great flood of Noah's day.

7 At your rebuke they fled;
   at the sound of your thunder they took to flight.
8 The mountains rose, the valleys sank down

The force of the water was so great that mountains were pushed upwards, causing valleys to sink lower.

   to the place that you appointed for them.
9 You set a boundary that they may not pass,
   so that they might not again cover the earth.
10 You make springs gush forth in the valleys;
   they flow between the hills;
11 they give drink to every beast of the field;
   the wild donkeys quench their thirst.
12 Beside them the birds of the heavens dwell;
   they sing among the branches.
13 From your lofty abode you water the mountains;
   the earth is satisfied with the fruit of your work.
14 You cause the grass to grow for the livestock
   and plants for man to cultivate,
   that he may bring forth food from the earth
15 and wine to gladden the heart of man,
   oil to make his face shine
   and bread to strengthen man's heart.
16 The trees of the LORD are watered abundantly,
   the cedars of Lebanon that he planted.
17 In them the birds build their nests;
   the stork has her home in the fir trees.
18 The high mountains are for the wild goats;
   the rocks are a refuge for the rock badgers.

Each place has its creature and each creature its place. Even the loneliest spots on earth abound with wildlife.

19 He made the moon to mark the seasons;
   the sun knows its time for setting.
20 You make darkness, and it is night,
   when all the beasts of the forest creep about.
21 The young lions roar for their prey,
   seeking their food from God.
22 When the sun rises, they steal away
   and lie down in their dens.
23 Man goes out to his work
   and to his labor until the evening.

---

[728] Psalm 104:1

Night and day each have their purpose. The wheels of providence[729] never stand still.

24 O Lord, how manifold are your works!
   In wisdom have you made them all;
   the earth is full of your creatures.
25 Here is the sea, great and wide,
   which teems with creatures innumerable,
   living things both small and great.
26 There go the ships,
   and Leviathan, which you formed to play in it.
27 These all look to you,
   to give them their food in due season.
28 When you give it to them, they gather it up;
   when you open your hand, they are filled with good things.
29 When you hide your face, they are dismayed;
   when you take away their breath, they die
   and return to their dust.
30 When you send forth your Spirit, they are created,
   and you renew the face of the ground.

God oversees all things, great or small. He has not left the world to mere laws and forces of nature. He is always working everywhere. Let us see his hand in all things and adore him.

31 May the glory of the Lord endure forever;
   may the Lord rejoice in his works,

If the Lord rejoices in his works, we would not be wise to close our eyes to nature's beauties or think they just happened by some huge accident.

32 who looks on the earth and it trembles,
   who touches the mountains and they smoke!
33 I will sing to the Lord as long as I live;
   I will sing praise to my God while I have being.
34 May my meditation be pleasing to him,
   for I rejoice in the Lord.
35 Let sinners be consumed from the earth,
   and let the wicked be no more!

For they alone damage creation and spoil the Maker's handiwork.

   Bless the Lord, O my soul!
   Praise the Lord!

October 13
Wait In Silence For God Alone[730]

This psalm is very typical of David. We are in the habit of calling it the Only Psalm, because it uses the word "only" or "alone" so often. David rejoiced to place his trust in God "only."

Psalm 62

1 For God alone *(or, "for God only")* my soul waits in silence;
   from him comes my salvation.

Our salvation comes to us only from the Lord. Therefore we should wait on or depend on him alone. If depending on God is worship, then depending on anything in creation is idolatry. If depending on God only is true faith, then thinking we need others to help us is reckless unbelief. Very few of us avoid this evil way of thinking and really depend on God only.

2 He only is my rock and my salvation,
   my fortress; I shall not be greatly shaken.

Shaken about, but not shaken off our foundation. Moved like a ship at anchor, which swings with the tide, but is not swept away by the current. Nothing keeps the soul secure like a faith that depends on God only. Faith stands alone. Faith is the only string in our bow, the one pillar for our house.

3 How long will all of you attack a man to batter him.
   like a leaning wall, a tottering fence?
4 They only plan to thrust him down from his high position.
   They take pleasure in falsehood.
   They bless with their mouths,
   but inwardly they curse.   *Selah*

The world is full of flatterers, but they secretly plan against our success. Let us run quickly away from them, to the only certain

---

[729] *Providence* - Usually, when used with a capital "P" it refers to God; when used with a lower case "p", it refers to God's will, his divine intervention, and his predetermination (predestination).

[730] From Psalm 62:5

hope of the saints. "If God is for us, who can be against us?"[731]

⁵ For God alone, O my soul, wait in silence,
   for my hope is from him.

Knock at no other door except that of your God. God is one. Let your hopes look toward him only. The eye that sees only God will be filled with the light of understanding.

⁶ He only is my rock and my salvation,
   my fortress; I shall not be shaken.
⁷ On God rests my salvation and my glory;
   my mighty rock, my refuge is God.

Notice how David brands his own initials on every title he gives to God. He rejoices in my hope, my rock, my salvation, my glory, and so on. There are seven my's in two verses and there can never be too many. The faith that applies divine blessings personally is the faith we all need.

⁸ Trust in him at all times, O people;
   pour out your heart before him;
   God is a refuge for us.   Selah

God has shown the fullness of his love to us. We should show our emptiness to him. Turn your soul upside down in his presence and let your innermost thoughts, desires, sorrows and sins be poured out like water. To keep our misery to our self just increases our hopelessness. The end of our deep distress is close when we freely acknowledge it to the Lord.

⁹ Those of low estate are but a breath;
   those of high estate are a delusion;
   in the balances they go up;
   they are together lighter than a breath.

Humans, whether great of small, are still only humans, and humans are dust. To trust what the majority thinks is foolishness, to depend on the advice of the famous is madness. To be controlled by the Lord's counsel is the only sanity.

¹⁰ Put no trust in extortion;
    set no vain hopes on robbery;
    if riches increase, set not your heart on them.

This is a difficult rule. Worldly wealth is a slimy thing and is too likely to stick to the heart. Maybe this is why so many of the saints are poor. Perhaps the Lord is protecting them from being tempted by growing riches. Our hope must be in God alone. Placing our confidence in the treasures of this life is as hopeless as trying to bottle the wind.

¹¹ Once God has spoken;
    twice have I heard this:
    that power belongs to God,

Do not look to people or their money for power. God is all powerful. Those who are wise will look only to him for help.

¹² and that to you, O Lord, belongs steadfast love.
   For you will render to a man
     according to his work.

The Lord gives us the strength we need for each day. All power is his and he will provide as much as our work requires. Let us go to God for our needs and to him only.

OCTOBER 14

Give Your Servant Therefore An Understanding Mind[732]

We will now return to the historical record with the beginning of the reign of Solomon.

1 Kings 3:1; 3-15

¹ Solomon made a marriage alliance with Pharaoh king of Egypt. He took Pharaoh's daughter and brought her into the city of David until he had finished building his own house and the house of the LORD and the wall around Jerusalem. *(A questionable beginning. A step full of danger.)*

³ Solomon loved the LORD, walking in the statutes of David his father, only he sacrificed and made offerings at the high places. *(Worshiping at the high places was expressly forbidden.[733] But the Lord saw that Solomon's heart was right and did not treat him harshly in this matter.)* ⁴ And the king went to Gibeon to sacrifice there, for that was the great high place. Solomon used to offer a thousand burnt offerings on that altar. ⁵ At Gibeon the LORD appeared to Solomon in a dream by night, and God said, "Ask what I shall give you." *(Solomon worships*

---
[731] Romans 8:31
[732] 1 Kings 3:9
[733] Deuteronomy 12:1-7

God by day and God appears to Solomon by night. The night must be happy when the day has been holy. The king had offered a thousand burnt sacrifices to God and now the Lord rewards him in a divine way with a wonderful gift. "Ask what I shall give you." God is no less generous to each of us today, for Jesus has said, "Whatever you ask of the Father in my name, he will give it to you."[734])

6 And Solomon said, "You have shown great and steadfast love to your servant David my father, because he walked before you in faithfulness, in righteousness, and in uprightness of heart toward you. And you have kept for him this great and steadfast love and have given him a son to sit on his throne this day. **7** And now, O Lord my God, you have made your servant king in place of David my father, although I am but a little child. I do not know how to go out or come in. **8** And your servant is in the midst of your people whom you have chosen, a great people, too many to be numbered or counted for multitude. **9** Give your servant therefore an understanding mind to govern your people, that I may discern between good and evil, for who is able to govern this your great people?"

It was a wise choice to choose wisdom. Young Solomon was already wise when he asked the Lord for wisdom. He did not ask for grace. That would have been the best gift of all. But he did choose the second best and his reasons for asking for wisdom should be applauded. He must have given this a lot of thought when he was awake to make such an excellent decision in his sleep.

10 It pleased the Lord that Solomon had asked this. **11** And God said to him, "Because you have asked this, and have not asked for yourself long life or riches or the life of your enemies, but have asked for yourself understanding to discern what is right, **12** behold, I now do according to your word. Behold, I give you a wise and discerning mind, so that none like you has been before you and none like you shall arise after you. **13** I give you also what you have not asked, both riches and honor, so that no other king shall compare with you, all your days. *(The greater includes the less. Wealth and honor may not bring wisdom, but wisdom brings wealth and honor. Let us first seek the kingdom of God and his righteousness, and all these things will be added to us.[735] Jesus Christ is infinite wisdom and is the choice of every believer.)* **14** And if you will walk in my ways, keeping my statutes and my commandments, as your father David walked, then I will lengthen your days."

15 And Solomon awoke, and behold, it was a dream. Then he came to Jerusalem and stood before the ark of the covenant of the Lord, and offered up burnt offerings and peace offerings, and made a feast for all his servants. *(Solomon showed his thankfulness by bringing his sacrifices to the right place—to Jerusalem. Our love to God should always lead us to pay closer attention to his commands. Solomon now had a spectacular life ahead of him and for many years he lived it in the right way. Those who begin life by seeking wisdom may expect success.)*

October 15

The Lord Reigns, Let the Earth Rejoice[736]

Solomon used his wisdom to bring great prosperity to his nation. Israel became a major center of trade and commerce. His royal government was conducted in a very expensive style.

1 Kings 4:22-34

22 Solomon's provision for one day was thirty cors *(over six tons)* of fine flour and sixty cors *(over twelve tons)*[737] of meal, **23** ten fat oxen, and twenty pasture-fed cattle, a hundred sheep, beside deer, gazelles, roebucks, and fattened fowl.

But what is this compared to what is piled high on the table of the King of kings from which all the saints are fed?

---

[734] John 16:23
[735] A reference to Matthew 6:33
[736] Psalm 97:1
[737] These are conservative estimates. The volume of a *cor* or *kor* is not certain.

24 For he had dominion over all the region west of the Euphrates from Tiphsah to Gaza, over all the kings west of the Euphrates. And he had peace on all sides around him. **25** And Judah and Israel lived in safety, from Dan even to Beersheba, every man under his vine and under his fig tree, all the days of Solomon. *(There was peace where Solomon ruled and there is peace that surpasses all understanding where Jesus reigns.)* **26** Solomon also had 40,000 stalls of horses for his chariots, and 12,000 horsemen. *(This was a forbidden luxury. The Hebrew kings were commanded not to acquire many horses.[738] Solomon was wrong to do this.)* **27** And those officers supplied provisions for King Solomon, and for all who came to King Solomon's table, each one in his month. They let nothing be lacking. **28** Barley also and straw for the horses and swift steeds they brought to the place where it was required, each according to his duty.

29 And God gave Solomon wisdom and understanding beyond measure, and breadth of mind like the sand on the seashore, **30** so that Solomon's wisdom surpassed the wisdom of all the people of the east and all the wisdom of Egypt. **31** For he was wiser than all other men, wiser than Ethan the Ezrahite, and Heman, Calcol, and Darda, the sons of Mahol, and his fame was in all the surrounding nations. **32** He also spoke 3,000 proverbs, and his songs were 1,005. **33** He spoke of trees, from the cedar that is in Lebanon to the hyssop that grows out of the wall. He spoke also of beasts, and of birds, and of reptiles, and of fish. **34** And people of all nations came to hear the wisdom of Solomon, and from all the kings of the earth, who had heard of his wisdom.

See how well the Lord fulfilled his promise. He gave him wisdom overflowing.

1 Kings 10:14-15; 18-23

14 Now the weight of gold that came to Solomon in one year was 666 talents *(about 25 tons)* of gold, **15** besides that which came from the explorers and from the business of the merchants, and from all the kings of the west and from the governors of the land. *(He built caravan rest stops and charged the merchants for their use. He also gained great wealth by buying the produce of the East, and selling it to the Western nations.)*

18 The king also made a great ivory throne and overlaid it with the finest gold. **19** The throne had six steps, and the throne had a round top, and on each side of the seat were armrests and two lions standing beside the armrests, **20** while twelve lions stood there, one on each end of a step on the six steps. The like of it was never made in any kingdom.

But how much more glorious will the throne of our Lord be in the day of his appearing?

21 All King Solomon's drinking vessels were of gold, and all the vessels of the House of the Forest of Lebanon were of pure gold. None were of silver; silver was not considered as anything in the days of Solomon. **22** For the king had a fleet of ships of Tarshish at sea with the fleet of Hiram. Once every three years the fleet of ships of Tarshish used to come bringing gold, silver, ivory, apes, and peacocks.

23 Thus King Solomon excelled all the kings of the earth in riches and in wisdom.

So again the promise was fulfilled and wealth followed wisdom. Who would not trust a God who is so faithful?

OCTOBER 16

We Are the Temple Of the Living God[739]

1 Kings 5:1-11; 13-18

1 Now Hiram king of Tyre sent his servants to Solomon when he heard that they had anointed him king in place of his father, for Hiram always loved David.

Close friends with a strong bond are rare. It was a happy thing for Solomon that his father passed on to him the love of such a useful ally.

2 And Solomon sent word to Hiram, **3** "You know that David my father could not build a house for the name of the Lord his God because of the warfare with which his

---

[738] Deuteronomy 17:16

[739] 2 Corinthians 6:16

enemies surrounded him, until the Lord put them under the soles of his feet. *(Like a good son who honored his father, he does not say that David could not build the temple because he had shed blood, but because he was busy with wars. We should always say the best things regarding our parents.)*

⁴ "But now the Lord my God has given me rest on every side. There is neither adversary nor misfortune. ⁵ And so I intend to build a house for the name of the Lord my God, as the Lord said to David my father, 'Your son, whom I will set on your throne in your place, shall build the house for my name.' ⁶ Now therefore command that cedars of Lebanon be cut for me. And my servants will join your servants, and I will pay you for your servants such wages as you set, for you know that there is no one among us who knows how to cut timber like the Sidonians." *(The tabernacle, which was temporary, was constructed by Jews only. But the temple, which was to be permanent, is not built without the help of Gentiles. Jews and Gentiles together make up the church that is the temple of God.)*

⁷ As soon as Hiram heard the words of Solomon, he rejoiced greatly and said, "Blessed be the Lord this day, who has given to David a wise son to be over this great people." ⁸ And Hiram sent to Solomon, saying, "I have heard the message that you have sent to me. I am ready to do all you desire in the matter of cedar and cypress timber. *(We should think very carefully about what we promise. Are we really willing and able to be true to our word? It is good when our hearts are full of liberality toward the work of God even after we have thoughtfully weighed the matter.)* ⁹ My servants shall bring it down to the sea from Lebanon, and I will make it into rafts to go by sea to the place you direct. And I will have them broken up there, and you shall receive it. And you shall meet my wishes by providing food for my household." *(Palestine was a fruitful agricultural country, so Solomon would do Hiram a service by paying him from the produce of the land.)*

¹⁰ So Hiram supplied Solomon with all the timber of cedar and cypress that he desired, *(When God's house is to be built, he will certainly find everything he needs for it.)* ¹¹ while Solomon gave Hiram 20,000 cors *(a little less than 2,000 tons)* of wheat as food for his household, and 20,000 cors *(over one million gallons)* of beaten oil. Solomon gave this to Hiram year by year.

¹³ King Solomon drafted forced labor out of all Israel, and the draft numbered 30,000 men. ¹⁴ And he sent them to Lebanon, 10,000 a month in shifts. They would be a month in Lebanon and two months at home. Adoniram was in charge of the draft. ¹⁵ Solomon also had 70,000 burden-bearers and 80,000 stonecutters in the hill country, ¹⁶ besides Solomon's 3,300 chief officers who were over the work, who had charge of the people who carried on the work. ¹⁷ At the king's command they quarried out great, costly stones in order to lay the foundation of the house with dressed stones.

Even the foundation stones were not rugged and rough, but cut and expensive. God would have everything that is done for him done well. He does not care so much for that which pleases human eyes; his delight is with the beauty of those living stones of his spiritual temple that are hidden from view.

¹⁸ So Solomon's builders and Hiram's builders and the men of Gebal did the cutting and prepared the timber and the stone to build the house. *(The stones and timbers arrived at the worksite already prepared. So, "When the house was built, it was with stone prepared at the quarry, so that neither hammer nor axe nor any tool of iron was heard in the house while it was being built."[740] Here below, the preparing us for heaven is a work of toil and noise, but in heaven all will be rest and quietness. May the Lord prepare us to be built into his temple above.)*

---

[740] 1 King 6:7

OCTOBER 17

You Yourselves Like Living Stones Are Being Built Up As a Spiritual House[741]

2 Chronicles 3

¹Then Solomon began to build the house of the LORD in Jerusalem on Mount Moriah, where the LORD had appeared to David his father, at the place that David had appointed, on the threshing floor of Ornan the Jebusite.

This was the place where Abraham offered up Isaac and near the spot where the Lord Jesus suffered as the Lamb that God had provided for sacrifice. It is a place that reminds us of sacrifice and atonement.[742] As the living temple of God, the Church should be a constant reminder of the sacrifice of Jesus Christ and the atonement he purchased for lost sinners.

²He began to build in the second month of the fourth year of his reign. ³These are Solomon's measurements for building the house of God: the length, in cubits of the old standard, was sixty cubits *(about ninety feet)*, and the breadth twenty cubits *(about thirty feet)*. ⁴The vestibule in front of the nave of the house was twenty cubits long, equal to the width of the house, and its height was 120 cubits *(about 180 feet)*. He overlaid it on the inside with pure gold. ⁵The nave he lined with cypress and covered it with fine gold and made palms and chains on it. ⁶He adorned the house with settings of precious stones. The gold was gold of Parvaim. *(The woodwork was expensive, but it was covered with pure gold of the best kind and then decorated with precious stones. The Lord's church is also built at a huge cost, because it is very precious in his eyes.)* ⁷So he lined the house with gold—its beams, its thresholds, its walls, and its doors—and he carved cherubim on the walls.

⁸And he made the Most Holy Place. Its length, corresponding to the breadth of the house, was twenty cubits, and its breadth was twenty cubits. He overlaid it with 600 talents *(over 20 tons)* of fine gold. ⁹The weight of gold for the nails was fifty shekels *(a little over one pound of gold for each nail)*. And he overlaid the upper chambers with gold.

¹⁰In the Most Holy Place he made two cherubim of wood and overlaid them with gold. ¹¹The wings of the cherubim together extended twenty cubits: one wing of the one, of five cubits *(about seven feet)*, touched the wall of the house, and its other wing, of five cubits, touched the wing of the other cherub, ¹²and of this cherub, one wing, of five cubits, touched the wall of the house, and the other wing, also of five cubits, was joined to the wing of the first cherub. ¹³The wings of these cherubim extended twenty cubits *(about thirty feet)*. The cherubim stood on their feet, facing the nave.

Did these symbolize angels? We think so. They are here represented as standing on their feet as servants and not as sitting on thrones like gods. We do not worship angels, but we worship with angels, joining in their holy song of praise to the Lord of all.

¹⁴And he made the veil of blue and purple and crimson fabrics and fine linen, and he worked cherubim on it. *(This curtain hid the Most Holy Place. The gospel of Christ had not been made clear yet.)*

¹⁵In front of the house he made two pillars thirty-five cubits *(about fifty-two feet)* high, with a capital of five cubits on the top of each. ¹⁶He made chains like a necklace and put them on the tops of the pillars, and made a hundred pomegranates and put them on the chains. ¹⁷He set up the pillars in front of the temple, one on the south, the other on the north; that on the south he called Jachin, *(the Lord will establish)* and that on the north Boaz *(in him is strength)*.

These pillars were enormous columns intended for glory and for beauty. The Church is the greatest design of the Great Architect. Holy Scripture gives us a full description of the various parts of the temple and the different pieces of furniture. Everything was decided by God and is full of instruction. Those seeing the completed

---

[741] 1 Peter 2:5
[742] *atonement* - A payment made to satisfy someone who has been wronged. An animal sacrificed as an offering to restore a relationship. Jesus is the Lamb of God and offered himself as a sacrifice to restore the relationship between God and man that was broken when Adam sinned in the Garden of Eden.

temple must have thought it was magnificent beyond compare.

OCTOBER 18
God Has Blessed You Forever[743]
Psalm 45

In this psalm, Solomon is just visible in the background as a type,[744] but the Lord Jesus fills the foreground in the fullness of loveliness and majesty.

1   My heart overflows with a pleasing theme;
      I address my verses to the king;
      my tongue is like the pen of a ready scribe

No subject can be as good as that which bubbles up from a warm heart and is about the King of saints. The psalmist decided to speak only from personal experience. He believed he could use his ability as a successful writer to deliver his message completely and with wisdom. Oh to have warm hearts whenever Jesus is the theme! Are we able to speak about King Jesus from personal experience? The question deserves an answer.

2   You are the most handsome of the sons of men;
      grace is poured upon your lips;
      therefore God has blessed you forever.

He speaks as if he had seen the Well-beloved One and the sight gives the psalmist great pleasure. He hears him speak and adores him. We will do the same if Jesus shows himself to us.

3   Gird your sword on your thigh, O mighty one,
      in your splendor and majesty!
4   In your majesty ride out victoriously
      for the cause of truth and meekness and righteousness;
      let your right hand teach you awesome deeds!

This should be our prayer: "Oh Immanuel, the mighty prince, display your power, conquer people and make them your servants. Oh most sweet Prince, as Solomon reigned over a wide-ranging kingdom, may you also."

5   Your arrows are sharp
      in the heart of the king's enemies;
      the peoples fall under you.

His gospel pierces the hearts of people and they surrender to his love.

6   Your throne, O God, is forever and ever.
      The scepter of your kingdom is a scepter of uprightness;
7   you have loved righteousness and hated wickedness.
    Therefore God, your God, has anointed you
      with the oil of gladness beyond your companions;

Here we see the divine and human natures combined in one person. As man, the Lord Jesus is like other men. But as God, his throne is for forever and ever. Let us make no mistake on this essential point and believe in Jesus as both God and man.

8   your robes are all fragrant with myrrh and aloes and cassia.
    From ivory palaces stringed instruments make you glad;
9   daughters of kings are among your ladies of honor;
      at your right hand stands the queen in gold of Ophir.

The church is dressed in the best of the best, the righteousness of God. How lovely she is in the loveliness of Jesus!

10 Hear, O daughter, and consider and incline your ear:
      forget your people and your father's house,
11   and the king will desire your beauty.
    Since he is your lord, bow to him.

The church must not be worldly. The kingdom of God must be her first priority. This must be the case for each one of us. And then, as the next verse teaches, all other things will be given to us.

12 The people of Tyre will seek your favor with gifts,
      the richest of the people.

---

[743] Psalm 45:2
[744] *type* - A type is something that represents something else, usually in the future. In this case, King Solomon represents, pictures, or, is a type of, the future King Jesus.

13 All glorious is the princess in her chamber, with robes interwoven with gold.
14 In many-colored robes she is led to the king,
    with her virgin companions following behind her.
15 With joy and gladness they are led along as they enter the palace of the king.
16 In place of your fathers shall be your sons; you will make them princes in all the earth.

May this household have many generations of those who are saved by grace. May holy children follow godly parents. May the King of our hearts have servants in this family as long as the world stands.

17 I will cause your name to be remembered in all generations;
    therefore nations will praise you forever and ever.

Jesus can never be forgotten. Solomon died, but Jesus lives on and reigns on, and will forever and ever. Blessed be his name.

OCTOBER 19

Will God Indeed Dwell On the Earth?[745]

1 Kings 8:1-6; 10-11; 22-30

1 Then Solomon assembled the elders of Israel and all the heads of the tribes, the leaders of the fathers' houses of the people of Israel, before King Solomon in Jerusalem, to bring up the ark of the covenant of the LORD out of the city of David, which is Zion.

Solomon prepared the temple before he brought the ark to it. An old writer observes that before we pray, we should prepare our heart as a temple of the Lord.

2 And all the men of Israel assembled to King Solomon at the feast in the month Ethanim, which is the seventh month. 3 And all the elders of Israel came, and the priests took up the ark. 4 And they brought up the ark of the LORD, the tent of meeting, and all the holy vessels that were in the tent; the priests and the Levites brought them up. 5 And King Solomon and all the congregation of Israel, who had assembled before him, were with him before the ark, sacrificing so many sheep and oxen that they could not be counted or numbered. *(They stopped at different spots along the way and offered sacrifices. Josephus[746] tells us, "The ground was moist with drink-offerings and sacrifices." It was the year of jubilee and the time of the feast of tabernacles. The crowds were great and the joy overflowing. When shall we see the whole earth celebrating and adoring the risen Savior?)* 6 Then the priests brought the ark of the covenant of the LORD to its place in the inner sanctuary of the house, in the Most Holy Place, underneath the wings of the cherubim.

10 And when the priests came out of the Holy Place, a cloud filled the house of the LORD, 11 so that the priests could not stand to minister because of the cloud, for the glory of the LORD filled the house of the LORD. *(The cloudy pillar was the sign that God was present. It filled the sanctuary to show that the Lord accepted the temple. We do not know whether the cloud was bright and awe-inspiring or dark and threatening. Either way, it overwhelmed the minds of the priests. It is a glorious thing to be so overcome by the presence of the Lord among his people that all our works become as nothing and we feel that we can no longer "stand to minister," because the Lord himself is there.)*

22 Then Solomon stood before the altar of the LORD in the presence of all the assembly of Israel and spread out his hands toward heaven, *(He was not a priest and therefore could not present the sacrifices on the altar. But as the king, he represented the nation and it was proper for him to offer up the national prayer.)* 23 and said, "O LORD, God of Israel, there is no God like you, in heaven above or on earth beneath, keeping covenant and showing steadfast love to your servants who walk before you with all their heart, 24 you have kept with your servant David my father what you declared to him. You spoke with your mouth, and with your hand have fulfilled it this day." *(Notice how he dwells*

---

[745] 1 Kings 8:27

[746] Flavius Josephus was a Jewish historian who lived during the first century A.D.

on the covenant. *Praying is more delightful when we can remind God of his promises.)*

25 "Now therefore, O Lord, God of Israel, keep for your servant David my father what you have promised him, saying, 'You shall not lack a man to sit before me on the throne of Israel, if only your sons pay close attention to their way, to walk before me as you have walked before me.' **26** Now therefore, O God of Israel, let your word be confirmed, which you have spoken to your servant David my father.

27 "But will God indeed dwell on the earth? Behold, heaven and the highest heaven cannot contain you; how much less this house that I have built! *(So even in the dim light of Judaism it was understood that the Lord does not live in temples made with hands. How astonishing it is that under the gospel people still cling to the idea of holy places.)* **28** Yet have regard to the prayer of your servant and to his pleas, O Lord my God, listening to the cry and to the prayer that your servant prays before you this day, **29** that your eyes may be open night and day toward this house, the place of which you have said, 'My name shall be there,' that you may listen to the prayer that your servant offers toward this place. **30** And listen to the plea of your servant and of your people Israel, when they pray toward this place. And listen in heaven your dwelling place, and when you hear, forgive."

In our highest joys we still have need to pray, "Forgive." Our hearts are out of order when that word does not rise to our lips. Let us plead with God to bless us throughout our lives and always to forgive.

October 20

Blessed Are Those Who Dwell In Your House[747]

The dedication of Solomon's temple makes us think about his father's delightful psalm, in which he expressed his love of worshiping the Lord his God.

Psalm 84

1 How lovely is your dwelling place,
O Lord of hosts!

The gathering for divine worship is more delightful than the tongue can describe. It is delightful to anticipate, delightful at the time and delightful to remember. Under heaven, no place is so heavenly as the church of the living God.

2 My soul longs, yes, faints
for the courts of the Lord;
my heart and flesh sing for joy
to the living God.

Do we feel the same burning desire after God? If so, we will not need urging to attend his worship. Some people need to be coaxed to worship, but David is crying for it here. He did not need to hear the clanging of a church bell to call him to worship. He carried his own bell in his heart.

3 Even the sparrow finds a home,
and the swallow a nest for herself,
where she may lay her young,
at your altars, O Lord of hosts,
my King and my God.

He envied the little birds that built their nests near the tabernacle. When he was far away from the Lord's altars, he wished he had wings to fly to them, as the sparrows did, or build near them like the swallows did.

4 Blessed are those who dwell in your house,
ever singing your praise!   Selah

He wished he could be like the Levites who worked for the Lord in the service of the tabernacle. He thought that even those in the lowest positions would always be praising him. The joy of those living so close to the presence of God would never stop; their praises could be heard both day and night.

5 Blessed are those whose strength is in you,
in whose heart are the highways to Zion.

Or, "whose heart is to do your will." Only those who put their whole heart into worshiping the Lord find joy in it. Neither prayer, nor praise, nor the hearing of the word will benefit people who have left their hearts behind.

6 As they go through the Valley of Baca
they make it a place of springs;

---

[747] Psalm 84:4

the early rain also covers it with pools.

The worshipers who traveled a long distance to the temple found water even in the driest parts of their journey. Even their gloomy trials became delightful to them. They even made the uninhabited desert valleys to be as cheerful as the town water well where men and women would meet to talk about the day's news. There is no end to what holy fellowship and wholehearted praise can do.

7   They go from strength to strength;
      each one appears before God in Zion.

God's people continue on their way, grow stronger, and at last reach the end of their journey. They have an almighty Helper who will not allow them to fail.

8   O LORD God of hosts, hear my prayer;
      give ear, O God of Jacob!   *Selah*
9   Behold our shield, O God;
      look on the face of your anointed!
10 For a day in your courts is better
      than a thousand elsewhere.
    I would rather be a doorkeeper in the
          house of my God
      than dwell in the tents of wickedness.

The doorkeeper is the first to arrive and the last to leave. He gets less sympathy than anyone. Yet David would rather have the lowest job in God's house that the highest position in the tents of sin. Quaint old Secker says, "Happy are those persons who God will use as brooms to sweep out the dust from his temple or who are allowed to pull at an oar of the boat where Christ and his people are on board."[748]

11 For the LORD God is a sun and shield;
      the LORD bestows favor and honor.
    No good thing does he withhold
      from those who walk uprightly.

What a great promise, or rather, what a great set of promises! Here we have all we need for all time and for all eternity. What an encouragement to pray! If all things are freely given to us by God, then let us open our mouths wide when making our requests.

What more can God himself say than he has said in this most precious verse?
12 O LORD of hosts,
      blessed is the one who trusts in you!

OCTOBER 21

My Beloved Is Mine, and I Am His[749]

It is possible that in those golden days when Solomon walked with God, he was inspired to write the matchless book of The Song of Solomon. It is the Holy of holies of the Scriptures, standing like the tree of life in the midst of the garden of inspiration. The song is highly allegorical or symbolic. It describes Christ and his church as a bride and bridegroom who sing to each other and about each other.[750] The passage we are about to read is a dialogue.

Song of Solomon 2
The Bridegroom speaks first.
1   I am a rose of Sharon,
      a lily of the valleys.
2   As a lily among brambles,
      so is my love among the young women.

Who can this person who is both a rose and lily be except Jesus?

   "White is his soul, from blemish free,
   Red with the blood he shed for me."[751]

He paints his church as a single lily growing in the middle of a wilderness of thorns. Among the thorns, but not of them. The beauty of his church is all the more easily seen in contrast to the prickly brambles of the world.

Then the Bride or the church exclaims:
3   As an apple tree among the trees of the
          forest,
      so is my beloved among the young men.

---

[748] William Secker (died about 1681). From *The Nonsuch Professor* first published in 1660.

[749] Song of Solomon 2:16
[750] This view is not held by all Christians. Most Jews saw the Song of Solomon as a picture of Jehovah and his chosen people, Israel. For the first eighteen centuries after Pentecost, most of the Church understood it as a love song about Christ and his Church. Many now view it as simply a historical love poem. In the New Testament, Christ alluded to himself as the groom and the Church as his bride. Perhaps in the future, the Church will once again more fully appreciate the intimate relationship between Christ and his bride.
—editor
[751] Believed to be quoted from a book of pulpit helps by William Nicholson (circa 1862).

With great delight I sat in his shadow,
   and his fruit was sweet to my taste,

Fruit trees are superior to other trees. They provide shade and fruit. Jesus is more excellent than all others. He provides protection and all our needs. To us who believe in him he is everything!

4 He brought me to the banqueting house,
    and his banner over me was love.
5 Sustain me with raisins;
    refresh me with apples,
  for I am sick with love.

Love to Jesus sometimes becomes such a strong feeling that the soul cannot handle it. The body is so frail, it is ready to faint under the supreme excitement.

6 His left hand is under my head,
    and his right hand embraces me!
7 I adjure you, O daughters of Jerusalem,
    by the gazelles or the does of the field,
  that you not stir up or awaken love
    until it pleases.

The bride now hears the voice of her husband. She rejoices to see him coming to her with all the sacred haste of omnipotent[752] love.

8 The voice of my beloved!
    Behold, he comes,
  leaping over the mountains,
    bounding over the hills.
9 My beloved is like a gazelle
    or a young stag.
  Behold, there he stands
    behind our wall,
  gazing through the windows,
    looking through the lattice.
10 My beloved speaks and says to me:
  "Arise, my love, my beautiful one,
    and come away,
11 for behold, the winter is past;
    the rain is over and gone.
12 The flowers appear on the earth,
    the time of singing has come,
  and the voice of the turtledove
    is heard in our land.
13 The fig tree ripens its figs,
    and the vines are in blossom;
  they give forth fragrance.
  Arise, my love, my beautiful one,
    and come away."

Dark days may come and go. Let us spend our joyful times walking with our Lord in the light while the light lasts. When doubts, fears, trials and distresses are over and the heart is full of music, we should make the most of it; rejoicing in holy fellowship and delighting ourselves in the Lord Jesus.

The Bridegroom continues speaking and calls to his beloved:

14 "O my dove, in the clefts of the rock,
    in the crannies of the cliff,
  let me see your face,
    let me hear your voice,
  for your voice is sweet,
    and your face is lovely.

Come out from the hiding places of fear or worldliness and acknowledge the Lord.

15 Catch the foxes for us,
    the little foxes
  that spoil the vineyards,
    for our vineyards are in blossom."

The church (the Bride) sings again:

16 My beloved is mine, and I am his;
    he grazes *(or pastures his flock)* among
      the lilies.
17 Until the day breathes
    and the shadows flee,
  turn, my beloved, be like a gazelle
    or a young stag on cleft mountains.

If we have lost our sense of the presence of the Lord, it is our duty and our privilege to cry to him to return swiftly; like the nimble deer that leaps over every barrier and obstacle.

OCTOBER 22

Let Me Sing For My Beloved My Love Song[753]

We continue in the poetic book of the Song of Solomon. This book is also known as Canticles which means songs or hymns.

        Song of Solomon 3:6-11

The first speakers are the Daughters of Jerusalem.

---

[752] *omnipotent, omnipotence* - all powerful, almighty, absolute and supreme power, having unlimited power.

[753] Isaiah 5:1

6 What is that coming up from the wilderness
　　like columns of smoke,
　perfumed with myrrh and frankincense,
　　with all the fragrant powders of a merchant?

The friends of the Bridegroom reply.

7 Behold, it is the litter[754] of Solomon!
　Around it are sixty mighty men,
　　some of the mighty men of Israel,
8 all of them wearing swords,
　　and expert in war,
　each with his sword at his thigh,
　　against terror by night.
9 King Solomon made himself a carriage
　　from the wood of Lebanon.
10 He made its posts of silver,
　　its back of gold, its seat of purple;
　its interior was inlaid with love
　　by the daughters of Jerusalem.
11 Go out, O daughters of Zion,
　　and look upon King Solomon,
　with the crown with which his mother crowned him
　　on the day of his wedding,
　　on the day of the gladness of his heart.

Then follows a song of The King, in which he praises the beauty of his bride.

Song of Solomon 4:1-7

1 Behold, you are beautiful, my love,
　　behold, you are beautiful!
　Your eyes are doves
　　behind your veil.
　Your hair is like a flock of goats
　　leaping down the slopes of Gilead.
2 Your teeth are like a flock of shorn ewes
　　that have come up from the washing,
　all of which bear twins,
　　and not one among them has lost its young.
3 Your lips are like a scarlet thread,
　　and your mouth is lovely.
　Your cheeks are like halves of a pomegranate
　　behind your veil.
4 Your neck is like the tower of David,
　　built in rows of stone;
　on it hang a thousand shields,
　　all of them shields of warriors.
5 Your two breasts are like two fawns,
　　twins of a gazelle,
　　that graze among the lilies.
6 Until the day breathes
　　and the shadows flee,
　I will go away to the mountain of myrrh
　　and the hill of frankincense.
7 You are altogether beautiful, my love;
　　there is no flaw in you.

In the first song, beginning with verse seven, the king is seen in his traveling palanquin or chariot, coming up from the wilderness. We may explain this scene as picturing our Lord and King going up to his glory from this wilderness world. His escort includes attending angels and warrior angels; or, as John Milton calls them, "the [guiding] cherubim and the sworded seraphim." They have kept watch around him in the wilderness of this world and continue with him to increase the magnificence of his ascension.[755] Jesus will return to earth a second time the same way he left. Then his church will see him in all his glory. The purple of that glorious chariot of love represents the atoning blood. The church will ride with him, rejoicing in his salvation. Happy are those who by faith are part of this event.

In chapter four, the king sings about the beauty of his bride. Believers understand that this beauty is the righteousness of the Lord Jesus that he has given to them. In the sight of God, the saints are "altogether beautiful." That is, they are perfect and without sin. Every single line in this book has special meaning. Spiritual minds will find great delight in discovering them.

---

[754] *litter* - That is, the sedan chair on which servants carry a king.

[755] *ascension* - Refers to the resurrected King Jesus leaving the earth to take his rightful place on the throne of heaven.

Sedan Chair
Also called a Palanquin and Litter (Song of Solomon 3:7). An enclosed chair for conveying one person, carried between horizontal poles by porters.

October 23

Come With Me From Lebanon, My Bride[756]

Our last reading gave us two parts of a delightful Canticle. We will now read the third part, where the King is the main speaker. He happily praises his bride, even as the Lord Jesus rejoices over his church.

Song of Solomon 4:8-16; 5:1

The King speaks.

8 Come with me from Lebanon, my bride;
    come with me from Lebanon.
  Depart from the peak of Amana,
    from the peak of Senir and Hermon,
    from the den of lions,
    from the mountain of leopards.

Jesus wants us to look above the highest earthly pleasures and withdraw from all earthly loves for his sake. Will he say, "Come with me," and will we refuse to follow him? Hear how he directs his love to us and the joy he has over us.

9 You have captivated my heart, my sister, my bride;
    you have captivated my heart with one glance of your eyes,
    with one jewel of your necklace.

Jesus lowers himself to love even lowly us. If he spies out even one good thing about us, he is charmed with it.

10 How beautiful is your love, my sister, my bride!
    How much better is your love than wine,
    and the fragrance of your oils than any spice!
11 Your lips drip nectar, my bride;
    honey and milk are under your tongue;
    the fragrance of your garments is like the fragrance of Lebanon.

In Jesus' eyes, the love, the spirit, the words, and the outward conduct of his people are all received with joy.

12 A garden locked is my sister, my bride,
    a spring locked, a fountain sealed.
13 Your shoots are an orchard of pomegranates
    with all choicest fruits,
    henna with nard,
14 nard and saffron, calamus and cinnamon,
    with all trees of frankincense,
    myrrh and aloes,
    with all chief spices—
15 a garden fountain, a well of living water,
    and flowing streams from Lebanon.

Jesus praises his beloved Church, but then he prays for her that the Holy Spirit may visit her, because what would she be without him? Listen to the Redeemer's prayer.

16 Awake, O north wind,
    and come, O south wind!
  Blow upon my garden,
    let its spices flow.

Inspired by the love of her Lord and influenced by the Holy Spirit, the Church begs the Lord to come nearer to her.

  Let my beloved come to his garden,
    and eat its choicest fruits.

The King lovingly responds.

5:1 I came to my garden, my sister, my bride,
    I gathered my myrrh with my spice,
    I ate my honeycomb with my honey,
    I drank my wine with my milk.
  Eat, friends, drink,
    and be drunk with love!

---

[756] Song of Solomon 4:8

Jesus accepts us and the fruit of the Spirit we bring. Therefore let us rejoice in him and feast on him.[757]

OCTOBER 24

And He Is Altogether Desirable[758]

We will again read from the Song. The bride hears the Bridegroom knocking at her door, but she excuses herself from getting up and letting him in. She acts in an unkind way to him .Sadly, we have too often done the same to our Lord Jesus. The whole story is told using graceful singing.

Song of Solomon 5:2-16

The bride speaks.

2 I slept, but my heart was awake.
   A sound! My beloved is knocking.
   "Open to me, my sister, my love,
     my dove, my perfect one,
   for my head is wet with dew,
     my locks with the drops of the night."

She then continues by giving poor excuses. How cruel she is to her friend! How selfish! How self-indulgent! Her excuses are embarrassing! But do we not see ourselves in her?

3 I had put off my garment;
     how could I put it on?
   I had bathed my feet;
     how could I soil them?
4 My beloved put his hand to the latch,
     and my heart was thrilled within me.
5 I arose to open to my beloved,
     and my hands dripped with myrrh,
   my fingers with liquid myrrh,
     on the handles of the bolt.
6 I open to my beloved,
     but my beloved had turned and gone.
   My soul failed me when he spoke.
   I sought him, but found him not;
     I called him, but he gave no answer.
7 The watchmen found me
     as they went about in the city;
   they beat me, they bruised me,
     they took away my veil,
     those watchmen of the walls.
8 I adjure you, O daughters of Jerusalem,
     if you find my beloved,
   that you tell him
     I am sick with love.

Sadly, the spouse had neglected her duty and in doing so she grieved her Lord. She made him hide his face from her. However, she still loved him and became very anxious about finding him again. She hoped that her Lord might listen to others, even if he had closed his ear to her for a time. She begged the daughters of Jerusalem to speak to him for her. When we are in darkness, the prayers of our fellow believers may be of great help to us.

The Daughters of Jerusalem question the Bride.

9 What is your beloved more than another
       beloved,
     O most beautiful among women?
   What is your beloved more than another
       beloved,
     that you thus adjure us?

The Bride responds to these questions.

10 My beloved is radiant and ruddy,
      distinguished among ten thousand.
11 His head is the finest gold;
      his locks are wavy,
      black as a raven.
12 He eyes are like doves
      beside streams of water,
    bathed in milk,
      sitting beside a full pool.
13 His cheeks are like beds of spices,
      mounds of sweet-smelling herbs.
    His lips are lilies,
      dripping liquid myrrh.
14 His arms are rods of gold,
      set with jewels.
    His body is polished ivory,
      bedecked with sapphires.
15 His legs are alabaster columns,

---

[757] Galatians 5:22-23a "The fruit of the Spirit is love, joy, peace, patience, kindness, goodness, faithfulness, gentleness, self-control." John 6:53-58, "So Jesus said to them, 'Truly, truly, I say to you, unless you eat the flesh of the Son of Man and drink his blood, you have no life in you. Whoever feeds on my flesh and drinks my blood has eternal life, and I will raise him up on the last day. For my flesh is true food, and my blood is true drink. Whoever feeds on my flesh and drinks my blood abides in me, and I in him. As the living Father sent me, and I live because of the Father, so whoever feeds on me, he also will live because of me. This is the bread that came down from heaven, not as the fathers ate and died. Whoever feeds on this bread will live forever'."

[758] Song of Solomon 5:16

set on bases of gold.
His appearance is like Lebanon,
choice as the cedars.
16 His mouth is most sweet,
and he is altogether desirable.
This is my beloved and this my friend,
O daughters of Jerusalem.

October 25
Hear, That Your Soul May Live[759]

It was in the days of his glory, before sin had darkened his sun, that Solomon collected and composed the Book of Proverbs. It is a goldmine of wisdom, a treasure chest of instruction.

Proverbs 1:20-31

20 Wisdom cries aloud in the street,
in the markets she raises her voice;

The right way is not to be kept secret or mentioned to only a few. Wise teaching and counsel should overflow whether it is popular or not. The Bible and those who faithfully preach it should not be avoided. If any perish, it should not be because the plan of salvation was not made public. Wisdom is among us and speaks clearly and in earnest.

21 at the head of the noisy streets she cries out;
at the entrance of the city gates she speaks:
22 "How long, O simple ones, will you love being simple?
How long will scoffers delight in their scoffing
and fools hate knowledge?
23 If you turn at my reproof,
behold, I will pour out my spirit to you;
I will make my words known to you."

The Lord Jesus, represented by wisdom, pleads with loving words from the heart. People are foolish and they love their foolishness. Some of them are so in love with sin that they sneer at the only instruction that can save their souls. The Lord reasons and pleads with them. It is not the will of the Redeemer that the sinner should die. His infinite love is put on display to prevent them from committing suicide of the soul. Notice how seriously he asks, "How long?" and how graciously he promises the help of his Holy Spirit so they can understand his instructions. Jesus pleads with each one of us. Have we obeyed his call?

24 "Because I have called and you refused to listen,
have stretched out my hand and no one has heeded,
25 because you have ignored all my counsel
and would have none of my reproof,
26 I also will laugh at your calamity;
I will mock when terror strikes you,
27 when terror strikes you like a storm
and your calamity comes like a whirlwind,
when distress and anguish come upon you.
28 Then they will call upon me, but I will not answer;
they will seek me diligently but will not find me.
29 Because they hated knowledge
and did not choose the fear of the Lord,
30 would have none of my counsel
and despised all my reproof,
31 therefore they shall eat the fruit of their way,
and have their fill of their own devices."

Not until calls of love have failed does the Lord change to words of stern rebuke. But when grace has been ignored, and even insulted, justice must speak in tones of thunder. The Lord Jesus wept over sinners in the days of his flesh. He continues, through his Church, to plead with them, warn them and offer his love to them. But he will not always do so. The time is coming when he will have no pity on those who reject him. Then he will reject the cries and pleas of his enemies. They say that the sweetest wine makes the sharpest vinegar. And so the very gentleness and tenderness of Jesus will make him the more terrible when his patience finally turns to wrath. Oh! may none of us ever be spoken to with the terrible words we have just read. They are full of weeping, and wailing, and gnashing of teeth.[760] Is it not right that the ones who perish are the ones

---

[759] Isaiah 55:3

[760] Matthew 13:42; Luke 13:28

who refused to be saved? Should not those be rejected at the last day who willfully rejected the Redeemer all through their day of grace? Is it not a most righteous rule that people should reap what they sow?[761] Is it not only fair that those who choose to follow their own fantasies will not be rewarded for turning their backs on the Savior?

Will any member of our family be so insanely wicked that they refuse to accept God's loving invitations to follow his Son? May God not let that happen!

OCTOBER 26
Those Who Seek Me Diligently Find Me[762]

In this chapter we once again hear the words of heavenly wisdom, in the person of the Son of God, warning us against foolishness. Let us not be unconcerned when God himself takes issue with us.

Proverbs 8:1-21

1 Does not wisdom call?
  Does not understanding raise her voice?
2 On the heights beside the way,
  at the crossroads she takes her stand;
3 beside the gates in front of the town,
  at the entrance of the portals she cries aloud:
4 "To you, O man, I call,
  and my cry is to the children of man."

All around, in his word, in providence, by his ministers, and by his Spirit, Wisdom still calls out to the children of man. In this country where Bibles are easily available, the Lord Jesus calls to young and old, rich and poor, to consider him and turn to him.

5 "O simple ones, learn prudence;
  O fools, learn sense."

Jesus invites the foolish to come to him. How kind he is. The masters of old wanted only wise men for students. Few teachers nowadays would invite fools to their schools. Jesus is gentle and lowly in heart. He includes those of humble means. He is ready to be the teacher of even slow learners. No one needs to stay away from Jesus because of their ignorance. It is even a good reason for coming to him. But for some who might ask, "Is his teaching worth hearing?" he goes on.

6 "Hear, for I will speak noble things,
  and from my lips will come what is right,"

But does he speak the truth? Yes! He does.

7 "for my mouth will utter truth;
  wickedness is an abomination to my lips.
8 All the words of my mouth are righteous;
  there is nothing twisted or crooked in them."

But can we understand his teaching? Can less educated people learn from him? Can little children respond to his teaching? Yes! His words are simplicity itself.

9 "They are all straight to him who understands,
  and right to those who find knowledge.
10 Take my instruction instead of silver,
  and knowledge rather than choice gold,"

Soul-saving knowledge is worth more than any amount of money.

11 "for wisdom is better than jewels,
  and all that you may desire cannot compare with her.
12 "I, wisdom, dwell with prudence,
  and I find knowledge and discretion."

Eternal Wisdom designed the Cross to bring peace between God and people. The plan of salvation—by using a substitute to pay for sin—is the very peak of wisdom. Let us make every effort to get this wisdom.

13 "The fear of the Lord is hatred of evil.
  Pride and arrogance and the way of evil
  and perverted speech I hate."

And what God hates, we must also hate with all our heart.

14 "I have counsel and sound wisdom;
  I have insight; I have strength.
15 By me kings reign,
  and rulers decree what is just;
16 by me princes rule,
  and nobles, all who govern justly.
17 I love those who love me,
  and those who seek me diligently find me."

---
[761] Galatians 6:7-8
[762] Proverbs 8:17

This is a thick slice of meat for the children of our families. Let boys and girls take hold of it and go to Jesus in complete confidence in this promise.

18 "Riches and honor are with me,
    enduring wealth and righteousness.
19 My fruit is better than gold, even fine gold,
    and my yield than choice silver."

Nothing can be so useful, so valuable, so really good for us as to know Christ and to be in fellowship with him.

20 "I walk in the way of righteousness,
    in the paths of justice,"

In the middle of the road, which is the path of safety.

21 "granting an inheritance to those who love me,
    and filling their treasuries."

They will be truly rich in grace. Even if they are poor in this world, they will be infinitely rich in the world to come, where there is a kingdom for the very least of them.

OCTOBER 27

The Hand Of the Diligent Makes Rich[763]

The first nine chapters are a kind of introduction to the Book of Proverbs. Its short, to-the-point sentences begin at the tenth chapter.

Proverbs 10:1-16

1 The proverbs of Solomon.

A wise son makes a glad father,
    but a foolish son is a sorrow to his mother.

This is the first of the proverbs. Let each child pay special attention to it. Who among us would wish to be a lifelong grief to father and mother? Yet such will be the case if we live in sin and despise heavenly wisdom.

2 Treasures gained by wickedness do not profit,
    but righteousness delivers from death.

Judas gained his thirty pieces of silver, but what good did they do him? Paul was given the righteousness of Christ and has the joy of heaven forever.

3 The LORD does not let the righteous go hungry,
    but he thwarts the craving of the wicked.

The godly may experience hunger, but not extreme hunger. The wicked may increase in wealth, but their hope for happiness will not be reached.

4 A slack hand causes poverty,
    but the hand of the diligent makes rich.

No pains, no gains. No sweat, no sweet.

5 He who gathers in summer is a prudent son,
    but he who sleeps in harvest is a son who brings shame.

Not using our time productively leads to sin. Our idle days are Satan's busy days. He who does not use his time wisely, will never have enough time.

6 Blessings are on the head of the righteous,
    but the mouth of the wicked conceals violence.
7 The memory of the righteous is a blessing,
    but the name of the wicked will rot.
8 The wise of heart will receive commandments,
    but a babbling fool will come to ruin.

Wise people listen more than they speak. They are willing to listen to practical instruction. Foolish people talk on and on until they prove their foolishness.

9 Whoever walks in integrity walks securely,
    but he who makes his ways crooked will be found out.
10 Whoever winks the eye causes trouble,
    and a babbling fool will come to ruin.

Cowards are afraid to say things they know they should not, but express their feelings with a clever wink of the eye. They cause much misery. No honest person will behave that way.

People who talk too much prove that their religion is not real. Their profession of faith will soon become a shipwreck.

11 The mouth of the righteous is a fountain of life,

---

[763] Proverbs 10:4

(sending out refreshing and saving streams from the water of life),
> but the mouth of the wicked conceals violence.

They are like stagnate ponds that are full of putrid water. They are deadly to others, as well as harmful to themselves.

12 Hatred stirs up strife,
> but love covers all offenses.

Loving spirits will not take offense, but will patiently endure for Christ's sake. Those who actually enjoy being evil, will take offense over the smallest thing. They are always fanning the flames of hostility. Let us not act like that.

13 On the lips of him who has understanding, wisdom is found,
> but a rod is for the back of him who lacks sense.

14 The wise lay up knowledge,
> (because they still feel their own lack of it),
> but the mouth of a fool brings ruin near.

They think they know it all and therefore will not learn. They blabber on to their own destruction.

15 A rich man's wealth is his strong city;
> the poverty of the poor is their ruin.

Sadly, this is often the case, even in our own country. Poor people are despised and few are willing to assist them. May the Lord send to us such a spirit of justice that we are always ready to stand with the weaker side and see to it that they are not treated unfairly. It is meanness itself to flatter the wealthy. True religion lifts us above such littleness.

16 The wage of the righteous leads to life,
> the gain of the wicked to sin.

Work, not idleness, is the badge of a servant of God. With the wicked, it is always "what's in it for me?" Their actions are sinful in the sight of the Lord.

Oh Lord, cause us to work because of the life of Christ within us and give us life even more abundantly.

OCTOBER 28

The Desire of the Righteous Will Be Granted[764]

Proverbs 10:17-32

17 Whoever heeds instruction is on the path to life,
> but he who rejects reproof leads others astray.

No one can do us a greater kindness than to instruct us in the right way and warn us of the wrong. But it is probably just as difficult to accept advice in the proper spirit as it is to give it wisely. A sensible person is always ready to listen to words of wisdom and never think they are above learning from anyone.

18 The one who conceals hatred has lying lips,
> and whoever utters slander is a fool.

The first part of this verse shows us that hiding hatred from someone is hypocritical as well as sinful. The last part is a harsh blow to many. Does it include any of us? Are not some of us far too ready to gossip by repeating things that are hurtful to others?

19 When words are many, transgression is not lacking,
> but whoever restrains his lips is prudent.

Talking too much is a common problem. People talk so much because they think so little. Drums make a great noise because they are hollow. There is one characteristic of a wise man that any of us can have. We can be quiet! Let us try it.

20 The tongue of the righteous is choice silver;
> the heart of the wicked is of little worth.

The ungodly person at their best is not worth much. That is God's opinion of them. That should humble them and make them think seriously about their life.

21 The lips of the righteous feed many,
> but fools die for lack of sense.

Fools cannot feed others with wisdom, because they are starving from a lack of truth and understanding.

22 The blessing of the LORD makes rich,
> and he adds no sorrow with it.

---

[764] Proverbs 10:24

Other riches always include sadness; only the Lord's roses do not have thorns.

23 Doing wrong is like a joke to a fool,
   but wisdom is pleasure to a man of understanding.
24 What the wicked dreads will come upon him,
   but the desire of the righteous will be granted.
25 When the tempest passes, the wicked is no more,
   but the righteous is established forever.

The tornado is only remembered by the destruction it leaves behind. The same is true of many bad people. But the reputation of good people is like an ancient castle. It remains strong for a very long time. People have good memories of them long after they have passed from this life.

26 Like vinegar to the teeth and smoke to the eyes,
   so is the sluggard to those who send him.

The sluggard is unpleasant and obnoxious, irritating and annoying. The person who wants to please their employer must be hard working, prompt, and cheerful.

27 The fear of the Lord prolongs life,
   but the years of the wicked will be short.

Anyone can see that the soberness, peacefulness and clean living of true religion tend to help a person live longer. It is just as easy to see that drunkenness, immorality, bad tempers and rough lifestyles tend to bring people to their graves sooner than would otherwise be expected. Godliness is often rewarded with more years in this life.

28 The hope of the righteous brings joy,
   but the expectation of the wicked will perish.
29 The way of the Lord is a stronghold to the blameless,
   but destruction to evildoers.
30 The righteous will never be removed,
   but the wicked will not dwell in the land.

There will come a day when wicked people will not be found on this earth. They will die and holy people will fill their places. We wait for the coming of the Lord and the new age of holiness.

31 The mouth of the righteous brings forth wisdom,
   but the perverse tongue will be cut off.
32 The lips of the righteous know what is acceptable,
   but the mouth of the wicked, what is perverse.

The tongues of the wicked try to make others mad and sad. They do not know how to be polite. They talk about anything that enters their mind without thinking first. May none of us have wild, uncontrollable tongues that hurt others for no good reason. Instead, let our conversations be holy and gentle, using words that bless both the hearer and the speaker. This would be a little heaven on earth for our family.

October 29

Do Not Boast About Tomorrow[765]

Proverbs 27:1-18

1 Do not boast about tomorrow,
   for you do not know what a day may bring.

Providing for the future is a duty, but to boast about the future is sin. Only an unbeliever would dare to brag about what he will accomplish tomorrow. Eternity is just around the corner. We may find ourselves brought to it before the sun goes down today or rises again tomorrow. The rich man thought he could relax, eat, drink and be merry for many years to come, but that very night, "God said to him, 'Fool! This night your soul is required of you.'"[766] Young people have no guarantee they will live to a ripe old age. There are little graves in the cemetery. Flowers in the bud are cut off from the bush. We are called today to repent and believe. To delay is to be like the rich man who boasted about tomorrow. It may result in our eternal ruin.

2 Let another praise you, and not your own mouth;
   a stranger, and not your own lips.
3 A stone is heavy, and sand is weighty,

---
[765] Proverbs 27:1
[766] Luke 12:20

but a fool's provocation is heavier than
both.

Because a fool will not forgive, thet are pouty and eager for revenge. Their anger crushes their own heart and they will crush the hearts of others if they can.

4 Wrath is cruel, anger is overwhelming,
but who can stand before jealousy?

Adam and Satan both fell because they envied God. If we give in to jealousy, it will certainly take away our happiness. Envy spits its venom on the best of people. It is a horrible and devilish emotion. Those who follow the loving Jesus must fight against resentment and overcome it.

5 Better is open rebuke
than hidden love.
6 Faithful are the wounds of a friend;
profuse are the kisses of an enemy.
7 One who is full loathes honey,
but to one who is hungry everything
bitter is sweet
8 Like a bird that strays from its nest
is a man who strays from his home.

Therefore we should avoid an aimless life that always hopes a change will make things better. If we have not succeeded where we are, let us try again. How can a tree grow if it is always being transplanted?

9 Oil and perfume make the heart glad,
and the sweetness of a friend comes
from his earnest counsel.
10 Do not forsake your friend and your
father's friend,

Jesus was our father's best friend; let us not turn our back on him. We will never find a better.

and do not go to your brother's house in
the day of your calamity.
Better is a neighbor who is near
than a brother who is far away.

Relatives should be close friends, but unfortunately, selfishness often gets in the way. Jonathan was a better friend to David than Joseph's brothers were to him.

11 Be wise, my son, and make my heart glad,
that I may answer him who reproaches
me.
12 The prudent sees danger and hides
himself,
but the simple go on and suffer for it.
13 Take a man's garment when he has put up
security for a stranger,
and hold it in pledge when he puts up
security for an adulteress.

Do not trust the immoral person. They are bad at heart and their faults will soon leave them begging for money. If you must do business with them, do it on the strictest terms, or they will rob you.

14 Whoever blesses his neighbor with a loud
voice,
rising early in the morning,
will be counted as cursing.

Sensible people find excessive praise distasteful. There is good reason to think it is given with a sinister motive in mind. We should wish our friends well, but to loudly sing their praises all the time is not doing them a favor. It is probably just the opposite!

15 A continual dripping on a rainy day
and a quarrelsome wife are alike;
16 to restrain her is to restrain the wind
or to grasp oil in one's right hand.

Arguing with a neighbor is like a spring shower and soon over. But quarreling with a wife at home is exhausting work and makes life miserable. Even worse, strong disagreements in the home cannot be hidden. The noise and bad temper of a bad woman become obvious to everyone. You might as well try to cover up the wind or hold oil in your hand. Let us never fight, unless it is fighting to make each other happy.

17 Iron sharpens iron,
and one man sharpens another.

*Good friendship is great help to growing in
grace. Fellowship with the saints
helps us in the service of God.*

18 Whoever tends a fig tree will eat its fruit,
and he who guards his master will be
honored.

And if Jesus is that Master, our honor will be great and long lasting; our reward will be sweet indeed.

OCTOBER 30

Something Greater Than Solomon Is Here[767]

1 Kings 10:1-13

1 Now when the queen of Sheba heard of the fame of Solomon concerning the name of the LORD, she came to him with hard questions. *(As far away as the queen of Sheba was, the glory of Solomon reached her and she was motivated to visit him. She was curious and wanted to see his splendor. She was also prompted for religious reasons and wanted to know more about Jehovah God. Sadly, there are thousands who show no interest in Jesus even though he is near them and the gospel is preached around them. It is sad that Solomon attracted a stranger from so far away and Jesus is overlooked by those who are nearby.)* **2** She came to Jerusalem with a very great retinue, with camels bearing spices and very much gold and precious stones. And when she came to Solomon, she told him all that was on her mind.

3 And Solomon answered all her questions; there was nothing hidden from the king that he could not explain to her. *(When sinners come to Jesus they will find solutions to all their difficult questions. He will both reveal and remove all their secret uneasiness. He is always ready to share his wisdom to all who come to him. There will never be a situation that he cannot work out.)* **4** And when the queen of Sheba had seen all the wisdom of Solomon, the house that he had built, **5** the food of his table, the seating of his officials, and the attendance of his servants, their clothing, his cupbearers, and his burnt offerings that he offered at the house of the LORD, there was no more breath in her.

6 And she said to the king, "The report was true that I heard in my own land of your words and of your wisdom, **7** but I did not believe the reports until I came and my own eyes had seen it. And behold, the half was not told me. Your wisdom and prosperity surpass the report that I heard. **8** Happy are your men! Happy are your servants, who continually stand before you and hear your wisdom! **9** Blessed be the LORD your God, who has delighted in you and set you on the throne of Israel! Because the LORD loved Israel forever, he has made you king, that you may execute justice and righteousness."

In the same way, although the good news about King Jesus seems unbelievably wonderful, the believer discovers his grace and goodness are even greater than they were told. Jesus must be known by each one of us personally or we will never know him. Oh that many who look down on the Redeemer now will see him for themselves. That would instantly change their indifference to adoration.

10 Then she gave the king 120 talents *(about four and one-half tons)* of gold, and a very great quantity of spices and precious stones. Never again came such an abundance of spices as these that the queen of Sheba gave to King Solomon.

When a heart truly knows King Jesus it brings gifts to him. Nothing is too good, too costly or too precious for Jesus. If we could lay the whole world at his feet, it would be "a present far too small."[768]

11 Moreover, the fleet of Hiram, which brought gold from Ophir, brought from Ophir a very great amount of almug wood and precious stones. **12** And the king made of the almug wood supports for the house of the LORD and for the king's house, also lyres and harps for the singers. No such almug wood has come or been seen to this day.

13 And King Solomon gave to the queen of Sheba all that she desired, whatever she asked besides what was given her by the bounty of King Solomon. So she turned and went back to her own land with her servants. *(And we may add with great confidence that our Lord Jesus will be in no one's debt. Everything that we can possible give to him, he will return a hundred times over. Yes, he will grant us whatsoever we ask, he will give us the desires of our heart.[769])*

---

[767] Matthew 12:42

[768] From the hymn *When I Survey the Wondrous Cross* by Isaac Watts (1707).

[769] Psalm 37:4, "Delight yourself in the LORD, and he will give you the desires of your heart." 1 John 5:14-15, "And this is the confidence that we have toward him, that if we ask anything according to his will he hears us. And if we

Matthew 12:42

The queen of the South will rise up at the judgment with this generation and condemn it, for she came from the ends of the earth to hear the wisdom of Solomon, and behold, something greater than Solomon is here.

The queen of Sheba came a great distance, with great difficulty, and ran great risks to see Solomon. Yet the majority of humanity is completely indifferent about a greater than Solomon. They will hardly ever even cross the street to see Jesus, who has power to bless them eternally.

OCTOBER 31
Abstain From the Passions Of the Flesh, Which Wage War Against Your Soul[770]

We now come to the sad part of Solomon's life, when the wise man played the fool to a great extreme. He proved that without the grace of God the greatest of people may lower themselves to commit the worst of sins. Who would have believed that Solomon could become so lustful and the son of David become a worshiper of idols?

1 Kings 11:1-5; 9-13

¹ Now King Solomon loved many foreign women, along with the daughter of Pharaoh: Moabite, Ammonite, Edomite, Sidonian, and Hittite women, ² from the nations concerning which the LORD had said to the people of Israel, "You shall not enter into marriage with them, neither shall they with you, for surely they will turn away your heart after their gods." Solomon clung to these in love. ³ He had 700 wives, who were princesses, and 300 concubines. And his wives turned away his heart. ⁴ For when Solomon was old his wives turned away his heart after other gods, and his heart was not wholly true to the LORD his God, as was the heart of David his father. ⁵ For Solomon went after Ashtoreth the goddess of the Sidonians, and after Milcom the abomination of the Ammonites.

⁹ And the LORD was angry with Solomon, because his heart had turned away from the LORD, the God of Israel, who had appeared to him twice ¹⁰ and had commanded him concerning this thing, that he should not go after other gods. But he did not keep what the LORD commanded. ¹¹ Therefore the LORD said to Solomon, "Since this has been your practice and you have not kept my covenant and my statutes that I have commanded you, I will surely tear the kingdom from you and will give it to your servant. ¹² Yet for the sake of David your father I will not do it in your days, but I will tear it out of the hand of your son. ¹³ However, I will not tear away all the kingdom, but I will give one tribe to your son, for the sake of David my servant and for the sake of Jerusalem that I have chosen."

Dr. James Hamilton has beautifully described the events of this part of Jewish history. "The people murmured. The monarch wheeled along with greater pomp than ever; but the popular prince had soured into the tyrant. The crown sat defiant on his unpredictable head. His subjects bowed down to him without feeling and their hearts were not in it when they sang his praises. The people of Zion were in mourning. The unused temple courts sprouted grass and weeds while mysterious groves and unholy shrines were popping up everywhere. The palace was defiled by lust. Chemosh and Ashtoreth, and other Gentile abominations, defiled the Holy Land.

"In the disastrous darkness in the land, beasts of the forest crept abroad. Hadad the Edomite ventured out of Egypt and became a lifelong torment to the God-forsaken king of Israel. Rezon the Syrian pounced on Damascus and made Syria his own. From the Pagan palaces of Thebes and Memphis harsh cries were soon heard; Pharaoh and Jeroboam taking counsel together, screeching forth their threats, and hooting insults at which Solomon could no longer laugh.

"Amidst all the gloom and misery a message comes from God: The kingdom is torn. Solomon's successor will have only an inferior piece and a fragment of Israel, while God hands ten tribes over to a rebel and a runaway.

---

know that he hears us in whatever we ask, we know that we have the requests that we have asked of him."
[770] 1 Peter 2:11

"Luxury and sinful wives made him an idolater, and idolatry made him yet more lustful. Finally, in the lazy exhaustion and idle daydreaming of the pleasure seeker, he lost the discernment of the wise man and the bravery of the sovereign. And when he rose from his drunken daze and picked up his tarnished crown from the mess, he woke to find his powers, once so clear and unclouded, all troubled and his strong reason paralyzed and his healthy imagination poisoned. He woke to find the world grown hollow, and himself grown old. He woke to see the sun in Israel's sky now dark. A special gloom surrounded him. Like one who falls asleep amidst the lights and music of the orchestra, and who awakes amidst empty benches and tattered programs; like a man who falls asleep in a flower garden, and who opens his eyes on an empty and locust-blackened wilderness; the life, the loveliness, was vanished, and all the remaining spirit of the mighty Solomon yawned forth that verdict of the tired pleasure seeker: 'Vanity of vanities! vanity of vanities! all is vanity!'"[771]

NOVEMBER 1
Vanity Of Vanities! All Is Vanity[772]

In the book of Ecclesiastes, or The Preacher, Solomon has left us his own biography. It is the life of a seeker after pleasure, the history of Solomon the prodigal, written by Solomon the preacher. In this first chapter, he gives us the introduction and the theme of its sad contents. It has well been called the saddest book in all the Bible.

Ecclesiastes 1:1-15

¹ The words of the Preacher, the son of David, king in Jerusalem.

² Vanity of vanities, says the Preacher,
 vanity of vanities! All is vanity.

This is Solomon speaking as the wise man, but we would love it better to hear the voice of Solomon the saint, who said, "Your love is better than wine."[773] "He brought me to the banqueting house, and his banner over me was love."[774] How dark are the forbidden ways! How sweet are the roads of holy fellowship!

³ What does man gain by all the toil
 at which he toils under the sun?
⁴ A generation goes, and a generation comes,
 but the earth remains forever.
⁵ The sun rises, and the sun goes down,
 and hastens to the place where it rises.
⁶ The wind blows to the south
 and goes around to the north;
around and around goes the wind,
 and on its circuits the wind returns.
⁷ All streams run to the sea,
 but the sea is not full;
to the place where the streams flow,
 there they flow again.
⁸ All things are full of weariness;
 a man cannot utter it;
the eye is not satisfied with seeing,
 nor the ear filled with hearing.
⁹ What has been is what will be,
 and what has been done is what will be done,
 and there is nothing new under the sun.
¹⁰ Is there a thing of which it is said,
 "See, this is new"?
It has been already
 in the ages before us.
¹¹ There is no remembrance of former things,
 nor will there be any remembrance
of later things yet to be
 among those who come after.

"As much as if he said, 'It is all a weary-go-round.' This system of things is an everlasting self-repetition and it is quite sickening. One generation goes, another comes. The sun rises, and the sun goes down. That was what the sun did yesterday, and what I expect it will do tomorrow. The wind blows north, and the wind blows south; and this is all it has been doing for these thousands of years. The rivers run into the sea, and it would be some relief to find that sea growing fuller; to spot the clear waters

---
[771] From the *Royal Preacher: Lectures on Ecclesiastes* by James Hamilton (1814-1867).
[772] Ecclesiastes 1:2
[773] Song of Solomon 1:2
[774] Song of Solomon 2:4

wetting the dry pebbles on the seashore, and reaching up to the green fields, and floating the boats and fishes up in the forest. But we are denied even that inconvenient novelty, because even after many streams and rivers have tumbled worlds of water into the sea, its tide will not overstep its boundary. The flood rises, but still refuses to cross its border.

"Words themselves are weariness. It would tire us to list their endless variations and their busy similarities that make up this endless weariness of existence. There are no novelties, no wonders, no discoveries. This universe does not provide an eye full or an arm full of newness to we who inhabit it. The present only repeats the past; the future will repeat them both. The inventions of today are the forgotten arts of yesterday; our children will forget our wisdom, only to have the pleasure of fishing up, as new geniuses, our outdated truisms. There is no new thing under the sun and yet no peace.

"Never ending responsibilities and momentary pleasures, the same atoms with minor alterations, sameness and yet constant change, make up this boring assortment. Woe is me for this weary world!"[775]

12 I the Preacher have been king over Israel in Jerusalem. **13** And I applied my heart to seek and to search out by wisdom all that is done under heaven. *(Solomon began his search by looking for supreme delight in knowledge, but his quest was useless. Had he used his efforts to know Christ, he would have found that knowledge to be a fountain of delight.)* It is an unhappy business that God has given to the children of man to be busy with. **14** I have seen everything that is done under the sun, and behold, all is vanity and a striving after wind.

15 What is crooked cannot be made straight,
 and what is lacking cannot be counted.

NOVEMBER 2
Seek First the Kingdom Of God and His Righteousness[776]

Solomon gives a description of the ways that he searched for the greatest pleasure, but without success. Everything seemed to be in his favor. He had a great mind and almost unlimited resources at his command. If Solomon could not find satisfaction when he had the whole world at his command, how much less can common people hope to find it with far less money and much more limited knowledge? There is no satisfaction apart from God.

Ecclesiastes 1:16-18

16 I said in my heart, "I have acquired great wisdom, surpassing all who were over Jerusalem before me, and my heart has had great experience of wisdom and knowledge." **17** And I applied my heart to know wisdom and to know madness and folly. I perceived that this also is but a striving after wind. *(He did not limit his research to serious subjects, but investigated all he could of the silly and insane things of human nature. Even if we assume that he gorged himself with the lighter as well as the heavier literature of his times, including the humorous side of life, the result was the same. The hunger of the soul was not satisfied with laughter any more than with hard study. It will always be that way. The library is not heaven. Neither are the amusements of the world a paradise.)* **18** For in much wisdom is much vexation,
 and he who increases knowledge
  increases sorrow.

Ecclesiastes 2:1-11

1 I said in my heart, "Come now, I will test you with pleasure; enjoy yourself." But behold, this also was vanity. **2** I said of laughter, "It is mad," and of pleasure, "What use is it?" *(In his mental madness, he tried one thing after another, from serious to carefree. From clearheaded thinking to wild excitement. But he did not find rest. How could he? True joy is found only in God.)* **3** I searched with my heart how to cheer my body with wine—my heart still guiding me

---

[775] From the *Royal Preacher: Lectures on Ecclesiastes* by James Hamilton (1814-1867).

[776] Matthew 6:33

with wisdom—and how to lay hold on folly, till I might see what was good for the children of man to do under heaven during the few days of their life. *(But in wine there is madness and not happiness. Drunkards prove this.)* ⁴ I made great works. I built houses and planted vineyards for myself. *(He became preoccupied with building. But it only amused him until the works were finished. Then he was as dissatisfied as before. If he had built as high as Babel's tower he would still not have reached heaven.)*

⁵ I made myself gardens and parks, and planted in them all kinds of fruit trees. ⁶ I made myself pools from which to water the forest of growing trees. *(But in all his gardens he could not grow the tree of life or the plant of content, and therefore he failed here also.)* ⁷ I bought male and female slaves, and had slaves who were born in my house. I had also great possessions of herds and flocks, more than any who had been before me in Jerusalem. ⁸ I also gathered for myself silver and gold and the treasure of kings and provinces. I got singers, both men and women, and many concubines, the delight of the sons of man.

But in all his treasure houses and halls of music, he could not possess the pearl of great value[777] or hear the song of sweet peace.[778] The poorest person of faith in Solomon's kingdom was far happier than he was. Alas, poor rich Solomon!

⁹ So I became great and surpassed all who were before me in Jerusalem. Also my wisdom remained with me. *(But it only remained to make him feel more deeply the emptiness of earthly joys. His wisdom only served to make him feel the hollowness in his heart more intensely. The light from his learning only helped him to see more clearly the "darkness visible"[779] in which he stumbled around.)* ¹⁰ And whatever my eyes desired I did not keep from them. I kept my heart from no pleasure, for my heart found pleasure in all my toil, and this was my reward for all my toil. ¹¹ Then I considered all that my hands had done and the toil I had expended in doing it, and behold, all was vanity and a striving after wind, and there was nothing to be gained under the sun. *(The little joy he felt in chasing after any one of his various desires vanished when he finally got hold of it. He became a worn out man; a man tired and bored, but unable to rest after getting what he thought would make him happy. He went round and round like a mill horse, harnessed to his work, but never getting beyond the weary circle of unrest. To know Jesus, to love God, to find satisfaction in heavenly things; this is wisdom. The foolishness of Solomon should force us to seek Jesus. May God allow that to be true about us.)*

Horse Harnessed to Grinding Mill

November 3

In the Day of Adversity Consider[780]

Ecclesiastes 7:1-14

1 A good name is better than precious ointment,
    and the day of death than the day of birth.

Almost everyone would like to have a good reputation. To be known as a righteous person is a good reason for choosing to live a life of integrity. And to have died as a martyr for the faith, or to have lived as a persecuted believer, or endured poverty rather than undermine Christian principles

---

[777] Matthew 13:45-46 , "The **kingdom of heaven** is like a merchant in search of fine pearls, who, on finding one pearl of great value, went and sold all that he had and bought it."
[778] Perhaps a reference to Luke 2:14, "and on earth peace among those with whom he is pleased!"
[779] "No light; but rather **darkness visible**, served only to discover sights of woe." From John Milton's *Hell in Paradise Lost*.

[780] Ecclesiastes 7:14

is a great blessing. To die being remembered for holiness and kindness means the difficult trials of life were worth it. To these, the day of death is the completing of a life of honor, the celebration of a life lived well.

2   It is better to go to the house of mourning
      than to go to the house of feasting,
   for this is the end of all mankind,
      and the living will lay it to heart.

3   Sorrow is better than laughter,
      for by sadness of face the heart is made glad.

4   The heart of the wise is in the house of mourning,
      but the heart of fools is in the house of mirth.

Experience has proved to all wise people that the trustworthy lessons they have learned in the house of mourning are more valuable, more strengthening, more comforting, and more joyous than the shallow, thoughtless activities of so many. People who live superficial and irresponsible lives are only wearing a mask to hide the sadness in their hearts. Their lives shined for an instant and then they were gone, leaving a deeper unhappiness behind. They are like thorns that blaze for a moment and leave only black spots where they once grew.

5   It is better for a man to hear the rebuke of the wise
      than to hear the song of fools.

6   For as the crackling of thorns under a pot,
      so is the laughter of the fools;
      this also is vanity.

7   Surely oppression drives the wise into madness,
      and a bribe corrupts the heart.

A bribe twists the judgment and kills the conscience.

8   Better is the end of a thing than its beginning,
      and the patient in spirit is better than the proud in spirit.

9   Be not quick in your spirit to become angry,
      for anger lodges in the heart of fools.

The best person feels the occasional flash of anger, but bad people feed the flame. Their anger smolders long. It is ready to burst forth whenever the breath of memory fans it. To be angry and not sin[781] is very difficult. May God give us grace to rule our temper, or it will be our ruin.

10   Say not, "Why were the former days better than these?"
      For it is not from wisdom that you ask this.

Those who wish for "the good old days" should think before they speak. It is a great question whether things were ever better than at this present moment. Let us stop pointless complaining and try to make our present days better. And if we cannot improve them, let us leave them to God.

11   Wisdom is good with an inheritance,
      an advantage to those who see the sun.

People who have an inheritance and no wisdom are in a sad situation. With wealth comes great responsibilities, but they have no grace to measure up to them. The truest wealth is true religion. The richest person is the one who has God for their inheritance.[782]

12   For the protection of wisdom is like the protection of money,
      and the advantage of knowledge is that wisdom preserves the life of him who has it.

If we understand that the wisdom Solomon is talking about is true wisdom, which is real godliness, then his meaning becomes clear. There is no real life apart from faith in the Lord Jesus. Faith is our best protection in this life, as well as the greatest way to live.

13   Consider the work of God:
      who can make straight what he has made crooked?

14 In the day of prosperity be joyful, and in the day of adversity consider: God has made the one as well as the other, so that man may not find out anything that will be after him.

Troubles and afflictions are part of this life. On this side of heaven there must be

---

[781] A reference to Ephesians 4:26
[782] Romans 11:33, "Oh, the depth of the riches and wisdom and knowledge of God!"

thorns with the roses and clouds with the sunshine. Wisdom acts correctly in all situations. We should bless the Lord when his mercies overflow and repent[783] when he strikes us with the rod. The Lord does not intend that his Birds of Paradise should build their nests on any of the trees of this life's forest. Therefore he sends his roughest winds to rock the branches back and forth so that his chosen may take wing and fly upward to the heavenly land where they may light on the tree of life and sing forever, never more to be disturbed*

NOVEMBER 4
Put Devious Talk Far From You[784]
Ecclesiastes 10:1-14

1 Dead flies make the perfumer's ointment give off a stench;
   so a little folly outweighs wisdom and honor.

No matter how beautiful the jar or how excellent the fragrance, dead flies will destroy the precious lotion. And even so, what seem like unimportant faults will spoil a fine character. Being rude, having a short temper, making jokes about serious matters, unwillingness to give or spend money, self-centeredness, and a thousand other harmful flies have often turned the wonderful perfume of a Christian's life into a destructive odor to those who were around him. Let us pray for grace to avoid the smaller errors, so that they will not do serious harm to us and the gospel. When something is really good it is a shame to spoil it by not correcting our small faults. Little things can ruin our influence for good. Watch out for little flies!

2 A wise man's heart inclines him to the right,
   but a fool's heart to the left.

The wise person is sensible and applies themselves to accomplishing their goals. The foolish person may have good intentions, but does not make the effort to achieve them.

3 Even when the fool walks on the road, he lacks sense,
   and he says to everyone that he is a fool.

4 If the anger of the ruler rises against you, do not leave your place,
   for calmness will lay great offenses to rest.

5 There is an evil that I have seen under the sun, as it were an error proceeding from the ruler: 6 folly is set in many high places, and the rich sit in a low place. 7 I have seen slaves on horses, and princes walking on the ground like slaves.

Kings are not always wise in choosing whom they honor. Sometimes the best people experience the pain of seeing less qualified people promoted over them. Sometimes God gives the least worthy people positions of power and influence, while people of character and grace are left to suffer in the cold shade of poverty. The Lord is behind this. He has wise reasons for bringing it about. Therefore we should cheerfully submit to his will. Let us not envy or flatter the great or be dissatisfied with our own situation. Wrongs will be righted in good time. God's people can afford to wait. Meanwhile it is better to be in the lowest condition and enjoy the love of God, than to sit among princes and live without our Father's presence.

8 He who digs a pit will fall into it,
   and a serpent will bite him who breaks through a wall.

Never set traps for others or disobey beneficial laws because they are unpleasant. Evil will come of it.

9 He who quarries stones is hurt by them,
   and he who splits logs is endangered by them.

There is some risk in any kind of job. This is a good reason to ask the Lord to keep us safe every day, however free from danger our work may seem to be.

10 If the iron is blunt, and one does not sharpen the edge,
   he must use more strength,
   but wisdom helps one to succeed.

---

[783] *repent, repentance* - The act or feeling of remorse, regret, sorrow or shame that results in a change of heart or purpose.
[784] Proverbs 4:24

Knowledge is power. A little common sense will save a lot of effort. It is good to have our wits about us. Christian people should never be stupid. Let us sharpen our axes.

¹¹ If the serpent bites before it is charmed,
   there is no advantage to the charmer.
¹² The words of a wise man's mouth win him favor,
   but the lips of a fool consume him.
¹³ The beginning of the words of his mouth is foolishness,
   and the end of his talk is evil madness.
¹⁴ A fool multiplies words,
   though no man knows what is to be,
   and who can tell him what will be after him?

Quiet rivers run deep, but the babbling brook is shallow. Great talkers are usually little doers. People of many words are rarely people of great deeds. No one person really knows all that much. If we talk a lot, we will most likely get into subjects that we do not understand and so reveal our foolishness. An ignorant person, if they are quiet, may pass for wise; but a talkative person advertises their own lack of common sense. A quiet tongue shows a wise head. We seldom get into trouble by silence, but noisy tongues often bring grief to their owners. "Let your speech always be gracious, seasoned with salt, so that you may know how you ought to answer each person."⁷⁸⁵ We should aim to edify with our words. However, this is often forgotten and people talk as if their tongues were their own. They forget Jesus said, "I tell you, on the day of judgment people will give account for every careless word they speak."⁷⁸⁶

Oh Lord, keep our lips, so that we will not sin against you.

---

⁷⁸⁵ Colossians 4:6
⁷⁸⁶ Matthew 12:36

NOVEMBER 5
At Evening Time There Shall Be Light⁷⁸⁷

We shall read once more in the book of Ecclesiastes. This selection is the wise man's famous words to young people.

Ecclesiastes 11:9-10

⁹ Rejoice, O young man, in your youth, and let your heart cheer you in the days of your youth. Walk in the ways of your heart and the sight of your eyes. But know that for all these things God will bring you into judgment. *(Solomon seems to dare the young man to throw caution to the wind and seek his own pleasure. But he warns him there is a price to be paid if he does. The cost will not be worth it! It never pays to sin, because the truth is, every sin will face punishment.)* ¹⁰ Remove vexation from your heart, and put away pain from your body, for youth and the dawn of life are vanity. *(There is a way for youth to have true joy. Let the wise young person try it. Our young days will soon be over, let us make them as happy as we can. Enjoy life while we have it. Everyone agrees with this advice, but few know that the best way of accomplishing it is to be given salvation by believing in Jesus.)*

Ecclesiastes 12:1-7; 13-14

¹ Remember also your Creator in the days of your youth, before the evil days come and the years draw near of which you will say, "I have no pleasure in them"; *(Youth is the best time for serious thinking about important things and deciding to believe in Jesus. Old age robs much of the incentive and ability to consider the crucial subject of eternity. The mind is not as sharp as it used to be and the body is weakening. Both make examining subjects that have been ignored for a long life all the more difficult to consider. Young people should beware of delay and give up the idea that they can wait until they are older to think about giving their lives to Jesus. No tree is so easily bent as the green sapling.)* ² before the sun and the light and the moon and the stars are darkened and the clouds return after the rain, *(meaning that in old age, sicknesses are many and are felt*

---

⁷⁸⁷ Zechariah 14:7

more sharply than when we are young.) ³ in the day when the keepers of the house tremble, *(the arms are no longer powerful)* and the strong men are bent, *(the old person's legs are unsteady beneath their weight)* and the grinders cease because they are few, *(their teeth are almost gone)* and those who look through the windows are dimmed, *(the eyes grow dim)* ⁴ and the doors on the street are shut—*(the senses are gradually fading, both ears and eyes become like doors closed to the outside world)* when the sound of the grinding is low, and one rises up at the sound of a bird, *(their nights are tiring, the first crowing of the rooster wakes them.)* and all the daughters of song are brought low—*(their own voice is gone, and they are no longer able to hear the voice of others)* ⁵ they are afraid also of what is high, and terrors are in the way; *(elderly people are full of worry; boldness and courage vanish)* the almond tree blossoms, the grasshopper drags itself along, and desire fails, because man is going to his eternal home, and the mourners go about the streets— ⁶ before the silver cord is snapped, or the golden bowl is broken, or the pitcher is shattered at the fountain, or the wheel broken at the cistern, *(The spinal cord, the skull, the heart, and the circulation of the blood are pictured here in beautiful imagery; all these fail us in death.)* ⁷ and the dust returns to the earth as it was, and the spirit returns to God who gave it.

¹³ The end of the matter; all has been heard. Fear God and keep his commandments, for this is the whole duty of man. ¹⁴ For God will bring every deed into judgment, with every secret thing, whether good or evil. *(This, then, is the heart of the matter. But the question is, how are we to fulfill "the whole duty of man?" We may rest assured that we are quite powerless to do it ourselves. Only in Christ Jesus can we find the law fulfilled. He is ours if we believe in him. This is true wisdom. Solomon would have been wiser even if this were all he knew.)*

NOVEMBER 6
Be Kind To Everyone[788]

2 Chronicles 9:31

³¹ And Solomon slept with his fathers and was buried in the city of David his father, and Rehoboam his son reigned in his place. *(The wisest man in the world died and so must we all. There is no getting around it. What a change came over the nation when the great ruler passed the scepter into the hands of his unfit successor. It is sad when great fathers have foolish children.)*

2 Chronicles 10:1-8; 10-16; 19

¹ Rehoboam went to Shechem, for all Israel had come to Shechem to make him king. ² And as soon as Jeroboam the son of Nebat heard of it (for he was in Egypt, where he had fled from King Solomon), then Jeroboam returned from Egypt. ³ And they sent and called him. *(The people had felt the government of Solomon had been too dictatorial. They had decided to demand more compassionate laws before they would allow Rehoboam to be their king. They hoped they would be given more liberty if they threatened to set up another king instead of him.)* And Jeroboam and all Israel came and said to Rehoboam, ⁴ "Your father made our yoke heavy. Now therefore lighten the hard service of your father and his heavy yoke on us, and we will serve you." ⁵ He said to them, "Come to me again in three days." So the people went away.

He did the right thing to take time for thinking about his decision. Important steps should not be taken in a hurry. We can do in an hour what we cannot undo in a lifetime.

⁶ Then King Rehoboam took counsel with the old men, who had stood before Solomon his father while he was yet alive, saying, "How do you advise me to answer this people?" ⁷ And they said to him, "If you will be good to this people and please them and speak good words to them, then they will be your servants forever." *(Lowering our expectations will often win over those who oppose our ideas. To give in a little in order to gain much is wise policy. The people had*

---
[788] 2 Timothy 2:24

a right to what they asked. If the young prince would have agreed to their demands with a graceful spirit, he would have been the beloved ruler of an enthusiastic people.)

⁸ But he abandoned the counsel that the old men gave him, and took counsel with the young men who had grown up with him and stood before him.

¹⁰ And the young men who had grown up with him said to him, "Thus shall you speak to the people who said to you, 'Your father made our yoke heavy, but you lighten it for us'; thus shall you say to them, 'My little finger is thicker than my father's thighs. ¹¹ And now, whereas my father laid on you a heavy yoke, I will add to your yoke. My father disciplined you with whips, but I will discipline you with scorpions.'"

These young advisors thought it would be dangerous to give the people what they asked for. If the king agreed to their request, would they not be encouraged to ask for more later? Let them be put in their place immediately with an iron fist. To consent to their demands would only inflate them with pride and lead to even more rebellion. We have heard men talk like this in our own day, but we judged them to be conceited fellows. If the people ask for right things, let them have them. No harm can come from it.

¹² So Jeroboam and all the people came to Rehoboam the third day, as the king said, "Come to me again the third day." ¹³ And the king answered them harshly; and forsaking the counsel of the old men, ¹⁴ King Rehoboam spoke to them according to the counsel of the young men, saying, "My father made your yoke heavy, but I will add to it. My father disciplined you with whips, but I will discipline you with scorpions." ¹⁵ So the king did not listen to the people, for it was a turn of affairs brought about by God that the LORD might fulfill his word, which he spoke by Ahijah the Shilonite to Jeroboam the son of Nebat.

¹⁶ And when all Israel saw that the king did not listen to them, the people answered the king, "What portion have we in David? We have no inheritance in the son of Jesse. Each of you to your tents, O Israel! Look now to your own house, David." So all Israel went to their tents.

¹⁹ So Israel has been in rebellion against the house of David to this day. *(The sin of Solomon inflicted his son Rehoboam, but God was not unjust. The unwise action of Rehoboam led naturally to the ten tribes breaking away. God's ways are always just. We may be confident that if he seems to act unjustly, it is not really the case. God's ways are fair and in the end men will confess that it is so.)*

NOVEMBER 7

Do Not Be Afraid Of Them, For I Am With You[789]

1 Kings 12:26-33

²⁶ And Jeroboam said in his heart, "Now the kingdom will turn back to the house of David. ²⁷ If this people go up to offer sacrifices in the temple of the LORD at Jerusalem, then the heart of this people will turn again to their lord, to Rehoboam king of Judah, and they will kill me and return to Rehoboam king of Judah" *(Jeroboam was afraid that when the ten tribes went up to the temple in Jerusalem every year, their old love for their fellow Israelites would return, that they would see the magnificence of David's palace and be sorry they had rebelled against the ancient line of kings. He thought that allowing his subjects to worship in the Lord's temple would endanger his position as king. He was a clever man, and like Ahithophel, he had no fear of God. So he decided to set up a new religion. God's honor meant nothing to him. Efforts to conform with worldly desires and other attempts to satisfy human nature have often been the reasons for starting false religions.)*

²⁸ So the king took counsel and made two calves of gold. And he said to the people, "You have gone up to Jerusalem long enough. Behold your gods, O Israel, who brought you up out of the land of Egypt." *(People naturally love things that require little effort. They prefer a religion that will not trouble them or interrupt their lives very much. That is the reason Jeroboam appealed*

---

[789] Jeremiah 1:8

to the shameful tendencies of their human nature. But how disgraceful it was for Israel to forsake the living God and bow before the image of a bull just as an excuse to not have to travel so far. May we never leave the good old paths of truth because it would be convenient, or give us a better chance of advancement in our job or better opportunities to make more money. Let us hold tightly to the Lord with all our heart.)

29 And he set one in Bethel, and the other he put in Dan. *(At both ends of the land, so that no one would have far to travel.)* **30** Then this thing became a sin, for the people went as far as Dan to be before one. **31** He also made temples on high places and appointed priests from among all the people, who were not of the Levites. *(The true priests remained faithful to the Lord, so Jeroboam appointed other men to be priests. This speaks well for the Levites. Even if all other people become idolaters, God's ministers must not.)* **32** And Jeroboam appointed a feast on the fifteenth day of the eighth month like the feast that was in Judah, and he offered sacrifices on the altar. So he did in Bethel, sacrificing to the calves that he made. And he placed in Bethel the priests of the high places that he had made.

33 He went up to the altar that he had made in Bethel on the fifteenth day in the eighth month, in the month that he had devised from his own heart. And he instituted a feast for the people of Israel and went up to the altar to make offerings. *(He dared to make himself a priest and change the seasons God had appointed for worship. He was not afraid to set up an altar to compete with the true one or to adore God by bowing down to the image of an animal. All of this is disgusting in the sight of God. We fear that many in our day are also guilty of Jeroboam's sin. They invent rituals and ceremonies of their own and desert the Lord, who is a Spirit, and must be worshiped in spirit and truth.[790] Oh for grace to be faithful to the Word of God in all things.)*

1 Kings 13:1-10

1 And behold, a man of God came out of Judah by the word of the Lord to Bethel. Jeroboam was standing by the altar to make offerings. **2** And the man cried against the altar by the word of the Lord and said, "O altar, altar, thus says the Lord: 'Behold, a son shall be born to the house of David, Josiah by name, and he shall sacrifice on you the priests of the high places who make offerings on you, and human bones shall be burned on you.'" **3** And he gave a sign the same day, saying, "This is the sign that the Lord has spoken: 'Behold, the altar shall be torn down, and the ashes that are on it shall be poured out.'" *(This was bravely spoken. The prophet did not fear the wrath of the king or the anger of the crowds around him. Messengers of God must not be afraid of how people might react to their message.)*

4 And when the king heard the saying of the man of God, which he cried against the altar at Bethel, Jeroboam stretched out his hand from the altar, saying. "Seize him." *(He was greatly irritated to have this first and greatest ceremony of his new religion interrupted by this zealous messenger of the Lord. "Seize him!" cries the king, as he puts forth his own hand to order the arrest.)* And his hand, which he stretched out against him, dried up, so that he could not draw it back to himself. **5** The altar also was torn down, and the ashes poured out from the altar, according to the sign that the man of God had given by the word of the Lord. **6** And the king said to the man of God, "Entreat now the favor of the Lord your God, and pray for me, that my hand may be restored to me." *(The Lord can soon bring down the strongest heart. This proud ruler went quickly from threatening to begging. The God who shriveled his hand could just as easily paralyzed his whole body, but in his wrath he remembered mercy.)* And the man of God entreated the Lord, and the king's hand was restored to him and became as it was before. *(God's servants are very willing to pray for their enemies and return good for evil.)*

7 And the king said to the man of God, "Come home with me, and refresh yourself, and I will give you a reward." *(Notice that*

---

[790] John 4:24

Jeroboam never said a word that indicated he had repented or was humbled by this experience. He was hardened in his proud rebellion against God. He might have been willing to reward the prophet, but he would not thank the Lord who sent him.) **8** And the man of God said to the king, "If you give me half your house, I will not go in with you. And I will not eat bread or drink water in this place, **9** for so was it commanded me by the word of the LORD, saying, 'You shall neither eat bread nor drink water nor return by the way that you came.'" **10** So he went another way and did not return by the way that he came to Bethel.

It was not proper for God's servant to have any fellowship with rebellious Israel. No, not even so much as eating a piece of bread or taking a sip of water with them. The true believer's duty is to avoid all unnecessary fellowship with people of sin. "What harmony has Christ with Belial?"[791]

NOVEMBER 8

The LORD Your God…Is a Jealous God[792]

1 Kings 13:11-30

11 Now an old prophet lived in Bethel. And his sons came and told him all that the man of God had done that day in Bethel. They also told to their father the words that he had spoken to the king. **12** And their father said to them, "Which way did he go?" And his sons showed him the way that the man of God who came from Judah had gone. **13** And he said to his sons, "Saddle the donkey for me." So they saddled the donkey for him and he mounted it. **14** And he went after the man of God and found him sitting under an oak. And he said to him, "Are you the man of God who came from Judah?" And he said, "I am." **15** Then he said to him, "Come home with me and eat bread." **16** And he said, "I may not return with you, or go in with you, neither will I eat bread nor drink water with you in this place, **17** for it was said to me by the word of the LORD, 'You shall neither eat bread nor drink water there, nor return by the way that you came.'" **18** And he said to him, "I also am a prophet as you are, and an angel spoke to me by the word of the LORD, saying, 'Bring him back with you into your house that he may eat bread and drink water.'" But he lied to him. **19** So he went back with him and ate bread in his house and drank water.

20 And as they sat at the table, the word of the LORD came to the prophet who had brought him back. **21** And he cried to the man of God who came from Judah, "Thus says the LORD, 'Because you have disobeyed the word of the LORD and have not kept the command that the LORD your God commanded you, **22** but have come back and have eaten bread and drunk water in the place of which he said to you, "Eat no bread and drink no water," your body shall not come to the tomb of your fathers.'" **23** And after he had eaten bread and drunk, he saddled the donkey for the prophet whom he had brought back. **24** And as he went away a lion met him on the road and killed him. And his body was thrown in the road, and the donkey stood beside it; the lion also stood beside the body. **25** And behold, men passed by and saw the body thrown in the road and the lion standing by the body. And they came and told it in the city where the old prophet lived.

26 And when the prophet who had brought him back from the way heard of it, he said, "It is the man of God who disobeyed the word of the LORD; therefore the LORD has given him to the lion, which has torn him and killed him, according to the word that the LORD spoke to him." **27** And he said to his sons, "Saddle the donkey for me." And they saddled it. **28** And he went and found his body thrown in the road, and the donkey and the lion standing beside the body. The lion had not eaten the body or torn the donkey. **29** And the prophet took up the body of the man of God and laid it on the donkey and brought it back to the city to mourn and to bury him. **30** And he laid the body in his own grave. And they mourned over him, saying, "Alas, my brother!"

This is a very frightful illustration of the great truth that the Lord our God is a jealous God. He expects those he honors, by making

---
[791] 2 Corinthians 6:15 NASB updated
[792] Deuteronomy 6:15

them his servants, to obey him. He has clearly stated, "Among those who are near me I will be sanctified."[793] To treat any of God's commands as unimportant may bring God's chastisement[794] on even the best of people. The old prophet at Bethel must have backslidden very far from God, or he would not have tempted the man of God so wickedly. However, the man of God should not have been so quick to believe a story that contradicted what God had personally commanded him. The Lord saw it necessary to take his life. Let us hope that as a righteous man he had hope in his death. Let us hope also that the death of the prophet from Judah became a warning to the old prophet at Bethel and was the means of restoring him to his right state before God. This may have been one of those terrible, but righteous acts where the Lord calls back his wandering followers. It is a lesson for all of us to walk before God with a fear of offending him and a holy jealousy that his name is honored.

NOVEMBER 9
The Root Of the Matter Is Found In Him[795]

1 Kings 14:1-10; 12-13; 17-18

1 At that time Abijah the son of Jeroboam fell sick. **2** And Jeroboam said to his wife, "Arise, and disguise yourself, that it not be known that you are the wife of Jeroboam, and go to Shiloh. Behold, Ahijah the prophet is there, who said of me that I should be king over this people. **3** Take with you ten loaves, some cakes, and a jar of honey, and go to him. He will tell you what shall happen to the child."

Bad people cannot help respecting God's true messengers. Why did Jeroboam not go to the prophets of the golden calves? In times of great need, the ungodly and those who follow false religions lose their faith in what they claimed to believe in. They begin to look around for something that will provide them more comfort. King Jeroboam had seen the power of the prophet's word before, so he wanted to hear what he had to say about his sick son. Many sinners are like Jeroboam. In his heart he knew Ahijah was a minister of the true God and that what he had to say was worth hearing.

4 Jeroboam's wife did so. She arose and went to Shiloh and came to the house of Ahijah. Now Ahijah could not see, for his eyes were dim because of his age. **5** And the LORD said to Ahijah, "Behold, the wife of Jeroboam is coming to inquire of you concerning her son, for he is sick. Thus and thus shall you say to her."

When she came, she pretended to be another woman. **6** But when Ahijah heard the sound of her feet, as she came in at the door, he said, "Come in, wife of Jeroboam. Why do you pretend to be another? For I am charged with unbearable news for you. *(Those who think they can hide from God will be absolutely amazed. God will unmask them and make them ashamed. Some sinners pretend they are saints, but "The Lord knows those who are his."[796])* **7** Go, tell Jeroboam, 'Thus says the LORD, the God of Israel: "Because I exalted you from among the people and made you leader over my people Israel **8** and tore the kingdom away from the house of David and gave it to you, and yet you have not been like my servant David, who kept my commandments and followed me with all his heart, doing only that which was right in my eyes, **9** but you have done evil above all who were before you and have gone and made for yourself other gods and metal images, provoking me to anger, and have cast me behind your back, **10** therefore behold, I will bring harm upon the house of Jeroboam and will cut off from Jeroboam every male, both bond and free in Israel, and will burn up the house of Jeroboam, as a man burns up dung until it is all gone."'" *(Jeroboam would have no living relatives to continue his name. His whole family was going to be wiped out and his name erased*

---
[793] Leviticus 10:3
[794] *chasten, chastening* or *chastisement* - The act of discipline which may include scolding, criticizing or pain inflicted for the purpose of correction or moral improvement.
[795] Job 19:28

[796] 2 Timothy 2:19

from the families of Israel. God knows how to punish as well as how to bless.)

¹² "Arise therefore, go to your house. When your feet enter the city, the child shall die. ¹³ And all Israel shall mourn for him and bury him, for he only of Jeroboam shall come to the grave, because in him there is found something pleasing to the LORD, the God of Israel, in the house of Jeroboam."

¹⁷ Then Jeroboam's wife arose and departed and came to Tirzah. And as she came to the threshold of the house, the child died. ¹⁸ And all Israel buried him and mourned for him, according to the word of the LORD, which he spoke by his servant Ahijah the prophet.

*Matthew Henry says this about this child: "Good people are those who have good things toward the Lord God of Israel. They have good tendencies, good intentions and good desires toward him. If there is only one good thing like that, God will find it. God looks for it. No matter how little it is, he is pleased with it. A little grace goes a great way with great folks. It is so rare to find princes who look with favor on religion, that when they are found, they are worthy of double honor. God fearing characteristics are very special and heart warming when they are found in those who are young. The image of God in miniature has an unusual glow and beauty in it. A good child in the house of Jeroboam is a miracle of divine grace. To be there and not be tainted is like being in the fiery furnace and not being burnt or injured. Observe the care taken of him. He is the only one of all Jeroboam's family that will be buried and mourned as one that lived an acceptable life. Those that are distinguished by divine grace will be distinguished by divine providence."*⁷⁹⁷

In this family we trust there are some who have hopeful signs of grace in them. If there are, let them be encouraged by knowing that the Lord notices the smallest amount of grace that may be found in any one of us.

NOVEMBER 10
God Is With Us At Our Head⁷⁹⁸

While the new kingdom of the ten tribes was under the rule of Jeroboam, Rehoboam died and was replaced by his son, Abijah.

2 Chronicles 13:1-16; 18; 20

¹ In the eighteenth year of King Jeroboam, Abijah began to reign over Judah. ² He reigned for three years in Jerusalem. His mother's name was Micaiah the daughter of Uriel of Gibeah.

Now there was war between Abijah and Jeroboam. ³ Abijah went out to battle, having an army of valiant men of war, 400,000 chosen men. And Jeroboam drew up his line of battle against him, with 800,000 chosen mighty warriors. *(The horrors of civil war are almost unimaginable. Surely every male in the two nations must have been drafted into one or the other army. We should be thankful when we are blessed with peace in our own country. A day is coming when the Lord will stop all wars on this earth.)*

⁴ Then Abijah stood up on Mount Zemaraim that is in the hill country of Ephraim and said, "Hear me, O Jeroboam and all Israel! ⁵ Ought you not to know that the LORD God of Israel gave the kingship over Israel forever to David and his sons by a covenant of salt? ⁶ Yet Jeroboam the son of Nebat, a servant of Solomon the son of David, rose up and rebelled against his lord, ⁷ and certain worthless scoundrels gathered about him and defied Rehoboam the son of Solomon, when Rehoboam was young and irresolute and could not withstand them.

⁸ "And now you think to withstand the kingdom of the LORD in the hand of the sons of David, because you are a great multitude and have with you the golden calves that Jeroboam made you for gods. *(Abijah was wise to explain the reason for the battle. When it comes to whether Jehovah or golden calves should be worshiped, the answer is clear.)* ⁹ Have you not driven out the priests of the LORD, the sons of Aaron, and the Levites, and made priests for yourselves like the peoples of other lands? Whoever comes

---

[797] Matthew Henry (1662-1714)

[798] 2 Chronicles 13:12

for ordination with a young bull or seven rams becomes a priest of what are not gods. ¹⁰ But as for us, the Lord is our God, and we have not forsaken him. We have priests ministering to the Lord who are sons of Aaron, and Levites for their service. ¹¹ They offer to the Lord every morning and every evening burnt offerings and incense of sweet spices, set out the showbread on the table of pure gold, and care for the golden lampstand that its lamps may burn every evening. For we keep the charge of the Lord our God, but you have forsaken him. ¹² Behold, God is with us at our head, and his priests with their battle trumpets to sound the call to battle against you. O sons of Israel, do not fight against the Lord, the God of your fathers, for you cannot succeed."

This speech was intended to prevent bloodshed. Abijah's motive was deserving of praise. We cannot be sure that Abijah was a spiritual man, but he and the nation of Judah still worshiped Jehovah and still had the Lord on their side.

¹³ Jeroboam had sent an ambush around to come upon them from behind. Thus his troops were in front of Judah, and the ambush was behind them. *(Jeroboam was not a man of words, but of deeds. While Abijah was delivering his speech, Jeroboam was surrounding his opponent.)* ¹⁴ And when Judah looked, behold, the battle was in front of and behind them. And they cried to the Lord, and the priests blew the trumpets. ¹⁵ Then the men of Judah raised the battle shout. And when the men of Judah shouted, God defeated Jeroboam and all Israel before Abijah and Judah. ¹⁶ The men of Israel fled before Judah, and God gave them into their hand. *(Prayer and praise are superior weapons. We should not be surprised that the Lord got involved when his people brought him into the fight by using prayer and praise.)*

¹⁸ Thus the men of Israel were subdued at that time, and the men of Judah prevailed, because they relied on the Lord, the God of their fathers.

²⁰ Jeroboam did not recover his power in the days of Abijah. And the Lord struck him down, and he died. *(He was made to feel how impossible it is to fight against God. But he would not quit and died without repenting[799] for his actions. He is remembered because the way he lived brought God's curse on him. May the good Lord save us from such an end.)*

November 11
Thanks Be To God, Who Gives Us the Victory[800]
2 Chronicles 14:1-15

¹ Abijah slept with his fathers, and they buried him in the city of David. And Asa his son reigned in his place. In his days the land had rest for ten years. *(Asa's reign was a change for the better. Abijah worshiped Jehovah, but he allowed idol worship in his kingdom. The godless group multiplied and polluted the nation with their idolatry and immoral behavior. Abijah and his favorite queens supported and helped these evil people and the nation grew worse. It is remarkable that even though his mother and father were bad, Asa did what was good. It is clear from this that children will not turn out wicked simply because their parents were.)*

² And Asa did what was good and right in the eyes of the Lord his God. ³ He took away the foreign altars and the high places and broke down the pillars and cut down the Asherim ⁴ and commanded Judah to seek the Lord, the God of their fathers, and to keep the law and the commandment. *(Asa made a complete change. He got rid of not only the images of the false gods, but the sacred groves where they were worshiped. Oh that we might live to see such a complete cleaning up of our own land! Let us pray for it.)* ⁵ He also took out of all the cities of Judah the high places and the incense altars. And the kingdom had rest under him.

⁶ He built fortified cities in Judah, for the land had rest. He had no war in those years, for the Lord gave him peace. ⁷ And he said to Judah, "Let us build these cities and surround them with walls and towers, gates and bars. The land is still ours, because we

---

[799] *repent, repentance* - The act or feeling of remorse, regret, sorrow or shame that results in a change of heart or purpose.
[800] 1 Corinthians 15:57

have sought the LORD our God. We have sought him, and he has given us peace on every side." So they built and prospered. *(They obeyed God and he blessed them. But even though this was obvious, their history shows their faithfulness did not last long.)* ⁸ And Asa had an army of 300,000 from Judah, armed with large shields and spears, and 280,000 men from Benjamin that carried shields and drew bows. All these were mighty men of valor.

⁹ Zerah the Ethiopian came out against them with an army of a million men and 300 chariots, and came as far as Mareshah. ¹⁰ And Asa went out to meet him, and they drew up their lines of battle in the Valley of Zephathah at Mareshah. *(The good king had his trials. His obedience brought prosperity, but it did not protect him from every trouble.)* ¹¹ And Asa cried to the LORD his God, "O LORD, there is none like you to help, between the mighty and the weak. Help us, O LORD our God, for we rely on you, and in your name we have come against this multitude. O LORD, you are our God; let not man prevail against you."

This is a great example of the prayer of faith. The million soldiers of Zerah are not enough to shake his faith. He knows they are nothing before the Lord and does not fear their large number. He is not discouraged because his army is not as strong as Zerah's. He knows the Lord is all powerful and does not depend on the strength of his people. It is a glorious thing to be able to call on the Lord our God and then to rest in him without concern or fear; knowing that our cause is safe because it is about the Lord's honor and it is in his own hands. Let us follow Asa's example. Let us trust God and not be afraid when we encounter great trails and difficulties.

¹² So the LORD defeated the Ethiopians before Asa and before Judah, and the Ethiopians fled. ¹³ Asa and the people who were with him pursued them as far as Gerar, and the Ethiopians fell until none remained alive, for they were broken before the LORD and his army. The men of Judah carried away very much spoil. ¹⁴ And they attacked all the cities around Gerar, for the fear of the LORD was upon them. They plundered all the cities, for there was much plunder in them. ¹⁵ And they struck down the tents of those who had livestock and carried away sheep in abundance and camels. Then they returned to Jerusalem. *(They were more than conquerors, as believers always are. They gained greatly by the very thing that threatened to destroy them. If we will only trust the Lord in the same way, the same experience will certainly be ours. Greater is he that is for us than all that are against us.[801])*

Charles Spurgeon with his twin sons Charles and Thomas. [In that culture very young boys frequently wore dresses or gowns.]

---

[801] See Romans 8:31 and 1 John 4:4

NOVEMBER 12
If You Seek Him, He Will Be Found By You[802]

2 Chronicles 15:1-17

¹ The Spirit of God came upon Azariah the son of Oded, ² and he went out to meet Asa and said to him, "Hear me, Asa, and all Judah and Benjamin: The LORD is with you while you are with him. If you seek him, he will be found by you, but if you forsake him, he will forsake you. *(While they were still thrilled with the victory it was a good time to remind them where their great strength came from. God sent them a prophet while the rewards of obeying him were before their eyes, to urge them to continue obeying the Lord. The prophet did not congratulate and flatter king Asa. Instead, he reminded him that he must continue to follow the Lord who had done so much for him. Pastors are not sent to please us, but to guide us.)*

³ "For a long time Israel was without the true God, and without a teaching priest and without law, ⁴ but when in their distress they turned to the LORD, the God of Israel, and sought him, he was found by them. ⁵ In those times there was no peace to him who went out or to him who came in, for great disturbances afflicted all the inhabitants of the lands. ⁶ They were broken in pieces. Nation was crushed by nation and city by city, for God troubled them with every sort of distress. ⁷ But you, take courage! Do not let your hands be weak, for your work shall be rewarded." *(Israel's history was clear. When they were faithful to God they prospered, when they turned their backs on him he did not bless them. They made or unmade their own fortunes. Have we not also learned by this time that we are happy when we live near to God and miserable when we fall back into our old evil habits? Let us not forget this remarkable truth.)*

⁸ As soon as Asa heard these words, the prophecy of Azariah the son of Oded, he took courage and put away the detestable idols from all the land of Judah and Benjamin and from the cities that he had taken in the hill country of Ephraim, and he repaired the altar of the LORD that was in front of the vestibule of the house of the LORD. *(The cleanest room can be cleaned even more. Asa investigated the situation and found there was more to be done. Here and there, the idol worshipers secretly kept their idols, but this time they must be found and destroyed.)* ⁹ And he gathered all Judah and Benjamin, and those from Ephraim, Manasseh, and Simeon who were residing with them, for great numbers had deserted to him from Israel when they saw that the LORD his God was with him.

¹⁰ They were gathered at Jerusalem in the third month of the fifteenth year of the reign of Asa. ¹¹ They sacrificed to the LORD on that day from the spoil that they had brought 700 oxen and 7,000 sheep. ¹² And they entered into a covenant to seek the LORD, the God of their fathers, with all their heart and with all their soul, ¹³ but that whoever would not seek the LORD, the God of Israel, should be put to death, whether young or old, man or woman. ¹⁴ They swore an oath to the LORD with a loud voice and with shouting and with trumpets and with horns. ¹⁵ And all Judah rejoiced over the oath, for they had sworn with all their heart and had sought him with their whole desire, and he was found by them, and the LORD gave them rest all around. *(The people were great at promising, but slow in performing. Their hearts were fickle. What they resolved on one day with great enthusiasm, they forgot the next. It was not long before they would again fall in love with their idols. They were a lot like we are!)*

¹⁶ Even Maacah, his mother, King Asa removed from being queen mother because she had made a detestable image for Asherah. Asa cut down her image, crushed it, and burned it at the brook Kidron. *(This was a masterstroke. He removed the queen-mother and destroyed her idol in the most humiliating manner. The king would not secretly allow sin even in those nearest and dearest to him. It must have caused him much pain, but he loved his God too well to back away from doing what he knew was right.)* ¹⁷ But the high places were not taken out of Israel. Nevertheless, the heart of Asa was wholly true all his days. *(There is*

---
[802] 2 Chronicles 15:2

imperfection in even the best work. Everything we do includes a "but." The false gods were torn down, but the forbidden altars to the true God were left untouched. This may be thought to be a lesser evil, but it would have been better to follow through with all the work. Still, we must admire Asa. His heart and intention were right before God.)

NOVEMBER 13
Cursed Is the Man Who Trusts In Man[803]

2 Chronicles 16:1-14

¹ In the thirty-sixth year of the reign of Asa, Baasha king of Israel went up against Judah and built Ramah, that he might permit no one to go out or come in to Asa king of Judah. *(The king of Israel was annoyed because the peace and prosperity of Judah, and the nation's faith in the true God, had inspired many of his subjects to move to the land under Asa's rule.)* ² Then Asa took silver and gold from the treasures of the house of the Lord and the king's house and sent them to Ben-hadad king of Syria, who lived in Damascus, saying, ³ "There is a covenant between me and you, as there was between my father and your father. Behold, I am sending to you silver and gold. Go, break your covenant with Baasha king of Israel, that he may withdraw from me." ⁴ And Ben-hadad listened to King Asa and sent the commanders of his armies against the cities of Israel, and they conquered Ijon, Dan, Abel-maim, and all the store cities of Naphtali. ⁵ And when Baasha heard of it, he stopped building Ramah and let his work cease. ⁶ Then King Asa took all Judah, and they carried away the stones of Ramah and its timber, with which Baasha had been building, and with them he built Geba and Mizpah.

What a proof this is that the best believers may fall into unbelief and sometimes place their trust in humans. Asa turned to Syria for help and for a while he was glad he did. The good outcome probably convinced him he was right in asking King Ben-hadad for help. But we are mistaken if we measure the correctness of our actions by their result. The Lord was angry with Asa and chastised[804] him with trouble for the rest of his life. He took the temple gold to bribe a heathen king to break his treaties, but his great fault was that he trusted in human power rather than in God.

⁷ At that time Hanani the seer came to Asa king of Judah and said to him, "Because you relied on the king of Syria, and did not rely on the Lord your God, the army of the king of Syria has escaped you. ⁸ Were not the Ethiopians and the Libyans a huge army with very many chariots and horsemen? Yet because you relied on the Lord, he gave them into your hand. ⁹ For the eyes of the Lord run to and fro throughout the whole earth, to give strong support to those whose heart is blameless toward him. You have done foolishly in this, for from now on you will have wars." *(Hanani was faithful to Asa and told him the truth. This godly king should have been touched in his conscience, but his soul was not in agreement with God. He did not receive the rebuke like a gracious person should have.)* ¹⁰ Then Asa was angry with the seer and put him in the stocks in prison, for he was in a rage with him because of this. And Asa inflicted cruelties upon some of the people at the same time.

His trust in physical means had apparently led to good results and so the king resented the prophet's warning. He became irritated and, sadly, the old nature in him took over. Until this time Asa had been a fair-minded king, but now he acted like a tyrant. We must not judge anyone by their isolated actions, but by the general course of their life. After all, Asa was one of the best kings in Judah's history.

¹¹ The acts of Asa, from first to last, are written in the Book of the Kings of Judah and Israel. ¹² In the thirty-ninth year of his reign Asa was diseased in his feet, and his disease became severe. Yet even in his disease he did not seek the Lord, but sought

---

[803] Jeremiah 17:5

[804] *chasten, chastening* or *chastisement* - The act of discipline which may include scolding, criticizing or pain inflicted for the purpose of correction or moral improvement

help from physicians. *(As a child of God he could not be left undisciplined for such sins. The disease in his feet became a heavy rod with which the Lord used to strike him. It is sad to see him at this time repeating his reckless trust in the creature instead of the Creator. We may call in the physician, but we must not forget our God. The most skillful doctor will do us no good unless God is in it.)* **13** And Asa slept with his fathers, dying in the forty-first year of his reign. **14** They buried him in the tomb that he had cut for himself in the city of David. They laid him on a bier that had been filled with various kinds of spices prepared by the perfumer's art, and they made a very great fire in his honor.

The people knew how to value a good king. His memory was very fragrant among them. May our names also "smell sweet and blossom in the dust."[805]

NOVEMBER 14
You Bless the Righteous, O LORD [806]

Asa evidently died in a backslidden condition. But the Lord had mercy on his people and gave them a good ruler in Jehoshaphat, the good son of a good father. Today, we read about his early days as king over Judah.

2 Chronicles 17:1-11

1 And Jehoshaphat his son reigned in his place and strengthened himself against Israel.

Ahab had been king over Israel for several years when Jehoshaphat became king. He was an active and warlike prince who needed to be guarded against. Jehoshaphat took normal precautions for the defense of his nation, but he did not place his trust in Syria like his father had.

2 He placed forces in all the fortified cities of Judah and set garrisons in the land of Judah, and in the cities of Ephraim that Asa his father had captured. **3** The LORD was with Jehoshaphat, because he walked in the earlier ways of his father David. He did not seek the Baals, *(Notice the difference between David's earlier ways and his last ways. What a pity that such a contrast had to be made. Sadly, many good people have their first warm, zealous, consistent ways, but gradually decline from their first love and grow cold and worldly. We should imitate that which is good in people, but avoid their faults that would have an evil influence over us. Jehoshaphat was not an idolater and was not tempted by the example of his neighbors to worship Baal.)* **4** but sought the God of his father and walked in his commandments, and not according to the practices of Israel.

5 Therefore the LORD established the kingdom in his hand. And all Judah brought tribute to Jehoshaphat, and he had great riches and honor. **6** His heart was courageous in the ways of the LORD. *(He was enthusiastic about following the Lord. His delight was to obey Jehovah.)* And furthermore, he took the high places and the Asherim out of Judah.

It is good when we can serve God with joy, because then our service is real and from the heart. The Lord made the king popular with his people and they gave him many presents, but this did not make him proud. Instead, by God's grace, the more they raised him up the more he rejoiced in the Lord.

7 In the third year of his reign he sent his officials, Ben-hail, Obadiah, Zechariah, Nethanel, and Micaiah, to teach in the cities of Judah; *(Princes and judges have great influence. When they give themselves over to promoting virtue they can accomplish great things. May God teach those who govern and those who are great. Then they will truly benefit the nation.)* **8** and with them the Levites, Shemaiah, Nethaniah, Zebadiah, Asahel, Shemiramoth, Jehonathan, Adonijah, Tobijah, and Tobadonijah, and with these Levites, the priests Elishama and Jehoram. **9** And they taught in Judah, having the Book of the Law of the LORD with them. They went about through all the cities of Judah and taught among the people.

The holy teaching of the priests and Levites supported the instruction given by the officials. Education is of small value if it is separated from true religion. There is more need for people to know their Bible than

---
[805] English poet James Shirley (1596-1666) from *The Contention of Ajax and Ulysses*
[806] Psalm 5:12

anything else. Ministers, when they teach, should carry their Bibles with them, to give weight to their words, and bring conviction on all who hear them.

10 And the fear of the LORD fell upon all the kingdoms of the lands that were around Judah, and they made no war against Jehoshaphat. *(When we are right with God he will make things right all around. He calms the raging of the sea and the unrest of the people. When the Lord gives peace no one can upset us.)*

11 Some of the Philistines brought Jehoshaphat presents and silver for tribute, and the Arabians also brought him 7,700 rams and 7,700 goats.

NOVEMBER 15
His Bread Will Be Given Him[807]

We now turn from the more peaceful history of Judah to the troubled history of their more sinful neighbor Israel. The family of Jeroboam was killed by Baasha. Baasha reigned over Israel for twenty-four years. "He did what was evil in the sight of the LORD and walked in the way of Jeroboam and in his sin which he made Israel to sin."[808] *Baasha's son, Elah, became king, but after two years he and all his descendants were murdered by his captain, Zimri, while he was "drinking himself drunk" in his palace at Tirzah.*[809] *Zimri reigned only seven days before he was overthrown by Omri, a rival commander. Omri attacked Tirzah and when Zimri knew all was lost, he set fire to the palace and died in the blaze. Omri had a troubled and wicked reign of twelve years and was then succeeded by the notorious Ahab, of whom we will now read.*

1 Kings 16:29-34

29 In the thirty-eighth year of Asa king of Judah, Ahab the son of Omri began to reign over Israel, and Ahab the son of Omri reigned over Israel in Samaria twenty-two years. **30** And Ahab the son of Omri did evil in the sight of the LORD, more than all who were before him. **31** And as if it had been a light thing for him to walk in the sins of Jeroboam the son of Nebat, he took for his wife Jezebel the daughter of Ethbaal king of the Sidonians, and went and served Baal and worshiped him. *(The strong-willed Jezebel completely mastered the indecisive Ahab. She became the real ruler of Israel. She killed the prophets of Jehovah and forced the people to worship her demon gods.)*

32 He erected an altar for Baal in the house of Baal, which he built in Samaria. **33** And Ahab made an Asherah. Ahab did more to provoke the LORD, the God of Israel, to anger than all the kings of Israel who were before him. **34** In his days Hiel of Bethel built Jericho. He laid its foundation at the cost of Abiram his firstborn, and set up its gates at the cost of his youngest son Segub, according to the word of the LORD, which he spoke by Joshua the son of Nun. *(It was a time of monstrous evil. God was not feared. The people ignored the Lord and even gloried in defying the Most High. Unbelief and superstition usually go hand in hand. Where some are worshiping a thousand false gods, others are always found who make fun of the one and only Lord. But even when this happens, the Lord's word is being fulfilled. After defeating Jericho, Joshua prophesied, "Cursed before the LORD be the man who rises up and rebuilds this city, Jericho. At the cost of his firstborn shall he lay its foundation, and at the cost of his youngest son shall he set up its gates."*[810] *In his arrogance, Hiel of Bethel did exactly what the Lord had proclaimed.)*

1 Kings 17:1-6

1 Now Elijah the Tishbite, of Tishbe in Gilead, said to Ahab, "As the LORD the God of Israel lives, before whom I stand, there shall be neither dew nor rain these years, except by my word." *(Elijah leaps onto the scene like a lion from the hills. Who he was, or what he had been, we are not told. He comes in thunder, and speaks lightning. The times were ready for an Elijah, and Elijah was ready for them.)* **2** And the word of the LORD came to him, **3** "Depart from here and

---
[807] Isaiah 33:16
[808] 1 Kings 15:34
[809] 1 Kings 16:9

[810] Joshua 6:26

turn eastward and hide yourself by the brook Cherith, which is east of the Jordan. ⁴ You shall drink from the brook, and I have commanded the ravens to feed you there." *(God is a good master and never allows his servants to starve. He will provide for his own, even if all the land is unfruitful because of drought.)*

⁵ So he went and did according to the word of the LORD. He went and lived by the brook Cherith that is east of the Jordan. ⁶ And the ravens brought him bread and meat in the morning, and bread and meat in the evening, and he drank from the brook.

He had plain food, but enough food. But what unlikely providers! Ravens are robbers of food, not providers. Yet they forgot their own hunger and the cries of their young to feed the prophet. Perhaps they brought the bread and meat from Ahab's kitchen. There was not much to be found anywhere else! An old writer observes, "Oh God! You that provide meat for the birds of the air, will make the birds of the air provide meat for man before you will allow man's dependence on you to be disappointed. Oh do not let our faith in you be inadequate, because your care can never be inadequate to us."[811]

NOVEMBER 16
Feed On His Faithfulness[812]
1 Kings 17:7-24

⁷ And after a while the brook dried up, because there was no rain in the land.

⁸ Then the word of the LORD came to [Elijah], ⁹ "Arise, go to Zarephath, which belongs to Sidon, and dwell there. Behold, I have commanded a widow there to feed you." *(When one door shuts, another opens. God is not limited to only one way of providing for his servants. It was wonderful that Elijah was fed by ravens. We now see a new wonder when he is fed by a widow who is both poor and a foreigner.)* ¹⁰ So he arose and went to Zarephath. *(He did not question the command, but obeyed it. This is the walk of faith.)* And when he came to the gate of the city, behold, a widow was there gathering sticks. *(As unlikely as it seemed that this poor woman could provide for the prophet, Elijah spoke to her with confidence.)* And he called to her and said, "Bring me a little water in a vessel, that I may drink." ¹¹ And as she was going to bring it, he called to her and said, "Bring me a morsel of bread in your hand."

¹² And she said, "As the LORD your God lives, I have nothing baked, only a handful of flour in a jar and a little oil in a jug. And now I am gathering a couple of sticks that I may go in and prepare it for myself and my son, that we may eat it and die." *(The good woman recognized Jehovah's servant and was ready to serve him, but his request for bread touched her in a tender place. She had barely enough for one small meal and then she expected to die with her child.)*

¹³ And Elijah said to her, "Do not fear; go and do as you have said. But first make me a little cake of it and bring it to me, and afterward make something for yourself and your son. ¹⁴ For thus says the LORD, the God of Israel, 'The jar of flour shall not be spent, and the jug of oil shall not be empty, until the day that the LORD sends rain upon the earth.'" *(She was to exercise obedient faith first. Then her needs would be supplied. Many try to reverse this order.)* ¹⁵ And she went and did as Elijah said. And she and he and her household ate for many days. ¹⁶ The jar of flour was not spent, neither did the jug of oil become empty, according to the word of the LORD that he spoke by Elijah. *(Our little will always be enough. We may often scrape the bottom of the barrel, but there will always be a handful left. It may be that we shall never have much in hand, but this is not a sin. Fulfillment of our needs will come to us fresh from our heavenly Father and never grow stale.)*

¹⁷ After this the son of the woman, the mistress of the house, became ill. And his illness was so severe that there was no breath left in him. ¹⁸ And she said to Elijah, "What have you against me, O man of God? You have come to me to bring my sin to remembrance and to cause the death of my son!" *(All too often we mistake the reasons for our troubles and place the blame on the*

---
[811] Author unknown.
[812] Psalm 37:3 NKJV

wrong causes. The prophet had kept the child from starving. How could the woman blame him for his death? Sorrow clouds our judgment and we may say or do things for which we are later sorry. Elijah knew this and was very tender toward her.)

19 And he said to her, "Give me your son." And he took him from her arms and carried him up into the upper chamber where he lodged, and laid him on his own bed. **20** And he cried to the Lord, "O Lord my God, have you brought calamity even upon the widow with whom I sojourn, by killing her son?" **21** Then he stretched himself upon the child three times and cried to the Lord, "O Lord my God, let this child's life come into him again." **22** And the Lord listened to the voice of Elijah. And the life of the child came into him again, and he revived. *(Prayers are often answered by what the world calls the laws of nature. In this case, the prophet prayed and was clearly answered by a miracle. Whether good things come to us by so-called laws of nature or by miracles, we know that if we pray like Elijah, we will have like Elijah.)*

23 And Elijah took the child and brought him down from the upper chamber into the house and delivered him to his mother. And Elijah said, "See, your son lives." **24** And the woman said to Elijah, "Now I know that you are a man of God, and that the word of the Lord in your mouth is truth."

November 17
I Will Speak Of Your Testimonies Before Kings[813]

1 Kings 18:1-15; 17-20

1 After many days the word of the Lord came to Elijah, in the third year, saying, "Go, show yourself to Ahab, and I will send rain upon the earth."

To unbelievers this would seem like a command to dive into the raging waves of the ocean or to walk into a lion's den. But soldiers of the Heavenly King do not hesitate. They obey.

2 So Elijah went to show himself to Ahab. Now the famine was severe in Samaria. **3** And Ahab called Obadiah, who was over the household. (Now Obadiah feared the Lord greatly, **4** and when Jezebel cut off the prophets of the Lord, Obadiah took a hundred prophets and hid them by fifties in a cave and fed them with bread and water.) *(Here was a dove living in the eagle's nest. Obadiah was not a half-and-half man, but feared the Lord fully. As a result, he won the respect of even the ungodly Ahab. The king trusted Obadiah more than any of the idol worshipers in his court. Obadiah lived in a wicked society, but he was still committed to God. He showed his zeal by feeding the prophets when food was scarce and being kind to them might have cost him his life. If Obadiah was so faithful when his circumstances were so difficult, what kind of people should we be who live in so much better situations?)*

5 And Ahab said to Obadiah, "Go through the land to all the springs of water and to all the valleys. Perhaps we may find grass and save the horses and mules alive, and not lose some of the animals." *(Judgment alone cannot soften the heart. God was punishing Ahab and all he thought about was saving his animals. He cared more for his horses than he did for the starving people over whom he ruled.)* **6** So they divided the land between them to pass through it. Ahab went in one direction by himself, and Obadiah went in another direction by himself.

7 And as Obadiah was on the way, behold, Elijah met him. And Obadiah recognized him and fell on his face and said, "Is it you, my lord Elijah?" **8** And he answered him, "It is I. Go, tell your lord, 'Behold, Elijah is here.'" **9** And he said, "How have I sinned, that you would give your servant into the hand of Ahab, to kill me? **10** As the Lord your God lives, there is no nation or kingdom where my lord has not sent to seek you. And when they would say, 'He is not here,' he would take an oath of the kingdom or nation, that they had not found you. **11** And now you say, 'Go tell your lord, "Behold, Elijah is here."' **12** And as soon as I have gone from you, the Spirit of the Lord will carry you I know not where. And so, when I come and tell Ahab and he cannot find you,

---
[813] Psalm 119:46

he will kill me, although I your servant feared the LORD from my youth. ¹³ Has it not been told my lord what I did when Jezebel killed the prophets of the LORD, how I hid a hundred men of the LORD's prophets by fifties in a cave and fed them with bread and water? ¹⁴ And now you say, 'Go tell your lord, "Behold, Elijah is here"'; and he will kill me."

The good man was afraid. He had not been living the life of separation from the world and therefore his faith was far inferior to that of lonely Elijah. But the prophet put up with his weakness, because he knew his heart was right. We who are strong must forgive the defects of the weak and not expect everyone to be equally bold.

¹⁵ And Elijah said, "As the LORD of hosts lives, before whom I stand, I will surely show myself to him today."

¹⁷ When Ahab saw Elijah, Ahab said to him, "It is you, you troubler of Israel?" ¹⁸ And he answered, "I have not troubled Israel, but you have, and your father's house, because you have abandoned the commandments of the LORD and followed the Baals. ¹⁹ Now therefore send and gather all Israel to me at Mount Carmel, and the 450 prophets of Baal and the 400 prophets of Asherah, who eat at Jezebel's table."

²⁰ So Ahab sent to all the people of Israel and gathered the prophets together at Mount Carmel. *(See the holy boldness of Elijah and how it awed the king. Elijah was far more royal than Ahab. His faith made him a king before the Lord. We should act with the same heroic spirit. Never fear the face of the Lord's enemies. Face them with unflinching bravery. Our highest aim should be to win the Lord's, "Well done, good and faithful servant."*[814]*)*

NOVEMBER 18
How Long Will You Go Limping Between Two Different Opinions?[815]

1 Kings 18:20-29

²⁰ So Ahab sent to all the people of Israel and gathered the prophets together at Mount Carmel. *(The whole band of 850 priests, in all their showy outfits, gathered on the mountaintop to confront the one lone prophet of the living God.)* ²¹ And Elijah came near to all the people and said, "How long will you go limping between two different opinions? If the LORD is God, follow him; but if Baal, then follow him." And the people did not answer him a word. *(In silent awe, the crowd listened to the one courageous man of God, as he offered them the great choice of God or Baal, and proposed one grand test to prove which was truly God.)* ²² Then Elijah said to the people, "I, even I only, am left a prophet of the LORD, but Baals's prophets are 450 men.

Some say there is safety in numbers, but numbers do not prove something is right. A brave person is someone who holds to the truth, when thousands love a lie.

²³ Let two bulls be given to us, and let them choose one bull for themselves and cut it in pieces and lay it on the wood, but put no fire to it. And I will prepare the other bull and lay it on the wood and put no fire to it. ²⁴ And you call upon the name of your god, and I will call upon the name of the LORD, and the God who answers by fire, he is God." And all the people answered, "It is well spoken."

> *"As when a wave,*
> *That rears itself, a wall of polished glass,*
> *For leagues along the shore, and hangs in air,*
> *Falls with one deafening crash, so rose the shout*
> *Of answering acclamation from the crowd*
> *White-faced, with restless lips and anxious eyes,*
> *Baal's prophets heard, their hundreds cowed and mute*
> *Before one man. They dared not, in mere shame,*
> *Decline the challenge."*[816]

²⁵ Then Elijah said to the prophets of Baal, "Choose for yourselves one bull and prepare it first, for you are many, and call upon the name of your god, but put no fire to it."

---

[814] Matthew 25:23
[815] 1 Kings 18:21
[816] From *The Days of Jezebel: An Historical Drama* by Peter Bayne, 1872.

He knew their tricks and that they would use sleight of hand to cheat if they could. So he said, "But put no fire to it."

26 And they took the bull that was given them, and they prepared it and called upon the name of Baal from morning until noon, saying, "O Baal, answer us!" But there was no voice, and no one answered. And they limped around the altar that they had made. *(They multiplied their prayers and showy gestures until they had performed every ritual in their religion. But the sun-god would not even lend them one spark from his fiery sphere.)* **27** And at noon Elijah mocked them, saying, "Cry aloud, for he is a god. Either he is musing, or he is relieving himself, or he is on a journey, or perhaps he is asleep and must be awakened." *(Idolatry deserves contempt. Elijah's sarcasm was holy, though it was a bitter truth for the prophets of Baal to hear. What would Elijah say today about the Roman Catholic religion that claims their communion bread actually turns into the body of Christ or of other groups who say they are Christian but claim their religious ceremonies are somehow magical? He would laugh them to scorn. As followers of Jesus, we mix pity with our outrage.)* **28** And they cried aloud and cut themselves after their custom with swords and lances, until the blood gushed out upon them. *(Many false religions involve a lot of self-torture. Our God takes no pleasure in the miseries of his children. Many false religions demand lives of pain, affliction and fasting until the bones stick out. These may be part of worshiping a demon god, but the true God has no love for such behavior.)* **29** And as midday passed, they raved on until the time of the offering of the oblation, but there was no voice. No one answered; no one paid attention.

> "They writhed and tore
> In ecstasies of grief and rage. At last
> They hung their heads in mute despair,
>   and looked
> Upon the ground."[817]

---

[817] Ibid (above)

Baal could do nothing. Our next reading will show us what Jehovah did.

NOVEMBER 19
The LORD, He Is God[818]

1 Kings 18:30-40

30 Then Elijah said to all the people, "Come near to me." And all the people came near to him. And he repaired the altar of the LORD that had been thrown down. *(It was now Elijah's turn. It was the time for Jehovah to work.)* **31** Elijah took twelve stones, according to the number of the tribes of the sons of Jacob, to whom the word of the LORD came, saying, "Israel shall be your name," **32** and with the stones he built an altar in the name of the LORD. *(Elijah had commanded Ahab to "gather all Israel."[819] The challenge was made to all Israel and therefore twelve stones were used to build the altar. The whole nation was about to see if Jehovah would answer by fire. The prophet would have nothing to do with Baal's altar. Christ has no harmony with Belial.[820])* And he made a trench about the altar, as great as would contain two seahs[821] of seed.

33 And he put the wood in order and cut the bull in pieces and laid it on the wood. And he said, "Fill four jars with water and pour it on the burnt offering and on the wood." **34** And he said, "Do it a second time." And they did it a second time. And he said, "Do it a third time." And they did it a third time. *(The twelve jars of water filled the trench and all the materials used for the sacrifice were soaking wet. Any thought that Elijah might start the fire by some trick was eliminated. All this water proved this was a fair and honest test.)* **35** And the water ran around the altar and filled the trench also with water.

36 And at the time of the offering of the oblation, Elijah the prophet came near and said, "O LORD, God of Abraham, Isaac, and Israel, let it be known this day that you are

---

[818] 1 Kings 18:39
[819] 1 Kings 18:19
[820] A reference to 2 Corinthians 6:15. Belial is another name for Satan or the devil.
[821] a *seah* was a little less than two gallons. The meaning appears to be that the trench was large enough to plant over three gallons of seed.

God in Israel, and that I am your servant, and that I have done all these things at your word. **37** Answer me, O Lord, answer me, that this people may know that you, O Lord, are God, and that you have turned their hearts back."

Bishop Hall[822] correctly observes, "The prayers of the priests of Baal were as long and boring as Elijah's was short and to the point. Elijah's prayer reminded God of his duty to keep his promises, to uphold truth and to receive glory and honor." The priests of Baal were full of outward strength and sensational action. Elijah's strength was inward. His method was straightforward, but reverent. His faith was the power of his prayer. His God helped him to pray with complete confidence. There was no question about the outcome. Superstition overflows with rituals and ceremonies. Faith has no use for them.

38 Then the fire of the Lord fell and consumed the burnt offering and the wood and the stones and the dust, and licked up the water that was in the trench.

The author of "The Days of Jezebel"[823] has described this with admirable language:

"Scarce had he spoken when a broad white glare,
Scattering earth's light, like darkness in its path,
Keener than lightning, calmer than the dawn,
The sword of God, that proves him by fire,
That proves him by fire in every age,
Stooped from above, and touched the sacrifice.
In the white blaze the sun grew dim, and hung
Like a pale moon upon the glimmering sky.
The fierce flame licked the water up, the wood
Crackled aloft, the very altar stones
Glowed fiery red!
Clear broke the shout from that great multitude,
'Yahweh is the God! Jehovah, he is God.'"

39 And when all the people saw it, they fell on their faces and said, "The Lord, he is God; the Lord, he is God." **40** And Elijah said to them, "Seize the prophets of Baal; let not one of them escape." And they seized them. And Elijah brought them down to the brook Kishon and slaughtered them there.

Elijah had the law of God to authorize this execution. The men were false prophets and were justly doomed to die. Elijah bared his arm for that terrible task and made the dry bed of Kishon run with blood! We do not strike at people in this way, but oh that every one of sin's errors and superstitions were put to death. Not one of them should be allowed to escape. Lord, do this killing work among evil systems in our day!

November 20
And He Said, "Go Again," Seven Times[824]

1 Kings 18:41-46

41 And Elijah said to Ahab, "Go up, eat and drink, for there is a sound of the rushing of rain." *(Only the prophet's ears heard that sound. Faith is quick to hear. There was not a cloud in the burning sky and no wind from the direction where the rains usually came from, but Elijah had no doubts and did not hesitate to declare to Ahab that rain was coming where drought had been. Faith never goes beyond God's promise, but is confident to declare that the Lord will fulfill his word.)* **42** So Ahab went up to eat and to drink. And Elijah went up to the top of Mount Carmel. *(Different men go to different appointments. Ahab to eat and drink; Elijah to wrestle and prevail with his God.[825])*

And he bowed himself down on the earth and put his face between his knees. **43** And he said to his servant, "Go up now, look toward the sea." *(Faith expects results. She bows to the earth in humility, but she assumes God will work and looks toward the sea.)* And he went up and looked and said, "There is

---

[822] Bishop Joseph Hall (1574-1656).
[823] *The Days of Jezebel: An Historical Drama* by Peter Bayne, 1872.
[824] 1 Kings 18:43
[825] A reference to Genesis 32:24-33 where Jacob wrestled and saw "God face to face."

nothing." And he said, "Go again," seven times. *(True faith can wait. Her persistence gains strength from her Lord's delays. She stays on the watchtower anticipating his arrival. It is a brave thing to be able to say, "Go again," seven times.)* **44** And at the seventh time he said, "Behold, a little cloud like a man's hand is rising from the sea." And he said, "Go up, say to Ahab, 'Prepare your chariot and go down, lest the rain stop you.'"

Prayer was heard, the little cloud was enough of a sign. Faith was now fully assured and made her boast even more courageously.

45 And in a little while the heavens grew black with clouds and wind, and there was a great rain. And Ahab rode and went to Jezreel. **46** And the hand of the LORD was on Elijah, and he gathered up his garment and ran before Ahab to the entrance of Jezreel. *(To show his loyalty, he acted as a running footman. Elijah was unyielding in his obedience to Jehovah, but he was still willing to serve the king if the king would serve the Lord.)*

1 Kings 19:1-8

1 Ahab told Jezebel all that Elijah had done, and how he had killed all the prophets with the sword. *(Ahab was easily influenced. His conceited wife was always compelling him toward evil. Woe to the man who marries a Jezebel.)* **2** Then Jezebel sent a messenger to Elijah, saying, "So may the gods do to me and more also, if I do not make your life as the life of one of them by this time tomorrow." **3** Then he was afraid, and he arose and ran for his life and came to Beersheba, which belongs to Judah, and left his servant there.

4 But he himself went a day's journey into the wilderness and came and sat down under a broom tree. And he asked that he might die, saying, "It is enough; now, O LORD, take away my life, for I am no better than my fathers." *(His intense excitement was followed by listlessness. The thrill of a great victory was followed by depression. We are only dust.[826] He prayed to die, and yet the Lord did not intend that he would ever die. Truly we often do not know what we ask.)* **5** And he lay down and slept under a broom tree. And behold, an angel touched him and said to him, "Arise and eat." **6** And he looked, and behold, there was at his head a cake baked on hot stones and a jar of water. And he ate and drank and lay down again. *(The Lord had pity on his weary and disappointed servant. Before he had fed him by ravens, then by a poor widow, and now he honors him by supplying his need by angels. We often receive our best encouragements in our worst times. And then how sweet they are!)*

7 And the angel of the LORD came again a second time and touched him and said, "Arise and eat, for the journey is too great for you." *(The holy refreshment came twice. When our sorrows are multiplied, the Lord doubles our comforts.)* **8** And he arose and ate and drank, and went in the strength of that food forty days and forty nights to Horeb, the mount of God.

A glorious journey, a heavenly fast, a divine assistance. The struggles on Mount Carmel and the disappointments in Samaria were about to be rewarded by holy fellowship at Horeb. "Blessed are all those who wait for [the Lord.]"[827] He will make them a people "who are near to him."[828]

NOVEMBER 21

There is a Remnant, Chosen by Grace[829]

Elijah fled from Jezebel to Horeb where he looked for fellowship with the Lord. He felt greatly annoyed and injured in his soul, because Israel remained idolatrous even after the decisive victory on Mount Carmel over the prophets of Baal. The people were still tremendously influenced by Jezebel and continued to worship Baal and the calves. Therefore Elijah went to Horeb where he could release his pent up emotions in private.

---

[826] Psalm 103:14, God "knows our frame; he remembers that we are dust."
[827] Isaiah 30:18
[828] Psalm 148:14
[829] Romans 11:5

1 Kings 19:9-18

⁹ There he came to a cave and lodged in it. And behold, the word of the LORD came to him, and he said to him, "What are you doing here, Elijah?" *(You, the brave Elijah. Why have you fled to this place? You, leader in Israel, why have you deserted your post? There is no one to teach or rebuke in this lonely, rocky place. What are you doing here?)* ¹⁰ He said, "I have been very jealous for the LORD, the God of hosts. For the people of Israel have forsaken your covenant, thrown down your altars, and killed your prophets with the sword, and I, even I only, am left, and they seek my life, to take it away." *(He was overcome with sorrow. He could have put up with hunger and thirst and even pain; but to see the Lord blasphemed was more than his great spirit could endure. He seems exasperated that the Lord had not stopped Jezebel from killing the prophets who served the Lord. He secretly hopes to see the Lord do terrible things that will strike fear in his ungodly nation and return them to worshiping the true God.)*

¹¹ And he said, "Go out and stand on the mount before the LORD." *(Come out of the cave, breathe the fresh air, and see what the Lord will teach you.)* And behold, the LORD passed by, and a great and strong wind tore the mountains and broke in pieces the rocks before the LORD, but the LORD was not in the wind. And after the wind an earthquake, but the LORD was not in the earthquake. ¹² And after the earthquake a fire, but the LORD was not in the fire. And after the fire the sound of a low whisper. *(This to teach Elijah that the hearts of people are not won to God by terrors and judgments, but by the gentler force of loving persuasion. Elijah was like earthquakes and fire. His ministry was powerful, but it was not successful. What was needed was a more gentle person; one whose expressive sorrow might win the rebellious people to their God.)*

¹³ And when Elijah heard it, he wrapped his face in his cloak and went out and stood at the entrance of the cave. And behold, there came a voice to him and said, "What are you doing here, Elijah?" ¹⁴ He said, "I have been very jealous for the LORD, the God of hosts. For the people of Israel have forsaken your covenant, thrown down your altars, and killed your prophets with the sword, and I, even I only, am left, and they seek my life, to take it away." ¹⁵ And the LORD said to him, "Go, return on your way to the wilderness of Damascus. And when you arrive, you shall anoint Hazael to be king over Syria. ¹⁶ And Jehu the son of Nimshi you shall anoint to be king over Israel, and Elisha the son of Shaphat of Abel-meholah you shall anoint to be prophet in your place. ¹⁷ And the one who escapes from the sword of Hazael shall Jehu put to death, and the one who escapes from the sword of Jehu shall Elisha put to death."

The best cure for depressed spirits is more work to do for God. Elijah soon recovered his cheerfulness when he had work to do for the Lord he loved so well. After this encounter with God, Elijah never again allowed the fear of Jezebel to discourage him from his labor for the Lord. He never stopped fighting the battles of the Lord until his time of service was over and the Lord took him home. In addition, he found great joy in learning there was still a faithful few, in this backsliding nation, who continued to worship the only true God. The Lord said to him, ¹⁸ "Yet I will leave seven thousand in Israel, all the knees that have not bowed to Baal, and every mouth that has not kissed him."

The Lord knows his own. They may be forced to hide themselves because of cruel persecution, but they are not hidden from him. In these evil days, when so many have set up false gods and turned the heart of our nation away from the gospel, let us remain faithful to the Lord. Let us in no way help or assist in promoting the miserable idols that are so popular today. Let us be among the thousands "that have not bowed to Baal."

NOVEMBER 22

Will Not God Give Justice To His Elect?[830]

1 Kings 21:1-16

¹ Now Naboth the Jezreelite had a vineyard in Jezreel, beside the palace of Ahab king of

---
[830] Luke 18:7

Samaria. ²And after this Ahab said to Naboth, "Give me your vineyard, that I may have it for a vegetable garden, because it is near my house, and I will give you a better vineyard for it; or, if it seems good to you, I will give you its value in money." ³But Naboth said to Ahab, "The LORD forbid that I should give you the inheritance of my fathers." *(Naboth did not refuse to sell his vineyard just because he had a natural attachment to it. It was the inheritance of his fathers and the law of God prohibited this kind of sale. The land could only be sold to someone from his tribe, not to someone who belonged to another tribe. Naboth knew this law and bravely decided to obey it.)*

⁴And Ahab went into his house vexed and sullen because of what Naboth the Jezreelite had said to him, for he had said, "I will not give you the inheritance of my fathers." And he lay down on his bed and turned away his face and would eat no food. *(Ahab acted like a spoiled, self-willed child. He was angry and upset because he could not have his way. Those who have not learned to control their desires are miserable people.)*

⁵But Jezebel his wife came to him and said to him, "Why is your spirit so vexed that you eat no food?" ⁶And he said to her, "Because I spoke to Naboth the Jezreelite and said to him, 'Give me your vineyard for money, or else, if it please you, I will give you another vineyard for it.' And he answered, 'I will not give you my vineyard.'" ⁷And Jezebel his wife said to him, "Do you now govern Israel? Arise and eat bread and let your heart be cheerful; I will give you the vineyard of Naboth the Jezreelite." *(A domineering woman is a tool ready for the Evil One to use. Ahab was bad enough, but he was a mere beginner in evil compared with his fierce pagan queen. Bad women are often very bad; even as good women are the best of the human race.)*

⁸So she wrote letters in Ahab's name and sealed them with his seal, and she sent the letters to the elders and the leaders who lived with Naboth in his city. ⁹And she wrote in the letters, "Proclaim a fast, and set Naboth at the head of the people. ¹⁰And set two worthless men opposite him, and let them bring a charge against him, saying, 'You have cursed God and the king.' Then take him out and stone him to death." ¹¹And the men of his city, the elders and the leaders who lived in his city, did as Jezebel had sent word to them. As it was written in the letters that she had sent to them, ¹²they proclaimed a fast and set Naboth at the head of the people. ¹³And the two worthless men came in and sat opposite him. And the worthless men brought a charge against Naboth in the presence of the people, saying, "Naboth cursed God and the king." So they took him outside the city and stoned him to death with stones. *(The leaders and the two men who pretended to be witnesses were entirely dishonest. They were willing and able disciples of the vicious court of Jezebel.)* ¹⁴Then they sent to Jezebel, saying, "Naboth has been stoned; he is dead."

A cold-blooded message indeed. Murder was no big deal in their eyes. Yet these very men had just celebrated a religious fast. Superstition has no conscience.

¹⁵As soon as Jezebel heard that Naboth had been stoned and was dead, Jezebel said to Ahab, "Arise, take possession of the vineyard of Naboth the Jezreelite, which he refused to give you for money, for Naboth is not alive, but dead." ¹⁶And as soon as Ahab heard that Naboth was dead, Ahab arose to go down to the vineyard of Naboth the Jezreelite, to take possession of it. *(Naboth had been accused of treason. They said he had "cursed God and the king." So Ahab claimed that Naboth's property now belonged to the king. How could he think his actions would be blessed? Never let us dare to take anything that does not belong to us. It will be a curse to us.)*

NOVEMBER 23
Evildoers Shall Be Cut Off[831]
1 Kings 21:17-29

¹⁷Then the word of the LORD came to Elijah the Tishbite, saying, ¹⁸"Arise, go down to meet Ahab king of Israel, who is in Samaria; behold, he is in the vineyard of Naboth, where he has gone to take

---
[831] Psalm 37:9

possession. *(The wicked will not enjoy their victories for long. Before Ahab can enjoy the land he obtained, he is served with an order from the court of God that was terrible to hear.)* **19** And you shall say to him, 'Thus says the LORD, "Have you killed and also taken possession?"' And you shall say to him, 'Thus says the LORD: "In the place where dogs licked up the blood of Naboth shall dogs lick your own blood."'" *(Let us applaud the fearless courage of Elijah. He does not hesitate to challenge the arrogant king in the very moment of his joy. Who would like to take the prey from between the lion's jaws? Yet this heroic man approaches his task with bravery.)*

20 Ahab said to Elijah, "Have you found me, O my enemy?" *(Ungodly people often consider faithful ministers to be their enemies, when they are actually their truest friends. We should consider the person who has the courage to tell us unpleasant truth to be our real friend.)* He answered, "I have found you, because you have sold yourself to do what is evil in the sight of the LORD. *(If Ahab had not committed a crime, Elijah would not have bothered him. Elijah offended the king, because the king offended the Lord. If people's consciences are troubled, they should not blame the preacher, but their own sins. Elijah went on to declare the complete elimination of the race of Ahab.)*

21 "Behold, I will bring disaster upon you. I will utterly burn you up, and will cut off from Ahab every male, bond or free, in Israel. **22** And I will make your house like the house of Jeroboam the son of Nebat, and like the house of Baasha the son of Ahijah, for the anger to which you have provoked me, and because you have made Israel to sin. *(The same sins were to be followed by the same judgments. Disaster was brought on Naboth and now disaster will be brought on Ahab. Pay attention! It is written, "But unless you repent, you will all likewise perish."[832])* **23** And of Jezebel the LORD also said, 'The dogs shall eat Jezebel within the walls of Jezreel.' *(Here was a special word for the proud queen, from the prophet who once feared her and fled from her. God makes his servants brave when they are on his errands. Human nature may fail them, but grace will not.)* **24** Anyone belonging to Ahab who dies in the city the dogs shall eat, and anyone of his who dies in the open country the birds of the heavens shall eat."

25 (There was none who sold himself to do what was evil in the sight of the LORD like Ahab, whom Jezebel his wife incited. {*Unconverted people will each have their price. Give them what they want and they will sin as Satan tells them to.*} **26** He acted very abominably in going after idols, as the Amorites had done, whom the LORD cast out before the people of Israel.)

27 And when Ahab heard those words, he tore his clothes and put sackcloth on his flesh and fasted and lay in sackcloth and went about dejectedly. **28** And the word of the LORD came to Elijah the Tishbite, saying, **29** "Have you seen how Ahab has humbled himself before me? Because he has humbled himself before me, I will not bring the disaster in his days; but in his son's days I will bring the disaster upon his house." *(Ahab's doom was most terrible. Evidently, the threat of it had a great impact on the double-minded king. He had no grace. His sorrow was not the repentance[833] of salvation. Yet even his natural fear had something about it that the Lord approved and therefore the doom was delayed for a little while. What power there is in humility and repentance! May God give us the grace to come to him through Jesus Christ in an even more acceptable way. If we add faith to our trembling, we may be quite certain that he who delayed Ahab's judgment will save us from his judgment completely!)*

---

[832] Luke 13:5

[833] *repent, repentance* - The act or feeling of remorse, regret, sorrow or shame that results in a change of heart or purpose.

NOVEMBER 24
What Accord Has Christ With Belial?[834]

1 Kings 22:1-9; 13-14; 23; 28; 30-35; 37-38

¹ For three years Syria and Israel continued without war.

This was evidently a remarkably long time of peace. What an unhappy condition for these poor but sinful people to be in a continual state of war. There was hardly a family that had not experienced the violence of war or the loss of a father or sons.

² But in the third year Jehoshaphat the king of Judah came down to the king of Israel. ³ And the king of Israel said to his servants, "Do you know that Ramoth-gilead belongs to us, and we keep quiet and do not take it out of the hand of the king of Syria?" ⁴ And he said to Jehoshaphat, "Will you go with me to battle at Ramoth-gilead?" And Jehoshaphat said to the king of Israel, "I am as you are, my people as your people, my horses as your horses." *(A good person should not join with an idolater so easily.)*

⁵ And Jehoshaphat said to the king of Israel, "Inquire first for the word of the LORD." ⁶ Then the king of Israel gathered the prophets together, about four hundred men, and said to them, "Shall I go to battle against Ramoth-gilead, or shall I refrain?" And they said, "Go up, for the Lord will give it into the hand of the king." *(There are always plenty of false prophets, because there is money to be made.)* ⁷ But Jehoshaphat said, "Is there not here another prophet of the LORD of whom we may inquire?" ⁸ And the king of Israel said to Jehoshaphat, "There is yet one man by whom we may inquire of the LORD, Micaiah the son of Imlah, but I hate him, for he never prophesies good concerning me, but evil." And Jehoshaphat said, "Let not the king say so." *(This rebuke was far too mild. Fellowship with evil people tends to lower the standards of even the best of people.)* ⁹ Then the king of Israel summoned an officer and said, "Bring quickly Micaiah the son of Imlah."

¹³ And the messenger who went to summon Micaiah said to him, "Behold, the words of the prophets with one accord are favorable to the king. Let your word be like the word of one of them, and speak favorably." *(This was an evil attempt to keep the prophet from doing the right thing. But Micaiah was a true disciple of Elijah and could not be tempted to join the crowd.)* ¹⁴ But Micaiah said, "As the LORD lives, what the LORD says to me, that I will speak."

²³ *(And Micaiah said to the king),* "Now therefore behold, The LORD has put a lying spirit in the mouth of all these your prophets; the LORD has declared disaster for you."

²⁸ "If you return in peace, the LORD has not spoken by me." And he said, "Hear, all you peoples!"

He spoke like a man of God and called on everyone who was there to be a witness of his prophecy.

³⁰ And the king of Israel said to Jehoshaphat, "I will disguise myself and go into battle, but you wear your robes." And the king of Israel disguised himself and went into battle. *(King Ahab was very cruel. It did not bother him to protect himself and leave his friend exposed to danger. If we keep company with bad people, we will discover they will not hesitate to see us ruined if they think doing so will be to their advantage.)* ³¹ Now the king of Syria had commanded the thirty-two captains of his chariots, "Fight with neither small nor great, but only with the king of Israel." ³² And when the captains of the chariots saw Jehoshaphat, they said, "It is surely the king of Israel." So they turned to fight against him. And Jehoshaphat cried out. ³³ And when the captains of the chariots saw that it was not the king of Israel, they turned back from pursuing him. *(This was a special deliverance. We read in 2 Chronicles 18:31 that, "Jehoshaphat cried out, and the LORD helped him; God drew them away from him." The great danger he found himself him in must have made him feel how wrong he was to associate with Ahab.)*

³⁴ But a certain man drew his bow at random and struck the king of Israel between

---
[834] 2 Corinthians 6:15

the scale armor and the breastplate. Therefore he said to the driver of his chariot, "Turn around and carry me out of the battle, for I am wounded." ³⁵ And the battle continued that day, and the king was propped up in his chariot facing the Syrians, until at evening he died. And the blood of the wound flowed into the bottom of the chariot.

³⁷ So the king died, and was brought to Samaria. And they buried the king in Samaria. ³⁸ And they washed the chariot by the pool of Samaria, and the dogs licked up his blood, and the prostitutes washed themselves in it, according to the word of the LORD that he had spoken.[835]

That arrow shot "at random" was guided by divine vengeance. Every syllable of Elijah's threatening prophecy proved true. "Who will not fear, O Lord, and glorify your name? For you alone are holy....Your righteous acts have been revealed."[836]

NOVEMBER 25
Should You Help the Wicked?[837]

2 Chronicles 19:1-11

¹ Jehoshaphat the king of Judah returned in safety to his house in Jerusalem. *(His rescue from being killed in the battle was very special. Let us hope he was deeply grateful for it. He had foolishly placed himself in danger. It was great mercy that saved him from almost certain death. However, we see that his behavior did not go unrebuked.)* ² But Jehu the son of Hanani the seer went out to meet him and said to King Jehoshaphat, "Should you help the wicked and love those who hate the LORD? Because of this, wrath has gone out against you from the LORD. ³ Nevertheless, some good is found in you, for you destroyed the Asheroth out of the land, and have set your heart to seek God."

Jehu's father had rebuked King Asa and was put in prison,[838] but this did not stop the son from doing his duty. He spoke personally and clearly to King Jehoshaphat. He did not hesitate to deliver the Lord's threatening message. The result was good. The king recognized his sin. He began to do all the good he could. This showed that his repentance was real.

⁴ Jehoshaphat lived at Jerusalem. And he went out again among the people, from Beersheba to the hill country of Ephraim, and brought them back to the LORD, the God of their fathers.

After we have turned to God, the best thing we can do is to use our influence to convert others.

⁵ He appointed judges in the land in all the fortified cities of Judah, city by city, ⁶ and said to the judges, "Consider what you do, for you judge not for man but for the LORD. He is with you in giving judgment. ⁷ Now then, let the fear of the LORD be upon you. Be careful what you do, for there is no injustice with the LORD our God, or partiality or taking bribes."

In all our interactions we are obligated to be absolutely fair. We should never allow the threats or smiles of anyone keep us from doing the right thing. Our heavenly Father is righteous and all his children should be too. Judges are not the only ones who can be bribed. Employees may be bribed to allow suppliers to rob their employers; employers may be tempted to treat their employees unfairly; and children may be persuaded by gifts or threats to tell lies. These things must not happen or we will grieve the Holy Spirit of God.[839]

⁸ Moreover, in Jerusalem Jehoshaphat appointed certain Levites and priests and heads of families of Israel, to give judgment for the LORD and to decide disputed cases. They had their seat at Jerusalem.

This was to be a central court where difficult cases would be decided. What a blessing it is that in the New Jerusalem we have one who is called Wonderful

---

[835] *New King James:* "and the dogs licked up the blood while the harlots bathed, according to the word of the LORD which he had spoken."
[836] Revelation 15:4
[837] 2 Chronicles 19:2
[838] 2 Chronicles 16:10

[839] Ephesians 4:29-30a: "Let no corrupting talk come out of your mouths, but only such as is good for building up, as fits the occasion, that it may give grace to those who hear. And do not grieve the Holy Spirit of God."

Counselor,[840] and no case is too hard for him.

⁹And he charged them: "Thus you shall do in the fear of the LORD, in faithfulness, and with your whole heart: ¹⁰whenever a case comes to you from your brothers who live in their cities, concerning bloodshed, law or commandment, statutes or rules, then you shall warn them that they may not incur guilt before the LORD and wrath may not come upon you and your brothers. Thus you shall do, and you will not incur guilt. *(And today it is still necessary to urge one another to do the right thing. What others think about us is not what is important. Disciples of Jesus should always be honest. If honor is expelled from all the rest of the world, it should still live in the heart of believers.)*

¹¹"And behold, Amariah the chief priest is over you in all matters of the LORD; and Zebadiah the son of Ishmael, the governor of the house of Judah, in all the king's matters, and the Levites will serve you as officers. Deal courageously, and may the LORD be with the upright!" *(Let this be our motto in everything we do. The person who acts uprightly never has a reason for fear, because God is with them. Children, learn this line by heart, "Deal courageously, and may the Lord be with the upright!")*

NOVEMBER 26
The Battle Is Not Yours But God's[841]
2 Chronicles 20:1-15; 17-19

¹After this *(the reforms of Jehoshaphat including the appointment of "certain Levites and priests and heads of families of Israel, to give judgment for the LORD and to decide disputed cases"[842])*, the Moabites and Ammonites, and with them some of the Meunites, came against Jehoshaphat for battle.

This was discipline against Jehoshaphat for joining with wicked Ahab. Now the wicked join against him. But it was sent in love and therefore it ended well.

²ᵃSome men came and told Jehoshaphat, "A great multitude is coming against you." ³Then Jehoshaphat was afraid and set his face to seek the LORD, and proclaimed a fast throughout all Judah. *(He not only feared these invaders because of their huge numbers, but because the Lord sent him the prophet to declare that God's anger would be shown. However, his fears drove him to prayer. When this is the case, things are certain to get better.)* ⁴And Judah assembled to seek help from the LORD; from all the cities of Judah they came to seek the LORD. *(Great troubles can only be met by great prayer. Let us use this certain cure when we meet with trials.)*

⁵And Jehoshaphat stood in the assembly of Judah and Jerusalem, in the house of the LORD, before the new court, ⁶and said, "O LORD, God of our fathers, are you not God in heaven? You rule over all the kingdoms of the nations. In your hand are power and might, so that none is able to withstand you. ⁷Did you not, our God, drive out the inhabitants of this land before your people Israel, and give it forever to the descendants of Abraham your friend? ⁸And they have lived in it and have built for you in it a sanctuary for your name, saying, ⁹'If disaster comes upon us, the sword, judgment, or pestilence, or famine, we will stand before this house and before you—for your name is in this house—and cry out to you in our affliction, and you will hear and save.' ¹⁰And now behold, the men of Ammon and Moab and Mount Seir, whom you would not let Israel invade when they came from the land of Egypt, and whom they avoided and did not destroy— ¹¹behold, they reward us by coming to drive us out of your possession, which you have given us to inherit. ¹²O our God, will you not execute judgment on them? For we are powerless against this great horde that is coming against us. We do not know what to do, but our eyes are on you."

This was a noble prayer. The king reminded the Lord of his mighty power and supremacy; and, of his favors to his people in times past. Then he reminded him of his promise and covenant with his people. This

---
[840] Isaiah 9:6 or *Wonderful Lawyer*
[841] 2 Chronicles 20:15
[842] 2 Chronicles 19:8

is the way we should pray too. The last sentence is especially sweet: "Our eyes are on you." They looked to the Lord alone for direction, help, protection and encouragement. We are sure to see good when our eyes are fixed on God alone.

13 Meanwhile all Judah stood before the Lord, with their little ones, their wives, and their children. *(The prayers of even little ones are powerful with God. All our family should learn to pray. And in times of distress each one should assist in calling on the Lord for help.)* **14** And the Spirit of the Lord came upon Jahaziel,…a Levite of the sons of Asaph, in the midst of the assembly.

When all his people humbly cry to him, God will soon send a loving word.

15 And he said, "Listen, all Judah and inhabitants of Jerusalem and King Jehoshaphat: Thus says the Lord to you, 'Do not be afraid and do not be dismayed at this great horde, for the battle is not yours but God's.'"

17 "'You will not need to fight in this battle. Stand firm, hold your position, and see the salvation of the Lord on your behalf, O Judah and Jerusalem.' Do not be afraid and do not be dismayed. Tomorrow go out against them, and the Lord will be with you." *(When the Lord takes up the battle for his people he makes short work of their enemies.)*

18 Then Jehoshaphat bowed his head with his face to the ground, and all Judah and the inhabitants of Jerusalem fell down before the Lord, worshiping the Lord.

God's great mercy humbled them to the point of adoration. They did not question the truth of the promise, but immediately worshiped him gratefully.

19 And the Levites, of the Kohathites and the Korahites, stood up to praise the Lord, the God of Israel, with a very loud voice.

This was real faith. Can we not also praise the Lord for favors yet to come? He will bless us, so we should bless him right now.

November 27
God Reigns Over the Nations[843]
2 Chronicles 20:20-30

20 And they rose early in the morning and went out into the wilderness of Tekoa. And when they went out, Jehoshaphat stood and said, "Hear me, Judah and inhabitants of Jerusalem! Believe in the Lord your God, and you will be established; believe his prophets, and you will succeed." **21** And when he had taken counsel with the people, he appointed those who were to sing to the Lord and praise him in holy attire, as they went before the army, and say,

"Give thanks to the Lord,
for his steadfast love endures forever."

They marched in faith, they sang in faith and they prepared in faith. Oh that we could meet our daily trials in the same way. We would then experience great deliverances from the Lord and praise him even more.

22 And when they began to sing and praise, the Lord set an ambush against the men of Ammon, Moab, and Mount Seir, who had come against Judah, so that they were routed. *(The people sang more or less all the way. They sang as they got started, but when they got close to the enemy they sang louder and louder. Then the Lord began to work. The Lord threw the various nations into confusion and they began to fight against one another.)* **23** For the men of Ammon and Moab rose against the inhabitants of Mount Seir, devoting them to destruction, and when they had made an end of the inhabitants of Seir, they all helped to destroy one another.

24 When Judah came to the watchtower of the wilderness, they looked toward the horde, and behold, there were dead bodies lying on the ground; none had escaped. *(They marched with hallelujahs and were more than conquerors. They did not need to strike a blow. Let us as a family make up a hallelujah band and continually magnify the Lord.[844])* **25** When Jehoshaphat and his people came to take their spoil, they found among them, in great numbers, goods, clothing, and

---
[843] Psalm 47:8
[844] Psalm 34:3, "Oh, magnify the Lord with me, and let us exalt his name together!"

precious things, which they took for themselves until they could carry no more. They were three days in taking the spoil, it was so much. *(Faith wins even more than she expects, a blessing that she does not have enough room to receive.)*

²⁶ On the fourth day they assembled in the Valley of Beracah *(or Valley of Blessing)*, for there they blessed the Lord. Therefore the name of that place has been called the Valley of Beracah to this day. ²⁷ Then they returned, every man of Judah and Jerusalem, and Jehoshaphat at their head, returning to Jerusalem with joy, for the Lord had made them rejoice over their enemies. ²⁸ They came to Jerusalem with harps and lyres and trumpets, to the house of the Lord. *(Those who praise before the blessing are sure to praise afterwards. What a glorious hymn of praise they sang before the Lord.)*

²⁹ And the fear of God came on all the kingdoms of the countries when they heard that the Lord had fought against the enemies of Israel. ³⁰ So the realm of Jehoshaphat was quiet, for his God gave him rest all around.

We will now read the Psalm that was very likely sung by the people on their triumphant return to the temple.

Psalm 47

1 Clap your hands, all peoples!
  Shout to God with loud songs of joy!
2 For the Lord, the Most High, is to be feared,
  a great king over all the earth.
3 He subdued peoples under us,
  and nations under our feet.
4 He chose our heritage for us,
  the pride of Jacob whom he loves.
    Selah
5 God has gone up with a shout,
  the Lord with the sound of a trumpet.
6 Sing praises to God, sing praises!
  Sing praises to our King, sing praises!
7 For God is the King of all the earth;
  sing praises with a psalm!
8 God reigns over the nations;
  God sits on his holy throne.
9 The princes of the peoples gather
  as the people of the God of Abraham.
  For the shields of the earth belong to God;
  he is highly exalted!

The Lord Jesus will come again a second time after he overcomes all his enemies and ours, and we will rejoice in words like these. We may sing to the Lord even now, because he has already won a glorious victory. His own right hand and his holy arm have already succeeded.

November 28

Our God Is a Consuming Fire[845]

2 Kings 1:2-13; 15-17

We now return to the history of the kingdom of Israel.

² Now Ahaziah *(the son of Ahab)* fell through the lattice in his upper chamber in Samaria, and lay sick; so he sent messengers, telling them, "Go, inquire of Baal-zebub, the god of Ekron, whether I shall recover from this sickness." *(Shame on an Israelite for going to a Philistine god and leaving the God of heaven for the god of flies.)* ³ But the angel of the Lord said to Elijah the Tishbite, "Arise, go up to meet the messengers of the king of Samaria, and say to them, 'Is it because there is no God in Israel that you are going to inquire of Baal-zebub, the god of Ekron? ⁴ Now therefore thus says the Lord, You shall not come down from the bed to which you have gone up, but you shall surely die.'" So Elijah went. *(He appeared to the messengers without warning, delivered his prophecy and left suddenly. The messengers of Ahaziah must have been astonished to meet with a man who knew their assignment and gave them an answer to a question they had never mentioned to him.)*

⁵ The messengers returned to the king, and he said to them, "Why have you returned?" ⁶ And they said to him, "There came a man to meet us, and said to us, 'Go back to the king who sent you, and say to him, Thus says the Lord, Is it because there is no God in Israel that you are sending to inquire of Baal-zebub, the god of Ekron? Therefore you shall not come down from the bed to which you have gone up, but you shall surely die.'" ⁷ He said to them, "What kind of man was he who came to meet you and told you these things?"

---

[845] Hebrews 12:29

⁸They answered him, "He wore a garment of hair, with a belt of leather about his waist." And he said, "It is Elijah the Tishbite."

Then, like a true son of Jezebel, he decided to have Elijah killed. Ahaziah was certain that he would never have rest as long as the troublesome prophet survived.

⁹Then the king sent to him a captain of fifty men with his fifty. He went up to Elijah, who was sitting on the top of a hill, and said to him, "O man of God, the king says, 'Come down.'" ¹⁰But Elijah answered the captain of fifty, "If I am a man of God, let fire come down from heaven and consume you and your fifty." Then fire came down from heaven and consumed him and his fifty.

We serve a prophet who is gentler than Elijah. The Lord Jesus rebuked his disciples when they talked about calling down fire from heaven on his enemies.[846] Elijah lived in a different age. He answered the anger of a king by a calm act of faith and the soldiers who came to arrest him lay dead at his feet.

¹¹And the king sent to him another captain of fifty men with his fifty. And he answered and said to him, "O man of God, this is the king's order, 'Come down quickly!'" *(This captain was more insistent than the first one. He ordered Elijah to surrender immediately. His approach was virtually asking for destruction.)* ¹²But Elijah answered them, "If I am a man of God, let fire come down from heaven and consume you and your fifty." Then the fire of God came down from heaven and consumed him and his fifty.

¹³Again the king sent the captain of a third fifty with his fifty. And the third captain of fifty went up and came and fell on his knees before Elijah and entreated him, "O man of God, please let my life, and the life of these fifty servants of yours, be precious in your sight. *(This captain was wise. Ahaziah had forced him to perform this dangerous mission, but he cast himself on the prophet's mercy. Humility turns the sword of vengeance away. It is wise to be humble before the Lord.)*

¹⁵Then the angel of the LORD said to Elijah, "Go down with him; do not be afraid of him." So he arose and went down with him to the king *(He came to the gates of Samaria with boldness. He entered the royal palace no longer afraid of Jezebel. The Lord had given his servant such a command of the situation that no one dared to stop him.)* ¹⁶and said to him, "Thus says the LORD, 'Because you have sent messengers to inquire of Baal-zebub, the god of Ekron—is it because there is no God in Israel to inquire of his word?—therefore you shall not come down from the bed to which you have gone up, but you shall surely die.'"

¹⁷ᵃSo he died according to the word of the LORD that Elijah had spoken.

NOVEMBER 29
We Shall Not All Sleep, But We Shall All Be Changed[847]

2 Kings 2:1-14

¹Now when the LORD was about to take Elijah up to heaven by a whirlwind, Elijah and Elisha were on their way from Gilgal. ²And Elijah said to Elisha, "Please stay here, for the LORD has sent me as far as Bethel." *(Gilgal was where a school for the prophets was located. Elijah's last earthly work was to visit these schools. No one can overestimate the importance of our theological colleges being filled with holy men. Do we pray for students as we should?)* But Elisha said, "As the LORD lives, and as you yourself live, I will not leave you." So they went down to Bethel. *(Elijah knew his time for leaving this world was near and he wanted time alone to pour out his soul before the Lord. He was also a humble man and did not wish others to see his glorious departure and perhaps think more of him than they should. However, God had arranged that Elisha would see his master's ascension to heaven. The Lord does not intend for his finest works to go unnoticed. Believers who would rather not have attention called to themselves are still "known and read by all."[848])*

³And the sons of the prophets who were in Bethel came out to Elisha and said to him,

---
[846] Luke 9:54-55
[847] 1 Corinthians 15:51
[848] 2 Corinthians 3:2

"Do you know that today the LORD will take away your master from over you?" And he said, "Yes, I know it; keep quiet."

⁴Elijah said to him, "Elisha, please stay here, for the LORD has sent me to Jericho." But he said, "As the LORD lives, and as you yourself live, I will not leave you." So they came to Jericho. ⁵The sons of the prophets who were at Jericho drew near to Elisha and said to him, "Do you know that today the LORD will take away your master from over you?" And he answered, "Yes, I know it; keep quiet."

⁶Then Elijah said to him, "Please stay here, for the LORD has sent me to the Jordan." But he said, "As the LORD lives, and as you yourself live, I will not leave you." So the two of them went on. *(Elisha could not be shaken off. He felt that he must see the last of his master and must obtain a parting blessing from him.)* ⁷Fifty men of the sons of the prophets also went and stood at some distance from them, as they both were standing by the Jordan. ⁸Then Elijah took his cloak and rolled it up and struck the water, and the water was parted to the one side and to the other, till the two of them could go over on dry ground. *(In the past, the river had been at flood stage or dried up at the command of the prophet as he opened or shut up heaven. Now it opened to give him a dry passage. In this, as in many other ways, Elijah was like Moses, who divided the waters of the Red Sea.)*

⁹When they had crossed, Elijah said to Elisha, "Ask what I shall do for you, before I am taken from you." And Elisha said, "Please let there be a double portion of your spirit on me."

Elisha understood how difficult it would be to be Elijah's successor. He concluded that he would need a double measure of grace to follow in his footsteps. His request shows that his heart was in his lifework and that he had forsaken every selfish desire. Hs only ambition was to serve his God.

¹⁰And he said, "You have asked a hard thing; yet, if you see me as I am being taken from you, it shall be so for you, but if you do not see me, it shall not be so." *(It was not in Elijah's power to give the Holy Spirit. But he could ask it for his friend and give him a sign that the request was granted.)* ¹¹And as they still went on and talked, behold, chariots of fire and horses of fire separated the two of them. And Elijah went up by a whirlwind into heaven. *(This was a proper departure for one whose fiery spirit and whirlwind force had made all Israel tremble. Elijah was the only mortal to be visibly carried to heaven. Remarkable faithfulness was honored by a remarkable departure.)*

¹²And Elisha saw it and he cried, "My father, my father! The chariots of Israel and its horsemen!" *(Elijah had been the protector of Israel, the chariot and horseman of the nation. Now that he is gone, what will Israel do? This was Elisha's main thought.)* And he saw him no more.

Then he took hold of his own clothes and tore them in two pieces. ¹³And he took up the cloak of Elijah that had fallen from him and went back and stood on the bank of the Jordan. ¹⁴Then he took the cloak of Elijah that had fallen from him and struck the water, saying, "Where is the LORD, the God of Elijah?" And when he had struck the water, the water was parted to the one side and to the other, and Elisha went over.

NOVEMBER 30
Whoever Receives You Receives Me[849]
2 Kings 4:1-14

¹Now the wife of one of the sons of the prophets cried to Elisha, "Your servant my husband is dead, and you know that your servant feared the LORD, but the creditor has come to take my two children to be his slaves."

This was the severe practice of that time. A man's sons were forced to serve his creditor until his debts were paid, even though their father was dead. The sorrows of this poor woman piled on. Her husband was dead, he left her in debt and her children were going to be taken from her to serve someone else.

²And Elisha said to her, "What shall I do for you? Tell me; what have you in the

---
[849] Matthew 10:40

house?" *(She would be forced to turn over anything of value to pay toward the debts)* And she said, "Your servant has nothing in the house except a jar of oil." *(She was extremely poor. She was a prophet's wife, but the people were too fond of their idols to give much to the Lord's servants.)* ³ Then he said, "Go outside, borrow vessels from all your neighbors, empty vessels and not too few. ⁴ Then go in and shut the door behind yourself and your sons and pour into all these vessels. And when one is full, set it aside." ⁵ So she went from him and shut the door behind herself and her sons. And as she poured they brought the vessels to her. ⁶ When the vessels were full, she said to her son, "Bring me another vessel." And he said to her, "There is not another." Then the oil stopped flowing.

If we have faith in God, his grace will fill up all our emptiness. When we are unable to receive more, the blessing will be put on hold. This is not because the Lord has used up his power, but because we are not able to hold any more. "According to your faith be it done to you."[850] *Great faith shall have great supplies. If we do not have enough, the fault lies completely with us.*

⁷ She came and told the man of God, and he said, "Go, sell the oil and pay your debts, and you and your sons can live on the rest."

She must pay her debts first and then the remainder will be hers. She had no right to any of the oil until the creditors were satisfied. It was not a sin for her not to pay her husband's debts when she had no way of paying them. But the moment it was in her power to pay them, she was obligated to do so. It would be good if all Christian people remember this. We are told to, "Pay to all what is owed to them,"[851] *but the shame is that debt is all too common among Christians.*

⁸ One day Elisha went on to Shunem, where a wealthy woman lived, who urged him to eat some food. So whenever he passed that way, he would turn in there to eat food. ⁹ And she said to her husband, "Behold now, I know that this is a holy man of God who is continually passing our way. ¹⁰ Let us make a small room on the roof with walls and put there for him a bed, a table, a chair, and a lamp, so that whenever he comes to us, he can go in there."

¹¹ One day he came there, and he turned into the chamber and rested there.

We read how Elisha had helped a poor woman. Now he is entertained by a rich woman. God repays those who show mercy. It was a great honor to this Shunammite woman to be allowed to show kindness to the Lord's servant. She showed her true godliness by doing this without being asked. She provided the good man with everything necessary and, even more, a quiet room all to himself where he would be undisturbed by the business of the household.

¹² And he said to Gehazi his servant, "Call this Shunammite." When he had called her, she stood before him. ¹³ And he said to him, "Say now to her, 'See, you have taken all this trouble for us; what is to be done for you? Would you have a word spoken on your behalf to the king or to the commander of the army?'" She answered, "I dwell among my own people." *(That is, she was content with her life. She did not wish for a special favor from the king.)* ¹⁴ And he said, "What then is to be done for her?" Gehazi answered, "Well, she has no son, and her husband is old."

Gehazi suggested to the prophet that the birth of a child would fill the house with joy and the Lord granted the generous woman her desire. Those who serve the Lord and are kind to his people will be honored by their Lord. May our house always be open to the ministers of Christ, as our way of showing appreciation for their Lord.

---

[850] Matthew 9:29
[851] Romans 13:7

The Music Hall in the Royal Surrey Gardens was home for Spurgeon and his congregation on Sunday mornings for three years beginning in 1856. There was seating for over 9,000 and the hall was filled virtually every Sunday with just as many turned away.

December 1

All Is Well[852]

2 Kings 4:18-23; 25-37

The greatest earthly blessings are never certain to last. The son who had brought joy to the Shunammite woman now became the cause of her grief.

18 When the child had grown, he went out one day to his father among the reapers. **19** And he said to his father, "Oh, my head, my head!" *(Perhaps the harvest sun was too hot for him and he suffered from sunstroke. This is common in the East.)* The father said to his servant, "Carry him to his mother." **20** And when he had lifted him and brought him to his mother, the child sat on her lap till noon, and then he died. **21** And she went up and laid him on the bed of the man of God and shut the door behind him and went out. *(She had lost her son and was full of grief. But she still had hope, because she had not lost her faith.)*

22 Then she called to her husband and said, "Send me one of the servants and one of the donkeys, that I may quickly go to the man of God and come back again." **23** And he said, "Why will you go to him today? It is neither new moon nor Sabbath." She said, "All is well."

She answered, "All is well." Her heart was full of sorrow and her faith was being greatly tried, so she said very little. She decided not to mention the crushing loss of their son until she appealed to the power of the prophet's God.

25 So she set out and came to the man of God at Mount Carmel.

When the man of God saw her coming, he said to Gehazi his servant, "Look, there is the Shunammite. **26** Run at once to meet her and say to her, 'Is all well with you? Is all well with your husband? Is all well with the child?'" And she answered, "All is well". **27** And when she came to the mountain to the man of God, she caught hold of his feet. And Gehazi came to push her away. *(She was in agony. Faith and fear battled within her. She did not act like herself, but fell anxiously at the prophet's feet.)* But the man of God said, "Leave her alone, for she is in bitter distress, and the Lord has hidden it from me and has not told me. **28** Then she said, "Did I ask my lord for a son? Did I not say, 'Do not deceive me?'"

She reasoned that the son was certainly not given to mock her and break her heart. But she felt that if he were taken from her so soon that is what it would look like. She refused to believe that this is what the Lord intended. Her faith and her distress pleaded with Elisha.

29 He said to Gehazi, "Tie up your garment and take my staff in your hand and go. If you meet anyone, do not greet him, and if anyone greets you, do not reply. And lay my staff on the face of the child." **30** Then the mother of the child said, "As the Lord lives and as you yourself live, I will not leave you." So he arose and followed her. **31** Gehazi went on ahead and laid the staff on the face of the child, but there was no sound or sign of life. Therefore he returned to meet him and told him, "The child has not awakened."

God would not grant this blessing in response to a mere act. There must be mighty prayer.

32 When Elisha came into the house, he saw the child lying dead on his bed. **33** So he went in and shut the door behind the two of them and prayed to the Lord. **34** Then he went up and lay on the child, putting his mouth on his mouth, his eyes on his eyes, and his hands on his hands. And as he

---

[852] 2 Kings 4:26

stretched himself upon him, the flesh of the child became warm. ³⁵ Then he got up again and walked once back and forth in the house, and went up and stretched himself upon him. The child sneezed seven times, and the child opened his eyes. *(By faith, this woman received her child raised to life again like the woman of Zarephath had before her.*⁸⁵³ *Although a miracle like this will not be worked for us, we should have the same faith. If we do, we shall then see things equally worthy of our gratitude.)*

³⁶ Then he summoned Gehazi and said, "Call this Shunammite." So he called her. And when she came to him, he said, "Pick up your son." ³⁷ She came and fell at his feet, bowing to the ground. Then she picked up her son and went out. *(We must imitate this good woman. In all times of trouble, go to the Lord and he will surely help us through. "Trust in the L*ORD *forever."*⁸⁵⁴*)*

December 2
He...Made the Iron Float[855]

2 Kings 4:38-44

³⁸ And Elisha came again to Gilgal when there was a famine in the land. And as the sons of the prophets were sitting before him, he said to his servant, "Set on the large pot, and boil stew for the sons of the prophets."

Even though there was only a little flour to put in the pot, Elisha was convinced that the Lord would provide a meal. Therefore he ordered that the pot be placed on the fire and be ready for what the Lord would provide. We have heard of someone who had no bread and much faith. He prayed and then had the tablecloth placed on the table in readiness for the Lord's provision to demonstrate how real his faith was. This was the faith Elisha had.

³⁹ One of them went out into the field to gather herbs, and found a wild vine, and gathered from it his lap full of wild gourds, and came and cut them up into the pot of stew, not knowing what they were. *(Unbelief always needs something to do. This person could not wait for the Lord to fill the pot. He felt he must come to the Lord's assistance and the result was trouble. Faith does better with her patient waiting than mistrust does with her conceited activity.)* ⁴⁰ And they poured out some for the men to eat. But while they were eating of the stew, they cried out, "O man of God, there is death in the pot!" And they could not eat it. ⁴¹ He said, "Then bring flour." And he threw it into the pot and said, "Pour some out for the men, that they may eat." And there was no harm in the pot. *(The Lord has an answer for every evil. There are deadly evils in this great pot of society, like superficial forms of worship and unbelief. The way to prevent their harmful influence is to throw in the flour of gospel truth until the error is made harmless by the wonder working grace of God.)*

⁴² A man came from Baal-shalishah, bringing the man of God bread of the firstfruits, twenty loaves of barley and fresh ears of grain in his sack. And Elisha said, "Give to the men, that they may eat." *(Elisha's faith had empowered him to believe that God could provide when there was nothing available. Now he was convinced that divine power could multiply even the little the man had brought.)* ⁴³ But his servant said, "How can I set this before a hundred men?" So he repeated, "Give them to the men, that they may eat, for thus says the L*ORD*, 'They shall eat and have some left.'" ⁴⁴ So he set it before them. And they ate and had some left, according to the word of the L*ORD*. *(We are to use what we have and then God will give us more. God will supply according to our needs. We are promised strength for each of our days here on earth.*⁸⁵⁶*)*

2 Kings 6:1-7

¹ Now the sons of the prophets said to Elisha, "See, the place where we dwell under your charge is too small for us. ² Let us go to the Jordan and each of us get there a log, and let us make a place for us to dwell there." And he answered, "Go." ³ Then one of them said, "Be pleased to go with your servants."

---

[853] This story is told in 1 Kings 17:8-24
[854] Isaiah 26:4
[855] 2 Kings 6:6

[856] Deuteronomy 33:25, "As your days, so shall your strength be."

And he answered, "I will go." *(His company would cheer them and his holy conversation would improve them. They loved him and so they wanted to have him with them. He loved them and so he agreed to join them in their work.)* **4** So he went with them. And when they came to the Jordan, they cut down trees.

5 But as one was felling a log, his axe head fell into the water, and he cried out, "Alas, my master! It was borrowed." *(He was poor and had borrowed the axe. But he was also honest and was doubly sorry to lose what had been lent to him.)* **6** Then the man of God said, "Where did it fall?" When he showed him the place, he cut off a stick and threw it in there and made the iron float. *(Yes, and God can still make iron float. Things that are impossible for us are possible to him. Our all-powerful God can rescue us from every difficulty. Let us cast all our anxieties on the Lord in childlike confidence.[857])* **7** And he said, "Take it up." So he reached out his hand and took it. *(Joy returned to this son of the prophets. May we have the same work, the same friendships, the same faith, and the same joy that he had!)*

DECEMBER 3

Wash, and Be Clean[858]

2 Kings 5:1-14

1 Naaman, commander of the army of the king of Syria, was a great man with his master and in high favor, because by him the LORD had given victory to Syria. He was a mighty man of valor, but he was a leper.

There is imperfection in even the best of people. No one can be described without including a "but." Naaman's "but" was one that made his life bitter. His disease was repulsive, deadly and incurable.

2 Now the Syrians on one of their raids had carried off a little girl from the land of Israel, and she worked in the service of Naaman's wife. **3** She said to her mistress, "Would that my lord were with the prophet who is in Samaria! He would cure him of his leprosy." *(Who knows how this girl came to know about the prophet of the true God? Perhaps a holy mother had made her familiar with the true faith and its ministers. Mothers cannot tell where their children may end up years from now. Therefore they should prepare them for the future by storing their minds with the truth of God.)*

4 So Naaman went in and told his lord, "Thus and so spoke the girl from the land of Israel. *(Naaman was a kind master. All his servants took an interest in him. It is very pleasant when each one in the family seeks the good of the rest. Parents should care for the good of their children and children should make their parent's concerns their own.)* **5** And the king of Syria said, "Go now, and I will send a letter to the king of Israel."

So he went, taking with him ten talents *(about 750 pounds)* of silver, six thousand shekels *(about 75 pounds)* of gold, and ten changes of clothes. **6** And he brought the letter to the king of Israel, which read, "When this letter reaches you, know that I have sent to you Naaman my servant, that you may cure him of his leprosy." *(This was a mistake. King Jehoram was an idolater and could do nothing to help Naaman.)* **7** And when the king of Israel read the letter, he tore his clothes and said, "Am I God, to kill and to make alive, that this man sends word to me to cure a man of his leprosy? Only consider and see how he is seeking a quarrel with me." *(He was alarmed and afraid that his powerful neighbor was looking for an excuse for another war.)*

8 But when Elisha the man of God heard that the king of Israel had torn his clothes, he sent to the king, saying, "Why have you torn your clothes? Let him come now to me, that he may know that there is a prophet in Israel." **9** So Naaman came with his horses and chariots and stood at the door of Elisha's house. *(He arrived in splendor and pride.)* **10** And Elisha sent a messenger to him, saying, "Go and wash in the Jordan seven times, and your flesh shall be restored, and you shall be clean." *(To cure Naaman of pride Elisha did not come out to meet him personally, but sent him a simple message.)*

11 But Naaman was angry and went away, saying, "Behold, I thought that he would

---

[857] 1 Peter 5:7, "Casting all your anxieties on him, because he cares for you."
[858] 2 Kings 5:13

surely come out to me and stand and call upon the name of the LORD his God, and wave his hand over the place and cure the leper. *(He wanted rituals and ceremonies, just as many do today.)* ¹²Are not Abana and Pharpar, the rivers of Damascus, better than all the waters of Israel? Could I not wash in them and be clean?" So he turned and went away in a rage. *(He was like those today who ignore the great gospel command, "Believe in the Lord Jesus Christ,"⁸⁵⁹ and look for a way to be saved by their own efforts or by the ritual of some so-called priest.)* ¹³But his servants came near and said to him, "My father, it is a great word the prophet has spoken to you; will you not do it? Has he actually said to you, 'Wash, and be clean'?"

This was good reasoning. If Jesus had said to us, "Go on a long journey to a holy place and you will be saved," we would have traveled across the world. Should we not obey him when he says, "Believe and live"?

¹⁴So he went down and dipped himself seven times in the Jordan, according to the word of the man of God, and his flesh was restored like the flesh of a little child, and he was clean.

God is always as good as his word, but he requires us to obey him. Faith will save us, but if we will not believe we will not inherit eternal life. How is it with each one of us? Have we washed in Jesus' blood or not?⁸⁶⁰

DECEMBER 4
He Who Tells Lies Will Perish⁸⁶¹
2 Kings 5:15-27

¹⁵Then [Naaman] returned to the man of God, he and all his company, and he came and stood before him. And he said, "Behold, I know that there is no God in all the earth but in Israel; so accept now a present from your servant. *(The stranger from Syria returned to give his heartfelt thanks. He was not like those who receive great help and then go away and forget the giver. His gratitude prompted him to reward the prophet as well as to praise his Master.)* ¹⁶But [Elisha] said, "As the LORD lives, before whom I stand, I will receive none." And he urged him to take it, but he refused.

He wanted Naaman to see that he was not like the greedy priests he was used to. Jesus taught his disciples, "You received without paying; give without pay."⁸⁶² Elisha accepted presents from others, but in this case he refused because he knew it was the best thing to do.

¹⁷Then Naaman said, "If not, please let there be given to your servant two mules' load of earth, for from now on your servant will not offer burnt offering or sacrifice to any god but the LORD. *(Did he want this earth to build an altar with, according to the law? We may suppose so, but we cannot be sure.)* ¹⁸In this matter may the LORD pardon your servant; when my master goes into the house of Rimmon to worship there, leaning on my arm, and I bow myself in the house of Rimmon, when I bow myself in the house of Rimmon, the LORD pardon your servant in this matter." *(His faith was very weak. He wanted some leeway granted regarding his responsibilities in the royal court in Syria. It was a wrong request and Elisha passed over it in silence. Perhaps Naaman outgrew his fear and became as decided for Jehovah as we could wish him to have been at the first.)* ¹⁹He said to him, "Go in peace."

But when Naaman had gone from him a short distance, ²⁰Gehazi, the servant of Elisha the man of God, said, "See, my master has spared this Naaman the Syrian, in not accepting from his hand what he brought. As the LORD lives, I will run after him and get something from him." *(How irreverent to mix up the name of the Lord with his greed and lie. Someone may live with a prophet and not be the better for it.)* ²¹So Gehazi followed Naaman. And when Naaman saw someone running after him, he got down from the chariot to meet him and said, "Is all well?" ²²And he said, "All is well. My master has sent me to say, 'There have just now come to me from the hill country of Ephraim two young men of the sons of the

---
⁸⁵⁹ Acts 16:31
⁸⁶⁰ Revelation 7:14b, "These are the ones coming out of the great tribulation. They have washed their robes and made them white in the blood of the Lamb."
⁸⁶¹ Proverbs 19:9 (NASB)
⁸⁶² Matthew 10:8

prophets. Please give them a talent of silver and two changes of clothing.'" *(Intentional falsehood, every word of it!)*

²³ And Naaman said, "Be pleased to accept two talents." And he urged him and tied up two talents *(about 150 pounds)* of silver in two bags, with two changes of clothing, and laid them on two of his servants. And they carried them before Gehazi. ²⁴ And when he came to the hill, he took them from their hand and put them in the house, and he sent the men away, and they departed.

What good could these things do him when he had to hide them and leave them? People lose their souls to get things that only cause them more trouble.

²⁵ He went in and stood before his master, and Elisha said to him, "Where have you been, Gehazi?" And he said, "Your servant went nowhere."

One lie requires another to back it up. The beginning of falsehood is like a fire that gets out of control. No one knows where it will end.

²⁶ But he said to him, "Did not my heart go when the man turned from his chariot to meet you? Was it a time to accept money and garments, olive orchards and vineyards, sheep and oxen, male servants and female servants? ²⁷ Therefore the leprosy of Naaman shall cling to you and to your descendants forever." So he went out from his presence a leper, like snow. *(May God, in his infinite mercy, keep us from provoking him by telling lies. Liars may not be punished with leprosy in these days, but they will have their part in the lake that burns with fire and sulfur.[863] Who can think about such a doom without trembling?)*

DECEMBER 5

The Glory of Israel Will Not Lie or Have Regret[864]

Some time after Naaman was cured of his leprosy, the king of Syria besieged Samaria. Food became so scarce that mothers actually ate their own children. At last the Lord directed Elisha to inform these people that they were about to be delivered from the Syrians.

2 Kings 7:1-17

¹ But Elisha said, "Hear the word of the LORD: thus says the LORD, Tomorrow about this time a seah *(about eight pounds)* of fine flour shall be sold for a shekel,[865] and two seahs of barley for a shekel, at the gate of Samaria." ² Then the captain on whose hand the king leaned said to the man of God, "If the LORD himself should make windows in heaven, could this thing be?" But he said, "You shall see it with your own eyes, but you shall not eat of it." *(The king's captain was scornful as well as unbelieving. This sarcasm was typical of the way he sneered at the Lord and his prophet.)*

³ Now there were four men who were lepers at the entrance to the gate. And they said to one another, "Why are we sitting here until we die? ⁴ If we say, 'Let us enter the city,' the famine is in the city, and we shall die there. And if we sit here, we die also. So now come, let us go over to the camp of the Syrians. If they spare our lives we shall live, and if they kill us we shall but die." ⁵ So they arose at twilight to go to the camp of the Syrians. But when they came to the edge of the camp of the Syrians, behold, there was no one there. ⁶ For the LORD had made the army of the Syrians hear the sound of chariots and of horses, the sound of a great army, so that they said to one another, "Behold, the king of Israel has hired against us the kings of the Hittites and the kings of Egypt to come against us." ⁷ So they fled away in the twilight and abandoned their tents, their horses, and their donkeys, leaving the camp as it was, and fled for their lives.

If the Lord wills it, the most courageous enemies of his church will run away like frightened rabbits. Why should we be afraid of those who can become afraid of themselves so quickly?

---

[863] Revelation 21:8, "But as for the cowardly, the faithless, the detestable, as for murderers, the sexually immoral, sorcerers, idolaters, and **all liars**, their portion will be in the lake that burns with fire and sulfur, which is the second death."

[864] 1 Samuel 15:29

[865] A *shekel* weighs about two-fifths of an ounce. A silver shekel might approximate an hour's wage.

⁸And when these lepers came to the edge of the camp, they went into a tent and ate and drank, and they carried off silver and gold and clothing and went and hid them. Then they came back and entered another tent and carried off things from it and went and hid them.

⁹Then they said to one another, "We are not doing right. This day is a day of good news. If we are silent and wait until the morning light, punishment will overtake us. Now therefore come; let us go and tell the king's household." ¹⁰So they came and called to the gatekeepers of the city and told them, "We came to the camp of the Syrians, and behold, there was no one to be seen or heard there, nothing but the horses tied and the donkeys tied and the tents as they were." ¹¹Then the gatekeepers called out, and it was told within the king's household. ¹²And the king rose in the night and said to his servants, "I will tell you what the Syrians have done to us. They know that we are hungry. Therefore they have gone out of the camp to hide themselves in the open country, thinking, 'When they come out of the city, we shall take them alive and get into the city.'"

¹³And one of his servants said, "Let some men take five of the remaining horses, seeing that those who are left here will fare like the whole multitude of Israel who have already perished. Let us send and see." *(The promise that God had given only a few hours earlier by his prophet Elisha seems to have already been forgotten. However they did the right thing to send men and see if the story the lepers told was true. Some people are so certain that a blessing from God cannot possibly happen, they will not bother to check out a story when they hear it.)* ¹⁴So they took two horsemen, and the king sent them after the army of the Syrians, saying, "Go and see." ¹⁵So they went after them as far as the Jordan, and behold, all the way was littered with garments and equipment that the Syrians had thrown away in their haste. And the messengers returned and told the king.

¹⁶Then the people went out and plundered the camp of the Syrians. So a seah of fine flour was sold for a shekel, and two seahs of barley for a shekel, according to the word of the LORD. *(God's word was fulfilled right down to the penny and the hour.)* ¹⁷Now the king had appointed the captain on whose hand he leaned to have charge of the gate. And the people trampled him in the gate, so that he died, as the man of God had said when the king came down to him.

God fulfills his threats as well as his promises. The fine flour is sold and the unbelieving captain is crushed. It will be terrible if any of us perish because we also refuse to believe. Yet that is what will happen if we see the blessings of the gospel all around us and lose them because we refuse to believe.

DECEMBER 6
The Heart Is Deceitful Above All Things[866]

2 Kings 8:1-15

¹Now Elisha had said to the woman whose son he had restored to life, "Arise, and depart with your household, and sojourn wherever you can, for the LORD has called for a famine, and it will come upon the land for seven years." *(She had been quite content to live among her own people and now she must undergo the trial of being away from them for a time. Undoubtedly she understood that the path of faith is not an easy one, but that it is always the safest one.)* ²So the woman arose and did according to the word of the man of God. She went with her household and sojourned in the land of the Philistines seven years. *(She submitted to this trial in the right spirit. She did not question "why?" and she did not complain.)*

³And at the end of the seven years, when the woman returned from the land of the Philistines, she went to appeal to the king for her house and her land. *(While she was gone, others had taken her property, so she went to the king to ask that it be returned to her)* ⁴Now the king was talking with Gehazi the servant of the man of God, saying, "Tell me all the great things that Elisha has done." ⁵And while he was telling the king how Elisha had restored the dead to life, behold,

---
[866] Jeremiah 17:9

the woman whose son he had restored to life appealed to the king for her house and her land. And Gehazi said, "My lord, O king, here is the woman, and here is her son whom Elisha restored to life."

This was an obvious act of providence. The odds were, as people would say, a million to one against these things happening at the same time. The king wanted to talk to Gehazi, the topic was about the woman's son being restored to life, and, just in time, the hero of the story shows up. Wonderful, was it not? Yet, if we will just open our eyes, we shall see wonders like this happen in our own lives more times than we can count.

⁶ And when the king asked the woman, she told him. So the king appointed an official for her, saying, "Restore all that was hers, together with all the produce of the fields from the day that she left the land until now." *(God repaid this woman a hundred times over for the cup of cold water that she gave to Elisha when she welcomed him as her guest. God will not be in debt to anyone.)*

⁷ Now Elisha came to Damascus. *(He marched right into the teeth of Israel's enemies. He carried out the Lord's errands with the same bravery that Elijah did before him.)* Ben-hadad the king of Syria was sick. And when it was told him, "The man of God has come here," ⁸ the king said to Hazael, "Take a present with you and go to meet the man of God, and inquire of the LORD through him, saying, 'Shall I recover from this sickness?'" ⁹ So Hazael went to meet him, and took a present with him, all kinds of goods of Damascus, forty camels' loads. When he came and stood before him, he said, "Your son Ben-hadad king of Syria has sent me to you, saying, 'Shall I recover from this sickness?'"

¹⁰ And Elisha said to him, "Go, say to him, 'You shall certainly recover,' but the LORD has shown me that he shall certainly die." *(He might recover as far as his illness was concerned, but he will die because Hazael would murder him. Both of Elisha's statements were correct.)* ¹¹ And he fixed his gaze and stared at him, until he was embarrassed. And the man of God wept.

¹² And Hazael said, "Why does my lord weep?" He answered, "Because I know the evil that you will do to the people of Israel. You will set on fire their fortresses, and you will kill their young men with the sword and dash in pieces their little ones and rip open their pregnant women." ¹³ And Hazael said, "What is your servant, who is but a dog, that he should do this great thing?" *(He denied that he could commit such a crime, but this was not the truth. In his heart he was already plotting the overthrow of his king.)* Elisha answered, "The LORD has shown me that you are to be king over Syria." ¹⁴ Then he departed from Elisha and came to his master, who said to him, "What did Elisha say to you?" And he answered, "He told me that you would certainly recover." ¹⁵ But the next day he took the bed cloth and dipped it in water and spread it over his face, till he died. And Hazael became king in his place.

Hazael proved that he was worse than a dog, even though he had pretended to be innocent. Words are worth nothing when the heart is wrong. We must have new hearts and right spirits or there is no predicting what crimes we may end up committing. Who knows the amount of evil that any one of us might do if grace does not stop us? Oh Lord, save us from ourselves.

DECEMBER 7

The LORD Has Made Himself Known; He Has Executed Judgment[867]

2 Kings 9:1-7; 14; 21-26; 30-37

¹ Then Elisha the prophet called one of the sons of the prophets and said to him, "Tie up your garments, and take this flask of oil in your hand, and go to Ramoth-gilead. ² And when you arrive, look there for Jehu the son of Jehoshaphat, son of Nimshi. And go in and have him rise from among his fellows, and lead him to an inner chamber. ³ Then take the flask of oil and pour it on his head and say, 'Thus says the LORD, I anoint you king over Israel.' Then open the door and flee; do not linger." *(He was not to wait for payment or reward. Those who do the Lord's business must not stand around idly or move*

---

[867] Psalm 9:16

slowly. God's angels fly swiftly and God's prophets must carry out their assignments with eagerness.)

⁴ So the young man, the servant of the prophet, went to Ramoth-gilead. ⁵ And when he came, behold, the commanders of the army were in council. And he said, "I have a word for you, O commander." And Jehu said, "To which of us all?" and he said, "To you, O commander." ⁶ So he arose and went into the house. And the young man poured the oil on his head, saying to him, "Thus says the LORD the God of Israel, I anoint you king over the people of the LORD, over Israel. ⁷ And you shall strike down the house of Ahab your master, so that I may avenge on Jezebel the blood of my servants the prophets, and the blood of all the servants of the LORD."

¹⁴ Thus Jehu the son of Jehoshaphat the son of Nimshi conspired against Joram. *(He was probably Joram's top general. It was not something new in Israel's history for a person in this position to overthrow the king.)* (Now Joram with all Israel had been on guard at Ramoth-gilead against Hazael king of Syria.)

King Joram had left Jehu in charge of the city of Ramoth-gilead while he went to Jezreel to recover from wounds he had received during a battle with the Syrians. Jehu chose this time to attack Joram. He came to Jezreel with his cavalry to attack the recuperating king. The watchman on the walls of the palace saw Jehu coming and King Joram sent messengers to find out why he was coming to Jezreel. But they immediately deserted Joram and joined Jehu's soldiers. Finally the king himself decided to ride out and confront his rebellious general. He acted foolishly and it ended in his death. The next verses describe the deadly encounter.

²¹ Joram said, "Make ready." And they made ready his chariot. Then Joram king of Israel and Ahaziah king of Judah set out, each in his chariot, and went to meet Jehu, and met him at the property of Naboth the Jezreelite. ²² And when Joram saw Jehu, he said, "Is it peace, Jehu?" *(He was asking Jehu whether the Syrians had defeated them or if he had conquered them and brought news of peace. Little did he dream of the doom to which he was rushing. The greatest sinners are usually the ones who feel no harm will come to them, even when they are on the edge of ruin.)* He answered, "What peace can there be, so long as the whorings and sorceries of your mother Jezebel are so many?" *(What peace can any sinner expect to have with God while they live in sin?)*

²³ Then Joram reined about and fled, saying to Ahaziah, "Treachery, O Ahaziah!" ²⁴ And Jehu drew his bow with his full strength, and shot Joram between the shoulders, so that the arrow pierced his heart, and he sank in his chariot. ²⁵ Jehu said to Bidkar his aide, "Take him up and throw him on the plot of ground belonging to Naboth the Jezreelite. For remember, when you and I rode side by side behind Ahab his father, how the LORD made this pronouncement against him. ²⁶ 'As surely as I saw yesterday the blood of Naboth and the blood of his sons—declares the LORD—I will repay you on this plot of ground.' Now therefore take him up and throw him on the plot of ground, in accordance with the word of the LORD." *(In this way, the Lord is known by the judgments he carries out. It is remarkable that the person who had heard the prophecy years before, as if by chance, should now become the one to fulfill the prophecy.)*

³⁰ When Jehu came to Jezreel, Jezebel heard of it. And she painted her eyes and adorned her head and looked out of the window. ³¹ And as Jehu entered the gate, she said, "Is it peace, you Zimri, murderer of your master?"

Her arrogant spirit did not back off. She sneered at the Lord's avenger. Maybe she hoped to frighten Jehu by showing him great disrespect. But he had a command from God and this made him bold to go forward and execute the wicked queen.

³² And he lifted up his face to the window and said, "Who is on my side? Who?" Two or three eunuchs looked out at him. ³³ He said, "Throw her down." So they threw her down. And some of her blood spattered on the wall and on the horses, and they trampled on her. *(Her murder of the Lord's prophets*

came home to her. The body that she pampered was now trampled on like "straw is trampled down in a dunghill."[868]) **34** Then he went in and ate and drank. And he said, "See now to this cursed woman and bury her, for she is a king's daughter."

35 But when they went to bury her, they found no more of her than the skull and the feet and the palms of her hands. **36** When they came back and told him, he said, "This is the word of the LORD, which he spoke by his servant Elijah the Tishbite, 'In the territory of Jezreel the dogs shall eat the flesh of Jezebel, **37** and the corpse of Jezebel shall be as dung on the face of the field in the territory of Jezreel, so that no one can say, This is Jezebel.'" *(This was heard in her pompous days. Her heralds proclaimed, "This is Jezebel," But they would say this no more. They could not even say, this is Jezebel's body, or this is Jezebel's tomb, or these are Jezebel's children. The name of the wicked will rot. Lord, we bow before you in reverence; we tremble at your justice.)*

DECEMBER 8
The Wicked Are Overthrown and Are No More[869]

We have seen the end of the house of Ahab. We will now glance at the kingdom of Judah. Jehoshaphat was a good king, but he was too friendly with the idol worshiping kings of Israel and the sad result was evil kings on the throne in Judah.

2 Chronicles 21:1, 4, 6; 18-20

1 Jehoshaphat slept with his fathers and was buried with his fathers in the city of David, and Jehoram his son reigned in his place.

4 When Jehoram had ascended the throne of his father and was established, he killed all his brothers with the sword, and also some of the princes of Israel. *(He followed the cruel policy of many oriental tyrants who are afraid of rivals. He put to death anyone who might rise to power through their position or influence. Jehoram's brothers were better than he was. Perhaps this was why he was so hardened against them.)*

6 And he walked in the way of the kings of Israel, as the house of Ahab had done, for the daughter of Ahab was his wife. And he did what was evil in the sight of the LORD. *(A lot about our future depends on whom we marry. Whether for good or evil, our spouse will influence our entire life. Jehoram acted wickedly. He married the daughter of wicked Ahab. May all the marriages of our family be "in the Lord.")*

Jehoram's sin resulted in his country being looted, his palace abandoned, and his wives and children carried off as prisoners. None of this caused him to repent of his wickedness.

18 And after all this the LORD struck him in his bowels with an incurable disease. **19** In the course of time, at the end of two years...he died in great agony. His people made no fire in his honor, like the fires made for his fathers. **20** He was thirty-two years old when he began to reign, and he reigned eight years in Jerusalem. And he departed with no one's regret. *(No one placed value in his life or mourned his death.)* They buried him in the city of David, but not in the tombs of the kings.

They did not think his body was worth burying with the godly kings. Those who despise God will not get much respect.

2 Chronicles 22:1-9

1 And the inhabitants of Jerusalem made Ahaziah, his youngest son, king in his place, for the band of men that came with the Arabians to the camp had killed all the older sons. So Ahaziah the son of Jehoram king of Judah reigned. **2** Ahaziah was twenty-two years old when he began to reign, and he reigned one year in Jerusalem. His mother's name was Athaliah, the granddaughter of Omri. **3** He also walked in the ways of the house of Ahab, for his mother was his counselor in doing wickedly.

Athaliah was the daughter of Ahab and Jezebel. She married Jehoram. She ruined her husband and influenced her son to be evil. Mothers have great influence in their

---

[868] Isaiah 25: 10, "For the hand of the LORD will rest on this mountain, and Moab shall be trampled down in his place, as straw is trampled down in a dunghill."
[869] Proverbs 12:7

families. They are the queens of the household and shape the future of their children.

⁴He did what was evil in the sight of the LORD, as the house of Ahab had done. For after the death of his father they were his counselors, to his undoing. *(His father's counselors became his advisors. Counselors to wickedness are counselors to destruction.)* ⁵He even followed their counsel and went with Jehoram the son of Ahab king of Israel to make war against Hazael king of Syria at Ramoth-gilead. And the Syrians wounded Joram, ⁶and he returned to be healed in Jezreel of the wounds that he received at Ramah, when he fought against Hazael king of Syria. And Ahaziah the son of Jehoram king of Judah went down to see Joram the son of Ahab in Jezreel, because he was wounded.

⁷But it was ordained by God that the downfall of Ahaziah should come about through his going to visit Joram. For when he came there, he went out with Jehoram to meet Jehu the son of Nimshi, whom the LORD had anointed to destroy the house of Ahab. ⁸And when Jehu was executing judgment on the house of Ahab, he met the princes of Judah and the sons of Ahaziah's brothers, who attended Ahaziah, and he killed them. ⁹ᵃHe searched for Ahaziah, and he was captured while hiding in Samaria, and he was brought to Jehu and put to death. *(Ahaziah had sinned like those in the house of Ahab and their overthrow also led to his destruction. His mother and his wife were both of the evil family of Ahab. He was twice cursed and the downfall of Ahab's family became his too. We should never have close associations on earth with those from whom we want to be separated on the day of judgment.)* They buried him, for they said, "He is the grandson of Jehoshaphat, who sought the LORD with all his heart." *(They buried him out of respect for his godly grandfather. Otherwise his body would have been left to the dogs. "The memory of the righteous is a blessing, but the name of the wicked will rot."*[870]*)*

DECEMBER 9
As For Me, I Have Set Up My King On Zion, My Holy Hill[871]
2 Kings 11:1-4; 10-18; 20

¹Now when Athaliah the mother of Ahaziah saw that her son was dead, she arose and destroyed all the royal family. *(Like a true descendant of Ahab, she stopped at nothing that could promote her own ambition. She earned the name, "Athaliah that wicked woman."*[872] *She almost succeeded in destroying David's descendants, but the Lord would not allow that to happen. The scepter could not be taken from the tribe of Judah until the Messiah came. The covenant promise to David was connected to the birth of Jesus Christ. It was not possible for God's word to be broken.)* ²But Jehosheba, the daughter of King Joram, sister of Ahaziah, took Joash the son of Ahaziah and stole him away from among the king's sons who were being put to death, and she put him and his nurse in a bedroom. Thus they hid him from Athaliah, so that he was not put to death. ³And he remained with her six years, hidden in house of the LORD, while Athaliah reigned over the land. *(Athaliah was not likely to go to the Lord's house to find the child, because she rarely visited that sacred place. David had lovingly cared for God's house and now the Lord protects the hope of his servant's race in the rooms of the temple.)*

⁴But in the seventh year Jehoiada sent and brought the captains of the Carites and of the guards, and had them come to him in the house of the LORD. And he made a covenant with them and put them under oath in the house of the LORD, and he showed them the king's son.

Jehoiada appointed these people to be the king's bodyguard when he brought him into the open to be crowned.

---
[870] Proverbs 10:7
[871] Psalm 2:6
[872] 2 Chronicles 24:7

Matthew Henry[873] remarks that Jehoiada was a man of great wisdom, because he kept the prince in the background until a time when the people were fed up with Athaliah's tyranny. He was a man of great influence; the Levites and all Judah did as he commanded. He was a man of great faith; in the darkest times he said, "Behold, the king's son! Let him reign, as the LORD spoke concerning the sons of David."[874] He was a man of great religion; he returned the worship of the Lord all over the land. He was a man of great determination; he went boldly through with his loyal plan and carried it out to final success.

10 And the priest gave to the captains the spears and shields that had been King David's, which were in the house of the LORD. **11** And the guards stood, every man with his weapons in his hand, from the south side of the house to the north side of the house, around the altar and the house on behalf of the king. **12** Then he brought out the king's son and put the crown on him and gave him the testimony. And they proclaimed him king and anointed him, and they clapped their hands and said, "Long live the king!"

13 When Athaliah heard the noise of the guard and of the people, she went into the house of the LORD to the people. **14** And when she looked, there was the king standing by the pillar, according to the custom and the captains and the trumpeters beside the king, and all the people of the land rejoicing and blowing trumpets. And Athaliah tore her clothes and cried, "Treason! Treason!" *(Yet she was herself the greatest traitor. Her cries were useless. Her tyranny and cruelty had lost her any friends she may have had. No one lifted a hand or voice in her defense.)*

15 Then Jehoiada the priest commanded the captains who were set over the army, "Bring her out between the ranks, and put to death with the sword anyone who follows her." For the priest said, "Let her not be put to death in the house of the LORD." **16** So they laid hands on her; and she went through the horses' entrance to the king's house, and there she was put to death.

The last of Ahab's family was put to death. Like Jezebel before her, this fierce and overbearing woman was rushed to her destruction.

17 And Jehoiada made a covenant between the LORD and the king and people, that they should be the LORD's people, and also between the king and the people. **18** Then all the people of the land went to the house of Baal and tore it down; his altars and his images they broke in pieces, and they killed Mattan the priest of Baal before the altars. And the priest posted watchmen over the house of the LORD.

20a So all the people of the land rejoiced, and the city was quiet. *(The holy influence of one great and good man brought the nation back to its previous condition. True worship of the Lord returned and the idols were removed. When God's Spirit is in a person they can sway the hearts of thousands. Lord, send us such people in both church and government.)*

DECEMBER 10

You Received Without Paying; Give Without Pay[875]

2 Kings 12:1-15

1a In the seventh year of Jehu, Jehoash *(an alternate spelling of Joash)* began to reign, and he reigned forty years in Jerusalem. **2** And Jehoash did what was right in the eyes of the LORD all his days, because Jehoiada the priest instructed him.

Unfortunately, Jehoash was controlled by those around him. He lacked strength of character. He was good only as long as the real reins of his actions were in godly hands. People should have minds of their own. They should have principles that will guide them no matter whose company they are in. Still, Jehoiada deserves great honor for the way he managed the affairs of the kingdom.

3 Nevertheless, the high places were not taken away; the people continued to sacrifice and make offerings on the high places.

---

[873] Matthew Henry (1662-1714). Pastor and Bible commentator.
[874] 2 Chronicles 23:3

[875] Matthew 10:8

⁴Jehoash said to the priests, "All the money of the holy things that is brought into the house of the LORD, the money for which each man is assessed—the money from the assessment of persons—and the money that a man's heart prompts him to bring into the house of the LORD, ⁵let the priests take, each from his donor, and let them repair the house wherever any need of repairs is discovered." *(The king had been brought up in the temple. Therefore he felt a great love for it. He had only an appearance of godliness,[876] but his appearance was very energetic. His zeal put even the priests to shame. Those who have nothing except external religion are often more passionate about it than those who possess the reality of godliness.)*

⁶But by the twenty-third year of King Jehoash, the priests had made no repairs on the house. ⁷Therefore King Jehoash summoned Jehoiada the priest and the other priests and said to them, "Why are you not repairing the house? Now therefore take no more money from your donors, but hand it over for the repair of the house." *(Pastors should not be burdened with the responsibility of raising money. They have higher duties. The priests managed the money poorly. They failed to keep contributions for the repairs in a separate fund, so the king decided on another plan. If we cannot come up with resources for a good work one way, we must try another.)* ⁸So the priests agreed that they should take no more money from the people, and that they should not repair the house.

⁹Then Jehoiada the priest took a chest and bored a hole in the lid of it and set it beside the altar on the right side as one entered the house of the LORD. And the priests who guarded the threshold put in it all the money that was brought into the house of the LORD. ¹⁰And whenever they saw that there was much money in the chest, the king's secretary and the high priest came up and they bagged and counted the money that was found in the house of LORD.

This was a new approach and the people liked the idea. It is most important that people should be sure that whatever is given to the cause of God is used honestly.

¹¹Then they would give the money that was weighed out into the hands of the workmen who had the oversight of the house of the LORD. And they paid it out to the carpenters and the builders who worked on the house of the LORD, ¹²and to the masons and the stonecutters, as well as to buy timber and quarried stone for making repairs on the house of the LORD, and for any outlay for the repairs of the house. ¹³But there were not made for the house of the LORD basins of silver, snuffers, bowls, trumpets, or any vessels of gold, or of silver, from the money that was brought into the house of the LORD, ¹⁴for that was given to the workmen who were repairing the house of the LORD with it.

This is a good place to stop and ask if each of us is doing our part for the support of God's worship and work. Let us not be content to live in well-maintained homes while the house of worship is in disrepair.

¹⁵And they did not ask an accounting from the men into whose hand they delivered the money to pay out to the workmen, for they dealt honestly. *(Faithfulness is a great virtue. Whatever may happen to us, we must keep an accurate account of expenses. A Christian should be someone who can be trusted with even very large amounts of money. Whether we seem to be unimportant or lords of the land, our first duty to other people is to be thoroughly honest.)*

DECEMBER 11
It is Good For the Heart To Be Strengthened By Grace[877]

2 Chronicles 24:2; 15-25

²And Joash did what was right in the eyes of the LORD all the days of Jehoiada the priest.

But Joash was not motivated by love to God. He did things to please Jehoiada, the man who had helped him to the throne. The religious party had put the crown on his

---

[876] 2 Timothy 3:5, "having the appearance of godliness, but denying its power."

[877] Hebrews 13:9

head and so as long as they were in power he followed their wishes. But when the idolaters became strong he went over to their side. The person who goes whichever way the wind blows will change direction when it does. It is very important to be guided by clearly established truth.

15 But Jehoiada grew old and full of days, and died. He was 130 years old at his death. **16** And they buried him in the city of David among the kings, because he had done good in Israel, and toward God and his house.

17 Now after the death of Jehoiada the princes of Judah came and paid homage to the king. Then the king listened to them.

No doubt the princes congratulated Joash on no longer needing to follow the wishes of an old priest. "Now," they said, "let us leave the dull and harsh religion of Jehovah for the fun and pleasurable worship of idols. We have had enough of this strict religion. Let us follow the ways of other nations. Let us enjoy the happy and more liberal ways of Baal and Ashtaroth." This king was very willing to listen to this kind of advice.

18 And they abandoned the house of the LORD, the God of their fathers, and served the Asherim and the idols. And wrath came upon Judah and Jerusalem for this guilt of theirs. **19** Yet he sent prophets among them to bring them back to the LORD. These testified against them, but they would not pay attention.

20 Then the Spirit of God clothed Zechariah the son of Jehoiada the priest, and he stood above the people, and said to them, "Thus says God, 'Why do you break the commandments of the LORD, so that you cannot prosper? Because you have forsaken the LORD, he has forsaken you.'" **21** But they conspired against him, and by command of the king they stoned him with stones in the court of the house of the LORD.

Their act of murder was done in the temple court and polluted the sanctuary of the Lord. They could not bear to be scolded for their faults. Some children show the same spirit and become very angry if a parent tries to correct them. Such bad anger and rage can lead to murder if it is not controlled. The person who is angry with someone for telling him about his faults will be judged (as a murderer).[878]

22 Thus Joash the king did not remember the kindness that Jehoiada, Zechariah's father, had shown him, but killed his son. And when he was dying, he said, "May the LORD see and avenge!"

An ungrateful man is capable of any crime. After the father had done so much for the king it was disgraceful to kill the son for doing his duty. Such a crime could not go unpunished.

23 At the end of the year the army of the Syrians came up against Joash. They came to Judah and Jerusalem and destroyed all the princes of the people from among the people and sent all their spoil to the king of Damascus.

The dying martyr's blood brought speedy vengeance on the land. The princes had been first in the sin and therefore they were prominent in the punishment. And the city where the murder took place was made to feel the full force of the war.

24 Though the army of the Syrians had come with few men, the LORD delivered into their hand a very great army, because Judah had forsaken the LORD, the God of their fathers. Thus they executed judgment on Joash.

25 When they had departed from him, leaving him severely wounded, his servants conspired against him because of the blood of the son of Jehoiada the priest, and killed him on his bed. So he died, and they buried him in the city of David, but they did not bury him in the tombs of the kings.

First, Joash was attacked by his enemies, then his land was looted and finally he was severely injured. Since all this did not bring him to repentance, the Lord put an end to his wicked reign by a well deserved punishment. He killed the sons of his greatest supporter and soon his own servants assassinated him in his bed. "Affliction will slay the wicked,

---

[878] Matthew 5:21-22, "You have heard that it was said to those of old, 'You shall not murder; and whoever murders will be liable to judgment.' But I say to you that everyone who is angry with his brother will be liable to judgment."

and those who hate the righteous will be condemned."[879]

DECEMBER 12
Where Shall I Flee From Your Presence?[880]

It was about the time of King Joash and Jehoiada the priest that the prophet Jonah made his visit to the city of Nineveh. As we read his story, we should pay attention to the honest way Jonah writes about himself. He is faithful to include his own shortcomings and faults.

Jonah 1:1-7

¹ Now the word of the LORD came to Jonah the son of Amittai, saying, ² "Arise, go to Nineveh, that great city, and call out against it, for their evil has come up before me." *(Nineveh has been described as being protected by a 60 mile wall surrounding the city and 1,000,000 people living in it. It was full of idols and its wealth was acquired by attacking and stealing from other nations. It was very gracious on the Lord's part to send a prophet to warn such a city. But it was no small task for one man to take on such an unwelcome assignment.)*

³ But Jonah rose to flee to Tarshish from the presence of the LORD. *(Who would have thought that a prophet would act so wickedly? "Let anyone who thinks that he stands take heed lest he fall."[881] We are much weaker than a prophet and more likely to fall. Therefore let us pray to the Lord to keep us from falling.)* He went down to Joppa and found a ship going to Tarshish. *(Some would think that Jonah finding a ship ready to sail away from his assignment was actually arranged by God so he would not need to follow the Lord's express command. Old Thomas Adams says, "If you will flee from God, the devil will loan you both spurs and a horse. Yes, a ready horse that will carry you swiftly."[882] It is our duty to follow God's orders and not the apparent leading of circumstances.)* So he paid the fare and went on board, to go with them to Tarshish, away from the presence of the LORD. *(Sin is expensive. A price must be paid. People will grumble about any little amount they are asked to give for the cause of God, but they do not care how much they have to pay to satisfy their wrong desires. Jonah took on a foolish mission when he tried to run away from the Lord. God is everywhere. He is just as present in Tarshish as in Nineveh!)*

⁴ But the LORD hurled a great wind upon the sea, and there was a mighty tempest on the sea, so that the ship threatened to break up.

If we run from God he will send rough deputies after us. We may flee when there is no apparent danger, but a storm will soon be sent as an officer from heaven to arrest us.

⁵ Then the mariners were afraid, and each cried out to his god. And they hurled the cargo that was in the ship into the sea to lighten it for them. *(On this, Adams remarks: "Mariners are as much at home in the sea as fish. They are fearless, adventurous and regard danger with contempt. Yet seeing the storm so violent all of a sudden and their large and tall ship tossed about like a little rowboat and cracked so that it was about to be torn to pieces, they were persuaded that it was no ordinary storm, but a revenging tempest, sent out by some great power that had been provoked. They trembled for fear, like little children when they are frightened, lest their ship break, or leak, and so sink, and they lose their ship, lives and all. These fearless fellows were brought down by danger, and quaked like a young soldier who jumps at the sound of a gun. They did well to pray, but they prayed not well, because they turned to idol gods that could not even help themselves.")* But Jonah had gone down into the inner part of the ship and had lain down and was fast asleep. *(He for whom the storm was sent was the last to hear its message. When good people fall into sin they are generally in such a sleepy state of heart that it is difficult to bring them to repentance.)*

⁶ So the captain came and said to him, "What do you mean, you sleeper? Arise, call out to your god! Perhaps the god will give a thought to us, that we may not perish." *(How*

---

[879] Psalm 34:21
[880] Psalm 139:7
[881] 1 Corinthians 10:12
[882] Thomas Adams (1583-1652). English clergyman known as "The Shakespeare of the Puritans."

well these words may be applied to those who are careless hearers of the gospel. They are asleep. Asleep in awful danger! Even an unbeliever might rebuke them as this ship's captain scolded Jonah. Oh that they would wake up and call on God for their own sakes and the sake of their families who are perishing with them.)

⁷ And they said to one another, "Come, let us cast lots, that we may know on whose account this evil has come upon us." So they cast lots, and the lot fell on Jonah. *(What people call chances are all in the hands of God. How sad that the best man on board the vessel should be convicted as being, at least at this time, the worst of all! When good people sin their offense is very great. Let us ask God to guard us, so that we will not also be put to shame before the ungodly.)*

December 13
Christ Also Suffered For You[883]
Jonah 1:8-16

⁸ Then [the mariners] said to [Jonah], "Tell us on whose account this evil has come upon us. *(They put the question to him and did not condemn him without a hearing. There was more justice among these idolatrous sailors than we often find among professed Christians, who will judge by appearances and condemn in haste.)* What is your occupation? And where do you come from? What is your country? And of what people are you?" ⁹ And he said to them, "I am a Hebrew, and I fear the Lord, the God of heaven, who made the sea and the dry land."

He spoke truthfully, like the honest man he was. He acknowledged that he was a Hebrew who feared the Lord. He did not hesitate to claim that his God was the supreme God who was greater than all the supposed gods to whom they had been praying. He was ashamed of himself, but not of his religion.

¹⁰ Then the men were exceedingly afraid and said to him, "What is this that you have done!" For the men knew that he was fleeing from the presence of the Lord, because he had told them.

They knew what he had done, but now they asked him "why?" What could have persuaded him to flee from the God who had made the sea and the dry land, and could therefore find him wherever he might try to escape?

¹¹ Then they said to him, "What shall we do to you, that the sea may quiet down for us?" For the sea grew more and more tempestuous.

The sailors were reluctant to lift up their hands against Jonah. They were afraid to injure him even though he was clearly guilty. They did not even insult him, as some would have done. Let us learn from this to never be harsh with our brothers and sisters in Christ, even if their faults result in trouble and great danger for us. Instead, let us allow them to condemn themselves and suggest what steps should be taken to correct the situation.

¹² He said to them, "Pick me up and hurl me into the sea; then the sea will quiet down for you, for I know it is because of me that this great tempest has come upon you."

Here, Jonah was a distinguished type of our Lord Jesus. He represents the doctrine[884] of substitution. Jonah is cast into the sea and it becomes calm. Jesus is cast into the sea of God's wrath and it becomes calm to us. This is the most glorious of all revealed truths and the most necessary to be believed and personally accepted. In this verse, Jonah is seen in a good light. He is humble and regrets the trouble he has caused the ship's crew and passengers. He is ready to be disciplined without any complaining.

¹³ Nevertheless, the men rowed hard to get back to dry land, but they could not, for the sea grew more and more tempestuous against them.

Jonah's tender response and his deep concern for their safety touched their hearts. They were determined to save him if they could, but their efforts were doomed to fail. This is a picture of the spiritual truth that no amount of our own effort can save us. It is only by the death of the Substitute that we can be saved.

---
[883] 1 Peter 2:21

[884] *doctrine* - the belief or teaching of a church or group.

14 Therefore they called out to the LORD, "O LORD, let us not perish for this man's life, and lay not on us innocent blood, for you, O LORD, have done as it pleased you."

They abandoned their false gods and prayed only to Jehovah. Their efforts to save Jonah were not effective. Therefore they were forced to throw him overboard, but they would not do it until they had made one last earnest request to heaven. What a sight it must have been, to see these men on their knees, in the fury of the storm, and what a pleasure to hear them cry, "O LORD. O LORD." Nor did they forget all this when the storm was removed. It is most pleasing to read, "They offered a sacrifice to the Lord and made vows."

15 So they picked up Jonah and hurled him into the sea, and the sea ceased from its raging.

This was one of the most solemn funerals that ever took place. Into the raging billows the living man was thrown as though it was his grave, and lo, all was still. The sacrifice was offered and peace returned. What a marvelous picture of our redemption! Do we all understand that it is by Jesus' death that we receive new life?

16 Then the men feared the LORD exceedingly, and they offered a sacrifice to the LORD and made vows. *(When men are saved from destruction they should give glory to God with both words and gifts. Let us honor the Lord with our songs and our thank-offerings, because he alone is the Rock of our salvation.)*

DECEMBER 14
Save Us, Lord; We Are Perishing[885]

Jonah 1:17

17 And the LORD appointed a great fish to swallow up Jonah. *(He who prepared the storm prepared the fish. It was prepared especially for this divine purpose. It is pointless to spend time investigating what species it belonged to.)* And Jonah was in the belly of the fish three days and three nights. *(Thomas Jones,[886] in his "Jonah's Portrait,"* points out, "He must be a preacher whether he wants to be or not. When he was sent to preach to one city only, he refused; and now the Lord compels him to preach, not to one city, but to the whole world, by making him a type of Christ in his death, burial, and resurrection. 'For just as Jonah was three days and three nights in the belly of the great fish, so will the Son of Man be three days and three nights in the heart of the earth.'[887] When the servants of God run away from an easy service, their Master frequently appoints them a harder task. If Jonah will not preach up and down the streets of Nineveh, he will preach from the bottom of the sea. Man's highest wisdom is to obey his God, whatever work he appoints for him to do. If they who are sent to preach will not preach willingly, storms and tempests will prepare them for their work. Many have fallen into dismal darkness and the deep, for lack of more zeal and dependability in their Master's service; when they are tried they come forth as gold. Let those who desert God and his service learn how necessary it is to return; and let those who repent see that 'with the LORD there is steadfast love, and with him is plentiful redemption.'[888]"*

Jonah 2

1 Then Jonah prayed to the LORD his God from the belly of the fish, *(He had lost his enthusiasm for prayer on board ship, but he began afresh when he was plunged into awful torment.)* **2** saying,

"I called out to the LORD, out of my
   distress,
   and he answered me;
out of the belly of Sheol I cried,
   and you heard my voice."

The belly of the fish must have seemed like the middle of an unseen world. Jonah sent up his heavyhearted cry to heaven and was heard. Prayer can reach the ear of God from the depths of the sea.

3 "For you cast me into the deep,
   into the heart of the seas,
   and the flood surrounded me;
all your waves and your billows

---

[885] Matthew 8:25
[886] Thomas Jones (1741-1803)
[887] Matthew 12:40
[888] Psalm 130:7

        passed over me.
4 Then I said, 'I am driven away
    from your sight;
  Yet I shall again look
    upon your holy temple'"

If you will not look on me, yet will I keep mine eyes on you. Perhaps I will still be shown grace.

5 "The waters closed in over me to take my life;
  the deep surrounded me;
  weeds were wrapped about my head"

He felt like the seaweed had become his burial shroud.

6   "at the roots of the mountains.
  I went down to the land
    whose bars closed upon me forever;
  yet you brought up my life from the pit,
    O LORD my God."

Jonah had sunk a long way, but he might have gone even lower except God's power and mercy stepped in. He was still alive and this made him glad. His thankfulness was heard even in the belly of the fish.

7 "When my life was fainting away,
    I remembered the LORD,
  and my prayer came to you,
    into your holy temple.
8 Those who pay regard to vain idols
    forsake their hope of steadfast love.
9 But I with the voice of thanksgiving
    will sacrifice to you;
  what I have vowed I will pay."

He expects to be delivered and begins to rejoice in it.

      "Salvation belongs to the LORD!"

This is a brief statement of trustworthy theology. Perhaps if more Christians had experienced the depth of soul trouble that was Jonah's, this rock hard Bible truth would be preached more and believed more. "Salvation belongs to the LORD!"

10 And the LORD spoke to the fish, and it vomited Jonah out upon the dry land.

A word from God was enough. The fish was glad to get rid of this trouble in its belly. When the enemies of the Lord's people persecute them, a word from God is enough to make them stop, so that they may escape the judgments that would otherwise come on them.

DECEMBER 15
Something Greater Than Jonah Is Here[889]

Jonah 3

1 Then the word of the LORD came to Jonah the second time, saying, 2 "Arise, go to Nineveh, that great city, and call out against it the message that I tell you." *(This was a gracious sign that the Lord had forgiven his servant's disobedience. But it also showed that the Lord would not change his purpose to please the whim of someone or change his servant's work because they quarreled with it. Jonah was forced to go to Nineveh after all. His rebellion had not freed him from his obligation.)* 3 So Jonah arose and went to Nineveh, according to the word of the LORD. *(This time there was no delay and no objection. Five hundred miles was not too long a trip, nor were rivers and deserts too difficult to cross. The prophet had learned to obey by the things that he had suffered.)* Now Nineveh was an exceedingly great city, three days' journey in breadth. 4 Jonah began to go into the city, going a day's journey. And he called out, "Yet forty days, and Nineveh shall be overthrown!"

The people of Nineveh must have been surprised to see this strange, demanding man and hear his unchanging words of warning. The news sped through the city and the people crowded to hear the terrible voice that declared to them their speedy doom.

5 And the people of Nineveh believed God. They called for a fast and put on sackcloth, from the greatest of them to the least of them.

6 For word reached the king of Nineveh, and he arose from his throne, removed his robe, covered himself with sackcloth, and sat in ashes. 7 And he issued a proclamation and published through Nineveh, "By the decree of the king and his nobles: Let neither man nor beast, herd nor flock, taste anything. Let them not feed or drink water, 8 but let man

---
[889] Matthew 12:41

and beast be covered with sackcloth, and let them call out mightily to God. Let everyone turn from his evil way and from the violence that is in his hands. **9** Who knows? God may turn and relent and turn from his fierce anger, so that we may not perish."

The kings of Assyria were looked on as gods and were adored by their people. It might have been thought that the king of Nineveh would strike off the prophet's head, but he was gripped with a sense of terror and became the humble servant of a higher authority. Jonah's message from God contained little hope for the doomed capital and yet they decided to see if repentance[890] might help. "Who knows?" was all they could say, even though the fierce messenger who warned them gave them no encouragement that it would help. Will these men rise up in judgment against us? They had only the law and yet they begged for mercy. What will be our fate if we remain unrepentant when the gospel is preached to us? They did not have a promise of mercy or an invitation to seek it. We have both! Will we refuse to come to that banquet of grace that they so eagerly hoped for? They made even their children and their cattle feel the bitterness of sin. Will we go on laughing and playing on the brink of eternal damnation? Woe to us if the men of Nineveh are better off than we are at the last great day.

10 When God saw what they did, how they turned from their evil way, God relented of the disaster that he had said he would do to them, and he did not do it. *(If threats will work, judgment will be avoided. God tries words before he comes to blows.)*

The Lord Jesus mentioned the repentance of the Ninevites when he spoke to the unbelievers of his own day. Let us read the passage in:

Matthew 12:38-41

38 Then some of the scribes and Pharisees answered him, saying, "Teacher, we wish to see a sign from you." **39** But he answered them, "An evil and adulterous generation seeks for a sign, but no sign will be given to it except the sign of the prophet Jonah. **40** For just as Jonah was three days and three nights in the belly of the great fish, so will the Son of Man be three days and three nights in the heart of the earth. **41** The men of Nineveh will rise up at the judgment with this generation and condemn it, for they repented at the preaching of Jonah, and behold, something greater than Jonah is here.

DECEMBER 16
Be Not Quick In Your Spirit To Become Angry[891]

Jonah 4

1 But it displeased Jonah exceedingly, and he was angry. *(His reputation as a prophet was everything in his eyes. What would become of it now that the city would be spared? Besides, he despised the idolatrous people of Nineveh. He thought sparing them was ridiculous. In his eyes it was only right for them to be destroyed.)* **2** And he prayed to the LORD and said, "O LORD, is not this what I said when I was yet in my country? That is why I made haste to flee to Tarshish; for I knew that you are a gracious God and merciful, slow to anger and abounding in steadfast love, and relenting from disaster. **3** Therefore now, O LORD, please take my life from me, for it is better for me to die than to live." *(We cannot love Jonah when we see him so irritable, but we must remember that he wrote this himself. He paints his own portrait in the blackest colors and does not try to excuse or explain away his gloomy temper. He was a man of serious integrity. He was extremely sensitive about being completely truthful about his personal character. He was afraid his reputation would be tarnished, so he fell into a very bad mood. A good person should not mope about like this.)*

4 And the LORD said, "Do you do well to be angry?" *(We should be critical enough about ourselves to ask these questions: Are we quick to become angry? Are we angry a lot of the time? Do we stay angry? Are we bitter in our anger? "Do you do well to be*

---

[890] *repent, repentance* - The act or feeling of remorse, regret, sorrow or shame that results in a change of heart or purpose.

[891] Ecclesiastes 7:9

angry?" How could it be right of Jonah to be angry because a million lives were spared?)

⁵Jonah went out of the city and sat to the east of the city and made a booth for himself there. He sat under it in the shade, till he should see what would become of the city.

Maybe he thought his prophecy would eventually be fulfilled. In any event, he lingered near the city with the harsh and horrible hope that the great city would be destroyed and his reputation saved.

⁶Now the LORD God appointed a plant and made it come up over Jonah, that it might be a shade over his head, to save him from his discomfort. So Jonah was exceedingly glad because of the plant. *(Jonah was a sensitive and nervous person. The great heat stressed him out. The cool shade that the leafy shelter gave him was a great comfort.)* ⁷But when dawn came up the next day, God appointed a worm that attacked the plant, so that it withered. *(The God who prepared a great fish prepared a plant and then prepared a worm to destroy it. All of this was done with the intention of preparing Jonah to submit to the will of God.)* ⁸When the sun rose, God appointed a scorching east wind, and the sun beat down on the head of Jonah so that he was faint. And he asked that he might die and said, "It is better for me to die than to live."

Jonah is like Elijah in his weak points. One is almost inclined to believe the tradition that says Jonah is the son of the widow of Zarephath and the student of Elijah.[892]

⁹But God said to Jonah, "Do you do well to be angry for the plant?" And he said, "Yes, I do well to be angry, angry enough to die. ¹⁰And the LORD said, "You pity the plant, for which you did not labor, nor did you make it grow, which came into being in a night and perished in a night. ¹¹And should not I pity Nineveh, that great city, in which there are more than 120,000 persons who do not know their right hand from their left, and also much cattle?" *(This was a convincing argument. No doubt it led the prophet to shake off his childishness. If Jonah did not want the plant destroyed, how much more should the Lord not want a great city with so many children in it destroyed? Perhaps some of us tend to be selfish or are overly sensitive or irritable. Let us turn to the Lord Jesus and learn. Take his yoke upon us, for he is gentle and lowly in heart.*[893] *We can never find rest until the demon of self-will is unconditionally cast out.)*

DECEMBER 17

They…Provoked the Holy One of Israel[894]

We will now take another glimpse at the guilty kingdom of Israel. King Jehu wiped out the worship of Baal from Israel and restored the worship of God. However, he kept the two golden calves in Bethel and Dan for the people to bow down to when they worshiped Jehovah.[895] *After he died, his sons continued to encourage the worship that the Lord had forbidden. Pretending to worship the true God by bowing down to images continues to this day in the Roman Catholic Church and other churches that call themselves "Christian."*

2 Kings 13:1-6; 9-11; 14-19

¹In the twenty-third year of Joash the son of Ahaziah, king of Judah, Jehoahaz the son of Jehu began to reign over Israel in Samaria, and he reigned seventeen years. ²He did what was evil in the sight of the LORD and followed the sins of Jeroboam the son of Nebat, which he made Israel to sin; he did not depart from them. ³And the anger of the LORD was kindled against Israel, and he gave them continually into the hand of Hazael king of Syria and into the hand of Ben-hadad the son of Hazael.

The Syrians reduced the population of Israel so low that no army was left to defend the country. The poor people are described as being made "like the dust at threshing."[896] *The devil is a poor paymaster. "The wicked are filled with trouble."*[897]

---

[892] Elijah was fed by this widow during a drought and he raised her son from the dead (1 Kings 17). The tradition that Jonah was this widow's son is, as far as we can discover, still told by Jewish rabbis to this day. –editor
[893] From Matthew 11:29
[894] Psalm 78:41
[895] 2 Kings 10:28-29
[896] 2 Kings 13:7
[897] Proverbs 12:21

⁴ Then Jehoahaz sought the favor of the Lord, and the Lord listened to him, for he saw the oppression of Israel, how the king of Syria oppressed them. ⁵ (Therefore the Lord gave Israel a savior, so that they escaped from the hand of the Syrians, and the people of Israel lived in their homes as formerly.)

Sometimes God will respond to the prayers of wicked people when they ask for earthly help. Who can tell God who he can extend his mercy to? This should encourage us to pray for spiritual blessings.

⁶ (Nevertheless, they did not depart from the sins of the house of Jeroboam, which he made Israel to sin, but walked in them; and the Asherah also remained in Samaria.) *(Maybe they did not destroy them because of their beauty. Even today, foolish people admire religious images because they are works of art.)*

⁹ So Jehoahaz slept with his fathers, and they buried him in Samaria, and Joash his son reigned in his place.

¹⁰ In the thirty-seventh year of Joash king of Judah, Jehoash the son of Jehoahaz began to reign over Israel in Samaria, and he reigned sixteen years. ¹¹ He also did what was evil in the sight of the Lord. He did not depart from all the sins of Jeroboam the son of Nebat, which he made Israel to sin, but he walked in them.

¹⁴ Now when Elisha had fallen sick with the illness of which he was to die, Joash king of Israel went down to him and wept before him, crying, "My father, my father! The chariots of Israel and its horsemen!"

After sixty or seventy years of service, rest came to the faithful prophet. Good people, when they come to die, are often honored by those who have rejected their living testimony. Bad as Joash was, he knew that Elisha was the only defense of the country and therefore wept at the likelihood of the prophet's death.

¹⁵ And Elisha said to him, "Take a bow and arrows." So he took a bow and arrows. ¹⁶ Then he said to the king of Israel, "Draw the bow," and he drew it. And Elisha laid his hands on the king's hands. ¹⁷ And he said, "Open the window eastward," and he opened it. Then Elisha said, "Shoot," and he shot. And he said, "The Lord's arrow of victory, the arrow of victory over Syria! For you shall fight the Syrians in Aphek until you have made an end of them." ¹⁸ And he said, "Take the arrows," and he took them. And he said to the king of Israel, "Strike the ground with them." And he struck three times and stopped. ¹⁹ Then the man of God was angry with him and said, "You should have struck five or six times; then you would have struck down Syria until you had made an end of it, but now you will strike down Syria only three times."

*Even though he was dying, Elisha was angry at unbelief. And why not? God is angry with it too. In this case unbelief robbed Israel of great victories and of all hope of permanent peace. If our faith can shoot many arrows by asking great things of God, expecting great things from God, and attempting great things for God,*⁸⁹⁸ *we will see mighty marvels. Lack of faith holds back blessing. We win only three times when we could have gone out "conquering and to conquer."*⁸⁹⁹ *People who stop short of this kind of faith rob themselves and stop the stream of blessing. Unfortunately, this kind of unbelief is common in our churches.*

Lord, send great blessings to our family. Convert every one of us. Bless our work for your sake and do great things for us and by us.

December 18
The Lord Is Able To Give You Much More Than This⁹⁰⁰

We now return to the history of the kingdom of Judah. Joash is succeeded by Amaziah.

2 Chronicles 25:1-11

¹ Amaziah was twenty-five years old when he began to reign, and he reigned twenty-nine years in Jerusalem. ² And he did what was right in the eyes of the Lord, yet not with a whole heart.

---
[898] "Expect great things from God. Attempt great things for God." William Carey (1793-1834) Baptist missionary to India.
[899] Revelation 6:2
[900] 2 Chronicles 25:9

Amaziah was like his father Joash. His views of right and wrong were changeable. He began well, but later he turned aside from doing what was right and suffered because of it.

3 And as soon as the royal power was firmly his, he killed his servants who had struck down the king his father. **4** But he did not put their children to death, according to what is written in the Law, in the Book of Moses, where the LORD commanded, "Fathers shall not die because of their children, nor children die because of their fathers, but each one shall die for his own sin." *(The king obeyed this righteous law even though it was common in those days for someone who took control of a kingdom by force to kill the reigning king and everyone in his family. Amaziah should be admired for obeying the law of the Lord and refusing to follow the custom of the time.)*

5 Then Amaziah assembled the men of Judah and set them by fathers' houses under commanders of thousands and of hundreds for all Judah and Benjamin. He mustered those twenty years old and upward, and found that they were 300,000 choice men, fit for war, able to handle spear and shield.

This was only one-fourth the size of his great-great-grandfather Jehoshaphat's army. The kingdom of Judah had suffered greatly from the wars that were the result of its sins.

6 He hired also 100,000 mighty men of valor from Israel for 100 talents *(about four tons)* of silver. *(This amount was paid to the king of Israel for agreeing to lend his troops to Amaziah. It was a relatively small amount and went directly to the king. The soldiers were not paid. They were expected to reward themselves by the spoils of war. What must war have been like under those kinds of rules? Human life was worth next to nothing and owning property meant even less.)* **7** But a man of God came to him and said, "O king, do not let the army of Israel go with you, for the LORD is not with Israel, with all these Ephraimites. **8** But go, act, be strong for the battle. Why should you suppose that God will cast you down before the enemy? For God has power to help or to cast down."

(God would not have his people joining with idolaters. All the help we can get from the ungodly will prove to be a handicap.)

9 And Amaziah said to the man of God, "But what shall we do about the hundred talents that I have given to the army of Israel?" The man of God answered, "The LORD is able to give you much more than this." *(These words should be remembered anytime it appears we will suffer loss for doing the right thing. God can make it up to us in many ways, both earthly and spiritual. We can compare the cost any way we please, but we will find that it is always best to obey the Lord.)* **10** Then Amaziah discharged the army that had come to him from Ephriam to go home again. And they became very angry with Judah and returned home in fierce anger. **11** But Amaziah took courage and led out his people and went to the Valley of Salt and struck down 10,000 men of Seir. *(He fought alone and was victorious. If we will trust in God and not rely on the arm of flesh, we will also be conquerors.[901] Any loss we endure for Christ's sake is a loss we may rejoice in.[902])*

DECEMBER 19
The Haughty Eyes You Bring Down[903]

2 Chronicles 25:14-24; 27-28

14 After Amaziah came from striking down the Edomites, he brought the gods of the men of Seir and set them up as his gods and worshiped them, making offerings to them.

This was madness itself. If the gods of Edom had been worth anything they would have helped their former worshipers. It is strange that a man will bow down before an idol he takes captive in battle. Is it not even more amazing that others will adore a piece of bread and then eat it?

15 Therefore the LORD was angry with Amaziah and sent to him a prophet, who said

---

[901] 2 Chronicles 32:8, "With him is an arm of flesh, but with us is the LORD our God, to help us and to fight our battles."
[902] Philippians 3:8, "Indeed, I count everything as loss because of the surpassing worth of knowing Christ Jesus my Lord. For his sake I have suffered the loss of all things and count them as rubbish, in order that I may gain Christ."
[903] Psalm 18:27

to him, "Why have you sought the gods of a people who did not deliver their own people from your hand?" ¹⁶ But as he was speaking, the king said to him, "Have we made you a royal counselor? Stop! Why should you be struck down?" So the prophet stopped, but said, "I know that God has determined to destroy you, because you have done this and have not listened to my counsel." *(Those who refuse to listen challenge God to use painful ways to make his point. Those who reject the Lord's warnings show that there is evil in their hearts. Victory made Amaziah proud and his pride became the mother of many sins. The less we admire ourselves and our accomplishments the better.)*

¹⁷ Then Amaziah king of Judah took counsel and sent to Joash the son of Jehoahaz, son of Jehu, king of Israel saying, "Come, let us look one another in the face."

This was an arrogant challenge to the king of Israel. The hired soldiers from Israel, who Amaziah had sent away, probably raided and robbed the towns and villages on their way home. This made proud Amaziah ready to start a war.

¹⁸ And Joash the king of Israel sent word to Amaziah king of Judah, "A thistle on Lebanon sent to a cedar on Lebanon, saying, 'Give your daughter to my son for a wife,' and a wild beast of Lebanon passed by and trampled down the thistle."

A proud challenge provoked an insulting answer. Joash as good as said, "You petty king, you are but a thistle. How dare you challenge such a powerful monarch like me? You are not worth getting our swords and spears bloody over."

¹⁹ "You say, 'See, I have struck down Edom,' and your heart has lifted you up in boastfulness. But now stay at home. Why should you provoke trouble so that you fall, you and Judah with you?"

²⁰ But Amaziah would not listen, for it was of God, in order that he might give them into the hand of their enemies, because they had sought the gods of Edom. ²¹ So Joash king of Israel went up, and he and Amaziah king of Judah faced one another in battle at Beth-Shemesh, which belongs to Judah. ²² And Judah was defeated by Israel, and every man fled to his home. ²³ And Joash king of Israel captured Amaziah king of Judah, the son of Joash, son of Ahaziah, at Beth-shemesh, and brought him to Jerusalem and broke down the wall of Jerusalem for 400 cubits *(about 600 feet)*, from the Ephraim Gate to the Corner Gate. ²⁴ And he seized all the gold and silver, and all the vessels that were found in the house of God, in the care of Obed-edom. He seized also the treasuries of the king's house, also hostages, and he returned to Samaria.

One intense battle and the war was over. Amaziah became a prisoner, the walls of Jerusalem were broken down, the temple was looted, and the nation was forced to live by the laws of king Joash to keep the peace. Proud King Amaziah was laid low. He lost the respect of everyone around him and before long there were plots against his position as king and his life.

²⁷ From the time when he turned away from the LORD they made a conspiracy against him in Jerusalem, and he fled to Lachish. But they sent after him to Lachish and put him to death there. ²⁸ And they brought him upon horses, and he was buried with his fathers in the city of David.

Amaziah was the unstable son of an unstable father. His life ended in disgrace. Many start well and appear to be heaven bound, but they fall short because there is no true life in their religion. It has not changed their nature. Nothing less than a new heart and a right spirit will equip a person to weather the storm and reach the shelter of eternal rest.

DECEMBER 20

Do Two Walk Together, Unless They Have Agreed To Meet?[904]

We take another glance at the kingdom of Israel. Jeroboam the Second is reigning with his father and will later succeed him on the throne.

---

[904] Amos 3:3

2 Kings 14:23-27; 29

23 In the fifteenth year of Amaziah the son of Joash, king of Judah, Jeroboam the son of Joash, king of Israel, began to reign in Samaria, and he reigned forty-one years. **24** And he did evil in the sight of the LORD. He did not depart from all the sins of Jeroboam the son of Nebat, which he made Israel to sin. **25** He restored the border of Israel from Lebo-hamath as far as the Sea of the Arabah, according to the word of the LORD, the God of Israel, which he spoke by his servant Jonah the son of Amittai, the prophet, who was from Gath-hepher.

We find Jonah still active after his return from Nineveh and his work is more pleasant. Those who fulfill difficult assignments will have easier work before long.

26 For the LORD saw that the affliction of Israel was very bitter, for there was none left, bond or free, and there was none to help Israel. **27** But the LORD had not said that he would blot out the name of Israel from under heaven, so he saved them by the hand of Jeroboam the son of Joash. *(God knows when his people are suffering. He is a tender father and is not unaffected by the miseries of his children. He will hold back his judgment for as long as it is in keeping with his righteous nature.)*

29 Now Jeroboam slept with his fathers, the kings of Israel, and Zechariah his son reigned in his place.

The prophet Amos delivered messages during the reign of Jeroboam. He was a shepherd and a farmer and these careers come out in his writings. His messages are short, sharp and decisive. We do not find flowery words and graceful style here. He uses short questions, sudden exclamations and claps of thundering alarming threats.

Amos 3:1-8

1 Hear this word that the LORD has spoken against you, O people of Israel, against the whole family that I brought up out of the land of Egypt:

2 "You only have I known
　　of all the families of the earth;
　therefore I will punish you
　　for all your iniquities."

Others sin with less understanding of God's law. Their faults may have little notice taken of them, but the justice of God becomes more terrible where sins are intentional and cruel.

3 "Do two walk together,
　　unless they have agreed to meet?
4 Does a lion roar in the forest,
　　when he has no prey?
　Does a young lion cry out from his den,
　　if he has taken nothing?"

God's voice is not mere noise. It means something and trouble comes to those who despise it. He does not threaten without a good reason.

5 "Does a bird fall in a snare on the earth,
　　when there is no trap for it?
　Does a snare spring up from the ground,
　　when it has taken nothing?"

God's judgments are not accidents. And he will not let up until his purposes have been accomplished.

6 "Is a trumpet blown in a city,
　　and the people are not afraid?
　Does disaster come to a city,
　　unless the LORD has done it?"

Do you think that God sends false alarms? Be sure of this; the Lord is behind the troubles that afflict the ungodly.

7 "For the Lord GOD does nothing
　　without revealing his secret
　　to his servants the prophets.
8 The lion has roared;
　　who will not fear?
　The Lord GOD has spoken;
　　who can but prophesy?"

The intention of this series of questions is to remind the people of their God, to notify them that the Lord is speaking to them through his prophets and by the judgments that have brought them so much suffering. We need the same wakeup call and if the Lord should send it by a shepherd, we should be ready to accept it. God chooses "what is low and despised in the world"[905] and was pleased to send a shepherd to warn a king. Who was more qualified to deal with such

---

[905] 1 Corinthians 1:28

violent people than someone responsible for difficult animals?

DECEMBER 21

Hate Evil[906]

Today's reading is from another portion of the prophecies of Amos.

Amos 5:14-27

14 "Seek good, and not evil,
    that you may live;
  and so the LORD, the God of hosts, will be with you,
    as you have said."

You brag that God is with you, but if you really want that to be true, you must seek him and follow his ways. Just because we go to a place of worship does not mean we are children of the heavenly Father. God lives in those who have a tender conscience before him.

15 "Hate evil, and love good,
    and establish justice in the gate;"

The gate was where courts of justice were held.

  "it may be that the LORD, the God of hosts,
    will be gracious to the remnant of Joseph."

If the Lord gives people only an "it may be," that should be enough to get them serious about seeking salvation. But how much more should we be eager for eternal life when we have the certain promise that, "everyone who calls on the name of the Lord WILL be saved."[907]

16 "Therefore thus says the LORD, the God of hosts, the Lord:

  In all the square there shall be wailing,
    and in all the streets they shall say, 'Alas! Alas!'
  They shall call the farmers to mourning
    and to wailing those who are skilled in lamentation,"

Farmers will be so disappointed in their harvest that they will mourn like those who bury the dead. The time for harvesting crops will be as sad as a funeral.

17 "and in all vineyards there shall be wailing,
    for I will pass through your midst,"
  says the LORD.

The place of great joy will become the place of great sorrow.

18 Woe to you who desire the day of the LORD!
    Why would you have the day of the LORD?
  It is darkness, and not light,

They will be bitterly sorry that they said, "Where is the promise of his coming?" They will find the day that they spoke about so jokingly will be overwhelmingly terrible to them.[908]

19   as if a man fled from a lion,
    and a bear met him,
  or went into the house and leaned his hand against the wall,
    and a serpent bit him.

For the wicked, the Day of the Lord will be going from bad to worse, from danger to destruction.

20 Is not the day of the LORD darkness and not light,
    and gloom with no brightness in it?

No gleams of mercy will be found on the day of his visitation, only justice. Pure terror will spread through the ranks of the rebellious.

21 "I hate, I despise your feasts,
    and I take no delight in your solemn assemblies."

The Lord is disgusted with those who seem to worship him, but cherish sin in their hearts. He is insulted by the outward ceremonies of those who love the pleasures of sin.

22 "Even though you offer me your burnt offerings and grain offerings,
    I will not accept them;
  and the peace offerings of your fattened animals,
    I will not look upon them.

---

[906] Amos 5:15
[907] Romans 10:13
[908] 2 Peter 3:3a-4, "Scoffers will come in the last days with scoffing, following their own sinful desires. They will say, 'Where is the promise of his coming? For ever since the fathers fell asleep, all things are continuing as they were from the beginning of creation.'"

²³ Take away from me the noise of your songs;
   to the melody of your harps I will not listen."

Expensive sacrifices and delightful music are not what God desires. A broken heart is the best offering and a holy life the best music.

²⁴ "But let justice roll down like waters,
   and righteousness like an ever-flowing stream."

This is what he wants and demands. Anything short of justice and righteousness is showing disrespect for God.

²⁵ "Did you bring to me sacrifices and offerings during the forty years in the wilderness, O house of Israel? *(They were idolaters from the beginning. After they left Egypt, they could not continue to worship God the right way for even one generation. Idol worship was deeply rooted. Nothing could keep them from it.)* ²⁶ You shall take up Sikkuth *(another name for Moloch)* your king, and Kiyyun your star-god—your images that you made for yourselves, *(They adored even Moloch, the most bloody of idols. No worship was too fiendish for them.)* ²⁷ and I will send you into exile beyond Damascus," says the LORD, whose name is the God of hosts.

Idolatry, injustice, and uncleanness provoke the Lord. He will not allow such evils to go unpunished.

Oh Lord God of hosts. Wash us in the blood of Jesus. Renew us by your Spirit. And, keep us true to you all our days.

DECEMBER 22
Fulfill Your Ministry[909]

Amos had many visions and he boldly told them to the people.

Amos 7

¹ This is what the Lord GOD showed me: behold, he was forming locusts when the latter growth was just beginning to sprout, and behold, it was the latter growth after the king's mowings. ² When they had finished eating the grass of the land, I said,

"O Lord GOD, please forgive!
   How can Jacob stand?
   He is so small!"

³ The LORD relented, concerning this;
   "It shall not be," said the LORD.

A food shortage was threatened by means of locusts, but Amos prayed and God's judgment was prevented. We cannot overestimate the value of the earnest prayers of holy people.

⁴ This is what the Lord GOD showed me: behold, the Lord GOD was calling for a judgment by fire, and it devoured the great deep and was eating up the land. ⁵ Then I said,

"O Lord GOD, please cease!
   How can Jacob stand?
   He is so small!"

⁶ The LORD relented concerning this:
   "This also shall not be," said the Lord GOD.

The judgment of fire would cause more loss than the locusts. Again the prophet prayed. This time he asked the Lord to consider the humble circumstances of Israel and for a second time his prayers were victorious. The prayers of the righteous protect the nation.

⁷ This is what he showed me: behold, the Lord was standing beside a wall built with a plumb line, with a plumb line in his hand. ⁸ And the LORD said to me, "Amos, what do you see?" And I said, "A plumb line." Then the Lord said,

"Behold, I am setting a plumb line
   in the midst of my people Israel;
   I will never again pass by them;
⁹ the high places of Isaac shall be made desolate,
   and the sanctuaries of Israel shall be laid waste,
and I will rise against the house of Jeroboam with the sword."

The Lord would judge the nation as a builder tests a wall to see if it is upright. He would then break down anything that was out of line and unfit to be left standing. The sinful house of Jehu had now ruled for four generations. There would be only one more king and then the family of Jehu would be

---
[909] 2 Timothy 4:5

swept away like Ahab's was. Amos made this prophecy in Bethel, the very center of the idol worship.

10 Then Amaziah the priest of Bethel sent to Jeroboam king of Israel, saying, "Amos has conspired against you in the midst of the house of Israel. The land is not able to bear all his words. **11** For thus Amos has said,

> "'Jeroboam shall die by the sword,
> and Israel must go into exile
> away from his land.'"

This was only partly true. Amos had not said that Jeroboam would be killed by the sword. We can never hope to have our positions represented fairly. Our enemies will twist our words to suit their desires.

12 And Amaziah said to Amos, "O seer, go, flee away to the land of Judah, and eat bread there, and prophesy there, **13** but never again prophesy at Bethel, for it is the king's sanctuary, and it is a temple of the kingdom." *(As much as to say, "You are not wanted here. Judah is the place for those of your way of thinking. Besides, your rough manners are not fit for this refined place." Little did the false priest dream of the response he would receive.)*

14 Then Amos answered and said to Amaziah, "I was no prophet, nor a prophet's son, but I was a herdsman and a dresser of sycamore figs. **15** But the LORD took me from following the flock, and the LORD said to me, 'Go, prophesy to my people Israel.' *(Amos did not speak out because he wanted to be popular. He was sent from God. Threats were not going to stop him.)* **16** Now therefore hear the word of the LORD.

> "You say, 'Do not prophesy against Israel,
> and do not preach against the house of Isaac.'

17 Therefore thus says the LORD:

> "Your wife shall be a prostitute in the city,
> and your sons and your daughters shall fall by the sword,
> and your land shall be divided up with a measuring line;
> you yourself shall die in an unclean land,
> and Israel shall surely go into exile away from its land.'"

In a few years these words came true. Woe to those who stand up against the Lord and oppose his servants.

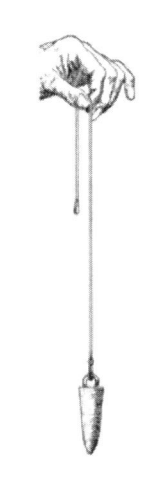

Plumb Line (Amos 7:8)

DECEMBER 23
Would Not God Discover This?[910]

We will read again in the book of Amos.

Amos 9

Chapter nine begins with Amos predicting the certain destruction of Israel.

1 I saw the LORD standing beside the altar, *(Trampling on the idolatrous altar at Bethel.)* and he said:

> "Strike the capitals until the thresholds shake,
> and shatter them on the heads of all the people;
> and those who are left of them I will kill with the sword;
> not one of them shall flee away;
> not one of them shall escape.
> **2** "If they dig into Sheol,
> from there shall my hand take them;
> if they climb up to heaven,
> from there I will bring them down.
> **3** If they hide themselves on the top of Carmel,
> from there I will search them out and take them;

---

[910] Psalm 44:21

and if they hide from my sight at the
 bottom of the sea,
 there I will command the serpent, and it
  shall bite them.
4 And if they go into captivity before their
  enemies,
 there I will command the sword, and it
  shall kill them;
 and I will fix my eyes upon them
  for evil and not for good."

The passage we have just read is one of the most wonderful descriptions of omnipresence[911] ever written, even by an inspired pen.

5 "The Lord GOD of hosts,
 he who touches the earth and it melts,
  and all who dwell in it mourn,
  and all of it rises like the Nile,
  and sinks again, like the Nile of Egypt;
6 who builds his upper chambers in the
  heavens
  and founds his vault upon the earth;
 who calls for the waters of the sea
  and pours them out upon the surface of
   the earth—
 the LORD is his name.
7 "Are you not like the Cushites to me,
  O people of Israel?" declares the LORD.
 "Did I not bring up Israel from the land of
  Egypt,
 and the Philistines from Caphtor and the
  Syrians from Kir?"

Amos warns them not to assume that God will always bless them like he had in the past. When they stopped seeing him as the one true God of Israel, the Lord mocked them and reminded them that he had done great things for other nations too.

8 "Behold, the eyes of the Lord GOD are
  upon the sinful kingdom,
  and I will destroy it from the surface of
   the ground,
  except that I will not utterly destroy the
   house of Jacob,"
 declares the LORD.
9 "For behold, I will command,
 and shake the house of Israel among all
  the nations
 as one shakes with a sieve,
  but no pebble shall fall to the earth.
10 All the sinners of my people shall die by
  the sword,
 who say, 'Disaster shall not overtake or
  meet us.'"

The prophecy we are now reading is not just about the evil things God has in store for his disobedient people. It also contains good news about glorious times to come.

11 "In that day I will raise up
  the booth of David that is fallen
 and repair it breaches,
  and raise up its ruins
  and rebuild it as in the days of old,
12 that they may possess the remnant of
   Edom
  and all the nations who are called by my
   name,"
 declares the LORD who does this.

In the person of the Lord Jesus, David's royal house will have more glory than it ever had in the past. Not only will the rebellious nation of Israel submit to the Son of David, but Gentiles[912] will also be ruled by King Jesus.

13 "Behold, the days are coming," declares
  the LORD,
 "when the plowman shall overtake the
  reaper
  and the treader of grapes him who sows
   the seed;
 the mountains shall drip sweet wine,
  and all the hills shall flow with it."

Palestine will become fruitful again. It will become the garden of the world when Jesus reigns over it.

14 "I will restore the fortunes of my people
  Israel,
  and they shall rebuild the ruined cities
   and inhabit them;
 they shall plant vineyards and drink their
  wine,
  and they shall make gardens and eat
   their fruit.
15 I will plant them on their land,
  and they shall never again be uprooted

---

[911] *omnipresence* - The teaching that God is present everywhere at the same time. There is no place where he is not there.

[912] *Gentile* - anyone who is not a Jew by natural birth.

out of the land that I have given them," says the LORD your God.

Is it not clear from this that Israel will be gathered under the reign of Jesus the Son of David and restored to their own land? There is a glorious future for the Lord's ancient people and also for us who have come to trust in the great Son of David.

DECEMBER 24
I Will Betroth You To Me In Righteousness[913]

In the days of the second Jeroboam, the prophet Hosea lived in Samaria. He prophesied about the sins and sufferings of Israel and Judah. His proclamations are made with strong feeling and intensity and might seem rough and almost rude. The first part of chapter two describes the sins of Israel. We will now read the second part and see how the Lord goes about lovingly and tenderly winning back the heart of Israel.

Hosea 2:14-23

14 "Therefore, behold, I will allure her,
and bring her into the wilderness,
and speak tenderly to her.
15 And there I will give her her vineyards
and make the Valley of Achor a door of hope.
And there she shall answer as in the days of her youth,
as at the time when she came out of the land of Egypt."

God had brought suffering to Israel as payment for her sins. He now brings the hope of returning to the joy she once had as the reward for her sincere return to him.

16 "And in that day, declares the LORD, you will call me 'My Husband,' and no longer will you call me 'My Baal.' *(Or call Baal, "My lord." Love will replace law. The spirit of the gospel will replace the spirit of cruel oppression.)* 17 For I will remove the names of the Baals from her mouth, and they shall be remembered by name no more. *(It is good when even talking about sin becomes disliked. The saints of God should want to avoid even talking about wicked behavior in which they once delighted.[914])* 18 And I will make for them a covenant on that day with the beasts of the field, the birds of the heavens, and the creeping things of the ground. And I will abolish the bow, the sword, and war from the land, and I will make you lie down in safety. 19 And I will betroth you to me forever. I will betroth you to me in righteousness and in justice, in steadfast love and in mercy. 20 I will betroth you to me in faithfulness. And you shall know the LORD." *(A marvelous verse! A bottomless gold mine of love. It is more appropriate to enjoy it in silence than to try to find words to explain it. Blessed are those who are married to the Lord. His love does not change. His wedding vows will never end in divorce.)*

21 "And in that day I will answer, declares the LORD,
I will answer the heavens,
and they shall answer the earth.
22 and the earth shall answer the grain, the wine, and the oil,
and they shall answer Jezreel,
23 and I will sow her for myself in the land.
And I will have mercy on No Mercy,
and I will say to Not My People, 'You are my people';
and he shall say, 'You are my God.'"

These are new covenant blessings. The will's and shall's of sovereign grace. The promises of overflowing mercy. Promises like these should lead sinners to repent and seek the Lord. Let us see how Hosea encouraged the people to do this.

Hosea 6:1-7

1 "Come, let us return to the LORD;
for he has torn us, that he may heal us;
he has struck us down, and he will bind us up.
2 After two days he will revive us;
on the third day he will raise us up.
that we may live before him."

---

[913] Hosea 2:19

[914] Ephesians 5:3-4, "But sexual immorality and all impurity or covetousness must not even be named among you, as is proper among saints. Let there be no filthiness nor foolish talk nor crude joking, which are out of place, but instead let there be thanksgiving."

When the Holy Spirit convicts of sin, he intends to show the love of God. His plan is to exhibit the Savior's healing power. God will not torment people before their time. If he brings terror to their consciences now, it is with the intention of leading them to the safety of his dear Son.

3 "Let us know; let us press on to know the Lord;
  his going out is sure as the dawn;
 he will come to us as the showers,
  as the spring rains that water the earth."

If we come to God, he will reveal himself to us in forgiving love.

4 What shall I do with you, O Ephraim?
  What shall I do with you, O Judah?
 Your love is like a morning cloud,
  like the dew that goes early away.

The problem with many who hear the gospel is that they are fickle. The message makes an impression on them, but the impression soon goes away.

5 Therefore I have hewn them by the prophets;
  I have slain them by the words of my mouth,
 and my judgment goes forth as the light.
6 For I desire steadfast love and not sacrifice,
  the knowledge of God rather than burnt offerings.
7 But like Adam they transgressed the covenant;
  there they dealt faithlessly with me.

Let us not be charged with being faithless. Instead, let our hearts be truly broken and let us seek the Lord of hosts through his Son, Jesus Christ.

December 25
Would That You Were Either Cold Or Hot![915]

Hosea 7

1 When I would heal Israel,
  the iniquity of Ephraim is revealed,
   and the evil deeds of Samaria;
  for they deal falsely;
   the thief breaks in,
 and the bandits raid outside.

In his goodness, God sent prophets to warn and teach the people of Israel. But in spite of this, they went on sinning like their idolatrous neighbors. They stole from each other. Justice was almost unknown.

2 But they do not consider
   that I remember all their evil.
  Now their deeds surround them;
   they are before my face.
3 By their evil they make the king glad,
   and the princes by their treachery.

It is sad when the leaders of a nation encourage sin and take pleasure in falsehood. What can we expect from common citizens when the leaders take delight in crime?

4 They are all adulterers;
   they are like a heated oven
  whose baker ceases to stir the fire,
   from the kneading of the dough
    until it is leavened.

They were as hot with wicked desires as a baker's oven is when it is ready for baking.

5 On the day of our king, the princes
   became sick with the heat of wine;
  he stretched out his hand with mockers.

Drunkenness and blasphemy were common in the king's court. Do we not see these sins all around us today at every level of society?

6 For with hearts like an oven they approach their intrigue;
  all night their anger smolders;
  in the morning it blazes like a flaming fire.

The baker may rest and sleep, but he knows he must get up early to add fuel to his fire. Even so, when they were quiet and resting, they thought about new ways to sin.

7 All of them are hot as an oven,
   and they devour their rulers.
  All their kings have fallen,
   and none of them calls upon me.
8 Ephraim mixes himself with the peoples;
   Ephraim is a cake not turned.

He is good for nothing. He says he fears God and yet he worships idols. This double-mindedness is common nowadays, and is

---

[915] Revelation 3:15

very distasteful to God, who says, "I wish that you were cold or hot."[916]

9 Strangers devour his strength,
   and he knows it not;
 gray hairs are sprinkled upon him,
   and he knows it not.

The nation did not know how rotten it had become, just as unbelievers do not know how sad their situation really is.

10 The pride of Israel testifies to his face;
    yet they do not return to the LORD their God,
  nor seek him, for all this.

As bad as they were, they still had a high opinion of themselves. They did not think it was necessary to repent or cry to God for mercy. This is the secret reason people are not ashamed of themselves and why they reject Christ.

11 Ephraim is like a dove,
    silly and without sense,
  calling to Egypt, going to Assyria.

They ran after many false religions. Instead of relying on God, they tried to be like one great nation after another.

12 As they go, I will spread over them my net;
   I will bring them down like birds of the heavens;
   I will discipline them according to the report made to their congregation.
13 Woe to them, for they have strayed from me!
   Destruction to them, for they have rebelled against me!
 I would redeem them,
   but they speak lies against me.

When God cries, "Woe," it is woe indeed! These words are leveled against every unrepentant sinner. It is a dreadful thing to remain opposed to the Lord.

14 They do not cry to me from the heart,
    but they wail upon their beds;
  for grain and wine they gash themselves;
    they rebel against me.

People can be loud enough when they are drinking, but when it comes to prayer or praise they are silent.

15 Although I trained and strengthened their arms,
    yet they devise evil against me.

God gave them power and ability, but they used them to rebel against him. Are any of us acting like this?

16 They return, but not upward (or to the Most High);
    they are like a treacherous bow;
    their princes shall fall by the sword
      because of the insolence of their tongue.
  This shall be their derision in the land of Egypt.

Their punishment would be mixed with shame. The idolatrous nation that they looked to for help would treat them with supreme contempt. If we will make earthly things our gods, we will be clothed with shame forever.

Lord save us from this. Amen.

DECEMBER 26
Unite My Heart To Fear Your Name[917]

Hosea 10

1 Israel is a luxuriant vine
    that yields its fruit.
  The more his fruit increased,
    the more altars he built;
  as his country improved,
    he improved his pillars.

If everything we do is for ourselves and to satisfy our sins, our lives are useless. But the lives of many very active and busy people deserve no better description. They work for self and toil for sin.

2 Their heart is false;
    now they must bear their guilt.
  The LORD will break down their altars
    and destroy their pillars.
3 For now they will say:
    "We have no king,
  for we do not fear the LORD;
    and a king—what could he do for us?"

For a time Israel had no king. Jeroboam the Second was dead, but civil strife kept his son Zechariah from immediately becoming the new king. Leadership is necessary to keep things running properly, but without

---

[916] Revelation 3:15 (NASB)

[917] Psalm 86:11

God even the best human arrangements fall apart.

4 They utter mere words;
>with empty oaths they make covenants;
>so judgment springs up like poisonous weeds
>>in the furrows of the field.

Israel had made an agreement with Shalmaneser king of Assyria when Hoshea was king and then shamefully broke it.[918] Their idea of fair play was no better than a poisonous weed. Their behavior was criminal.

5 The inhabitants of Samaria tremble
>for the calf of Beth-aven.

This was a mocking reference to their worship of the golden calf at Bethel.

>Its people mourn for it, and so do its idolatrous priests—
>>those who rejoiced over it and over its glory—
>for it has departed from them.

6 The thing itself shall be carried to Assyria
>as tribute to the great king.
>Ephraim shall be put to shame,
>>and Israel shall be ashamed of his idol.

7 Samaria's king shall perish
>like a twig on the face of the waters.

The king was like a stick floating on the water and just as easily destroyed.

8 The high places of Aven, the sin of Israel,
>shall be destroyed.
>Thorn and thistle shall grow up
>>on their altars,
>and they shall say to the mountains, "Cover us,"
>and to the hills, "Fall on us."

Then the only use for the mountains, where they built places for idol worship, will be to provide hiding places from the armies of the terrible king of Assyria.

9 From the days of Gibeah, you have sinned, O Israel;
>there they have continued.
>Shall not the war against the unjust
>>overtake them in Gibeah?

Israel once fought for God against the tribe of Benjamin, but from that day on they have only been found on the side of evil. Which side are we on?

10 When I please, I will discipline them,
>and nations shall be gathered against them
>when they are bound up for their double iniquity.

Israel and her sin are joined like two oxen plowing the field. As long as they are yoked together, they will not be able to escape.

11 Ephraim was a trained calf
>that loved to thresh,
>and I spared her fair neck;
>but I will put Ephraim to the yoke;

They had had a comfortable life, like oxen treading out grain, but now they will have a yoke placed on them and be forced to pull a heavy load.

>Judah must plow;
>Jacob must harrow for himself.

12 Sow for yourselves righteousness;
>reap steadfast love;
>break up your fallow ground,
>for it is the time to seek the LORD,
>that he may come and rain righteousness upon you.

13 You have plowed iniquity;
>you have reaped injustice;
>you have eaten the fruit of lies.
>Because you have trusted in your own way
>and in the multitude of your warriors,

14 therefore the tumult of war shall arise among your people,
>and all your fortresses shall be destroyed,
>as Shalman *(or Shalmaneser)* destroyed Beth-arbel on the day of battle;
>mothers were dashed in pieces with their children.

Evidently, the fierce Assyrian king made a terrible example of a certain city. And this is what would happen to all the land of Israel if they continued in their sin.

15 Thus it shall be done to you, O Bethel,
>because of your great evil.
>At dawn the king of Israel
>>shall be utterly cut off.

---

[918] 2 Kings 17:1-5

They worshiped the golden calf in Bethel. That idol would now be the reason for the sudden downfall of them and their king. This prophecy of Hosea was fulfilled when the Assyrians destroyed their land, carried away king Hoshea, left him in prison until he died, and put an end to the very existence of the kingdom of the ten tribes of Israel. God will deal out justice to those who sin against him. Let us cry to him for mercy and turn away from every evil way.

DECEMBER 27
I Will Heal Their Backsliding[919]

Hosea 11:1-11

1   When Israel was a child, I loved him,
      and out of Egypt I called my son.

God had shown his love and grace to Israel for centuries. That should have been a powerful reason for obeying him, but they still refused to pay attention to the Lord's warnings.

2   The more they were called,
      the more they went away;
    they kept sacrificing to the Baals
      and burning offerings to idols.

The more they were warned, the more they sinned. Sadly, many do the same in our day!

3   Yet it was I who taught Ephraim to walk;
      I took them up by their arms,
    but they did not know that I healed them.
4   I led them with cords of kindness,
      with the bands of love
    and I became to them as one who eases
      the yoke on their jaws,
    and I bent down to them and fed them.

Farmer rest their oxen. They take their yokes off and feed them. The Lord gives rest to his people. He sets them free and supplies their needs. But they returned his love by rebelling against him.

5   They shall not return to the land of Egypt,
      but Assyria shall be their king,
    because they have refused to return to me.
6   The sword shall rage against their cities,
      consume the bars of their gates,
    and devour them because of their own counsels.
    My people are bent on turning away from me,
      and though they call out to the Most High,
      he shall not raise them up at all.
8   How can I give you up, O Ephraim?
      How can I hand you over, O Israel?
    How can I make you like Admah?
      How can I treat you like Zeboiim?[920]
    My heart recoils within me;
      my compassion grows warm and tender.
9   I will not execute my burning anger;
      I will not again destroy Ephraim;
    for I am God and not a man
      the Holy One in your midst,
      and I will not come in wrath.

Note the tender love of God and his unwillingness to strike his people. The same conflict over sinners is still in his soul. His great concern should lead us to repentance.[921]

10 They shall go after the LORD;
      he will roar like a lion;
    when he roars,
      his children shall come trembling from the west;
11 they shall come trembling like birds from Egypt,
      and like doves from the land of Assyria,
    and I will return them to their homes,
      declares the LORD.

At last, aware of their danger, they would fly to God and he would save them. Even if sinners come to God entirely out of fear, he will not reject them.

Hosea 14

1   Return, O Israel, to the LORD your God,
      for you have stumbled because of your iniquity.

---

[919] Hosea 14:4 (New King James Version)

[920] Deuteronomy 29:23, "The whole land burned out with brimstone and salt, nothing sown and nothing growing, where no plant can sprout, an overthrow like that of Sodom and Gomorrah, **Admah** and **Zeboiim**, which the LORD overthrew in his anger and wrath."

[921] *repent, repentance* - The act or feeling of remorse, regret, sorrow or shame that results in a change of heart or purpose.

What gracious pleading! Can we reject it like Israel did? If we do, we will fall like they did.

2 Take with you words
    and return to the LORD;
  say to him,
    "Take away all iniquity;
  accept what is good,
    and we will pay with bulls
    the vows of our lips.
3 Assyria shall not save us;
    we will not ride on horses;
  and we will say no more, 'Our God,'
    to the work of our hands.
  In you the orphan finds mercy."

Here Hosea gives the words for sinners to pray. Will they use them? All they have to do is give up their sins and quit trusting in things and false gods, and God will pity them like he does suffering children. The next words are pure mercy written in capital letters.

4 I will heal their apostasy;
    I will love them freely,
    for my anger has turned from them.
5 I will be like the dew to Israel;
    he shall blossom like the lily;
    he shall take root like the trees of
      Lebanon;
  He shall be beautiful and strong.
6 his shoots shall spread out;
    his beauty shall be like the olive,
    and his fragrance like Lebanon.

He will thrive and give shade to others. He will be fruitful and therefore pleasant to look at. And the fame of his happiness and excellence will drift about like sweet perfume.

7 They shall return and dwell beneath my
      shadow;
    they shall flourish like the grain;
    they shall blossom like the vine;
      their fame shall be like the wine of
        Lebanon.

His children will also be blessed. They too will enjoy the sweet kindness of God.

8 O Ephraim, what have I to do with idols?
    It is I who answer and look after you.
  I am like an evergreen cypress;
    from me comes your fruit.

All our goodness comes from God's grace. We cannot produce spiritual fruit without him. We should study these passages of God's word deeply. The next verse should have our very special attention.

9 Whoever is wise, let him understand these
      things.
    whoever is discerning, let him know
      them;
  for the ways of the LORD are right,
    and the upright walk in them,
    but transgressors stumble in them.

DECEMBER 28

He Destroys You, O Israel, For You Are Against Me, Against Your Helper[922]

Hosea 13:1-14

1 When Ephraim spoke, there was
      trembling;
    he was exalted in Israel,
    but he incurred guilt through Baal and
      died.

To walk humbly before God brings honor, but to sin intentionally and proudly is deadly. Oh for grace to keep a humble spirit before the Lord.

2 And now they sin more and more,
    and make for themselves metal images,
    idols skillfully made of their silver,
    all of them the work of craftsmen.
  It is said of them,
    "Those who offer human sacrifice kiss
      calves!"
3 Therefore they shall be like the morning
      mist
    or like the dew that goes early away,
    like the chaff that swirls from the
      threshing floor
    or like smoke from a window.

If people trust in things that are here today and gone tomorrow, their joys will be here today and gone tomorrow. If we love gold, our joy will melt. If we live for fame, which is the breath of man praising us, it will disappear and be gone like the morning mist. Only God provides what truly lasts, yet only a few open their hearts to him!

---

[922] Hosea 13:9

4 But I am the LORD your God
    from the land of Egypt;
  you know no God but me,
    and besides me there is no savior.

Looking to our own works is useless. So is looking to false priests. Only Jesus can save and only Jesus alone.

5 It was I who knew you in the wilderness,
    in the land of drought;

The Lord has not let us down in hardship or suffering. We have tried him and proved his faithfulness in times of great need. We should return his kindness by being faithful to him.

6 but when they had grazed, they became full,
    they were filled, and their heart was lifted up;
  therefore they forgot me.

What shameful ungratefulness! The more mercies they enjoyed the more wickedly they behaved! Because God remembered them in his goodness they forgot him and grew proud.

7 So I am to them like a lion;
    like a leopard I will lurk beside the way.
8 I will fall upon them like a bear robbed of her cubs;
    I will tear open their breast,
  and there I will devour them like a lion,
    as a wild beast would rip them open.

Our God is completely fair and his punishment is terrible. Sin makes him angry. The Lord is slow to anger, but when the time of his vengeance arrives, he is mighty to punish.

9 He destroys you, O Israel,
    for you are against me, against your helper.

This is the beginning and the end of the whole matter. People bring their ruin upon themselves. God alone saves them. Damnation is completely the result of sin. Salvation is completely the result of grace.

10 Where now is your king, to save you in all your cities?
     Where are all your rulers—
   those of whom you said,
     "Give me a king and princes"?

11 I gave you a king in my anger,
     and I took him away in my wrath.

Saul is an example of a king they asked for and who God gave them in his anger. People often wish for useless things.

12 The iniquity of Ephraim is bound up;
     his sin is kept in store.

Sin is not forgotten. God stores it up for future judgment like people take the deed to their home and keep it in a safe. All our sins will be remembered at the last great day, unless they are covered by the blood of Jesus.

13 The pangs of childbirth come for him,
     but he is an unwise son,
   for at the right time he does not present himself
     at the opening of the womb.

He is slow to be born again. He delays coming to Christ. Many sinners know they should trust in Jesus, but make excuses not to. "How long will you go limping between two different opinions? If the LORD is God, follow him."[923] Death and judgment are coming soon. Hurry, Oh sinner, and be wise before it is too late.

14 I shall ransom them from the power of Sheol;
     I shall redeem them from Death.
   O Death, where are your plagues?
   O Sheol, where is your sting?
   Compassion is hidden from my eyes.

These words apply first to Israel becoming a nation again, but they also refer to the great resurrection of the dead and God's final judgment. We believe in this promise, we hate our sins and know that we are pardoned. We face death with joy, because we expect to rise from the grave in the glorious likeness of the Redeemer.

DECEMBER 29

The Day Of the LORD Is Great and Very Awesome[924]

Joel probably prophesied to Judah about the same time Amos and Hosea were the Lord's messengers to Israel. One of his most

---

[923] 1 Kings 18:21
[924] Joel 2:11

unforgettable prophecies is about a plague of locusts that was sent to the nation.

Joel 2:1-14

1 Blow a trumpet in Zion;
   sound an alarm on my holy mountain!
   Let all the inhabitants of the land tremble,
   for the day of the LORD is coming; it is near,

This was an event worth getting alarmed about. It was also a visit from the Lord that should have humbled his people and caused them to pray.

2 a day of darkness and gloom,
   a day of clouds and thick darkness!
   Like blackness there is spread upon the mountains
   a great and powerful people;
   their like has never been before,
   nor will be again after them
   through the years of all generations.

There were so many locusts that they were like thick clouds covering the sun. They caused darkness in the middle of the day. Huge swarms of these destructive creatures are not unusual, but Joel's prophecy was about a special and unusual plague of locusts.

3 Fire devours before them,
   and behind them a flame burns.
   The land is like the garden of Eden before them,
   but behind them a desolate wilderness,
   and nothing escapes them.

Locusts devour every green thing as completely as a raging fire.

4 Their appearance is like the appearance of horses,
   and like war horses they run.
5 As with the rumbling of chariots,
   they leap on the tops of the mountains,
   like the crackling of a flame of fire
   devouring the stubble,
   like a powerful army
   drawn up for battle.

The Italians call a locust "little horse" because their numbers, speed, noise and even the way they advance across the land remind them of troops of cavalry.

6 Before them peoples are in anguish;
   all faces grow pale.

7 Like warriors they charge;
   like soldiers they scale the wall.
   They march each on his way;
   they do not swerve from their paths.
8 They do not jostle one another;
   each marches in his path;
   they burst through the weapons
   and are not halted.

Their attack is marvelous in every way. No disciplined troops could possibly maintain their ranks more accurately.

9 They leap upon the city,
   they run upon the walls,
   they climb up into the houses,
   they enter through the windows like a thief.

Nothing can stop them. Their march is onward, over walls and fences, hills and valleys.

10 The earth quakes before them;
    the heavens tremble.
    The sun and the moon are darkened,
    and the stars withdraw their shining.

This is the misery of the poor people who see the crops of their fields devoured before their eyes by this relentless and irresistible force. They are full of terror and make it seem like the end of the world has come.

11 The LORD utters his voice
    before the army,
    for his camp is exceedingly great;
    he who executes his word is powerful.
    For the day of the LORD is great and very awesome;
    who can endure it?

The human ear does not hear, but their Commander-in-chief makes his voice heard by his battalions of devouring locusts. The Lord of hosts commands them to push forward in their awful advance. It is not hard to understand why the prophet says, "Who can endure it?"

12 "Yet even now," declares the LORD,
    "return to me with all your heart,
    with fasting, with weeping, and with mourning;
13 and rend your hearts and not your garments."
    Return to the LORD, your God,
    for he is gracious and merciful,

slow to anger, and abounding in steadfast
love;
and he relents over disaster.
14 Who knows whether he will not turn and
relent,
and leave a blessing behind him,
a grain offering and a drink offering
for the LORD your God?

If anything could prevent such a terrible disaster, prayer would do it. True repentance is the only way to remove God's rod of correction from any people.

Oh Lord, help us to drive out our sins, before they require you to discipline us with painful affliction. Accept us, for our hope is in your Son.

DECEMBER 30
There Is One Mediator Between God and Men[925]

We now return to the history of Judah and are glad to find that a good man was crowned king and that he ruled for many years.

2 Chronicles 26:1; 4-8; 16-21

1 And all the people of Judah took Uzziah, who was sixteen years old, and made him king instead of his father Amaziah.

4 And he did what was right in the eyes of the LORD, according to all that his father Amaziah had done. *(But he did not worship idols like his father had foolishly done. Children should follow the example of their parents as far as they follow the commands of God, but no further.)* 5 He set himself to seek God in the days of Zechariah, who instructed him in the fear of God, and as long as he sought the LORD, God made him prosper. *(Only God can give true success and seeking the Lord with all our heart is the surest way to be blessed.)*

6 He went out and made war against the Philistines and broke through the wall of Gath and the wall of Jabneh and the wall of Ashdod, and he built cities in the territory of Ashdod and elsewhere among the Philistines. 7 God helped him against the Philistines and against the Arabians who lived in Gurbaal and against the Meunites. 8 The Ammonites paid tribute to Uzziah, and his fame spread even to the border of Egypt, for he became very strong. *(Uzziah was a skilled man. He was a great inventor of instruments of war as well as a soil expert. The country achieved a high level of prosperity under his rule.[926])*

16 But when he was strong, he grew proud, to his destruction. *(What a warning this is to Christians who are well off. When we are weak we depend on the Lord and are safe. But when we are strong the temptation is to become proud and then a fall is near. More fall among the strong than among the timid and trembling. Uzziah's fall came when he decided he could be a priest as well as a king.)* For he was unfaithful to the LORD his God and entered the temple of the LORD to burn incense on the altar of incense.

Most of the idolatrous kings combined the role of king and priest into one. No doubt Uzziah thought that his own influence would become stronger if he did too. But this was a wicked thing for him to do and it angered the Lord.

17 But Azariah the priest went in after him, with eighty priests of the LORD who were men of valor, 18 and they withstood King Uzziah and said to him, "It is not for you, Uzziah, to burn incense to the LORD, but for the priests the sons of Aaron, who are consecrated to burn incense. Go out of the sanctuary, for you have done wrong, and it will bring you no honor from the LORD God." *(They boldly told the intruding king that his act was not right and was not safe for him. Korah and his followers paid dearly for offering incense,[927] because it was the work of the priests only. The king would also find that taking over the office of priest would not bring him honor either. The incense of our prayers and praises must rise up before the Lord from the hand of our great High Priest Jesus. Any other way will not be accepted by the Lord.)*

19 Then Uzziah was angry. Now he had a censer in his hand to burn incense, and when he became angry with the priests, leprosy

---

[925] 1 Timothy 2:5

[926] See 2 Chronicles 26:9-15
[927] This story is told in Numbers 16

broke out on his forehead in the presence of the priests in the house of the LORD, by the altar of incense.

The Lord ended the disagreement once and for all. If the king would not listen to the Lord's word, then he would feel the Lord's anger. Woe to those who pretend to offer a sacrifice for sin now that the one offering of Jesus has put away our sin. The leprosy of false teaching is on their foreheads even now. Let us steer clear of fellowship with them.

20 And Azariah the chief priest and all the priests looked at him, and behold, he was leprous in his forehead! And they rushed him out quickly, and he himself hurried to go out, because the LORD had struck him. **21** And King Uzziah was a leper to the day of his death, and being a leper lived in a separate house, for he was excluded from the house of the LORD. And Jotham his son was over the king's household, governing the people of the land. *(His punishment was merciful, because it gave him time to repent. But it was an appropriate penalty for his sin. He was proud and the disease humbled him. He had invaded the office of the priests and now he became their subject, because lepers were under the care of the priests. He coveted an honor to which he had no right and he ended up losing his legitimate honor as king. Let us have the greatest respect for the priesthood of our Lord Jesus and never dream of intruding into it.)*

Posing for Another Photographer
Spurgeon's instant and overwhelming success in London brought severe criticism from both the secular and religious press. The most devastating harassment came on the morning of October 19, 1856, as he began preaching in the Surrey Gardens Music Hall. Several hundred people had apparently conspired to sound a false alarm. A stampede to the exits followed and seven people lost their lives. Many believe this event affected Spurgeon's health for the rest of his life—resulting in his death in 1892.

DECEMBER 31
Here Am I! Send Me[928]

Uzziah was confined as a leper for some time. The year he died was also a year Isaiah received one of his visions. The ministry of this renowned prophet extended over the reign of Uzziah and the next three kings.

Isaiah 6

1 In the year that King Uzziah died I saw the Lord sitting upon a throne, high and lifted up; and the train of his robe filled the temple. *(We learn from John 12:41 that Isaiah saw the Messiah. His marvelous clothing and majesty filled the Holy of Holies with glory.)* **2** Above him stood the seraphim. *(Those holy angels stood around the throne of glory, adoring and waiting as servants to obey their King's instructions.)* Each had six

---
[928] Isaiah 6:8

wings: with two he covered his face, and with two he covered his feet, and with two he flew.

Milton poetically describes a seraph in this way:

> *"Six wings he wore to shade*
> *His lineaments divine; the pair that clad*
> *Each shoulder broad, came mantling o'er his breast*
> *With regal ornament; the middle pair*
> *Girt like a starry zone his waist, and round*
> *Skirted his loins and thighs with downy gold,*
> *And colors dipped in heaven; the third his feet*
> *Shadowed from either heel with feathered mail,*
> *Sky tinctured grain."*[929]

3 And one called to another and said:

"Holy, holy, holy is the LORD of hosts;
the whole earth is full of his glory!"

4 And the foundations of the thresholds shook at the voice of him who called, and the house was filled with smoke. 5 And I said: "Woe is me! For I am lost; for I am a man of unclean lips, and I dwell in the midst of a people of unclean lips; for my eyes have seen the King, the LORD of hosts!" *(A sense of the Lord's presence humbles even the best of people. We cannot see the glory of God and continue to glory in ourselves. Humility is absolutely necessary in preparing for the Lord's work. Isaiah must first feel his sinfulness before the live coal can touch his lips.)*

6 Then one of the seraphim flew to me, having in his hand a burning coal that he had taken with tongs from the altar. 7 And he touched my mouth and said: "Behold, this has touched your lips; your guilt is taken away, and your sin atoned for.

8 And I heard the voice of the Lord saying, "Whom shall I send, and who will go for us?" Then I said, "Here am I! Send me."

When a person's lips have felt the flame from the altar of Jesus' sacrifice, they are bold to go the ends of the earth in the Lord's service.

9 And he said, "Go, and say to this people:

"'Keep on hearing, but do not understand;
keep on seeing, but do not perceive,'
10 Make the heart of this people dull,
and their ears heavy,
and blind their eyes;
lest they see with their eyes,
and hear with their ears,
and understand with their hearts,
and turn and be healed."
11 Then I said, "How long, O Lord?"
And he said:
"Until cities lie waste
without inhabitant,
and houses without people
and the land is a desolate waste,
12 and the LORD removes people far away,
and the forsaken places are many in the midst of the land."

The people could find no blessing in Isaiah's ministry because of their sin. Even the voice of God brought the smell of death to them.[930]

13 "And though a tenth remain in it,
it will be burned again,
like a terebinth or an oak,
whose stump remains
when it is felled."
The holy seed is its stump.

As a tree has life even when it is chopped down, so the nation will still live. When the time is right, Israel will be restored to the glory it once had.

The evangelist John applied these words of Isaiah to the times of our Lord as a fulfillment of this prophecy.

John 12:37-41

37 Though he had done so many signs before them, they still did not believe in him, 38 so that the word spoken by the prophet Isaiah might be fulfilled:

"Lord, who has believed what he heard from us,
and to whom has the arm of the Lord been revealed?"

---

[929] From John Milton's (1608-1674) *Paradise Lost* circa 1667.

[930] 2 Corinthians 2:15-16, "For we are the aroma of Christ to God among those who are being saved and among those who are perishing, to one a fragrance from death to death, to the other a fragrance from life to life.

⁣³⁹ Therefore they could not believe. For again Isaiah said,

⁴⁰ "He has blinded their eyes
  and hardened their heart,
 lest they see with their eyes,
  and understand with their heart, and turn,
   and I would heal them."

⁴¹ Isaiah said these things because he saw his glory and spoke of him.

Scripture Index For Year One

Genesis 1:1-5	January 1
Genesis 1:6-13	January 2
Genesis 1:14-23	January 3
Genesis 1:26-31	January 4
Genesis 2:1-3	January 6
Genesis 2:7-24	January 4
Genesis 3:1-19	January 7
Genesis 4:1-15	January 10
Genesis 5:21-24	January 11
Genesis 6:5-22	January 12
Genesis 7:1-5; 11-23	January 13
Genesis 8:1-12; 15-22	January 15
Genesis 9:8-17	January 16
Genesis 11:19	January 17
Genesis 12:1-8	January 18
Genesis 12:10-20	January 19
Genesis 13:1-4	January 19
Genesis 13:5-18	January 20
Genesis 14:1-3; 10-12; 14-24	January 21
Genesis 15:1-18	January 23
Genesis 16:1-15	January 25
Genesis 18:1-15	January 27
Genesis 18:16-17	January 28
Genesis 18:22-33	January 28
Genesis 19:1-3; 15-26	January 30
Genesis 21:1-21	January 31
Genesis 2 2:1-19	February 2
Genesis 23:1-19	February 5
Genesis 24:1-4; 10-31	February 7
Genesis 24:50-67	February 8
Genesis 25:27-34	February 11
Genesis 27:1-5; 17-29	February 12
Genesis 28:10-22	February 13
Genesis 31:36-44	February 14
Genesis 32:6-13; 21-31	February 15
Genesis 37:2-14; 18-24; 31-35	February 16
Genesis 39:1-6; 16-23	February 17
Genesis 40:1; 3-23	February 18
Genesis 41:1; 8-16; 25-36	February 19
Genesis 41:37-43; 46-57	February 20
Genesis 42:1-4; 6-10; 13-24	February 21
Genesis 43:1-14	February 22
Genesis 43:15, 16; 18-23; 26-34	February 23
Genesis 44:14-34	February 24
Genesis 45:1-15	February 25
Genesis 45:16-28	February 26
Genesis 46:1, 2-3; 26; 29-34	February 27
Genesis 47:2-10; 12	February 27
Genesis 48:1-5; 8-21	February 29
Genesis 49:1-15	March 1
Genesis 49:16-33	March 2
Exodus 1:1-14; 22	March 12
Exodus 2:1-10	March 13
Exodus 3:1-8; 10-20	March 14
Exodus 4:1-16	March 15
Exodus 5:1-4; 6-23	March 16
Exodus 7:1-5; 10-22	March 17
Exodus 12:1-15	March 19
Exodus 12:21-36	March 20
Exodus 13:17,18; 20-22	March 21
Exodus 14:1-5; 8-14	March 21
Exodus 14:15-31	March 22
Exodus 15:1-21	March 23
Exodus 15:22-27	March 25
Exodus 16:1-10	March 25
Exodus 16:11-31	March 26
Exodus 16:32-35	March 27
Exodus 17:1-7	March 29
Exodus 17:8-16	March 30
Exodus 19:1-6; 10-11; 16-18; 20-23	April 1
Exodus 20:1-17	April 2
Exodus 20:8-11	January 6
Exodus 24:1-15, 18	April 5
Exodus 30:11-16	April 6
Exodus 32:1-14	April 7
Exodus 32:15-20; 30-35	April 8
Exodus 33:1-7; 12-23	April 9
Exodus 34:15; 28-35	April 11
Exodus 35:4-5b; 20-29	April 13
Leviticus 4:1-12	April 14
Leviticus 10:1-11	April 15
Leviticus 13:12-17, 45, 46	April 16
Leviticus 14:1-7	April 17
Leviticus 16:1-10; 15-22	April 18
Leviticus 23:26-32; 37-43	April 19
Leviticus 24:10-16; 23	April 20
Leviticus 25:8-17; 25-28; 39-42	April 21
Numbers 10:29-36	April 22
Numbers 11:4-5; 10-23	April 23
Numbers 11:24-34	April 24
Numbers 12:1-15	April 25
Numbers 13:1-2; 17-21; 23-33	April 26
Numbers 14:1-21	April 27
Numbers 14:26-32; 36-45	April 29
Numbers 16:1-4; 16-24; 26-34	May 2
Numbers 16:41-50	May 3
Numbers 17:1-13	May 4
Numbers 20:1-13	May 5
Numbers 21:4-8	May 7
Numbers 22:1-20	May 9
Numbers 22:21-35	May 10
Numbers 23:13-24	May 11
Numbers 35:9-12; 14-16; 19; 22-28	May 17
Deuteronomy 1:34-38	May 20
Deuteronomy 2:26-37	May 8
Deuteronomy 3:1-5	May 8
Deuteronomy 3:23-28	May 20
Deuteronomy 4:9-20, 23, 24	May 13
Deuteronomy 8	May 14
Deuteronomy 14:1-21	May 1
Deuteronomy 21:22-23	May 15
Deuteronomy 22:1-12	May 15
Deuteronomy 25:17-19	March 30
Deuteronomy 32:1-20	May 16
Deuteronomy 33:1-3; 6-17	May 18
Deuteronomy 33:18-29	May 19

Deuteronomy 34	May 21
Joshua 1:1-9	June 2
Joshua 2:1-21	June 3
Joshua 3:1-13	June 4
Joshua 3:14-17	June 5
Joshua 4:4-11; 18	June 5
Joshua 5:1, 10-15	June 6
Joshua 6:1-5; 12-21; 23, 25	June 7
Joshua 7:1-13; 15	June 9
Joshua 7:16-26	June 10
Joshua 9:3-21	June 11
Joshua 10:1-6; 8-14	June 13
Joshua 14:6-14	June 15
Joshua 15:13-19	June 16
Joshua 18:1-10	June 17
Joshua 21:3; 10-13	June 16
Joshua 22:1-6; 10-20	June 18
Joshua 22:21-34	June 19
Joshua 23:1-15	June 20
Joshua 24:11-26	June 21
Judges 2:1-5	June 30
Judges 2:6-16	June 30
Judges 3:1-15; 31	July 1
Judges 4:1-23	July 2
Judges 5:1-18	July 3
Judges 5:19-31	July 4
Judges 6:1-16	July 6
Judges 6:17-32	July 7
Judges 6:33-40	July 8
Judges 7:1-8	July 8
Judges 7:9-21; 23-25	July 9
Judges 8:1-3; 22-27; 32-35	July 10
Judges 10:6, 7; 9-18	July 11
Judges 11:5-7; 9-10; 12-21; 23-28	July 12
Judges 11:29-40	July 13
Judges 14	July 14
Judges 15:9-20	July 15
Judges 16:6-20	July 16
Judges 16:21-31	July 17
Judges 17	July 19
Judges 18:1-6; 14-20; 22-26	July 20
Ruth 1:1-11; 13b-18	July 25
Ruth 1:19-22	July 26
Ruth 2:1-7	July 26
Ruth 2:8-23	July 27
Ruth 4:1-17	July 28
1 Samuel 1:1-3; 9-18	July 31
1 Samuel 1:19-28	August 1
1 Samuel 2:1-11	August 2
1 Samuel 2:12-21; 23-26	August 3
1 Samuel 3:1-18	August 4
1 Samuel 3:19-21	August 5
1 Samuel 4:1-11	August 5
1 Samuel 5:1-4; 6-12	August 7
1 Samuel 6:1-10; 12-15; 19-21	August 8
1 Samuel 7:1-13; 15-17	August 9
1 Samuel 8: 1; 3-22	August 10
1 Samuel 9:1-6; 14-21, 26, 27	August 11
1 Samuel 10:1, 17-27	August 12
1 Samuel 12	August 13
1 Samuel 13:1-14	August 14
1 Samuel 15:1-3; 9-11; 13-23	August 15
1 Samuel 16:1; 4-14; 22, 23	August 17
1 Samuel 17:1-12; 14-18	August 19
1 Samuel 17:20-37	August 20
1 Samuel 17:38-51	August 21
1 Samuel 17:55-58	August 22
1 Samuel 18:3-4	August 23
1 Samuel 18:6-16; 28-30	August 22
1 Samuel 19:1, 4-18	August 23
1 Samuel 21:1-3; 6-7	August 25
1 Samuel 21:10-15	August 27
1 Samuel 22:1, 2	August 29
1 Samuel 22:9-23	August 25
1 Samuel 23:1-13	August 31
1 Samuel 23:19-29	September 1
1 Samuel 24:1-7; 17-19	September 4
1 Samuel 26:1-22; 25	September 7
1 Samuel 30:1-13; 15-18	September 8
1 Samuel 31:1-5; 7-13	September 9
1 Samuel 34:12-18; 20-22	August 6
2 Samuel 1:1-16	September 10
2 Samuel 1:17-27	September 11
2 Samuel 5:1-3; 4-9	September 12
2 Samuel 5:17-25	September 13
2 Samuel 6:12-23	September 17
2 Samuel 7:1-17	September 18
2 Samuel 7:18-29	September 19
2 Samuel 9	September 22
2 Samuel 11:1-3; 6-10; 12-17; 26-27	September 23
2 Samuel 12:1-10; 13, 14	September 24
2 Samuel 12:15-23	September 25
2 Samuel 15:1-12	September 28
2 Samuel 15:13-15; 17-26	September 29
2 Samuel 15:29-37	September 30
2 Samuel 16:5-14	October 1
2 Samuel 17:22, 24; 27-29	September 30
2 Samuel 18:1; 5-18	October 3
2 Samuel 18:24-33	October 5
2 Samuel 19:2, 4-8	October 5
2 Samuel 24:1-4; 9-15	October 6
2 Samuel 24:16-25	October 7
1 Kings 3:1, 3-15	October 14
1 Kings 4:22-34	October 15
1 Kings 5:1-11; 13-18	October 16
1 Kings 8:1-6; 10-11; 22-30	October 19
1 Kings 10:1-13	October 30
1 Kings 10:14-15; 18-23	October 15
1 Kings 11:1-5; 9-13	October 31
1 Kings 12:26-33	November 7
1 Kings 13:1-10	November 7
1 Kings 13:11-30	November 8
1 Kings 14:1-10; 12-13; 17-18	November 9
1 Kings 16:29-34	November 15
1 Kings 17:1-6	November 15
1 Kings 17:7-24	November 16
1 Kings 18:1-15; 17-20	November 17
1 Kings 18:20-29	November 18
1 Kings 18:30-40	November 19
1 Kings 18:41-46	November 20

1 Kings 19:1-8	November 20
1 Kings 19:9-19	November 21
1 Kings 21:1-16	November 22
1 Kings 21:17-29	November 23
1 Kings 22:1-9; 13-14; 23; 28; 30-35; 37-38	November 24
2 Kings 1:2-13; 15-17	November 28
2 Kings 2:1-14	November 29
2 Kings 4:1-14	November 30
2 Kings 4:18-23; 25-37	December 1
2 Kings 4:38-44	December 2
2 Kings 5:1-14	December 3
2 Kings 5:15-27	December 4
2 Kings 6:1-7	December 2
2 Kings 7:1-17	December 5
2 Kings 8:1-15	December 6
2 Kings 9:1-7; 14; 21-26; 30-37	December 7
2 Kings 11:1-4; 10-18; 20	December 9
2 Kings 12:1-15	December 10
2 Kings 13:1-6; 9-11; 14-19	December 17
2 Kings 14:23-27; 29	December 20
1 Chronicles 10:13,14	September 9
1 Chronicles 11:10-14	August 29
1 Chronicles 11:15-19	August 29
1 Chronicles 12:39-40	September 12
1 Chronicles 13	September 16
1 Chronicles 29:1-9; 20-23	October 9
2 Chronicles 3	October 17
2 Chronicles 9:31	November 6
2 Chronicles 10:1-8; 10-16; 19	November 6
2 Chronicles 13:1-16; 18; 20	November 10
2 Chronicles 14:1-15	November 11
2 Chronicles 15:1-17	November 12
2 Chronicles 16:1-14	November 13
2 Chronicles 17:1-11	November 14
2 Chronicles 19:1-11	November 25
2 Chronicles 20:1-15; 17-19	November 26
2 Chronicles 20:20-30	November 27
2 Chronicles 21:1, 4, 6; 18-20	December 8
2 Chronicles 22:1-9	December 8
2 Chronicles 24:2; 15-25	December 11
2 Chronicles 25:1-11	December 18
2 Chronicles 25:14-24, 27-28	December 19
2 Chronicles 26:1; 4-8; 16-21	December 30
Job 1:1-12	March 3
Job 1:13-22	March 4
Job 2:1-13	March 5
Job 4:12-21	March 6
Job 5:17-27	March 6
Job 14:1-15	February 6
Job 19:21-27	May 23
Job 23:1-17	March 7
Job 28	March 8
Job 38:1-11; 16, 17; 22, 23; 31-41	March 9
Job 39:19-30	March 10
Job 40:1-14	March 10
Job 42:1-13	March 11
Psalm 7	September 3
Psalm 8	January 5
Psalm 15	June 12
Psalm 17	September 2
Psalm 18:1-24	September 14
Psalm 18:30-50	September 15
Psalm 20	September 20
Psalm 21	September 21
Psalm 23	March 28
Psalm 32	September 27
Psalm 33:10-22	January 17
Psalm 34	August 28
Psalm 38	October 2
Psalm 45	October 18
Psalm 47	November 27
Psalm 51	September 26
Psalm 52	August 26
Psalm 54	September 1
Psalm 55	October 4
Psalm 56	August 27
Psalm 57	September 5
Psalm 59	August 24
Psalm 62	October 13
Psalm 63	September 6
Psalm 68:1-8	April 22
Psalm 72	October 10
Psalm 77	March 24
Psalm 78:13-32	March 31
Psalm 78:58-66	August 7
Psalm 78:67-72	August 18
Psalm 80	July 24
Psalm 81	May 6
Psalm 83	July 5
Psalm 84	October 20
Psalm 90	April 30
Psalm 91	January 14
Psalm 95	April 10
Psalm 101	September 13
Psalm 103	October 11
Psalm 104	October 12
Psalm 105:1-23	February 28
Psalm 105:24-38	March 18
Psalm 106:13-33	May 12
Psalm 106:34-48	July 23
Psalm 115	July 21
Psalm 119:1-16	May 27
Psalm 119:17-32	June 22
Psalm 119:33-48	June 23
Psalm 119:49-64	July 29
Psalm 119:65-80	July 30
Psalm 124	February 14
Psalm 132	October 8
Psalm 136	June 14
Psalm 139	January 26
Psalm 141	August 30
Psalm 142	August 30
Psalm 148	January 3
Proverbs 1:20-31	October 25
Proverbs 7:1-18; 21-27	July 18
Proverbs 8:1-21	October 26
Proverbs 8:22-36	January 2
Proverbs 10:1-16	October 27
Proverbs 10:17-32	October 28
Proverbs 16:1-16	June 25

Proverbs 16:17-33	June 26
Proverbs 23:13-18	August 6
Proverbs 26:1-16	May 28
Proverbs 26:17-28	May 29
Proverbs 27:1-18	October 29
Ecclesiastes 1:1-15	November 1
Ecclesiastes 1:16-18	November 2
Ecclesiastes 2:1-11	November 2
Ecclesiastes 7:1-14	November 3
Ecclesiastes 10:1-14	November 4
Ecclesiastes 11:9-10	November 5
Ecclesiastes 12:1-7; 13-14	November 5
Song of Solomon 2	October 21
Song of Solomon 3:6-11	October 22
Song of Solomon 4:1-7	October 22
Song of Solomon 4:8-16	October 23
Song of Solomon 5:1	October 23
Song of Solomon 5:2-16	October 24
Isaiah 1:10-20	August 16
Isaiah 6	December 31
Isaiah 11:1-10	August 18
Isaiah 26:19-21	May 23
Isaiah 41:17, 18	March 29
Isaiah 43:18-21	March 29
Isaiah 44:9-20	July 22
Isaiah 53	February 3
Isaiah 54:4-10	January 16
Isaiah 55	May 30
Jeremiah 1:6-9	March 15
Daniel 12:2-3; 13	May 23
Hosea 2:14-23	December 24
Hosea 6:1-7	December 24
Hosea 7	December 25
Hosea 10	December 26
Hosea 11:1-11	December 27
Hosea 13:1-14	December 28
Hosea 14	December 27
Joel 2:1-14	December 29
Amos 3:1-8	December 20
Amos 5:14-27	December 21
Amos 7	December 22
Amos 9	December 23
Jonah 1:1-7	December 12
Jonah 1:8-16	December 13
Jonah 1:17	December 14
Jonah 2	December 14
Jonah 3	December 15
Jonah 4	December 16
Micah 6:6-8	August 16
Matthew 6:25-34	March 28
Matthew 12:38-41	December 15
Matthew 12:42	October 30
Mark 1:40-45	April 17
Mark 2:23-28	January 6
Mark 15:16-38	May 24
Luke 13:1-9	January 29
Luke 14:1-5	January 6
Luke 18:1-14	June 24
John 1:1-14	January 1
John 3:14-17	May 7
John 6:47-58	March 27
John 12:37-41	December 31
John 15:1-15	May 31
John 15:16-27	June 1
Acts 7:22-29	March 13
Acts 7:37-41; 44, 45	May 22
Romans 3:9-26	January 9
Romans 4:1-25	January 24
Romans 5:12-21	January 8
Romans 9:1-13	February 10
Romans 10:1-21	April 3
1 Corinthians 1:18-31	June 8
1 Corinthians 5:6-8	March 19
1 Corinthians 10:1-12	April 10
1 Corinthians 13	June 27
1 Corinthians 16:2	April 13
2 Corinthians 3:7-18	April 12
2 Corinthians 6:14-18	January 18
2 Corinthians 9:6-8	April 13
Galatians 3:6-18	February 4
Galatians 4:21-31	February 1
Galatians 5:1-6	February 1
Ephesians 6:1-10	May 26
1 Thessalonians 4:13-18	June 29
1 Thessalonians 5:1-10	June 29
Hebrews 3:1-6	May 22
Hebrews 7:1-17; 20-25	January 22
Hebrews 9:1-14	April 4
Hebrews 10:28-31	April 20
Hebrews 11:5-6	January 11
Hebrews 11:8-19	February 9
Hebrews 11:24-26	March 13
Hebrews 11:31	June 3
Hebrews 12:15-17	February 11
Hebrews 12:18-26	April 1
Hebrews 13:10-14	April 14
James 2:25-26	June 3
1 Peter 1:15-21	April 6
1 Peter 2:1-10	May 25
1 Peter 2:13-25	June 28
1 John 3:10-15	January 10
Jude 14-15	January 11
Revelation 7:1-10	April 28